THE IRAN NUCLEAR ISSUE

Controversy over the Iranian nuclear policy has been mounting in both legal and political circles since the early 2000s. Most recently, the IAEA, tasked with verifying compliance of member states with the NPT, has been expressing concern that Iran's nuclear efforts are directed not solely at peaceful uses but also at military purposes. In response, various states have tried, individually and collectively, to engage Iran in agreed frameworks of action that would include an Iranian self-imposed restraint on its nuclear development. This volume documents the Iranian nuclear issue, tracing the evolution of international interest and concern with Iran's nuclear policy. It covers the period beginning in the 1970s, when Iran began earnest efforts to acquire nuclear capabilities; through the early 2000s, when it was established that Iran had concealed certain aspects of its nuclear activities from the IAEA; until the end of 2009, by which time it has been subject to three years of enforcement measures by the UN Security Council, aimed at inducing Iran to suspend or terminate its nuclear development.

This volume analyses the legal aspects of the Iran nuclear issue by reference to documents of the UN Security Council, IAEA, dedicated ad hoc bodies, individual states and more.

DOCUMENTS IN INTERNATIONAL LAW

GENERAL EDITOR: PROFESSOR STEFAN TALMON
Professor of Public International Law in the University of
Oxford and Fellow of St. Anne's College

ALSO IN THIS SERIES

THE LEGAL ORDER OF THE OCEANS
Vaughan Lowe and Stefan Talmon (2009)

THE IRAN NUCLEAR ISSUE

Yaël Ronen

·HART·
PUBLISHING

OXFORD AND PORTLAND, OREGON
2010

Published in the United Kingdom by Hart Publishing Ltd
16C Worcester Place, Oxford, OX1 2JW
Telephone: +44 (0)1865 517530
Fax: +44 (0)1865 510710
E-mail: mail@hartpub.co.uk
Website: http://www.hartpub.co.uk

Published in North America (US and Canada) by
Hart Publishing
c/o International Specialized Book Services
920 NE 58th Avenue, Suite 300
Portland, OR 97213-3786
USA
Tel: +1 503 287 3093 or toll-free: (1) 800 944 6190
Fax: +1 503 280 8832
E-mail: orders@isbs.com
Website: http://www.isbs.com

British Library Cataloguing in Publication Data
Data Available

ISBN: 978-1-84113-756-8

Typeset by Tatiana Galarza
Printed and bound in Great Britain by
TJ International Ltd, Padstow, Cornwall

Credits:

- Doc. 4-Doc. 6, Doc. 22-97, Doc. 100, Doc. 107, Doc. 109, Doc. 111-Doc. 113, Doc. 115,
  Doc. 116, Doc. 119, Doc. 120, Doc. 124, Doc. 125, Doc. 130, Doc. 133, Doc. 134, Doc.
  147 – courtesy of IAEA.
- Doc. 9-Doc. 21, Doc. 98, Doc. 99, Doc. 101, Doc. 102, Doc. 110, Doc. 114, Doc. 117, Doc.
  118, Doc. 121, Doc. 141-Doc. 145 – by permission of ODS
- Doc. 128, Doc. 129, Doc. 131, Doc. 132, Doc. 155-Doc. 161 - courtesy of the EU
- Doc. 136, Doc. 137 – courtesy of the US Department of State
- Doc. 108 – courtesy of the British American Security Information Council (BASIC)
- Doc. 139 – courtesy of Reaching Critical Will

CONTENTS

PREFACE

This book is concerned with legal aspects of the Iranian nuclear dispute. It does not deal directly with the question whether Iran is carrying out a military nuclear programme, or what its intentions are. This is not for lack of material; indeed there is vast literature on these questions. However, at the time of writing, whether Iran is pursuing non-peaceful objectives remains a matter for assessment rather than established fact. The legal process, with which this book is concerned, is driven and governed by this factual uncertainty.

The Iranian nuclear dispute raises questions from a variety of legal spheres: the law relating to non-proliferation, treaty interpretation in general and the interpretation of the Treaty on the Non-Proliferation of Nuclear Weapons (NPT) in particular, the law of international organizations, most notably of the UN Security Council, international responsibility of states, use of force (*ius ad bellum*) in general and specifically with regard to weapons of mass destruction, and more. The analysis addresses these areas of law as they relate to the treatment of the Iranian dossier in the International Atomic Energy Agency (IAEA) and its referral to the Security Council. It also briefly touches upon on issues that at least at the time of writing are still in the realm of the speculative, such as use of force against Iran.

The purpose of the analysis is to present the legal questions that have arisen and relate them to the documents included in the compilation. As a roadmap for readers wishing to make use of the primary sources, it does not purport to present a definitive position on the correct application of the law, but rather to delineate the parameters which inform the debate.

The documents are organised according to international players, and within each category of players, chronologically. Each document is allocated a unique number in the table of contents and thereafter navigation within the book is by document number, not page number. References to documents in the footnotes and subject index also use this document number, which can be found at the top outside corner of each page and next to each document's title.

In preparing the compilation I benefited from the kind assistance of the Media and Outreach Section of the IAEA. The Feinberg Fund of the Hebrew University of Jerusalem generously funded the research. Many people offered me their insights and counsel, including Dr. Hans Blix, Dr. Daniel Joyner and Dr. Eitan Barak, as well as Prof. Moshe Hirsch, Dr. Emily Landau, Dr. Robbie Sabel, Prof. Yuval Shany and Prof. Stefan Talmon. Moria Cohen and Akiva Miller also assisted in bringing the manuscript to print. Last but not least, Richard Hart and the Hart Publishing team have been patient and helpful throughout the project. I am grateful to them all.

The manuscript was signed on 15 September 2009.

Yaël Ronen
Jerusalem, September 2009

ABBREVIATIONS

1737 Committee	Committee established by Security Council Resolution 1737
AEOI	Atomic Energy Organization of Iran
CTBT	Comprehensive Test Ban Treaty
EU3	France and Germany and the United Kingdom
EU3+3	China, France, Germany, Russia, the UK and the US (also referred to as P5+1)
FEP	Fuel Enrichment Facility
HEU	High Enriched Uranium
IAEA BOG	International Atomic Energy Agency Board of Governors
IAEA DG	International Atomic Energy Agency Director General
IAEA	International Atomic Energy Agency
LEU	Low Enriched Uranium
NAM	Non-Aligned Movement
NNWS	Non-Nuclear-Weapon States
NPT	Treaty on the Non-Proliferation of Nuclear Weapons
NSG	Nuclear Supply Group
NWS	Nuclear-Weapon States
PFEP	Pilot Fuel Enrichment Facility
UCF	Uranium Conversion Facility
UNSC	United Nations Security Council
WMDs	Weapons of Mass Destruction

Analytical Introduction

1. Introduction

The present dispute over Iran's nuclear programme erupted in August 2002, when an Iranian opsposition group revealed in Washington, DC, the existence of two previously-undisclosed nuclear facilities under construction in Iran: a fuel enrichment plant in Natanz and a heavy water reactor in Arak. In December 2002 the United States published satellite pictures of the two facilities, as proof of its long-held suspicions that Iran was pursuing both weapons of mass destruction and long-range missile capabilities. Iran reacted by stating repeatedly that it was committed to the prevailing international legal regimes on weapons of mass destruction, including the Treaty on the Non-Proliferation of Nuclear Weapons, not merely on the basis of its contractual obligations but, more importantly, because of its religious convictions and historical experience.[1] Iran maintained that its programme, which was aimed at mastering the complete fuel cycle, was intended solely to support a civilian nuclear energy programme.[2] It explained that it had operated clandestinely because of obstructions by the US and other countries to its overt activities.[3]

Suspicion nonetheless arose and increased among various governments[4] that the Iranian nuclear programme was run clandestinely for reasons other than evading obstruction of peaceful activities, and that particularly the uranium enrichment work which Iran was carrying out was intended not solely for use in peaceful energy production but also for the manufacturing of nuclear weapons. The matter was taken up by the international Atomic Energy Agency (IAEA), which began an intensive inspection and verification operation in Iran. The IAEA found that Iran had made substantial efforts over the previous two decades to master an independent nuclear fuel cycle, had performed some laboratory-scale experiments related to the reprocessing of irradiated fuel, and was carrying out research and development activities related to the treatment, storage and disposal of radioactive waste.[5] In June 2003, and several times subsequently, the IAEA Director-General (IAEA DG), Mohamed ElBaradei, declared that Iran had failed to comply with its obligations under its NPT Safeguards Agreement.[6]

Amid calls on the one hand to take decisive measures against Iran, including referral to the Security Council,[7] and on the other hand to give it a chance to rectify its conduct,[8] the UK, France and Germany (EU3) undertook to negotiate directly with Iran. In October 2003 the two sides issued the Tehran Statement, in which Iran agreed to cooperate fully with the IAEA to settle all outstanding issues and to correct any failures to comply with its Safeguards Agreement. To that end, Iran announced its willingness to sign and commence

---

[1] Doc. 15; Doc. 98-Doc. 101.
[2] Doc. 99; Doc. 100.
[3] Eg Doc. 63 para 8.
[4] Eg Doc. 149; Doc. 150.
[5] Doc. 33; Doc. 35.
[6] Doc. 35 para 50; Doc. 39 para 107; Doc. 40 para 42.
[7] Canada: Doc. 62 para 19.
[8] Doc. 60-Doc. 63.

the ratification process of a protocol additional to its Safeguards Agreement. The protocol would enable the IAEA to conduct a wider scope of verification activities, throughout Iran and with regard to undeclared material and activities. It also agreed to 'voluntarily suspend all uranium enrichment and reprocessing activities as defined by the IAEA'. On their part, the EU3 informed Iran that 'in their view, full implementation of Iran's decisions, confirmed by the IAEA's Director General, should enable the immediate situation to be resolved by the IAEA Board'.[9] This sentence was understood to mean that if Iran complied with its commitments, the EU3 would not seek referral of Iran's dossier to the Security Council.[10]

In mid-2004 Iran resumed work on uranium conversion, which is the preparatory process for uranium enrichment. The IAEA informed it that given the quantity of nuclear material involved, this testing would technically amount to production of feed material for enrichment processes, which Iran had undertaken to suspend. Iran responded that its voluntary suspension had not at any time covered the production of feed material for the enrichment process.[11] The IAEA Board of Governors (BOG) nonetheless called on Iran to suspend this activity.[12] To defuse the crisis, the EU3 engaged in negotiations with Iran, and on 15 November 2004, the EU3 and Iran signed the Paris Agreement, outlining how negotiations were to proceed. Iran agreed to continue and extend its suspension to include all tests or production at any uranium conversion installation. The EU3 recognised that this suspension was a voluntary confidence-building measure and not a legal obligation. The EU3 and Iran agreed that during the suspension they would negotiate long-term arrangements. According to the Paris Agreement, the aim of the negotiations was to produce objective guarantees that Iran's nuclear programme was exclusively for peaceful purposes, as well as firm guarantees on nuclear, technological and economic cooperation, and firm commitments on security issues.[13]

Negotiations did not progress well. In April 2005 Iran threatened that unless negotiations progressed, it would start up uranium conversion.[14] In June 2005 Mahmoud Ahmadinejad was elected Iran's president. On 1 August 2005 Iran announced the resumption of uranium conversion at the Esfahan facility.[15] This was shortly before, and in anticipation of, the EU3's delivery on 5 August of a proposal for a framework for a long-term agreement with Iran.[16] Iran explained its step as a result of its disappointment with the EU3's broken promises, procrastination and bad faith.[17] The EU3 considered the Iranian step a retraction from previous commitments.[18] Consequently, they aligned with the US, which had already been pressing the IAEA BOG to refer the Iranian issue to the Security Council.[19] The IAEA BOG urged Iran to re-establish full, IAEA-verified suspension of all enrichment-related and reprocessing activities, including research and development.[20]

In January 2006 Iran began to enrich uranium in centrifuges at the Natanz plant.[21] On 4 February, the IAEA BOG adopted a resolution in which it demanded of Iran that

---

[9] Doc. 7.
[10] Pierre Goldschmidt, 'Exposing Nuclear Non-Compliance' (2009) 51 *Survival* 143, 150.
[11] Doc. 39 paras 118-132.
[12] Doc. 27.
[13] Doc. 8 paras 5, 6.
[14] Sharon Squassoni, 'The Iranian Nuclear Program' in Nathan E Busch and Daniel H Joyner (eds) *Combating Weapons of Mass Destruction* (University of Georgia Press 2009) 281, 287-288.
[15] Doc. 107.
[16] Doc. 126.
[17] Doc. 106.
[18] Doc. 127; Doc. 128.
[19] Doc. 72 para 82.
[20] Doc. 29 operative para 3; Doc. 30 operative para 4(II); Doc. 32 operative para 1.
[21] Doc. 42.

it re-establish full and sustained suspension of all enrichment-related and reprocessing activities; reconsider the construction of the heavy-water research reactor in Arak; ratify the Additional Protocol, and pending its ratification, act in accordance with the Additional Protocol's provisions; and implement the transparency measures requested by the IAEA DG. The BOG also requested the IAEA DG to report to the Security Council that these steps were required, and to convey to the Security Council all IAEA reports and resolutions relating to the issue.[22] The matter was thus referred to the Security Council.

In March 2006 the Security Council issued a presidential statement calling on Iran to take the steps requested by the IAEA BOG.[23] On 31 July 2006 the Security Council adopted resolution 1696(2006), in which, acting under Article 40 of the UN Charter, it demanded of Iran to take those steps.[24] Iran's refusal to do so[25] led the Security Council on 23 December 2006 to adopt Resolution 1737(2006) under Article 41 of the UN Charter. This Resolution imposed enforcement measures on Iran until it complied with the previous demands of the Security Council and the requests of the IAEA BOG, to which the Security Council added the suspension of work on all heavy-water-related projects, including the construction of the heavy-water research reactor in Arak.[26] The enforcement measures included a trade embargo on items and technologies which could contribute to the activities which Iran was ordered to suspend, a prohibition on provision to Iran of technical or financial assistance related to these activities, and a travel notification requirement and asset freeze with respect to designated individuals and entities involved in the activities which Iran was ordered to suspend. The measures provided for exceptions on humanitarian grounds. In light of Iran's unyieldingness, Resolution 1747(2007) of 24 March 2007, also adopted under Article 41 of the UN Charter, expanded the trade embargo to certain conventional arms and widened the travel restraints and asset freeze to additional individuals and entities.[27]

In August 2007 the IAEA Secretariat and Iran negotiated a work plan to address a limited number of issues regarding Iran's past nuclear programme. The plan states that 'after the implementation of the above work plan and the agreed modalities for resolving the outstanding issues, the implementation of safeguards in Iran will be conducted in a routine manner'.[28] This formulation limited the mandate of the IAEA, which normally encompasses on-going verification activities to ensure that there are no undeclared nuclear material and activities in Iran and that its declarations to the IAEA are correct and complete, to an exhaustive set of specific questions.[29] The consequences of this formulation became apparent when Iran argued that other than the six issues listed as outstanding, which it regarded as having been resolved, the IAEA was not in a position to make further demands upon it, not even with regard to issues mentioned in the plan under a different heading, such as the 'alleged studies'.[30]

In November 2007 the IAEA announced that it had been able to verify that the material that Iran had previously not declared but owned up to since 2003 had not been diverted from

---

[22] Doc. 32.
[23] Doc. 9.
[24] Doc. 10 operative para 1.
[25] Doc. 114; Doc. 115.
[26] Doc. 11 operative para 2(b).
[27] Doc. 12.
[28] Doc. 6.
[29] Pierre Goldschmidt, 'Verifying Iran's Nuclear Program: Is the International Community Up to the Task?' Lamont Lecture at the Belfer Center, Harvard University (30 October 2007), www.carnegieendowment.org/files/lamontlecture_goldschmidt.pdf. All URLs accessed 15 September 2009 unless otherwise noted.
[30] Doc. 125.

peaceful to non-peaceful purposes.[31] Since then, the IAEA has continuously reported that it was able to verify the non-diversion of this material, but was unable to provide credible assurances about the absence of any other undeclared nuclear material and activities in Iran.[32]

Outstanding issues have by the time of writing largely been addressed through the process established in the IAEA-Iran work plan. However, the IAEA is still requesting that Iran account for and explain a series of documents found in its possession which point to nuclear weapons-related research, and respond fully to queries on weapons studies that Iran had allegedly conducted. Iran denies the existence of any such studies.[33] These outstanding issues, in addition to Iran's continued refusal to suspend uranium enrichment and construction of the heavy-water reactor, and to adhere to the Additional Protocol, form the basis for maintaining its dossier before the UN Security Council and pursuing the sanctions against it. Iran argues that the work plan issues have been resolved satisfactorily, and that even under the Security Council's own terms there is no basis for continuing the sanctions regime or maintaining its case before the Security Council.[34]

On 3 March 2008, Security Council Resolution 1803(2008) expanded the scope of the enforcement measures further.[35] Resolution 1835(2008) of 27 September 2008 reiterated the demands on Iran but did not change the scope of enforcement measures.[36] By September 2009, no further action has been taken by the Security Council.

2. Scientific Background

Nuclear energy is used for both civilian and military purposes. In civilian nuclear reactors it is used primarily to generate electricity and for research. As of 2009, there were over 400 reactors operating in 30 countries, and over 40 more reactors under construction (among them the Bushehr reactor in Iran).[37]

Nuclear energy is produced when fissile isotopes of heavy elements are bombarded with neutrons, until they split into atoms of lighter elements. This process releases large quantities of energy and neutrons. The most frequently used fissile materials are uranium 235 (U-235) and plutonium 239 (Pu-239). U-235 forms only 0.7% of natural uranium ore, which is mostly made up of U-238, which is not naturally-fissile. In order to be used in certain reactor types and in weapons, uranium must therefore be enriched, i.e. the concentration of fissile U-235 must be increased through physical processes. Pu-239 does not exist naturally at all. It is produced from uranium and separated from it. Most civilian nuclear-power reactors in the world use as fuel U-235 enriched to about 4%. Production of a nuclear weapon requires a minimum of 15 kilograms of U-235 enriched to a level of around 90%, or 4 kilograms of plutonium of which 93% or above is Pu-239.[38]

---

[31] Doc. 50.

[32] Doc. 56.

[33] Doc. 52.

[34] Doc. 118; Doc. 119 Section E; Doc. 124.

[35] Doc. 13.

[36] Doc. 14.

[37] IAEA Power Reactor Information System, www.iaea.org/programmes/a2/.

[38] Bomb Facts: How Nuclear Weapons are Made, www.wisconsinproject.org/pubs/articles/2001/bomb%20 facts.htm. The 'significant quantities' which the IAEA safeguards have as a goal to discover are 25 kg of U-235 and 8 kg of Pu-239, David Fischer, *History of the International Atomic Energy Agency, the First forty Years* (Vienna, IAEA, 1997) 285; MCIS/CNS *NPT Briefing Book* (Southampton, Mountbatten Center for International Studies, 2009).

2.1 Iran's Nuclear Fuel Cycle

The first stage ('front end') of the nuclear fuel cycle consists of mining the uranium and processing it into a uranium concentrate called yellowcake. In February 2003 Iranian President Mohammad Khatami declared that his government intended to extract uranium from a mine at Saghand, in the province of Yazd.[39] Iranian authorities also admitted to producing yellowcake at a milling plant near the city of Yazd.[40]

Once mined and concentrated, the uranium is converted into uranium hexafluoride gas (UF_6), which serves as the feed material for enrichment. In 2000, the Iranian government informed the IAEA that a uranium conversion facility (UCF) was being constructed at Esfahan.[41] According to Iran, the UCF is intended to have additional process lines, for converting low enriched UF_6 into low-enriched uranium metal (UO_2), depleted UF_6 into uranium tetrafluoride (UF_4), and depleted UF_4 into depleted uranium metal.[42]

The UCF began operating in June 2006. However, although Iran's production of material from indigenously-mined uranium is growing, as of August 2009 the UO_2 it introduces into the UCF is still foreign-supplied.[43] Analysts further question the economic rationale of Iran's investment in front-end nuclear fuel cycle facilities. The scale of facilities required to reach market competitiveness in these technologies is inconsistent with the scale of Iran's uranium sources as estimated by the Iranian government, and the expected timetable for operational completion of these facilities makes an a recovery of this significant investment in an economic rate of return almost impossible. This lack of economic merit of the venture casts doubt on the credibility of Iran's justification for its programme, namely energy independence;[44] the latter would be better served by conservation and stewardship of national oil and natural gas resources. Iran has proven reserves of about 90 years' worth of oil at its current production rate, and the compatible statistic is 220 years for natural gas reserve. Iran's proven uranium reserves represent slightly more than one year's consumption for the declared nuclear programme.[45]

2.1.1 Uranium Enrichment

There are a number of different ways to enrich uranium, and enrichment plants exist in a dozen countries. Iran currently engages in enrichment by centrifuges. In this process UF_6 is spun at high speed, causing molecules of the denser U-238 isotope to separate from the lighter U-235 molecules. The dense U-238 is drawn towards the walls of the centrifuge and extracted; the gas containing higher concentration of the lighter U-235 clusters near the centre and is collected. It is then fed into another centrifuge. The process is repeated many times through a chain of centrifuges known as a cascade, until the desired concentration of U-235 (i.e. the level of enrichment) is achieved.

[39] —— 'Nuclear energy for peaceful purposes, a right of nations: Khatami' (Presidency of the Islamic Republic of Iran website 9 February 2003), former.president.ir/khatami/eng/cronicnews/1381/8111/811120/811120.htm.

[40] —— 'Latest Developments in the Nuclear Program of Iran, in Particular on the Plutonium Way', (Presentation by France at the Nuclear Suppliers Group Information Exchange Meeting, May, 2003), www.iranwatch.org/government/france/france-nsgpaper-2003-.htm.

[41] Doc. 33 para 21.

[42] Doc. 35 Annex I para 3.

[43] Paul K Kerr, 'Iran's Nuclear Program: Status' Congressional Research Service Report for Congress (11 August 2009) 10.

[44] Doc. 17, Doc. 110.

[45] Thomas W Wood, Matthew D Milazzo, Barbara A Reichmuth and Jeffrey Bedell, 'The Economics of Energy Independence for Iran' (2007) 14 *Nonproliferation Review* 89, 90-92.

The difficulty in mastering the technique of enrichment by centrifuge lies in the production of pure UF_6 and in its maintenance in optimal conditions, as well as in setting up accurate and efficiently-operating centrifuge cascades. Once these obstacles are overcome, the difference between enrichment to reactor-fuel and enrichment to weapon-grade level is merely quantitative, not qualitative.

Iran has embarked on an ambitious large-scale uranium-enrichment programme, allegedly intended to supply low-enriched uranium (LEU) as nuclear fuel for its nuclear power reactor in Bushehr. Since 2002 this activity has been carried out at an underground facility near the town of Natanz, which houses a 1,000-centrifuge pilot fuel-enrichment plant (PFEP), as well as a commercial-scale fuel-enrichment plant (FEP), which is expected to house over 50,000 centrifuges.

The capacity of a machine to accomplish the separation of U-235 from U-238 is expressed in Separative Work Units (SWU). The centrifuges that are currently being used are estimated to have a maximum SWU of 3, and appear to be working at a level of between 1 and 2 SWU per year. In comparison, state-of-the-art centrifuges operating in the US and Europe boast SWU of between 40 and several hundred.[46] When completed, the FEP could supply nuclear fuel for a nuclear power reactor, albeit at an economically-inefficient cost. Because of its size, the completed enrichment facility will also have the potential to produce highly-enriched uranium (HEU).

Iran first used UF_6 to test a centrifuge at the PFEP in June 2003.[47] By September 2007 it had installed 18 cascades of 164 centrifuges each. As of August 2009, over 4500 centrifuges have been operating at the FEP, while over 3,700 more being installed.[48] Iran has accumulated some 1,500 kg of LEU.[49] It is not believed to have produced any weapon-grade HEU. Analysts suggest that Iran has accumulated LEU that could have been enriched to enough weapon-grade material for one nuclear weapon by February 2008, and two nuclear weapons by February 2010.[50]

Iran has also pursued two types of laser enrichment technology. After conducting laboratory-scale work, and before informing the IAEA of this work, Iran dismantled the relevant equipment and moved it to a storage facility.[51]

2.1.2 Plutonium Production

Iran is constructing a 40-megawatt heavy-water reactor in Arak (the IR-40). The reactor will use natural UO_2 fuel, which will be made at the UCF at Esfahan. In August 2009, following repeated requests by the IAEA, Iran provided the Agency with access to the IR-40 reactor at Arak, at which time the Agency was able to carry out a design information verification. The IAEA verified that the construction of the facility was ongoing. In particular, the IAEA noted that no reactor vessel was yet present. The operator stated that the reactor vessel was still being manufactured, and that it would be installed in 2011.[52]

---

[46] ISIS, 'NuclearIran FAQ', www.isisnucleariran.org/nuclear-faq/.

[47] Doc. 34 para 33.

[48] Doc. 57 para 2.

[49] Doc. 57 para 3.

[50] David Albright, Paul Brannan, Jacqueline Shire, 'ISIS Analysis of the August 2009 IAEA Report on Iran' (28 August 2009) 3, www.isis-online.org/publications/iran/Analysis_IAEA_Report.pdf.

[51] Doc. 35 Annex I para 61.

[52] Doc. 57 para 11.

According to Iranian authorities, the IR-40 will be used for research and development and for the production of radioisotopes for medical and industrial use.[53] However, analysts argue that smaller, light-water research reactors are fully satisfactory for the kinds of applications in which Iran says it is interested, and interpret the Iranian activity as aimed at producing weapon-grade plutonium.[54] The EU3 have offered to replace the heavy-water reactor with a light-water research reactor,[55] but Iran has rejected the offer.

Plutonium can also be produced by reprocessing spent nuclear fuel, although spent fuel is not the material of choice for nuclear-weapon producers. Although the light-water reactor at Bushehr is capable of providing spent fuel, Russia, which agreed to supply all the nuclear fuel for Bushehr, signed in 2005 an agreement with Iran that would require Iran to return all spent fuel from Bushehr to Russia. The spent fuel will initially be stored in Iran for several years, pending sufficient radioactive decay to allow the fuel's safe transport.[56] The Arak reactor can be operated with natural uranium, which means it will not be dependent on foreign-supplied enriched uranium.[57]

Before it can be used in a nuclear weapon, plutonium must be separated from the uranium in a processing plant.[58] At present, no construction in Iran of a reprocessing plant has been reported.[59] Reprocessing plants exist in over a dozen countries.[60]

2.2 Weaponization

In addition to fissile material, manufacturing nuclear weapons requires the production of a device that could cause the uranium or plutonium to explode in a nuclear chain reaction. This process is called weaponization. There is no conclusive evidence that Iran has worked on weaponization. However, Iran has conducted a number of activities and experiments that could be related to attempts at producing a nuclear device. These include production of polonium-210,[61] which may be used as a neutron initiator in nuclear weapons but also has civilian applications, as well as Iran's seeking of deuterium gas,[62] which is used with tritium to boost the yield of fission bombs. Iran is also routinely engaged in experimentation with long-range missiles that are regarded as capable of carrying a nuclear device.

---

[53] Doc. 119 section E.

[54] Eg Robert J Einhorn and Daryl G Kimball, 'Iran's Heavy-Water Reactor: A Plutonium Bomb Factory', (Arms Control Association, Press Room Report 9 November 2006), www.armscontrol.org/pressroom/2006/20061109_Einhorn.

[55] Doc. 131; Doc. 133.

[56] —— 'Russia-Iran nuclear deal signed' *BBC World News* (27 February 2005), news.bbc.co.uk/2/hi/middle_east/4301889.stm.

[57] *Kerr* (n 43) 12.

[58] ISIS, 'Arak IR-40 Heavy Water Reactor', www.isisnucleariran.org/sites/facilities/arak-ir-40/.

[59] Ephraim Asculai, 'How Iran Can Attain its Nuclear Capability - and Then Use It' in Ephraim Kam (ed), *Israel and a Nuclear Iran: Implications for Arms Control, Deterrence, and Defense*, ed. Memorandum No 94 (Institute for National Security Studies, Tel Aviv, 2008) 13, 15.

[60] US Congress, Office of Technology Assessment, *Nuclear Safeguards and the International Atomic Energy Agency*, OTA-ISS-615, 113-114 (1995).

[61] Doc. 6 section II.A; Doc. 40 para 48.

[62] Intelligence report citing Russian sources, Circulated at the IAEA, July 2004, www.iranwatch.org/international/iaea/iaea-iran_report_d_t.pdf.

3. The NPT Regime

The Treaty on the Non-Proliferation of Nuclear Weapons (NPT),[63] which entered into force in 1970, is the cornerstone of the global non-proliferation regime. It identifies two classes of states, Nuclear-Weapon States (NWS) and Non-Nuclear-Weapon States (NNWS). The former are defined as those which have manufactured and exploded a nuclear weapon or other nuclear explosive device prior to 1 January 1967 (China, France, the Soviet Union (today the Russian Federation), the UK and the US).[64] The Treaty provides a delicate balance between three sets of commitments: non-acquisition of nuclear weapons by the NNWS; nuclear disarmament by the NWS; and the right of NNWS parties to develop or acquire peaceful nuclear technology alongside acceptance of IAEA safeguards over all fissile materials within their jurisdiction. As of September 2009, only four states are not parties to the NPT – India, Israel, Pakistan and, since 2003, North Korea.

3.1 Article IV.1: The Right to Develop Production of Nuclear Energy for Peaceful Purposes

NPT Article IV contains the principal provisions relating to the development and sharing of nuclear technology for peaceful purposes. It provides:

> 1. Nothing in this Treaty shall be interpreted as affecting the inalienable right of all the Parties to the Treaty to develop research, production and use of nuclear energy for peaceful purposes without discrimination and in conformity with articles I and II of this Treaty.
> 2. All the Parties to the Treaty undertake to facilitate, and have the right to participate in, the fullest possible exchange of equipment, materials and scientific and technological information for the peaceful uses of nuclear energy. Parties to the Treaty in a position to do so shall also cooperate in contributing alone or together with other States or international organizations to the further development of the applications of nuclear energy for peaceful purposes, especially in the territories of non-nuclear-weapon States Party to the Treaty, with due consideration for the needs of the developing areas of the world.

One of Iran's recurring arguments is that given that its nuclear programme is entirely peaceful, it is legitimately pursuing its inalienable right under NPT Article IV, which without possession of the nuclear fuel cycle is 'an empty proposition'. Any attempt to limit Iran's endeavors by circumscribing the scope of its activities or by demanding suspension of its activities, in particular the enrichment of uranium, would therefore be an infringement upon its right.[65]

The *travaux préparatoires* of the NPT reflect a variety of opinions as to the content of the right to peaceful nuclear development, ranging from an expansive interpretation, encompassing anything short of a nuclear explosion, to a limited one, encompassing only activities which cannot in any way lead to military uses.[66] Traditionally it has been the accepted view that NNWS acting in full conformity with Article II of the Treaty may

---

[63] Doc. 1.

[64] Doc. 1 art XI.3.

[65] Doc. 110; Doc. 119.

[66] Xinjun Zhang, 'The Riddle of "Inalienable Right" in Article IV of the Treaty on the Non-Proliferation of Nuclear Weapons: Intentional Ambiguity' (2006) 5 *Chinese Journal of International Law* 647.

engage in all stages of fuel-cycle activity,[67] including uranium enrichment and reprocessing of spent fuel.[68] However, the rise of regional security agendas, an illicit market in nuclear technology and the threat of nuclear terrorism, have led to renewed interest in proposals for limiting civilian uranium enrichment and plutonium reprocessing to a handful of fully-transparent fuel-cycle facilities, operating under international control and monitoring.[69]

Iran and its supporters emphasise the 'inalienable' character of the right under NPT Article IV, suggesting that peremptory norms may be at issue. Iran emphasises that the 'inalienable right of the states to develop nuclear technology for peaceful purposes emanates from the universally accepted proposition that scientific and technological achievements are the common heritage of mankind'.[70] This statement may allude to the international community's collective interest in the right, which would strengthen the argument that it is a peremptory one.[71] Other statements contend that the right cannot be denied or changed, must always be respected, and cannot be undermined or curtailed under any pretext,[72] again implying a peremptory character. In contrast, the *travaux préparatoires* of the NPT reveal that the term 'inalienable' was a purely rhetorical tool with no specific meaning, used to alleviate concerns of NNWS on the relationship between Article IV and Articles I and II.[73] Moreover, while international law knows of peremptory obligations, the notion of a peremptory right would be a novel one.

Furthermore, the right under Article IV to 'develop research, production and use of nuclear energy for peaceful purposes' is 'in conformity with Article I and II of this Treaty',[74] suggesting that it is conditional upon compliance with the obligation to refrain from pursuing nuclear weapons. These two parts of Article IV appear contradictory. One possible interpretation to reconcile this apparent contradiction is to regard Articles I and II as carving out a limited conventional exception to the inalienable right, in the case of the existence of clear evidence that a NNWS party to the NPT is using its right to assistance in development of peaceful nuclear application in order to contribute to the development of a nuclear weapons programme.[75] The proviso in Article IV is thus significant with respect to

---

[67] NAM: Doc. 82 para 62, but see Henry Sokolski, 'After Iran: Article IV, Peaceful Nuclear Energy, and the NPT', (Livermore, California, Lawrence Livermore National Laboratory, 1 June 2005), www.npec-web.org/ Projects.asp; Robert Zarate, 'The NPT, IAEA Safeguards and Peaceful Nuclear Energy: An "Inalienable Right," But Precisely To What?' in Henry D Sokolski (ed), *Falling Behind: International Scrutiny of the Peaceful Atom* (Pennsylvania, Strategic Studies Institute, 2008) 221, 259.

[68] Weapons of Mass Destruction Commission, *Weapons of Terror: Freeing the Worlds of Nuclear, Biological, and Chemical Arms* (Stockholm, Weapons of Mass Destruction Commission, 2006) 70-71.

[69] Shannon N Kile, 'The controversy over Iran's nuclear programme' in Shannon N Kile (ed), *Europe and Iran: Perspectives on Non-proliferation* SIPRI Research Report No 21 (Oxford, Oxford University Press, 2005) 1, 20; IAEA, 'Multilateral approaches to the nuclear fuel cycle: Expert Group Report Submitted to the Director General of the International Atomic Energy Agency', IAEA Doc INFCIRC/640, 22 February 2005, www.iaea. org/NewsCenter/News/2005/fuelcycle.html.

[70] Doc. 102; Doc. 106.

[71] See the ILC: '...obligations imposed on States by peremptory norms necessarily affect the vital interests of the international community as a whole'. ILC 'Draft Articles on Responsibility of States for Internationally Wrongful Acts', UN Doc A/56/10 commentary to art 12 para 7 (ILC DASR).

[72] Iran: Doc. 107; Qatar and Indonesia: Doc. 17.

[73] *Zhang* (n 66) 659. Significantly, the Vienna Convention on the Law of Treaties, which introduced the concept of peremptory norms, was still being negotiated when the NPT text was adopted. Vienna Convention on the law of Treaties (adopted May 23, 1969, entered into force 27 January 1980) 1155 UNTS 331 (VCLT).

[74] *MCIS/CNS* (n 38) I-6 (2009), *Zhang* (n 66); Cf. Eileen Denza, 'Non-proliferation of Nuclear Weapons: The European Union and Iran' (2005) 10 *European Foreign Affairs Review* 289, 309.

[75] Daniel H Joyner, *International Law and the Proliferation of Weapons of Mass Destruction* (Oxford, Oxford University Press, 2009) 46; Darryl Howlett and John Simpson, 'Nuclear Non- proliferation: How to Ensure an Effective Compliance Mechanism', in Burkard Schmitt (ed), Effective Non-Proliferation: the European Union and the 2005 NPT Review Conference, Chaillot Papers No 77 (European Union Institute for Security Studies 2005) 12, www.iss.europa.eu / index.php?id=143.

dual-use activities. The difference between peaceful and other uses lies exclusively in the intentions of the state undertaking these activities. UK Foreign Secretary Jack Straw has expressed the significance of this difference with respect to Iran:[76]

> …we wouldn't be engaged in this kind of very tough negotiation with the Iranians, nor would the IAEA board have passed the resolutions that it has passed, if there was not a perceived risk by the international community… that the civil nuclear programme, to which in principle Iran is entitled under the Non-Proliferation Treaty to pursue, is being used as a cover for a programme to build and develop a nuclear weapons programme, which it most surely is banned by the NPT from pursuing.

3.2 Article II: The Non-proliferation Commitment of NNWS

NPT Article II contains the key non-proliferation commitment of NNWS. It provides:

> Each non-nuclear-weapon State Party to the Treaty undertakes not to receive the transfer from any transferor whatsoever of nuclear weapons or other nuclear explosive devices or of control over such weapons or explosive devices directly, or indirectly; not to manufacture or otherwise acquire nuclear weapons or other nuclear explosive devices; and not to seek or receive any assistance in the manufacture of nuclear weapons or other nuclear explosive devices.

In line with the rules of treaty interpretation,[77] the term 'nuclear weapon or explosive devices' must be interpreted in accordance with its ordinary meaning in its context and in the light of the NPT's object and purpose. These clearly indicate that the prohibition pertains not only to obtaining a complete nuclear explosive device, but extends to obtaining its components. Otherwise, NNWS could develop a full fuel cycle and construct all the parts of a nuclear explosive, and then withdraw from the NPT before assembling the device.[78] However, it is not clear how far the prohibition extends. Some argue that as long as a state complies with its safeguards obligations and thus with Article III (discussed below in section 3.3), it cannot be regarded as violating Article II.[79] Others argue that Article III safeguards are essential but not sufficient guarantees of compliance with Article II.[80] The US, for example, holds that whether or not there has been a safeguards violation under Article III, it is also important to determine whether all the facts of a case tend to point toward an intent to manufacture or acquire nuclear weapons. Such facts could include seeking certain fuel cycle facilities of direct relevance to nuclear weapons, enrichment or reprocessing of uranium with no clear economic or peaceful justification, hiding clandestine facilities and procurements, committing safeguards violations and failing to cooperate with the IAEA to remedy them, and using denial and deception tactics to conceal nuclear-related activities.[81] The US relies

---

[76] Straw Meets US Secretary of State Condoleezza Rice (06/02/2005), 4 February 2005, www.fco.gov.uk/resources/en/news/2005/02/fco_not_040205_strawcondirice.

[77] VCLT (n 73) art 31. Although the NPT precedes the Vienna Convention, the provisions of the latter are generally regarded as customary law.

[78] Lawrence Scheinman, 'Article IV of the NPT: Background, Problems, Some Prospects' Weapons of Mass Destruction Commission Publication No 5 (2004) p 5; IAEA Director General Dr. Mohamed ElBaradei, 'Addressing Verification Challenges, Symposium on International Safeguards', 16-20 October 2006, Vienna, Austria (16 October 2006).

[79] Michael Spies, 'Iran and the Limits of the Nuclear Non-Proliferation Regime' (2006-2007) 22 *American University International Law Review* 401, 409, citing Mohamed Shaker, *The Nuclear Non-Proliferation Treaty: Origin and Implementation 1959-1979* (London, Oceana Publications, 1980) 251.

[80] *Howlett and Simpson* (n 75) 15.

[81] Doc. 137. The US has articulated this position already in 1968, *Joyner* (n 75), 16 footnote 41.

heavily on the notion that a state's apparent intentions underlying certain nuclear-related activities can be used to determine violations of Article II. This interpretation is not shared by all experts.[82]

Iran has in its possession a document on the production of uranium metal hemispheres, a process related to the fabrication of nuclear weapon components.[83] It has been argued that the possession of this document is, *stricto sensu*, a breach of NPT Article II.[84] However, ordinarily there are, at best, only indirect indications of Article II violations rather than hard evidence. Since the distinction between peaceful and non-peaceful nuclear development is for the most part a matter of purpose,[85] it is difficult to prove that a state is violating Article II. The only definite proof that a state's intention is to obtain nuclear weapons is when it declares so openly[86] or when it becomes known that the state already has nuclear weapons in its possession. Reaching this point is considered too dangerous.[87] The NPT regime therefore focuses on prevention of a state's ability to seek or develop nuclear weapons capabilities from its earliest stages through a mechanism designed to verify that there is no clandestine production or diversion of nuclear material to military purposes, rather than on enforcement of the ban on nuclear weapons proliferation by *ex post facto* measures and sanctions.

3.3 Article III.1: the IAEA Safeguards System

NPT Article III.1 stipulates:

> Each non-nuclear-weapon State Party to the Treaty undertakes to accept safeguards, as set forth in an agreement to be negotiated and concluded with the International Atomic Energy Agency in accordance with the Statute of the International Atomic Energy Agency and the Agency's safeguards system, for the exclusive purpose of verification of the fulfilment of its obligations assumed under this Treaty with a view to preventing diversion of nuclear energy from peaceful uses to nuclear weapons or other nuclear explosive devices. Procedures for the safeguards required by this Article shall be followed with respect to source or special fissionable material whether it is being produced, processed or used in any principal nuclear facility or is outside any such facility. The safeguards required by this Article shall be applied on all source or special fissionable material in all peaceful nuclear activities within the territory of such State, under its jurisdiction, or carried out under its control anywhere.

The NPT regime's principal tool for verifying the compliance by member states with their non-proliferation obligations is the safeguards system.[88] The political objective of the safeguard system is to provide credible assurances to the international community of the

---

[82] Paul K Kerr, 'Iran's Nuclear Program: Tehran's Compliance with International Obligations' Congressional Research Service Report for Congress (31 March 2009) 9.

[83] Doc. 32 operative para 3.

[84] Pierre Goldschmidt, 'Rule of Law, Politics and Nuclear Nonproliferation' Presentation to the Ecole Internationale de Droit Nucléaire, the University of Montpellier, France (7 September 2007), www.carnegieendowment.org/publications/index.cfm?fa=print&id=19564.

[85] James Crawford and Philippe Sands, 'Legal Aspects of a Nulcear Weapons Convention' (1998) 6 *African Yearbook of International Law* 153, 165.

[86] Eg the exceptional case of the Democratic People's Republic of Korea, which declared on 10 February 2005 that it has a nuclear weapon arsenal, www.nuclearfiles.org/menu/key-issues/nuclear-weapons/issues/proliferation/north-korea/foreign-affairs-ministry-statement.htm.

[87] US: Doc. 71 para 62.

[88] The safeguards system is not part of the NPT mechanism and is therefore available to non-member states.

peaceful nature of safeguarded nuclear activity.[89] Its technical objectives are the timely detection of diversion of significant quantities of nuclear material from peaceful nuclear activities to the manufacture of nuclear weapons or of other nuclear explosive devices or for purposes unknown, and deterrence of such diversion by the risk of the countermeasures that ultimately follow an early detection of a serious breach of the safeguards.[90]

NPT Article III requires each NNWS to conclude a safeguards agreement with the IAEA, 'with a view to preventing diversion of nuclear energy from peaceful uses to nuclear weapons'. According to Article 26 of the standard safeguards agreement, if the state party withdraws from the NPT, the safeguards agreement is automatically terminated. Most of the agreements under which the IAEA applies safeguards, including the Safeguards Agreement with Iran, which entered into force in 1974,[91] are of the comprehensive type.[92] Under such an agreement, the state undertakes to accept Agency safeguards on all source or special fissionable material in all peaceful nuclear activities within its territory, under its jurisdiction, or carried out under its control anywhere. The IAEA has a corresponding right and obligation to ensure that safeguards are applied on all such material for the exclusive purpose of verifying that such material is not diverted to nuclear weapons or other nuclear explosive devices.[93]

Safeguards agreements set out the states' and IAEA's basic rights and obligations with respect to the application of safeguards. Detailed implementation procedures are concluded in confidential 'subsidiary arrangements' between the IAEA Secretariat and the state, simultaneously with, or subsequent to, the conclusion of the safeguards agreement, and are tailored to the specific requirements of safeguarded facilities.

Under a comprehensive safeguards agreement, the state is obliged to provide the IAEA with an initial report on all nuclear material that must be declared under the terms of that agreement. From this report the Secretariat establishes an inventory of nuclear material for the state, which it maintains through subsequent reports and oversees through verification activities. In February 1992 the IAEA BOG confirmed that the Agency must verify not only that state declarations of nuclear material subject to safeguards are 'correct' (i.e. they accurately describe the types and quantities of the state's declared nuclear material holdings), but also that they are 'complete' (i.e. they include everything that should have been declared). The Agency verifies both the correctness and completeness of the initial inventory declaration, including through inspections. If discrepancies or anomalies arise during verification, the Secretariat acts to resolve them through consultations with the state or through additional inspections. If the situation is not resolved through follow-up action, the Secretariat recommends corrective actions. Where appropriate, the Secretariat assesses the qualitative significance of the failure, to determine whether there is any indication of diversion of declared nuclear material or misuse of declared facilities. Where there is no indication of diversion, the conclusion is drawn that the declared nuclear material for the state in question remained in peaceful use. The Secretariat reports its safeguards conclusions in a Safeguards Implementation Report (SIR) to the IAEA BOG, including any cases of non-compliance.[94]

---

[89] Mohamed ElBaradei, Edwin Nwogugu and John Rames, 'International law and nuclear energy: Overview of the legal framework' 3/1995 *IAEA Bulletin* 16, 22.

[90] Doc. 4 para 28.

[91] Doc. 4.

[92] As of 9 July 2009, all but 26 NPT member states have comprehensive safeguards agreements in force, www.iaea.org/Publications/Factsheets/English/nptstatus_overview.html.

[93] Doc. 4 paras 1, 2.

[94] IAEA, 'The Safeguards System of the International Atomic Energy Agency' (2003).

The IAEA BOG may call on a state to take urgent action if it decides, pursuant to Article 18 of the Safeguards Agreement, that such action is essential and urgent in order to ensure verification of non-diversion. Urgent action may include special inspections, not only in declared nuclear sites but also in undeclared sites that may contain nuclear material.[95] The BOG cannot force the inspection on a state but the refusal itself may give rise to suspicion that the state has something to hide.

The discovery in 1991 of Iraq's clandestine nuclear weapons programme highlighted the shortcomings of safeguards mechanisms, in particular the focus on declared nuclear material and safeguards conclusions drawn at the facility – rather than state-level. This realization led to the adoption by the IAEA BOG of a model protocol additional to agreements between states and the IAEA for the application of safeguards (additional protocol).[96] As of July 2009, 91 states have additional protocols in force.[97] The implementation of an additional protocol strengthens the Agency's ability to detect undeclared nuclear material and activities, by obliging a state to provide the Agency with broader information and access rights. Thus, both timely detection of diversion and deterrence are pursued for all states with comprehensive safeguards agreements, but it is only for states with both comprehensive safeguards agreements and additional protocols in force that the Secretariat can provide credible assurance of both non-diversion of declared nuclear material from peaceful activities, and the absence of undeclared nuclear material and activities for a state as a whole. For a state with a comprehensive safeguards agreement but no additional protocol, the conclusion drawn relates only to no indication of diversion of declared nuclear material, since the Secretariat does not have a sufficient basis on which to draw a conclusion related to the absence of undeclared nuclear material or activities for the state as a whole.

Iran signed the Additional Protocol in December 2003 and began to implement it pending its ratification. However, following the IAEA BOG resolution of September 2005 finding Iran in non-compliance,[98] Iran informed the IAEA that it will cease to implement the Additional Protocol. In February 2006 Iran repeated this notice, explaining that this change was pursuant to an Iranian bill passed in 2005, which required cessation of implementation if the Iranian dossier is referred to the Security Council.[99]

NPT Article III.1 stipulates that 'Procedures for the safeguards required by this Article shall be followed with respect to source or special fissionable material'. It also provides that '[t]he safeguards required by this Article shall be applied on all source or special fissionable material...'. These phrases have been interpreted by some commentators as linking compliance with the safeguards agreement to compliance with the NPT itself. According to this reading, a violation of an applicable safeguards agreement is by implication a violation of NPT Article III. While the IAEA's mandate does not include verification of compliance with the NPT but only with IAEA safeguards agreements, when it does find a case of non-compliance with a safeguards agreement, *ipso facto* there is also an implied of violation of the NPT.[100] A different reading of this provision

[95] IAEA Press Release 92/12 (26 February 1992) (reporting an IAEA BOG decision); Lawrence Scheinman, 'the Role of Muitilateral Regimes in Non-Proliferation' (1992) 2 *Transnational Law and Contemporary Problems* 569, 578; *Asculai* (n 59) 22.

[96] Doc. 5.

[97] www.iaea.org/OurWork/SV/Safeguards/sg_protocol.html.

[98] Doc. 30.

[99] Doc. 84 para 149.

[100] Thomas B Cochran, 'Adequacy of IAEA's Safeguards for Achieving Timely Detection' in *Sokolski* (n 67) 121-122; *Fischer* (n 38) 294.

is that it delineates the scope of the potential safeguards agreement rather than creates an independent obligation to comply with the terms of that agreement.

3.4 Article III.2: Export Controls

NPT Article III.2 contains the undertaking of states parties not to provide NNWS with fissionable material and equipment for processing such material unless those are under IAEA safeguards. It provides:

> Each State Party to the Treaty undertakes not to provide: (a) source or special fissionable material, or (b) equipment or material especially designed or prepared for the processing, use or production of special fissionable material, to any non-nuclear-weapon State for peaceful purposes, unless the source or special fissionable material shall be subject to the safeguards required by this Article.

In order to give effect to this provision, various groups of countries have agreed voluntarily to restrict the export of dual-use sensitive materials and technologies, among them the Zangger Committee[101] and the Nuclear Suppliers Group (NSG).[102] These groups formulated non-binding export control guidelines under which recipient states must meet certain security standards to be eligible to participate in nuclear trade. The guidelines help prevent the export of items that would assist other states in producing nuclear weapons. The guidelines thereby enhance compliance of the trading states with legal non-proliferation obligations.[103] The guidelines are implemented by each participating government in accordance with its domestic laws and practices.

The compatibility of the export controls with the provisions of the NPT has been a matter of debate. On the one hand, although export control regimes are not directly stipulated by the Treaty, they give effect to the prohibition in Article III.2 on transferring to NNWS fissionable material or technologies that are not covered by safeguards. Thus, at the 2005 NPT Review Conference, attempts were made to tie export controls into the broader issue of nuclear proliferation and to strengthen them. On the other hand, several developing nations, led, *inter alia*, by Iran, criticise export control regimes as contrary to the inalienable right to the peaceful use of nuclear energy under NPT Article IV. These countries object to the discriminatory nature of these regimes which place the non-proliferation objective above that of promoting international co-operation in the peaceful use of nuclear energy, and claim that these regimes harm their economic development.[104]

---

[101] The Zangger Committee was formed in 1971 to draft a 'trigger list' of special fissionable materials and equipment or materials especially designed or prepared for the processing, use, or production of special fissionable materials, INFCIRC/209/Rev.2 (9 March 2000). Its 37 members include 22 EU member states, the US, Russia, China, South Africa, Republic of Korea, and others, www.zanggercommittee.org/Zangger/Members/default.htm.

[102] The NSG is a voluntary group created in 1975 of supplier countries. It has designed and implemented two guidelines for nuclear exports and nuclear related exports, including dual-use items, INFCIRC/254/Rev.8/Part 1 (20 March 2006); INFCIRC/254/Rev.7/Part 2 (20 March 2006). Its 44 member states include 18 EU member states (excluding Germany and France), the US, Russia, Ukraine, Belarus, South Africa, Republic of Korea and others, www.nuclearsuppliersgroup.org/Leng/03-member.htm. A third, related group is the Wassenaar Arrangement, which addresses conventional and dual-use goods and technologies. It was was formed in 1995 and comprises 40 states, including all EU member states except Cyprus, and also the US, Russia, Ukraine, South Africa and the Republic of Korea. For its control lists see www.wassenaar.org/index.html.

[103] Doc. 137.

[104] Doc. 95; Doc. 96.

Moreover, since not all NPT members are parties to these regimes, the effectiveness of the regimes in halting proliferation is limited.[105]

3.5 Compliance with the NPT

The NPT lacks a mechanism for overseeing its implementation. The IAEA's treaty-monitoring role is limited to the safeguards agreement (although its findings may imply a violation of NPT Article III, or, in certain circumstances, also of NPT Article II). Monitoring of NPT compliance therefore falls to state parties, acting through the periodic review conferences. However, in 1991 the Security Council determined that Iraq had acted in violation of its obligations under the NPT and that Iraq's breach of the Treaty constituted a threat to peace and international security.[106] In a sense the Council thus became the guardian of the Treaty, through its general powers under Chapter VII.[107]

The 1995 NPT Review and Extension Conference and the 2000 NPT Review Conference attempted to expand the compliance mechanism of the NPT by linking a violation of NPT Article III, possibly including a violation by failure to comply with the safeguards agreement,[108] with the right under NPT Article IV. Both documents emphasise[109]

> the inalienable right of all the parties to the Treaty to develop research, production and use of nuclear energy for peaceful purposes without discrimination and in conformity with articles I, II as well as III of the Treaty.

Various countries have endorsed this non-binding formulation, under which the right to peaceful development of nuclear energy is contingent upon compliance not only with NPT Articles I and II but also with the safeguards agreement.[110] This limitation goes beyond the letter of the NPT, which specifically provides that *nothing* in the treaty shall be interpreted as limiting the right under Article IV except Articles I and II. Although statements have been made in the context of Iran's nuclear programme, they did not go so far as to expressly claim that Iran had violated either Article II or III, and thus do not call to deny Iran its Article IV rights. The UK has also suggested that violation of Article III may lead to forfeiture of Article IV rights, but has linked the two articles through Article II:[111]

> ... states which fail to comply with their safeguards obligations inevitably lose the confidence of the international community. The bargain which is at the heart of the Treaty is then called

---

[105] On the export control regimes see Daniel H Joyner (ed), *Non-Proliferation Export Controls* (Burlington, Ashgate, 2006); Harald Müller, 'National and International Export Control Systems and Supplier States' Commitments under the NPT' (Programme for Promoting Nuclear Non-Proliferation 8 Issue Review, September 2006).

[106] Security Council Resolution 707(1991) (15 August 1992) operative para 2.

[107] *Fischer* (n 38) 281-282. The Security Council never adopted a resolution on North Korea's violation of the NPT, partly because North Korea withdrew from the NPT in 2003, before it openly admitted to having engaged in a weapons program.

[108] text to n 100.

[109] Decision 2: Principles and Objectives for Nuclear Non-Proliferation and Disarmament Para 14, NPT/CONF.1995/32 (Part I) p. 11, almost identical wording in 2000 Review Conference of the Parties to the Treaty on the Non-Proliferation of Nuclear Weapons, Final Document, NPT/CONF.2000/28 (Parts I and II) 8 para 2 disarmament.un.org/library.nsf; see also Fourteenth Summit Conference of the Heads of State or Government of the Non-Aligned Movement, Final Document, NAM 2006/Doc.1/Rev.3 (September, 16, 2006) para 95.

[110] Eg US: Doc. 63, para 47; France: Doc. 17; Doc. 59 para 1; Doc. 62 para 34; Canada: Doc. 72, para 46; South Africa: Doc. 17; Costa Rica: Doc. 18.

[111] UK Foreign Secretary Jack Straw, 'Countering the Proliferation of Weapons of Mass Destruction', Written Ministerial Statement (25 February 2004), www.fco.gov.uk/resources/en/news/2004/02/fco_nst_250204_ counterprolifwmd.

into question. We should consider whether such states should not forfeit the right to develop the nuclear fuel cycle, particularly the enrichment and reprocessing capabilities which are of such proliferation sensitivity.

Other states continue to emphasise that the right under Article IV is subject only to compliance with Articles I and II.[112]

Loss of Article IV.2 benefits might not be a sufficient incentive for a deviant state to return to compliance with Article II. General treaty law offers other remedies, such as termination and suspension. Those also offer little incentive to a deviant state. Be that as it may, it is worth recalling that the right to develop nuclear technology does not emanate from the NPT. A state which violates Articles I and II might lose international trust, might not enjoy the benefits of Article IV.2, but its right to develop nuclear technology remains intact.[113]

4. Referral of Iran's Dossier to the Security Council

The IAEA statute and the safeguards agreement allow the IAEA BOG to refer the case of a state to the Security Council under any one of three sets of circumstances, which are legally distinct but may be factually linked: (a) a state's non-compliance with the safeguards agreement (IAEA Statute Article XII.C), (b) a matter which falls within the competence of the Security Council, i.e. the maintenance of international peace and security (IAEA Statute Article III.B.4), or (c) IAEA inability to verify non-diversion (safeguards agreement Article 19). The BOG's referral of Iran's dossier to the Security Council in 2006 relied on the first two grounds.[114]

4.1 Non-compliance under IAEA Statute Article XII.C

The first ground for the IAEA BOG's referral of Iran's dossier to the Security Council was that Iran's 'many failures and breaches of its obligation to comply with its NPT Safeguards Agreement, as detailed in GOV/2003/75 [of November 2003], constitute non compliance in the context of Article XII.C of the Agency's Statute'.[115]

Iran claims that the determination that it was non-compliant, and consequently the referral of its dossier to the Security Council, were both procedurally and substantively improper. First, some of the activities which had not been declared had not been subject to a duty of declaration.[116] Second, with respect to other activities, Iran claims that its omission to report was inadvertent and insignificant.[117] Both of Iran's claims refer mostly to design information, but do not address the acquisition of materials and experimentation. Iran also argues that it did not meet its safeguards obligations as a consequence of violations of the NPT by other state parties. One alleged violation is the obstruction of its endeavours through export control regimes and unilateral US measures, contrary to its right under NPT Article IV. The other alleged violation is the failure of the NWS to disarm in accordance with NPT Article VI. These arguments are considered below.

[112] Eg Norway: Doc. 85 para 33.

[113] But interestingly see Iran's assertion that the UN Charter does not require states to give up their 'basic rights emanating from treaties', Doc. 17.

[114] Doc. 30; Doc. 32.

[115] Doc. 30 operative para 1; 32 preambular para (g). See also Doc. 22-Doc. 24; Doc. 28; Doc. 30.

4.1.1 The Procedure for Determining Non-compliance

Iran argues that it 'has been referred to the UNSC in contravention of the provision of the Statute of the IAEA and the NPT' because 'the inspectors have not reached or concluded any non-compliance'.[118] Similar claims have been made by Cuba and Venezuela, who argue that only the IAEA may determine non-compliance.[119]

According to Article XII.C of the IAEA Statute, reporting a state to the Security Council for non-compliance with its safeguards undertakings is a process comprising numerous steps. First, the inspectors have the responsibility to determine whether there is compliance with the safeguards agreement. They report any non-compliance to the IAEA DG, who thereupon transmits the report to the IAEA BOG. The Board calls upon the state in question 'to remedy forthwith any non-compliance which *it (the IAEA BOG) finds* to have occurred' (emphasis added). The Board then reports the non-compliance to all members and to the UN Security Council and General Assembly.

Thus, under Article XII.C the determination of non-compliance begins with the inspectors, but is ultimately in the hands of the IAEA BOG.[120] Contrary to Iran's claim, the IAEA DG has in fact reported to the BOG that Iran was non-compliant, when he stated that Iran's conduct resulted in 'breaches of its obligation to comply' with the provisions of the Safeguards Agreement,[121] a term which within the IAEA Secretariat is synonymous with 'non-compliance'.[122]

4.1.2 What Constitutes Non-compliance

Iran and other countries claim that a determination of non-compliance requires a positive finding of diversion towards military purposes, and that there has been no such finding.[123] Both Iran and Venezuela inaccurately[124] claim that the IAEA had concluded that no diversion had taken place.[125] The Non-Aligned Movement (NAM) specifically argues that a failure to declare does not amount to non-compliance.[126] Libya argues that referral cannot be based on 'doubts'.[127]

These arguments ignore the fact that the safeguards regime is a preventive mechanism, not one of *ex post facto* enforcement and sanctions. To require a positive finding of diversion in order to trigger the Article XII.C mechanism would be to render Article XII.C largely superfluous, as such a finding might indicate that a violation of NPT Article II has already occurred, while compliance monitoring aims to prevent such an eventuality.

---

[116] Doc. 77 para 66; Doc. 109. Iran suggests that it did not report feeding UF_6 into the UCF because this was an obvious use of the facility, Doc. 59 para 51.

[117] Doc. 66 para 44.

[118] Doc. 116.

[119] Doc. 63 para 29; Doc. 78 para 17.

[120] Doc. 64 para 63; *Goldschmidt* (n 84).

[121] Doc. 35 para 50; Doc. 39 para 107; Doc. 40 para 42.

[122] *Goldschmidt* (n 10) 146. The IAEA BOG's Legal Advisor has indicated that 'non-compliance' as used in the IAEA Statute has only a generic meaning and may vary to fit the circumstances, Statement by the Legal Adviser, IAEA BOG March 2009, para 10, www.armscontrolwonk.com/file_download/162/Legal_Adviser_Iran.pdf.

[123] Iran: Doc. 83 para 44; Doc. 119 section D; Venezuela: Doc. 78 para 17; Doc. 82 para 125.

[124] See clarification by the IAEA DG, Doc. 64 para 78, that 'no finding of diversion' is not synonymous with 'a finding of no diversion'.

[125] Doc. 82 para 125.

[126] Doc. 58 para 94.

[127] Doc. 84.

Moreover, the IAEA's 2001 Glossary provides that non-compliance is any 'violation by a state of its safeguards agreement with the IAEA'. Examples of non-compliance include the 'diversion of nuclear material from declared nuclear activities, or the failure to declare nuclear material required to be placed under safeguards'; but also 'violation of the agreed recording and reporting system, obstruction of the activities of IAEA inspectors, interference with the operation of safeguards equipment, or prevention of the IAEA from carrying out its verification activities'. The Glossary specifically notes that diversion of nuclear material is only 'a particular case of non-compliance'.[128] The Glossary is not a binding instrument but it is significant in guiding state practice.[129]

Under Article XII.C, every case of non-compliance *shall* be referred to the Security Council.[130] Yet since not every discrepancy in reporting merits the attention of the Security Council, the determination of non-compliance by the IAEA BOG has been interpreted as a matter of discretion.[131] It is the BOG's role to determine if what is at issue is a small technical reporting mistake or a meaningful omission that has actual or potential proliferation significance.[132] Thus, it is not failure to declare *per se* that triggers the obligation to notify the Security Council of non-compliance, but the absence of declaration when in view of the surrounding circumstances, a military purpose is plausible.[133]

The purpose accompanying a technical failure is an elusive parameter as it depends on intent. The IAEA has no legal basis on which to draw conclusions about intent,[134] the standard safeguards agreement focusing exclusively on 'the timely detection of diversion of significant quantities of nuclear material'.[135] The difficulties of proving intent are borne out by the experience with Iran. Iran has made available to the IAEA a '15-page document', which describes how uranium can be cast into hemispheres, a process that is unambiguously associated with the manufacture of nuclear weapons.[136] Yet even then the proof as to Iran's intentions was not in the proverbial pudding, since Iran claimed in its defense that the document was given to it, unsolicited, by the Pakistan-based AQ Khan network.[137]

Alongside intent, there are other parameters for assessing whether a failure amounts to non-compliance.[138] These may include the quantity and strategic significance of the nuclear material involved; the capability of a state's undeclared programme to manufacture fissile material in militarily significant quantities; the intensity of efforts to develop fuel-cycle technology; the involvement of the military and experiments with potential relevance to

[128] IAEA Safeguards Glossary (2001) 13-14.

[129] Eg Canada: Doc. 66 para 31.

[130] John Bolton, Keynote speech at the AEI conference 'The International Atomic Energy Agency: The World's Enforcer or Paper Tiger?' (28 September 2004), www.aei.org/event/911; Russia: Doc. 71 para 84; US: Doc. 72 para 45. Goldschmidt argues that referral to the Security Council should be automatic upon finding of non-compliance, see Pierre Goldschmidt, 'IAEA Safeguards: Dealing Preventively with Non-Compliance' (12 July 2008) 3, www.carnegieendowment.org/files/Goldschmidt_Dealing_Preventively_7-12-08.pdf. *Squassoni* (n 14) 292.

[131] Statement by the IAEA BOG Legal Advisor (n 122) para 10. But see NAM arguing that the determination of non-compliance should be only scientific, and made by the IAEA only, Doc. 82 para 65.

[132] *Goldschmidt* (n 10) 147, John Carlson, 'Defining Noncompliance: NPT Safeguards Agreements' 8 May 2009, www.armscontrol.org/act/2009_5/Carlson.

[133] *Goldschmidt* (n 84); Andrew J Grotto, 'Iran, the IAEA and the UN' ASIL Insight (November 2004), www.asil.org/insights/2004/10/insight041105.htm; Australia: Doc. 62 para 57.

[134] IAEA DG: Doc. 94 para 91.

[135] Doc. 4 art 28. An exception may exist when the IAEA investigates weaponisation activities, James M Acton, 'The Problem with Nuclear Mind Reading' (2009) 51 *Survival* 119, 123.

[136] Doc. 41 para 6.

[137] Doc. 82 para 16.

[138] For a contrary position see Iran: Doc. 72 para 100. For a discussion of the effectiveness of indicia of diversion to military purposes see Annette Schaper, 'Implementing Safeguards in Countries under Suspicion' in Erwin Häckel and Gotthard Stein (eds), *Tightening the Reins* (Springer 2000) 151.

weaponization; active attempts to conceal non-compliance; whether the failure is on-going and if not, the circumstances of its termination;[139] the extent of cooperation with the IAEA; and compliance with IAEA BOG or Security Council resolutions.[140] Some of these criteria undoubtedly correlate with intent, but unlike intent they can be measured objectively by the IAEA within its current mandate, and are in fact already routinely assessed by the Agency. The presence of these indicators may lead to different responses to failures that are similar in terms of amounts of material and processes.[141]

In light of these indicators, the motive or purpose of Iran's non-compliance is regarded as suspect because of the pattern of concealment;[142] the perceived technical and economic inutility of the Iranian programme;[143] the potential involvement of the military;[144] the potential military dimensions as evidenced in the documents;[145] Iran's lackluster record of cooperation with the IAEA once its activities had been revealed;[146] its bellicose attitude towards Israel and hostility towards other states in the Middle East; and its support of organisations that practice terrorism.[147]

Yet Iran and others claim that Iran's case is no graver than that of other countries' cases in which discrepancies have been found, and which have not been referred to the Security Council.[148] Iran is correct that there have been a few instances of severe non-compliance which have not led to Security Council action, most notoriously the cases of Libya and South Korea. In late 2003 Libya admitted to having engaged in a programme to manufacture nuclear weapons. It had violated not only the Safeguards Agreement but also Article II of the NPT. Its nuclear weapons pursuit was exacerbated by its sponsorship of international terrorism. Yet its case was referred to the Security Council 'for information purposes only'.[149] The reason given for the mildness of this rebuke was that by the time the international community had learned the full details of its efforts, Libya was already on the road to eliminating its WMD programmes.[150] South Korea's case came to light in

---

[139] Iran argues that non-compliance may only be referred to the Security Council if it is on-going. In view of the wide definition of non-compliance, there seems to be no reason to limit the power of referral in this way. Iran: Doc. 71 para 142; US: Doc. 64 para 67; Australia: Doc. 76 para 75. Compare with BOG Resolution GOV/2004/18 (10 March 2004) operative para 4, which 'finds under Article XII.C of the Statute, that the past failures to meet the requirements of the relevant Safeguards Agreement (INFCIRC/282), identified by the Director General constituted non-compliance…'.

[140] Australia: Doc. 65 para 45; Korea: Doc. 66 para 12; *Acton* (n 135) 130-131; *Carlson* (n 132).

[141] Christopher A Ford, 'Compliance Assessment and Compliance Enforcement: the Challenge of Nuclear Noncompliance' (2006) 12 *ILSA Journal of International and Comparative Law* 583, 587-588. Eg Canada, after arguing that Iran was in non-compliance, was willing to reconsider its position in light of Iran's cooperation with the IAEA, Doc. 65 para 4; *Carlson* (n 132); Harald Müller, 'WMD Crisis: Law Instead of Lawless Self-Help', Weapons of Mass Destruction Commission Publication No 37 (August 2005) 5.

[142] US: Doc. 64 paras 57-58; 60; Doc. 70 paras 63-64; Canada: Doc. 58 para 111; Doc. 62 para 59; Australia: Doc. 59 para 37; Doc. 62 para 59.

[143] US: Doc. 59 para 14; Doc. 64 para 65; Doc. 69 para 77; Canada: Doc. 76 para 81; EU: Doc. 76 para 55; EU3: Doc. 127. *Kerr* (n 43) 14.

[144] Doc. 32 operative para 1.

[145] Doc. 32 preambular paras (i), (j), operative para 3.

[146] *Grotto* (n 133). *Kerr* (n 43) 14

[147] G8: Doc. 152; US: Doc. 17; George Perkovich and James Acton, 'Abolishing Nuclear Weapons' Adelphi Paper 396 in George Perkovich and James Acton (eds), *Abolishing Nuclear Weapons: A Debate* (Washington DC, Carnegie Endowment for Peace, 2009) 44.

[148] Iran: Doc. 58 para 101; NAM: Doc Doc. 58 para 94; Cuba: Doc. 59 para 6. The IAEA BOG has determined on four prior occasions that a State was in non-compliance with its NPT Safeguards Agreement: Iraq (1991), Romania (1992), DPRK (1993) and Libya (2004). Only the cases of Iraq and DPRK were referred to the Security Council for further action.

[149] IAEA BOG, 'Implementation of the NPT Safeguards Agreement of the Socialist People's Libyan Arab Jamahiriya' (10 March 2004) GOV/2004/18.

[150] UK: Doc. 68 para 63; *Ford* (n 141) 588.

2004, when IAEA inspectors discovered that it had secretly conducted reprocessing and enrichment experiments at various times during the previous 22 years, during which it had enriched uranium to 77%. This violation of safeguards obligations was never referred to the Security Council. The justifications given for this inaction included the fact that South Korea had terminated its activities voluntarily before non-compliance was revealed and the uncertainty whether the activities were concealed intentionally.[151]

4.1.3 Iran's Exculpatory Arguments

The willingness to consider mitigating circumstances for Libya and South Korea's non-compliance in a wider context invites a similar approach with regard to Iran. It is in this context that Iran's justification of the clandestine nature of its activities, namely the violations of the NPT by other countries, becomes relevant, as it offers an innocuous and peaceful explanation to an otherwise-suspect conduct. As noted earlier, Iran argues that it has been subject to illegal restrictions imposed upon it by export control regimes, contrary to its right under NPT Article IV.[152] It also argues that by failing to disarm, the NWS violate their obligation under NPT Article VI,[153] although it has not explicitly claimed that this justified its own clandestine programme. Both assertions are controversial. First, it is not clear whether Article IV creates a binding obligation on NWS to assist NNWS to acquire peaceful nuclear capabilities.[154] It is also not clear that Article VI sets an obligation on states to achieve a result of disarmament, rather than an obligation of conduct.[155] The ICJ has said in its advisory opinion on the legality of the use of nuclear weapons that '[t]he legal import of that obligation [Article VI] goes beyond that of a mere obligation of conduct; the obligation involved here is an obligation to achieve a precise result – nuclear disarmament in all its aspects – by adopting a particular course of conduct, namely, the pursuit of negotiations on the matter in good faith'.[156] This opinion has nonetheless been challenged by those who hold that the obligation in Article VI extends only to negotiating in good faith.[157] Yet another interpretation of Article VI emphasises the political commitment in Article VI, as elaborated in the Thirteen Steps,[158] but despite the concretization of the obligation to act towards disarmament, it is unclear whether what was agreed to was a series of commitments to act or a number of yardsticks to measure progress towards disarmament.[159]

---

[151] *Acton* (n 135) 132-134.

[152] Doc. 63; Doc. 98 para 8; Doc. 64 para 93; Doc. 66 para 45; Doc. 98; Doc. 102; Doc. 106; Doc. 107; Doc. 110.

[153] Doc. 97; Doc. 99.

[154] Joyner argues that Article IV creates a binding obligation, in exchange for the NNWS's obligation under Article II, Joyner (n 75) 46-49. Greig argues to the contrary. D W Greig, 'The Interpretation of Treaties and Article IV.2 of the Nuclear Non-Proliferation Treaty' (1974-1975) *Australian Yearbook of International Law* 77. Similarly see Harald Müller, 'Peaceful uses of Nuclear Energy and the Stability of the Non-Proliferation Regime' in *Schmitt* (n 75) 43, 47.

[155] *Crawford and Sands* (n 85) 161-162.

[156] *Legality of the Threat or Use of Nuclear Weapons* (Advisory Opinion) [1996] ICJ Rep 226 para 99.

[157] Christopher A Ford, 'Debating Disarrmament: Interpreting Article VI of the treaty on the Non-Proliferaiton of Nuclear Weapons' (2007) 14 *Nonporliferation Review* 401. For the US position see 'Deputy Legal Adviser Bettauer's address before Lawyer's Committee on Nuclear Policy re U.S. compliance with nuclear policy' (10 October 2006) in Sally J Cummins, *Digest of United States Practice in International Law 2006* (Oxford University Press and International Law Institute, 2008) 1255, 1257-1260.

[158] 2000 Review Conference of the Parties to the Treaty on the Non-Proliferation of Nuclear Weapons, Final Document, NPT/CONF.2000/28 (Parts I and II) para 15.

[159] Thomas Graham Jr 'The Origin and Interpretation of Article VI' (2008) 15 *Nonproliferation Review* 7, but also John Simpson, 'The Future of the NPT' in Nathan E Busch and Daniel H Joyner (eds), *Combating Weapons of Mass Destruction* (University of Georgia Press 2009) 45, 65.

Assuming for present purposes that Article IV has been violated by states capable of but unwilling to engage in an Article IV exchange with Iran, and that Article VI has been violated by the NWS, Iran has not clarified what it considers to be the legal implications of these breaches on its own obligations: do they exempt it from the obligation to declare its activities as a matter of treaty law, preclude the wrongfulness of its own failure under the law of state responsibility, or constitute mitigating circumstances with regard to its own transgression within the framework of non-compliance procedures.[160]

The Law of Treaties:

Under the Vienna Convention on the Law of Treaties, a material breach of a multilateral treaty by one party entails a party specially affected by the breach to suspend the operation of the treaty in whole or in part in the relations between itself and the defaulting state.[161] Since Articles IV and VI form part of the political 'grand bargain' underlying the NPT, their violation can be regarded as material breaches, i.e. breaches of provisions that are essential to the accomplishment of the object or purpose of the treaty.[162] Iran can be said to be 'specially affected' by the alleged breach of Article IV because the refusal to engage with it in the exchange envisaged in Article VI and the pressure by the US on other states not to engage with Iran has a direct effect on Iran. Article 60(2)(b) therefore permits it to suspend or terminate its treaty relations with the breaching states.

Iran is not 'specially affected' by the alleged breach of Article VI, but the Vienna Convention also provides that 'any party other than the defaulting state [is entitled] to invoke the breach as a ground for suspending the operation of the treaty in whole or in part with respect to itself if the treaty is of such a character that a material breach of its provisions by one party radically changes the position of every party with respect to the further performance of its obligations under the treaty'.[163] This raises the question of the relationship between the various obligations under the NPT and Safeguards Agreement.

The obligations in disarmament treaties are ordinarily regarded as interdependent, in a manner which renders each country an injured state if the other fails to comply with its obligations.[164] To the extent that Article VI obligates NWS to disarm, failure to do so may therefore entitle every other party to invoke the breach as ground for suspension, at least the NNWS, which undertook to refrain from pursuing nuclear weapons on the assumption that the world was moving towards total disarmament. However, given the unique asymmetry in the structure of the NPT regime as a disarmament treaty, it is doubtful whether the obligations of the NWS under Article VI and the obligations of the NNWS under Article III (the adherence to with which may be considered affected by non-compliance with the Safeguards Agreement), should be regarded as legally (rather than politically) interdependent.[165]

Thus, the law of treaties may permit Iran to suspend or terminate its treaty relations with the defaulting parties (in the case of an Article IV violation) or with all parties (in the case of an Article VI violation). If it does so, the Safeguards Agreement between Iran

---

[160] Doc. 75 para 44.
[161] VCLT (n 73) art 60(2)(b).
[162] VCLT (n 73) art 60(3).
[163] VCLT (n 73) art 60(2)(c).
[164] ILC 'Report of the International Law Commission on the work of its eighteenth session' (4 May-19 July 1966), UN Doc A/6309/Rev.1 commentary to art 57 [later adopted as Article 60] para 8.
[165] See also *Weapons of Mass Destruction Commission* (n 68) 48, and Cf *Joyner* (n 75) 66-67.

and the IAEA would also be suspended or terminated.[166] However, although Iran has occasionally insinuated that it might withdraw from the NPT,[167] it has never declared that it was suspending the Treaty's application with respect to a specific breaching party or with respect to itself. Unless it does so, it remains bound by the NPT and by the Safeguards Agreement.

A different line of argument is that under the principle *inadimplenti non est adimplendum*, an injured state may not only suspend or terminate a treaty in the case of non-performance by another party, but also engage in non-compliance with its obligations deriving from the treaty.[168] Indeed, Iran merely posits that other states' violations of the NPT exempt itself from compliance.[169] This position is held, more on political than on legal grounds, by the majority of NAM states, which generally treat non-compliance as a procedural matter. Since acceptance of safeguards is contingent upon receipt of benefits, it is only a short step to perceive it reasonable for a state to withhold compliance with safeguards if the expected benefits are withheld. Since non-compliance is both justified and merely a procedural matter, coming back into compliance is a simple matter of completing the appropriate reports and allowing the necessary inspections. Past inaccuracies or lack of information do not reflect on the confidence in future performance. In contrast, westerns states consider safeguards obligations as contingent only upon accession to the NPT and conclusion of an agreement with the IAEA. Compliance is not dependent on any action on the part of others or on the receipt of any benefits. Past conduct, in this case, creates a confidence deficit that can only be addressed by extraordinary levels of cooperation and transparency.[170] The alleged violation by the NWS of Article VI hardly provides the necessary legitimisation for Iran: if failure of the NWS to disarm were seen as justifying non-compliance, the entire NPT regime would fail, as no state (at least not NNWS) would be obligated by its own undertakings. As for the violation of Article IV, the context for the refusal to cooperate with Iran must also be taken into consideration. In essence, the refusal to assist Iran in its peaceful pursuit of nuclear energy is based on fear that this pursuit is a cover for a nuclear

---

[166] Doc. 4 art 26. For an analysis of this question, sparked by the withdrawal of North Korea from the NPT, see Antonio F Perez, 'Survival of Rights under the Nuclear Non-Proliferation Treaty: Withdrawal and the Continuing Right of the International Atomic Energy Agency Safeguards ' (1993-1994) 34 *Virginia Journal of International Law* 749.

[167] Doc. 95 para 19. It has also insinuated that it might respond this way to the referral of its dossier to the Security Council, see Doc. 61 para 89.

[168] Elisabeth Zoller, *Peacetime Unilateral Remedies: An Analysis of Countermeasures* (New York, Transnational Publishers, 1984) 15, 28. The principle has been invoked in the context of international responsibility, rather than of substantive obligations: *Diversion of Water from the Meuse* (Merits) PCIJ Series A/B, No 70, Dissenting opinion of Judge Anzilotti, 50. But see ILC 'Fourth Report on the Law of treaties of Special Rapporteur Fitzmaurice', UN Doc A/CN.4/120, 43-47, rejecting the notion of non-performance based on treaty law falling short of suspension or termination. Even under this controversial view, non-compliance is limited to the same treaty and to the same parties. ILC 'Third report on State responsibility by Mr. Gaetano Arangio-Ruiz, Special Rapporteur' UN Doc A/CN.4/440 and Add.1 13 para 33. Thus, Iran might be permitted not to comply with its obligations under the NPT as against the NWS and the member states of the export regimes. But it would not be exempt from compliance as against other parties, nor as against the IAEA under the Safeguards Agreement. However, since the Safeguards Agreement exists to support the NPT, exemption from compliance with the NPT would presumably mean exemption from compliance with the Safeguards Agreement. For an opposing view see D W Greig, 'Reciprocity, Proportionality and the Law of Treaties', (1993-1994) 34 *Virginia Journal of International Law* 295.

[169] Joyner and Garvey contend that the violation by the NWS does entitle Iran not to perform its own obligations. Joyner suggests that as a matter of treaty law, Article II has become 'void'. Neither author provides a clear explanation for his position. *Joyner* (n 75) 10-11; Jack I Garvey, 'A New Architecture for the Non-Proliferation of Nuclear Weapons' (2008) 12 *Journal of Conflict and Security Law* 339, 348.

[170] Russell Leslie, 'The Good Faith Assumption: Different Paradigmatic Approaches to Nonproliferation Issues' (2008) 15 *Nonproliferation Review* 479, 485-486.

weapons programme or, at best, a jumping board towards such a programme should Iran choose to go that way at a later stage.

Preclusion of Wrongfulness Analogies:

Reliance on a claim of breach of the NPT by other states as circumstances precluding the wrongfulness of Iran's conduct under the laws of state responsibility raises different issues. It is questionable whether such preclusion is pertinent to a finding of non-compliance under Article XII.C. The referral from the IAEA to the Security Council is not an invocation of international responsibility for failure to comply with treaty provisions, but an implementation of an internal treaty mechanism which aims to remove a proliferation problem. It is a preventive rather than an enforcement tool. Terminological support for this interpretation lies in the fact that Article XII.C refers to 'non-compliance' rather than to 'violation' of the safeguards agreements. Another factor is the fact that Article XII.C concerns the authority of the IAEA BOG rather than the rights and obligations of the state concerned. All these factors suggest that the international responsibility of a state for non-compliance as an internationally-wrongful act is of little significance for the IAEA BOG's execution of its authority.

The alleged breaches of the NPT are probably most pertinent as mitigating circumstances for Iran's non-compliance, which depends on a subjective assessment of purpose. Iran's exculpatory explanation is important inasmuch as it offers a non-military purpose for its actions. The plausibility and quality of this explanation may be assessed by analogy to circumstances precluding wrongfulness under the law of state responsibility, since Iran essentially claims that it failed to comply out of necessity in view of the violation by other states of NPT Article IV. Necessity is a ground recognised by customary international law for precluding the wrongfulness of an act not in conformity with an international obligation. It can only be accepted on an exceptional basis. A 'state of necessity' is the situation of a state whose sole means of safeguarding an essential interest threatened by a grave and imminent peril is to adopt conduct not in conformity with what is required of it by an international obligation to another state.[171] The threat to the state interest need not emanate from a violation of an international obligation. Thus, the success of an Iranian plea of necessity does not depend on the export controls constituting a violation of NPT Article IV, but on whether they made clandestine activity the only means to safeguard an essential Iranian interest against a grave and imminent peril.[172] Iran argues that the clandestine nature of its programme was aimed at protecting the country's self-sufficiency with respect to energy resources,[173] the pursuit of which would have been obstructed by other states had it been overt. This claim is based on Iran's experience: In the 1980s, when Iran began to revive its pre-revolutionary nuclear activities, the US adopted a policy of denial and pressured other states so that various contracts with Iran were unilaterally abrogated, and nuclear material rightfully purchased and owned by Iran was in some cases illegally withheld.[174] Thus, the perceived economic inutility of the programme, based on calculations that Iran can

---

[171] *Gabčíkovo-Nagymaros Project* (*Hungary v Slovakia*) (Judgment) [1997] ICJ Rep 7, [50]-[51].

[172] Even then, a plea of necessity may only be invoked if the otherwise-wrongful conduct does not seriously impair an essential interest of the states towards which the obligation exists. ILC DASR (n 75) art 25.

[173] Doc. 15.

[174] Doc. 83 para 31; Doc. 95 para 18; Doc. 102; Doc. 109 part 1; see also Cuba: Doc. 82 para 111; Kaveh L Afrasiabi, 'Iran, Nuclear Challenges' (25 August 2007) *Iranian Journal of International Affairs*; Squassoni (n 14) 283.

achieve the same result through alternative routes that are not only permissible but more cost-effective, does not take account of the reality in which these routes proved unavailable to Iran.[175] Necessity may not be invoked if the state has contributed to the situation of necessity.[176] Western states argue that Iran has contributed to the situation, thereby denying itself the right to rely on any 'necessity' that may have emerged.

Another analogy from the laws of international responsibility concerns countermeasures by injured states to induce a violating state to revert to compliance.[177] As with regard to suspension of a treaty under the law of treaties, Iran is entitled as an injured state to take countermeasures against a breaching state if it is specially affected (in the context of an Article IV violation) or when the obligation breached is of such a character as radically to change the position of all the other states to which the obligation is owed with respect to the further performance of the obligation (in the context of an Article VI violation).[178] As noted above, the relevance of this provision to the NPT is not free of doubt.[179] Even if Iran is entitled to take countermeasures, it may only take such measures as may induce the internationally-responsible state to comply with its obligations.[180] Whether the breach is of Article IV or VI, clandestine activities have no potential of inducing a breaching state to return to a condition of legality,[181] nor does Iran claim that it intended to induce the NWS to disarm.[182] There are other requirements for conduct to be regarded as lawful countermeasures, which do not appear to be fulfilled in the case of Iran. Countermeasures may be taken only against a state which is responsible for an internationally wrongful act, and they must be preceded by notification and an offer to negotiate.[183]

Iran claims that the strict standard to which it is being held and the disregard of the circumstances that led to its conduct reflect a politically-imposed double standard.[184] This critique may not be entirely misplaced, if one considers the light treatment by the IAEA BOG and the Security Council of other states which have been found in non-compliance, such as Libya and South Korea; or the willingness of the Security Council to accept IAEA findings with respect to Iraq in the early 2000s, but its disregard of IAEA reports which gradually narrow the scope of uncertainty with respect to Iran.[185] It may be that the IAEA BOG has in the past been led by national idiosyncrasies and prejudices, particularly those of the US.[186] The same may be true with respect to the Iranian dispute. However, it is hard to accept an argument that inadequate treatment of some states entitles others to be treated in the same manner.

---

[175] For a comment on the economic inutility of the Arak research reactor see Burton Richter, 'Iran's Other Nuclear Reactor' 56 (7) *New York Times Review of Books* (30 April 2009), www.nybooks.com/articles/22648.

[176] ILC DASR (n 71).art 25.

[177] ILC DASR (n 71) art 49(1).

[178] ILC DASR (n 71) art 42(b)(i),(ii).

[179] ILC DASR (n 71) commentary to art 42 paras 13, 14.

[180] ILC DASR (n 71) art 49(1).

[181] ILC DASR (n 71) art 49(2).

[182] In Doc. 119 section E para 9 Iran claims that suspending the implementation of Modified Code 3.1 of the Subsidiary Arrangements is a countermeasure.

[183] ILC DASR (n 71) arts 49(1), 52(1).

[184] Iran: Doc. 17; Doc. 66 para 42; Cuba: Doc. 59 para 9; Doc. 82 para 112; Venezuela: Doc. 77 para 59; Doc. 78 para 16; Doc. 82 para 122; Indonesia: Doc. 82 para 144; Morocco: Doc. 84 para 42; NAM: Doc. 77 para 20; OIC: Doc. 148 para 2. See also Tanya Ogilvie-White, 'International Responses to Iranian Nuclear Defiance: The Non-Aligned Movement and the Issue of Non-Compliance' (2007) 18 *European Journal of International Law* 453, 462-464; *Ford* (n 141) 587; *Joyner* (n 75) 25-26; and *Goldschmidt* (n 10) 152-155, who laments the politicization of substantively-appropriate decisions.

4.2 Peace and Security Concerns under IAEA Statute Article III.B.4

The IAEA BOG's second ground for referring the Iranian dossier to the Security Council was that[187]

> the history of concealment of Iran's nuclear activities referred to in the Director General's report, the nature of these activities, issues brought to light in the course of the Agency's verification of declarations made by Iran since September 2002 and the resulting absence of confidence that Iran's nuclear programme is exclusively for peaceful purposes have given rise to questions that are within the competence of the Security Council, as the organ bearing the main responsibility for the maintenance of international peace and security.

This ground invokes Article III.B.4 of the IAEA Statute, which provides:

> If in connection with the activities of the Agency there should arise questions that are within the competence of the Security Council, the Agency shall notify the Security Council, as the organ bearing the main responsibility for the maintenance of international peace and security.

There are still divergent views as to whether the exercise of authority under Article III.B.4 depends on the existence of a violation of the Safeguards Agreement, and specifically on a finding of diversion.[188] The understanding of the delegations negotiating the IAEA Statute was that a violation of international law is not a *sine qua non* for referral,[189] although such a violation could be evidence that a question of international peace and security has arisen. Furthermore, since even non-NPT states may refer a situation to the Security Council if a question arises within the latter's competence, it is difficult to read Article III.B.4 as placing limitations on the comparable powers of member states when acting through the IAEA BOG. Finally, the power to refer such a question to the Security Council may be an implied power of the IAEA as an international organization. Inaction on the part of the Security Council in one case cannot give rise to any legitimate expectations on the part of other states that the Security Council will not act in their case.

A determination that a question arises within the competence of the Security Council is a political step, and therefore cannot be made by the IAEA staff, but only by the IAEA BOG.[190] Where a question arises that implicates international peace and security, notification of the Security Council is mandatory.[191]

Iran argues that since its programme is peaceful, its activities do not constitute a threat to international peace and security.[192] It further claims that the IAEA DG has confirmed the peaceful nature of its programme.[193] Moreover, singling it out is discriminatory, in view of the past inaction against Iraq and present inaction against Israel.[194]

---

[185] Eg Doc. 16; Doc. 50 para 41; Doc. 51 para 53; Doc. 83 para 37; Doc. 118; South Africa: Doc. 18; Venezuelea: Doc. 82 para 123; *Müller* (n 141) 9-12; Hans Blix, 'A world Community on the Path to Peace?' (Lecture at Bergen's Student Society, Bergen 22 March 2007) 7, www.wmdcommission.org. Iran most often refers to the double standard with respect to Israel. It should be recalled that Israel is not a party to the NPT, and has no comprehensive Safeguards Agreement. There is no claim that it is in non-compliance with regard to the agreement relating to the IRR-I reactor in Soreq.

[186] *Müller* (n 141); Iran: Doc. 15-Doc. 17; Doc. 59 para 53; Doc. 63 para 3; Doc. 77 para 65; Doc. 86 para 72; Doc. 99; Doc. 109; Doc. 117; Doc. 119 part B; Cuba: Doc. 59 para 6; Doc. 77 paras 57, 59; Doc. 84 para 60;.

[187] Doc. 30 operative para 2.

[188] This is the position advocated by Iran, Doc. 115 para 134; Doc. 119 sections D, E. See also *Spies* (n 79) 427.

[189] *Fischer* (n 38) 45; *Bolton* (n 130).

[190] But see Iran: Doc. 119 section D.

[191] *Grotto* (n 133) citing *Bolton* (n 130).

[192] Doc. 15; Doc. 17; Doc. 18. See also India: Doc. 78 para 62.

[193] Doc. 18.

[194] Iran: Doc. 15; Doc. 16; Doc. 17; Doc. 94 para 70; Doc. 95 para 21; Doc. 121; Libya: Doc. 84 para 110; Cuba: Doc. 84 para 60.

There are opinions according to which not every pursuit of nuclear armament poses a threat to international peace and security. Müller, for example, suggests that a distinction is in order among states which arm themselves for defensive purposes, for the acquisition of status, or for aggressive ends. Müller argues that referral to the Security Council under IAEA Statute Article III.B.4 or through other routes of states motivated by these interests may be ineffective and even counterproductive.[195] Undoubtedly, such a distinction is made as a matter of practice. An example (not involving a matter of non-compliance) is the case of Japan, which is said to be very close to potentially becoming a NWS, but is regarded as having peaceful intentions and is therefore not regarded as a threat to international peace and security.[196] Iran's renewed interest in nuclear energy may have arisen out of defensive interests,[197] and there is no doubt that it strives to acquire regional and international status, including through its nuclear capability (although it denies that this capability is military).[198]

But many states maintain that Iran's activities do constitute a threat.[199] One ground for this position is the belief or at least concern that Iran is in fact pursuing nuclear weapons capabilities,[200] in the face of which the international community cannot take the risk that Iran would develop even the capability of producing weapon-grade material.[201] Analysts suggest that if Iran's enrichment programme is not delayed, it may achieve a level of self-sufficiency that would enable it to hide its activities from international inspectors and foreign intelligence agencies far more effectively,[202] and undermine the balance of power in the region and the viability of the global nonproliferation regime.[203] Once Iran acquires a nuclear weapon, not only might it attack a state (a scenario mentioned in particular with respect to Israel) or purposely provide nuclear weapons to terrorists,[204] but it may feel unconstrained in its willingness to engage in terrorism, subversion and other unacceptable methods of advancing its foreign policy.[205] More generally, the Security Council has

---

[195] *Müller* (n 141) 2-3. This is not to say that such armament is lawful. In adition to violation of the NPT, armament as a deterrent may be a violation of UN Charter art 2(4). *Legality of the Threat or Use of Nuclear Weapons* (Advisory Opinion) (n 156) para 41, and separate opinions by Judges Shi, Ferrari Bravo, Guillaume and Schwebel.

[196] Toshi Yoshihara and James R. Holmes, 'Thinking about the Unthinkable: Tokyo's Nuclear Option' (2009) 62 *Naval War College Review* 61.

[197] Mustafa Kibaroglu, 'Good for the Shah, Banned for the Mullahs: The West and Iran's Quest for Nuclear Power' (2006) 60 *Middle East Journal* 207, 216, 220.

[198] Kaveh Afrasiabi and Mustafa Kibaroglu, 'Negotiating Iran's Nuclear Populism' (2005) XII *Brown Journal of World Affairs* 255, 257; *Weapons of Mass Destruction Commission* (n 68) 71; Emily B Landau, 'One Size Does Not Fit All: Confronting Iran and North Korea' INSS Insight No 102 (16 April 2009), www.inss.org.il/publications.php?cat=21&incat=&read=2815.

[199] UK: Doc. 78 para 4; Doc. 80 para 154; US: Doc. 15; Doc. 18; Doc. 80 para 248; Australia: Doc. 76 para 75.

[200] Doc. 10 preambular paras 4, 9; Doc. 11 preambular paras 4, 9; Doc. 12 preambular paras 3, 4, 9; Doc. 13 preambular para 12; Doc. 32 opeartive para 5.

[201] UK: Doc. 15. For early statements on this by the US and Israel see statements by Robert Speier and Robbie Sabel, in Joseph Cirincione, Kathleen Newland (eds), *Reparing the Regime: Preventing the Spread of Weapons of Mass Destruction* (Carnegie Endowment for International Peace and Routledge, 2000) ch 12.

[202] But others argue that Iran's ability to act covertly is severely limited. *Kerr* (n 43) 11.

[203] Joseph Cirincione and Andrew Grotto, 'Contain and Engage: A New Strategy for Resolving the Nuclear Crisis with Iran' (Center for American Progress, 28 February 2007) 6, www.americanprogress.org/issues/2007/02/iran_report.html; Mark Fitzpatrick, 'The World After: Proliferation, Deterrence and Disarmament if the Nuclear Taboo is Broken' IFRI Proliferation Paper (Spring 2009) 25, www.ifri.org/frontDispatcher/ifri/publications/proliferation_papers_1090224187156/publi_P_publi_sec_cea_fitzpatrick_1244565613914.

[204] James Timbie, 'Iran's Nuclear Program' (2007) 57 *Syracuse Law Review* 433, 434.

[205] George Perkovich, Joseph Cirincione, Rose Gottemoeller, Joh B Wolfsthal, Jessica T Mathews, *Universal Compliance: A Strategy for Nuclear Security* (Washington, DC, Carnegie Endowment for Peace, 2004) 26.

declared in 1992 that proliferation of all weapons of mass destruction constitutes a threat to international peace and security.[206] The Weapons of Mass Destruction Commission, while admitting the possibility that Iran's engagement in nuclear technology might be influenced by its experience in the war with Iraq and by a presently perceived threat in its region,[207] emphatically rejected the suggestion that the pursuit of nuclear weapons by some pose no threat while it places the world in mortal jeopardy when carried out by others. For one, the intentions of governments may change, and with them the danger posed by their possession of nuclear weapons.[208] Second, and pertinently in the case of Iran, the threat to international peace and security may exist even before the nuclear weapons capability is achieved. An Iranian nuclear arsenal or even progress toward nuclear capability might unleash a cascade of proliferation across the Middle East.[209] Even if the nuclear programme is at present entirely peaceful, it may already threaten international peace and security, since parts of its programme, notably the enrichment of uranium, dramatically raises the tension in the Middle East.[210] Various states have already embarked on nuclear projects: Abu Dhabi concluded in 2008 a multi-billion deal with France to build nuclear power reactors,[211] the United Arab Emirates signed a deal with the US,[212] Jordan signed an agreement with the UK,[213] and Egypt announced that it was resurrecting its decades-old plans to build nuclear power reactors along its Mediterranean coast.[214] While these are all peaceful, civilian enterprises, the risk of proliferation is ever-present.[215] Therefore, even if Iran's programme is at present peaceful, its potential to transform into a military one and its effect on the region render it a threat to international peace and security.

---

[206] UN Doc S/23500 (31 January 1992). This was reaffirmed in UNSC Res 1540 (2004) (28 April 2004) UN Doc S/RES/1540(2004).

[207] *Weapons of Mass Destruction Commission* (n 68) 71.

[208] *Weapons of Mass Destruction Commission* (n 68) 60.

[209] US: Doc. 15; Doc. 18; EU: Doc. 160; Orde F Kittrie, 'Emboldened by Impunity: The History and Consequences of Failure to Enforce Iranian Violations of International Law' (2007) 57 *Syracuse Law Review* 531; *Timbie* (n 207) 434; See comments of Kenneth M. Pollack, Director of Research, Saban Center for Middle East Policy, Brookings Institution, in 'Iran's Nuclear Program Symposium: Policy Options for the United States' (Council on Foreign Relations, Rush Transcript, Federal News Service, Inc. 5 April 2006), www.cfr. org/publication/10388/irans_nuclear_program_symposium.html. See in general on the danger of a cascade of proliferation: 'A more secure world: our shared responsibility', Report of the High-Level Panel on Threats, Challenges and Change, UN Doc A/59/565 (2 December 2004) [39]-[40].

[210] Hans Blix, 'Disarmament Visions and the Prospects for a WMD-free Zone in the Middle East' (Lecture in Berlin, 24 June 2008, on file with the author); *Fitzpatrick* (n 200) 24, *Perkovich et al* (n 205) 27.

[211] AFP, 'France and UAE Sign Defence, Nuclear Deals' *ABC News* (16 January 2008), www.abc.net.au/news/stories/2008/01/16/2139245.htm?site=news.

[212] Golnaz Esfandiari, 'New U.S.-U.A.E. Deal Raises Eyebrows Amid Concern Over Iran's Nuclear Program' *Radio Free Europe/Radio Liberty* (8 September 2008), www.rferl.org/content/New_US_UAE_Deal_Raises_Eyebrows_Amid_Concern_Over_Irans_Nuclear_Program/1370983.html.

[213] 'UK-Jordan Nuclear Cooperation Agreement' (22 June 2009), ukinromania.fco.gov.uk/en/newsroom/?view=News&id=19946255.

[214] For Egypt's stance towards the Iranian nuclear issue see Ephraim Kam, 'Egypt's View of the Threat: Iran-Hizbollah-Hamas' INSS Insight No 101 (20 April 2009), www.inss.org.il/research.php?cat=3&incat=&read=2837.

[215] Ephraim Asculai, 'The Pros and Cons of Nuclear Power in the Middle East' INSS Insight No 118 (6 July 2009) www.inss.org.il/publications.php?cat=21&incat=&read=3068; *Kibaroglu* (n 196) 224-225.

4.3 Inability to Verify Under Safeguards Agreement Article 19

Article 19 of Iran's Safeguards Agreement provides:[216]

> If the Board, upon examination of relevant information reported to it by the Director General, finds that the Agency is not able to verify that there has been no diversion of nuclear material required to be safeguarded under this Agreement, to nuclear weapons or other nuclear explosive devices, it may make the reports provided for in paragraph C of Article XII of the Statute of the Agency (hereinafter referred to as 'the Statute') and may also take, where applicable, the other measures provided for in that paragraph. In taking such action the Board shall take account of the degree of assurance provided by the safeguards measures that have been applied and shall afford the Government of Iran every reasonable opportunity to furnish the Board with any necessary reassurance.

Article 19 concerns a situation where the information provided by the state and findings by IAEA inspectors do not add up to a coherent picture of legitimate conduct, in a manner that suggests that nuclear material required to be safeguarded may have been diverted elsewhere.

Diversion typically means removal of nuclear material from safeguarded activities, conduct in which Iran has engaged.[217] It has also been interpreted as encompassing failure to declare nuclear material for safeguards.[218] Iran's failures to declare importation of nuclear material and use of the material in undeclared nuclear activities, and its denial of the importation when questioned by the Agency, thus would constitute 'diversion', so that not only was the IAEA not able to verify non-diversion, but it actually had positive findings of diversion.

Iran rejects reliance on Article 19 to refer its case to the Security Council because the IAEA Director General 'has constantly stated in all his reports that the Agency has been able to verify that the declared nuclear materials and activities in Iran have not been diverted towards military purposes, and that they have remained absolutely under peaceful use'.[219] As a matter of fact, the BOG did not rely on Article 19 in referring the Iranian dossier to the Security Council.[220] It nonetheless could have.[221] The IAEA DG's assurances of non-diversion addressed only material that Iran had since 2003 admitted to having and put under safeguards. In all other respects, the IAEA DG has repeatedly reported that the Agency was unable, and without cooperation on the part of Iran would not be able, to provide assurances about the absence of undeclared nuclear material and activities in Iran or about the exclusively peaceful nature of that programme.[222]

What is not clear is what threshold level of discrepancy should trigger a finding of inability to verify under Article 19.[223] Some argue that Article 19's standard of 'not able to

---

[216] Doc. 4. The text is standard for all safeguards agreements.

[217] Iran has 'carried out UF_4 conversion experiments … using depleted uranium which had been imported in 1977 and exempted from safeguards upon receipt, and which Iran had declared in 1998 (when the material was de-exempted) as having been lost during processing' (Doc. 39 para 14). *Goldschmidt* (n 84) considers this a clear case of diversion of declared nuclear material.

[218] *Carlson* (n 132); *Goldschmidt* (n 84).

[219] Doc. 119 section D.

[220] Several states mention Article 19 together with IAEA Statute XII.C, on which the BOG did rely. Australia: Doc. 62 para 58; Brazil: Doc. 65 para 28; the Netherlands: Doc. 66 para 25.

[221] UK: Doc. 62 para 13.

[222] Doc. 40 para 51; Doc. 42 para 53; Doc. 47 para 29; Doc. 48 para 19; Doc. 50 para 43; Doc. 51 para 57; Doc. 53 para 23; Doc. 54 para 18; Doc. 55 para 21; Doc. 56 para 22; *Goldschmidt* (n 84).

[223] Gary Milhollin, statement at 2004 at AEI conference 'The International Atomic Energy Agency: The World's Enforcer or Paper Tiger?' (28 September 2004), www.aei.org/event/911.

verify' is too low and therefore incompatible with respect of the right under NPT Article IV.[224] Others warn that to demand evidence that undeclared material and activities were related to a nuclear weapons programme would be setting a standard of proof for the IAEA that is too high.[225] According to the IAEA BOG legal advisor, Article 19 may be triggered by any action by a state that is inconsistent with its safeguards agreement and which rises to a level where the agency cannot verify non-diversion.[226]

It has been argued that the problem of 'inability to verify' is not unique to Iran and applies equally to other states that have not entered into an additional protocol, because with respect to them there are also no means of verifying the absence of undeclared materials.[227] Indeed, the IAEA has certified correctness and completeness of declarations with respect to the absence of undeclared material and activity of only 24 countries. A diversion is defined by an element of purpose – 'to nuclear weapons or other nuclear explosive devices'.[228] Again, the quantitative element is examined in light of the qualitative assessment.[229] In this respect, Iran's case is unique.[230] Unlike other states, it is known for a fact to have held undeclared nuclear material and to have engaged in undeclared activities for two decades.[231] As a result, it suffers from an exceptional trust deficit. This is why it has been requested to ratify the Additional Protocol, which enables the IAEA to explore whether there are non-declared material and activities. Only then – and in fact only if Iran goes even beyond the Additional Protocol[232] – will the IAEA be able to fill the knowledge gap in order to work towards a conclusion on whether there are undeclared nuclear materials or activities in Iran.

5. IAEA BOG Suspension of Privileges

In the event of failure by the state to take fully corrective action with respect to the safeguards agreement within a reasonable time, IAEA statute Article XII.C permits the BOG to directly curtail or suspend assistance being provided by the Agency or by a member, and to call for the return of materials and equipment made available to the recipient member or group of members. These powers have rarely been used due to high levels of resistance among member states, especially members of the NAM, and an IAEA culture of permissiveness.[233]

---

[224] *Joyner* (n 75) 50.

[225] *Goldschmidt* (n 84) section C.

[226] Statement by the IAEA BOG Legal Advisor (n 122) para 10.

[227] Iran: Doc. 15; *Spies* (n 79) 429.

[228] Doc. 4 arts 1, 2. Article 28 speaks of the objective of the Safeguards Agreement as detecting and deterring diversion also to 'purposes unknown'. However, Article 19 does not refer to this alternative. Instead it sets a higher standard of proof as to the suspected purpose of diversion.

[229] Algeria: Doc. 84 para 23; *US Congress, Office of Technology Assessment* (n 60) 30; Statement by the IAEA BOG Legal Advisor (n 122) para 10.

[230] Doc. 32 preambular para (e); Doc. 40; Doc. 94 para 85;

[231] IAEA DG in Doc. 94 para 87.

[232] IAEA: Doc. 33 para 35; Doc. 39 para 112; Doc. 40 para 50; Doc. 42 para 54; Doc. 43 para 34; Doc. 50 para 43; Doc. 62 para 68; Doc. 63 para 48; UK: Doc. 62 para 14; France: Doc. 59 para 5; US:Doc. 59 para 26; EU: Doc. 61 para 84; Doc. 156; Doc. 157; Japan: Doc. 61 para 119; G8: Doc. 151; South Africa: Doc. 71 para 121; *Carlson* (n 132); *Spies* (n 79) 431, 434.

[233] *Ogilvie-White* (n 184) 467. For previous practice see the BOG's resolution regarding DPRK (10 June 1994) operative para 6, www.globalsecurity.org/wmd/library/news/dprk/un/pr94-25.htm.

The same permissiveness was apparent in the IAEA's approach to Iran. In November 2006, the IAEA BOG examined a request by Iran for technical assistance for the Arak facility as well as for seven other projects. According to the Statute, the BOG could have rejected all eight applications in an effort to maximise pressure on Iran.[234] Various governments opined that to allow the Security Council resolutions to affect the IAEA's deliberations on the technical assistance would inappropriately politicise the agency.[235] The IAEA BOG eventually decided to block Iran's request regarding the Arak facility for a period of at least two years, but approved technical assistance for the seven other, less contentious, projects submitted by Iran.

6. The IAEA's Call for Suspension of Enrichment-related and Reprocessing Activities

Iran and others claim that the demand for suspension of uranium enrichment and reprocessing activities by both the IAEA BOG and the Security Council constitutes nuclear apartheid, and a violation of NPT Article IV, the UN Charter, and the rights to development and education. In this context Iran has argued that the Paris Agreement,[236] in which it undertook to suspend its activities, is not a binding treaty but a statement of principles to guide negotiations; divergence from it is no more than a breakdown in negotiations.[237]

The Paris Agreement refers to Iran's decision to continue and extend the suspension 'on a voluntary basis', and to continue implementing the Additional Protocol 'voluntarily'. The EU3 expressly recognised 'that this suspension is a voluntary confidence-building measure and not a legal obligation'. This was acknowledged by Iran's interlocutors and by the IAEA numerous times subsequently.[238] On the other hand, Iran itself has referred to the Paris Agreement as binding, at least with respect to the EU3. It thus refers to the EU3's 'violation' of it.[239] The EU3 also regard the Paris Agreement as legally binding, referring to Iran's 'obligations', its 'breaking' the Agreement and its 'breach' of 'commitments' under it.[240]

Be that as it may, the 2005 resumption of enrichment processes generated concern not because it violated a bilateral legal undertaking to suspend enrichment,[241] but because of its implications for dealing with Iran's non-compliance, namely for the assessment whether Iran's earlier failure to declare material and activities amounted to non-compliance in terms of Article XII.C of the IAEA Statute, which should be referred to the Security Council. Suspension did not change the objective finding as to Iran's failure to meet its obligations under the Safeguards Agreement. However, Iran's stance towards suspension directly affected the subjective, qualitative assessment of its failure. Iran is suffering from

---

[234] Doc. 89, EU: paras 33-34, Canada: paras 74-78, US: para 98.

[235] Doc. 89, Egypt: para 107, Indonesia: para 147, South Africa: para 157. For an analysis of NAM member policy see *Ogilvie-White* (n 184) 469-470.

[236] Doc. 8

[237] Iran: Doc. 17; Doc. 18; Farhang Jahanpour, 'Iran's Nuclear Threat: Exploring the Politics', Oxford Research Group (July 2006) 4; *Spies* (n 79) 429, 440.

[238] BOG: Doc. 28 preambular para (h), operative para 1; Doc. 29 operative para 3; Doc. 32 operative para 5; EU: Doc. 7 para 2(b)(II); UK: Doc. 71 para 18; EU3: Doc. 75 para 3; Doc. 127; Iran: Doc. 116; NAM: Doc. 71 para 17; Doc. 146 para 5; Doc. 147 para 2.

[239] Doc. 83 para 39; Doc. 108; Doc. 109; but see also Doc. 111.

[240] EU3: Doc. 127; EU3+3: Doc. 128; US: Doc. 72 para 82; EU: Doc. 82 para 31.

[241] Iran regards the suspension as a bilateral issue: Doc. 83 para 40; Doc. 109. For a response see France: Doc. 75 para 4; EU: Doc. 82 para 77; EU3+3: Doc. 128.

an international trust deficit because of its record of concealment and failure to report as required under its Safeguards Agreement. It bears the extraordinary onus of proving the peaceful nature of its intentions. For this it is called upon to act not only lawfully but also in a confidence-building manner. Maintaining the suspension acted towards building this confidence.[242] Thus, the initial BOG call on Iran to suspend its nuclear activities was a political call on a state to refrain from exercising the full scope of its legal rights.[243] As long as Iran suspended its nuclear-related activities, it increased the confidence in its peaceful intention and contained the potential consequences of its failure to declare. It enabled the BOG to avoid determining that Iran was in non-compliance and referring the matter to the Security Council.[244] Once Iran resumed its activities, the level of confidence in its peaceful intentions decreased, and once again the qualitative significance of its failure grew. In other words, the referral of Iran to the Security Council was not the result of its refusal to suspend enrichment,[245] but the renewed loss of confidence that its intentions were peaceful.

The loss of confidence on the ground of Iran's refusal to suspend its uranium conversion and enrichment activities is only justifiable if the request for suspension was reasonable. This is a matter of controversy, particularly insofar as the expected duration of the suspension is concerned. The 2004 negotiations on suspension were fraught with distrust and controversy from the outset. The EU3 reportedly focused on the need for Iran to cease use of, and dismantle, 'sensitive parts' of the fuel cycle,[246] while the Iranians stressed that a solution should be sought in the framework of its legal rights and obligations under IAEA safeguards and the Additional Protocol, stressing the importance of respecting Iran's right to research and develop nuclear energy for peaceful purposes.[247] The principal stumbling block was the requirement in the Paris Agreement to negotiate 'objective guarantees that Iran's nuclear programme is exclusively for peaceful purposes'. The EU3 position, later echoed by others,[248] was that the only acceptable guarantee for them was the indefinite cessation of uranium enrichment and reprocessing activities. Iran clearly objected to this, as did its supporters.[249] This difference of opinions was temporarily glossed over but in reality could not be spanned.[250] It was exposed when Iran claimed that the EU3 were intentionally

[242] Security Council: Doc. 9-Doc. 11; EU3 and Iran: Doc. 7 para 2(b)(II); Doc. 8; Iran: Doc. 102; Doc. 104; EU3+3: Doc. 134; France: Doc. 18; Doc. 68 para 85; IAEA BOG: Doc. 22-Doc. 24; Doc. 26-Doc. 28; Doc. 30; IAEA DG: Doc. 36; Japan: Doc. 61 para 118; Canada: Doc. 65 para 6, Doc. 69 para 71; South Africa: Doc. 59 para 30; New Zealand: Doc. 71 para 314; UK: Doc. 15; Russia: Doc. 15; Doc. 63 para 39; Doc. 64 para 112; US: Doc. 66 para 48; Doc. 71 para 66; Doc. 68.

[243] Russia: Doc. 71 para 75; Hans Blix, Comments made at the conference 'Breaking the U.S.-Iran Stalemate' (Lecture organized by the National Iranian American Council, Washington, 8 April 2008) (on file with the author).

[244] EU: Doc. 72 para 18, Doc. 76 para 54; Canada: Doc. 71 para 84, Doc. 76 para 80; US: Doc. 72 paras 82-85, France: Doc. 75 para 4; Canada: Doc. 82 paras 43-46; Argentina: Doc. 84 para 84; George Perkovich, 'Defining Iran's Nuclear Rights' Proliferation Analysis (7 October 2006).

[245] Iran: Doc. 106; Cuba: Doc. 78 para 79.

[246] The EU3 was apparently referring to uranium conversion and enrichment since light water power reactors, reactors with no significant capacity to produce plutonium, waste storage sites, uranium mines, or concentration plants, could be maintained by Iran. 'Summary of the Latest Round of Nuclear Talks between Iran and The European Union as Seen and Transcribed by Reuters' (26 January 26 2005), www.iranwatch.org/international/EU/eu-summaryoftalks-reuters-012605.htm.

[247] Andreas Persbo, 'Raising the stakes: Iran's resumption of nuclear activities', BASIC Notes (20 September 2005) www.basicint.org/pubs/Notes/BN050920.htm.

[248] Eg Canada: Doc. 74 para 75.

[249] NAM: Doc. 71 para 38; Doc. 72 para 26; Doc. 82 paras 69.

[250] Emily B Landau, 'A Nuclear Iran: Implications for Arms Control in the Nuclear Realm', in Ephraim Kam (ed), *Israel and a Nuclear Iran: Implications for Arms Control, Deterrence, and Defense*, Memorandum No 94 (Tel Aviv, Institute for National Security Studies, 2008) 33, 38.

protracting the negotiations in an attempt to make the suspension a *fait accompli* and refused to cooperate further.[251]

In addition to confidence building, some states emphasise the role of suspension in enabling inspectors to retrace past activities,[252] possibly in the context of Safeguards Agreement Article 18, which authorises the BOG to demand any necessary and urgent actions on the part of the Iran to ensure verification of non-diversion. Without suspension, the IAEA cannot verify that there had not been past diversion of nuclear materials and activities.

7. Security Council Action

Referral of a matter to the Security Council under IAEA Statute Article III.B.4, namely because it raises a question of international peace and security, does not necessarily indicate that there is already a threat to, international peace and security. The case of Iran may well be one which falls within the scope of UN Charter Chapter VI, which may be triggered by parties to a dispute, if the continuance of the dispute is likely to endanger the maintenance of international peace and security. The Security Council may investigate any dispute, or any situation which might lead to international friction.[253]

Nonetheless, until 2006 the Security Council was not at all involved in the dispute over Iran's nuclear programme, not even by taking note of the situation.[254] When it did step in, it resorted directly to Chapter VII measures. Indeed, Blix suggests that a main purpose of the US initiative to refer the case of Iran to the Security Council was to seek authorization for enforcement measures.[255]

7.1 Legality of the Security Council's Demand for Suspension

Security Council Resolutions 1737(2006), 1747(2007) and 1803(2008) were adopted under UN Charter Chapter VII. Although none of them expressly declares that Iran's nuclear programme constituted a threat to the peace, a breach of the peace or an act of aggression under UN Charter Article 39, nor invokes Article 39 itself, they all note the Security Council's concern over the proliferation risks that the programme presents and the Security Council's primary responsibility under the UN charter for the maintenance of international peace and security. The reference to 'risks' does not invoke the threat as articulated in the Security Council's 1992 statement, but the implicit reference to such a threat through the recourse to Articles 40 and 41 is common practice in the Security Council.

As a matter of positive law, UN Charter Article 39 authorises the Security Council to 'decide what measures shall be taken... to maintain or restore international peace and security'. These measures typically involve demanding actions on the part of the target

[251] Doc. 107.

[252] Russia: Doc. 15; Doc. 71 para 75; US: Doc. 18; Doc. 59 para 16.

[253] UN Charter arts 33, 34; Hans Blix, 'International Law Relating to the Use of Armed Force and Weapons of Mass Destruction (Presentation to the International Law Association, Toronto, 5 June 2006) 12, www. wmdcommission.org.

[254] See critique by *Müller* (n 141) 11.

[255] Hans Blix, 'Revive Disarmament' (Statement at Middle Powers Initiative's Article VI Forum, Ottawa (27 September 2006), 6 www.middlepowers.org/docs/A6F_Ottawa_Blix.pdf.

state to bring itself into compliance with preexisting legal obligations, but may also require the target state to go beyond those obligations.[256] The authority of the Security Council to impose demands that are incompatible with other obligations of states is provided for in UN Charter Articles 25 and 103, which give precedence to Security Council demands over other obligations.[257] These Articles do not mention rights and liberties, such as the one asserted by Iran under NPT Article IV. This is hardly surprising: if the Security Council may require a state to act in a manner which under ordinary circumstances is prohibited, *a fortiori* it may require a state to act in a manner which is permitted.

The authority of the Security Council may, in principle, be limited by the impermissibility of violating peremptory norms.[258] As discussed above, although Article IV refers to the right to develop nuclear capability as 'inalienable', this term does not have the legal meaning alleged by Iran. Moreover, if Iran has violated NPT Article II by pursuing nuclear weapons, then under the terms of Article IV itself Iran no longer benefits from the right to participate in exchange of material and technology insofar as it is guaranteed by Article IV.[259] If the Security Council prohibits a state from exercising its NPT Article IV right in the context of preventing or putting an end to an Article II violation, it is not infringing upon the right. As noted above, Article IV is also increasingly being interpreted as limited by the obligation of adherence to Article III, which Iran has violated by its non-compliance with the Safeguards Agreement. It should be emphasised, however, that no authoritative international body has declared Iran to be in violation of any provision of the NPT. In fact, one may query whether the Security Council could make a legal determination on this issue; if it could, a further question is whether it is bound to accept the IAEA findings for this purpose.[260]

In short, once the Security Council stepped in with an obligatory demand under Chapter VII, the failure by Iran to suspend its enrichment and reprocessing activities took on a different dimension. It not only affected the assessment regarding non-compliance, but became an independent breach of the obligation under the UN Charter to comply with a binding Security Council demand.

The purpose of the demand for suspension also changed once it emanated from the Security Council. The Security Council resolutions emphasise that the Council is acting to reinforce the efforts of the IAEA.[261] They demand suspension both in order to enable resolution of outstanding questions and as a confidence-building measure.[262] On this basis the Security Council endorsed the dual track-approach of the EU3+3 (China, France, Germany, Russia, the UK and the US), namely that Iran should choose between suspension and the maintenance of its dossier before the Security Council.[263] However, suspension

---

[256] Orde F Kittrie, 'Averting Catastrophe: Why the Nuclear Nonproliferation Treaty is Losing its Deterrence Capacity and How to Restore It' (2007) 28 *Michigan Journal of International Law* 337, 364.

[257] Joyner (n 75); Bruno Simma (ed), *The Charter of the United Nations, A Commentary* Vol II (2nd ed Oxford, 2002) 1292, 1295-1296; *Questions of Interpretation and Application of the 1971 Montreal Convention Arising from the Aerial Incident at Lockerbie* (*Libyan Arab Jamahiriya v United States*) (Request for the Indication of Provisional Measures: Order) [1992] ICJ Rep 114 para 42.

[258] Generally on the powers of the Security Council see Mohammed Bedjaoui, *The New World Order and the Security Council, Testing the Legality of its Acts* (1994).

[259] *Goldschmidt* (n 84).

[260] *Müller* (n 141) 14.

[261] Doc. 9 para 5; Doc. 10 preambular para 6, operative para 1; Doc. 11 preambular para 8, operative paras 4, 22; Doc. 12 preambular para 7, operative paras 1, 11; Doc. 13 preambular paras 6, 11, operative para 1; Doc. 14 operative para 4.

[262] Doc. 9 para 5; Doc. 10 operative para 1; Doc. 11 operative para 1; Doc. 12 operative para 1; Doc. 13 operative para 1.

[263] Doc. 11 operative para 19; Doc. 12 operative para 13; Doc. 13 preambular para 24.

has also been tied to the Security Council's mandate to maintain international peace and security.[264] In addition, while all the Security Council statements and resolutions emphasise that suspension will contribute towards achievement of a long-term solution to the mutual benefit of all parties,[265] the later resolutions expressly demand suspension as a precondition for the resumption of negotiations.[266] This demand is puzzling: which player in a game should be expected to give the other side its trump card before the game begins?[267] Both as a measure of ensuring international peace and security and as a precondition for negotiation, suspension seems to have become, contrary to the expectations of at least some states,[268] a goal in itself rather than a means.

7.2 Security Council Enforcement Measures

Resolutions 1737(2006), 1747(2007) and 1803(2008) were adopted under UN Charter Article 41, which authorises the Security Council to take measures not involving the use of armed force, in order to give effect to its decisions. These resolutions target Iranian officials and entities directly involved in Iran's sensitive nuclear programmes in order to focus pressure on those responsible for wrongdoing.[269]

While the Security Council's authority to impose Article 41 measures is beyond question, one could query whether the recourse to Chapter VII measures was appropriate in the first place. At one end of the spectrum are those who claim that since there is no likelihood that diplomacy will progress far enough to make any real difference, there is no point in waiting for negotiations to play out.[270] A different approach is that a policy of negotiating and *quid pro quo* may be more helpful than one of threats and punishment.[271] There is no legal mechanism to ensure that Article 41 measures are taken only after other means of resolving a dispute have been exhausted. Even if enforcement measures under Article 41 prove ineffective in the case of Iran,[272] other non-forcible means of resolving the dispute, whether or not they include Iran abandoning its nuclear programme, could have been explored even prior to the adoption of Resolution 1737(2007) and may still offer a solution. The Weapons of Mass Destruction Commission, for example, proposed that negotiations continue to induce Iran to suspend its activities through reliable assurances regarding the supply of fuel-cycle services, suspension or renouncement of sensitive fuel-cycle activities for a prolonged period of time by all states in the Middle East, assurances against attacks and subversion aiming at regime change, and facilitation of international trade and investment.[273] Some of these incentives were included in the EU3's proposals.

[264] Doc. 10 preambular para 9; Doc. 11 preambular para 9; Doc. 12 preambular para 9; Doc. 13 preambular para 12.

[265] Doc. 9 para 5, 6; Doc. 10 operative para 3; Doc. 11 operative para 20; Doc. 12 preambular para 9; Doc. 13 preambular para 7.

[266] Doc. 12 operative para 24(a); Doc. 13 operative para 15; Doc. 14 operative para 3; see statements by China: Doc. 15; Doc. 17; France: Doc. 15; EU3+3: Doc. 132.

[267] *Blix* (n 251) 7.

[268] South Africa and Indonesia: Doc. 18

[269] On non-forcible enforcement measures see Vera Gowlland-Debbas (ed), *United Nations Sanctions and International Law* (The Hague, Kluwer Law International, 2001); *Kittrie* (n 209) 539-548.

[270] John R Bolton 'Time for an Israeli Strike?' *Washington Post* (2 July 2009), www.washingtonpost.com/wp-dyn/content/article/2009/07/01/AR2009070103020.html?hpid=opinionsbox1.

[271] *Blix* (n 255) 6.

[272] Indonesia and Libya: Doc. 18; Andrew Grotto, 'Smarter Sanctions for Iran' (12 July 2007), www.americanprogress.org/issues/2007/07/grotto_sanctions.html.

[273] *Weapons of Mass Destruction Commission* (n 68) 72, recommendation 6.

However, they were never discussed at the Security Council level. In stark contrast with the case of North Korea, Iran was offered no assurances against outside attacks and subversion, nor did the US offer resumption of diplomatic relations.[274] Even in the US, proposals have been made to engage Iran in a deal that would allow it to enrich uranium but expand inspections.[275]

The Obama administration in the US appeared to introduce a change of policy. In a speech in June 2009, Obama adopted a relatively conciliatory approach towards Iran. First, he openly admitted that the United States played a role in the overthrow of a democratically-elected Iranian government, although he stopped short of apologizing for that intervention. With respect to the nuclear issue, he hinted that the direct dialogue expected to begin after the Iranian elections will touch on 'many issues', suggesting a possible relaxation of the urgency for which the US was calling earlier.[276] Obama also expressed willingness 'to move forward without preconditions', conceding the demand for suspension as a precondition for negotiations. He made no mention whatsoever of other enforcement measures, instead speaking of global nuclear disarmament and of all the region's nations joining the NPT.[277] Statements following the June 2009 elections in Iran have been less cordial.[278] By early 2010, US rhetoric had heated up again.

The resolutions have been criticised for not making full use of the range of possible available measures.[279] Any assessment of the resolutions must nonetheless account for the need to compromise between the strong proponents of enforcement, led by the US, and their opponents, particularly Russia and China, who were reluctant to involve the Security Council in the first place,[280] and subsequently urged to limit the scope of enforcement measures.[281] Both Russia and China have strategic and economic interests in Iran, including in its peaceful nuclear programme. Indeed, Resolution 1737(2007) exempts the provision of Russian equipment to Bushehr from the scope of enforcement measures.[282]

At the same time, the Security Council is legally bound to exhaust the potential of Article 41 measures before proceeding to considering Article 42 forcible measures, although it need not go through the formal motions of pursuing Article 41 measures if it considers that they 'would be inadequate or have proved to be inadequate'. Theoretically, the potential for non-forcible enforcement measures is still far from exhausted. At the time of writing, the sanctions only relate to Iran's nuclear programme. They can be expanded to other areas, such as the oil industry, or even to a total trade embargo, as that which was imposed

---

[274] *Blix* (n 255) 6. For an analysis of the political differences surrounding the disputes with Iran and with the DPRK see *Landau* (n 197).

[275] Luers, Pickering and Walsh propose an international consortium for enrichment-related activities and reprocessing on Iranian soil. William Luers, Thomas R. Pickering, Jim Walsh, 'A Solution for the US-Iran Nuclear Standoff' 55(4) *New York Times Review of Books* (20 March 2008). Iran has expressed a willingness to consider an international consortium, although on its own terms, Doc. 114; Doc. 120.

[276] Roni Bart, 'Obama's Speech in Cairo' INSS Insight No 111 (8 June 2009) www.inss.org.il/publications. php?cat=21&incat=&read=2980.

[277] Doc. 140.

[278] Emily B Landau, 'Red Light, Green Light: Establishing US Levers of Pressure on Iran' INSS Insight No 119 (13 July 2009) www.inss.org.il/research.php?cat=3&incat=&read=3084.

[279] *Kittrie* (n 209) 547.

[280] Russia: Doc. 82 para 38; Norway: Doc. 82 para 88. See also peculiar statements by Russia and China, that 'the relevant provisions that pertained to reporting to the Security Council should not be construed as an exercise based on Articles XII.C or III.B of the Statute' Doc. 84 paras 130, 135.

[281] Russia: Doc. 16.

[282] On Russia's dilemma see Zvi Magen, 'Russia's Iranian Dilemma' INSS Insight No 120 (4 August 2009) www.inss.org.il/research.php?cat=268&incat=&read=3145.

on Iraq.[283] In July 2009 the EU3 and the US were reportedly considering investment bans, additional curbs on Iranian banks and businesses, bans on insurance for companies trading with Iran, and a possible effort to cut off Iran's gasoline imports, which account for 40% of annual consumption. A ban on Iranian ships and planes docking and landing in western countries is reportedly another longer-term option.[284]

At the time of writing a Security Council-authorised use of force is not a realistic option. Russia has repeatedly emphasised that the resolutions do not even contemplate this possibility,[285] and conventional wisdom suggests that should a military option be raised, Russia and China will veto it.

8. Unilateral Use of Force

From an early stage there have been insinuations that states, particularly Israel or the US, may unilaterally take military action in order to destroy Iran's nuclear-related facilities and thus halt its nuclear programme.[286] The US under both the Bush administration and the Obama administration, has not rejected the possibility of military intervention, although it has never openly engaged with it.[287]

Although the focus of the present analysis is on the dealing with the Iranian nuclear issue in the framework of the NPT regime and the UN, and analysis of aspects of the use of force exceeds it and in certain respects may be regarded as premature, some essential aspects can be highlighted.[288] The main obstacle to lawful military action against Iran is that the right to self-defense may be invoked under UN Charter Article 51 only following an armed attack. It is widely, although by no means universally, accepted that the right to self-defense also includes the use of force in order to avert the threat of an imminent attack, often referred to as anticipatory or preemptive self-defense.[289] Yet despite different estimates as to how close Iran is to producing a nuclear weapon, experts concur in that Iran does not yet possess such a weapon. Military action against it would fall at best within the category of 'preventive self-defense', that is military action aimed at preventing the threat from even crystallizing.

In its 2002 National Security Strategy, the US has advocated a doctrine according to which[290]

> [w]e must be prepared to stop rogue states and their terrorist clients before they are able to threaten or use weapons of mass destruction against the United States and our allies and friends.

[283] UNSC Res 661(1990) (6 August 1990) UN Doc S/RES/661(1990).

[284] Simon Tisdall, 'Time's running out for Obama in Iran' *The Guardian* (3 August 2009) www.guardian.co.uk/commentisfree/cifamerica/2009/aug/03/barack-obama-iran.

[285] Russia: Doc. 15-Doc. 18; Argentina: Doc. 16.

[286] Israeli then-deputy prime minister Shaul Mofaz was reported to have told the media that 'If Iran continues with its programme for developing nuclear weapons, we will attack it. The sanctions are ineffective', and that '[a]ttacking Iran, in order to stop its nuclear plans, will be unavoidable'. —— 'Israeli Minister Threatens Iran' *BBC World News* news.bbc.co.uk/2/hi/middle_east/7440472.stm. Iran responded to this statement in Doc. 118.

[287] For an analysis of the nuances of the US position, including whether it is willing to back an Israel operation, see *Landau* (n 278).

[288] General questions include whether states may act when the Security Council is seized of a matter. Malvina Halberstam, 'The Rights to Self-defense Once the Security Council Takes Action' (1996) 17 *Michigan Journal of International Law* 229.

[289] UN Doc A/59/565 (n 209) para 188.

[290] The National Security Strategy of the United States of America (September 2002) 41 *International Legal Materials* 1478.

The National Security Strategy sparked immediate controversy, in part because it was articulated by the world's sole superpower and by an administration with a reputation for acting unilaterally and seemingly eager to advance US interests through the use of military force, particularly in the then-looming confrontation with Iraq. The doctrine misfired badly in Iraq, where the US-led intervention was justified as essential to destroy Saddam Hussein's WMDs programmes, which were later found not to exist.[291]

Israel has also relied on the notion of preventive self-defence when on 7 June 1981 its air force bombed the French-supplied, nearly completed Osiraq research nuclear reactor in Iraq. Two days later Israeli Prime Minister Menachem Begin justified the attack both on moral and legal grounds. Begin referred to the strike as an act of 'anticipatory self-defense at its best'. However, the substance of his argument was on preventive self-defence:[292]

> We chose this moment: now, not later, because later may be too late, perhaps forever. And if we stood by idly, two, three years, at the most four years, and Saddam Hussein would have produced his three, four, five bombs.... Then, this country and this people would have been lost...we shall defend our people with all the means at our disposal. We shall not allow any enemy to develop weapons of mass destruction turned against us.

The Israeli attack met with near-universal condemnation from the international community. The UN Security Council unanimously and 'strongly' condemned Israel for the strike.[293] Its resolution characterised the Israeli action as a 'clear violation of the UN charter and the norms of international conduct'. The IAEA BOG was equally condemnatory.[294] The UN General Assembly adopted a resolution harshly critical of the Israeli attack,[295] with only Israel and the United States voting against it. Nonetheless, some argue that the import of these resolutions must not be overestimated: since the resolutions are not, by themselves, norm-creating, the states adopting them were afforded a diplomatic opportunity to condemn the attack while secretly applauding it. D'Amato points out that the Security Council resolution did not mention punishment, did not call for reparations to be paid by Israel, and did not set in motion any enforcement machinery under the UN Charter.[296]

Reactions were entirely different when on 6 September 2007 Israeli warplanes destroyed an industrial facility near al-Kibar, Syria, later identified by the CIA as a nearly-completed nuclear reactor secretly under construction since 2001. According to the CIA, the unit was built with North Korean assistance and was modeled on one used by North Korea to produce plutonium for nuclear weapons. In the aftermath of the attack, there was near total lack of international comment or criticism of Israel's action. The lack of reaction contrasted starkly with the international outcry that followed the 1981 strike. To be sure, foreign governments may have reserved comment because of the lack of information after the attack. The Israeli and US governments imposed virtually total news blackouts immediately after the raid, that held for seven months, and Syria was initially silent on the matter and then subsequently denied that the bombed target was a nuclear facility. Yet, the international silence continued even after the CIA on 24 April 2008, provided a 12-minute

---

[291] Leonard S Spector and Avner Cohen, 'Israel's Airstrike on Syria's Reactor: Implications for the Nonproliferation Regime' *Arms Control Today* (July/August 2008).

[292] *Spector and Cohen* (n 291).

[293] UNSC Res 487 (19 June 1981) UN Doc S/RES/487 (1981).

[294] IAEA General Conference, 'Military attack on Iraqi nuclear research centre and its implications for the Agency' Resolution GC(25)/RES/381 (19 October 1981).

[295] UNGA Res 36/27 (13 November 1981) UN Doc A/RES/36/27, adopted 109-2-34.

[296] Anthony D'Amato, 'Israel's Air Strike Against The Osiraq Reactor: A Retrospective' (1996) 10 *Temple International and Comparative Law Journal* 259, 262.

video and an extensive briefing that made a strong case that the target was a North Korean-built reactor designed for production of weapons-usable plutonium. The attack was not even discussed at either the Security Council, the 2009 Preparatory Committee for the 2010 review conference of the NPT, or the IAEA BOG. It would probably be an overstatement to interpret this silence as an endorsement of the right to preventive self-defence; silence is a convenient reaction that avoids the need for a government to openly take sides in a potentially incendiary international controversy. Nonetheless, the persistence of the silence suggests that states are becoming increasingly concerned about the weakness of the NPT regime and are therefore cautiously more tolerant of an affected state using force preventively.[297] At the same time, articulated *opinio juris* still seems to coalesce around the impermissibility of use of force to respond to threats which have not yet crystallised but which might materialise at some time in the future, even when at issue are WMDs.[298] This is also the prevalent opinion of scholars,[299] who warn that if the requirement of an imminent attack is foregone, the prohibition on the use of force loses much of its force as regards actions to stop the development of nuclear weapons.[300]

To bridge the emerging gap between positive law and the emerging challenge, new substantive and procedural paradigms have been proposed for the use of force when the international community is faced with WMDs. Some propose more lenient interpretations of the requisite of 'imminence'.[301] Others emphasise the characteristics of the holder of the WMDs, namely whether it is an 'aggressive' state.[302] However, as pointed out earlier, the interests of states are prone to change, and it is doubtful whether different standards should apply on the basis of such characterizations. A more revolutionary proposal is to re-characterise the law on the use of force as non-binding.[303]

---

[297] *Spector and Cohen* (n 291).

[298] *Blix* (n 253) 10.

[299] For sample opinions see Thomas M Franck, 'The Future of Force: Waging War in the 21st Century: Preemption, Prevention and Anticipatory Self-Defence: New Law Regarding Recourse to Force' (2004) 27 *Hastings International and Comparative Law Review* 425; Richard N Gardner, 'Neither Bush nor the Jusiprudes' (2003) 97 *American Journal of International Law* 585; Miriam Sapiro, 'Iraq: the Shifting Sands of Preemptive Self-Defence' (2003) 97 *American Journal of International Law* 599; Tom J Farer, 'Beyond the Charter Frame: Unilateralism or Condominium?' (2002) 96 *American Journal of International Law* 359; Thomas Graham, 'National Self-Defense, International Law, and Weapons of Mass Destruction' (2003) 4 *Chicago Journal of International Law* 1, and sources cited therein; Elizabeth Wilmshurst, 'Chatham House Principles of International Law on the Use of Force by States In Self-Defence', International Law Program Working Paper 1/05 (October 2005); Mary Ellen O'Connell and Maria Alevra-Chen, 'The Ban on the Bomb - and Bombing: Iran, the U.S., and the International Law of Self-Defense' (2007) 57 *Syracuse Law Review* 497, 503; Yoram Dinstein, *War Aggression and Self-Defence* (4th ed, Cambridge University Press, Cambridge, 2005) 185-186; Richard Dalton (ed), 'Iran: Breaking the Nuclear deadlock' Chatham House Report (2008) 36.

[300] *Blix* (n 253) 9.

[301] Kristen Eichensehr, 'Targeting Tehran: Assessing the Lawfulness of Preemptive Strikes against Nuclear Facilities' (2006) 11 *UCLA Journal of International Law and Foreign Affairs* 59; Mark L Rockefeller, 'The "Imminent Threat" Requirement for the Use of Preemptive Military Force: Is it Time for a Non-Temporal Standard?' (2004-2005) 13 *Denver Journal of International Law and Policy* 131.

[302] D'Amato (n 296) 263; Eyal Benvenisti, 'The US and the Use of Force: Double-edged Hegemony and the Management of Global Emergencies' (2004) 15 *European Journal of International Law* 677; Colonel Guy B Roberts, 'The Counterproliferation Self-Help Paradigm: A Legal Regime for Enforcing the Norm Prohibiting the Proliferation of Weapons of Mass Destruction' (1998-1999) 27 *Denver Journal of International Law and Policy* 483; *Timbie* (n 204); Prof Robert F Turner, Presentation at 'A Nuclear Iran: The Legal Implications of a Preemptive National Security Strategy', Syarcuse University College of Law (27 October 2006), webdev. maxwell.syr.edu/insct/archive/Miscellaneous%20Pages/Research_SWP0607.htm.

[303] Daniel H Joyner, '*Jus ad Bellum* in the Age of WMD Proliferation' (2008) 40 *George Washington International Law Review* 233, 274-288.

Any unilateral military action would have to comply with the requirements of necessity and proportionality.[304] As with respect to resort to force under Article 42, in the case of unilateral self-defence again the question arises whether all peaceful means of resolving the dispute have been exhausted. In this context the effectiveness or otherwise of Article 41 measures is even less controlling.

Analysts debate the political wisdom of military action. Others doubt the effectiveness of military intervention in halting a nuclear research programme, in which case its necessity is doubtful.[305] This concern also affects the requirement of proportionality: if a military attack is non-conducive to its aim, it would also be disproportionate.[306]

Finally, the *ius in bello* aspects of any military action should be considered. Iran has dispersed its nuclear sites throughout the country, near civilian population concentrations, and possibly also underground.[307] Some scholars express concern that given the dispersal and structure of Iran's nuclear facilities, any military attack which could effectively neutralise these facilities would also cause disproportionate incidental injury to civilians.[308]

9. Conclusion

Iran argues that the issues raised since 2003 have for the most part been resolved in a manner which supports or at least does not contradict its explanations, yet this has been largely disregarded by the Security Council.[309] It claims that nothing short of its total capitulation will satisfy the western powers, and regards this as extortion.[310] Others accuse Iran of being the one engaging in blackmail, in its demand for economic assistance permitted under Articles III and IV of the NPT and the release of sanctions as conditions for returning to the path of non-proliferation.[311] Western states argue that given Iran's past record of concealment and its overall policy, it cannot benefit from the doubt as to its ultimate goal.[312] It seems that any stance adopted by Iran which falls short of complete acquiescence is regarded not only as an act of defiance but also as an indication that Iran has something to hide.[313]

The debate remains, however, to what extent the lack of trust can generate legal consequences. Some argue that without a 'smoking gun', there is no ground to act against Iran. They warn of the danger in relying on strategic assessment, which may prove to be misguided, as was the case of Iraq in 2003. Others emphasise the severity of the risks on the one hand and the ability of proliferators to hide the evidence, concluding that while comprehensive and logical assessments with regard to nuclear proliferation need to include as much hard evidence as possible, in the interest of non-proliferation they should

---

[304] *Military and Paramilitary Activities in and against Nicaragua (Nicaragua v United States of America)* (Merits) [1986] ICJ Rep 94 [176]; *Legality of Threat or Use of Nuclear Weapons* (advisory opinion) (n 156) [41].

[305] *Ciricione and Grotto* (n 203) 30-33; Patrick Clawson and Michael Eisenstadt, 'Halting Iran's Nuclear Programme: The Military Option' (2008) 50 *Survival* 13; *O'Connell and Alevra-Chen* (n 299) 509, 511.

[306] *O'Connell and Alevra-Chen* (n 299) 515.

[307] *O'Connell and Alevra-Chen* (n 299) 515.

[308] *O'Connell and Alevra-Chen* (n 299) 509; *Afraziabi and Kibaroglu* (n 197) 261.

[309] Sources at n 185.

[310] Iran: Doc. 15; Doc. 129 para 12; Libya: Doc. 81 para 59.

[311] *Garvey* (n 169) 344.

[312] Shahram Chubin, *Iran's Nuclear Ambitions* 4 (Washington, DC, Carnegie Endowment for International Peace, 2006).

[313] US: Doc. 18.

not be held hostage to the absence of such evidence.[314] The wording of the international instruments allows account to be taken of risks and evaluations rather than rely exclusively on hard evidence. Opinions continue to differ on just how far the international community may proceed in acting against a state in the absence of any hard evidence.

No less significant is the question of how to deal with a state once it is identified as a suspected proliferator. Clearly the NPT regime is ill-equipped to deal with cases such as Iran's. Its provisions are not geared to seeking out and stopping suspected defectors, as the lack of precise criteria for dealing with such suspicions when they arise demonstrates. The NPT drafters devoted little attention to the prospect that a state may develop an interest in becoming a nuclear-weapon state without first withdrawing from the Treaty.[315] But in a world of new instabilities, where nuclear technology is increasingly accessible, the NPT is failing to achieve containment.[316] The consensual regime of the NPT was established during the cold war, which encouraged adherence to the Treaty and the IAEA safeguards regime. Some argue that this consensual regime is not only increasingly ill-fitted to address nuclear weapons proliferation risk, but actually enhances the incentive to proliferate.

There are various initiatives and proposals attempting to escape this impasse. Some propose to strengthen the existing non-proliferation regime from the inside, both substantively and institutionally. These initiatives include, among other, strengthening the IAEA BOG, creating standing institutions for the NPT and limiting the nuclear fuel cycle.[317] In 2004 the Secretary-General's High-level Panel Report on Threats, Challenges and Change, put forward proposals for meeting the challenge of preventing the proliferation of WMDs. These recommendations contained both political and legal incentives for compliance. They included the NWS honoring their commitments under NPT Article VI, universal adherence to the NPT, establishment of nuclear-weapon-free zones, making the additional protocol a standard for IAEA safeguards (with Security Council action in case of serious concern over non-compliance), self-imposed moratoria, and IAEA verification for states withdrawing from the NPT.[318] These recommendations were not adopted by the heads of states when they endorsed the Report in General Assembly Resolution 60/1.[319] Johnson suggests that this rejection was linked to the emphasis on disarmament as part of the 'package deal' of recommendations. He nonetheless argues that the recommendations are non-problematic in themselves and may be adopted gradually and individually.[320]

Other proposals move away from consensual mechanisms for encouraging compliance, and towards effective enforcement. As Fidler and other point out, the traditional reliance on the consensual arms control regimes is fading away, giving way to regulation of

---

[314] Emily B Landau, 'Assessing Nuclear Activity in Syria and Iran: The Elusive Smoking Gun' INSS Insight No 54 (4 May 2008), www.inss.org.il/research.php?cat=3&incat=&read=1785.

[315] *Landau* (n 250) 36.

[316] *Garvey* (n 169) 341.

[317] *Howlett and Simpson* (n 75) 17, 19-20. For a comparison of the US and European approaches to dealing with the proliferation WMDs see Milagros Alvarez-Verdugo 'Comparing U.S. and E.U. Strategies against Weapons of Mass Destruction: Some Legal Consequences' (2005) 11 *Annual Survey of International and Comparative Law* 119.

[318] UN Doc A/59/565 (n 209) ch 5, particularly paras 120-134; many of these recommendations (and others) are also included in the *Weapons of Mass Destruction Commission* (n 68) 188-204. Müller proposes to strengthen the authority of the Conference of the Parties to the NPT to address violations of the Treaty, *Müller* (n 141) 13-14.

[319] A/RES/60/1 (24 October 2005).

[320] Larry D Johnson, 'Protecting the World from Weapons of Mass Destruction: Reflections on the High-level Panel Report on Threats, Challenges and Change' (2007-2008) 28 *California Western International Law Journal* 63, 73-74.

proliferation through the international law on the use of force.[321] Indeed, even initiatives related directly to strengthening compliance with safeguard agreements invest in non-consensual mechanisms for strengthening the existing regime.[322] Thus, Goldschmidt proposes a generic Security Council resolution to address the case of a state that has been found by the Agency to be deliberately in non-compliance with its safeguards undertakings. Such a resolution would obligate the non-compliant state to suspend all sensitive nuclear fuel cycle activities until the IAEA has drawn the conclusion that the state's declaration is correct and complete, and to provide the Agency with the additional verification authority necessary to reach that conclusion without undue delay. The proposed resolution would also prohibit delivery of nuclear material to the non-compliant state unless it guarantees that it would remain under IAEA safeguards even if it withdraws from the NPT.[323] Garvey proposes a different generic Security Council resolution, which would declare nuclear weapons proliferation a 'threat to the peace', thereby engaging the sanctions regime of UN Charter Chapter VII in every case of non-compliance with the IAEA. Garvey's proposed resolution would also include benchmarks, such as uranium enrichment and spent fuel reprocessing; refer to prior resolutions adopting targeted sanctions; stipulate the obligation of every state to declare its nuclear weapons or non-nuclear weapons status; and formalise the function of the IAEA to notify the Security Council of evidence of proliferation.[324] Kittrie proposes to maintain the central role of the NPT but to amend the Treaty through a Security Council resolution, and to buttress the regime by Security Council measures.[325]

These and other proposals[326] have been put forward in response to challenges to the NPT regime, reflected, *inter alia*, in the Iranian nuclear dispute. None of them address what is perhaps the greatest obstacle to success of the NPT regime - its unique formal asymmetry and the legacy of international practice. Whatever the legal extent of the obligation to disarm, undoubtedly the political legitimacy of the regime is being undermined by what is perceived as abuse of status by the NWS.[327]

It remains to be seen whether effective legal tools will be adopted in a timely manner to prevent Iran's nuclear programme from maturing into a nuclear threat, or whether international law will continue to play a merely responsive role to that threat.

---

[321] David P Fidler, 'International Law and Weapons of Mass Destruction: End of the Arms Control Approach?' (2004) 14 *Duke Journal of Comparative and International Law* 39, 43; *Milagros Alvarez-Verdugo* (n 317) identifies a similar trend with respect to the US.

[322] Eg the Proliferation Security Initiative, see Jack I Garvey, 'The International Institutional Imperative for Countering the Spread of Weapons of Mass Destruction: Assessing the Proliferation Security Initiative' (2005) 10 *Journal of Conflict and Security Law* 125.

[323] Pierre Goldschmidt, 'Priority Steps to Strengthen the Nonproliferation Regime' (February 2007) Carnegie Endowment Policy Outlook; Vik Kanwar, 'Two Crises of Confidence: Securing Non-Proliferation and the Rule of Law through Security Council Resolutions' (2009) 35 *Ohio Northern University Law Review* 171.

[324] *Garvey* (n 169) 346.

[325] *Kittrie* (n 256) 419-423.

[326] *Perkovich et al* (n 205) 77-80.

[327] *Weapons of Mass Destruction Commission* (n 68) 61; *Müller* (n 141) 6; *Blix* (n 253) 4.

Chronology

1968-1990

1 July 1968

Iran signs the NPT.[1]

February-March 1970

Iran deposits instruments of ratification of the NPT with the Governments of the United States (2 February 1970), the Soviet Union (10 February 1970) and the United Kingdom of Great Britain and Northern Ireland (5 March 1970). The NPT enters into force, including with respect to Iran, on 5 March 1970.

19 June 1973

Iran signs an agreement with the IAEA for the application of safeguards in connection with the NPT. The Agreement enters into force on 15 May 1974.[2]

12 February 1976

Iran and the IAEA conclude Subsidiary Agreements to the Safeguards Agreement.[3]

1991-1995

Late October 1991

A US National Intelligence Estimate concludes that Iran is seeking to develop a nuclear weapons capability. It adds that Iran's nuclear programme appears disorganised and in its early stages.[4]

7-12 February 1992

The IAEA visits facilities in Iran[5] following US and Israeli allegations that Iran has a secret nuclear weapons programme. Concluding the visit, at sites which the IAEA has selected, the IAEA declares that the activities reviewed by the team 'were found to be consistent with the peaceful application of nuclear energy and ionizing radiation'.[6]

24 September 1993

In a speech before the IAEA 37th General Conference, Iran says that its nuclear programme is completely peaceful and that it is the first country to promote a nuclear-weapon-free zone for the Middle East. It invites the IAEA to visit its nuclear facilities.[7]

November 1993

The IAEA visits facilities in Iran following further allegations by the US. The IAEA reports that the officials 'found no evidence which was inconsistent with Iran's declaration that all its nuclear activities are peaceful'. These findings are said to be inconclusive because of the size of these sites and because Iran does not allow the inspectors to perform the full range of inspection methods including environmental monitoring.[8]

20 September 1994

Speaking at the IAEA 38th General Conference, Iran hints that it would consider ceasing cooperation with the Agency and even withdrawing from the NPT if US sanctions and export control regimes prevent it from benefiting from the peaceful application of nuclear energy under international instruments.[9]

10 January 1995

The IAEA says it has no evidence that Iran is constructing nuclear weapons. The report comes after allegations by the US and Israel that Iran will have a nuclear bomb within 7-15 years.[10]

---

[1] INFCIRC/140 (22 April 1970).

[2] Doc. 4.

[3] Date mentioned in IAEA, 'Communication dated 18 April 2007 from the Secretariat to the Resident Representative of the Islamic Republic of Iran' (18 April 2007) GOV/INF/2007/10. The Subsidiary Arrangements are kept confidential.

[4] Elaine Sciolino 'Report Says Iran Seeks Atomic Arms' *New York Times* (31 October 1991) A7.

[5] UNGA 'Report of the International Atomic Energy Agency' UN GAOR 49th session UN Doc A/49/PV.34 9.

[6] IAEA 'Communication Received from the Islamic Republic of Iran' (14 July 1992) INFCIRC/406.

[7] IAEA GC(XXXVII)/OR.354.

[8] Mark D Skootsky 'US Nuclear Policy toward Iran' (1 June 1995) people.csail.mit.edu/boris/iran-nuke.text.

[9] Doc. 95 paras 16-19.

[10] Reuters, 'Iran Gets Nuclear All-Clear' *The Independent* (11 January 1995) International 15.

18 April 1995

At the 1995 NPT Review and Extension Conference, the UK says that export controls only affect states like Iran, 'about whose ultimate intentions there were widespread doubts'.[11] Iran deplores this statement and says that parties to the NPT which fulfill their obligations should be able to exercise their inalienable right under Article IV of the Treaty and have free access to the peaceful use of nuclear energy.[12]

17 June 1995

Concluding a G7 Summit, the Chairman's Statement calls on all states to avoid any collaboration with Iran which might contribute to the acquisition of a nuclear weapons capability.[13] This call is reiterated in the 1996, 1997 and 1998 summits.[14]

4 July 1995

According to Iranian media, the IAEA DG says that Iran has adhered to all its international commitments, and that there has not been the slightest obstruction preventing IAEA experts from familiarising themselves with Iran's atomic installations.[15]

1996-2000

July 1996

The Wassenaar Arrangement becomes operative. It controls dual-use exports of technologies that can facilitate the proliferation of WMDs, complementing the controls of the NSG.

24 September 1996

Iran signs the Comprehensive Test Ban Treaty (CTBT). It has not ratified it.

28 October 1996

At the UN General Assembly debate on the IAEA annual report, Iran objects to the 'unilateral evaluation and certification of the activities' of IAEA members through the export control regimes. It says that the IAEA remains the competent authority to verify and assure compliance with the NPT. Export control regimes are inconsistent with the letter and spirit of the NPT, and with the principles of sovereign equality of states and non-intervention.[16] This statement is repeated in subsequent UN General Assembly debates.[17]

20-21 July 1997

The IAEA DG carries out inspections in Iran. Iranian media later report that the IAEA has repeatedly stressed the peaceful nature of Iran's nuclear programmes and that all of Iran's nuclear activities are conducted under the supervision of IAEA.[18]

9 May 1998

The G8 foreign ministers call on Iran 'to respect the international conventions or arrangements it has signed regarding the development of weapons of mass destruction and urge all states to avoid providing assistance to Iran that might contribute to its ability to develop these weapons or missile capabilities in violation of international conventions or arrangements'.[19]

---

[11] 1995 Review and Extension Conference of the Parties to the NPT, Summary Record of the 3rd Meeting, (18 April 1995) NPT/Conf.1995/SR.3 para 36.

[12] NPT/CONF.1995/SR.3 para 167.

[13] Doc. 149 para 19.

[14] G7 Lyon Summit Chairman's Statement [Political Declaration]: Toward Greater Security and Stability in a More Cooperative World, Part II para 3 (29 June 1996), www.g8.fr/evian/english/navigation/g8_documents/archives_from_previous_summits/lyons_summit_-_1996/toward_greater_security_and_stability_in_a_more_cooperative_world.html; G8 Denver Summit Communiqué para 86 (22 June 1997) www.g7.utoronto.ca/summit/1997denver/g8final.htmm; G8 Birmingham Summit, Conclusions of G8 Foreign Ministers, para 41 (London 9 May 1998), www.g8.utoronto.ca/foreign/fm980509.htm.

[15] —— 'IAEA's Blix gives Iran clean bill of health' *Vision of the Islamic Republic of Iran Network 1*(Tehran 4 July 1995); *BBC Summary of World Broadcasts* (5 July 1995).

[16] Doc. 98.

[17] Eg 12 November 1997: A/52/PV.49 3-4; 2 November 1998: A/53/PV.51 5.

[18] —— 'IAEA chief in Tehran to inspect research facilities' *Associated Press* (20 July 1997); *BBC Summary of World Broadcasts* (21 August 1997); 'IAEA official denies The Times' report on Iran's nuclear activities' (Tehran 19 August 1997); *BBC Summary of World Broadcasts* (19 August 1997); —— 'Iranian Atomic Energy Chief Holds Talks With IAEA's Blix' *IRNA* (Tehran 2 October 1997).

[19] G8 Birmingham Summit, Conclusions of G8 Foreign Ministers (9 May 1998), www.g8.utoronto.ca/foreign/fm980509.htm.

2 April 2000

According to Iranian media, IAEA official David Kyd has stated that the IAEA has regularly inspected Iranian nuclear facilities and has never observed anything that would indicate that the Iranian nuclear programme has any military purposes.[20]

13 July 2000

The G8 Foreign Ministers 'call on Iran to sign with the IAEA an additional safeguards protocol. The G8 calls on Iran to cooperate fully in not developing and in preventing the proliferation of weapons of mass destruction and missiles for their delivery'.[21]

2001

2001

A revised General Part of the Subsidiary Arrangements to the Safeguards Agreement enters into force for Iran.[22]

7 February 2001

The European Commission recommends to the European Council to develop closer relations with Iran on the basis of, *inter alia*, strengthening the Common Foreign and Security Policy dialogue in areas such as regional security, WMDs and nuclear proliferation.[23]

3 July 2001

The IAEA DG says 'We have not seen any violation of [Iran's] obligation under the Non-Proliferation Treaty'.[24]

13 December 2001

The European Parliament adopts a resolution following up on the European Commission's communication of February 2001, in which it advocates a two-pronged policy for cooperation with Iran, comprising on the one hand a critical dialogue to raise issues including nuclear, chemical and biological WMDs; and, on the other hand, cooperation in various fields to provide a more solid base for cooperation.[25]

14 December 2001

Former Iranian President Akbar Hashemi Rafsanjani gives a speech in Tehran. Pointing out that the survival of Israel depends on the interests of western powers, Rafsanjani says:[26]

Of course, you can see that the Americans have kept their eyes peeled and they are carefully looking for even the slightest hint that technological advances are being made by an independent Islamic country. If an independent Islamic country is thinking about acquiring other kinds of weaponry, then they will do their utmost to prevent it from acquiring them. Well, that is something that almost the entire world is discussing right now.

Now, even if that does not happen, they can still inflict greater costs on the imperialists. That is possible as well. Developments over the last few months really frightened the Americans. That is a cost in itself. Under special circumstances, such costs may be inflicted on the imperialists by people who are fighting for their rights or by Muslims. Then they will compare them to see how they could advance their interests better or what they can do. However, we cannot engage in such debates for too long. We cannot encourage that sort of thing either. I am only talking about the natural course of developments. The natural course of developments is such that such things may happen.

---

[20] Agence France Presse, 'IAEA Spokesman: Iran's Nuclear Program Peaceful' *Tehran Times* (Tehran 2 April 2000).

[21] Doc. 150 para 37.

[22] IAEA Annual Report for 2001 GC(46)/2 100.

[23] Doc. 161.

[24] —— 'Nuclear Threats' *National Public Radio* (3 July 2001), www.npr.org/templates/story/story.php?storyId=1125297.

[25] European Parliament resolution on the communication from the Commission to the European Parliament and the Council on EU relations with the Islamic Republic of Iran (COM(2001) 71 - C5-0338/2001 - 2001/2138(COS)).

[26] *Voice of the Islamic Republic of Iran*, Tehran, in Persian (14 December 2001). Translation by BBC Monitoring, reprinted by permission from the BBC.

27 December 2001

In a letter to the Security Council, Israel alleges that Rafsanjani's sermon on 14 December indicated that the Islamic world is arming itself with nuclear weapons.[27]

2002

9 January 2002

Iran rejects the Israeli allegation as a misrepresentation of Rafsanjani's sermon. Iran says that its practice of rejecting WMDs through the position of its officials, including Rafsanjani's, is well known.[28]

29 January 2002

In his State of the Union address, US President George W Bush accuses Iran of pursuing WMDs.[29]

4 February 2002

In response to US President Bush's State of the Union Address Iran says that it does not seek WMDs but is pursuing disarmament. Iran vigorously pursues its inalienable right to develop its nuclear, chemical and biological industries for peaceful purposes. It says that the deliberate campaign by the United States to arbitrarily deprive Iran of this right is a further violation of the non-proliferation regimes.[30]

26 May 2002

Iran successfully completes its fourth test of the Shahab-3 medium-range ballistic missile, with a range of 1,300 kilometres when equipped with a 700-kilogram payload. Shahab-3 is liquid-fueled and road-mobile.[31]

17 June 2002

The EU Council asks the European Commission to launch negotiations with Iran on a Trade and Co-operation Agreement, which is linked to separate instruments on political dialogue and counter-terrorism. The EU encourages Iran to sign, ratify and fully implement international instruments relevant to non-proliferation.[32]

14 August 2002

The Iranian opposition group National Council of Resistance of Iran (NCRI) reveals a report in Washington DC,[33] according to which Iran is carrying out many secret nuclear programmes. The leading ones are a nuclear fuel production plant and research lab in Natanz,[34] and a heavy water facility in Arak. The report lists other planned and active nuclear centers in Iran and discloses details on front companies of the Atomic Energy Organization of Iran (AEOI), which facilitate the Organization's contacts and exchanges with foreign companies to procure technical needs without using its official title. During subsequent months, the NCRI reveals additional information on sites that might be used for uranium enrichment to complement Natanz.[35]

16 September 2002

Speaking before the IAEA 46th General Conference, Iran declares that ever since the inception of the IAEA, it has submitted all its nuclear activities to the IAEA's supervision. Without express reference to the sites in Natanz and Arak it also announces that it is embarking on a long-term plan to construct within two decades nuclear power plants with a total capacity of 6000 MW. It says that such a sizable project entails all-out planning, well in advance, in various fields of nuclear technology such as fuel cycle, safety and waste management. It reiterates its ideological opposition to WMDs.[36]

---

[27] UN Doc A/56/758-S/2001/1262.

[28] UN Doc S/2007/37 Letter dated 8 January 2002 from the Permanent Representative of the Islamic Republic of Iran to the United Nations addressed to the UN Secretary-General.

[29] stateoftheunionaddress.org/2002-george-w-bush.

[30] Doc. 99.

[31] —— 'Iran Conducts Fourth Shahab-3 Test' *Arms Control Today* (1 June 2002).

[32] Doc. 155.

[33] News Bulletin of the Foreign Affairs Committee of the National Council of Resistance of Iran (19 August 2002).

[34] Iran later confirmed that it was constructing a pilot fuel enrichment plant (PFEP) and a large commercial-scale fuel enrichment plant (FEP), Doc. 33 para 5.

[35] Sharon Squassoni, 'Iran's Nuclear Program: Recent Developments' (Congressional Research Service, Report for Congress 15 August 2003).

[36] Doc. 100.

During the General Conference, Iranian Vice President Aghazadeh confirms to the IAEA DG that Iran is building a number of nuclear fuel cycle facilities.[37] He agrees to a visit by the DG to the two sites later in 2002, accompanied by safeguards experts, and to a discussion on Iran's nuclear development plans. The visit is later postponed to February 2003.[38]

12 December 2002

The EU and Iran begin negotiations on a trade and cooperation agreement and on political dialogue and cooperation against terrorism.[39]

12-14 December 2002

CNN shows satellite pictures of the nuclear facilities in Natanz and Arak.[40] The US says[41] that the circumstances of the particular nuclear sites lead to the conclusion that Iran's nuclear programme is neither peaceful nor transparent. It says that it will continue its longstanding effort to get agreement from all countries to refrain from nuclear cooperation with Iran and to thwart Iran's covert efforts to buy or acquire sensitive nuclear equipment and expertise. Iran responds that its activities are totally transparent, clear and peaceful, and that had it engaged in the alleged activities, it would have been impossible to conceal them.[42]

2003

February 2003

The IAEA begins verification of Iran's newly-revealed nuclear programme.[43]

9 February 2003

Iranian President Khatami announces that Iran has adopted plans to exploit the uranium mines 200 km off Yazd and set up plants in Esfahan and Kashan (Near Natanz) to extract uranium composites to provide fuel for generating electricity. He says that for Iran to produce electricity from its nuclear power plants, it must complete the fuel cycle from discovering uranium to managing remaining spent fuel.[44]

21-26 February 2003

The IAEA DG and other officials visit sites in Iran, including Natanz, originally scheduled for October 2002. During the visit Iran discloses the existence of a pilot fuel enrichment plant (PFEP) and a commercial-scale fuel enrichment plant (FEP) in Natanz, and confirms that a heavy-water production plant is under construction in Arak.[45] Iran acknowledges receipt in 1991 of natural uranium from a foreign source.[46] The IAEA DG stresses the value of bringing an additional protocol into force as an important tool for enabling the IAEA to provide comprehensive assurances of Iran's peaceful intentions. Iran affirms its obligations under the NPT to use all nuclear technology in the country exclusively for peaceful purposes and to follow a policy of transparency. To this end it accepts modification to the Subsidiary Arrangements of the Safeguards Agreement. The modified Code 3.1 of the General Part requires Iran to inform the IAEA of new facilities and on modification to existing facilities, through provision of preliminary design information, at a much earlier date than under the existing Subsidiary Arrangements, namely as soon as the decision to construct, to

---

[37] Interview with Mohamed ElBaradei *CNN* (13 December 2002), edition.cnn.com/TRANSCRIPTS/0212/13/lt.01.html.

[38] Doc. 33 paras 3-4.

[39] EU Presidency and Commission Joint Press Release at the opening of negotiations with Iran (Brussels, 12 December 2002).

[40] David Albright and Corey Hinderstein 'Iran Building Nuclear Fuel Cycle Facilities: International Transparency Needed' (ISIS Issue Brief 12 December 2002), www.isis-online.org/publications/iran/iranimages.html.

[41] US Department of State Daily Press Briefing, Richard Boucher, Spokesman (Washington DC 13 December 2002), 2001-2009.state.gov/r/pa/prs/dpb/2002/15976.htm.

[42] —— 'Iranian FM dismisses US charge of building secret nuclear facilities' *Xinhua News Agency* (Tehran 14 December 2002), www.highbeam.com/doc/1P2-13359714.html.

[43] IAEA DG report to the UN General Assembly, A/59/PV.47, page 5.

[44] —— 'Nuclear Energy for Peaceful Purposes, a Right of Nations: Khatami' *IRNA* (9 February 2003), former. president.ir/khatami/eng/cronicnews/1381/8111/811120/811120.htm.

[45] Doc. 33.

[46] Doc. 33 para 7. The source appears to have been China, see Thérèse Delpech, *Iran and the Bomb: The Abdication of International Responsibility* (New York, Columbia University Press, 2006) 123.

authorise construction or to modify has been taken, and to provide the IAEA with further design information as it is developed.[47]

12 March 2003

Iran's ambassador to the UN reveals that Iran is seeking to establish its own fuel cycle, out of concern that US pressure may affect foreign suppliers.[48]

3 June 2003

The G8 foreign ministers stress the importance of Iran's full compliance with its obligation under the NPT, urge Iran to sign and implement an IAEA Additional Protocol without delay or conditions, and offer their strongest support to comprehensive IAEA examination of Iran's nuclear programme.[49]

6 June 2003

The IAEA DG reports to the BOG on implementation of the NPT Safeguards Agreement in Iran. The report says that 'Iran has failed to meet its obligations under its Safeguards Agreement with respect to the reporting of nuclear material, the subsequent processing and use of that material and the declaration of facilities where the material was stored and processed'.[50] While the quantities of nuclear material involved are not large, the number of failures is a matter of concern. The DG encourages Iran to conclude an Additional Protocol, without which the Agency's ability to provide credible assurances regarding the absence of undeclared nuclear activities is limited.[51]

7-13 June 2003

IAEA experts visit Iran. Samples reveal possible presence in Iran of high enriched uranium (HEU). Iran claims that this results from contamination of imported centrifuge components.[52]

16 June 2003

The EU Council expresses concern at some aspects of Iran's programme as reported by the IAEA DG, and reiterates that progress in this area and strengthened dialogue and cooperation are interdependent, essential and mutually reinforcing elements of the EU-Iran relations.[53]

18-19 June 2003

The IAEA BOG considers the report of the DG. Summing up the discussion, the Chairperson says that the Board shares the concern expressed by the Director General in his report at the number of Iran's past failures to report as required by its safeguards obligations. The Board urges Iran to promptly rectify all safeguards problems identified in the report and to resolve questions that remain open. The Board expects Iran to grant the Agency all access deemed necessary by it, in order to create the necessary confidence in the international community. The Board also encourages Iran, pending the resolution of related outstanding issues, not to introduce nuclear material at the pilot enrichment plant as a confidence-building measure. The Board urges Iran promptly and unconditionally to conclude and implement an additional protocol to its Safeguards Agreement in order to enhance the Agency's ability to provide credible assurances regarding the peaceful nature of Iran's nuclear activities, particularly the absence of undeclared material and activities.[54]

25 June 2003

Iran first uses UF_6 to test a centrifuge at the PFEP in June 2003.[55]

19 August 2003

Iran acknowledges that in the early 1990s it had carried out uranium conversion experiments that should have been reported under the Safeguards Agreement. This contradicts its previous statements that no research or development of

---

[47] Iranian letter of 26 February 2003, reported in Doc. 33 paras 6, 15.
[48] Colum Lynch, 'Envoy: Iran To Continue Its Nuclear Power Effort' *Washington Post* (13 March 2003) A11.
[49] Doc. 150.
[50] Doc. 33 para 32.
[51] Doc. 33.
[52] Doc. 34.
[53] Doc. 151.
[54] Doc. 60 paras 52-58.
[55] Doc. 34 para 33.

uranium conversion had been conducted using nuclear material.[56]

26 August 2003

The IAEA DG reports to the IAEA BOG on implementation of the NPT Safeguards Agreement in Iran. According to the report, environmental sampling at the PFEP in Natanz revealed the presence of two types of HEU, which suggest that Iran might have carried out undeclared enrichment experiments. In addition, IAEA inspectors report that Iran had made extensive efforts to clean up a centrifuge research and development facility at the Kalaye Electric Company, making environmental sampling more difficult; and that some of Iran's statements to the IAEA are inconsistent with previous ones that it had made. Finally, the Agency reports that Iran had begun to introduce UF_6 into the PFEP. The report notes an increased degree of cooperation by Iran, although some of the information and access have at times been slow in coming and incremental. It also points out that it requires information from states that may have provided assistance to Iran.[57]

August-September 2003

According to media reports, the UK, Germany and France, acting together with the High Representative of the EU (EU3) offer to assist Iran with nuclear technology if Iran stops its nuclear fuel enrichment programme and agrees to sign the Additional Protocol. Iran rejects the offer, leading the EU3 to adopt a tougher stance at the IAEA BOG meeting.[58]

8-12 September 2003

The IAEA BOG considers the report of the DG, and adopts without a vote Resolution GOV/2003/69, which reiterates the call for Iran to suspend all further uranium enrichment-related activities; and, as a confidence-building measure, to also suspend any reprocessing activities until the IAEA DG provides the assurances that Iran's nuclear activities have all

been declared. The Board presents Iran with a deadline for the end of October 2003 to remedy all failures and to cooperate fully with the IAEA to ensure verification of its compliance with the Safeguards Agreement.

Iran says that for the preceding 24 years, it has been subject to severe sanctions and export restrictions on material and technology related to the peaceful use of nuclear energy. Consequently it has had no choice but to exercise discretion, as any previous attempts to procure or produce what it needed for its peaceful programme had been relentlessly suppressed. Iran says that full co-operation with the Agency depends on avoiding politicization of the situation. Iran is fully prepared to take remedial action where necessary to ensure that its programme remains peaceful. It says that the adoption of the resolution will force it to undertake a far-reaching review of the existing level and extent of its involvement with the Agency, hinting that it would consider withdrawal from the NPT.[59]

25 September 2003

At the UN General Assembly Iran says it 'will not give in to unreasonable, discriminatory and selective demands that go beyond the requirements of non-proliferation under existing IAEA instruments'.[60] It thus rejects the calls for suspension of its nuclear programme.

5 October 2003

Iran says that it does not consider itself bound by the 31 October deadline, as it has not formally accepted the IAEA BOG's resolution; however, Iran intends to cooperate with the IAEA and give answers as quickly as possible.[61]

16 October 2003

Iran expresses its readiness to conclude an Additional Protocol and, pending its entry into force, to act in accordance with the Protocol and with a policy of full transparency.[62]

---

[56] Doc. 34 paras 14-15; Doc. 35 Annex I para 6.
[57] Doc. 34 paras 47-52.
[58] Dan De Luce, 'Europeans fail to end Iranian nuclear crisis' *Guardian* (London, 20 September 2003).
[59] Doc. 61-Doc. 63.
[60] Doc. 101.
[61] —— 'Iran says "not bound" by IAEA deadline, but promises quick answers' *AFP* (Tehran, 5 October 2003).
[62] Doc. 35 para 13.

17 October 2003

The EU Council says that the EU remains ready to explore ways to develop a wider cooperation with Iran. This can only be achieved through increased international confidence in the peaceful nature of Iran's nuclear programme, and improvements in the areas of human rights, fight against terrorism and Iran's position on the Middle East peace process.[63]

21 October 2003

Iran and the EU3 issue the Tehran Statement in which Iran declares that it has decided to cooperate fully with the IAEA and to sign and ratify the Additional Protocol; as a confidence-building measure it will act in accordance with the Additional Protocol until its ratification. It has also decided 'voluntarily to suspend all uranium enrichment and reprocessing activities as defined by the IAEA'. The EU3 declare that they recognise the right of Iran to enjoy peaceful use of nuclear energy in accordance with the NPT, and that full implementation of Iran's decision, confirmed by the IAEA DG, will open the way to a dialogue on a basis for longer term cooperation, which will provide all parties with satisfactory assurances relating to Iran's nuclear programme and subsequently easier access for Iran to modern technology and supplies in a range of areas.[64]

On the same day Iran admits to having carried out enrichment-related activities in 1991 and 2002 additional to those declared previously.[65]

Late October 2003

The IAEA DG writes to Iran in an attempt to define clearly the activities that require suspension. The first request is that Iran put a stop to testing and operating gas centrifuges, installation of centrifuges at Natanz, and stop laser-enrichment and plutonium-reprocessing activities. Secondly, the DG considers that Iran should cease the production and assembly of centrifuges and their components in sites other than Natanz. Thirdly, the DG suggests that Iran consider additional measures, including a stop to the import of equipment relevant to its nuclear programme.[66]

3 November 2003

At the UN General Assembly's debate on the IAEA annual report, Russia says that it is convinced that in the future all the problems between Iran and IAEA should be resolved through cooperation. It says that the issue of Iran's nuclear programme is excessively politicised, and hopes that it will be possible to move this issue back within the area of regular IAEA inspection activities. Russia adds that it sees no reason to reduce its cooperation with the Islamic Republic of Iran in the nuclear field, which is fully transparent and does not violate either Russia's or Iran's international obligations.[67]

Iran warns that 'arbitrary and often politically motivated limitations and restrictions' on exports will lead targeted states to acquire the same peaceful technology from unofficial channels and in a less than fully transparent fashion, thus exacerbating mutual suspicions and mistrust. It reiterates that nuclear and other WMDs have no place in its defense doctrine, and that the information it provided the IAEA will enable the Agency to verify that all Iranian activities are exclusively in the peaceful domain and in compliance with the NPT and the Safeguards Agreement.[68]

10 November 2003

Iran formally informs the IAEA that it suspends with immediate effect all enrichment related and reprocessing in Iran, and specifically all activities on the site in Natanz, including production of feed material for enrichment processes, and importation of enrichment related materials.[69] It also declares that it accepts and is preparing to sign an Additional Protocol, and that pending the entry into force of the

---

[63] 15188/03 POLGEN 77, issued 25 November 2003, para 68.

[64] Doc. 7.

[65] Doc. 35 para 16

[66] Bronwen Maddox, 'One Small Sliver of Hope From a Recalcitrant Tehran' *The Times* (11 November 2003), www.timesonline.co.uk/tol/news/world/middle_east/article1014278.ece.

[67] Doc. 141.

[68] Doc. 102.

[69] Doc. 35 para 19; Doc. 36 para 58.

Additional Protocol, it will act in accordance with the Additional Protocol's provisions.[70] The US and the EU3 consider that Iran has not fully responded to the requests of IAEA DG with respect to suspension, which they also regard as overly narrow.[71]

10 November 2003

The IAEA DG reports to the BOG on implementation of the NPT Safeguards Agreement in Iran. The report says Iran has 'breached its obligation to comply with the provisions of the Safeguards Agreement', through additional failures, identified since the June 2003 report. It lists failure to report enrichment and reprocessing experiments, uranium importation, laser experiments and uranium conversion; failure to provide design information for various facilities; and failure to cooperate to facilitate the implementation of safeguards, through concealment.[72] It summarises that 'there is no evidence that the previously undeclared nuclear material or activities referred to above were related to a nuclear weapons programme, but given Iran's past pattern of concealment, it will take some time before the Agency can conclude that Iran's nuclear programme is exclusively for peaceful purposes'. The IAEA DG stresses that an Additional Protocol, coupled with a policy of full transparency and openness on the part of Iran, is indispensable for reaching such a conclusion.[73]

12 November 2003

Iran shuts down all centrifuges at Natanz.[74]

21-26 November 2003

The IAEA BOG considers the report of the DG and adopts without a vote Resolution GOV/2003/81, which deplores Iran's failures to report as required by its Safeguards Agreement and its breaches of its obligations under the Safeguards Agreement through a pattern of concealment. The Board decides that should

any further serious Iranian failures come to light, it would immediately consider all options at its disposal. It welcomes Iran's voluntary suspension of all enrichment-related and reprocessing activities and requests Iran to adhere to the suspension completely and in a verifiable manner.[75]

Iran reiterates that its concealment of its programme was due to illegal sanctions and suppression to which it had been and still was subject.[76]

29 November 2003

Iran informs the IAEA, that, with immediate effect:

– it will suspend the operation and/or testing or any centrifuges, either with or without nuclear material, at the PFEP at Natanz;

– it will suspend further introduction of nuclear material into any centrifuges;

– it will suspend installation of new centrifuges at PFEP and installation of centrifuges at the FEP at Natanz; and

– it will withdraw nuclear material from any centrifuge enrichment facility if and to the extent practicable.

Iran also declares that it does not have any type of gas centrifuge enrichment facility at any location in Iran other than the facility at Natanz; that it is not constructing, nor does it have plans to construct, during the suspension period, new facilities capable of isotopic separation; that it has dismantled its laser enrichment projects and removed all related equipment; and that it is neither constructing nor operating any plutonium separation facility.

In addition, Iran states that during the period of suspension it does not intend to make new contracts for the manufacture of centrifuge machines and their components; the Agency can fully supervise storage of all centrifuge machines assembled during the suspension period; Iran does not intend to import centrifuge machines or their components, or feed material for enrichment processes. It also says that there

---

[70] Doc. 35 para 18; IAEA Press Release 2003/13, Vienna 10 November 2003.
[71] Bronwen Maddox (n 66).
[72] Doc. 35 para 48.
[73] Doc. 35.
[74] Doc. 36 para 63.
[75] Doc. 24 operative paragraphs 2, 8, 10.
[76] Doc. 65; Doc. 66.

is no production of feed material for enrichment processes in Iran.[77]

On 29 December 2003 Iran specifies the scope of suspension of its enrichment and reprocessing activities that the IAEA is invited to verify.[78]

18 December 2003

Iran signs the Additional Protocol.[79]

2004

10-18 January 2004

IAEA inspectors in Iran visit a number of military sites.[80]

20 January 2004

Iran acknowledges that it had received P-2 centrifuge drawings from foreign sources in 1994 and that it has conducted some mechanical tests, without nuclear material, using domestically-manufactured rotors. It had not, however, obtained any P-2 centrifuges or their components from abroad, and any centrifuge components it has in its possession have been produced domestically.[81]

24 February 2004

Iran expands the scope of its suspension, begun in November 2003, to cover also the assembly and testing of centrifuges, and domestic manufacture of centrifuge components. Iran also confirms that the suspension of enrichment activities applies to all facilities in Iran.[82]

24 February 2004

The IAEA DG reports to the BOG on implementation of the NPT Safeguards Agreement in Iran. The report says that Iran's

earlier supposedly complete declaration of past activities had failed to provide information on Iran's earlier research on advanced P-2 centrifuge designs and experiments with polonium-210 (Po-210). The report also notes concern over the purpose of Iran's activities related to Po-210. It adds that the production of centrifuge components continues, because, according to Tehran, contracts with private manufacturers of the parts could not be broken.[83]

13 March 2004

The IAEA BOG considers the report of the DG. It adopts without a vote Resolution GOV/2004/21, deferring the consideration of progress made by the IAEA in Iran and the decision on how to respond to the omissions until its June meeting.[84]

Iran says that the resolution had been imposed on the Board by the US and its associates. It threatens to halt cooperation with the IAEA if the latter fails to resist US pressure.[85]

31 March 2004

The EU3 foreign ministers react to an Iranian announcement that it intends to put into service a uranium conversion facility (UCF) in Esfahan, saying that it 'sends the wrong signal regarding Iran's readiness to implement a suspension of its activities'.[86] Iran rejects the criticism, saying that 'the plant is a totally separate issue from our commitment to the suspension of uranium enrichment'.[87]

6 April 2004

Iran agrees to accelerate cooperation with the Agency on a number of outstanding matters identified by the IAEA DG with a view to

---

[77] Doc. 36 paras 58-61.

[78] Doc. 36 para 6.

[79] Doc. 36 para 5; Doc. 5.

[80] Doc. 36 para 8.

[81] Doc. 36 para 44.

[82] Doc. 36 para 62.

[83] Doc. 36.

[84] Doc. 25.

[85] Iranian Ministry of Foreign Affairs, 'Dr. Kharrazi's Statements to the Reporters on the Fringe of Cabinet Meeting, on IAEA Decisions' (10 March 2004), web-srv.mfa.gov.ir/output/english/documents/doc3875.htm (broken link).

[86] FCO Response to Iranian Announcement on Nuclear Facility in Esfahan (31 March 2004), www.fco.gov.uk/en/newsroom/latest-news/?view=PressR&id=2004358.

[87] —— 'Iran Uranium Plant Sparks New Row' *BBC News* (1 April 2004), news.bbc.co.uk/2/hi/middle_east/3589737.stm.

achieving progress on their resolution prior to the June 2004 meeting of the IAEA BOG.[88]

29 April 2004

Iran informs the IAEA that it intended to test the UF_6 production line at Esfahan. The Agency responds[89] that given the amounts of nuclear material involved, this would technically amount to the production of feed material for enrichment processes (which in November 2003 Iran has declared would be covered by its suspension). Iran informs the Agency[90] that 'the decision taken for voluntary and temporary suspension is based on clearly defined scope which does not include suspension of production of UF_6'.[91]

21 May 2004

Iran submits initial declarations pursuant to its Additional Protocol (concerning sites where nuclear material is kept, and fuel cycle activities). It informs the IAEA that as it had signed the Additional Protocol and has decided voluntarily to apply it as a confidence-building measure prior to its formal entry into force, the declarations were being submitted prior to the due date of 18 June 2004, following the IAEA DG's request.[92]

1 June 2004

The IAEA DG reports to the BOG on implementation of the NPT Safeguards Agreement in Iran. The report notes that the verification of Iran's suspension is not comprehensive and that the Iranian decision to proceed with production of UF_6 is at variance with the IAEA understanding as to the scope of the voluntary suspension. It further notes as outstanding issues the origin of HEU and the extent of activity regarding P-1 and P-2 centrifuges.[93]

9 June 2004

The G8 Sea Island Summit Action Plan on Nonproliferation acknowledges the areas of progress reported by the IAEA DG, but expresses deep concern that Iran's suspension of enrichment-related activity is not yet comprehensive. It deplores Iran's delays, deficiencies in cooperation, and inadequate disclosures. It urges Iran promptly and fully to comply with its commitments and with all IAEA Board requirements.[94]

18 June 2004

The IAEA BOG meets to consider the IAEA DG's report and adopts without a vote Resolution GOV/2004/49, drafted and sponsored by the EU3. In the resolution the Board deplores Iran's incomplete cooperation and calls on Iran to take all steps to resolve outstanding questions. The Board welcomes Iran's voluntary suspension but regrets that it is not implemented comprehensively. It urges Iran to ratify without delay its Protocol. It calls on Iran immediately to follow the Agency's understanding of the scope of Iran's decisions regarding suspension, including by refraining from UF_6 production and from all production of centrifuge components. It also calls on Iran to reconsider its decision to begin production testing at UCF at Esfahan and construction of a research heavy water reactor.[95]

Iran says that the provisions concerning UF_6 production and construction of a heavy water research reactor violate the letter and spirit of the NPT and the IAEA Statute, and constitute the first time in the Agency's history that a member state is being asked to suspend the exercise of its right with regard to a declared facility under comprehensive Agency safeguards.

The IAEA DG says that the Agency is not able to certify either that Iran's programme was exclusively for peaceful purposes or that it had a military component.[96]

---

[88] Doc. 37 para 7.
[89] on 7 May 2004.
[90] on 18 May 2004.
[91] Doc. 37 para 14, Doc. 38.
[92] Doc. 37 para 19.
[93] Doc. 37.
[94] G8 Sea Island Summit Action Plan on Nonproliferation para 4 (9 June 2004), www.g8.utoronto.ca/summit/2004seaisland/nonproliferation.html.
[95] Doc. 26.
[96] Doc. 70 paras 10, 13, 34.

23-29 June 2004

Iran informs the IAEA that it intends to suspend the expanded voluntary measures of suspension conveyed on 24 February 2004, and to resume on 29 June manufacturing of centrifuge components and assembly and testing of centrifuges, under IAEA supervision.[97]

8 July 2004

Speaking in Israel, the IAEA DG says that taking Iran to the Security Council runs the risk that Iran might withdraw from the NPT. In the absence of a 'smoking gun', he expresses preference for diplomatic action.[98]

1 September 2004

The IAEA DG reports to the BOG on implementation of the NPT Safeguards Agreement in Iran. The report says that Iran has been providing information, although not always at the pace expected of it. The source of uranium contamination and the extent of Iran's effort to procure and use P-1 and P-2 centrifuges remain key issues. Other matters under examination include plutonium experiments and Po-210 activities.[99]

13-18 September 2004

The IAEA BOG considers the report of the IAEA DG and adopts without a vote Resolution GOV/2004/79. In it the Board regrets that the Iran's voluntary suspension of enrichment-related and reprocessing activities fell significantly short of the Agency's understanding of the scope of those commitments and that it has been partially reversed; considers it necessary, to promote confidence, that Iran immediately suspend all enrichment-related activities, including the manufacture or import of centrifuge components, the assembly and testing of centrifuges, and the production of feed material, including through tests or production at the UCF; and calls again on Iran, as a further confidence-building measure, voluntarily to reconsider the construction of the heavy-water reactor in Arak.

The IAEA BOG decides that at its November session it will decide whether or not further steps are appropriate in relation to Iran's obligations under its NPT Safeguards Agreement, and the requests made of Iran, as confidence-building measures, by the Board in this and previous resolutions.[100] The Board's implicit intention is to consider referral to the Security Council.[101]

Iran says that it has implemented the agreement on suspension fully, while the other side has not met its commitments. Thus the scope of the suspension had to be, and was, readjusted.[102]

1 November 2004

At the UN General Assembly debate on the IAEA annual report, China and Russia emphasise their support for resolving the Iran nuclear issue within the framework of the IAEA. Russia also notes the importance of prompt Agency action to switch its monitoring activities in Iran into normal, routine channels, and views the 18 September resolution of the IAEA BOG as a 'plan of action'.[103]

10 November 2004

Iranian negotiating official Sirus Naseri hints that Iran will pull out of the NPT and develop its atomic programme in secret if pressure to cease uranium enrichment persists.[104]

15 November 2004

The EU3 and Iran conclude the Paris Agreement, which builds on the Tehran Statement of 21 October 2003. Under the Paris Agreement, the EU3 'recognize Iran's rights under the NPT exercised in conformity with its obligations under the Treaty, without discrimination', and Iran reaffirms that 'it does not and will not seek to acquire nuclear weapons'. Iran will, on a voluntary basis, continue and extend its suspension to include 'all enrichment related and reprocessing activities, and specifically: the manufacture and import of gas centrifuges and their components; the assembly, installation, testing or operation of gas centrifuges; work

---

[97] Doc. 38 para 7.
[98] Louis Charbonneau, 'ElBaradei Wary of Taking Iran to Security Council' *Reuters* (8 July 2004).
[99] Doc. 38 paras 56-63.
[100] Doc. 27 paras 7-9.
[101] *Delpech* (n 368) 127.
[102] Doc. 71 paras 17, 18, 41, 45, 67, 71, 64, 123, 142.
[103] Doc. 141; Doc. 143.
[104] Interview with Sirus Naseri, Nuclear Affairs Advisor to the Iranian Government and Senior Negotiator with Europe *Jaam E Jam TV* (10 November 2004), www.memritv.org/clip/en/351.htm.

to undertake any plutonium separation, or to construct or operate any plutonium separation installation; and all tests or production at any uranium conversion installation'. This suspension will be implemented before the IAEA DG's November report and will be sustained while negotiations proceed on a mutually-acceptable agreement on long-term arrangement. That arrangement will provide objective guarantees that Iran's nuclear programme is exclusively for peaceful purposes. It will equally provide firm guarantees on nuclear, technological and economic cooperation and firm commitments on security issues. The EU3 recognise that the suspension is a voluntary confidence-building measure and not a legal obligation. Once suspension has been verified, the negotiations with the EU on a trade and cooperation agreement will resume.[105]

15 November 2004

The IAEA DG reports to the BOG on implementation of the NPT Safeguards Agreement in Iran. The report says that Iran's policy of concealment continued until October 2003, and has resulted in many breaches of its obligation to comply with that Agreement, through failures to report and declare, as well as failure on many occasions to facilitate the implementation of safeguards.[106] Good progress has been made in Iran's correction of those breaches and in the Agency's ability to confirm certain aspects of Iran's current declarations, which will be followed up as a routine safeguards implementation matter.

There remain two important issues relevant to the Agency's investigation in order to provide assurances that there are no undeclared enrichment activities in Iran: the origin of uranium contamination found in Iran; and the extent of Iran's efforts to import, manufacture and use centrifuges of both the P-1 and P-2 designs. The Agency is also still assessing other aspects of Iran's past nuclear programme.[107]

The report indicates that all the declared nuclear material in Iran has been accounted for, and that such material is not diverted to prohibited activities. The IAEA is however still not in a position to conclude that there are no undeclared nuclear materials or activities in Iran. In view of Iran's past concealment of significant aspects of its nuclear programme, this conclusion can be expected to take longer than in normal circumstances.[108]

29 November 2004

The IAEA BOG considers the report of the DG. It adopts without a vote Resolution GOV/2004/90, in which it welcomes Iran's decision to continue and extend its suspension of all enrichment related and reprocessing activities, and underlines that the full and sustained implementation of the suspension, which is a voluntary, non-legally-binding confidence-building measure, is essential to addressing outstanding issues. The Board welcomes Iran's continuing voluntary commitment to act in accordance with the provisions of the Additional Protocol, as a confidence-building measure that facilitates the resolution of the questions that have arisen, and calls on Iran once again to ratify the Protocol. The Board also requests the IAEA DG to inform it should the suspension not be fully sustained.[109]

Iran says that the resolution is a start towards normalisation of its case.[110]

13 December 2004

Negotiations begin between the EU and Iran for the long-term arrangement envisaged in the Paris Agreement of 15 November 2004. The Council of the EU stresses that this arrangement will have to provide objective guarantees that Iran's nuclear programme is exclusively for peaceful purposes. In light of the IAEA's confirmation that Iran has instituted a full suspension of enrichment activities, the EU confirms that it will resume negotiations with Iran on trade and

---

[105] Doc. 8.
[106] Doc. 39 paras 85-86, 87-88.
[107] Doc. 39 paras 107-108.
[108] Doc. 39 para 132 and Statement of the IAEA DG to the IAEA Board of Governors (29 November 2004), www.iaea.org/NewsCenter/Statements/2004/ebsp2004n017.html.
[109] Doc. 28.
[110] Doc. 72 paras 26-27, 47-48, 51, 72, 77, 82-92, 100-101.

cooperation agreement as well as on a political agreement.[111]

2005

12 January 2005

Iran discloses a one-page document reflecting an offer made to it in 1987 by a foreign intermediary for the delivery of centrifuge-related design, technology and sample components. It says that the components were never requested nor delivered.[112] It later acknowledges that some had been delivered.[113] It insists that the document is the only remaining documentary evidence relevant to the scope and content of the 1987 offer.[114] It later offers documents related to earlier stages of the same offer.[115]

17 January 2005

Iran presents the Political and Security Working Group set up following the November 2004 Paris Agreement with a draft joint statement concerning general principles of non-use of force, non-intervention and peaceful settlement of disputes; elimination and non-proliferation of weapons of mass destruction; combating terrorism; sustainable partnership on regional issues, security and defense cooperation; and cooperation in export control.

According to the draft, Iran would remain 'committed not to purse nuclear weapons and others weapons of mass destruction under any circumstances', while the EU3 would undertake to reject the use or threat of use of nuclear weapons against Iran and to take all appropriate measures to prevent it. The two sides would underline the inviolability of peaceful and safeguarded nuclear facilities and agree that any direct or indirect attack or threat against Iranian nuclear facilities would warrant action by the Security Council in accordance it the provision of the UN Charter. Under the draft the EU3 would reaffirm Iran's inherent right to acquire legitimate means for self-defense under Article 51 of the UN Charter, and decide to remove restrictions on the transfer of conventional armaments and their relevant sensitive dual use goods and technology to Iran. Iran would undertake to adopt measures to prevent unauthorised access to its nuclear capability and enrichment technology, and the two sides would to cooperate actively towards this goal.[116]

According to reports, Iran offers additional assurances of the peaceful nature of is nuclear programme, such as increased verification and certain restrictions on the level and extent of the uranium enrichment programme. The EU3 firmly reject this, stressing that suspension is vital for the process. They clarify that Iran's aspiration to maintain the fuel cycle is unacceptable, since the fuel cycle programme is the core of the problem. They request that Iran be more precise in defining its proposals for objective guarantees. The EU3 call for cessation and dismantlement of the sensitive part of Iran's nuclear programme, including the fuel cycle.[117]

4 February 2005

Responding to a press question whether there could be circumstances in which the US would attack Iran, US Secretary of State Rice says:

> The question is simply not on the agenda at this point in time. You know, we have diplomatic means to do this... we believe, particularly in regard to the nuclear issue, that while no one ever asks the American President to take... any option off the table, that there are plenty of diplomatic means at our disposal to get the Iranians to finally live up to their international obligations.[118]

---

[111] Doc. 158 paras 4, 5.

[112] Doc. 40 para 14.

[113] Doc. 40 para 14; Doc. 41 para 5.

[114] 25 January 2006, Developments in the Implementation of the NPT Safeguards Agreement in the Islamic Republic of Iran and Agency Verification of Iran's Suspension of Enrichment-related and Reprocessing Activities, Update Brief by the Deputy Director General for Safeguards (31 January 2006).

[115] Doc. 41 para 6.

[116] Doc. 103.

[117] Summary of the Latest Round of Nuclear Talks between Iran and The European Union as Seen and Transcribed by Reuters (26 January 2005), www.iranwatch.org/international/EU/eu-summaryoftalks-reuters-012605.htm; 'Crunch time at Iran nuclear talks' *BBC* (26 January 2005), news.bbc.co.uk/2/hi/middle_east/4210257.stm.

[118] Remarks With British Foreign Secretary Jack Straw After Meeting, Secretary Condoleezza Rice, Foreign and Commonwealth Office (London, United Kingdom, 4 February 2005), www.state.gov/secretary/rm/2005/41834.htm.

27 February 2005

Iran and Russia sign an agreement under which Russia will provide nuclear fuel to Iran for the operation of the Bushehr nuclear reactor for ten years. Iran will return the spent fuel to Russia.[119] The final conclusion of the agreement is delayed until December 2007.

2 March 2005

The IAEA BOG discusses the Iranian issue but adopts no resolution.[120]

5 March 2005

Iranian chief nuclear negotiator Hassan Rohani warns that Iran will suspend all its voluntary confidence-building measures and resume nuclear fuel production if its case is referred to the UN Security Council. Mr. Rohani indicates further repercussions could include withdrawing from the NPT.[121]

11 March 2005

The US declares that it will make an effort to actively support the EU3's negotiations with Iran. In this context it will, *inter alia*, lift its objection to an Iranian application to the WTO.[122] Iran is expected to live up to its international commitments.

23 March 2005

Iranian officials offer the EU3 a 'General Framework for Objective Guarantees, Firm Guarantees, and Firm Commitments'. The four-phased plan, beginning in April 2005, includes excluding spent-fuel reprocessing from the Iranian nuclear programme, imposing a ceiling of enrichment at a low level, and limiting the extent of the programme's immediate conversion of all enriched uranium to fuel rods. Iran offers to ratify the Additional Protocol and adopt a permanent ban on the development, stockpiling and use of nuclear weapons.

Under the proposal, the EU3 will guarantee Iran's access to advanced and nuclear technology, act towards building new nuclear power plants in Iran by EU3 members and guarantee the supply of nuclear fuel necessary to complement Iran's domestic production, normalise Iran's status under G8 export control regulations, and follow up actively towards establishing a WMD-free zone in the Middle East.

The proposal also calls for phased cooperation in counter-terrorism, export control and regional security matters.[123]

Because the framework does not specifically refer to the suspension of the uranium enrichment activities as stated in the Paris Agreement, the EU3 call the offer 'unacceptable'.

29 April 2005

Iran proposes to implement the first phase of its 23 March 2005 proposal, including ratification of the Additional Protocol, resumption of work at Esfahan and a six-month extension of the suspension of all other enrichment related activities. In exchange it expects the EU3 to implement its part under the proposal before the end of 2005.[124]

25 May 2005

Iran presents an offer to the EU3, which it characterises as 'most flexible' and intended to salvage the negotiations. The offer includes: resumption of the work of the Esfahan UCF plant at low capacity and under full scope monitoring; negotiations on an initial limited operation at Natanz; and negotiations for full-scale operation of Natanz on the premise that it would be synchronised with the fuel requirements of light-water reactors.[125]

The EU3 commit to presenting a proposal by early August.[126] Iran agrees to a two-month extension of the suspension, pending receipt of the European proposal.

---

[119] Doc. 73 para 18.

[120] Doc. 73.

[121] Paul Hughes, 'Iran Says to Make Atomic Fuel if Sent to UN Council' *Reuters* (5 March 2005).

[122] Doc. 136.

[123] Doc. 107.

[124] Doc. 105.

[125] Doc. 107.

[126] Edited transcript of statement by the Foreign Secretary, Jack Straw, at a press conference in Geneva (25 May 2005), www.fco.gov.uk/en/newsroom/latest-news/?view=News&id=1540693.

28 May 2005

Iran's Guardian Council approves a law that calls on the government to develop a nuclear fuel cycle, including uranium enrichment. The law does not compel the government to immediately resume uranium enrichment, but insists that Iran pursue its nuclear goals even as international pressure over its ambitions increases.[127]

16 June 2005

The IAEA BOG hears a report on Iran by the Deputy Director-General for Safeguards. The Board emphasises that it is essential that Iran act with transparency and proactive cooperation with the Agency by providing it in a prompt manner with fully-detailed information that could shed light on the outstanding issues, in order to build the required confidence and permit the Agency to complete its assessment of all outstanding issues related to Iran's nuclear programme. The Board reiterates its call for Iran to ratify the Additional Protocol as a matter of urgency.[128]

23-24 June 2005

The 15th Plenary Meeting of the Nuclear Suppliers Group (NSG) agrees to establish a procedure towards suspending, through national decisions, nuclear transfers to countries that are non-compliant with their safeguards agreements. In addition, it agrees that supplier and recipient states should elaborate appropriate measures to invoke fall-back safeguards if the IAEA can no longer undertake its safeguard mandate in a recipient state.[129]

24 June 2005

Mahmoud Ahmadinejad is elected president of Iran.

1-2 August 2005

Iran informs the IAEA of its decision to resume uranium conversion activities at the UCF at Esfahan, since the EU3 policy is 'to protract negotiations without the slightest attempt to move forward in fulfilling their commitments under the Tehran or the Paris Agreements [of 21 October 2003 and 15 November 2004 respectively], in order to keep the suspension in place for as long as it takes to make it a *fait accompli*. This is contrary to the letter and spirit of the Paris Agreement and to the principle of good faith negotiations'. Finally, Iran says that the IAEA BOG has recognised that suspension is a voluntary, non-legally-binding confidence-building measure. Accordingly the IAEA BOG has 'no factual or legal ground, nor any statutory power, to make or enforce such a demand, or impose ramifications as a consequence of it'.[130]

The EU3 inform Iran that resumption of nuclear work in Esfahan would be a breach of the Paris Agreement and of the IAEA BOG resolution of 29 November 2004, and would heighten international concern about the real objective of Iran's nuclear programme. This would bring the negotiations for a long-term arrangement to an end.[131] They call on Iran not to take this step, only days before the EU3 presents its proposal for a long-term agreement.

5 August 2005

The EU3 transmit to Iran their proposals for a Framework for a Long-Term Agreement. In the nuclear area, the proposals include a reaffirmation of Iran's inalienable rights to the peaceful use of nuclear energy, exercised in conformity with the NPT, and assurances for Iran of fuel supply for its light-water power and research reactors. Iran's undertakings include a commitment not to pursue fuel-cycle activities other than construction and operation of light water reactors, ending construction of the heavy-water reactor in Arak, ratification of the Additional Protocol by the end of 2005 and its implementation in the interim, continued cooperation with the IAEA, and a binding commitment not to withdraw from the NPT.

[127] 'Iran Law Mandates Nuclear Program' *Los Angeles Times* (29 May 2005), articles.latimes.com/2005/may/29/world/fg-iran29.

[128] Doc. 74 paras 64, 75, 77, 84, 87, 89, 110-1-17.

[129] NSG Plenary Meeting (Oslo Norway 23-24 June 2005) NSG_OSL/PRESS/FINAL. These decisions are reflected in the NSG's updated Guidelines for the Export of Nuclear Material, equipment and Technology and for Transfers of Nuclear-related Dual-use Equipment, Materials, Software and Related Technology (20 March 2006) INFCIRC/254/Rev.7/Parts 1 and 2.

[130] Doc. 107.

[131] INFCIRC/649.

In view of Iran's expected resumption of uranium convention at the UCF at Esfahan, the EU3 introduce the two-track policy. They say they have no choice but to set in motion procedures for the convening of an extraordinary meeting of the IAEA BOG. However, if Iran were to make clear that it will not proceed as it has indicated and will enter into discussion on the enclosed proposal, the EU3 are ready not to continue with this process. They reiterate that the Tehran Statement of October 2003 and the Paris Agreement of November 2004 remain the basis for work.[132]

Iran rejects the proposal as an insulting violation of international law, the UN Charter, the NPT, the Tehran Statement and the Paris Agreement. It claims that the proposal seeks to intimidate it into accepting illegal inspections beyond existing international instruments and abandoning most of its peaceful nuclear programme. It says that the proposal is a shortened version of an offer rejected by Iran in October 2004, that it makes the EU3's commitment to general principles of international law under the UN charter optional, partial and conditional, and that it fails to indicate the EU3's readiness to ease its violations of international law with regard to Iran's access to technology.[133]

8 August 2005

Iran resumes uranium conversion activities in Esfahan.[134]

11 August 2005

The IAEA BOG meets in an extraordinary session at the request of the EU3, in view of Iran's resumption of uranium conversion activities at Esfahan. It adopts without a vote Resolution GOV/2005/64 in which it: expresses serious concern at Iran's resumption of uranium conversion activities in Esfahan; underlines the importance of rectifying the situation; urges Iran to re-establish full suspension of all enrichment related activities including the production of feed material, including through tests or production at UCF; and notes that such suspension would be on the same voluntary, non-legally-binding basis as requested in previous Board resolutions.[135]

Iran says that the Board may not react to an action which was in full conformity with the NPT and safeguards. It says it will not yield. It will be a nuclear fuel producer and supplier within a decade. It is prepared to engage in negotiations without preconditions and in a spirit of good will.[136]

2 September 2005

The IAEA DG reports to the BOG that interim results tend on balance to support Iran's statement on the foreign origin of uranium contamination.[137] He reiterates that all the declared nuclear material in Iran has been accounted for, but that the Agency is still not in a position to conclude that there are no undeclared nuclear materials or activities in Iran. In view of the past undeclared nature of significant aspects of Iran's nuclear programme, and its past pattern of concealment, this conclusion can be expected to take longer than in normal circumstances. Also, transparency measures should extend beyond the formal requirements of the Safeguards Agreement and Additional Protocol; otherwise, the Agency's ability to verify the correctness and completeness of the statements made by Iran will be restricted.[138]

17 September 2005

Speaking before the UN General Assembly, Iranian President Ahmadinejad outlines the main elements of Iran's initiative regarding the nuclear issue. These include reaffirmation that in accordance with its religious principles, the pursuit of nuclear weapons is prohibited. In addition, as a most far-reaching further confidence-building measure, Iran is prepared to engage in serious partnerships with the private and public sectors of other countries in the implementation of an uranium enrichment programme in Iran.

---

[132] Doc. 126.
[133] Doc. 108.
[134] Doc. 32; IAEA 'Report of the Director-General' (10 August 2005) GOV/2005/62; Doc. 41.
[135] Doc. 29; Compare the EU3 drafts GOV/2005/63 and GOV/2005/63 Rev.1.
[136] Doc. 75 paras 2-5, 15-16, 21-22, 29, 43-48.
[137] Doc. 40 paras 45-48
[138] Doc. 40 paras 50-51.

In keeping with Iran's inalienable right to have access to a nuclear fuel cycle, cooperation with the IAEA will be the centerpiece of Iran's nuclear policy. Negotiations with other countries will be carried out based on Iran's legitimate rights in its pursuit of peaceful nuclear technology without discrimination and to receive objective guarantees for uranium enrichment in the nuclear fuel cycle.[139]

22 September 2005

The EU3 foreign ministers elaborate the EU3 position in an op-ed in the Wall Street Journal. They consider the Iranian president's speech a rejection of negotiations, and the resumption of suspended activities a rejection of its 5 August proposal.[140]

21-24 September 2005

The IAEA BOG considers the DG's report on Iran. It adopts Resolution GOV/2005/77 by 22 votes of approval, one opposing vote (Venezuela), and 12 abstentions, including Russia and China. The resolution expresses uncertainty as to Iran's motives in pursuing a policy of concealment up to October 2003, and deplores the fact that Iran has failed 'to heed the call by the Board in its resolution of 11 August 2005 to re-establish full suspension of all enrichment related activities including the production of feed material, including through tests or production at the Uranium Conversion Facility'. The Board finds that that Iran's many failures and breaches of the Safeguards Agreement as detailed in the Director-General's report of November 2003 constitute non-compliance in the context of Article XII.C of the IAEA Statute. It also finds 'that the history of concealment of Iran's nuclear activities in the Director-General's report, the nature these activities', issues brought to light since September 2002 'and the resulting absence of confidence that Iran's nuclear programme is

exclusively for peaceful purposes have given rise to questions that are within the competence of the Security Council, as the organ bearing the main responsibility for the maintenance of international peace and security'. The IAEA BOG requests a further report from the DG and decides to 'address the timing and content of the report required under Article XII.C and the notification required under Article III.B.4'.[141]

Iran says that the threat of referral to the Security Council does not deter it from pursuing its right to a complete nuclear fuel cycle for its peaceful nuclear programme.[142]

28 September 2005

Iran warns that unless the BOG's resolution is amended, and if there is insistence on its implementation, Iran will terminate all previous voluntary and temporary concessions, including implementation of the Additional Protocol without ratification.[143]

UK Foreign Secretary Jack Straw says that military action against Iran 'is not on the agenda' and is 'inconceivable'.[144] This follows US President George W Bush's remarks the previous day to the effect that 'all options are open'.

13 October 2005

The European Parliament adopts a resolution in which it, *inter alia*, stresses the importance of cooperation with the US, Russia, China and non-aligned countries in order to achieve a comprehensive agreement with Iran; reaffirms that no military options should be taken into consideration in order to reach a solution to the present crisis; and underlines that the conclusion of a cooperation and trade agreement between Iran and the EU depends on the substantial improvement of Iran's human rights situation as well as on Iran's full cooperation with the IAEA and objective guarantees regarding the peaceful nature of its nuclear programme.[145]

---

[139] Doc. 110, paras 8-9.

[140] Doc. 127.

[141] Doc. 30 preambular paras (d), (e), (h), (k), operative paras 1, 2, 3.

[142] Doc. 78 paras 15-17, 20, 24-25, 36, 43, 84-89.

[143] Iranian Ministry of Foreign Affairs Statement on the Resolution of IAEA Adopted by a Group of Members of the Board of Governors (28 September 2005) web-srv.mfa.gov.ir/output/English/documents/doc5654.htm.

[144] —— 'UK rules out Iran military action' *BBC News* (28 September 2005), news.bbc.co.uk/1/hi/world/middle_east/4289470.stm.

[145] European Parliament resolution on Iran (13 October 2005) P6_TA(2005)0382 Iran, www.europarl.europa.eu/activities/plenary/ta/sidesSearch.do#.

17-18 October 2005

The NSG holds an extraordinary plenary meeting to consider the Iran issue in light of the IAEA BOG's resolution declaring Iran in non-compliance with its safeguards obligations. The EU announces that it would make no transfers of NSG trigger-list items to Iran, and would exercise special vigilance with regard to non-listed items that could nonetheless be useful in enrichment and reprocessing.[146]

26 October 2005

In a speech to an Islamic Student Associations conference on 'The World Without Zionism' held in Tehran at the Interior Ministry, Iranian President Ahmadinejad says with respect to Israel:[147]

> Our dear Imam said that the occupying regime must be wiped off the map and this was a very wise statement. We cannot compromise over the issue of Palestine. Is it possible to create a new front in the heart of an old front. This would be a defeat and whoever accepts the legitimacy of this regime has in fact, signed the defeat of the Islamic world. Our dear Imam targeted the heart of the world oppressor in his struggle, meaning the occupying regime. I have no doubt that the new wave that has started in Palestine, and we witness it in the Islamic world too, will eliminate this disgraceful stain from the Islamic world. But we must be aware of tricks.

Controversy ensues over whether the Persian text was correctly translated, and whether Ahmadinejad called for the annihilation of Israel.[148] President Ahmadinejad later avoids giving a direct response to the question of his intention in this statement. In an interview on NPR on 23 October 2008 the following exchange takes place:[149]

> NPR: Do you accept the label of the man who wants to wipe Israel off the map?...
> Ahmadinejad: ...Let me create an analogy here — where exactly is the Soviet Union today? It did disappear — but exactly how? It was through the vote of its own people. So therefore in Palestine too we must allow the people, the Palestinians, to determine their own future... Let's ask ourselves, where exactly did the Zionist regime come from? Palestine has existed historically with people who live there for thousands of years. Then at gunpoint several million of the indigenous people there were forced out of their homes and became displaced. And it didn't stop there; others were brought from elsewhere in the world to replace them. How can you accept this regime?

31 October 2005

At the General Assembly debate on the IAEA annual report, Russia stresses that the IAEA's potential is far from exhausted, and that this allows keeping the settlement process of the Iran issue within the Agency.[150]

2 November 2005

Russia proposes that Iran enrich uranium in Russia. The plan is rejected by Iran, which says it is contrary to its right to enrich uranium in its own territory.[151]

18 November 2005

The IAEA DG reports to the BOG that since September 2005 Iran has been more forthcoming in providing access information. Issues remain to be resolved, including documents on production of uranium metal as part of the 1987 offer by a foreign intermediary for certain centrifuge components. The DG reiterates that Iran's full transparency is indispensable and overdue.[152]

---

[146] Christopher A Ford, 'Compliance Assessment on Compliance Enforcement: the Challenge of Nuclear Noncompliance'(2006) 12 *ILSA Journal of International and Comparative Law* 583, 590.

[147] Text of Mahmoud Ahmadinejad's Speech, translated by Nazila Fathi in the New York Times Tehran Bureau, New York Times, 30 October 2005. The text of the speech was posted online, in Persian, by the Iranian Student News Agency www.isnagency.com.

[148] The crux of controversy revolved over the fact that the literal translation of Ahmadinejad's words is 'wiped off the page of time'; however, his words were a quotation of Ayatollah Khomeini, who had said 'wiped off the map'.

[149] 'Iranian President Sounds Off on Israel' *National Public Radio* (23 October 2008), www.npr.org/templates/story/story.php?storyId=94900645.

[150] Doc. 143.

[151] *Delpech* (n 46) 133-134.

[152] Doc. 41.

Commentators say that the material described in the report points heavily in the direction of weapons research.[153]

24 November 2005

The IAEA BOG considers the DG's report on Iran. It reiterates its call that Iran ratify its Additional Protocol as a matter of urgency. It also reiterates its support for the resumption of negotiations between Iran and the EU3. The Board encourages Iran to provide further supporting documentation as requested by the Agency and to expand transparency towards the Agency.[154]

3 December 2005

Iran's Guardian Council approves a law which provides that if Iran's nuclear file is referred or reported to the UN Security Council, the government will be required to cancel all voluntary measures it has taken and implement all scientific, research and executive programmes to enable the rights of the nation under the NPT.[155]

25-30 December 2005

Iran refuses to resume negotiations with the EU3. Iranian President Ahmadinejad again rejects the Russian proposal to enrich uranium in Russia, and then agrees to reconsider it. At the end of January 2006 Iran rejects the Russian offer saying it is not sufficient for Iran's nuclear technology.[156]

2006

3-10 January 2006

Iran informs the IAEA that: 'in benefiting full privilege and inalienable rights for research and development on nuclear energy as recognised in article III of the Agency Statute and article IV of the NPT, the AEOI has decided to resume from 9 January 2006 those R&D on the peaceful nuclear energy programme which has [*sic*] been suspended as part of its expanded voluntary and non-legally binding suspension'.[157] Iran resumes enrichment testing and other activities in Natanz and elsewhere.[158] On 6 January 2006 Iran informs the IAEA that it ceases to voluntarily apply the Additional Protocol.[159]

12-16 January 2006

The EU3 declare that the Iranian resumption of enrichment activity is a clear rejection of the process that the EU3 and Iran have been engaged in, and that discussions have reached an impasse. It is time for the Security Council to become involved to reinforce the authority of IAEA resolutions.[160]

On 16 January 2006 the EU requests an emergency meeting of the IAEA to vote on a draft resolution to refer Iran to the UN Security Council.

26 January 2006

President Bush declares support for the Russian proposal for a civil nuclear plant in Iran as long as the material used to power the plant is manufactured in Russia, delivered under IAEA surveillance to Iran to be used only in that plant, and spent fuel is returned to Russia.[161]

30 January 2006

The foreign ministers of the EU3, US, China, and Russia, and the High Representative of the EU (EU3+3) meet in London. They jointly call on Iran to restore in full the suspension of enrichment-related activity, including research and development, under the supervision of the

[153] Richard Bernstein, 'Atomic Agency Delays Action on Iran' *New York Times* (25 November 2005), www.nytimes.com/2005/11/25/international/europe/25vienna.html?fta=y.

[154] Doc. 80 paras 175-184.

[155] —— 'Iran Votes to Block Nuclear Inspections' *Associated Press* (20 November 2005), www.foxnews.com/story/0,2933,176145,00.html.

[156] *Delpech* (n 46) 135; David E Sanger and Elaine Sciolino 'Iran says Russia's Nuclear Plan is "not sufficient"' *New York Times* (27 January 2006); —— 'Russia plan not enough for Iran' *BBC News* (27 January 2006), news.bbc.co.uk/2/hi/middle_east/4653376.stm.

[157] GOV/INF/2006/1.

[158] Deputy Director General (Safeguards) report of 31 Jan 2006, Doc. 32; Doc. 42 paras 41-45.

[159] Doc. 42 para 30-31.

[160] Doc. 127.

[161] Press Conference of the President, James S. Brady Briefing Room (26 January 2006), georgewbush-whitehouse.archives.gov/news/releases/2006/01/20060126.html.

IAEA; agree that the Extraordinary IAEA BOG meeting should report to the Security Council its decision on the steps required from Iran; agree that the Security Council should await the IAEA DG's report to the March meeting of the IAEA BOG, and any resolution from that meeting, before deciding to take action to reinforce the authority of the IAEA process; and confirm their resolve to continue to work for a diplomatic solution to the Iran problem.[162]

2-4 February 2006

Briefing the press on the upcoming IAEA BOG's resolution, the IAEA DG says:

We are reaching a critical phase but it is not a crisis situation. It is about confidence building and it is not about an imminent threat... All who have spoken on the issue, even those who are supporting Security Council reporting, are making it very clear that the Security Council is not asked, at this stage to take any action, definitely not before I submit my report in March. All of them are saying that this is simply a continuation of diplomacy.[163]

Iran informs the IAEA that it considers the imminent BOG's decision to report the issue of its nuclear programme to the Security Council illegal and without technical basis, since Iran is acting strictly within the IAEA legal framework.

The IAEA BOG adopts Resolution GOV/2006/14 by 27 votes of approval (including China and Russia), 3 objections (Cuba, Syria and Venezuela), and five abstentions (Algeria, Belarus, Indonesia, Libya and South Africa). The resolution recalls 'Iran's many failures and breaches of its obligations to comply with its NPT Safeguards Agreement and the absence of confidence that Iran's nuclear programme is exclusively for peaceful purposes resulting from the history of concealment', and requests the DG to report in March to the Security Council

of the steps that the Board has required of Iran (namely: re-establishment of full suspension, reconsideration of constructing a heavy water reactor, ratification of the Additional Protocol, and until then continued action in accordance with the Additional Protocol, and implementation of transparency measures which extend beyond the formal requirements of the Safeguards Agreement) and on the implementation by Iran of the Board's resolutions, including any resolution that may be adopted in the March session.[164]

Following the vote Russia expresses satisfaction that the work on the Iranian nuclear programme will continue within the IAEA framework.[165]

The DG reports to the Security Council the steps required of Iran by the Board and all IAEA reports and resolutions relating to this issue.[166]

6 February 2006

Iran informs the IAEA that in view of the BOG's decision to report it to the Security Council, all voluntarily-suspended non-legally-binding measures, including the provisions of the Additional Protocol and even beyond that, will be suspended.[167]

11-14 February 2006

Iran starts enrichment tests in Natanz.[168]

15 February 2006

The European Parliament adopts a resolution in which it affirms that the Iranian issue must be resolved in accordance with the rules of international law, and considers that the involvement of the UN Security Council is a necessary step in that regard.[169]

20 February 2006

Speaking before the EU Parliament, Iranian Foreign Minister Mottaki says that Iran is ready to accept the Russian proposal to have uranium

---

[162] Doc. 129.

[163] 'IAEA Director General Briefs Press on Iran Nuclear Issue' (2 February 2006), www.iaea.org/NewsCenter/News/2006/dg_bog020206.html.

[164] Doc. 32.

[165] Statement by Mikhail Kamynin, the Spokesman of Russia's Ministry of Foreign Affairs, Regarding the Adoption by IAEA Governing Board of a Resolution on Iran's Nuclear Program (4 February 2006), www.mid.ru/brp_4.nsf/e78a48070f128a7b43256999005bcbb3/20c4da9279eef1dec325710d0040942a?OpenDocument.

[166] Doc. 42 para 3.

[167] Doc. 42 para 31 quoting GOV/INF/2006/3; Doc. 43 para 23.

[168] Doc. 42 para 44.

[169] European Parliament resolution on the confrontation between Iran and the international community (15 February 2006) P6_TA(2006)0060, Iran.

enriched in Russia on certain conditions, but that in the meanwhile it will continue its nuclear research. Iran is ready to negotiate on safeguards against the possible use of its nuclear technology to develop weapons, but it will not give up its right to develop a nuclear capacity for peaceful purposes.[170]

27 February 2006

The IAEA DG report reaffirms that all the declared nuclear material in Iran has been accounted for, but the Agency is not in a position to conclude that there are no undeclared nuclear materials or activities in Iran.[171]

27 February 2006

Iran requests the EU3 to meet prior to the March session of the IAEA BOG. The EU3 respond that for such a meeting to be productive, it must conclude with a clear public commitment to re-establish full and sustained suspension of all enrichment-related and reprocessing activities; and to fully cooperate with the IAEA, including the resumption of the voluntary application of the Additional Protocol. Anything short of this would result in a public disagreement.[172]

7 March 2006

Iran responds to the IAEA DG's report, which it says is politically biased.[173]

8 March 2006

The IAEA BOG meets to consider the DG's report.[174]

12 March 2006

Iran declares that the Russian nuclear proposal 'is not on the agenda any more'.[175]

29 March 2006

The UN Security Council unanimously and without formal debate adopts a presidential statement. According to reports, this follows weeks of heated negotiations among the permanent members of the Security Council. Russia and China were concerned that Security Council involvement could lead to sanctions against Iran and wanted the IAEA to take the lead. To enable the adoption of the text, some of the detailed demands of suspension of uranium enrichment activities were omitted, as well as a statement that the proliferation of nuclear weapons is a threat to international peace and security.[176] The statement recalls the right of states parties under the NPT, notes with serious concern Iran's decision to resume enrichment-related activities and suspend cooperation with the IAEA under the Additional Protocol, calls upon Iran to take the steps required by the IAEA BOG, including re-establishing the suspension, and to resume cooperation in order to build confidence in the peaceful purpose of its nuclear programme, and requests the IAEA DG to report within 30 days on the process of Iranian compliance.[177]

30 March 2006

Iran's Foreign Minister Mottaki says with respect to the possibility of UN Security Council sanctions that Iran prefers reaching agreement, but has raised its capacity and potential in different fields in the past. It has practically made itself 'compatible with the present sanctions'.[178]

11 April 2006

Iranian president Ahmadinejad announces that Iran has produced enriched uranium at Natanz, and has joined the group of countries possessing

[170] Meeting of MEPS with Iranian Foreign Minister Manoochehr Mottaki, European Union Parliament, www.iranwatch.org/international/EU/eu-parliament-meps-mottaki-022106.htm.

[171] Doc. 42 paras 49-50, 53-54.

[172] Doc. 130.

[173] Doc. 113.

[174] Doc. 85.

[175] Iranian Ministry of Foreign Affairs, 'Russian nuclear offer not on agenda any more: Asefi' (12 March 2006), web-srv.mfa.gov.ir/output/english/documents/doc6328.htm (broken link).

[176] Comments by US Ambassador John Bolton, Russian Ambassador Konstantin Doglov, and Chinese Ambassador Wang Guangya, John Shovelan 'Security Council tells Iran to stop uranium program', *ABC Radio The World Today* (30 March 2006), www.abc.net.au/reslib/200603/r79170_227203.ram.

[177] Doc. 9.

[178] Iranian Ministry of Foreign Affairs, 'Mottaki: Reporting Iran's nuclear case to UNSC a mistake' (30 March 2006), web-srv.mfa.gov.ir/output/English/documents/doc6379.htm (broken link).

nuclear technology. This announcement is confirmed in a television appearance by AEOI head Gholamreza Aghazadeh, who says that scientists at Natanz have successfully enriched uranium to the 3.5% level, using a small cascade of 164 gas centrifuges.[179] This seems to be confirmed by samples taken by IAEA.[180]

25 April 2006

Iran's chief nuclear negotiator Ali Larijani says that Iran will suspend contacts with the IAEA if sanctions are imposed. He adds that military actions against Iran will lead Iran not to close the programme but to hide it.[181]

27 April 2006

Iran offers to continue allowing IAEA inspections under the Safeguards Agreement if the Iranian nuclear dossier remains in the framework of the IAEA, and to provide a timetable for resolving outstanding issues within three weeks.[182]

28 April 2006

The IAEA DG reports to the BOG and in parallel to the Security Council that the IAEA cannot exclude the possibility that the plutonium analysed by the IAEA was derived from sources other than those declared by Iran. The report reiterates the inability of the IAEA to progress in clarifying outstanding issues, including the absence of undeclared materials and activities, without transparency measures by Iran. It notes that safeguards obligations and confidence-building measures are distinct and not interchangeable.[183]

17 May 2006

The Iranian foreign Minister says that Iran will welcome any proposal which will officially recognise Iran's inalienable rights to access nuclear technology and to uphold this right; any call for suspension or interruption of Iran's nuclear programme will be rejected.[184]

31 May-1 June 2006

The US announces that it will join talks with Iran if the latter suspends its enrichment and reprocessing activities. The move is meant to 'give new energy' to the negotiating track.[185] This is the first time since 1979 that the US is offering direct negotiations with Iran. Russia welcomes this initiative.[186] Iranian Foreign Minister Manouchehr Mottaki says that the US has presented no 'new and rational solution' to Iran's nuclear case.[187]

6 June 2006

The EU3+3 present a proposal to Iran, including offers of cooperation in the political, economic and nuclear areas. They stress, however, that should Iran decide not to engage, further steps would have to be taken in the Security Council.

In the nuclear area, the proposal includes: reaffirmation of Iran's right to develop nuclear energy for peaceful purposes, support for Iran to build light-water reactors, cooperation on research and development, fuel guarantees, suspension of discussion of Iran's nuclear programme in the Security Council upon the resumption of negotiations, and cooperation in other fields (trade, regional security, civil aviation, etc). In

---

[179] Mike Shuster, 'Iran Enriches Uranium, Plans New Expansion' *National Public Radio* (11 April 2006), www.npr.org/templates/story/story.php?storyId=5336802.

[180] Doc. 43 para 31.

[181] —— 'Iran threatens to end UN contacts' *BBC News* (25 April 2006), news.bbc.co.uk/2/hi/middle_east/4941438.stm.

[182] GOV/2006/38; Doc. 44 para 10.

[183] Doc. 43 paras 35-36.

[184] Iranian Ministry of Foreign Affairs, 'FM: we are resolved to safeguard our nuclear rights' (17 May 2006), web-srv.mfa.gov.ir/output/English/documents/doc6561.htm (broken link); 'Iran welcomes proposals to settle nuclear issue that recognize its N-rights; FM' (17 May 2006), web-srv.mfa.gov.ir/output/English/documents/doc6574.htm (broken link).

[185] Press Conference on Iran, Secretary Condoleezza Rice, (Benjamin Franklin Room Washington DC (31 May 2006) wwwk.state.gov/secretary/rm/2006/67103.htm2006 (broken link).

[186] President Vladimir Putin, Transcript of Meeting with the Leaders of the News Agencies of G8 Member Countries (Novo-Ogaryovo 2 June 2006), www.kremlin.ru/eng/speeches/2006/06/02/1121_type82914type82917type84779_106433.shtml.

[187] Iranian Ministry of Foreign Affairs, 'US offer no new solution, says Mottaki' (1 June 2006), web-srv.mfa.gov.ir/output/english/documents/doc6719.htm (broken link).

exchange, Iran will commit to addressing all of the outstanding concerns of IAEA through full cooperation with IAEA, suspending all enrichment-related and reprocessing activities to be verified by IAEA and continuing this during these negotiations, and resuming the implementation of the Additional Protocol.[188]

15 June 2006

In an initial response to the EU3+3 proposal, Iranian Foreign Minister Mottaki describes the new proposal as a 'step forward' in the negotiation process, but calls for the EU3+3 to continue in their efforts to remove ambiguities in the proposal, and warns that 'lack of flexibility' and 'insistence on certain unacceptable points' may prevent parties from achieving their goal.[189]

21 June 2006

Iran offers to respond to the 6 June proposal by 22 August 2006.[190]

12 July 2006

The EU3+3 reiterate the two-track policy: Since Iran did not respond to the 6 June proposal and has not taken the steps needed under it, they will seek a Security Council resolution which would make the IAEA-required suspension mandatory. Should Iran refuse to comply, they will work for the adoption of measures under Article 41 of Chapter VII of the UN Charter. Should Iran implement the decisions of the IAEA and the UN Security Council and enter into negotiations, they will hold back from further action in the UN Security Council.[191]

16-17 July 2006

The G8 leaders declare that they stand fully behind the EU3+3 proposal of 6 June 2006, as well as behind the EU3+3 decision to return the issue to the Security Council.[192]

31 July 2006

Acting under Article 40 of Chapter VII of the UN Charter, the Security Council adopts Resolution 1696(2006) (14-1-0, Qatar against). According to the resolution, the Security Council is concerned by the proliferation risks that the Iranian nuclear programme presents. It calls on Iran to take steps required by the IAEA BOG; demands the suspension of all enrichment-related and reprocessing activities, including research and development; endorses the EU3+3 proposal of June 2006; calls upon all states to exercise vigilance and prevent the transfer of items that could contribute to Iran's enrichment-related and reprocessing activities and ballistic missile programmes; supports the role of the IAEA and underlines the necessity of its work; and expresses its intention, in the event that Iran does not comply with the resolution by 31 August, to adopt measures under Article 41.[193]

Qatar votes against the resolution despite its agreement with the need to verify Iran's activities, because it does not want to proceed when its region 'is inflamed'. In addition, it says that a few more days could help identify Iran's real intentions, especially since it has not rejected the diplomatic initiatives but has only asked for more time.[194]

Iran says that the demand that it suspend uranium enrichment violates the fundamental principles of international law, the NPT and IAEA BOG resolutions. It also runs counter to the views of the majority of UN member states, which the Security Council is obliged to represent.[195]

22 August 2006

Iran responds to the EU3+3 proposal of June 2006.[196] It says that it accepts the core idea of a renewed process of negotiations to replace all other means to resolve the nuclear issue, but demands certain assurances and clarifications,

[188] Doc. 131.
[189] Iranian Ministry of Foreign Affairs, 'FM calls on 5+1 Group to remove ambiguities in new proposal' (15 June 2006), web-srv.mfa.gov.ir/output/english/documents/doc6802.htm (broken link).
[190] *Delpech* (n 46) 137.
[191] Doc. 132.
[192] G8 St. Petersburg Summit, Chair's Summary (17 July 2006), en.g8russia.ru/docs/25.html.
[193] Doc. 10.
[194] Doc. 15.
[195] UN Doc S/2003/603 circulated 2 August 2006.
[196] Doc. 114.

in particular on the scope of exercise of its right to peaceful nuclear activity. Iran also requires guarantees on access to nuclear know-how and technology. It rejects the two-track policy, namely the suspension of Security Council action in exchange for its suspension of enrichment-related and reprocessing activities, saying that Security Council involvement is intrinsically inconsistent with negotiations.[197] Iran rejects the demand for suspension of its nuclear activities, saying that it is disruptive for negotiations.[198] Iran is nonetheless willing to discuss bilateral voluntary confidence-building measures. It demands, *inter alia*, the removal of its dossier from the Security Council, normalization of its case in the IAEA, and an end to limitation on its peaceful activities and to export controls.[199] In exchange it will voluntarily implement the Additional Protocol. It is furthermore willing to guarantee that it would not withdraw from the NPT if measures are taken with respect to Israel's nuclear programme.[200]

30 August 2006

Shortly before the IAEA DG is to report to the BOG, Iran provides the IAEA with information to which it has previously refused access. It also provides visas for inspectors following refusal to do so from the end of July 2006.

The DG's report to the BOG and to the Security Council says that the IAEA remains unable to verify the correctness and completeness of Iran's declaration with a view to confirming the peaceful nature of Iran's nuclear programme.[201]

15-16 September 2006

The 14th NAM Summit in Havana, Cuba, issues a statement on Iran. The heads of state or government emphasise the fundamental distinction between the legal obligations of states to their respective safeguards agreements and any confidence-building measures voluntarily undertaken to resolve difficult issues. They further express their conviction that all issues on safeguards and verification, including those of Iran, should be resolved within the IAEA framework, and be based on technical and legal grounds.[202]

18 September 2006

At the IAEA 50th General Conference Iran says that if the IAEA restricts its access to peaceful nuclear capabilities and undermines its inalienable rights, Iran would be under no legal obligation to comply with IAEA safeguards. Furthermore, any hostile action by the Security Council will lead to a limitation of cooperation with the IAEA.[203]

19 September 2006

Speaking before the UN General Assembly, Iranian President Ahmadinejad raises Iran's grievance against the abuse of the Security Council as an instrument of threat and coercion by some of its permanent members. He concludes that 'as long as the Council is unable to act on behalf of the entire international community in a transparent, just and democratic manner, it will be neither legitimate nor effective'.[204]

21 September 2006

The EU presidency says that a compromise proposal has been discussed with Iran, which would include the suspension of uranium enrichment by Iran for a specific period or during the negotiations.[205]

13 October 2006

Iran begins testing a 164-centrifuge cascade with UF_6 gas.[206]

---

[197] Doc. 114 point 7 and specifically 7-1.
[198] Doc. 114 point 7-5.
[199] Doc. 114 point 7-6.
[200] Doc. 114 point 9.
[201] Doc. 44 paras 27-29.
[202] Doc. 146.
[203] Doc. 115.
[204] UN Doc A/61/PV.11 p 38-39
[205] Ministry of Foreign Affairs of Finland 'Negotiated settlement with Iran still in the cards, says Foreign Minister Tuomioja' (21 September 2006), www.formin.fi/public/default.aspx?contentid=80800&nodeid=17409&contentlan=2&culture=en-US.
[206] Doc. 45 para 2.

14 November 2006

The IAEA DG issues a report on implementation of the NPT Safeguards Agreement in Iran, reiterating that the IAEA is unable to progress in verifying the absence of undeclared nuclear material and activities and consequently the peaceful nature of Iran's nuclear programme, unless Iran addresses the longstanding verification issues.[207]

20-23 November 2006

The IAEA BOG examines a request by Iran for technical assistance for its Arak facility and for seven other projects. Most member states agree to refuse assistance, citing the Security Council resolutions. A number of NAM representatives argue that it is the Agency's duty to promote the civilian application of nuclear energy, and that technical cooperation is an inalienable right under Article IV of the NPT and one of the fundamental privileges of IAEA membership.[208] In an attempt to compromise, the Board decided to block Iran's request for a period of at least two years. During the same meeting the IAEA BOG approves technical assistance for the seven, less contentious, projects submitted by Iran.[209] The IAEA BOG decides to reject the cooperation project concerning the heavy-water reactor at Arak requested by Iran.[210]

23 December 2006

The Security Council unanimously adopts resolution 1737(2006) under Article 41 of the UN Chapter. It decides that Iran must suspend the 'proliferation sensitive nuclear activities', including all enrichment-related and reprocessing activities and work on all heavy water-related projects. Both these steps are to be verified by the IAEA. The resolution imposes an embargo and targeted measures relating to proliferation-sensitive nuclear activities and nuclear-weapon delivery systems. These include an asset freeze and a travel notification requirement with respect

to persons and entities designated in the annex to the resolution and on any additional persons and entities designated by the Security Council or the Committee established within the Resolution the in order to monitor compliance (the '1737 Committee'). The asset freeze also applies to persons or entities acting on behalf of or at the direction of designated persons or entities and of entities owned or controlled by them. In addition, the Council calls upon all states to prevent specialised teaching or training of Iranian nationals in disciplines that would contribute to Iran's proliferation sensitive nuclear activities and the development of nuclear weapon delivery systems.

The resolution confirms that the June 2006 proposal by the EU3+3 is still on the table and calls on Iran to engage in negotiations on its basis. Finally, the Security Council introduces the two-track or freeze-for-freeze policy: it will suspend implementation of UN Charter Article 41 measures, if and for so long as Iran suspends all enrichment-related and reprocessing activities. It will terminate the measures under Article 41 if Iran fully complies with its obligations, or adopt additional measures under Article 41 if Iran does not.[211]

Iran says that the resolution represents only the latest in a decades-long history of bias against itself. it says that bringing Iran's peaceful nuclear programme to the Council is merely an instrument of pressure and intimidation to compel Iran to abandon its rights.[212]

27 December 2006

The Iranian Parliament adopts a bill according to which the government should 'revise its cooperation with the International Atomic Energy Agency based on the interests of Iran and its people'. The measure is considered by some moderate members of Parliament to be less severe than earlier proposals to the effect that Iran withdraw from the NPT and ban all inspectors.[213]

---

[207] Doc. 45 paras 20-21.

[208] Doc. 89.

[209] Doc. 91; Tanya Ogilvie-White, 'International Responses to Iranian Nuclear Defiance: The Non-Aligned Movement and the Issue of Non-Compliance' (2007) 18 *European Journal of International Law* 453, 469-70.

[210] French Ministry of Foreign Affairs, 'Chronology/Iranian Nuclear Question', www.diplomatie.gouv.fr/en/country-files_156/iran_301/the-iranian-nuclear-issue_2724/chronology-iranian-nuclear-question_9205.html.

[211] Doc. 11.

[212] Doc. 16; UN Doc S/2006/1024, Letter dated 23 December 2006 from the Permanent Representative of the Islamic Republic of Iran to the United Nations addressed to the President of the Security Council.

[213] Nazila Fathi, 'Iran to "Revise" Any Relations with Monitors in Nuclear Area', *New York Times* (28 December 2006), www.nytimes.com/2006/12/28/world/middleeast/28nuke.html.

2007

23 January 2007

Iran refuses the IAEA's request for remote monitoring and challenges the IAEA to provide a detailed legal basis for implementing such a measure, as well as examples of its existing use in sensitive facilities in other states.[214]

29 January 2007

The IAEA DG calls for a timeout with respect to both Iran's nuclear programme and the UN Security Council sanctions of December 2006, so that the parties resume negotiations immediately.[215]

22 February 2007

The IAEA DG reports to the BOG that the Agency is still unable to verify the absence of undeclared nuclear material and activities in Iran unless Iran addresses the long outstanding verification issues through the implementation of the Additional Protocol and the required transparency measures. He says that there has been no indication of reprocessing-related activities at any declared sites in Iran.[216]

9 March 2007

The IAEA BOG approves the recommendation in the DG's report of 9 February 2004[217] for suspension of 22 nuclear technical aid projects to Iran as part of imposed UN Security Council sanctions. It exempts programmes with medical, agricultural or humanitarian purposes. Iran rejects the decision as the work of a 'few countries…to deprive Iran from its inalienable rights for [the] peaceful use of nuclear energy'. It stresses that none of the suspended projects are related to the enrichment programme, which will continue.[218]

23 March 2007

The 1737 Committee submits to the Security Council its first report, according to which 58 member states and the EU have submitted reports on implementation of resolution 1737(2006). Of those, 51 states reported that they already have legislation in place that covered the relevant paragraphs of the resolution and seven others reported that they were taking steps to put the necessary frameworks into place.[219]

24 March 2007

The Security Council, again acting under Article 41 of the UN Charter, unanimously adopts Resolution 1747(2007), widening the scope of sanctions against Iran. These include a ban on the export of arms and related materiel from Iran, and the designation of additional entities and persons as subject to the asset freeze and to the travel notification requirement. In addition, the Council calls upon all states to exercise vigilance and restraint in the supply of the seven categories of conventional weapons and related services to Iran, and calls upon all states and international financial institutions not to enter into new commitments for grants, financial assistance and concessional loans to Iran, except for humanitarian and development purposes. The resolution reiterates the two-track policy.

Iran's Foreign Minister Mottaki rejects the resolution as illegitimate. Iran's nuclear programme is entirely peaceful and therefore outside the Council's mandate. He again charges that the sanctions are aimed at depriving the Iranian people of their inalienable rights.[220]

29 March 2007

Iran suspends the implementation of modified Code 3.1 under the Subsidiary Arrangements of 2003, and reverts to the 1976 version of the Code. It explains that the modified code in 2003 has not been ratified by the Iranian Parliament.[221]

13-18 April 2007

Iran refuses the IAEA request to carry out an inspection at Arak. It contends that this

---

[214] Doc. 47 para 8.

[215] IAEA, 'Dr. ElBaradei Calls for 'Timeout' on Iran Nuclear Issue' (CNN interview, Davos, 26 January 2007), www.iaea.org/NewsCenter/Multimedia/Videos/Davos_26.01.2007/index.html.

[216] Doc. 47.

[217] Doc. 46.

[218] Molly Moore, 'U.N. Nuclear Agency Curtails Technical Assistance to Iran' *Washington Post* (9 March 2007), www.washingtonpost.com/wp-dyn/content/article/2007/03/08/AR2007030801108.html.

[219] UN Doc S/PV.5646, Doc. 20.

[220] Doc. 17.

[221] Doc. 48; Doc. 50 footnote 2.

verification is in excess of its obligations under the 1976 version of Code 3.1, to which it has reverted. The IAEA responds that in accordance with Article 39 of Iran's Safeguards Agreement, agreed Subsidiary Arrangements cannot be modified unilaterally; nor is there a mechanism in the Safeguards Agreement for the suspension of provisions agreed upon in Subsidiary Arrangements. Moreover, Code 3.1 is related to the provision of design information and not to the frequency or timing of verification by the Agency of such information, which is not dependent on the stage of construction of a facility, or the presence of nuclear material therein.[222]

24 April 2007

Iranian foreign minister Mottaki says Iran will not accept suspension of uranium enrichment as a topic or outcome of the upcoming talks with the EU.[223]

1 May 2007

At the first session of the Preparatory Committee for the 2010 NPT Review Conference, Iran deplores incursion of the Security Council into issues that are within the exclusive authority of the IAEA.[224]

23 May 2007

The IAEA DG reports to the IAEA BOG and in parallel to the Security Council that because the IAEA has not been receiving for over a year information that Iran had used to provide, the Agency's level of knowledge of certain aspects of Iran's nuclear related activities has deteriorated.[225]

8 June 2007

The G8 leaders express support for additional measures if Iran further refuses to comply with Security Council resolutions.[226]

18 June 2007

The EU council resolves to adopt further appropriate measures under Article 41 Chapter VII of the UN Charter should Iran continue not to comply with its international obligations.[227]

21 June 2007

The 1737 Committee submits to the Security Council its second report.[228]

21 August 2007

The IAEA and Iran sign Understandings on the Modalities of Resolution of the Outstanding Issues. The understandings contain a detailed work plan for cooperation between the two sides: for Iran to respond to questions about its nuclear activities and to provide for more effective inspections of facilities, and for the IAEA to declare certain issues closed. The Understandings list present and past outstanding issues, including the enrichment programme, heavy-water research reactor in Arak, plutonium experiments, P-1 and P-2 centrifuges, source of contamination, the 15-page uranium metal document, Po-210, the Ghachine Mine, and alleged weapons studies. The IAEA confirms that there are no other remaining issues and ambiguities regarding Iran's past nuclear programme and activities, and that it will not provide Iran with questions beyond those envisaged in the work plan. The IAEA and Iran agree that after the implementation of the work plan for resolving the outstanding issues, the implementation of safeguards in Iran will be conducted in a routine manner.[229]

30 August 2007

The IAEA DG reports to the IAEA BOG on implementation of the NPT Safeguards Agreement and resolutions 1737(2006) and 1747(2007) in Iran, reiterating the IAEA's inability to verify certain aspects relevant to the scope and nature of Iran's nuclear programme.

---

[222] Doc. 48.

[223] Iranian Ministry of Foreign Affairs, 'Iran Not to Accept Suspension as Topic of Talks: FM' (24 April 2007), web-srv.mfa.gov.ir/output/english/documents/doc8417.htm (broken link).

[224] Doc. 116.

[225] Doc. 48.

[226] Doc. 152.

[227] Doc. 159.

[228] UN Doc S/PV.5702.

[229] Doc. 6.

The DG notes that the work plan is a significant step forward. If Iran finally addresses the long outstanding verification issues, the Agency should be in a position to reconstruct the history of Iran's nuclear programme. Finally the report notes that contrary to the decisions of the Security Council, Iran has not suspended its enrichment-related activities. Iran is also continuing with its heavy water-related projects.[230]

12 September 2007

The IAEA DG reiterates his call for a timeout, under which Iran will suspend its current enrichment activities as a show of goodwill, and the international community will refrain from sanctions, in order to create space for negotiations. Following an IAEA BOG meeting he says that the EU3, China, and South Africa support this proposal.[231]

19 September 2007

The 1737 Committee submits to the Security Council its third report.[232]

25 September 2007

Speaking before the UN General Assembly, Iranian President Ahmadinejad says that certain big powers are attempting to prevent Iran's scientific progress under that pretext of possible deviation. Iran will pursue the issue through its appropriate legal path through the IAEA and disregard unlawful and political impositions by the arrogant powers. Because of the resistance of the Iranian nation, the issue is back with the Agency, and the nuclear issue of Iran is now closed and has turned into an ordinary Agency matter.[233]

28 September 2007

The EU3+3 declare that since Iran has not fulfilled the requirements of UN Security Council Resolutions 1737(2006) and 1747(2007), including the suspension of its enrichment and reprocessing activities, they agree to bring to a vote a third Security Council sanctions resolution under Article 41 of Chapter VII of the UN Charter, unless the November reports of the EU High Representative and IAEA DG show a positive outcome of their efforts.[234]

23 October 2007

The EU High Representative Javier Solana and the new Iranian nuclear negotiator Saeed Jalili meet. The EU High Representative reiterates the two-track policy and recalls that measures against Iran will only be lifted when Iran fully complies with Security Council resolutions.[235]

In a statement made on the same day, Iranian President Ahmadinejad says that Iran would not retreat 'one iota' from its nuclear programme.[236]

15 November 2007

The IAEA DG reports to the IAEA BOG on measures for implementation by Iran of the work plan agreed upon on 21 August 2007, noting that Iran's cooperation has been reactive rather than proactive. The report reiterates the IAEA's inability to provide assurances on the exclusively peaceful nature of Iran's nuclear programme and the absence of undeclared nuclear material and activities in Iran without Iranian transparency.[237]

3 December 2007

The US National Intelligence Estimate judges with high confidence that Iran halted its nuclear weapons programme in the fall of 2003; assesses with moderate-to-high confidence that Iran is, at a minimum, keeping open the option to develop nuclear weapons; judges with high confidence that the halt, as well as Iran's announcement of its decision to suspend its declared uranium enrichment programme and sign an Additional

---

[230] Doc. 49.

[231] IAEA 'Board of Governors Considers Safeguards Implementation in Iran' (IAEA Chief Talked to the Press on Latest Developments, 12 September 2007), www.iaea.org/NewsCenter/Multimedia/Audio/mp3/bog_091207_dg.mp3.

[232] UN Doc S/PV.5743.

[233] Doc. 117.

[234] Statement on Iran, New York (28 September 2007) S267/07.

[235] Javier Solana, EU High Representative for the CFSP, met the Iranian negotiators in Rome (23 October 2007) S312/07.

[236] Elaine Sciolino and Peter Kiefer, 'Iran Has New Nuclear Negotiator, but Similar Stance' *New York Times* (24 October 2007), www.nytimes.com/2007/10/24/world/middleeast/24iran.html.

[237] Doc. 50.

Protocol, were primarily in response to increasing international pressure; and estimates with moderate confidence that Iran's ongoing uranium enrichment efforts would allow it to produce a weapon between 2010 and 2015.[238]

13-16 December 2007

Russia and Iran agree on a schedule for completion of the Bushehr nuclear plant.[239] Russia begins nuclear fuel deliveries. Under the Russian-Iranian agreement, spent fuel will be returned to Russia for further processing and storage, and will be under IAEA control for the duration of its presence on Iranian territory. Iran has given additional written assurances that the fuel will be used only for the Bushehr nuclear power plant. Russia says that the cooperation on the Bushehr plant demonstrates that it is possible effectively and reliably to develop a civilian nuclear power sector in full accordance with the rights and obligations under the NPT.[240] Nuclear fuel deliveries required for the operation of the plant are reportedly completed in early 2008.[241]

14 December 2007

The EU Council expresses regret that there has been no positive outcome in their negotiations with Iran, particularly on its compliance with Security Council resolutions. The EU Council renews support for additional UN sanctions as well as for additional unilateral EU measures.[242]

18 December 2007

The 1737 Committee submits to the Security Council its fourth report.[243]

31 December 2007

The 1737 Committee submits to the Council an annual report, according to which it has received 88 reports under Resolution 1737(2006) and 72 reports under Resolution 1747(2007). Of those, 17 are combined reports under both resolutions. A majority of the reporting states have indicated that they already had legislation in place that covered the relevant paragraphs of the resolutions. Most others reported on the steps they had taken or would be taking to put the necessary legal framework into place.[244] The Committee has received one notification concerning the travel of a listed individual. It received and granted ten requests for exemptions under Resolution 1737(2006). It also received 30 notifications by states of the intention to make or receive payments, or to authorise the unfreezing of funds, in connection with contracts entered into prior to the listing of persons and entities in the annexes to the two resolutions.

2008

11-12 January 2008

The IAEA DG visits Iran and meets Iran's leaders. Iran agrees to accelerate implementation of the August 2007 work plan.[245]

31 January 2008

The European Parliament calls on 'the US Administration and all other actors involved to renounce all rhetoric on military options and regime change policies against Iran', and calls on the US to 'participate directly in negotiations with Iran along with the EU'.[246]

15 February 2008

Media reports reveal that the US has shared intelligence data with the IAEA on weapon studies by Iran, especially information on the 'green salt project'. Iran's envoy to the IAEA

---

[238] Doc. 138.

[239] —— 'Russia, Iran agree nuclear deal" *BBC News* (13 December 2007), news.bbc.co.uk/2/hi/middle_east/7142117.stm.

[240] Ministry of Foreign Affairs of the Russian Federation, Press Release in Relation to Start of Russian Fuel Deliveries for Iranian Nuclear Power Plant at Bushehr 2034-17-12-2007, www.mid.ru/brp_4.nsf/e78a48070f128a7b43256999005bcbb3/7041b5f6601d564dc32573b50021b5b4?OpenDocument.

[241] 'Iran receives final shipment of fuel for Bushehr' *WNN* (28 January 2008), www.world-nuclear-news.org/Iran_receives_final_shipment_of_fuel_for_Bushehr_from_Russia-280108.html.

[242] European Council 14 December 2007 Presidency Conclusions 16616/1/07 REV 1 CONCL para 83, 86.

[243] UN Doc S/PV.5807.

[244] Doc. 20.

[245] Doc. 51.

[246] PE 401.026 European Parliament resolution of 31 January 2008 on Iran, P6_TA(2008)0031, www.europarl.europa.eu/sides/getDoc.do?pubRef=-//EP//TEXT+TA+P6-TA-2008-0031+0+DOC+XML+V0//EN&language=EN.

calls the data '100 percent fabricated and forged'.[247]

22 February 2008

The IAEA DG reports to the BOG on implementation of Iran's Safeguards Agreement and of Security Council Resolutions 1737(2006) and 1747(2007). According to the report, the answers provided by Iran in accordance with the work plan are consistent with IAEA findings with respect to some issues (e.g. Po-210 experiments) or are not inconsistent with its findings with respect to others (e.g. contamination sources and procurement activities). Therefore, the Agency considers these questions no longer outstanding. However, the Agency continues, in accordance with its procedures and practices, to seek corroboration of its findings and to verify these issues as part of its verification of the completeness of Iran's declarations.

The one major remaining issue is the alleged studies on weapons, with respect to which Iran has provided no information. These studies are a matter of serious concern and critical to an assessment of a possible military dimension to Iran's nuclear programme. With the exception of this issue, the Agency has no concrete information about possible current undeclared nuclear material and activities in Iran.[248]

25 February 2008

In identical letters to the UN Secretary-General and to the President of the Security Council, Iran states that the recent IAEA DG report, which declares all work plan issues resolved, vindicates its claim as to the exclusively peaceful nature of its nuclear programme. Accordingly, the IAEA is the sole pertinent international organization to deal with its nuclear issue and, as envisaged in the work plan, safeguards implementation in Iran should be carried out in a routine manner from now on.[249]

3 March 2008

The Security Council considers the situation of Iran. Iran says that the attempt to make the suspension mandatory through the Security Council contravenes the fundamental principles of international law, the NPT and IAEA BOG resolutions, and is a gross violation of Article 25 of the UN Charter. It also flouts the stated position of the overwhelming majority of the international community. With the resolution of the outstanding issues, with the IAEA's repeated conclusions of non-diversion in Iran's nuclear activities, and with Iran's nuclear activities under the full and continuous monitoring of the Agency, there remains no pretext for the illegal request for suspension.[250]

The Security Council adopts Resolution 1803(2008) (14-0-1, Indonesia abstaining), imposing further measures relating to Iran. These included the broadening of the scope of the proliferation-sensitive nuclear activities and nuclear weapons delivery systems-related embargo, the introduction of a travel ban on persons designated in an annex to the resolution as well as on any additional persons designated by the Council or the 1737 Committee, and the expansion of the lists of persons and entities subject to the asset freeze and travel notification requirement. The Security Council calls upon all states to exercise vigilance with regard to publicly-provided financial support for trade with Iran and activities of their financial institutions with banks in Iran, and to inspect the cargoes to and from Iran of aircraft and vessels, at their airports and seaports, owned or operated by two Iranian companies, provided that there were reasonable grounds to believe that the aircraft or vessel is transporting goods prohibited under the Security Council Resolution 1737(2006), Resolution 1747(2007) or Resolution 1803(2008). Finally, the Council reiterates its two-track policy.[251]

Following the vote, the EU3+3 reconfirm their proposal to Iran of June 2006.[252]

[247] —— 'Iran says work plan closed and U.S. intelligence fake' *Reuters* (Vienna 24 February 2008), uk.reuters.com/article/worldNews/idUKL2460705720080224.
[248] Doc. 51.
[249] Doc. 118.
[250] Doc. 18.
[251] Doc. 13.
[252] Doc. 18, also circulated as INFCIRC/723.

Speaking to the press after the debate, the Security Council President stresses that at no time during the debates of the new resolution and its precursors was the use of force suggested.[253]

5 March 2008

The IAEA BOG meets to consider the IAEA DG's report. Agreeing not to pursue a formal resolution, members of the Board criticise Iran for its reluctance to disclose more information about its nuclear activities.[254]

17 March 2008

The 1737 Committee submits its fifth report to the Security Council.[255]

20 March 2008

Russian Foreign Minister Lavrov says that the best method of guaranteeing compliance with the NPT Treaty is 'to continue the work of IAEA observers in Iran, as in any other country. Whatever may be done, it should not interfere with the possibility of continued IAEA work in Iran... Any attempts to resolve this situation by non-peaceful methods will bring to naught all the efforts that have been undertaken in respect of the Iranian nuclear program to date'.[256]

26 March 2008

Iran submits a detailed critique of Security Council Resolution 1803(2008) to the UN Secretary-General, repeating its claims regarding the illegality of the referral of the issue to the Security Council as well as of the Security Council's action. Iran says that in view of this illegality, it does not regard itself obliged to implement the Security Council resolutions. The letter then addresses specific paragraphs of Security Council Resolution 1803(2008). Concluding, Iran says that the breaches of its

rights has led to damages, including interruption of its right to develop and use nuclear energy for peaceful purposes under NPT Article IV, interruption of technical cooperation projects under IAEA Statute Article XI, and injury to its intellectual and reputation rights.[257]

29 April 2008

US President George W Bush explains that his administration chose to reveal intelligence on the Syrian nuclear facility in order to advance 'certain policy objectives', including a message to Iran 'about just how destabilizing a nuclear proliferation would be in the Middle East'. He also says that it is essential to work together to enforce Security Council resolutions aimed at getting Iran to stop their enrichment programmes.[258]

13 May 2008

In a letter addressed to the UN Secretary-General as well as to the EU3+3, Iran proposes a 'package for constructive negotiations' covering political and security issues, economic issues and nuclear issues.[259] The proposal makes no mention of the specific demands made of Iran by the IAEA BOG and the Security Council.

26 May 2008

The IAEA DG reports to the UN Security Council and to the IAEA BOG on the implementation of the NPT Safeguards Agreement and relevant provisions of Security Council Resolutions 1737(2006), 1747(2007) and 1803(2008) in Iran.

The report, which shows continued non-compliance with these resolutions, says that the alleged weapons studies remain a matter of serious concern.[260] The DG emphasises that the Agency currently has no information, apart

---

[253] Webcast, available on UN News Centre 'Security Council will not endorse use of force to deal with Iran – President', www.un.org/apps/news/story.asp?NewsID=25849&Cr=iran&Cr1=&Kw1=Iran&Kw2=&Kw3=.

[254] Greg Webb, 'Iran Weathers Rhetorical Storm at IAEA Over Nuclear Program' (5 March 2008), www.nti.org/d_newswire/issues/2008/3/5/dbf30474-97c8-4f93-a0c3-00b9346d9447.html.

[255] UN Doc S/PV.5853.

[256] Ministry of Foreign Affairs of the Russian Federation, 'Transcript of Remarks and Replies to Media Questions by Russian Minister of Foreign Affairs Sergey Lavrov at Joint Press Conference with Israeli Minister of Foreign Affairs Tzipi Livni' (Tel Aviv, 20 March 2008), www.mid.ru/brp_4.nsf/e78a48070f128a7b43256999005bcbb3/b7ec84b5bb108d6bc3257416004635c2?OpenDocument.

[257] Doc. 119.

[258] Press Conference by the President, Rose Garden (29 April 2008), georgewbush-whitehouse.archives.gov/news/releases/2008/04/20080429-1.html.

[259] Doc. 120.

[260] Doc. 52.

from the uranium metal document, related to the actual design or manufacture by Iran of nuclear material components, or of other key components of a nuclear weapon. Likewise, the Agency has not seen indications of the actual use of nuclear material in connection with the alleged studies.[261]

6 June 2008

Iran delivers a letter to the UN Secretary General referring to a reported statement of the Israeli Deputy Prime Minister that Israel 'will attack Iran... attacking Iran, in order to stop its nuclear plans, will be unavoidable'. Iran says that this threat constitutes a manifest violation of international law and contravenes the most fundamental principles of the Charter of the United Nations. The letter reserves Iran's right to act in self-defense to respond to any attack against the Iranian nation and to take appropriate defensive measures to protect itself'.[262]

13 June 2008

The 1737 Committee presents to the Security Council its sixth report.[263]

12-14 June 2008

The EU3+3 present an offer to Iran, building upon their June 2006 proposal. The EU3+3 are ready to fully recognise Iran's rights to have nuclear energy for peaceful purposes; to cooperate in the nuclear energy, political, economic and other fields, including in the development of a modern nuclear energy programme based on the most modern generation of light-water reactors (an offer which the US has long resisted); and to offer legally-binding fuel supply guarantees. In return, the EU3+3 demand that Iran restore the confidence of the international community in its programme, by fully cooperating with the IAEA and implementing Security Council resolutions.[264]

5 July 2008

Labeling the offers made to it as outdated 'discriminatory language' and 'condescension', Iran proposes a new round of negotiations towards a comprehensive agreement on the basis of commonalities in the EU3+3 and Iranian proposals. It does not indicate those commonalities beyond the general areas of cooperation.[265]

6 July 2008

The EU3+3 express disappointment at Iran's failure to respond positively to their package and agree that while informal contacts with Iran's chief nuclear negotiator will continue, they have no choice but to pursue further sanctions against Iran, as part of their two-track strategy.[266]

8 July 2008

The G8 leaders declare that they firmly support and cooperate with the efforts by the EU3+3 to 'resolve the issue innovatively through negotiation'.[267]

9-11 July 2008

Iran conducts major missile tests, including an intermediate-range Shahab 3 ballistic missile, which may be capable of carrying a nuclear warhead. The EU says that such missile tests can only heighten the concern of the international community at a time when Iran has still not implemented relevant Security Council Resolutions, and, in particular, has not suspended its sensitive nuclear activities.[268]

16 July 2008

Iranian state television quotes Iran's supreme leader Ayatollah Ali Khamenei as saying that Iran is ready for negotiations over the nuclear crisis but would not suspend uranium enrichment activities.[269]

[261] Introductory Statement to the Board of Governors by IAEA Director General Dr. Mohamed ElBaradei (2 June 2008).

[262] Doc. 121.

[263] UN Doc S/PV. 5909.

[264] Doc. 133.

[265] Doc. 122, also circulated as S/2006/806.

[266] Statement by UK Foreign Office Minister Dr. Kim Howells (6 August 2008), www.fco.gov.uk/en/newsroom/latest-news/?view=PressR&id=5072905.

[267] Doc. 153.

[268] Declaration by the Presidency on behalf of the EU on the Iranian missile tests (Brussels 11 July 2008) 11755/08 (Presse 209) P 084.

[269] —— 'Iran accepts nuclear talks but has 'red lines': Khamenei:' *AFP* (Tehran 16 July 2008), afp.google.com/article/ALeqM5jxCjXq_M-0IVJK5a6WbjX5E4x1qw.

19 July 2008

The EU3+3 discuss the 12 June proposal with Iranian negotiators. US Under Secretary of State for Political Affairs is present in the meeting. This is the first time that the US participates directly in negotiations with Iran since 1979.[270] The EU3+3 allow Iran two weeks to respond formally to their proposal before it is withdrawn.[271]

23 July 2008

Iranian president Ahmadinejad says that Iran will not 'retreat one iota' in its nuclear activities.[272]

27 July 2008

Iranian president Ahmadinejad declares that Iran has 6,000 centrifuges.[273]

Iran's former chief nuclear negotiator Ali Larijani says that the two sides 'should find out a third model which will be of benefit to both sides'. Commentators interpret this as a compromise that would allow Iran to proceed with all its nuclear-related activities at a slower pace and with closer international supervision.[274]

30 July 2008

The NAM ministers declare that they believe 'that all safeguards and verification issues, including those of Iran, should be resolved within the IAEA framework, and be based on technical and legal grounds'.[275]

5 August 2008

Iran delivers a three-day late response to the EU3+3 proposal of 12 June, but gives no concrete reply to the demand to freeze its nuclear activity. It says: 'Now the Islamic Republic of Iran is ready to provide a "clear response" to your proposal at the earliest opportunity while simultaneously expecting to receive your "clear response" to our questions and ambiguities as well'.[276] The European foreign ministers say that this response is inadequate, and reiterate their two-track approach to resolving this issue.[277]

25 August 2008

Russian Foreign Minister Lavrov says that the efforts of the EU3+3 have succeeded in creating some definite possibilities for the start of negotiations on the basis of the proposals of the two sides. The EU3+3 are focusing on realizing these possibilities based on a two-track approach. He notes that no one calls into question Iran's lawful right to peaceful uses of nuclear power in accordance with the NPT. If and when trust in the peaceful character of the Iranian nuclear programme is restored, attitude towards it will be the same as to similar programmes of any other non-nuclear weapon state party to the NPT. This broadens opportunities for Iran to actively develop political, economic and other cooperation with the international community, particularly in the area of peaceful utilization of nuclear energy. Russia supports resolving the situation solely by politico-diplomatic methods, at the negotiating table.[278]

11 September 2008

The 1737 Committee submits to the Security Council its seventh report.[279]

---

[270] Summary of remarks by Javier Solana, EU High Representative for the CFSP, after the meeting with Saeed Jalili, Secretary of the Iranian Supreme National Security Council on the Iranian nuclear issue, Geneva (19 July 2008) S259/08.

[271] US Department of State, 'Secretary of State Condoleezza Rice's remarks en route to Abu Dhabi, United Arab Emirates' (21 July 2008), merln.ndu.edu/archivepdf/iran/State/107286.pdf .

[272] —— 'Iran vows no nuclear concessions' *BBC News* (23 July 2008), news.bbc.co.uk/2/hi/middle_east/7520854.stm.

[273] —— 'Report: Iran says it now has 6,000 centrifuges' *Associated Press* (27 July 2008), www.msnbc.msn.com/id/25859051/.

[274] —— 'Iran Favors N. Talks' Fars News Agency (Tehran 27 July 2008), www.farsnews.com/English/newstext.php?nn=8705061492.

[275] Doc. 147.

[276] Doc. 123.

[277] Doc. 123; Mike Nizza, 'Iran Letter Proves Disappointing' *New York Times* (5 August 2008), thelede.blogs.nytimes.com/2008/08/05/iran-letter-proves-disappointing/.

[278] Interview of Russian Minister of Foreign Affairs Sergey Lavrov, *Al-Hayat* (25 August 2008), www.mid.ru/brp_4.nsf/e78a48070f128a7b43256999005bcbb3/b6f85edb742084e3c32574b1001ef91d?OpenDocument.

[279] UN Doc S/PV. 5973.

15 September 2008

The IAEA DG reports to the BOG that the Agency has been able to continue to verify the non-diversion of declared nuclear material in Iran. Iran has provided the Agency with access and information related to declared nuclear material but has not implemented the modified Code 3.1 of its Subsidiary Arrangements General Part.

There remain a number of outstanding issues which give rise to concerns about possible military dimensions to Iran's nuclear programme. For the Agency to provide assurances regarding the absence of undeclared nuclear material and activities in Iran, it is essential that Iran, *inter alia*, provide information and access requested of it.[280]

27 September 2008

The Security Council unanimously adopts Resolution 1835(2008). The Resolution calls on Iran to fully and without delay comply with Council resolutions that demanded an end to that programme and to meet the requirements of the IAEA BOG. The Council reaffirms its commitment to the two-track policy.[281]

Before the vote, Indonesia says that it would not have supported the resolution had it provided for additional sanctions against Iran.[282] Following the vote, Russia says that one of the values of the Resolution is that it reaffirms previous resolutions, which were carefully drafted so as to avoid even the possibility of encouraging or contemplating military solution to the Iranian nuclear issue.[283]

5 October 2008

Iranian Foreign Minister Mottaki says that Iran's uranium enrichment policy remains unchanged. Enrichment will continue until Iran becomes self-sufficient in fuel production for nuclear plants.[284]

19 November 2008

The IAEA DG reports to the BOG on the implementation of the NPT Safeguards Agreement and of relevant Security Council resolutions in Iran, reporting little change.[285]

3 December 2008

Egypt's Foreign Minister says that Egypt supports international efforts aimed at preventing Iran from acquiring nuclear weapons. He also warns against taking military action against Iran.[286]

10 December 2008

The 1737 Committee presents its eighth report to the Security Council.[287]

16 December 2008

The EU3+3 meet with representatives from Bahrain, Kuwait, Saudi Arabia, the UAE, Egypt, Iraq, and Jordan. Following the meeting US Secretary of State Rice says that all participants expressed their concern about Iran's nuclear policies and its regional ambitions, and expressed support for the ongoing work of the UN Security Council, the EU3+3, and the IAEA regarding the Iranian nuclear file.[288]

23 December 2008

Arab League Leader Amr Moussa says that Arabs and Iranians should sit together to try to resolve regional disputes, including Iran's nuclear ambitions. Moussa warned that Arabs should not let the Iranians and foreign powers decide the 'fate of the region' without an Arab say.[289]

---

[280] Doc. 53.

[281] Doc. 14

[282] Doc. 19.

[283] Informal comments to the media by the Permanent Representative of the Russian Federation, H.E. Mr. Vitaly Churkin, on the issue of non-proliferation (Webcast 27 September 2008), www.un.int/russia/new/MainRoot/interviews2008.html.

[284] _____ 'Iran says it will not halt uranium enrichment' *Reuters* (5 October 2008), www.reuters.com/article/worldNews/idUSTRE4941KO20081005.

[285] Doc. 54.

[286] _____ 'Egypt against Iran "developing nuclear weapons"' *AFP* (3 Dec 2008), www.google.com/hostednews/afp/article/ALeqM5ju-AHI_NntJ3siqbNBy5RGJ6Twhw.

[287] UN Doc S/PV. 6036.

[288] Secretary Condoleezza Rice, Remarks Following Meeting Concerning Iran (New York City 16 December 2008) available on lexis-nexis news.

[289] Associated Press, 'Arab League chief urges member states to talk to Iran' *Haaretz* (29 December 2008), www.haaretz.com/hasen/spages/1049381.html.

31 December 2008

The 1737 Committee presents the Security Council with its annual report. According to the report, the Committee had received 90 reports pursuant to Resolution 1737(2006), 77 reports pursuant to Resolution 1747(2007) and 63 reports pursuant to Resolution 1803(2008). Of those reports, some were combined under two or three resolutions.[290]

2009

4 March 2009

The EU3+3 issue a joint statement calling on Iran to cooperate with the IAEA. The statement does not mention the possibility of further sanctions.[291]

10 March 2009

The 1737 Committee presents its ninth report to the Security Council.[294]

19 March 2009

The IAEA DG reports to the BOG that as a result of the continued lack of cooperation by Iran in connection with the remaining issues which give rise to concerns about possible military dimensions of Iran's nuclear programme, the Agency has not made any substantive progress on these issues.[292]

8 April 2009

Following the US willingness to participate fully in the EU3+3 process, the EU3+3 invite Iran to meet.[293]

11 April 2009

Iran's President Ahmadinejad announces that Iran has tested two types of new high-capacity centrifuges. AEOI Head Aghazadeh says that the centrifuges were 5 to 6 times faster than the older

ones. He also says that around 7000 centrifuges have been installed in Natanz facilities.[295]

According to press reports, Iran and the European Union agree to resume talks over Iran's controversial nuclear programme.[296]

20 May 2009

Iran successfully tests the Sajjil-2 two-staged missile with a range of about 2,000 kilometers and which uses solid fuel.[297]

4 June 2009

Speaking in Cairo on the rights and responsibilities of nations on nuclear weapons, US President Obama says that he has 'made it clear to Iran's leaders and people that my country is prepared to move forward. The question now is not what Iran is against, but rather what future it wants to build'. He says that the US is

... willing to move forward without preconditions on the basis of mutual respect. But it is clear to all concerned that when it comes to nuclear weapons, we have reached a decisive point. This is not simply about America's interests. It's about preventing a nuclear arms race in the Middle East that could lead this region and the world down a hugely dangerous path. I understand those who protest that some countries have weapons that others do not. No single nation should pick and choose which nation holds nuclear weapons. And that's why I strongly reaffirmed America's commitment to seek a world in which no nations hold nuclear weapons. And any nation – including Iran – should have the right to access peaceful nuclear power if it complies with its responsibilities under the nuclear Non-Proliferation Treaty. That commitment is at the core of the treaty, and it must be kept for all who fully abide by

---

[290] Doc. 21.

[291] Doc. 134.

[292] Doc. 55.

[293] Doc. 135.

[294] UN Doc S/PV.6090.

[295] —— 'Iran new centrifuges both of one generation: official' *ISNA* (11 April 2009), isna.ir/ISNA/NewsView. aspx?ID=News-1315373&Lang=P.

[296] DPA, 'Iran and European Union reach formula for nuclear talks' *Haaretz* (14 April 2009), www.haaretz. com/hasen/spages/1078373.html.

[297] Peter Crail, 'Progress Seen in Iranian Missile Test' (4 June 2009), www.armscontrol.org/act/2009_6/ IranMissile.

it. And I'm hopeful that all countries in the region can share in this goal.[298]

5 June 2009

The IAEA DG report to the BOG reflects a continued stalemate between IAEA inspectors and Iran. The Report confirms that the IAEA continues to verify the non-diversion of declared nuclear material in Iran. According to the Report, nearly 5,000 centrifuges are being fed UF_6 to enrich uranium at Natanz, with more than 2,000 more ready to start enriching.[299]

12 June 2009

Mahmoud Ahmadinejad is re-elected president of Iran. The opposition claims the elections were rigged.[300]

15 June 2009

In a BBC interview, IAEA DG ElBaradei says in response to a question whether Iran wants nuclear weapons:

My gut feeling is that Iran definitely would like to have the technology… that would enable it to have nuclear weapons if they decide to do so. It wants to send a message to its neighbours, it wants to send a message to the rest of the world, that 'yes, don't mess up with us, we can have nuclear weapons if we want to'. But the ultimate aim of Iran, as I understand it, is they want to be recognised as a major power in the Middle East, and they are, and this is to them the road to get that recognition, to power and prestige and… pretty much an insurance policy against what they heard in the past, about regime change, axis of evil, what have you.[301]

The 1737 Committee presents its tenth report to the Security Council.[302]

3 July 2009

Elected IAEA DG Yukiya Amano says he has not seen any hard evidence that Iran was trying to gain the ability to develop nuclear arms.[303]

8 July 2009

The G8 issue a joint statement urging Iran to pursue a peaceful settlement to the nuclear standoff. They declare their intention to review Iran's behaviour during the Group of 20's global economic summit on 24 and 25 September 2009, with a view to considering new sanctions.[304]

17 July 2009

Iranian President Ahmadinejad appoints Ali Akbar Salehi, Iran's former envoy to the IAEA, head of the AEOI. This follows the resignation of Gholam Reza Aghazadeh. No official reason is given for Aghazadeh's resignation, but he is said to be close to reformist opposition leader Mir Hossein Mousavi, who claims to be the victor in the June presidential elections.[305] Salehi's first comments to the media following his appointments are that 'legal and technical discussions about Iran's nuclear case have finished', and 'there is no room left to keep this case open'. He adds the Iranian hope that 'more efforts will be made to obtain mutual confidence, instead of the last six years of hostility'.[306]

28 August 2009

The IAEA DG reports to the BOG that Iran has cooperated with the Agency in improving safeguards measures at the Fuel Enrichment Plant and in providing the required access to

---

[298] The White House, Office of the Press Secretary, 'Remarks by the President on a New Beginning' (Cairo University, Cairo, Egypt 4 June 2009), www.whitehouse.gov/the_press_office/Remarks-by-the-President-at-Cairo-University-6-04-09/.

[299] Doc. 56

[300] —— 'Mousavi letter to Iran's supreme leader' *BBC News* (14 June 2009), news.bbc.co.uk/2/hi/middle_east/8099876.stm.

[301] —— 'ElBaradei urges Iran nuclear talks' *BBC Radio 4*(17 June 2009), news.bbc.co.uk/today/hi/today/newsid_8104000/8104455.stm.

[302] UN Doc S/PV.6142.

[303] 'No sign Iran seeks nuclear arms: new IAEA head' *Reuters* (3 July 2009), www.reuters.com/article/worldNews/idUSL312024420090703.

[304] Doc. 154.

[305] Ali Akbar Dareini, 'Ahmadinejad appoints new nuclear chief, *Associated Press* (17 July 2009), www.google.com/hostednews/ap/article/ALeqM5jG7bnyWWJfgaYD-JwcqmImlpRujwD99G2F100.

[306] Edward Yeranian, 'New Iranian Nuclear Head Urges Mutual Trust with West' *VOA News* (18 July 2009), www.voanews.com/english/2009-07-18-voa13.cfm.

the Nuclear Research Reactor (IR-40) at Arak for purposes of design information verification. On all other issues relevant to Iran's nuclear programme, however, there is a stalemate. Iran has not suspended its enrichment related activities or its work on heavy water related projects as required by the Security Council, nor has Iran implemented the Additional Protocol. Likewise, Iran has not cooperated with the Agency in connection with the remaining issues, detailed fully and completely in the Agency's reports, which need to be clarified in order to exclude the possibility of there being military dimensions to Iran's nuclear programme.[307]

3 September 2009

French Foreign Minister Bernard Kouchner accuses the IAEA of withholding information about Iran's nuclear programme. He says the IAEA has put key information about Iran's programme in unpublished annexes of the report published the previous week. He says that he thinks 'that in the annexes there are elements that would make us question the military aspect of Iran's nuclear program'.[308]

7 September 2009

The IAEA DG says that *all* information made available to the Agency relevant to Iran's nuclear programme which has been critically assessed by the Agency in accordance with its standard practices has been brought to the attention of the Board. He expresses dismay by the allegations of some member states, which have been fed to the media, that information has been withheld from the Board. He says that these allegations are politically motivated and totally baseless, and that such attempts to influence the work of the Secretariat and undermine its independence and objectivity are in violation of Article VII.F of the IAEA Statute and should cease forthwith.[309]

9 September 2009

Iran hands a package of proposals to the EU3+3, which, it says, address 'various global issues' and represent a 'new opportunity for talks and cooperation'.[310] Diplomatic sources say that the document does not really answer the questions raised with the Iranians, and proposes talks but not on Iran's nuclear program *per se*.[311]

21 September 2009

Iran discloses to the IAEA that since 2007 it has been constructing another, as-yet undeclared enrichment plant at Fordow. It explains that the enrichment facility was intended to serve as a contingency in case the Natanz enrichment plant were attacked.[312]

1 October 2009

During talks with the EU3+3, Iran agrees to allow inspectors to view the Fordow enrichment facility and to participate in follow-up discussions about its overall nuclear enrichment program. There is discussion about the possibility of Iran sending its LEU to Russia and France for further enrichment for the purpose of ultimately fueling a Tehran-based medical research reactor operating under IAEA safeguards. The plan would enable Iran to continue operation of the research reactor beyond 2011, but would also reduce its current LEU stocks at Natanz significantly.[313]

16 December 2009

Iran announces that it had successfully test-launched an improved version of its long-range Sajjil 2 missile, thought to have a range of about 1,250 miles.[314]

---

[307] Doc. 57.

[308] Gregory Viscusi, 'France's Kouchner Says UN Body Withheld Iran Nuclear Evidence' Bloomberg (3 September 2009), www.bloomberg.com/apps/news?pid=20601090&sid=aLq6XbWch_Qo.

[309] Introductory Statement to the Board of Governors by IAEA Director General Dr. Mohamed ElBaradei (7 September 2009), www.iaea.org/NewsCenter/Statements/2009/ebsp2009n009.html#iran.

[310] Fredrik Dahl and Reza Derakhshi, 'Iran presents proposals as West ups nuclear pressure' *Reuters* (9 September 2009), ca.reuters.com/article/topNews/idCAL768384720090909?pageNumber=1&virtualBrandChannel=0.

[311] Laura Rosen, 'Iran's Response' *Politico* (9 September 2009), http://www.politico.com/blogs/laurarozen/0909/Irans_response.html.

[312] GOV/2009/94 (16 November 2009) paras 7, 12.

[313] Julian Borger, 'Iran agrees to send uranium abroad after talks breakthrough' *The Guardian* (2 October 2009) 21.

[314] Reuters, 'Iran Launches Long-Range Missile in Test' NTI (16 December 2009) http://gsn.nti.org/gsn/nw_20091216_9437.php.

INTERNATIONAL AGREEMENTS

1. Multilateral Agreements

Document 1: Treaty on the Non-Proliferation of Nuclear Weapons (NPT)

729 UNTS 161, in force for Iran from 5 March 1970

By letters addressed to the Director General on 5, 6 and 20 March 1970 respectively, the Governments of the United Kingdom of Great Britain and Northern Ireland, the United States of America and the Union of Soviet Socialist Republics, which are designated as the Depositary Governments in Article IX.2 of the Treaty on the Non-Proliferation of Nuclear Weapons, informed the Agency that the Treaty had entered into force on 5 March 1970.

The States concluding this Treaty, hereinafter referred to as the Parties to the Treaty,

Considering the devastation that would be visited upon all mankind by a nuclear war and the consequent need to make every effort to avert the danger of such a war and to take measures to safeguard the security of peoples,

Believing that the proliferation of nuclear weapons would seriously enhance the danger of nuclear war,

In conformity with resolutions of the United Nations General Assembly calling for the conclusion of an agreement on the prevention of wider dissemination of nuclear weapons,

Undertaking to co-operate in facilitating the application of International Atomic Energy Agency safeguards on peaceful nuclear activities,

Expressing their support for research, development and other efforts to further the application, within the framework of the International Atomic Energy Agency safeguards system, of the principle of safeguarding effectively the flow of source and special fissionable materials by use of instruments and other techniques at certain strategic points,

Affirming the principle that the benefits of peaceful applications of nuclear technology, including any technological by-products which may be derived by nuclear-weapon States from the development of nuclear explosive devices, should be available for peaceful purposes to all Parties to the Treaty, whether nuclear-weapon or non-nuclear-weapon States,

Convinced that, in furtherance of this principle, all Parties to the Treaty are entitled to participate in the fullest possible exchange of scientific information for, and to contribute alone or in co-operation with other States to, the further development of the applications of atomic energy for peaceful purposes,

Declaring their intention to achieve at the earliest possible date the cessation of the nuclear arms race and to undertake effective measures in the direction of nuclear disarmament,

Urging the co-operation of all States in the attainment of this objective,

Recalling the determination expressed by the Parties to the 1963 Treaty banning nuclear weapons tests in the atmosphere, in outer space and under water in its Preamble to seek to achieve the discontinuance of all test explosions of nuclear weapons for all time and to continue negotiations to this end,

Desiring to further the easing of international tension and the strengthening of trust between States in order to facilitate the cessation of the manufacture of nuclear weapons, the liquidation of all their existing stockpiles, and the elimination from national arsenals of nuclear weapons and the means of their delivery pursuant to a Treaty on general and complete disarmament under strict and effective international control,

Recalling that, in accordance with the Charter of the United Nations, States must refrain in their international relations from the threat or use of force against the territorial integrity or political independence of any State, or in any other manner inconsistent with the Purposes of the United Nations, and that the establishment and maintenance of international peace and security are to be promoted with the least diversion for armaments of the world's human and economic resources,

Have agreed as follows:

Article I

Each nuclear-weapon State Party to the Treaty undertakes not to transfer to any recipient whatsoever nuclear weapons or other nuclear explosive devices or control over such weapons or explosive devices directly, or indirectly; and not in any way to assist, encourage, or induce any non-nuclear-weapon State to manufacture or otherwise acquire nuclear weapons or other nuclear explosive devices, or control over such weapons or explosive devices.

Article II

Each non-nuclear-weapon State Party to the Treaty undertakes not to receive the transfer from any transferor whatsoever of nuclear weapons or other nuclear explosive devices or of control over such weapons or explosive devices directly, or indirectly; not to manufacture or otherwise acquire nuclear weapons or other nuclear explosive devices; and not to seek or receive any assistance in the manufacture of nuclear weapons or other nuclear explosive devices.

Article III

1. Each non-nuclear-weapon State Party to the Treaty undertakes to accept safeguards, as set forth in an agreement to be negotiated and concluded with the International Atomic Energy Agency in accordance with the Statute of the International Atomic Energy Agency and the Agency's safeguards system, for the exclusive purpose of verification of the fulfilment of its obligations assumed under this Treaty with a view to preventing diversion of nuclear energy from peaceful uses to nuclear weapons or other nuclear explosive devices. Procedures for the safeguards required by this Article shall be followed with respect to source or special fissionable material whether it is being produced, processed or used in any principal nuclear facility or is outside any such facility. The safeguards required by this Article shall be applied on all source or special fissionable material in all peaceful nuclear activities within the territory of such State, under its jurisdiction, or carried out under its control anywhere.

2. Each State Party to the Treaty undertakes not to provide: (a) source or special fissionable material, or (b) equipment or material especially designed or prepared for the processing, use or production of special fissionable material, to any non-nuclear-weapon State for peaceful purposes, unless the source or special fissionable material shall be subject to the safeguards required by this Article.

3. The safeguards required by this Article shall be implemented in a manner designed to comply with Article IV of this Treaty, and to avoid hampering the economic or technological development of the Parties or international co-operation in the field of peaceful nuclear activities, including the international exchange of nuclear material and equipment for the processing, use or production of nuclear material for peaceful purposes in accordance with the provisions of this Article and the principle of safeguarding set forth in the Preamble of the Treaty.

4. Non-nuclear-weapon States Party to the Treaty shall conclude agreements with the International Atomic Energy Agency to meet the requirements of this Article either individually or together with other States in accordance with the Statute of the International Atomic Energy Agency. Negotiation of such agreements shall commence within 180 days from the original entry into force of this Treaty. For States depositing their instruments of ratification or accession after the 180-day period, negotiation of such agreements shall commence not later than the date of such deposit. Such agreements shall enter into force not later than eighteen months after the date of initiation of negotiations.

Article IV

1. Nothing in this Treaty shall be interpreted as affecting the inalienable right of all the Parties to the Treaty to develop research, production and use of nuclear energy for peaceful purposes without discrimination and in conformity with Articles I and II of this Treaty.

2. All the Parties to the Treaty undertake to facilitate, and have the right to participate in, the fullest possible exchange of equipment, materials and scientific and technological information for the peaceful uses of nuclear energy. Parties to the Treaty in a position to do so shall also co-operate in contributing alone or together with other States or international organizations to the further development of the applications of nuclear energy for peaceful purposes, especially in the territories of non-nuclear-weapon States Party to the Treaty, with due consideration for the needs of the developing areas of the world.

Article V

Each Party to the Treaty undertakes to take appropriate measures to ensure that, in accordance with this Treaty, under appropriate international observation and through appropriate international procedures, potential benefits from any peaceful applications of nuclear explosions will be made available to non-nuclear-weapon States Party to the Treaty on a non-discriminatory basis and that the charge to such Parties for the explosive devices used will be as low as possible and exclude any charge for research and development. Non-nuclear-weapon States Party to the Treaty shall be able to obtain such benefits, pursuant to a special international agreement or agreements, through an appropriate international body with adequate representation of non-nuclear-weapon States. Negotiations on this subject shall commence as soon as possible after the Treaty enters into force. Non-nuclear-weapon States Party to the Treaty so desiring may also obtain such benefits pursuant to bilateral agreements.

Article VI

Each of the Parties to the Treaty undertakes to pursue negotiations in good faith on effective measures relating to cessation of the nuclear arms race at an early date and to nuclear disarmament, and on a treaty on general and complete disarmament under strict and effective international control.

Article VII

Nothing in this Treaty affects the right of any group of States to conclude regional treaties in order to assure the total absence of nuclear weapons in their respective territories.

Article VIII

1. Any Party to the Treaty may propose amendments to this Treaty. The text of any proposed amendment shall be submitted to the Depositary Governments which shall circulate it to all Parties to the Treaty. Thereupon, if requested to do so by one-third or more of the Parties to the Treaty, the Depositary Governments shall convene a conference, to which they shall invite all the Parties to the Treaty, to consider such an amendment.

2. Any amendment to this Treaty must be approved by a majority of the votes of all the Parties to the Treaty, including the votes of all nuclear-weapon States Party to the Treaty and all other Parties which, on the date the amendment is circulated, are members of the Board of Governors of the International Atomic Energy Agency. The amendment shall enter into force for each Party that deposits its instrument of ratification of the amendment upon the deposit of such instruments of ratification by a majority of all the Parties, including the instruments of ratification of all nuclear-weapon States Party to the Treaty and all other Parties which, on the date the amendment is circulated, are members of the Board of Governors of the International Atomic Energy Agency. Thereafter, it shall enter into force for any other Party upon the deposit of its instrument of ratification of the amendment.

3. Five years after the entry into force of this Treaty, a conference of Parties to the Treaty shall be held in Geneva, Switzerland, in order to review the operation of this Treaty with a view to assuring that the purposes of the Preamble and the provisions of the Treaty are being realised. At intervals of five years thereafter, a majority of the Parties to the Treaty may obtain, by submitting a proposal to this effect to the Depositary Governments, the convening of further conferences with the same objective of reviewing the operation of the Treaty.

Article IX

1. This Treaty shall be open to all States for signature. Any State which does not sign the Treaty before its entry into force in accordance with paragraph 3 of this Article may accede to it at any time.

2. This Treaty shall be subject to ratification by signatory States. Instruments of ratification and instruments of accession shall be deposited with the Governments of the United Kingdom of Great Britain and Northern Ireland, the Union of Soviet Socialist Republics and the United States of America, which are hereby designated the Depositary Governments.

3. This Treaty shall enter into force after its ratification by the States, the Governments of which are designated Depositaries of the Treaty, and forty other States signatory to this Treaty and the deposit of their instruments of ratification. For the purposes of this Treaty, a nuclear-weapon State is one which has manufactured and exploded a nuclear weapon or other nuclear explosive device prior to 1 January 1967.

4. For States whose instruments of ratification or accession are deposited subsequent to the entry into force of this Treaty, it shall enter into force on the date of the deposit of their instruments of ratification or accession.

5. The Depositary Governments shall promptly inform all signatory and acceding States of the date of each signature, the date of deposit of each instrument of ratification or

of accession, the date of the entry into force of this Treaty, and the date of receipt of any requests for convening a conference or other notices.

6. This Treaty shall be registered by the Depositary Governments pursuant to Article 102 of the Charter of the United Nations.

Article X

1. Each Party shall in exercising its national sovereignty have the right to withdraw from the Treaty if it decides that extraordinary events, related to the subject matter of this Treaty, have jeopardized the supreme interests of its country. It shall give notice of such withdrawal to all other Parties to the Treaty and to the United Nations Security Council three months in advance. Such notice shall include a statement of the extraordinary events it regards as having jeopardized its supreme interests.

2. Twenty-five years after the entry into force of the Treaty, a conference shall be convened to decide whether the Treaty shall continue in force indefinitely, or shall be extended for an additional fixed period or periods. This decision shall be taken by a majority of the Parties to the Treaty.[1]*

Article XI

This Treaty, the English, Russian, French, Spanish and Chinese texts of which are equally authentic, shall be deposited in the archives of the Depositary Governments. Duly certified copies of this Treaty shall be transmitted by the Depositary Governments to the Governments of the signatory and acceding States.

IN WITNESS WHEREOF the undersigned, duly authorized, have signed this Treaty.

DONE in triplicate, at the cities of London, Moscow and Washington, the first day of July, one thousand nine hundred and sixty-eight.

Document 2: United Nations Charter

…

Article 24

In order to ensure prompt and effective action by the United Nations, its Members confer on the Security Council primary responsibility for the maintenance of international peace and security, and agree that in carrying out its duties under this responsibility the Security Council acts on their behalf.

In discharging these duties the Security Council shall act in accordance with the Purposes and Principles of the United Nations. The specific powers granted to the Security Council for the discharge of these duties are laid down in Chapters VI, VII, VIII, and XII.

The Security Council shall submit annual and, when necessary, special reports to the General Assembly for its consideration.

Article 25

The Members of the United Nations agree to accept and carry out the decisions of the Security Council in accordance with the present Charter.

…

[1] On 11 May 1995, in accordance with article X, paragraph 2, the Review and Extension Conference of the Parties to the Treaty on the Non-Proliferation of Nuclear Weapons decided that the Treaty should continue in force indefinitely (decision 3).

Article 39

The Security Council shall determine the existence of any threat to the peace, breach of the peace, or act of aggression and shall make recommendations, or decide what measures shall be taken in accordance with Articles 41 and 42, to maintain or restore international peace and security.

Article 40

In order to prevent an aggravation of the situation, the Security Council may, before making the recommendations or deciding upon the measures provided for in Article 39, call upon the parties concerned to comply with such provisional measures as it deems necessary or desirable. Such provisional measures shall be without prejudice to the rights, claims, or position of the parties concerned. The Security Council shall duly take account of failure to comply with such provisional measures.

Article 41

The Security Council may decide what measures not involving the use of armed force are to be employed to give effect to its decisions, and it may call upon the Members of the United Nations to apply such measures. These may include complete or partial interruption of economic relations and of rail, sea, air, postal, telegraphic, radio, and other means of communication, and the severance of diplomatic relations.

Article 42

Should the Security Council consider that measures provided for in Article 41 would be inadequate or have proved to be inadequate, it may take such action by air, sea, or land forces as may be necessary to maintain or restore international peace and security. Such action may include demonstrations, blockade, and other operations by air, sea, or land forces of Members of the United Nations.

Document 3: Statute of the IAEA

ARTICLE I: Establishment of the Agency

The Parties hereto establish an International Atomic Energy Agency (hereinafter referred to as 'the Agency') upon the terms and conditions hereinafter set forth.

ARTICLE II: Objectives

The Agency shall seek to accelerate and enlarge the contribution of atomic energy to peace, health and prosperity throughout the world. It shall ensure, so far as it is able, that assistance provided by it or at its request or under its supervision or control is not used in such a way as to further any military purpose.

ARTICLE III: Functions

A. The Agency is authorized:

1. To encourage and assist research on, and development and practical application of, atomic energy for peaceful uses throughout the world; and, if requested to do so, to act as an intermediary for the purposes of securing the performance of

services or the supplying of materials, equipment, or facilities by one member of the Agency for another; and to perform any operation or service useful in research on, or development or practical application of, atomic energy for peaceful purposes;

2. To make provision, in accordance with this Statute, for materials, services, equipment, and facilities to meet the needs of research on, and development and practical application of, atomic energy for peaceful purposes, including the production of electric power, with due consideration for the needs of the under-developed areas of the world;

3. To foster the exchange of scientific and technical information on peaceful uses of atomic energy;

4. To encourage the exchange of training of scientists and experts in the field of peaceful uses of atomic energy;

5. To establish and administer safeguards designed to ensure that special fissionable and other materials, services, equipment, facilities, and information made available by the Agency or at its request or under its supervision or control are not used in such a way as to further any military purpose; and to apply safeguards, at the request of the parties, to any bilateral or multilateral arrangement, or at the request of a State, to any of that State's activities in the field of atomic energy;

6. To establish or adopt, in consultation and, where appropriate, in collaboration with the competent organs of the United Nations and with the specialized agencies concerned, standards of safety for protection of health and minimization of danger to life and property (including such standards for labour conditions), and to provide for the application of these standards to its own operation as well as to the operations making use of materials, services, equipment, facilities, and information made available by the Agency or at its request or under its control or supervision; and to provide for the application of these standards, at the request of the parties, to operations under any bilateral or multilateral arrangements, or, at the request of a State, to any of that State's activities in the field of atomic energy;

7. To acquire or establish any facilities, plant and equipment useful in carrying out its authorized functions, whenever the facilities, plant, and equipment otherwise available to it in the area concerned are inadequate or available only on terms it deems unsatisfactory.

B. In carrying out its functions, the Agency shall:

1. Conduct its activities in accordance with the purposes and principles of the United Nations to promote peace and international co-operation, and in conformity with policies of the United Nations furthering the establishment of safeguarded worldwide disarmament and in conformity with any international agreements entered into pursuant to such policies;

2. Establish control over the use of special fissionable materials received by the Agency, in order to ensure that these materials are used only for peaceful purposes;

3. Allocate its resources in such a manner as to secure efficient utilization and the greatest possible general benefit in all areas of the world, bearing in mind the special needs of the under-developed areas of the world;

4. Submit reports on its activities annually to the General Assembly of the United Nations and, when appropriate, to the Security Council: if in connection with the activities of the Agency there should arise questions that are within the competence of the Security Council, the Agency shall notify the Security Council, as the organ bearing the main responsibility for the maintenance of international peace and security, and may also take the measures open to it under this Statute, including those provided in paragraph C of Article XII;

5. Submit reports to the Economic and Social Council and other organs of the United Nations on matters within the competence of these organs.

C. In carrying out its functions, the Agency shall not make assistance to members subject to any political, economic, military, or other conditions incompatible with the provisions of this Statute.

D. Subject to the provisions of this Statute and to the terms of agreements concluded between a State or a group of States and the Agency which shall be in accordance with the provisions of the Statute, the activities of the Agency shall be carried out with due observance of the sovereign rights of States.

...

ARTICLE XII: Agency safeguards

A. With respect to any Agency project, or other arrangement where the Agency is requested by the parties concerned to apply safeguards, the Agency shall have the following rights and responsibilities to the extent relevant to the project or arrangement:

1. To examine the design of specialized equipment and facilities, including nuclear reactors, and to approve it only from the view-point of assuring that it will not further any military purpose, that it complies with applicable health and safety standards, and that it will permit effective application of the safeguards provided for in this article;

2. To require the observance of any health and safety measures prescribed by the Agency;

3. To require the maintenance and production of operating records to assist in ensuring accountability for source and special fissionable materials used or produced in the project or arrangement;

4. To call for and receive progress reports;

5. To approve the means to be used for the chemical processing of irradiated materials solely to ensure that this chemical processing will not lend itself to diversion of materials for military purposes and will comply with applicable health and safety standards; to require that special fissionable materials recovered or produced as a by-product be used for peaceful purposes under continuing Agency safeguards for research or in reactors, existing or under construction, specified by the member or members concerned; and to require deposit with the Agency of any excess of any special fissionable materials recovered or produced as a by-product over what is needed for the above-stated uses in order to prevent stockpiling of these materials, provided that thereafter at the request of the member or members concerned special fissionable materials so deposited with the Agency shall be returned promptly to the member or members concerned for use under the same provisions as stated above.

6. To send into the territory of the recipient State or States inspectors, designated by the Agency after consultation with the State or States concerned, who shall have access at all times to all places and data and to any person who by reason of his occupation deals with materials, equipment, or facilities which are required by this Statute to be safeguarded, as necessary to account for source and special fissionable materials supplied and fissionable products and to determine whether there is compliance with the undertaking against use in furtherance of any military purpose referred to in sub-paragraph F-4 of article Xl, with the health and safety measures referred to in sub-paragraph A-2 of this article, and with any other conditions prescribed in the agreement between the Agency and the State or States concerned. Inspectors designated by the Agency shall be accompanied by representatives of the authorities of the State concerned, if that State so requests, provided that the inspectors shall not thereby be delayed or otherwise impeded in the exercise of their functions;

7. In the event of non-compliance and failure by the recipient State or States to take requested corrective steps within a reasonable time, to suspend or terminate assistance and withdraw any materials and equipment made available by the Agency or a member in furtherance of the project.

B. The Agency shall, as necessary, establish a staff of inspectors. The Staff of inspectors shall have the responsibility of examining all operations conducted by the Agency itself to determine whether the Agency is complying with the health and safety measures prescribed by it for application to projects subject to its approval, supervision or control, and whether the Agency is taking adequate measures to prevent the source and special fissionable materials in its custody or used or produced in its own operations from being used in furtherance of any military purpose. The Agency shall take remedial action forthwith to correct any non-compliance or failure to take adequate measures.

C. The staff of inspectors shall also have the responsibility of obtaining and verifying the accounting referred to in sub paragraph A-6 of this article and of determining whether there is compliance with the undertaking referred to in sub paragraph F-4 of article XI, with the measures referred to in sub-paragraph A-2 of this article, and with all other conditions of the project prescribed in the agreement between the Agency and the State or States concerned. The inspectors shall report any non-compliance to the Director General who shall thereupon transmit the report to the Board of Governors. The Board shall call upon the recipient State or States to remedy forthwith any non-compliance which it finds to have occurred. The Board shall report the non-compliance to all members and to the Security Council and General Assembly of the United Nations. In the event of failure of the recipient State or States to take fully corrective action within a reasonable time, the Board may take one or both of the following measures: direct curtailment or suspension of assistance being provided by the Agency or by a member, and call for the return of materials and equipment made available to the recipient member or group of members. The Agency may also, in accordance with article XIX, suspend any non-complying member from the exercise of the privileges and rights of membership.

...

ARTICLE XIX: Suspension of privileges

A. A member of the Agency which is in arrears in the payment of its financial contributions to the Agency shall have no vote in the Agency if the amount of its arrears equals or exceeds the amount of the contributions due from it for the preceding two years.

The General Conference may, nevertheless, permit such a member to vote if it is satisfied that the failure to pay is due to conditions beyond the control of the member.

B. A member which has persistently violated the provisions of this Statute or of any agreement entered into by it pursuant to this Statute may be suspended from the exercise of the privileges and rights of membership by the General Conference acting by a two-thirds majority of the members present and voting upon recommendation by the Board of Governors.

ARTICLE XX: Definitions

As used in this Statute:

1. The term 'special fissionable material' means plutonium-239; uranium-233; uranium enriched in the isotopes 235 or 233; any material containing one or more of the foregoing; and such other fissionable material as the Board of Governors shall from time to time deter mine; but the term 'special fissionable material' does not include source material.

2. The term 'uranium enriched in the isotopes 235 or 233' means uranium containing the isotopes 235 or 233 or both in an amount such that the abundance ratio of the sum of these isotopes to the isotope 238 is greater than the ratio of the isotope 235 to the isotope 238 occurring in nature.

3. The term 'source material' means uranium containing the mixture of isotopes occurring in nature; uranium depleted in the isotope 235; thorium; any of the foregoing in the form of metal, alloy, chemical compound, or concentrate; any other material containing one or more of the foregoing in such concentration as the Board of Governors shall from time to time determine; and such other material as the Board of Governors shall from time to time determine.

2. Agreements between Iran and the IAEA

Document 4: Agreement between Iran and the International Atomic Energy Agency for the Application of Safeguards in Connection with the Treaty on the Non-Proliferation of Nuclear Weapons, 954 UNTA 91

Signed by Iran 19 June 1973, entered into force on 15 May 1974

AGREEMENT BETWEEN IRAN AND THE INTERNATIONAL ATOMIC ENERGY AGENCY FOR THE APPLICATION OF SAFEGUARDS IN CONNECTION WITH THE TREATY ON THE NON-PROLIFERATION OF NUCLEAR WEAPONS

WHEREAS Iran is a party to the Treaty on the Non-Proliferation of Nuclear Weapons (hereinafter referred to as 'the Treaty') opened for signature at London, Moscow and Washington on 1 July 1968 and which entered into force on 5 March 1970:

WHEREAS paragraph 1 of Article III of the Treaty reads as follows:

'Each non-nuclear-weapon State Party to the Treaty undertakes to accept safeguards, as set forth in an agreement to be negotiated and concluded with the International Atomic

Energy Agency in accordance with the Statute of the International Atomic Energy Agency and the Agency's safeguards system, for the exclusive purpose of verification of the fulfilment of its obligations assumed under this Treaty with a view to preventing diversion of nuclear energy from peaceful uses to nuclear weapons or other nuclear explosive devices. Procedures for the safeguards required by this Article shall be followed with respect to source or special fissionable material whether it is being produced, processed or used in any principal nuclear facility or is outside any such facility. The safeguards required by this Article shall be applied on all source or special fissionable material in all peaceful nuclear activities within the territory of such State, under its jurisdiction, or carried out under its control anywhere'.

WHEREAS the International Atomic Energy Agency (hereinafter referred to as 'the Agency') is authorized, pursuant to Article III of its Statute, to conclude such agreements;

NOW THEREFORE the Government of Iran and the Agency have agreed as follows:

PART I
BASIC UNDERTAKING

Article 1

The Government of Iran undertakes, pursuant to paragraph 1 of Article III of the Treaty, to accept safeguards, in accordance with the terms of this Agreement, on all source or special fissionable material in all peaceful nuclear activities within its territory, under its jurisdiction or carried out under its control anywhere, for the exclusive purpose of verifying that such material is not diverted to nuclear weapons or other nuclear explosive devices.

APPLICATION OF SAFEGUARDS

Article 2

The Agency shall have the right and the obligation to ensure that safeguards will be applied, in accordance with the terms of this Agreement, on all source or special fissionable material in all peaceful nuclear activities within the territory of Iran, under its jurisdiction or carried out under its control anywhere, for the exclusive purpose of verifying that such material is not diverted to nuclear weapons or other nuclear explosive devices.

CO-OPERATION BETWEEN THE GOVERNMENT OF IRAN
AND THE AGENCY

Article 3

The Government of Iran and the Agency shall co-operate to facilitate the implementation of the safeguards provided for in this Agreement.

IMPLEMENTATION OF SAFEGUARDS

Article 4

The safeguards provided for in this Agreement shall be implemented in a manner designed:

(a) To avoid hampering the economic and technological development of Iran or international co-operation in the field of peaceful nuclear activities, including international exchange of nuclear material;

(b) To avoid undue interference in Iran's peaceful nuclear activities, and in particular in the operation of facilities; and

(c) To be consistent with prudent management practices required for the economic and safe conduct of nuclear activities.

...

NATIONAL SYSTEM OF MATERIALS CONTROL

Article 7

(a) The Government of Iran shall establish and maintain a system of accounting for and control of all nuclear material subject to safeguards under this Agreement.

(b) The Agency shall apply safeguards in such a manner as to enable it to verify, in ascertaining that there has been no diversion of nuclear material from peaceful uses to nuclear weapons or other nuclear explosive devices, findings of Iran's system. The Agency's verification shall include, inter alia, independent measurements and observations conducted by the Agency in accordance with the procedures specified in Part II of this Agreement. The Agency, in its verification, shall take due account of the technical effectiveness of Iran's system.

PROVISION OF INFORMATION TO THE AGENCY

Article 8

(a) In order to ensure the effective implementation of safeguards under this Agreement, the Government of Iran shall, in accordance with the provisions set out in Part II of this Agreement, provide the Agency with information concerning nuclear material subject to safeguards under this Agreement and the features of facilities relevant to safeguarding such material.

    (b) (i)   The Agency shall require only the minimum amount of information and data consistent with carrying out its responsibilities under this Agreement.

          (ii)   Information pertaining to facilities shall be the minimum necessary for safeguarding nuclear material subject to safeguards under this Agreement.

(c) If the Government of Iran so requests, the Agency shall be prepared to examine on premises of Iran design information which the Government of Iran regards as being of particular sensitivity. Such information need not be physically transmitted to the Agency provided that it remains readily available for further examination by the Agency on premises of Iran.

AGENCY INSPECTORS

Article 9

    (a) (i)   The Agency shall secure the consent of the Government of Iran to the designation of Agency inspectors to Iran.

          (ii)   If the Government of Iran, either upon proposal of a designation or at any other time after a designation has been made, objects to the designation, the Agency shall propose to the Government of Iran an alternative designation or designations.

(iii) If, as a result of the repeated refusal of the Government of Iran to accept the designation of Agency inspectors, inspections to be conducted under this Agreement would be impeded, such refusal shall be considered by the Board, upon referral by the Director General of the Agency (hereinafter referred to as 'the Director General'), with a view to its taking appropriate action.

(b) The Government of Iran shall take the necessary steps to ensure that Agency inspectors can effectively discharge their functions under this Agreement.

(c) The visits and activities of Agency inspectors shall be so arranged as:

(i) To reduce to a minimum the possible inconvenience and disturbance to the Government of Iran and to the peaceful nuclear activities inspected; and

(ii) To ensure protection of industrial secrets or any other confidential information coming to the inspectors' knowledge.

...

INTERNATIONAL RESPONSIBILITY

Article 17

Any claim by the Government of Iran against the Agency or by the Agency against the Government of Iran in respect of any damage resulting from the implementation of safeguards under this Agreement, other than damage arising out of a nuclear incident, shall be settled in accordance with international law.

MEASURES IN RELATION TO VERIFICATION OF NON-DIVERSION

Article 18

If the Board, upon report of the Director General, decides that an action by the Government of Iran is essential and urgent in order to ensure verification that nuclear material subject to safeguards under this Agreement is not diverted to nuclear weapons or other nuclear explosive devices, the Board may call upon the Government of Iran to take the required action without delay, irrespective of whether procedures have been invoked pursuant to Article 22 of this Agreement for the settlement of a dispute.

Article 19

If the Board, upon examination of relevant information reported to it by the Director General, finds that the Agency is not able to verify that there has been no diversion of nuclear material required to be safeguarded under this Agreement, to nuclear weapons or other nuclear explosive devices, it may make the reports provided for in paragraph C of Article XII of the Statute of the Agency (hereinafter referred to as 'the Statute') and may also take, where applicable, the other measures provided for in that paragraph. In taking such action the Board shall take account of the degree of assurance provided by the safeguards measures that have been applied and shall afford the Government of Iran every reasonable opportunity to furnish the Board with any necessary reassurance.

...

ENTRY INTO FORCE AND DURATION

Article 25

    This Agreement shall enter into force on the date upon which the Agency receives from the Government of Iran written notification that Iran's statutory and constitutional requirements for entry into force have been met. The Director General shall promptly inform all Member States of the Agency of the entry into force of this Agreement.

Article 26

    This Agreement shall remain in force as long as Iran is party to the Treaty.

PART II
INTRODUCTION

Article 27

    The purpose of this part of the Agreement is to specify the procedures to be applied in the implementation of the safeguards provisions of Part I.

OBJECTIVE OF SAFEGUARDS

Article 28

    The objective of the safeguards procedures set forth in this part of the Agreement is the timely detection of diversion of significant quantities of nuclear material from peaceful nuclear activities to the manufacture of nuclear weapons or of other nuclear explosive devices or for purposes unknown, and deterrence of such diversion by the risk of early detection.

...

DONE in Vienna on the 19th day of June 1973 in duplicate in the English language.
For the GOVERNMENT OF IRAN: (signed) Dr. M. Sadri
For the INTERNATIONAL ATOMIC ENERGY AGENCY: (signed) Sigvard Eklund

Document 5: Model Additional Protocol, INFCIRC/540 Corr.1

Signed by Iran 18 December 2003, Not Ratified

MODEL PROTOCOL ADDITIONAL TO THE AGREEMENT(S) BETWEEN ... AND THE INTERNATIONAL ATOMIC ENERGY AGENCY FOR THE APPLICATION OF SAFEGUARDS

Preamble

    WHEREAS ... (hereinafter referred to as '...') is a party to (an) Agreement(s) between ... and the International Atomic Energy Agency (hereinafter referred to as the 'Agency')

for the application of safeguards [full title of the Agreement(s) to be inserted] (hereinafter referred to as the 'Safeguards Agreement(s)'), which entered into force on ...;

AWARE OF the desire of the international community to further enhance nuclear non-proliferation by strengthening the effectiveness and improving the efficiency of the Agency's safeguards system;

RECALLING that the Agency must take into account in the implementation of safeguards the need to: avoid hampering the economic and technological development of ... or international co-operation in the field of peaceful nuclear activities; respect health, safety, physical protection and other security provisions in force and the rights of individuals; and take every precaution to protect commercial, technological and industrial secrets as well as other confidential information coming to its knowledge;

WHEREAS the frequency and intensity of activities described in this Protocol shall be kept to the minimum consistent with the objective of strengthening the effectiveness and improving the efficiency of Agency safeguards;

NOW THEREFORE ... and the Agency have agreed as follows:

RELATIONSHIP BETWEEN THE PROTOCOL AND THE SAFEGUARDS AGREEMENT

Article 1

The provisions of the Safeguards Agreement shall apply to this Protocol to the extent that they are relevant to and compatible with the provisions of this Protocol. In case of conflict between the provisions of the Safeguards Agreement and those of this Protocol, the provisions of this Protocol shall apply.

PROVISION OF INFORMATION

Article 2

a. ... shall provide the Agency with a declaration containing:

(i) A general description of and information specifying the location of *nuclear fuel cycle-related research and development activities*[2] not involving *nuclear material* carried out anywhere that are funded, specifically authorized or controlled by, or carried out on behalf of, ...

(ii) Information identified by the Agency on the basis of expected gains in effectiveness or efficiency, and agreed to by ..., on operational activities of safeguards relevance at *facilities* and at *locations outside facilities where nuclear material* is customarily used.

(iii) A general description of each building on each *site*, including its use and, if not apparent from that description, its contents. The description shall include a map of the *site*.

(iv) A description of the scale of operations for each location engaged in the activities specified in Annex I to this Protocol.

(v) Information specifying the location, operational status and the estimated annual production capacity of uranium mines and concentration plants and thorium concentration plants, and the current annual production of such mines and concentration plants for ... as a whole. ... shall provide, upon request by the

---

[2] Terms in italics have specialized meanings, which are defined in Article 18 below (footnote in the original).

Agency, the current annual production of an individual mine or concentration plant. The provision of this information does not require detailed *nuclear material* accountancy.

(vi) Information regarding source material which has not reached the composition and purity suitable for fuel fabrication or for being isotopically enriched, as follows:

(a) The quantities, the chemical composition, the use or intended use of such material, whether in nuclear or non-nuclear use, for each location in … at which the material is present in quantities exceeding ten metric tons of uranium and/or twenty metric tons of thorium, and for other locations with quantities of more than one metric ton, the aggregate for … as a whole if the aggregate exceeds ten metric tons of uranium or twenty metric tons of thorium. The provision of this information does not require detailed *nuclear material* accountancy;

(b) The quantities, the chemical composition and the destination of each export out of … of such material for specifically non-nuclear purposes in quantities exceeding:

(1) Ten metric tons of uranium, or for successive exports of uranium from … to the same State, each of less than ten metric tons, but exceeding a total of ten metric tons for the year;

(2) Twenty metric tons of thorium, or for successive exports of thorium from … to the same State, each of less than twenty metric tons, but exceeding a total of twenty metric tons for the year;

(c) The quantities, chemical composition, current location and use or intended use of each import into … of such material for specifically non-nuclear purposes in quantities exceeding:

(1) Ten metric tons of uranium, or for successive imports of uranium into … each of less than ten metric tons, but exceeding a total of ten metric tons for the year;

(2) Twenty metric tons of thorium, or for successive imports of thorium into … each of less than twenty metric tons, but exceeding a total of twenty metric tons for the year; it being understood that there is no requirement to provide information on such material intended for a non-nuclear use once it is in its non-nuclear end-use form.

(vii) (a) Information regarding the quantities, uses and locations of *nuclear material* exempted from safeguards pursuant to [paragraph 37 of INFCIRC/153][3];

(b) Information regarding the quantities (which may be in the form of estimates) and uses at each location, of *nuclear material* exempted from safeguards pursuant to [paragraph 36(b) of INFCIRC/153] but not yet in a non-nuclear end-use form, in quantities exceeding those set out in [paragraph 37 of INFCIRC/153]. The provision of this information does not require detailed nuclear material accountancy.

(viii) Information regarding the location or further processing of intermediate or high-level waste containing plutonium, *high enriched uranium* or uranium-

---

[3] The reference to the corresponding provision of the relevant Safeguards Agreement should be inserted where bracketed references to INFCIRC/153 are made (footnote in the original).

233 on which safeguards have been terminated pursuant to [paragraph 11 of INFCIRC/153] . For the purpose of this paragraph, 'further processing' does not include repackaging of the waste or its further conditioning not involving the separation of elements, for storage or disposal.

(ix) The following information regarding specified equipment and non-nuclear material listed in Annex II:

(a) For each export out of ... of such equipment and material: the identity, quantity, location of intended use in the receiving State and date or, as appropriate, expected date, of export;

(b) Upon specific request by the Agency, confirmation by ... as importing State, of information provided to the Agency by another State concerning the export of such equipment and material to ... .'.

(x) General plans for the succeeding ten-year period relevant to the development of the nuclear fuel cycle (including planned nuclear fuel cycle-related research and development activities) when approved by the appropriate authorities in ....

b. ... shall make every reasonable effort to provide the Agency with the following information:

(i) A general description of and information specifying the location of nuclear fuel cycle-related research and development activities not involving nuclear material which are specifically related to enrichment, reprocessing of nuclear fuel or the processing of intermediate or high-level waste containing plutonium, high enriched uranium or uranium-233 that are carried out anywhere in ... but which are not funded, specifically authorized or controlled by, or carried out on behalf of, ... For the purpose of this paragraph, 'processing' of intermediate or high-level waste does not include repackaging of the waste or its conditioning not involving the separation of elements, for storage or disposal.

(ii) A general description of activities and the identity of the person or entity carrying out such activities, at locations identified by the Agency outside a site which the Agency considers might be functionally related to the activities of that site. The provision of this information is subject to a specific request by the Agency. It shall be provided in consultation with the Agency and in a timely fashion.

c. Upon request by the Agency, ... shall provide amplifications or clarifications of any information it has provided under this Article, in so far as relevant for the purpose of safeguards.

Article 3

a. ... shall provide to the Agency the information identified in Article 2.a.(i), (iii), (iv), (v), (vi)(a), (vii) and (x) and Article 2.b.(i) within 180 days of the entry into force of this Protocol.

b. ... shall provide to the Agency, by 15 May of each year, updates of the information referred to in paragraph a. above for the period covering the previous calendar year. If there has been no change to the information previously provided, ... shall so indicate.

c. ... shall provide to the Agency, by 15 May of each year, the information identified in Article 2.a.(vi)(b) and (c) for the period covering the previous calendar year.

d. ... shall provide to the Agency on a quarterly basis the information identified in Article 2.a.(ix)(a). This information shall be provided within sixty days of the end of each quarter.

e. ... shall provide to the Agency the information identified in Article 2.a.(viii) 180 days before further processing is carried out and, by 15 May of each year, information on changes in location for the period covering the previous calendar year.

f. ... and the Agency shall agree on the timing and frequency of the provision of the information identified in Article 2.a.(ii).

g. ... shall provide to the Agency the information in Article 2.a.(ix)(b) within sixty days of the Agency's request.

COMPLEMENTARY ACCESS

Article 4

The following shall apply in connection with the implementation of complementary access under Article 5 of this Protocol:

a. The Agency shall not mechanistically or systematically seek to verify the information referred to in Article 2; however, the Agency shall have access to:

> (i) Any location referred to in Article 5.a.(i) or (ii) on a selective basis in order to assure the absence of undeclared nuclear material and activities;
>
> (ii) Any location referred to in Article 5.b. or c. to resolve a question relating to the correctness and completeness of the information provided pursuant to Article 2 or to resolve an inconsistency relating to that information;
>
> (iii) Any location referred to in Article 5.a.(iii) to the extent necessary for the Agency to confirm, for safeguards purposes, ...'s declaration of the decommissioned status of a *facility* or of a *location outside facilities* where *nuclear material* was customarily used.

b. (i) Except as provided in paragraph (ii) below, the Agency shall give ... advance notice of access of at least 24 hours;

> (ii) For access to any place on a *site* that is sought in conjunction with design information verification visits or ad hoc or routine inspections on that *site*, the period of advance notice shall, if the Agency so requests, be at least two hours but, in exceptional circumstances, it may be less than two hours.

c. Advance notice shall be in writing and shall specify the reasons for access and the activities to be carried out during such access.

d. In the case of a question or inconsistency, the Agency shall provide ... with an opportunity to clarify and facilitate the resolution of the question or inconsistency. Such an opportunity will be provided before a request for access, unless the Agency considers that delay in access would prejudice the purpose for which the access is sought. In any event, the Agency shall not draw any conclusions about the question or inconsistency until ... has been provided with such an opportunity.

e. Unless otherwise agreed to by ..., access shall only take place during regular working hours.

f. ... shall have the right to have Agency inspectors accompanied during their access by representatives of ..., provided that the inspectors shall not thereby be delayed or otherwise impeded in the exercise of their functions.

Article 5

... shall provide the Agency with access to:

a.   (i) Any place on a *site*;
(ii) Any location identified by ... under Article 2.a.(v)-(viii);
(iii) Any *decommissioned facility or decommissioned location outside facilities* where *nuclear material* was customarily used.

b. Any location identified by ... under Article 2.a.(i), Article 2.a.(iv), Article 2.a.(ix) (b) or Article 2.b, other than those referred to in paragraph a.(i) above, provided that if ... is unable to provide such access, ... shall make every reasonable effort to satisfy Agency requirements, without delay, through other means.

c. Any location specified by the Agency, other than locations referred to in paragraphs a. and b. above, to carry out *location-specific environmental sampling*, provided that if ... is unable to provide such access, ... shall make every reasonable effort to satisfy Agency requirements, without delay, at adjacent locations or through other means.

...

Article 7

a. Upon request by ..., the Agency and ... shall make arrangements for managed access under this Protocol in order to prevent the dissemination of proliferation sensitive information, to meet safety or physical protection requirements, or to protect proprietary or commercially sensitive information. Such arrangements shall not preclude the Agency from conducting activities necessary to provide credible assurance of the absence of undeclared *nuclear material* and activities at the location in question, including the resolution of a question relating to the correctness and completeness of the information referred to in Article 2 or of an inconsistency relating to that information.

b. ... may, when providing the information referred to in Article 2, inform the Agency of the places at a *site* or location at which managed access may be applicable.

c. Pending the entry into force of any necessary Subsidiary Arrangements, ... may have recourse to managed access consistent with the provisions of paragraph a. above.

Article 8

Nothing in this Protocol shall preclude ... from offering the Agency access to locations in addition to those referred to in Articles 5 and 9 or from requesting the Agency to conduct verification activities at a particular location. The Agency shall, without delay, make every reasonable effort to act upon such a request.

Article 9

... shall provide the Agency with access to locations specified by the Agency to carry out *wide-area environmental sampling*, provided that if ... is unable to provide such access it shall make every reasonable effort to satisfy Agency requirements at alternative locations. The Agency shall not seek such access until the use of *wide-area environmental sampling* and the procedural arrangements therefore have been approved by the Board and following consultations between the Agency and ....

...

DEFINITIONS

Article 18

For the purpose of this Protocol:

a. *Nuclear fuel cycle-related research and development activities* means those activities which are specifically related to any process or system development aspect of any of the following:

- conversion of *nuclear material*,
- enrichment of *nuclear material*,
- nuclear fuel fabrication,
- reactors,
- critical facilities,
- reprocessing of nuclear fuel,
- processing (not including repackaging or conditioning not involving the separation of elements, for storage or disposal) of intermediate or high-level waste containing plutonium, *high enriched uranium* or uranium-233, but do not include activities related to theoretical or basic scientific research or to research and development on industrial radioisotope applications, medical, hydrological and agricultural applications, health and environmental effects and improved maintenance.

b. *Site* means that area delimited by ... in the relevant design information for a facility, including a *closed-down facility*, and in the relevant information on a *location outside facilities* where *nuclear material* is customarily used, including a *closed-down location outside facilities* where *nuclear material* was customarily used (this is limited to locations with hot cells or where activities related to conversion, enrichment, fuel fabrication or reprocessing were carried out). It shall also include all installations, co-located with the *facility* or location, for the provision or use of essential services, including: hot cells for processing irradiated materials not containing *nuclear material*; installations for the treatment, storage and disposal of waste; and buildings associated with specified activities identified by ... under Article 2.a.(iv) above.

c. *Decommissioned facility* or *decommissioned location outside facilities* means an installation or location at which residual structures and equipment essential for its use have been removed or rendered inoperable so that it is not used to store and can no longer be used to handle, process or utilize *nuclear material*.

d. *Closed-down facility* or *closed-down location outside facilities* means an installation or location where operations have been stopped and the *nuclear material* removed but which has not been decommissioned.

e. *High enriched uranium* means uranium containing 20 percent or more of the isotope uranium-235.

f. *Location-specific environmental sampling* means the collection of environmental samples (e.g., air, water, vegetation, soil, smears) at, and in the immediate vicinity of, a location specified by the Agency for the purpose of assisting the Agency to draw conclusions about the absence of undeclared *nuclear material* or nuclear activities at the specified location.

g. Wide-area environmental sampling means the collection of environmental samples (e.g., air, water, vegetation, soil, smears) at a set of locations specified by the Agency for the purpose of assisting the Agency to draw conclusions about the absence of undeclared nuclear material or nuclear activities over a wide area.

h. Nuclear material means any source or any special fissionable material as defined in Article XX of the Statute. The term source material shall not be interpreted as applying to ore or ore residue. Any determination by the Board under Article XX of the Statute of the Agency after the entry into force of this Protocol which adds to the materials considered to be source material or special fissionable material shall have effect under this Protocol only upon acceptance by ...

i. *Facility* means:

(i) A reactor, a critical facility, a conversion plant, a fabrication plant, a reprocessing plant, an isotope separation plant or a separate storage installation; or

(ii) Any location where *nuclear material* in amounts greater than one effective kilogram is customarily used.

j. *Location outside facilities* means any installation or location, which is not a facility, where *nuclear material* is customarily used in amounts of one effective kilogram or less.

Document 6: Understanding of the Islamic Republic of Iran and the IAEA on the Modalities of Resolution of the Outstanding Issues

Tehran, 21 August 2007, INFCIRC/711, 27 August 2007

Pursuant to the negotiations between H.E. Dr. Larijani, I. R. of Iran's Secretary of Supreme National Security Council and H.E. Dr. ElBaradei, Director General of the IAEA, in Vienna; following the initiative and good will of the Islamic Republic of Iran and the agreement made, a high ranking delegation consisting of the directors of technical, legal and political departments of the IAEA, paid a visit to Tehran from 11 to 12 July 2007 during which 'Understandings of The Islamic Republic of Iran and the IAEA on the Modalities of Resolution of the Outstanding Issues, Tehran 12 July 2007' were prepared. A second meeting took place in Vienna on 24 July 2007 followed by a further meeting in Iran from 20 to 21 August 2007. The Agency's delegation had the opportunity to have meetings with H.E. Dr. Larijani during both visits to Tehran. Following these three consecutive meetings, both Parties reached the following understandings:

I. Latest Developments:

Based on the modalities agreed upon on 12 July 2007, the following decisions were made:

1. Present Issues:

A. Enrichment Programme

The Agency and Iran agreed to cooperate in preparing the safeguards approach for the Natanz Fuel Enrichment Plant in accordance with Iran's Comprehensive Safeguards Agreement.[4] The draft text of the safeguards approach paper, and the facility attachment of IRN- were provided to Iran on 23 July 2007. The safeguards approach and the facility attachment were discussed during technical meetings in Iran between the Agency and the AEOI from 6 to 8 August 2007. Further discussions will be held with the aim of finalizing the facility attachment by the end of September 2007.

---

[4] Doc. 4.

B. Heavy Water Research Reactor in Arak

Iran agreed with the Agency's request to visit the heavy water research reactor (IR40) site in Arak. A successful visit took place on 30 July 2007.

C. Designation of new inspectors

On 12 July 2007, Iran accepted the designation of five additional inspectors.

D. Issue of multiple entry visas

On 12 July 2007, Iran agreed to issue one year multiple entry visas for 14 inspectors and staff of the Agency.

2. Past Outstanding Issues:

A. Plutonium Experiments

In order to conclude and close the file of the issue of plutonium (Pu), the Agency provided Iran with the remaining questions on 23 July 2007. During a meeting in Iran between representatives of the Agency and Iran, Iran provided clarifications to the Agency that helped to explain the remaining questions. In addition, on 7 August 2007, Iran sent a letter to the Agency providing additional clarifications to some of the questions. On 20 August 2007 the Agency stated that earlier statements made by Iran are consistent with the Agency's findings, and thus this matter is resolved. This will be communicated officially by the Agency to Iran through a letter.

B. Issue of P1-P2:

Based on agreed modalities of 12 July 2007, Iran and the Agency agreed the following procedural steps to resolve the P1-P2 issue. The proposed timeline assumes that the Agency announces the closure of the Pu-experiments outstanding issue by 31 August 2007, and its subsequent reporting in the Director General's report to the September 2007 Board of Governors.[5]

The Agency will provide all remaining questions on this issue by 31 August 2007. Iran and the Agency will have discussions in Iran on 24-25 September 2007 to clarify the questions provided. This will be followed up by a further meeting in mid-October 2007 to further clarify the written answers provided. The Agency's target date for the closure of this issue is November 2007.

C. Source of Contamination

Based on the agreed modalities on 12 July 2007 and given the Agency's findings which tend, on balance, to support Iran's statement about the foreign origin of the observed HEU contamination, the only remaining outstanding issue on contamination is the contamination found at a Technical University in Tehran.

Iran and the Agency agreed on the following procedural steps to address this issue, starting once the P1-P2 issue is concluded and the file is closed. The Agency will again provide Iran with the remaining questions regarding the contamination found at a Technical University in Tehran by 15 September 2007. After 2 weeks of the closure of the P1-P2 issue Iran and the Agency will have discussions in Iran on this issue.

D. U Metal Document

Upon the request of the Agency, Iran agreed to cooperate with the Agency in facilitating the comparison of the relevant sections of the document. Iran is presently reviewing the proposals already made during the first meeting on 12 July 2007. After taking this step by Iran, the Agency undertakes to close this issue.

---

[5] Doc. 49.

II. Modalities of Resolution of other Outstanding Issues

A. Po210

Based on agreed modalities of 12 July 2007, Iran agreed to deal with this issue, once all the above mentioned issues are concluded and their files are closed. Iran and the Agency agreed upon the following procedural steps: regarding this issue, the Agency will provide Iran in writing with all its remaining questions by 15 September 2007. After 2 weeks from conclusion and closure of the issues of the source of contamination and U-metal, reflected in the Director General's report to the Board of Governors, Iran and the Agency will have discussions in Iran where Iran will provide explanations on the Po210.

B. Ghachine Mine

Based on agreed modalities of 12 July 2007, Iran agreed to deal with this issue, once the issue of Po210 is concluded and its file is closed. Iran and the Agency agreed upon the following procedural steps: regarding this issue, the Agency will provide Iran in writing with all its remaining questions by 15 September 2007.

After 2 weeks from conclusion and closure of the issue of Po210, reflected in the Director General's report to the Board of Governors, Iran and the Agency will have discussions in Iran where Iran will provide explanations to the Agency about Ghachine Mine.

III. Alleged Studies

Iran reiterated that it considers the following alleged studies as politically motivated and baseless allegations. The Agency will however provide Iran with access to the documentation it has in its possession regarding: the Green Salt Project, the high explosive testing and the missile re-entry vehicle.

As a sign of good will and cooperation with the Agency, upon receiving all related documents, Iran will review and inform the Agency of its assessment.

IV. General Understandings

1. These modalities cover all remaining issues and the Agency confirmed that there are no other remaining issues and ambiguities regarding Iran's past nuclear program and activities.

2. The Agency agreed to provide Iran with all remaining questions according to the above work plan. This means that after receiving the questions, no other questions are left. Iran will provide the Agency with the required clarifications and information.

3. The Agency's delegation is of the view that the agreement on the above issues shall further promote the efficiency of the implementation of safeguards in Iran and its ability to conclude the exclusive peaceful nature of the Iran's nuclear activities.

4. The Agency has been able to verify the non-diversion of the declared nuclear materials at the enrichment facilities in Iran and has therefore concluded that it remains in peaceful use.

5. The Agency and Iran agreed that after the implementation of the above work plan and the agreed modalities for resolving the outstanding issues, the implementation of safeguards in Iran will be conducted in a routine manner.

3. Agreements between the EU3/EU3+3 and Iran

Document 7: Agreed Statement at the End of a Visit to the Islamic Republic of Iran by the Foreign Ministers of Britain, France and Germany ('Tehran Statement')

21 October 2003

1. Upon the invitation of the Government of the Islamic Republic of Iran, the Foreign Ministers of Britain, France and Germany paid a visit to Tehran on 21 October 2003. The Iranian authorities and the Ministers, following extensive consultations, agreed on measures aimed at the settlement of all outstanding IAEA issues with regard to the Iranian nuclear programme and at enhancing confidence for peaceful cooperation in the nuclear field.

2. The Iranian authorities reaffirmed that nuclear weapons have no place in Iran's defence doctrine and that its nuclear programme and activities have been exclusively in the peaceful domain. They reiterated Iran's commitment to the nuclear non-proliferation regime, and informed the Ministers that:

(a) The Iranian Government has decided to engage in full co-operation with the IAEA to address and resolve, through full transparency, all requirements and outstanding issues of the Agency, and clarify and correct any possible failures and deficiencies within the IAEA.

(b) To promote confidence with a view to removing existing barriers for cooperation in the nuclear field:

(i) Having received the necessary clarifications, the Iranian Government has decided to sign the IAEA Additional Protocol,[6] and commence ratification procedures. As a confirmation of its good intentions, the Iranian Government will continue to co-operate with the Agency in accordance with the Protocol in advance of its ratification.

(ii) While Iran has a right within the nuclear non-proliferation regime to develop nuclear energy for peaceful purposes, it has decided voluntarily to suspend all uranium enrichment and reprocessing activities as defined by the IAEA.

3. The Foreign Ministers of Britain, France and Germany welcomed the decisions of the Iranian Government and informed the Iranian authorities that:

(a) Their Governments recognize the right of Iran to enjoy peaceful use of nuclear energy in accordance with the NPT.

(b) In their view, the Additional Protocol is in no way intended to undermine the sovereignty, national dignity or national security of its States Parties.

(c) In their view, the full implementation of Iran's decisions, confirmed by the IAEA Director-General, should enable the immediate situation to be resolved by the IAEA Board.

(d) The three Governments believe that this will open the way to a dialogue on a basis for longer term cooperation, which will provide all parties with satisfactory

---

[6] Doc. 5.

assurances relating to Iran's nuclear power generation programme. Once international concerns, including those of the three Governments, are fully resolved, Iran could expect easier access to modern technology and supplies in a range of areas.
(e) They will co-operate with Iran to promote security and stability in the region, including the establishment of a zone free from weapons of mass destruction in the Middle East in accordance with the objectives of the United Nations.

Document 8: Agreement, Paris, 15 November 2004 ('Paris Agreement')

IFCIRC/637, 26 November 2004

The Government of the Islamic Republic of Iran and the Governments of France, Germany and the United Kingdom, with the support of the High Representative of the European Union (E3/EU), reaffirm the commitments in the Tehran Agreed Statement of 21 October 2003[7] and have decided to move forward, building on that agreement.

The E3/EU and Iran reaffirm their commitment to the NPT.

The E3/EU recognise Iran's rights under the NPT exercised in conformity with its obligations under the Treaty, without discrimination.

Iran reaffirms that, in accordance with Article II of the NPT, it does not and will not seek to acquire nuclear weapons. It commits itself to full cooperation and transparency with the IAEA. Iran will continue to implement the Additional Protocol[8] voluntarily pending ratification.

To build further confidence, Iran has decided, on a voluntary basis, to continue and extend its suspension to include all enrichment related and reprocessing activities, and specifically: the manufacture and import of gas centrifuges and their components; the assembly, installation, testing or operation of gas centrifuges; work to undertake any plutonium separation, or to construct or operate any plutonium separation installation; and all tests or production at any uranium conversion installation. The IAEA will be notified of this suspension and invited to verify and monitor it. The suspension will be implemented in time for the IAEA to confirm before the November Board that it has been put into effect. The suspension will be sustained while negotiations proceed on a mutually acceptable agreement on long-term arrangement.

The E3/EU recognize that this suspension is a voluntary confidence-building measure and not a legal obligation.

Sustaining the suspension, while negotiations on a long-term agreement are under way, will be essential for the continuation of the overall process. In the context of this suspension, the E3/EU and Iran have agreed to begin negotiations, with a view to reaching a mutually acceptable agreement on long term arrangements. The agreement will provide objective guarantees that Iran's nuclear programme is exclusively for peaceful purposes. It will equally provide firm guarantees on nuclear, technological and economic cooperation and firm commitments on security issues.

A steering committee will meet to launch these negotiations in the first half of December 2004 and will set up working groups on political and security issues, technology

[7] Doc. 7.
[8] Doc. 5.

and cooperation, and nuclear issues. The steering committee shall meet again within three months to receive progress reports from the working groups and to move ahead with projects and/or measures that can be implemented in advance of an overall agreement.

In the context of the present agreement and noting the progress that has been made in resolving outstanding issues, the E3/EU will henceforth support the Director General reporting to the IAEA Board as he considers appropriate in the framework of the implementation of Iran's Safeguards Agreement and Additional Protocol.

The E3/EU will support the IAEA Director General inviting Iran to join the Expert Group on Multilateral Approaches to the Nuclear Fuel Cycle.

Once suspension has been verified, the negotiations with the EU on a Trade and Cooperation Agreement will resume. The E3/EU will actively support the opening of Iranian accession negotiations at the WTO.

Irrespective of progress on the nuclear issue, the E3/EU and Iran confirm their determination to combat terrorism, including the activities of Al Qa'ida and other terrorist groups such as the MeK. They also confirm their continued support for the political process in Iraq aimed at establishing a constitutionally elected Government.

SECURITY COUNCIL DOCUMENTS

1. Security Council Resolutions and Presidential Statements

Document 9: Statement by the President of the Security Council

S/PRST/2006/15, 29 March 2006

At the 5403rd meeting of the Security Council, held on 29 March 2006, in connection with the Council's consideration of the item entitled 'Non-proliferation', the President of the Security Council made the following statement on behalf of the Council:

'The Security Council reaffirms its commitment to the Treaty on the Non-proliferation of Nuclear Weapons and recalls the right of States Party, in conformity with Articles I and II of that Treaty, to develop research, production and use of nuclear energy for peaceful purposes without discrimination.

'The Security Council notes with serious concern the many IAEA reports and resolutions related to Iran's nuclear programme, reported to it by the IAEA Director General, including the February IAEA Board Resolution (GOV/2006/14).[9]

'The Security Council also notes with serious concern that the Director General's report of 27 February 2006 (GOV/2006/15)[10] lists a number of outstanding issues and concerns, including topics which could have a military nuclear dimension, and that the IAEA is unable to conclude that there are no undeclared nuclear materials or activities in Iran.

'The Security Council notes with serious concern Iran's decision to resume enrichment-related activities, including research and development, and to suspend cooperation with the IAEA under the Additional Protocol.[11]

'The Security Council calls upon Iran to take the steps required by the IAEA Board of Governors, notably in the first operative paragraph of its resolution GOV/2006/14, which are essential to build confidence in the exclusively peaceful purpose of its nuclear programme and to resolve outstanding questions, and underlines, in this regard, the particular importance of re-establishing full and sustained suspension of all enrichment-related and reprocessing activities, including research and development, to be verified by the IAEA.

'The Security Council expresses the conviction that such suspension and full, verified Iranian compliance with the requirements set out by the IAEA Board of Governors would contribute to a diplomatic, negotiated solution that guarantees Iran's nuclear programme is for exclusively peaceful purposes, and underlines the willingness of the international community to work positively for such a solution which will also benefit nuclear non-proliferation elsewhere.

'The Security Council strongly supports the role of the IAEA Board of Governors and commends and encourages the Director General of the IAEA and its secretariat

---

[9] Doc. 32.
[10] Doc. 42.
[11] Doc. 5.

for their ongoing professional and impartial efforts to resolve outstanding issues in Iran, and underlines the necessity of the IAEA continuing its work to clarify all outstanding issues relating to Iran's nuclear programme.

'The Security Council requests in 30 days a report from the Director General of the IAEA on the process of Iranian compliance with the steps required by the IAEA Board, to the IAEA Board of Governors and in parallel to the Security Council for its consideration.'

Document 10: Security Council Resolution 1696(2006)

31 July 2006

The Security Council,

Recalling the Statement of its President, S/PRST/2006/15, of 29 March 2006,[12]

Reaffirming its commitment to the Treaty on the Non-proliferation of Nuclear Weapons, and recalling the right of States Party, in conformity with Articles I and II of that Treaty, to develop research, production and use of nuclear energy for peaceful purposes without discrimination,

Noting with serious concern the many reports of the IAEA Director General and resolutions of the IAEA Board of Governors related to Iran's nuclear programme, reported to it by the IAEA Director General, including IAEA Board resolution GOV/2006/14,[13]

Noting with serious concern that the IAEA Director General's report of 27 February 2006 (GOV/2006/15)[14] lists a number of outstanding issues and concerns on Iran's nuclear programme, including topics which could have a military nuclear dimension, and that the IAEA is unable to conclude that there are no undeclared nuclear materials or activities in Iran,

Noting with serious concern the IAEA Director General's report of 28 April 2006 (GOV/2006/27)[15] and its findings, including that, after more than three years of Agency efforts to seek clarity about all aspects of Iran's nuclear programme, the existing gaps in knowledge continue to be a matter of concern, and that the IAEA is unable to make progress in its efforts to provide assurances about the absence of undeclared nuclear material and activities in Iran,

Noting with serious concern that, as confirmed by the IAEA Director General's report of 8 June 2006 (GOV/2006/38) Iran has not taken the steps required of it by the IAEA Board of Governors, reiterated by the Council in its statement of 29 March and which are essential to build confidence, and in particular Iran's decision to resume enrichment-related activities, including research and development, its recent expansion of and announcements about such activities, and its continued suspension of cooperation with the IAEA under the Additional Protocol,

Emphasizing the importance of political and diplomatic efforts to find a negotiated solution guaranteeing that Iran's nuclear programme is exclusively for peaceful purposes, and noting that such a solution would benefit nuclear nonproliferation elsewhere,

[12] Doc. 9.
[13] Doc. 32.
[14] Doc. 42.
[15] Doc. 43.

Welcoming the statement by the Foreign Minister of France, Philippe Douste-Blazy, on behalf of the Foreign Ministers of China, France, Germany, the Russian Federation, the United Kingdom, the United States and the High Representative of the European Union, in Paris on 12 July 2006 (S/2006/573),[16]

Concerned by the proliferation risks presented by the Iranian nuclear programme, mindful of its primary responsibility under the Charter of the United Nations for the maintenance of international peace and security, and being determined to prevent an aggravation of the situation,

Acting under Article 40 of Chapter VII of the Charter of the United Nations in order to make mandatory the suspension required by the IAEA,

1. *Calls* upon Iran without further delay to take the steps required by the IAEA Board of Governors in its resolution GOV/2006/14, which are essential to build confidence in the exclusively peaceful purpose of its nuclear programme and to resolve outstanding questions;

2. *Demands*, in this context, that Iran shall suspend all enrichment-related and reprocessing activities, including research and development, to be verified by the IAEA;

3. *Expresses* the conviction that such suspension as well as full, verified Iranian compliance with the requirements set out by the IAEA Board of Governors, would contribute to a diplomatic, negotiated solution that guarantees Iran's nuclear programme is for exclusively peaceful purposes, underlines the willingness of the international community to work positively for such a solution, encourages Iran, in conforming to the above provisions, to re-engage with the international community and with the IAEA, and stresses that such engagement will be beneficial to Iran;

4. *Endorses*, in this regard, the proposals of China, France, Germany, the Russian Federation, the United Kingdom and the United States, with the support of the European Union's High Representative, for a long-term comprehensive arrangement which would allow for the development of relations and cooperation with Iran based on mutual respect and the establishment of international confidence in the exclusively peaceful nature of Iran's nuclear programme (S/2006/521);

5. *Calls* upon all States, in accordance with their national legal authorities and legislation and consistent with international law, to exercise vigilance and prevent the transfer of any items, materials, goods and technology that could contribute to Iran's enrichment-related and reprocessing activities and ballistic missile programmes;

6. *Expresses* its determination to reinforce the authority of the IAEA process, strongly supports the role of the IAEA Board of Governors, commends and encourages the Director General of the IAEA and its secretariat for their ongoing professional and impartial efforts to resolve all remaining outstanding issues in Iran within the framework of the Agency, underlines the necessity of the IAEA continuing its work to clarify all outstanding issues relating to Iran's nuclear programme, and calls upon Iran to act in accordance with the provisions of the Additional Protocol and to implement without delay all transparency measures as the IAEA may request in support of its ongoing investigations;

7. *Requests* by 31 August a report from the Director General of the IAEA primarily on whether Iran has established full and sustained suspension of all activities mentioned in this resolution, as well as on the process of Iranian compliance with all the steps required by the IAEA Board and with the above provisions of this resolution, to the IAEA Board of Governors and in parallel to the Security Council for its consideration;

---

[16] Doc. 132.

8. *Expresses* its intention, in the event that Iran has not by that date complied with this resolution, then to adopt appropriate measures under Article 41 of Chapter VII of the Charter of the United Nations to persuade Iran to comply with this resolution and the requirements of the IAEA, and underlines that further decisions will be required should such additional measures be necessary;

9. *Confirms* that such additional measures will not be necessary in the event that Iran complies with this resolution;

10. *Decides* to remain seized of the matter.

Document 11: Security Council Resolution 1737(2006)

23 December 2006

The Security Council,

Recalling the Statement of its President, S/PRST/2006/15, of 29 March 2006,[17] and its resolution 1696(2006) of 31 July 2006,[18]

Reaffirming its commitment to the Treaty on the Non-Proliferation of Nuclear Weapons, and recalling the right of States Party, in conformity with Articles I and II of that Treaty, to develop research, production and use of nuclear energy for peaceful purposes without discrimination,

Reiterating its serious concern over the many reports of the IAEA Director General and resolutions of the IAEA Board of Governors related to Iran's nuclear programme, reported to it by the IAEA Director General, including IAEA Board resolution GOV/2006/14,[19]

Reiterating its serious concern that the IAEA Director General's report of 27 February 2006 (GOV/2006/15)[20] lists a number of outstanding issues and concerns on Iran's nuclear programme, including topics which could have a military nuclear dimension, and that the IAEA is unable to conclude that there are no undeclared nuclear materials or activities in Iran,

Reiterating its serious concern over the IAEA Director General's report of 28 April 2006 (GOV/2006/27)[21] and its findings, including that, after more than three years of Agency efforts to seek clarity about all aspects of Iran's nuclear programme, the existing gaps in knowledge continue to be a matter of concern, and that the IAEA is unable to make progress in its efforts to provide assurances about the absence of undeclared nuclear material and activities in Iran,

Noting with serious concern that, as confirmed by the IAEA Director General's reports of 8 June 2006 (GOV/2006/38), 31 August 2006 (GOV/2006/53)[22] and 14 November 2006 (GOV/2006/64), Iran has not established full and sustained suspension of all enrichment-related and reprocessing activities as set out in resolution 1696(2006), nor resumed its cooperation with the IAEA under the Additional Protocol,[23] nor taken the other steps required of it by the IAEA Board of Governors, nor complied with the provisions of

---

[17] Doc. 9.
[18] Doc. 10.
[19] Doc. 32.
[20] Doc. 42.
[21] Doc. 45.
[22] Doc. 44.
[23] Doc. 5.

Security Council resolution 1696(2006) and which are essential to build confidence, and *deploring* Iran's refusal to take these steps,

Emphasizing the importance of political and diplomatic efforts to find a negotiated solution guaranteeing that Iran's nuclear programme is exclusively for peaceful purposes, and *noting* that such a solution would benefit nuclear non-proliferation elsewhere, and *welcoming* the continuing commitment of China, France, Germany, the Russian Federation, the United Kingdom and the United States, with the support of the European Union's High Representative to seek a negotiated solution,

Determined to give effect to its decisions by adopting appropriate measures to persuade Iran to comply with resolution 1696(2006) and with the requirements of the IAEA, and also to constrain Iran's development of sensitive technologies in support of its nuclear and missile programmes, until such time as the Security Council determines that the objectives of this resolution have been met,

Concerned by the proliferation risks presented by the Iranian nuclear programme and, in this context, by Iran's continuing failure to meet the requirements of the IAEA Board of Governors and to comply with the provisions of Security Council resolution 1696(2006), *mindful* of its primary responsibility under the Charter of the United Nations for the maintenance of international peace and security,

Acting under Article 41 of Chapter VII of the Charter of the United Nations,

1. *Affirms* that Iran shall without further delay take the steps required by the IAEA Board of Governors in its resolution GOV/2006/14, which are essential to build confidence in the exclusively peaceful purpose of its nuclear programme and to resolve outstanding questions;

2. *Decides*, in this context, that Iran shall without further delay suspend the following proliferation sensitive nuclear activities:

> (a) all enrichment-related and reprocessing activities, including research and development, to be verified by the IAEA; and
>
> (b) work on all heavy water-related projects, including the construction of a research reactor moderated by heavy water, also to be verified by the IAEA;

3. *Decides* that all States shall take the necessary measures to prevent the supply, sale or transfer directly or indirectly from their territories, or by their nationals or using their flag vessels or aircraft to, or for the use in or benefit of, Iran, and whether or not originating in their territories, of all items, materials, equipment, goods and technology which could contribute to Iran's enrichment-related, reprocessing or heavy water-related activities, or to the development of nuclear weapon delivery systems, namely:

> (a) those set out in sections B.2, B.3, B.4, B.5, B.6 and B.7 of INFCIRC/254/Rev.8/Part 1 in document S/2006/814;[24]
>
> (b) those set out in sections A.1 and B.1 of INFCIRC/254/Rev.8/Part 1 in document S/2006/814, except the supply, sale or transfer of:
>
>> (i) equipment covered by B.1 when such equipment is for light water reactors;
>>
>> (ii) low-enriched uranium covered by A.1.2 when it is incorporated in assembled nuclear fuel elements for such reactors;
>
> (c) those set out in document S/2006/815,[25] except the supply, sale or transfer of items covered by 19.A.3 of Category II;

---

[24] List of items, materials, equipment, goods and technology related to nuclear programmes, 13 October 2006.
[25] List of items, materials, equipment, goods and technology related to ballistic missile programmes, 13 October 2006.

(d) any additional items, materials, equipment, goods and technology, determined as necessary by the Security Council or the Committee established by paragraph 18 below (herein 'the Committee'), which could contribute to enrichment-related, or reprocessing, or heavy water-related activities, or to the development of nuclear weapon delivery systems;

4. *Decides* that all States shall take the necessary measures to prevent the supply, sale or transfer directly or indirectly from their territories, or by their nationals or using their flag vessels or aircraft to, or for the use in or benefit of, Iran, and whether or not originating in their territories, of the following items, materials, equipment, goods and technology:

(a) those set out in INFCIRC/254/Rev.7/Part2 of document S/2006/814 if the State determines that they would contribute to enrichment-related, reprocessing or heavy water-related activities;

(b) any other items not listed in documents S/2006/814 or S/2006/815 if the State determines that they would contribute to enrichment-related, reprocessing or heavy water-related activities, or to the development of nuclear weapon delivery systems;

(c) any further items if the State determines that they would contribute to the pursuit of activities related to other topics about which the IAEA has expressed concerns or identified as outstanding;

5. *Decides* that, for the supply, sale or transfer of all items, materials, equipment, goods and technology covered by documents S/2006/814 and S/2006/815 the export of which to Iran is not prohibited by subparagraphs 3 (b), 3 (c) or 4 (a) above, States shall ensure that:

(a) the requirements, as appropriate, of the Guidelines as set out in documents S/2006/814 and S/2006/985 have been met; and

(b) they have obtained and are in a position to exercise effectively a right to verify the end-use and end-use location of any supplied item; and

(c) they notify the Committee within ten days of the supply, sale or transfer; and

(d) in the case of items, materials, equipment, goods and technology contained in document S/2006/814, they also notify the IAEA within ten days of the supply, sale or transfer;

6. *Decides* that all States shall also take the necessary measures to prevent the provision to Iran of any technical assistance or training, financial assistance, investment, brokering or other services, and the transfer of financial resources or services, related to the supply, sale, transfer, manufacture or use of the prohibited items, materials, equipment, goods and technology specified in paragraphs 3 and 4 above;

7. *Decides* that Iran shall not export any of the items in documents S/2006/814 and S/2006/815 and that all Member States shall prohibit the procurement of such items from Iran by their nationals, or using their flag vessels or aircraft, and whether or not originating in the territory of Iran;

8. *Decides* that Iran shall provide such access and cooperation as the IAEA requests to be able to verify the suspension outlined in paragraph 2 and to resolve all outstanding issues, as identified in IAEA reports, and *calls upon* Iran to ratify promptly the Additional Protocol;

9. *Decides* that the measures imposed by paragraphs 3, 4 and 6 above shall not apply where the Committee determines in advance and on a case-by-case basis that such supply,

sale, transfer or provision of such items or assistance would clearly not contribute to the development of Iran's technologies in support of its proliferation sensitive nuclear activities and of development of nuclear weapon delivery systems, including where such items or assistance are for food, agricultural, medical or other humanitarian purposes, provided that:

(a) contracts for delivery of such items or assistance include appropriate end-user guarantees; and

(b) Iran has committed not to use such items in proliferation sensitive nuclear activities or for development of nuclear weapon delivery systems;

10. *Calls upon* all States to exercise vigilance regarding the entry into or transit through their territories of individuals who are engaged in, directly associated with or providing support for Iran's proliferation sensitive nuclear activities or for the development of nuclear weapon delivery systems, and *decides* in this regard that all States shall notify the Committee of the entry into or transit through their territories of the persons designated in the Annex to this resolution (herein 'the Annex'), as well as of additional persons designated by the Security Council or the Committee as being engaged in, directly associated with or providing support for Iran's proliferation sensitive nuclear activities and for the development of nuclear weapon delivery systems, including through the involvement in procurement of the prohibited items, goods, equipment, materials and technology specified by and under the measures in paragraphs 3 and 4 above, except where such travel is for activities directly related to the items in subparagraphs 3 (b) (i) and (ii) above;

11. *Underlines* that nothing in the above paragraph requires a State to refuse its own nationals entry into its territory, and that all States shall, in the implementation of the above paragraph, take into account humanitarian considerations as well as the necessity to meet the objectives of this resolution, including where Article XV of the IAEA Statute is engaged;

12. *Decides* that all States shall freeze the funds, other financial assets and economic resources which are on their territories at the date of adoption of this resolution or at any time thereafter, that are owned or controlled by the persons or entities designated in the Annex, as well as those of additional persons or entities designated by the Security Council or by the Committee as being engaged in, directly associated with or providing support for Iran's proliferation sensitive nuclear activities or the development of nuclear weapon delivery systems, or by persons or entities acting on their behalf or at their direction, or by entities owned or controlled by them, including through illicit means, and that the measures in this paragraph shall cease to apply in respect of such persons or entities if, and at such time as, the Security Council or the Committee removes them from the Annex, and *decides further* that all States shall ensure that any funds, financial assets or economic resources are prevented from being made available by their nationals or by any persons or entities within their territories, to or for the benefit of these persons and entities;

13. *Decides* that the measures imposed by paragraph 12 above do not apply to funds, other financial assets or economic resources that have been determined by relevant States:

(a) to be necessary for basic expenses, including payment for foodstuffs, rent or mortgage, medicines and medical treatment, taxes, insurance premiums, and public utility charges or exclusively for payment of reasonable professional fees and reimbursement of incurred expenses associated with the provision of legal services, or fees or service charges, in accordance with national laws, for routine holding or maintenance of frozen funds, other financial assets and economic resources, after notification by the relevant States to the Committee of the intention to authorize, where appropriate, access to such funds, other financial assets or economic resources and in the absence of a negative decision by the Committee within five working days of such notification;

(b) to be necessary for extraordinary expenses, provided that such determination has been notified by the relevant States to the Committee and has been approved by the Committee;

(c) to be the subject of a judicial, administrative or arbitral lien or judgement, in which case the funds, other financial assets and economic resources may be used to satisfy that lien or judgement provided that the lien or judgement was entered into prior to the date of the present resolution, is not for the benefit of a person or entity designated pursuant to paragraphs 10 and 12 above, and has been notified by the relevant States to the Committee;

(d) to be necessary for activities directly related to the items specified in subparagraphs 3 (b) (i) and (ii) and have been notified by the relevant States to the Committee;

14. *Decides* that States may permit the addition to the accounts frozen pursuant to the provisions of paragraph 12 above of interests or other earnings due on those accounts or payments due under contracts, agreements or obligations that arose prior to the date on which those accounts became subject to the provisions of this resolution, provided that any such interest, other earnings and payments continue to be subject to these provisions and are frozen;

15. *Decides* that the measures in paragraph 12 above shall not prevent a designated person or entity from making payment due under a contract entered into prior to the listing of such a person or entity, provided that the relevant States have determined that:

(a) the contract is not related to any of the prohibited items, materials, equipment, goods, technologies, assistance, training, financial assistance, investment, brokering or services referred to in paragraphs 3, 4 and 6 above;

(b) the payment is not directly or indirectly received by a person or entity designated pursuant to paragraph 12 above;

and after notification by the relevant States to the Committee of the intention to make or receive such payments or to authorize, where appropriate, the unfreezing of funds, other financial assets or economic resources for this purpose, ten working days prior to such authorization;

16. *Decides* that technical cooperation provided to Iran by the IAEA or under its auspices shall only be for food, agricultural, medical, safety or other humanitarian purposes, or where it is necessary for projects directly related to the items specified in subparagraphs 3 (b) (i) and (ii) above, but that no such technical cooperation shall be provided that relates to the proliferation sensitive nuclear activities set out in paragraph 2 above;

17. *Calls upon* all States to exercise vigilance and prevent specialized teaching or training of Iranian nationals, within their territories or by their nationals, of disciplines which would contribute to Iran's proliferation sensitive nuclear activities and development of nuclear weapon delivery systems;

18. *Decides* to establish, in accordance with rule 28 of its provisional rules of procedure, a Committee of the Security Council consisting of all the members of the Council, to undertake the following tasks:

(a) to seek from all States, in particular those in the region and those producing the items, materials, equipment, goods and technology referred to in paragraphs 3 and 4 above, information regarding the actions taken by them to implement effectively the measures imposed by paragraphs 3, 4, 5, 6, 7, 8, 10 and 12 of this resolution and whatever further information it may consider useful in this regard;

(b) to seek from the secretariat of the IAEA information regarding the actions taken by the IAEA to implement effectively the measures imposed by paragraph 16 of this resolution and whatever further information it may consider useful in this regard;

(c) to examine and take appropriate action on information regarding alleged violations of measures imposed by paragraphs 3, 4, 5, 6, 7, 8, 10 and 12 of this resolution;

(d) to consider and decide upon requests for exemptions set out in paragraphs 9, 13 and 15 above;

(e) to determine as may be necessary additional items, materials, equipment, goods and technology to be specified for the purpose of paragraph 3 above;

(f) to designate as may be necessary additional individuals and entities subject to the measures imposed by paragraphs 10 and 12 above;

(g) to promulgate guidelines as may be necessary to facilitate the implementation of the measures imposed by this resolution and include in such guidelines a requirement on States to provide information where possible as to why any individuals and/or entities meet the criteria set out in paragraphs 10 and 12 and any relevant identifying information;

(h) to report at least every 90 days to the Security Council on its work and on the implementation of this resolution, with its observations and recommendations, in particular on ways to strengthen the effectiveness of the measures imposed by paragraphs 3, 4, 5, 6, 7, 8, 10 and 12 above;

19. *Decides* that all States shall report to the Committee within 60 days of the adoption of this resolution on the steps they have taken with a view to implementing effectively paragraphs 3, 4, 5, 6, 7, 8, 10, 12 and 17 above;

20. *Expresses* the conviction that the suspension set out in paragraph 2 above as well as full, verified Iranian compliance with the requirements set out by the IAEA Board of Governors, would contribute to a diplomatic, negotiated solution that guarantees Iran's nuclear programme is for exclusively peaceful purposes, *underlines* the willingness of the international community to work positively for such a solution, *encourages* Iran, in conforming to the above provisions, to reengage with the international community and with the IAEA, and *stresses* that such engagement will be beneficial to Iran;

21. *Welcomes* the commitment of China, France, Germany, the Russian Federation, the United Kingdom and the United States, with the support of the European Union's High Representative, to a negotiated solution to this issue and encourages Iran to engage with their June 2006 proposals (S/2006/521),[26] which were endorsed by the Security Council in resolution 1696(2006), for a long-term comprehensive agreement which would allow for the development of relations and cooperation with Iran based on mutual respect and the establishment of international confidence in the exclusively peaceful nature of Iran's nuclear programme;

---

[26] Doc. 131.

22. *Reiterates* its determination to reinforce the authority of the IAEA, strongly supports the role of the IAEA Board of Governors, *commends* and *encourages* the Director General of the IAEA and its secretariat for their ongoing professional and impartial efforts to resolve all remaining outstanding issues in Iran within the framework of the IAEA, *underlines* the necessity of the IAEA continuing its work to clarify all outstanding issues relating to Iran's nuclear programme;

23. *Requests* within 60 days a report from the Director General of the IAEA on whether Iran has established full and sustained suspension of all activities mentioned in this resolution, as well as on the process of Iranian compliance with all the steps required by the IAEA Board and with the other provisions of this resolution, to the IAEA Board of Governors and in parallel to the Security Council for its consideration;

24. *Affirms* that it shall review Iran's actions in the light of the report referred to in paragraph 23 above, to be submitted within 60 days, and:

(a) that it shall suspend the implementation of measures if and for so long as Iran suspends all enrichment-related and reprocessing activities, including research and development, as verified by the IAEA, to allow for negotiations;

(b) that it shall terminate the measures specified in paragraphs 3, 4, 5, 6, 7, 10 and 12 of this resolution as soon as it determines that Iran has fully complied with its obligations under the relevant resolutions of the Security Council and met the requirements of the IAEA Board of Governors, as confirmed by the IAEA Board;

(c) that it shall, in the event that the report in paragraph 23 above shows that Iran has not complied with this resolution, adopt further appropriate measures under Article 41 of Chapter VII of the Charter of the United Nations to persuade Iran to comply with this resolution and the requirements of the IAEA, and underlines that further decisions will be required should such additional measures be necessary;

25. *Decides* to remain seized of the matter.

Annex

A. Entities involved in the nuclear programme
… (7 entities)

B. Entities involved in the ballistic missile programme
… (3 entities)

C. Persons involved in the nuclear programme
… (7 person)

D. Persons involved in the ballistic missile programme
… (4 persons)

E. Persons involved in both the nuclear and ballistic missile programmes
… (1 person)

Document 12: Security Council Resolution 1747(2007)

24 March 2007

The Security Council,

Recalling the Statement of its President, S/PRST/2006/15, of 29 March 2006,[27] and its resolution 1696(2006) of 31 July 2006,[28] and its resolution 1737(2006) of 23 December 2006,[29] and reaffirming their provisions,

Reaffirming its commitment to the Treaty on the Non-Proliferation of Nuclear Weapons, the need for all States Party to that Treaty to comply fully with all their obligations, and recalling the right of States Party, in conformity with Articles I and II of that Treaty, to develop research, production and use of nuclear energy for peaceful purposes without discrimination,

Recalling its serious concern over the reports of the IAEA Director General as set out in its resolutions 1696(2006) and 1737(2006),

Recalling the latest report by the IAEA Director General (GOV/2007/8) of 22 February 2007[30] and deploring that, as indicated therein, Iran has failed to comply with resolution 1696(2006) and resolution 1737(2006),

Emphasizing the importance of political and diplomatic efforts to find a negotiated solution guaranteeing that Iran's nuclear programme is exclusively for peaceful purposes, and noting that such a solution would benefit nuclear non-proliferation elsewhere, and welcoming the continuing commitment of China, France, Germany, the Russian Federation, the United Kingdom and the United States, with the support of the European Union's High Representative to seek a negotiated solution,

Recalling the resolution of the IAEA Board of Governors (GOV/2006/14),[31] which states that a solution to the Iranian nuclear issue would contribute to global non-proliferation efforts and to realizing the objective of a Middle East free of weapons of mass destruction, including their means of delivery,

Determined to give effect to its decisions by adopting appropriate measures to persuade Iran to comply with resolution 1696(2006) and resolution 1737(2006) and with the requirements of the IAEA, and also to constrain Iran's development of sensitive technologies in support of its nuclear and missile programmes, until such time as the Security Council determines that the objectives of these resolutions have been met,

Recalling the requirement on States to join in affording mutual assistance in carrying out the measures decided upon by the Security Council,

Concerned by the proliferation risks presented by the Iranian nuclear programme and, in this context, by Iran's continuing failure to meet the requirements of the IAEA Board of Governors and to comply with the provisions of Security Council resolutions 1696(2006) and 1737(2006), mindful of its primary responsibility under the Charter of the United Nations for the maintenance of international peace and security,

Acting under Article 41 of Chapter VII of the Charter of the United Nations,

---

[27] Doc. 9.
[28] Doc. 10.
[29] Doc. 11.
[30] Doc. 47.
[31] Doc. 32.

1. *Reaffirms* that Iran shall without further delay take the steps required by the IAEA Board of Governors in its resolution GOV/2006/14, which are essential to build confidence in the exclusively peaceful purpose of its nuclear programme and to resolve outstanding questions, and, in this context, affirms its decision that Iran shall without further delay take the steps required in paragraph 2 of resolution 1737(2006);

2. *Calls* upon all States also to exercise vigilance and restraint regarding the entry into or transit through their territories of individuals who are engaged in, directly associated with or providing support for Iran's proliferation sensitive nuclear activities or for the development of nuclear weapon delivery systems, and decides in this regard that all States shall notify the Committee established pursuant to paragraph 18 of resolution 1737(2006) (herein 'the Committee') of the entry into or transit through their territories of the persons designated in the Annex to resolution 1737(2006) or Annex I to this resolution, as well as of additional persons designated by the Security Council or the Committee as being engaged in, directly associated with or providing support for Iran's proliferation sensitive nuclear activities or for the development of nuclear weapon delivery systems, including through the involvement in procurement of the prohibited items, goods, equipment, materials and technology specified by and under the measures in paragraphs 3 and 4 of resolution 1737(2006), except where such travel is for activities directly related to the items in subparagraphs 3 (b) (i) and (ii) of that resolution;

3. *Underlines* that nothing in the above paragraph requires a State to refuse its own nationals entry into its territory, and that all States shall, in the implementation of the above paragraph, take into account humanitarian considerations, including religious obligations, as well as the necessity to meet the objectives of this resolution and resolution 1737(2006), including where Article XV of the IAEA Statute is engaged;

4. *Decides* that the measures specified in paragraphs 12, 13, 14 and 15 of resolution 1737(2006) shall apply also to the persons and entities listed in Annex I to this resolution;

5. *Decides* that Iran shall not supply, sell or transfer directly or indirectly from its territory or by its nationals or using its flag vessels or aircraft any arms or related materiel, and that all States shall prohibit the procurement of such items from Iran by their nationals, or using their flag vessels or aircraft, and whether or not originating in the territory of Iran;

6. *Calls* upon all States to exercise vigilance and restraint in the supply, sale or transfer directly or indirectly from their territories or by their nationals or using their flag vessels or aircraft of any battle tanks, armoured combat vehicles, large calibre artillery systems, combat aircraft, attack helicopters, warships, missiles or missile systems as defined for the purpose of the United Nations Register on Conventional Arms to Iran, and in the provision to Iran of any technical assistance or training, financial assistance, investment, brokering or other services, and the transfer of financial resources or services, related to the supply, sale, transfer, manufacture or use of such items in order to prevent a destabilizing accumulation of arms;

7. *Calls* upon all States and international financial institutions not to enter into new commitments for grants, financial assistance, and concessional loans, to the Government of the Islamic Republic of Iran, except for humanitarian and developmental purposes;

8. *Calls* upon all States to report to the Committee within 60 days of the adoption of this resolution on the steps they have taken with a view to implementing effectively paragraphs 2, 4, 5, 6 and 7 above;

9. *Expresses* the conviction that the suspension set out in paragraph 2 of resolution 1737(2006) as well as full, verified Iranian compliance with the requirements set out by the IAEA Board of Governors would contribute to a diplomatic, negotiated solution that guarantees Iran's nuclear programme is for exclusively peaceful purposes, underlines the willingness of the international community to work positively for such a solution, encourages Iran, in conforming to the above provisions, to re-engage with the international community and with the IAEA, and stresses that such engagement will be beneficial to Iran;

10. *Welcomes* the continuous affirmation of the commitment of China, France, Germany, the Russian Federation, the United Kingdom and the United States, with the support of the European Union's High Representative, to a negotiated solution to this issue and encourages Iran to engage with their June 2006 proposals (S/2006/521),[32] attached in Annex II to this resolution, which were endorsed by the Security Council in resolution 1696(2006), and acknowledges with appreciation that this offer to Iran remains on the table, for a long-term comprehensive agreement which would allow for the development of relations and cooperation with Iran based on mutual respect and the establishment of international confidence in the exclusively peaceful nature of Iran's nuclear programme;

11. *Reiterates* its determination to reinforce the authority of the IAEA, strongly supports the role of the IAEA Board of Governors, commends and encourages the Director General of the IAEA and its secretariat for their ongoing professional and impartial efforts to resolve all outstanding issues in Iran within the framework of the IAEA, underlines the necessity of the IAEA, which is internationally recognized as having authority for verifying compliance with safeguards agreements, including the non-diversion of nuclear material for non-peaceful purposes, in accordance with its Statute, to continue its work to clarify all outstanding issues relating to Iran's nuclear programme;

12. *Requests* within 60 days a further report from the Director General of the IAEA on whether Iran has established full and sustained suspension of all activities mentioned in resolution 1737(2006), as well as on the process of Iranian compliance with all the steps required by the IAEA Board and with the other provisions of resolution 1737(2006) and of this resolution, to the IAEA Board of Governors and in parallel to the Security Council for its consideration;

13. *Affirms* that it shall review Iran's actions in light of the report referred to in paragraph 12 above, to be submitted within 60 days, and:

(a) that it shall suspend the implementation of measures if and for so long as Iran suspends all enrichment-related and reprocessing activities, including research and development, as verified by the IAEA, to allow for negotiations in good faith in order to reach an early and mutually acceptable outcome;

(b) that it shall terminate the measures specified in paragraphs 3, 4, 5, 6, 7 and 12 of resolution 1737(2006) as well as in paragraphs 2, 4, 5, 6 and 7 above as soon as it determines, following receipt of the report referred to in paragraph 12 above, that Iran has fully complied with its obligations under the relevant resolutions of the Security Council and met the requirements of the IAEA Board of Governors, as confirmed by the IAEA Board;

(c) that it shall, in the event that the report in paragraph 12 above shows that Iran has not complied with resolution 1737(2006) and this resolution, adopt further appropriate measures under Article 41 of Chapter VII of the Charter of the United Nations to persuade Iran to comply with these resolutions and the requirements

---

[32] Doc. 131.

of the IAEA, and underlines that further decisions will be required should such additional measures be necessary;

14. *Decides* to remain seized of the matter.

Annex I
Entities involved in nuclear or ballistic missile activities
... (10 entities)
Iranian Revolutionary Guard Corps entities
... (3 entities)
Persons involved in nuclear or ballistic missile activities
... (8 persons)
Iranian Revolutionary Guard Corps key persons
... (7 persons)
Annex II Elements of a long-term agreement
...

Document 13: Security Council Resolution 1803(2008)

3 March 2008

The Security Council,

Recalling the Statement of its President, S/PRST/2006/15, of 29 March 2006,[33] and its resolution 1696(2006) of 31 July 2006,[34] its resolution 1737(2006) of 23 December 2006[35] and its resolution 1747(2007) of 24 March 2007,[36] and reaffirming their provisions,

Reaffirming its commitment to the Treaty on the Non-Proliferation of Nuclear Weapons, the need for all States Party to that Treaty to comply fully with all their obligations, and recalling the right of States Party, in conformity with Articles I and II of that Treaty, to develop research, production and use of nuclear energy for peaceful purposes without discrimination,

Recalling the resolution of the IAEA Board of Governors (GOV/2006/14),[37] which states that a solution to the Iranian nuclear issue would contribute to global non-proliferation efforts and to realizing the objective of a Middle East free of weapons of mass destruction, including their means of delivery,

Noting with serious concern that, as confirmed by the reports of 23 May 2007 (GOV/2007/22),[38] 30 August 2007 (GOV/2007/48),[39] 15 November 2007 (GOV/2007/58)[40] and 22 February 2008 (GOV/2008/4)[41] of the Director General of the International Atomic Energy Agency (IAEA), Iran has not established full and sustained suspension of all enrichment related and reprocessing activities and heavy water-related projects as set out in resolution 1696(2006), 1737(2006), and 1747(2007), nor resumed its cooperation with

---

[33] Doc. 9.
[34] Doc. 10.
[35] Doc. 11.
[36] Doc. 12.
[37] Doc. 32.
[38] Doc. 48.
[39] Doc. 49.
[40] Doc. 50.
[41] Doc. 51.

the IAEA under the Additional Protocol,[42] nor taken the other steps required by the IAEA Board of Governors, nor complied with the provisions of Security Council resolution 1696(2006), 1737(2006) and 1747(2007) and which are essential to build confidence, and deploring Iran's refusal to take these steps,

Noting with concern that Iran has taken issue with the IAEA's right to verify design information which had been provided by Iran pursuant to the modified Code 3.1, emphasizing that in accordance with Article 39 of Iran's Safeguards Agreement[43] Code 3.1 cannot be modified nor suspended unilaterally and that the Agency's right to verify design information provided to it is a continuing right, which is not dependent on the stage of construction of, or the presence of nuclear material at, a facility,

Reiterating its determination to reinforce the authority of the IAEA, strongly supporting the role of the IAEA Board of Governors, commending the IAEA for its efforts to resolve outstanding issues relating to Iran's nuclear programme in the work plan between the Secretariat of the IAEA and Iran (GOV/2007/48, Attachment), welcoming the progress in implementation of this work plan as reflected in the IAEA Director General's reports of 15 November 2007 (GOV/2007/58) and 22 February 2008 (GOV/2008/4), underlining the importance of Iran producing tangible results rapidly and effectively by completing implementation of this work plan including by providing answers to all the questions the IAEA asks so that the Agency, through the implementation of the required transparency measures, can assess the completeness and correctness of Iran's declaration,

Expressing the conviction that the suspension set out in paragraph 2 of resolution 1737(2006) as well as full, verified Iranian compliance with the requirements set out by the IAEA Board of Governors would contribute to a diplomatic, negotiated solution, that guarantees Iran's nuclear programme is for exclusively peaceful purposes,

Stressing that China, France, Germany, the Russian Federation, the United Kingdom and the United States are willing to take further concrete measures on exploring an overall strategy of resolving the Iranian nuclear issue through negotiation on the basis of their June 2006 proposals (S/2006/521),[44] and noting the confirmation by these countries that once the confidence of the international community in the exclusively peaceful nature of Iran's nuclear programme is restored, it will be treated in the same manner as that of any Non-Nuclear Weapon State party to the Treaty on the Non-Proliferation of Nuclear Weapons,

Having regard to States' rights and obligations relating to international trade,

Welcoming the guidance issued by the Financial Actions Task Force (FATF) to assist States in implementing their financial obligations under resolution 1737(2006),

Determined to give effect to its decisions by adopting appropriate measures to persuade Iran to comply with resolution 1696(2006), resolution 1737(2006), resolution 1747(2007) and with the requirements of the IAEA, and also to constrain Iran's development of sensitive technologies in support of its nuclear and missile programmes, until such time as the Security Council determines that the objectives of these resolutions have been met,

Concerned by the proliferation risks presented by the Iranian nuclear programme and, in this context, by Iran's continuing failure to meet the requirements of the IAEA Board of Governors and to comply with the provisions of Security Council resolutions 1696(2006), 1737(2006) and 1747(2007), mindful of its primary responsibility under the Charter of the United Nations for the maintenance of international peace and security,

---

[42] Doc. 5.
[43] Doc. 4.
[44] Doc. 131.

Acting under Article 41 of Chapter VII of the Charter of the United Nations,

1. *Reaffirms* that Iran shall without further delay take the steps required by the IAEA Board of Governors in its resolution GOV/2006/14, which are essential to build confidence in the exclusively peaceful purpose of its nuclear programme and to resolve outstanding questions, and, in this context, affirms its decision that Iran shall without delay take the steps required in paragraph 2 of resolution 1737(2006), and underlines that the IAEA has sought confirmation that Iran will apply Code 3.1 modified;

2. *Welcomes* the agreement between Iran and the IAEA to resolve all outstanding issues concerning Iran's nuclear programme and progress made in this regard as set out in the Director General's report of 22 February 2008 (GOV/2008/4), encourages the IAEA to continue its work to clarify all outstanding issues, stresses that this would help to re-establish international confidence in the exclusively peaceful nature of Iran's nuclear programme, and supports the IAEA in strengthening its safeguards on Iran's nuclear activities in accordance with the Safeguards Agreement between Iran and the IAEA;

3. *Calls* upon all States to exercise vigilance and restraint regarding the entry into or transit through their territories of individuals who are engaged in, directly associated with or providing support for Iran's proliferation sensitive nuclear activities or for the development of nuclear weapon delivery systems, and decides in this regard that all States shall notify the Committee established pursuant to paragraph 18 of resolution 1737(2006) (herein 'the Committee') of the entry into or transit through their territories of the persons designated in the Annex to resolution 1737(2006), Annex I to resolution 1747(2007) or Annex I to this resolution, as well as of additional persons designated by the Security Council or the Committee as being engaged in, directly associated with or providing support for Iran's proliferation sensitive nuclear activities or for the development of nuclear weapon delivery systems, including through the involvement in procurement of the prohibited items, goods, equipment, materials and technology specified by and under the measures in paragraphs 3 and 4 of resolution 1737(2006), except where such entry or transit is for activities directly related to the items in subparagraphs 3 (b) (i) and (ii) of resolution 1737(2006);

4. *Underlines* that nothing in paragraph 3 above requires a State to refuse its own nationals entry into its territory, and that all States shall, in the implementation of the above paragraph, take into account humanitarian considerations, including religious obligations, as well as the necessity to meet the objectives of this resolution, resolution 1737(2006) and resolution 1747(2007), including where Article XV of the IAEA Statute is engaged;

5. *Decides* that all States shall take the necessary measures to prevent the entry into or transit through their territories of individuals designated in Annex II to this resolution as well as of additional persons designated by the Security Council or the Committee as being engaged in, directly associated with or providing support for Iran's proliferation sensitive nuclear activities or for the development of nuclear weapon delivery systems, including through the involvement in procurement of the prohibited items, goods, equipment, materials and technology specified by and under the measures in paragraphs 3 and 4 of resolution 1737(2006), except where such entry or transit is for activities directly related to the items in subparagraphs 3 (b) (i) and (ii) of resolution 1737(2006) and provided that nothing in this paragraph shall oblige a State to refuse its own nationals entry into its territory;

6. *Decides* that the measures imposed by paragraph 5 above shall not apply where the Committee determines on a case-by-case basis that such travel is justified on the grounds of humanitarian need, including religious obligations, or where the Committee concludes that an exemption would otherwise further the objectives of the present resolution;

7. *Decides* that the measures specified in paragraphs 12, 13, 14 and 15 of resolution 1737(2006) shall apply also to the persons and entities listed in Annexes I and III to this resolution, and any persons or entities acting on their behalf or at their direction, and to entities owned or controlled by them and to persons and entities determined by the Council or the Committee to have assisted designated persons or entities in evading sanctions of, or in violating the provisions of, this resolution, resolution 1737(2006) or resolution 1747(2007);

8. *Decides* that all States shall take the necessary measures to prevent the supply, sale or transfer directly or indirectly from their territories or by their nationals or using their flag vessels or aircraft to, or for use in or benefit of, Iran, and whether or not originating in their territories, of:

> (a) all items, materials, equipment, goods and technology set out in INFCIRC/254/Rev.7/Part 2 of document S/2006/814,[45] except the supply, sale or transfer, in accordance with the requirements of paragraph 5 of resolution 1737(2006), of items, materials, equipment, goods and technology set out in sections 1 and 2 of the Annex to that document, and sections 3 to 6 as notified in advance to the Committee, only when for exclusive use in light water reactors, and where such supply, sale or transfer is necessary for technical cooperation provided to Iran by the IAEA or under its auspices as provided for in paragraph 16 of resolution 1737(2006);
>
> (b) all items, materials, equipment, goods and technology set out in 19.A.3 of Category II of document S/2006/815[46];

9. *Calls* upon all States to exercise vigilance in entering into new commitments for public provided financial support for trade with Iran, including the granting of export credits, guarantees or insurance, to their nationals or entities involved in such trade, in order to avoid such financial support contributing to the proliferation sensitive nuclear activities, or to the development of nuclear weapon delivery systems, as referred to in resolution 1737(2006);

10. *Calls* upon all States to exercise vigilance over the activities of financial institutions in their territories with all banks domiciled in Iran, in particular with Bank Melli and Bank Saderat, and their branches and subsidiaries abroad, in order to avoid such activities contributing to the proliferation sensitive nuclear activities, or to the development of nuclear weapon delivery systems, as referred to in resolution 1737(2006);

11. *Calls* upon all States, in accordance with their national legal authorities and legislation and consistent with international law, in particular the law of the sea and relevant international civil aviation agreements, to inspect the cargoes to and from Iran, of aircraft and vessels, at their airports and seaports, owned or operated by Iran Air Cargo and Islamic Republic of Iran Shipping Line, provided there are reasonable grounds to believe that the aircraft or vessel is transporting goods prohibited under this resolution or resolution 1737(2006) or resolution 1747(2007);

12. *Requires* all States, in cases when inspection mentioned in the paragraph above is undertaken, to submit to the Security Council within five working days a written report on the inspection containing, in particular, explanation of the grounds for the inspection, as well as information on its time, place, circumstances, results and other relevant details;

---

[45] List of items, materials, equipment, goods and technology related to nuclear programmes, 13 October 2006.
[46] List of items, materials, equipment, goods and technology related to ballistic missile programmes, 13 October 2006.

13. *Calls* upon all States to report to the Committee within 60 days of the adoption of this resolution on the steps they have taken with a view to implementing effectively paragraphs 3, 5, 7, 8, 9, 10 and 11 above;

14. *Decides* that the mandate of the Committee as set out in paragraph 18 of resolution 1737(2006) shall also apply to the measures imposed in resolution 1747(2007) and this resolution;

15. *Stresses* the willingness of China, France, Germany, the Russian Federation, the United Kingdom and the United States to further enhance diplomatic efforts to promote resumption of dialogue, and consultations on the basis of their offer to Iran, with a view to seeking a comprehensive, long-term and proper solution of this issue which would allow for the development of all-round relations and wider cooperation with Iran based on mutual respect and the establishment of international confidence in the exclusively peaceful nature of Iran's nuclear programme, and inter alia, starting direct talks and negotiation with Iran as long as Iran suspends all enrichment-related and reprocessing activities, including research and development, as verified by the IAEA;

16. *Encourages* the European Union High Representative for the Common Foreign and Security Policy to continue communication with Iran in support of political and diplomatic efforts to find a negotiated solution including relevant proposals by China, France, Germany, the Russian Federation, the United Kingdom and the United States with a view to create necessary conditions for resuming talks;[47]

17. *Emphasizes* the importance of all States, including Iran, taking the necessary measures to ensure that no claim shall lie at the instance of the Government of Iran, or of any person or entity in Iran, or of persons or entities designated pursuant to resolution 1737(2006) and related resolutions, or any person claiming through or for the benefit of any such person or entity, in connection with any contract or other transaction where its performance was prevented by reason of the measures imposed by the present resolution, resolution 1737(2006) or resolution 1747(2007);

18. *Requests* within 90 days a further report from the Director General of the IAEA on whether Iran has established full and sustained suspension of all activities mentioned in resolution 1737(2006), as well as on the process of Iranian compliance with all the steps required by the IAEA Board and with the other provisions of resolution 1737(2006), resolution 1747(2007) and of this resolution, to the IAEA Board of Governors and in parallel to the Security Council for its consideration;

19. *Reaffirms* that it shall review Iran's actions in light of the report referred to in the paragraph above, and:

   (a) that it shall suspend the implementation of measures if and for so long as Iran suspends all enrichment-related and reprocessing activities, including research and development, as verified by the IAEA, to allow for negotiations in good faith in order to reach an early and mutually acceptable outcome;

   (b) that it shall terminate the measures specified in paragraphs 3, 4, 5, 6, 7 and 12 of resolution 1737(2006), as well as in paragraphs 2, 4, 5, 6 and 7 of resolution 1747(2007), and in paragraphs 3, 5, 7, 8, 9, 10 and 11 above, as soon as it determines, following receipt of the report referred to in the paragraph above, that Iran has fully complied with its obligations under the relevant resolutions of the Security Council and met the requirements of the IAEA Board of Governors, as confirmed by the IAEA Board;

---

[47] Doc. 131.

(c) that it shall, in the event that the report shows that Iran has not complied with resolution 1696(2006), resolution 1737(2006), resolution 1747(2007) and this resolution, adopt further appropriate measures under Article 41 of Chapter VII of the Charter of the United Nations to persuade Iran to comply with these resolutions and the requirements of the IAEA, and underlines that further decisions will be required should such additional measures be necessary;

20. *Decides* to remain seized of the matter.

Annex I
... (13 persons)
Annex II
A. Individuals listed in resolution 1737(2006)
... (3 persons)
B. Individuals listed in resolution 1747(2007)
... (2 persons)
Annex III
... (12 entities)

Document 14: Security Council Resolution 1835(2008)

27 September 2008

The Security Council,

Taking note of the 15 September 2008 Report by the Director General of the International Atomic Energy Agency on the Implementation of the NPT Safeguards Agreement and relevant provisions of Security Council resolutions (GOV/2008/38),[48]

Reaffirming its commitment to the Treaty on the Non-Proliferation of Nuclear Weapons (NPT),

1. *Reaffirms* the Statement of its President, S/PRST/2006/15, of 29 March 2006,[49] and its resolution 1696(2006) of 31 July 2006,[50] its resolution 1737(2006) of 23 December 2006,[51] its resolution 1747(2007) of 24 March 2007,[52] and its resolution 1803(2008) of 3 March 2008;[53]

2. *Takes note* of the 3 March 2008 Statement of the Foreign Ministers of China, France, Germany, the Russian Federation, the United Kingdom, the United States of America, with the support of the High Representative of the European Union, describing the dual-track approach to the Iranian nuclear issue;[54]

3. *Reaffirms* its commitment within this framework to an early negotiated solution to the Iranian nuclear issue and welcomes the continuing efforts in this regard;

---

[48] Doc. 53.
[49] Doc. 9.
[50] Doc. 10.
[51] Doc. 11.
[52] Doc. 12.
[53] Doc. 13.
[54] Doc. 18.

4. *Calls upon* Iran to comply fully and without delay with its obligations under the above-mentioned resolutions of the Security Council, and to meet the requirements of the IAEA Board of Governors;

5. *Decides* to remain seized of the matter.

2. Provisional Verbatim Records of the Security Council

*Numbers in square brackets indicate page numbers in
the Security Council verbatim record.*

Document 15: Security Council Debate on Resolution 1696(2006)

S/PV.5500, 31 July 2006

[2] **The President**: The Security Council will now begin its consideration of the item on its agenda. The Security Council is meeting in accordance with the understanding reached in its prior consultations.

Members of the Council have before them document S/2006/589, which contains a draft resolution submitted by France, Germany and the United Kingdom of Great Britain and Northern Ireland.

I should like to draw the attention of members of the Council to two letters from the representative of France contained in documents S/2006/521[55] and S/2006/573.[56]

I should like also to draw the attention of Council members to the reports of the Director-General of the International Atomic Energy Agency dated 27 February and 28 April 2006, contained in documents S/2006/150[57] and S/2006/270,[58] respectively.

It is my understanding that the Council is ready to proceed to the vote on the draft resolution. Unless I hear any objection, I shall put the draft resolution to the vote now.

There being no objection, it is so decided.

A vote was taken by show of hands.

In favour: Argentina, China, Congo, Denmark, France, Ghana, Greece, Japan, Peru, Russian Federation, Slovakia, United Kingdom of Great Britain and Northern Ireland, United Republic of Tanzania, United States of America

Against: Qatar

The President (*spoke in French*): The result of the voting is as follows: 14 votes in favour and one against. The draft resolution has been adopted as resolution 1696(2006).[59]

...

Mr. Al-Nasser (**Qatar**):

...

---

[55] Doc. 131.
[56] Doc. 132.
[57] Doc. 42.
[58] Doc. 43.
[59] Doc. 10.

Ever since the question of Iran's nuclear programme was brought before the Council, we have repeatedly underscored the importance of finding a political solution to this problem and of giving diplomacy enough time to bring about a peaceful solution. Such a solution can be reached only if all parties concerned show flexibility, wisdom and a sense of responsibility.

We are grateful for the efforts made by the six States in order to reach a peaceful solution through offering Iran a comprehensive package. We deem this a bold and commendable step. However, we believe that [3] Iran is also called upon seriously to address the concerns of the international community about the very nature of its nuclear programme, to ensure that it is used exclusively for peaceful purposes.

There is no doubt that this is a legitimate demand that we all are making. However, we do not agree with the submission of this draft resolution at a time when our region is inflamed. We would have seen no harm in waiting a few days so as to exhaust all possible ways and means in order to determine Iran's real intentions and the degree of its willingness to cooperate, particularly since Iran has not rejected the package that was offered to it; it has simply asked for a period of time in which to consider it. This prompts us to ask members of the Council to accede to this request. We have been patient, and, indeed, our Council has waited longer to act on much more burning issues.

The State of Qatar is fully committed to the unity of the Council, particularly when it comes to very sensitive issues. We have reiterated our intention to join in this unity. However, the fact that this draft resolution was submitted at this critical time serves to achieve neither the stability of the region nor the unity of the Council. On the contrary, whether we like it or not, it will only intensify the conflagration in our region. Do we really want to see another volcano erupting in this region?

My country, which is not very far away from this area - no more than 200 kilometres from the nuclear reactors - is fully committed to ensuring that the Middle East becomes a nuclear-weapon-free zone. But given the special circumstances surrounding our region, the failure to take on board our concerns and to take account of the issues to which I have just referred will not help us to achieve the unity of the Council to which we all aspire.

Mr. Bolton (**United States of America**): Four months have passed since the Security Council called upon Iran to fully and verifiably suspend its nuclear programmes,[60] and nearly two months have passed since the European Union three (EU-3) plus three made its generous offer, inviting Iran to enter into negotiations and avoid further Security Council action.[61] Let us not forget that this diplomatic activity was preceded by more than three years of Iranian non-compliance with the Treaty on the Non-Proliferation of Nuclear Weapons and its International Atomic Energy Agency (IAEA) Safeguards Agreement.[62] Sadly, Iran has consistently and brazenly defied the international community by continuing its pursuit of nuclear weapons, and the continued intransigence and defiance of the Iranian leadership demands a strong response from the Council. The resolution adopted today does just that.

We are pleased that the Council has taken clear and firm action in adopting this resolution. The pursuit of nuclear weapons by Iran constitutes a direct threat to international peace and security and demands a clear statement from the Council in the form of a binding resolution.

---

[60] Doc. 9.
[61] Doc. 131.
[62] Doc. 4.

This resolution also demands action. It sends an unequivocal and unambiguous message to Tehran: Take the steps required by the IAEA Board of Governors, including full and sustained suspension of all enrichment-related and reprocessing activities, including research and development, and suspend construction of your heavy-water reactor. It also calls upon Member States to prevent the transfer of resources to Iran's nuclear and missile programmes, and Iran should understand that the United States and others will ensure that the financial transactions associated with these proliferation activities will be subject to scrutiny as well. The United States expects that Iran and all other States Members of the United Nations will immediately act in accordance with the mandatory obligations of this resolution.

This is the first Security Council resolution on Iran in response to its nuclear weapons programme, reflecting the gravity of the situation and the determination of the Council. We hope the resolution will demonstrate to Iran that the best way to end its international isolation is to simply give up the pursuit of nuclear weapons. We look forward to Iran's full, unconditional and immediate compliance with the resolution. We hope that Iran makes the strategic decision that the pursuit of programmes of weapons of mass destruction makes it less, not more, secure. We need to be prepared, however, that Iran might choose a different path. That is why it is important that the United States and other member States have expressed their intention to adopt measures under Article 41 in the event that Iran does not comply with the resolution.

...

[4] Sir Emyr Jones Parry (**United Kingdom**): .... The United Kingdom commends the continuing investigation of the International Atomic Energy Agency (IAEA) and is very deeply concerned about Iran's failure to cooperate fully with the Agency. As today's resolution notes, after more than three years, the Agency is still unable to conclude that there are no undeclared nuclear materials or activities in Iran. Important questions, including on activities with a possible military nuclear dimension, remain unanswered.

The international community has shown great patience. We have given Iran many opportunities to show that it has no intention to develop nuclear weapons. Regrettably, Iran has not taken the steps required by the IAEA Board and the Security Council that would help build confidence.

The United Kingdom remains fully committed to working for a negotiated solution. On 6 June, the European Union High Representative, Javier Solana, presented to Iran, on behalf of China, France, Germany, Russia, the United Kingdom and the United States, a new set of far-reaching and imaginative proposals for a comprehensive agreement that we would negotiate with Iran. The proposals offer Iran a way forward that would enable a solution based on mutual respect and cooperation. They would give Iran everything it needs to achieve its stated ambition of developing a modern, civil nuclear power industry, including active support in the building of light-water power reactors in Iran, participation in a uranium enrichment facility in Russia and legally binding assurances relating to the supply of nuclear material; address Iran's concern that it should not depend on a single foreign supplier; and provide a substantive package of cooperation in less proliferation-sensitive nuclear research and development. In addition, the proposals would also offer Iran significant political and economic benefits, including a trade and cooperation agreement with the European Union.

... Suspension will not hinder Iran's development of a modern, civil nuclear power industry in any way, but the continuation of enrichment-related and reprocessing activities, including research and development, would allow Iran to develop the know-how to produce fissile material suitable for use in nuclear weapons. Given the concern about Iran's ambitions, that is not a risk that we can afford to take. Our proposals suggest a procedure for reviewing the moratorium once international confidence in Iran's intentions has been restored.

The United Kingdom is deeply disappointed that Iran has neither given any indication that it is ready to engage seriously on our proposals nor taken the steps needed to allow negotiations to begin. We concluded that there was no alternative but to seek today's resolution, which creates a mandatory obligation on Iran to suspend fully all uranium enrichment-related and reprocessing activities, including research and development, to be verified by the IAEA. A full suspension is required to help build confidence and to create the atmosphere of trust necessary for negotiations. Negotiations cannot succeed if Iran is continuing the activities that are the main source of international concern.

We have adopted a Security Council resolution that makes the IAEA-required suspension mandatory. Should Iran refuse to comply, we will work for the adoption of measures under Article 41 of Chapter VII of the Charter. Should Iran implement the decisions of the IAEA and the Security Council and enter into negotiations, we would be ready to hold back from further action in the Security Council.

We reaffirm that the proposals that were conveyed to Iran by the six countries on 6 June 2006 remain valid. The choice is now for Iran to make. We urge and encourage Iran to take the positive path by implementing the steps required by the IAEA Board and the Security Council and to return to talks on the basis of the ambitious package which we have put forward.

[5] Mr. Churkin (**Russian Federation**): ... The main goal of the resolution is to support the efforts of the IAEA to resolve Iran's nuclear problems. The Agency possesses all the necessary capacity to that end and should continue to play a central role in resolving non-proliferation issues in the context of Iran's nuclear programme. We hope that, with the support of the Security Council in the form of today's resolution, it will be easier for the IAEA to do that job.

By acting under Article 40 of the Charter, the resolution makes mandatory the demand of the IAEA regarding Tehran's suspension of all uranium enrichment and reprocessing activities. If Iran does not comply with the provisions of the resolution, members of the Security Council have expressed the intention to take appropriate action under Article 41 of Chapter VII Charter. It is crucial that, as follows unambiguously from the resolution, any additional measures that could be required in the future in order to implement the resolution rule out the use of military force. The suspension by Iran of all enrichment and reprocessing activities, which is called for in the resolution, is not a goal in itself. It should help to clarify outstanding issues with regard to the nuclear activities of Iran and to restore trust in its nuclear programme. Thus, this measure, in accordance with Article 40 of the Charter, should be viewed as an interim measure during the period necessary for resolving the issue. If Iran, as we hope, complies with the Security Council resolution and the demands of the IAEA and enters into negotiations, members of the Security Council would be prepared to refrain from any further action in this context. We believe that, if negotiations yield a positive - solution to the problem in terms of the implementation of the demands of the IAEA, then no additional action against Iran would be taken in the Security Council.

It is important that the resolution has a provision that opens the door for Tehran's establishment of broad international cooperation to meet Iran's energy requirements on the basis of the peaceful uses of nuclear energy. We reaffirm the proposals that were transmitted to Iran by the six countries on 6 June 2006. We hope that Tehran will properly and seriously view the contents of this resolution and will take the necessary steps to redress the situation regarding Iran's nuclear programme. We call upon Teheran to respond positively to the proposals of the six countries.

Mr. Liu Zhenmin (**China**):

…

China has all along indicated that purpose of the Security Council reviewing this issue is to safeguard the international nuclear non-proliferation mechanism, strengthen the authority and role of the IAEA, support the endeavours of the IAEA Director General and his team to clarify the outstanding issues relating to Iran's nuclear programme, promote diplomatic efforts and resolutely commit itself to finding an appropriate solution to this issue through political and diplomatic means.

…

This resolution stresses in many of its paragraphs the importance of finding a negotiated solution through political and diplomatic efforts. It underlines the irreplaceable key role of the IAEA in handling this issue. It endorses the package of proposals put forward by China, France, Germany, Russia, the United Kingdom and the United States in early June. It also emphasizes that these proposals constitute an important [6] effort for a comprehensive arrangement which would allow for the development of bilateral relations and cooperation based on mutual respect and the establishment of international confidence in the exclusively peaceful nature of Iran's nuclear programme.

The fact that an appropriate solution to the Iran nuclear issue is late in coming is due to lack of trust among the main parties involved. It needs to be emphasized that, whether it is now or in the future, the Security Council cannot handle this issue single-handedly. Dialogue and negotiations are the only way out. The IAEA should always be the main mechanism for dealing with this issue. The solution requires all-around diplomatic efforts; any measures adopted by the Security Council should serve the purpose of diplomatic efforts.

According to Article 25 of the United Nations Charter, all United Nations Member States are obliged to accept and carry out Security Council resolutions. In the current circumstances, China urges Iran to practice restraint, attach importance to the extensive appeals and expectations of the international community, earnestly implement the requirements of this resolution and make early response to the package of proposals, so as to create conditions for increasing trust and promoting dialogue and negotiations.

We also wish to call upon all the other parties to adopt a highly responsible attitude towards world peace, security and stability and the international nuclear non-proliferation mechanism, and to remain confident and calm, practice restraint, explore new ways of thinking and continue to creatively carry out diplomatic efforts for the settlement of the Iran nuclear issue. We welcome any ideas and efforts conducive to conducting talks, breaking the stalemate and reaching compromises.

During this sensitive period, it is essential for Iran and all the other parties concerned not to take any steps that will harm the aforementioned diplomatic efforts and that may lead to complications or even loss of control. We call upon all the parties to resume dialogue and negotiations as soon as possible for the proper solution of the Iran nuclear issue.

…

[7] **The President**: I shall now make a statement in my capacity as representative of **France**.

Resolution 1696(2006), which the Security Council has just adopted, was made necessary by the fact that Iran, despite three meetings between Mr. Javier Solana and Mr. Ali Larijani, has shown no willingness to seriously discuss the substance of the proposals made on 6 June on behalf of China, France, Germany, the Russian Federation, the Russian Federation and the United States. Under such conditions, the six countries had no choice but to resume the activity that had been suspended in the Security Council. We welcome the international community's support, through this vote, for the efforts of our countries.

France – in a position shared by Germany, which co-sponsored the text – emphasizes the following elements.

The resolution that we have just adopted makes mandatory the suspension requested by the International Atomic Energy Agency (IAEA); it does not mean an end to negotiations. We reaffirm the proposals made to Iran on 6 June by our six countries. If Iran should refuse to comply with the resolution, we will then work to adopt measures under Article 41 of Chapter VII of the Charter of the United Nations. If Iran should implement the decisions of the IAEA and the Security Council and enter into negotiations, we will be prepared to abstain from further action in the Council.

Once again, we appeal to Iran to respond positively to the substantive proposals that we made last month.

I now resume my functions as President of the Security Council.

…

Mr. Zarif (**Islamic Republic of Iran**):

…

[8] This is not the first time that Iran's endeavours to stand on its own feet and make technological advances have faced stiff resistance and concerted pressure from some Powers permanently represented in the Security Council. In fact, contemporary Iran has been subjected to numerous injustices and prejudicial approaches by those Powers. In a draft resolution submitted on 12 October 1951 by the United Kingdom and supported in the Council by the United States and France, the Iranian people's struggle to nationalize their oil industry was touted as a threat to international peace and security…

More recently, Saddam Hussein's aggression against the Islamic Republic of Iran on 22 September 1980 and his swift advance to occupy 30,000 square kilometres of Iranian territory did not trouble the same permanent members of the Security Council enough to make them consider it a threat to international peace and security or even to make the routine call for a ceasefire and withdrawal…

Over the past several weeks, this body has been prevented from moving to stop the massive aggression against the Palestinian and Lebanese peoples and the resulting terrible humanitarian crisis…

Likewise, the Security Council has been prevented from reacting to the daily threats of resort to force against Iran, even threats of using nuclear weapons uttered at the highest levels by representatives of the United States, the United Kingdom and the lawless Israeli regime, in violation of Article 2(4) of the Charter.

On the other hand, over the past few years, a few big Powers have spared no effort in turning the Security Council, or the threat of resorting to it, into a tool for attempting to prevent Iran from exercising its inalienable right to nuclear technology for peaceful purposes, recognized explicitly under the Treaty on the Non-Proliferation of Nuclear

Weapons. The intention to use the Council only as a tool for that or even more dangerous ends could not have been made clearer than in the statement by the permanent representative of the United States at the meeting of the American Israel Public Affairs Committee on 5 March this year:

'It is critical that we use the Council to help mobilize international public opinion.
Rest assured, though, we are not relying on the Security Council as the only tool in our toolbox to address this problem.'

The people and the Government of the Islamic Republic of Iran are determined to exercise their inalienable right to nuclear technology for peaceful purposes and to build on their own scientific advances in developing various peaceful aspects of that technology. At the same time, as the only victims of the use of weapons of mass destruction in recent history, [9] they reject the development and use of all those inhuman weapons on ideological as well as strategic grounds. The leader of the Islamic Republic has issued a public and categorical religious decree against the development, production, stockpiling and use of nuclear weapons.[63]

Iran has also clearly and continuously stressed that nuclear weapons have no place in its military doctrine. The President of the Islamic Republic of Iran, in his statement before the General Assembly last September, also underlined Iran's fundamental rejection of nuclear weapons, as well as the need to strengthen and revitalize the non-proliferation Treaty. He also stressed that 'continued interaction and technical and legal cooperation with the International Atomic Energy Agency will be the centerpiece of our nuclear policy'.[64]

In order to dispel any doubt about our peaceful nuclear programme, we enabled the International Atomic Energy Agency (IAEA) to carry out a series of inspections that amounts to the most robust inspection of any IAEA member State. It included more than 2,000 inspector-days of scrutiny over the past three years; the signing of the Additional Protocol[65] on 18 December 2003 and its immediate implementation until 6 February 2006; the submission of more than 1,000 pages of declaration under the Additional Protocol; allowing over 53 instances of complementary access to different sites across the country; and permitting inspectors to investigate baseless allegations by taking the unprecedented step of providing repeated access to military sites.

Consequently, all reports of the IAEA since November 2003 have been indicative of the peaceful nature of the Iranian nuclear programme. In November 2003 and in the wake of sensational media reports on the so-called 18-years of concealment by Iran, the Agency confirmed that '[t]o date, there is no evidence that the previously undeclared nuclear material and activities... were related to a nuclear weapons programme'.[66] We all remember how that statement was received by the United States Under-Secretary of State of the time.

The same conclusion can be found in other IAEA reports, even as recently as that of February 2006, which states that, '[a]s indicated to the Board in November 2004, and again in September 2005, all the declared nuclear material in Iran has been accounted for'.[67] The Agency reaffirmed once again in paragraph 53 of the same report that it 'has not seen any diversion of nuclear material to nuclear weapons or other nuclear explosive devices'.

---

[63] Kayhan, 6 November 2004.
[64] Doc. 110.
[65] Doc. 5.
[66] Doc. 35 para 52.
[67] Doc. 41 para 53.

Much has been made, including in today's resolution, of a statement by the IAEA that it is not yet in a position 'to conclude that there are no undeclared nuclear materials or activities in Iran'.[68] But the sponsors have conveniently ignored the repeated acknowledgment by the Director-General of the IAEA that 'the process of drawing such a conclusion... is a time consuming process'.[69] They also ignored the addendum to the 2005 IAEA safeguards implementation report, released in June 2006, which indicates that 45 other countries are in the same category as Iran, including 14 Europeans and several members of this Council. I might add that, out of three sponsors of today's resolution, two are obviously in the privileged class, self-immunized from any scrutiny, but the third is in the same category as Iran.

Iran's peaceful nuclear programme poses no threat to international peace and security, and therefore dealing with that issue in the Security Council is unwarranted and void of any legal basis or practical utility. Far from reflecting, as advertised, the concerns of the international community, the approach of the sponsors flouts the stated position of the overwhelming majority of the international community, clearly reflected in the most recent statements by the foreign ministers of the Non-Aligned Movement and of the Organization of the Islamic Conference (OIC), and partly reflected in the June 2006 IAEA Board Chairman's conclusion.[70]

The 57 members of the OIC, in their recent ministerial meeting in Baku, expressed their 'conviction that the only way to resolve Iran's nuclear issue is to resume negotiations without preconditions'.[71] They welcomed 'the readiness of the Islamic Republic of Iran to settle all remaining outstanding issues peacefully'; recognized that 'any attempt aimed at limiting the application of peaceful uses of nuclear energy would affect the sustainable development of developing countries'; rejected 'discrimination and double standards in peaceful uses of nuclear energy'; and, finally, expressed [10]

> 'concern over any unwanted consequences on the peace and security of the
> region and beyond of threats and pressures on Iran by certain circles to renounce
> its inalienable right to develop nuclear energy for peaceful purposes'.

The Non-Aligned Movement, comprising an overwhelming majority of the Members of the Organization, in the recent statement of its ministers, meeting in Putrajaya, 'stressed that there should be no undue pressure or interference in the Agency's activities, especially its verification process, which would jeopardize the efficiency and credibility of the Agency' and that 'nothing should be interpreted in a way as inhibiting or restricting this right of States to develop atomic energy for peaceful purposes'. They also reaffirmed that 'States' choices and decisions in the field of peaceful uses of nuclear technology and its fuel-cycle policies must be respected'.[72]

But, claiming to represent the international community itself, the European Union three (EU-3), in their so-called package of incentives last August, asked Iran to 'make a binding commitment not to pursue fuel cycle activities'.[73] A cursory look at the chronology of events since last August indicates that Iran's rejection of that illegal and unwarranted demand has been, and continues to be, the sole reason for the imposition of resolutions and

---

[68] Doc. 39 para 51.
[69] Doc. 39 para 51.
[70] Doc. 87.
[71] OIC/33-ICFM/2006/BAKU-DC, annex, enclosure 2, para 12, circulated in UN Doc A/60/915 (19 July 2006).
[72] Ministerial Meeting of the Coordinating Bureau of the Non-Aligned Movement, Putrajaya, Statement on the Islamic Republic of Iran's Nuclear Issue 30 May 2006 NAM/MM/COB/9 paras, 2, 3
[73] Doc. 126 para 34.

statements on the Board of the International Atomic Energy Agency and on the Security Council.[74] Today's proposed action by the Council - which is the culmination of those efforts aimed at making the suspension of uranium enrichment mandatory - violates the fundamental principles of international law, the Treaty on the Non-Proliferation of Nuclear Weapons (NPT) and IAEA Board resolutions. It also runs counter to the views of the majority of Member States, which the Security Council is obliged to represent.

The IAEA Board, in its November 2004 resolution,[75] ironically drafted by the very same sponsors of today's resolution, declared that suspension 'is a voluntary, non-legally binding, confidence-building measure'. That was repeated as recently as 15 June 2006, in the IAEA Board Chairman's conclusion.

The Non-Aligned Movement, in its recent ministerial statement referred to earlier, stressed 'the fundamental distinction between the legal obligations of States to their respective safeguards agreements and any confidence-building measures voluntarily undertaken to resolve difficult issues' and 'that such voluntary undertakings are not legal safeguards obligations'.[76]

The sole reason for pushing the Council to take action, as highlighted in the resolution, is that Iran decided, after over two years of negotiations, to resume the exercise of its inalienable right to nuclear technology for peaceful purposes by partially reopening its fully safeguarded facilities and ending a voluntary suspension. Iran's right to enrich uranium is recognized under the NPT. Upholding the rights of States parties to international treaties is as essential as ensuring respect for their obligations. Those regimes, including the NPT, are sustained by a balance between rights and obligations. Threats will not sustain the NPT or other international regimes; ensuring that members can draw rightful benefits from membership, and that non-members are not rewarded for their intransigence, will.

Yet, exactly the opposite is the trend today. Today we are witness to an extremely dangerous trend. While members of the NPT are denied their rights and are punished, those who defy the NPT, particularly the perpetrators of the current carnage in Lebanon and Palestine, are rewarded with generous nuclear cooperation agreements. This goes so far that, when it suits the United States, even the acquisition of nuclear weapons by non-NPT members becomes 'legitimate', to quote the United States Ambassador. That is one awkward way to strengthen the NPT or ensure its universality.

That trend has reached such a horrendous, and indeed ridiculous, state that the Israeli regime – a non-member of the NPT, whose nuclear arsenal, coupled with its expansionist, repressive and State-terror policies and behaviour are repeatedly recognized, including by NPT Review Conferences, as the single most serious threat to regional and international peace and security – finds the audacity to cry wolf about Iran's peaceful nuclear programme and to lead a global campaign of threats, lies, deception, pressure, blackmail and outright extortion. Yet, in spite of the massive political and propaganda machine, no one in today's world can accept the convoluted logic that it is okay for some to have nuclear weapons while others are prevented from developing nuclear energy.

[11] Another destructive trend is the imposition of arbitrary thresholds, which are often a function of bilateral considerations rather than objective or technical criteria. It should be interesting to recall that the United States began by trying to deny Iran any kind

---

[74] —— 'Leaked letter in full: UK diplomat outlines Iran strategy' *Times Online* (22 March 2006), www. timesonline.co.uk/tol/news/uk/article744070.ece.

[75] Doc. 28 operative para 1.

[76] Ministerial Meeting of the Coordinating Bureau of the Non-Aligned Movement, Putrajaya, Statement on the Islamic Republic of Iran's Nuclear Issue 30 May 2006 NAM/MM/COB/9 para 5.

of nuclear activity. Even as late as 31 January 2003, the State Department spokesman was saying that 'we have consistently urged Russia to cease all such cooperation with Iran, including its assistance to the light water reactor at Bushehr'.

The new threshold regarding enrichment is as arbitrary as the previous ones, and is simply another excuse to begin a trend to prevent the realization of the rights of the members of the NPT to peaceful use while, according to the United States Ambassador, nonmembers could legitimately continue producing nuclear bombs.

It has been argued that intervention by the Security Council is needed to ensure cooperation by Iran with the Agency and to bring Iran back to the negotiating table. I suggest that Security Council involvement is not needed to achieve that goal. In fact, involvement by the Council hinders rather than helps this ongoing process, because it is designed as an instrument of pressure.

As I indicated earlier, Iran's cooperation with the Agency was far more extensive and comprehensive before action was imposed on the IAEA Board to engage the Security Council. That cooperation enabled the Agency to conclude, last September, that good progress had been made 'in the Agency's ability to confirm certain aspects of Iran's current declarations, which will be followed up as a routine safeguards implementation matter'.[77]

As for returning to the negotiating table, Iran has always been ready for negotiations. For almost three years, Iran tried to sustain, and even to resuscitate, negotiations with the EU-3. Iran offered far-reaching proposals to address concerns as well as to usher in a new era of cooperation: in August 2004, in January 2005, in March 2005, in April 2005, in July 2005, in September 2005, in January 2006, in February 2006 and in March 2006. Throughout that period, Iran adopted extensive and extremely costly confidence-building measures, including the suspension of its rightful enrichment activities for two years, to ensure the success of those negotiations. All along, it has been the persistence of some in drawing arbitrary red lines and deadlines that has closed the door to any compromise. This tendency has single-handedly blocked success and in most cases killed proposals in their infancy. This has been Washington's persistent strategy ever since Iran and the EU-3 started their negotiations in October 2003. Only the tactics have changed.

All along, the threats by some to bring this issue before the Council and to take it out of its proper technical and negotiated structure have loomed large over the negotiations and have impeded progress, derailed discussions and prevented focus on a mutually acceptable resolution. The manner in which negotiations over the recently proposed package have been conducted is a further indication of the same propensity to resort to threats and the lack of genuine will to reach a mutually acceptable resolution.

Iran, publicly and in a show of good faith, reacted positively to this initiative and indicated its readiness to engage in fair, non-discriminatory and result-oriented negotiations about the package within a mutually agreed time frame and without preconditions. Yet, an arbitrary deadline was set, ex post facto, without any justification and only to serve the totally ulterior objective of maximizing pressure.[78]

Indeed, it is informative to note that it took the EU-3 nearly five months, from March to August 2005, to consider a very serious proposal made by Iran last year. And even then the EU-3 came up with a response that did not address any elements of that proposal. And yet, while the Islamic Republic of Iran has clearly stated that it requires three more weeks to conclude its evaluation of the proposed package and come up with a substantive reaction,

---

[77] Doc. 39, para 43.
[78] See n 75.

it is astonishing - and indeed telling - to see that the EU-3 and the United States are in such a rush to prematurely hamper the path of negotiations by imposing a destructive and totally unwarranted Security Council resolution. This rush becomes even more suspect if one takes into account repeated statements of the Director-General of the IAEA, numerous United States experts and even the United States intelligence community about the absence of any urgency.

Compare this rush to the fact that some of the very same Powers have for the past three weeks prevented any action — not even a 72-hour humanitarian truce — by the Security Council on the [12] urgent situation in Lebanon, which has been officially and publicly interpreted by the aggressors as a green light to continue their onslaught, unfortunately including the recent carnage in Qana. Security Council members can be the judge of how much credibility this leaves for the Council. Millions of people around the world have already passed their judgement.

So, it is pertinent to ask: What is the motive behind this long-standing urge of some permanent members to bring Iran before the Security Council? And what is the current rush? Is it anything but pressure and coercion? I would suggest that this approach will not lead to any productive outcome and that in fact it can only exacerbate the situation. The people and the Government of the Islamic Republic of Iran are not seeking confrontation and have always shown their readiness to engage in serious and result-oriented negotiations based on mutual respect and on an equal footing. They have also shown, time and again, their resilience in the face of pressure, threat, injustice and imposition.

…

Document 16: Security Council Debate on Resolution 1737(2006)

S/PV.5612, 23 December 2006

[2] **The President**: The Security Council will now begin its consideration of the item on its agenda. The Council is meeting in accordance with the understanding reached in its prior consultations.

Members of the Council have before them document S/2006/1010, which contains the text of a draft resolution submitted by France, Germany and the United Kingdom of Great Britain and Northern Ireland.

…

It is my understanding that the Council is ready to proceed to the vote on the draft resolution before it. Unless I hear any objection, I shall put the draft resolution to the vote now.

There being no objection, it is so decided.

…

Mr. Churkin (**Russian Federation**): The Russian Federation will support the draft resolution before us relating to Iran's nuclear programme. We will do so because we believe that the draft, the outcome of lengthy and complex consultations, focuses on the affirmation of measures that Iran must take in order to produce confidence in its nuclear programme, formulated by the Board of Governors of the International Atomic Energy Agency (IAEA). In other words, the main thrust of the draft resolution we are to adopt today is the support of the Security Council, through its authority, of the Agency's activities in that area.

It is crucial that the restrictions being introduced on cooperation with Iran apply to those areas that are the cause of the IAEA's concern. In that regard, we firmly believe that cooperation with Iran in areas and using resources that are not restricted by the draft resolution shall not be subject to the draft resolution's restrictions.

We believe that some of the draft resolution's wording could have been made clearer.

We are convinced that ways effectively to resolve the Iranian nuclear problem are to be found exclusively in the political, diplomatic and legal framework. In that context, it is important that the measures provided for in the draft resolution be taken in accordance with Article 41 of the United Nations Charter and commit no use of force. In strengthening the global non-proliferation regime for nuclear weapons, it is necessary to seek the establishment of solid regional and international security and stability.

Russia views the draft resolution as a serious message to Iran regarding the need to cooperate more actively and more openly with the IAEA to resolve the remaining concerns and questions relating to its nuclear programme. The parameters for the required cooperation have been set forth in the resolutions of the IAEA Board of Governors and supported by the Security Council.

[3] The draft resolution clearly reaffirms that, if Iran suspends all activities relating to the enrichment and chemical reprocessing of uranium, the measures spelled out in the draft resolution will be suspended. That will make it possible to launch the negotiating process in the interests of a solid political settlement of the Iranian nuclear problem. The proposals that have been transmitted to the Iranian Government on behalf of the 'six' remain valid.

We hope that Iran will correctly and most earnestly consider the contents of the draft resolution and take the measures necessary to redress the situation. Constructive steps by Tehran to comply with the draft resolution will make it possible to mitigate the urgency of the questions relating to Iran's nuclear programme.

Mr. Wolff (**United States of America**): Iran's pursuit of nuclear weapons capability constitutes a grave threat and demands a clear statement from this Council. Today we are placing Iran in the small category of States under Security Council sanctions and sending it an unambiguous message that there are serious repercussions to its continued disregard of its obligations and defiance of this body.

…

The United States expects that Iran and all other United Nations Member States will immediately act under their Charter obligations to implement the requirements of this draft resolution.

This will be the second Security Council resolution under Chapter VII on Iran in response to that country's efforts to obtain a nuclear weapons capability, reflecting the gravity of this situation and the determination of the Council. We hope this draft resolution will convince Iran that the best way to ensure its security and end its international isolation is to abandon the pursuit of nuclear weapons and take steps needed to restore international confidence. In this draft resolution the Council has clearly affirmed its intention to review Iran's actions based on the IAEA report and to adopt further measures if Iran has not complied fully with its obligations.

We look forward to Iran's full, unconditional and immediate compliance with this draft resolution. Iran's cooperation would pave the way for a negotiated solution. We hope that the Iranian leadership comes to [4] understand that the pursuit of a nuclear weapons capability makes it less, not more, secure.

…

The President: I shall now make a statement in my capacity as the representative of **Qatar**.

...

The State of Qatar considers that Iran has the right to undertake research on nuclear technology and to use that technology and produce nuclear energy for peaceful purposes. No one can invoke articles I and II of the NPT to take away that right. But atomic concepts designed for destruction have given rise to advanced technologies that can be turned to peaceful purposes, provided that standards for safety, including the safety of nuclear reactors, are in place. Such standards would avert accidents. Great benefits can come of cooperation with the IAEA in this sphere, because the Agency is a centre for exchanging information and for establishing guidelines.

With respect to this difficult issue, Qatar has no suspicions concerning the sincerity of Iran's intentions as regards the peaceful nature of its nuclear programme. But we must not risk the potential benefits of cooperation with the IAEA in guaranteeing nuclear safety, particularly since this draft resolution would impede delivery of equipment necessary for the Iranian nuclear programme, which could have dangerous repercussions for the nuclear safety issue. That is why we appeal once again to our sisterly neighbour Iran and urge it to respond to this draft resolution. We know that the draft resolution is tough, but we are confident that there is wide scope for diplomatic cooperation, given that Iran has expressed readiness to continue to permit inspection activities under IAEA safeguards, including settling outstanding questions, so long as the issue remains within the IAEA's purview, in conformity with Iran's letter dated 27 April 2006 addressed to the Director General of the IAEA.

The Council's draft resolution also states that the measures to be enforced would be suspended to provide an opportunity for negotiations. These are issues that can be overcome, so long as we act in good faith. Iran can use its wisdom to address the situation with the rationality that is required. Our vote is prompted by our concerns over the safety of Iranian nuclear facilities.

Finally, we hope that the Council will stand united in the search for a peaceful settlement and that it will use such a settlement to limit nuclear proliferation [5] in other regions, in accordance with existing resolutions, in particular with respect to the Middle East region, and especially with respect to Israel, which has recently made statements concerning its nuclear deterrence capability.

For all those reasons, the State of Qatar will vote in favour of the draft resolution.

I now resume my functions as President of the Security Council.

I now put to the vote the draft resolution contained in document S/2006/1010.

A vote was taken by show of hands.

In favour: Argentina, China, Congo, Denmark, France, Ghana, Greece, Japan, Peru, Qatar, Russian Federation, Slovakia, United Kingdom of Great Britain and Northern Ireland, United Republic of Tanzania, United States of America

The President: There were 15 votes in favour. The draft resolution has been adopted unanimously as resolution 1737(2006).[79]

I now give the floor to those members of the Council who wish to make statements following the voting.

---

[79] Doc. 11.

Sir Emyr Jones Parry (**United Kingdom**): On 31 July, the Security Council adopted resolution 1696(2006)[80] which made mandatory the suspension required by the International Atomic Energy Agency (IAEA) of enrichment-related and reprocessing activities in Iran. The Council called upon Iran, without further delay, to take the steps required by the IAEA Board of Governors to act in accordance with the provision of the Additional Protocol[81] and to implement all transparency measures as the IAEA may request.

The resolution set a deadline of 31 August for Iranian compliance. Iran's response was to step up its sensitive activities and offer to export the technologies it developed to other countries. The IAEA reported in November that Iran continued to provide insufficient transparency to help the Agency resolved outstanding issues and remove uncertainties.

In sum, Iran has simply thumbed its nose at the Council and defied international law. Bearing in mind the Council's primary responsibility for the maintenance of international peace and security, and in this regard taking with utmost seriousness the threat from the proliferation of weapons of mass destruction, the Council unequivocally expressed its intention in resolution 1696(2006) to adopt measures under Article 41 of the Charter of the United Nations in the event of Iranian non-compliance.

And that is what we have done today. We have adopted resolution 1737(2006) under Chapter VII of the Charter, and in this we reiterate and expand the Council's mandatory suspension of Iran's proliferation-sensitive activities. We have also established an embargo aimed at preventing Iran from importing the items and material that will sustain its proliferation-sensitive activities.

In addition to taking steps to inhibit Iran's proliferation-sensitive activities, the Council has introduced a set of measures intended to persuade Iran to stop pursuing activities of concern. This resolution underlines the seriousness of the situation, including the international community's lack of confidence about the direction of Iran's policies.

But, importantly, the door is not closed for Iran. The United Kingdom, France and Germany, with the European Union High Representative, Javier Solana, have led negotiations with Iran. We remain committed to seeking a diplomatic, negotiated solution with Iran, based on cooperation. A new relationship between the European Union and Iran is on the table, but it must be with an Iran which eschews nuclear weapons.

In resolution 1737(2006), the Council makes clear that Iran's suspension of enrichment and reprocessing activities will permit negotiations to resume and intensify, this time with the United States, Russia and China engaged alongside France, Germany and the United Kingdom.

For this reason, in the pursuit of a negotiated agreement to resolve the situation, it is vital that all States implement the resolution as fully and comprehensively as possible. This means taking immediate action, including by adopting the necessary legislation to pave the way for rapid and robust implementation. Without that, we cannot expect the Council to be able to meet its objectives.

In the event that Iran does not change course, the Council has committed itself in this resolution to the adoption of further measures. Iran, therefore, faces a choice. The vote today illustrates the gravity of that [6] choice and the seriousness with which we, as a Council, view Iran's behaviour.

...

---

[80] Doc. 10.
[81] Doc. 5.

Mr. De La Sablière (**France**):

...

This resolution, adopted on the basis of a draft presented by Germany, the United Kingdom and France, confirms the mandatory nature of the suspension of sensitive activities in the nuclear field, which are of concern to the international community, because they do not have a credible civilian application in Iran today. These include enrichment, reprocessing, the manufacture of heavy water and the construction in Arak of a reactor moderated by heavy water capable of producing plutonium of military grade quality.

...

These sanctions are proportionate and reversible. The Security Council states, without ambiguity, that if Iran re-establishes the suspension of all its enrichment and reprocessing activities, including research and development, the measures that the Council has just adopted will be suspended. If it conforms to all provisions of resolution 1696(2006) and 1733(2006) [*sic*], as well as those of the resolutions of the IAEA Board of Governors, these sanctions will be lifted; but if it persists on its current path, there will be other measures under Article 41 of Chapter VII.

This resolution sends out a clear message on the part of the international community to Iran, which is now facing a strategic choice, which was recalled by President Jacques Chirac on 12 December: cooperation with the international community or growing isolation. We hope that Tehran will choose dialogue and that it will take decisions that will allow for a resumption of negotiations based on resolutions 1696(2006) and 1733(2006) [*sic*]. France, with its partners, remains ready for this at all times.

Mr. Oshima (**Japan**): It is a matter of great regret that the Council has been compelled to act in this Chamber on another resolution regarding Iran's nuclear issue only five months after adopting resolution 1696(2006). Over the course of this year, we have had intensive discussions on the Iranian nuclear issue in the Council as concerted international efforts continued for the purpose of seeking a peaceful and diplomatic resolution of this problem by the States concerned, including my own. These efforts, however, have failed to produce positive results.

In defiance of resolution 1696(2006), Iran has refused to take any steps required of it to comply with the measures set out by the International Atomic Energy Agency (IAEA) and the Security Council, including the suspension of enrichment- and reprocessing-related activities. On the contrary, the situation has worsened, with Iran's expansion of its enrichment- and reprocessing-related activities.

Japan attaches great importance to the non-proliferation of nuclear weapons as an issue that can affect its own national peace and security and that of the international community. Proliferation of nuclear and other weapons of mass destruction, along with their means of delivery, is a clear and present global [7] challenge posing a great threat and must be handled with firm determination. It is our strong belief that, in order to counter such a threat, actual or potential, the international community must act appropriately, resolutely and in a timely manner wherever it occurs, be it in the Middle East, North-East Asia or elsewhere in the world. We believe that Iran's case, where it has failed to comply with the requirements set out by the IAEA and the Security Council, must be dealt with based on the basis of a principled stand.

At the same time, the right to the peaceful use of nuclear energy by all States is also important and must be fully respected and protected. Iran has that right, just as much as any other country. We hope and expect that, in the exercise of that right, Iran will fully comply with its international obligations and give its utmost cooperation to the IAEA so that it will be able to enjoy fully the fruits of the peaceful use of nuclear energy.

...

Mr. Wang Guangya (**China**) (*spoke in Chinese*): Since the beginning of this year, Iran's nuclear issue has attracted more and more attention in the world. Regrettably and disappointingly, Iran has yet to respond positively to the requirements of the International Atomic Energy Agency (IAEA) and the Security Council and show flexibility on the suspension of enrichment-related activities.

After issuing a presidential statement (S/PRST/2005/15)[82] in March and adopting resolution 1696(2006) in July on Iran's nuclear issue, the Security Council has today adopted another resolution, aiming at safeguarding the international nuclear non-proliferation mechanism, reinforcing the IAEA's authority and role, and promoting diplomatic efforts to seek peaceful solutions to Iran's nuclear issue. The Chinese delegation has therefore voted in favour of the draft resolution before us.

China wishes to emphasize that sanctions are not the end, but are a means to urge Iran to resume negotiations. The sanction measures adopted by the Security Council this time are limited and reversible, and they target proliferation-sensitive nuclear activities and the development of nuclear-weapon delivery systems. There are also explicit provisions indicating that if Iran suspends its enrichment-related and reprocessing activities, complies with the relevant resolutions of the Security Council and meets the requirements of the IAEA, the Security Council would suspend and even terminate the sanction measures.

The Security Council cannot handle Iran's nuclear issue single-handedly. The IAEA remains the principal mechanism for dealing with this issue. Dialogue and negotiations are the fundamental, indeed the only, way out. The solution to Iran's nuclear issue requires all-around diplomatic efforts.

Diplomatic efforts outside the Security Council in particular should be strengthened. The resolution welcomes the commitment of China, France, Germany, the Russian Federation, the United Kingdom and the United States to a negotiated solution to this issue, and encourages Iran to engage with those six countries' proposals for a long-term comprehensive agreement.[83] Such an accord would allow for the development of relations and cooperation with Iran based on mutual respect and the establishment of international confidence in the peaceful nature of Iran's nuclear programme. All these aspects would be conducive to reactivating a new round of diplomatic efforts.

All along, China has supported safeguarding the international nuclear non-proliferation mechanism and opposed the proliferation of nuclear weapons. We do not wish to see new turbulence in the Middle East. We are in favour of a peaceful solution to Iran's nuclear issue through political and diplomatic efforts and negotiations.

Under the current circumstances, we wish to call upon all the parties concerned to adopt a highly responsible and constructive attitude, remain calm, [8] practice restraint, and refrain from taking any steps that would harm diplomatic efforts and lead to a deterioration of the situation. At the same time, we hope that the parties will seek to resume negotiations in a creative and forward-looking manner and continue to spare no effort in seeking to enhance diplomatic endeavours in favour of the comprehensive and peaceful solution of Iran's nuclear issue.

...

[82] Doc. 9.
[83] Doc. 131.

Mr. Mayoral (**Argentina**): At the outset, I should like to state that Argentina voted in favour of resolution 1737(2006), just adopted, because the resolution reaffirms the inalienable right enjoyed by all States parties to the Treaty on the Non-Proliferation of Nuclear Weapons under articles I and II of the Treaty to develop, research, produce and use nuclear energy for peaceful purposes without discrimination.

At the same time, on behalf of my Government, I express our confidence that the Government of Iran will in the future pursue its nuclear programme exclusively for peaceful purposes, following the parameters established by the International Atomic Energy Agency and the relevant resolutions of the Security Council. Moreover, on a different point, we note our satisfaction that the resolution was adopted unanimously and under article 41 of the United Nations Charter. In other words, there is no possibility under resolution 1737(2006) of recourse to the use of force.

...

Mr. Zarif (**Islamic Republic of Iran**): Today is a sad day for the non-proliferation regime. Only a few days ago, the Prime Minister of the Israeli regime boasted about his regime's nuclear weapons, but [9] instead of even raising an eyebrow, let alone addressing that serious threat to international peace and security and to the non-proliferation regime, the Security Council is imposing sanctions on a party to the Treaty on the Non-Proliferation of Nuclear Weapons (NPT) that, unlike Israel, has never attacked or threatened to use force against any Member of the United Nations; has categorically rejected the development, stockpiling and use of nuclear weapons on ideological and strategic grounds;[84] was prepared to provide guarantees that it would never withdraw from the NPT; has placed all its nuclear facilities under the safeguards of the International Atomic Energy Agency (IAEA); fully implemented the Additional Protocol for over two years, and stated its readiness to resume its implementation; allowed over 2,000 person days of IAEA scrutiny of all its related and unrelated facilities, resulting in repeated statements by the Agency on the absence of any evidence of diversion; voluntarily suspended its lawful enrichment activities for over two years, as verified by the IAEA, in order to build confidence and provide ample opportunity to find a mutually acceptable solution, if that ever were the intention of its negotiating partners; presented various far-reaching proposals to ensure permanent non-diversion; and has consistently called for time-bound and unconditional negotiations to find a mutually acceptable solution - a call that was repeated yesterday by the Iranian Foreign Minister.

...

The reaction of the Security Council to the Israeli regime's unlawful possession of nuclear weapons will show whether the Council is even considering to act – as it is obliged to do under Article 24 of the Charter – on behalf of the members of the international community that have made their views on that issue abundantly clear, or whether it is merely a tool in the toolbox of a few of its permanent members, which only misuse it to fix their foreign policy problems and to serve their short-sighted perceived interests.

With such tendencies, it is not at all surprising that a nation is being punished for exercising its inalienable rights, primarily at the behest of a dangerous regime with aggression and war crimes as its signature brand of behaviour, which is apparently being rewarded today for having clandestinely developed and unlawfully possessed nuclear weapons. Does anyone expect that to enhance the credibility of the Council or to strengthen the authority of the NPT?

---

[84] Religious Fatwa by the leader of the Islamic Republic reflected in Kayhan, 6 November 2004 and Doc. 99, pp. 2, 13 (partial references in the original).

Put into perspective, today's resolution can only remind the Iranian people of the historic injustices that this Security Council has done to them over the past six decades...
[10] ...

The bringing of Iran's peaceful nuclear programme to the Council by a few of its permanent members, particularly the United States, is not aimed at seeking, nor will it help to find, a solution or at encouraging negotiations. Even their stated objective is not to achieve that. Their stated objective has always been to use the Council as an instrument of pressure and intimidation to compel Iran to abandon its rights. Knowing their bright recent history, we can all assume what the unstated objective has been. Allow me to provide just two examples of the stated objective.

An informal paper entitled 'Options for Addressing Iran's Nuclear Programme at the United Nations Security Council', circulated by the United States mission in October 2004 - exactly when the United States three European Union (EU) allies were ostensibly engaged in negotiations with Iran - states:

'The United States has long believed that Iran's nuclear activities must be reported to the United Nations Security Council ... The United Nations Security Council has the legal authority to require Iran to stop its enrichment programme.'

That was the intention. As to our negotiating partners, the Political Director of the British Foreign Office, in a letter dated 16 March 2006 addressed to his counterparts in France, Germany and the United States[85] revealed the more conniving British plan:

'We may also need to remove one of the Iranian arguments that the suspension called for is 'voluntary'. We could do [that] by making the voluntary suspension a mandatory requirement to the Security Council.'

The letter gets even more interesting as we read on:

'I agreed to circulate a short paper which we might use as a sort of speaking note with the Russians and Chinese. Implicit in the paper is a recognition that we are not going to bring the Russians and Chinese to accept significant sanctions over the coming months, certainly not without further efforts to bring the Iranians around ... In return for the Russians and Chinese agreeing to [a Chapter VII resolution], we would then want to put together a package that could be presented to the Iranians as a new proposal.'

Now we see what motivated the presentation of the infamous package of incentives presented to Iran on 6 June 2006, and now we see why the United States and its EU three partners never even took the trouble to study various Iranian proposals. They were from the very beginning bent on abusing this Council and the threat of referral and sanctions as an instrument of pressure to compel Iran to abandon the exercise of its NPT-guaranteed right to peaceful nuclear technology. It is now an open secret that their sole objective in the negotiations has always been to impose and then prolong and perpetuate the suspension of Iran's rights, in line with their arbitrary and fluctuating red lines. Finding solutions has never even been among the objectives.

Suspension is not a solution. It is at best a temporary - one might call it a stop-gap-measure to allow time to find a real solution. Such a suspension was in place for over two years and, contrary to the excuse that the proponents of the resolution have presented here and there, the IAEA repeatedly verified that Iran fully suspended what it had agreed to suspend in each and every report from November 2003 to February 2006.[86] So, we had a

---

[85] See n 75.
[86] Doc. 35-Doc. 42.

suspension for two years and on-and-off negotiations for three. The question is: What has been done during those three years to find an agreement?

Have the EU three or the United States presented any proposal on what measures - short of outright revision of the NPT - would remove their so-called proliferation concerns? Having failed to do so, did they ever consider the far-reaching proposals that were offered by Iran in Paris on 23 March, 2005,[87] which the EU three negotiators initially considered to contain positive elements? Did they ever propose how those positive elements could be enhanced or how the points of divergence could be bridged? Or did they, after consultations with a certain absent party, come back and simply say 'It is not good enough. Continue to suspend'? Did they even bother to read our proposal of 18 July 2005,[88] which suggested: [11]

> 'Allow the Agency to develop an optimized arrangement on numbers, monitoring mechanism and other specifics for an initial limited operation at Natanz, which would address our needs and allay [their] concerns'?

Did they ponder the far-reaching non-proliferation potential of the proposal by the President of the Islamic Republic of Iran in his address to the General Assembly on 17 September 2005? Let me refresh the memory of Council members. On that occasion, he said,

> 'in order to provide the greatest degree of transparency, the Islamic Republic of Iran is prepared to engage in serious partnerships with the private and public sectors of other countries in the implementation of a uranium enrichment programme in Iran'.[89]

Did they respond to the concrete proposal by the Iranian Foreign Minister at the Conference on Disarmament on 30 March 2006? Allow me to quote what he said.

> 'In our view, one option to resolve the issue could be the establishment of regional consortia on fuel cycle development with the participation of regional countries... Of course, countries outside the region may also participate in such regional arrangements... The facility would also be jointly owned by the sharing countries, and the work could be divided based on the expertise of the participants'.[90]

Were these suggestions not an exact replica of the main proposal of the IAEA experts on multinational approaches to nuclear fuel cycle activities published on 22 February 2005? For those members who may have not seen the report, it suggests

> 'promoting voluntary conversion of existing facilities to [multilateral nuclear approaches (MNAs)], and pursuing them as confidence-building measures, with the participation of NPT non-nuclear-weapon States and nuclear-weapon States, and non-NPT States... [and] creating, through voluntary agreements and contracts, multinational, and in particular regional, MNAs for new facilities based on joint ownership, drawing rights or co-management for front-end and back-end nuclear facilities, such as uranium enrichment'.[91]

Did the Iranian readiness to implement these ideas almost verbatim not present a unique opportunity to create a global model to strengthen the NPT and remove concerns about fuel cycle activities based on the recommendation of the best international experts

---

[87] Doc. 104.
[88] www.un.int/iran/facts_about_peaceful_nuclear_program.pdf, page 53.
[89] Doc. 110.
[90] UN Doc CD/PV.1015, pp. 6-7.
[91] IAEA Doc. INFCIRC/640, 22 February 2005.

brought together by the IAEA for this exact purpose? Was any other country with similar technology prepared to be as flexible as Iran? Did the United States and its European allies seriously consider our detailed reply of 22 August 2006,[92] which, unlike their practice, provided a point-by-point reply to their 6 June package and made genuine proposals to address its shortcomings? All I know is that they even refused to refer to it in the present resolution.

Did they discuss the offer of an international consortium which was presented by Iran in the course of the September and October 2006[93] negotiations in Vienna and Berlin and was initially considered very promising, leading to public statements of progress after those meetings - a prognosis that was rapidly and astonishingly reversed even before the ministerial meeting of the five-plus-one?

Many other similar questions may be asked. But the answer to all of them will be the same, because what the United States, and apparently the EU-3 - in spite of what they told us during the negotiations - wanted, and the only outcome that they were and are ready to accept from these so-called negotiations, was - and still is - that Iran should 'make a binding commitment not to pursue fuel cycle activities', as it is phrased in package proposed by the EU3, of August 2005.[94]

We are here because we did not accept that unlawful demand, which, as many here already know, would not have been their last demand. At the same time, we were prepared to go to any length to allay their so-called proliferation concerns, in spite of the fact that we all know that these are no more than sheer unfounded and self-serving excuses. Indeed, old-hand proliferators and suppliers of chemical weapons and nuclear weapon technology can hardly have proliferation concerns.

The sponsors tell you that they do not trust our intentions. But the problem is that their 'intentionometer' has a rather abysmal record of chronic malfunction. Suffice it to say that the former United States Director of Central Intelligence, Robert Gates, in testimony before Congress in March 1992, [12] claimed that Iran was trying to acquire a nuclear weapons capability and added that this goal was unlikely to be achieved before the year 2000 - seven years ago. Later, in November of the same year, a draft National Intelligence Estimate by the same Central Intelligence Agency concluded that Iran was making progress on a nuclear arms programme and could develop a nuclear weapon by 2000 - seven years ago. Now, the same intelligence establishment is saying, not before 2015.

Accusing Iran of having 'the intention' of acquiring nuclear weapons has, since the early 1980s, been a tool used to deprive Iran of any nuclear technology, even a light water reactor or fuel for the American-built research reactor. I wonder which 'Iranian intention' or which 'proliferation concern' has prompted the main proponents of today's resolution to prevent Iran, for the past 27 years, from even acquiring civilian aircraft - or even spare parts for the civilian aircraft they sold to Iran, thereby jeopardizing the lives and safety of Iranian civilians, whom they hypocritically try to court these days - and, I might add, to no avail.

As IAEA Director General ElBaradei recently said,

'A lot of what you see about Iran right now is assessment of intentions… But one of the lessons we learned from Iraq is that we really need to be very, very

---

[92] Doc. 99.

[93] —— 'EU's Solana reports progress in Iran nuclear talks' *USA Today* (15 September 2006), www.usatoday.com/news/world/2006-09-15-iran-eu_x.htm?csp=34.

[94] IAEA Doc. INFCIRC/651.

careful coming to conclusions, because these issues make the difference between war and peace'.[95]

As we are talking about intentions, while the main proponents of the resolution may have self-servingly claimed that they doubt ours, they themselves have said and done plenty so that nobody in Iran or elsewhere in the world could have any illusions about theirs: one need only read the recent dangerously divisive statement by the Prime Minister of the United Kingdom. Or take a look at the 23 August report by the staff of the Intelligence Committee of the United States House of Representatives on Iran's nuclear programme.[96] That report was so dangerously misleading and so illustrative of the extent to which some war-mongers are prepared to go that it compelled the IAEA to officially dispute its allegations against Iran. In its letter, the IAEA called parts of the report 'outrageous and dishonest' and containing 'incorrect and misleading assertions', and it offered evidence to refute the report's central claims. The Agency stressed that the report even seriously distorted IAEA findings on Iran's nuclear activities.[97]

Let me conclude by reiterating that the Islamic Republic of Iran firmly believes that the days of weapons of mass murder have long passed, that these inhumane instruments of indiscriminate slaughter have not brought about internal stability or external security for anyone and that they will not be able to do so in the future.

Unlike some who despise the NPT and international law in general, we have a high stake in preserving, fully implementing, strengthening and universalizing the NPT. Today's decision does exactly the opposite; That should be no surprise because it was championed by a non-member of the NPT, coupled with its main benefactor, which made no secret of its contempt for this and other disarmament instruments. None of us has forgotten last year's World Summit when even the word 'disarmament' was removed by the famous 'red pen'.

By the same token, we believe that the days of bullying, pressure and intimidation by some nuclear weapon holders are long gone. We are told that we need to build confidence. Indeed, we all do in this tumultuous world. But confidence can only be built through respect for and the non-discriminatory application of the law. Those are the only objective criteria. Anything else would be to accept the whims of the powerful. International law and international treaties cannot be the subject of arbitrary, fluctuating and self-serving reinterpretations, readjustments or red lines even if they are connivingly imposed through resolutions. Such a precedent is dangerous for everyone.

The Security Council would go a long way in addressing its own confidence deficit by truly acting on behalf of the United Nations membership, as mandated by Article 24 of the Charter. Nearly two thirds of them are members of the Non-Aligned Movement or the Organization of Islamic Conference which, at the summit level, have reaffirmed that 'States' choices and decisions in the field of peaceful uses of nuclear technology and its fuel cycle policies must be respected',[98] and have 'expressed concern over… threats and pressures on Iran by certain circles to renounce its inalienable right to develop nuclear energy for peaceful purposes'.[99] They have also clarified where [13] the real threat to international peace and security does in fact lie, by, again at the summit level, 'expressing

---

[95] Newsweek Interview with Mohamed ElBaradei, 20 October 2006.
[96] 'Recognizing Iran as a Strategic Threat: An Intelligence Challenge for the United States' Staff Report of the House Permanent Select Committee on Intelligence Subcommittee on Intelligence Policy (23 August 2006), intelligence.house.gov/Media/PDFS/IranReport082206v2.pdf.
[97] Dan Glaister, 'IAEA says Congress report on Iran's nuclear capacity is erroneous and misleading' *The Guardian* (15 September 2006) www.guardian.co.uk/iran/story/0,,1873114,00.html.
[98] Doc. 146 (reference in the original).
[99] OIC Resolution 18/33-P (reference in the original).

grave concern over the acquisition of nuclear capability by Israel, which poses a serious and continuing threat to the security of neighbouring and other States'.

That is the real issue that States Members of the United Nations expected the Security Council to be seized of.

Document 17: Security Council Debate on Resolution 1747(2007)

S/PV.5647, 24 March 2007

[2] **The President**: The Security Council will now begin its consideration of the item on its agenda. The Council is meeting in accordance with the understanding reached in its prior consultations.

Members of the Council have before them document S/2007/170, which contains the text of a draft resolution submitted by France, Germany and the United Kingdom of Great Britain and Northern Ireland.

…

Mr. Al-Nasser (**Qatar**) (*spoke in Arabic*): The State of Qatar believes that Iran has the right to nuclear energy research and production for peaceful purposes. That is an inalienable right of Iran under articles I and II of the Treaty on the Non-Proliferation of Nuclear Weapons, that no one can deny. We do not doubt Iran's genuine intentions as regards the peaceful purposes of its nuclear programme.

We are deeply saddened that the Security Council is being forced to impose new sanctions on the Islamic Republic of Iran. We do not view sanctions as an appropriate means of pressure. On the contrary, sanctions can sometimes complicate matters and, in our opinion, signal another failure at diplomatic efforts. Continued pressure does not help to build confidence, which is already lost between the two parties; rather, it can sometimes have serious consequences, given the already volatile situation in that region of the world. The dead end that has been reached in the negotiations between the countries concerned and Iran makes it necessary for us to seek new prospects and to explore all possible means that could pave the way to a peaceful solution to this impasse through diplomatic means.

The State of Qatar is keen to see all States adhere to the Treaty on the Non-Proliferation of Nuclear Weapons. We believe that to be a bedrock principle from which we cannot deviate. Even as we voted against resolution 1696(2006),[100] we were absolutely clear that we were not expressing an opinion opposed to that principle; rather, we wanted to allow Iran more time to study the offer put to it by the group of six countries. We look forward to seeing specific proposals from both parties that can contribute to revitalizing the prospects for a diplomatic solution.

Addressing non-proliferation issues, which is the basis for the positive vote to be cast by the State of Qatar, should not be done selectively. We do not see the Council dealing with those issues with different criteria. In our view, the Council is required to follow the same approach towards countries that do not comply with their obligations under the NPT, as well as towards those that do not respect it in the first place. That is why we introduced a clear and direct proposal regarding the draft resolution on the establishment in the Middle East of a zone free of nuclear weapons and their means of delivery. We regret that the sponsors of that draft resolution did not take that proposal on board.

---

[100] Doc. 10.

[3] ...

Mr. Jenie (**Indonesia**): Indonesia is of the view that the purpose of the draft resolution is not to punish the Government or people of Iran, but to be a vehicle for persuading the Iranian Government to comply with previous resolutions of the Council and resolve outstanding issues with the International Atomic Energy Agency (IAEA). It must therefore be clear that the draft resolution is not a final, irrevocable position, but a reversible one.

...

Should Iran feel it to be necessary to move ahead towards a negotiated solution, the draft resolution provides that opportunity in accordance with the proposals made in June 2006,[101] which are still on the table and serve as the basis for operative paragraph 10 of the draft resolution. We therefore enjoin the Government of Iran to keep that door open, because through it lies a comprehensive negotiated agreement based on mutual respect and international confidence in the exclusively peaceful nature of Iran's nuclear programme.

The delegation of Indonesia notes that the draft resolution has accommodated some of the concerns of my Government and that several of our amendments were taken on board. Those include the reference to a Middle East free of weapons of mass destruction that firmly notes that we are concerned about the problem of non-proliferation in general and in the region in particular...

[4] ...

Finally, I wish to stress that the solution to the issue of Iran should in no way affect or change the inalienable rights of all parties to the NPT, including Iran, to develop and research the production and use of nuclear energy for peaceful purposes, without discrimination, in accordance with the Treaty. That remains an inalienable right of all State parties to the Treaty that should always be respected.

...

The President: I should like to make a statement in explanation of vote in my national capacity, as the representative of **South Africa**.

South Africa will vote in favour of the resolution before the Council today. Although far from ideal, it is a consequence of concern about the need to build international confidence in Iran's nuclear programme.

...

While South Africa recognizes that the Security Council may be called upon to impose coercive measures such as sanctions, we believe those measures should be utilized with great caution and only to support the resumption of political dialogue and negotiations to achieve a peaceful solution. South Africa's interventions in the Council have therefore focused on trying to de-escalate tensions, promote dialogue to establish confidence in the nuclear programme of Iran and ensure that the IAEA inspectors remain on the ground in Iran and that Iran remains part of the Nuclear Non-Proliferation Treaty.

South Africa has always been very clear, as a matter of principle, that the Security Council must remain within its mandate of addressing threats to international peace and security. If the sponsors of the resolution were convinced that the Iranian programme was a threat to international peace, then the Security Council should have been asked to take a decision on a draft that would have concentrated on that, and not to act as if the Iranian Government itself posed a threat to international peace and security.

South Africa proposed a number of constructive amendments to the draft resolution. Our purpose was to assist the Security Council to find language for a new resolution that

---

[101] Doc. 131.

matched the stated objectives of the sponsors that the resolution would be 'proportionate, incremental and reversible'.

[5] We remain deeply disappointed that not all our proposals were accommodated. The resolution does, however, correctly acknowledge that there is a need to respect the right of all countries, including Iran, to exploit the peaceful uses of nuclear technology, subject to appropriate safeguards. We are particularly pleased with the fact that the resolution now reaffirms the need of all States parties to the NPT to comply fully with all their obligations, which corresponds to our view that the twin obligations of nuclear disarmament and nuclear non-proliferation require our equal attention. After all, there is no basis for arguing that weapons of mass destruction are safe in some hands and not in others.

We note that the IAEA has been able to verify the non-diversion of declared nuclear material in Iran. However, we share the concern of the IAEA Director General that the Agency continues to be unable 'to reconstruct fully the history of Iran's nuclear programme and some of its components' because the necessary level of transparency and cooperation have not been provided by Iran.

...

Every effort must be made to resume dialogue and enter into meaningful negotiations to find a sustainable long-term solution to this matter, since no one will win through a process of confrontation that could lead to disastrous consequences in a highly volatile region.

...

A vote was taken by show of hands.

In favour: Belgium, China, Congo, France, Ghana, Indonesia, Italy, Panama, Peru, Qatar, Russian Federation, Slovakia, South Africa, United Kingdom of Great Britain and Northern Ireland, United States of America

The President: There were 15 votes in favour. The draft resolution has been adopted unanimously as resolution 1747(2007).[102]

...

Sir Emyr Jones Parry (**United Kingdom**): I would like to begin by reading out the text of a statement that has been agreed by the Foreign Ministers of China, France, Germany, Russia, the United Kingdom and the United States of America, with the support of the High Representative of the European Union. The statement reads as follows:

'The unanimous adoption of Security Council resolution 1747(2007) reflects the international community's profound concerns over Iran's nuclear programme. We deplore Iran's failure to comply with the earlier resolutions of the Security Council and the International Atomic Energy Agency, and we call upon Iran once again to comply fully with all its international obligations.

'We are committed to seeking a negotiated solution that would address the international community's concerns. The purpose of negotiations would be to reach a comprehensive agreement with Iran, based on mutual respect, that would re-establish international confidence in the exclusively peaceful nature of Iran's nuclear programme and would open the way to [6] improving relations and developing wider cooperation between Iran and all our countries.

'We recognize Iran's rights under the Treaty on the Non-Proliferation of Nuclear Weapons (NPT) to develop research, production and use of nuclear energy for peaceful purposes in conformity with its NPT obligations. In that respect, future arrangements, modalities and timing will be dealt with in negotiations.

---

[102] Doc. 12.

'Full transparency and cooperation by Iran with the International Atomic Energy Agency is essential in order to address outstanding concerns. We reiterate our full support for the Agency and its staff.

'We stand by our suspension-for-suspension proposal. That means that for the duration of negotiations - which would take place within an agreed time frame, extendable by mutual agreement - Iran would maintain an Agency-verified suspension, as required by Security Council resolution 1737(2006)[103] and, now, resolution 1747(2007). Security Council discussion of Iran's nuclear programme would also be suspended, as would the implementation of the measures adopted under the relevant Council resolutions.

'We reconfirm that the proposals we presented to Iran in June 2006 stay on the table. They include cooperation with Iran on civil nuclear energy, legally binding guarantees on the supply of nuclear fuel and wider political, security and economic cooperation. Those proposals remain on the table.

'We urge Iran to take this opportunity to engage with us all to find a negotiated way forward. Our proposals would bring far-reaching benefits to Iran and to the region, and they provide a means to address the international community's concerns while taking account of Iran's legitimate interests.

'In a region that has known too much instability and violence, let us find an agreed way forward that builds confidence and promotes peace and mutual respect. In that spirit, we propose further talks with the Islamic Republic of Iran to see if a mutually acceptable way can be found to open negotiations.'

That concludes the statement on behalf of the six Foreign Ministers. I should like now to make some remarks in my national capacity.

It is just short of a year since the Security Council first took action on the Iranian nuclear issue, following the referral of the issue to the Council by the International Atomic Energy Agency. Our concern throughout has been twofold: to promote prospects for a negotiated solution, on which suspension of enrichment by Iran depends; and, secondly, to reinforce the role of the Agency, as our resolution today again does.

Those concerns led to the elaboration of a detailed offer of long-term cooperation from the six nations whose Ministers' statement I have just read. But those Ministers also agreed to seek further Security Council action on Iran should our demands not be met.

Iran's continuing defiance prompted the adoption of resolution 1696(2006) in July 2006, setting the framework for the Council's actions, including a binding Chapter VII decision that Iran should suspend its enrichment-related and reprocessing activities. Despite that, Iran ignored the Council.

That led in turn to further Council action. On 23 December, the Security Council adopted - as today, by unanimity - resolution 1737(2006), reaffirming the mandatory requirement that Iran suspend its enrichment-related and reprocessing activities, and clarifying that Iran must also suspend construction of the heavy-water research reactor at Arak. It also introduced a number of measures aimed at restricting Iran's development of sensitive nuclear technologies and its development of ballistic missiles that could deliver them.

Those measures were an incremental and proportionate response to Iran's continued failure to comply with the requirements of resolution 1696(2006), aimed at persuading Iran that its interests were best served by putting in place the conditions necessary for discussions to seek a negotiated resolution of the issue.

---

[103] Doc. 11.

As requested in resolution 1737(2006), the Director General of the Agency, Mohamed ElBaradei, reported on 22 February that Iran had continued to pursue these sensitive technologies in defiance of its obligations under international law. This situation was a backdrop to the intensive and constructive [7] deliberations that have led to this resolution unanimously adopted today.

By adopting this resolution, we have continued our incremental and proportionate approach, increasing gradually the pressure on Iran to address the concerns shared across the international community. We have strengthened the restrictions on individuals closely associated with Iran's sensitive nuclear activities and with its ballistic missile programme. We have prohibited arms sales from Iran and urge vigilance over the supply of heavy weapons to Iran. We have also urged restraint in making finance available to the Government of Iran.

I should clarify that the United Kingdom's undertaking and understanding that the new resolution does not introduce any changes to the provisions in paragraph 15 of resolution 1737(2006). The asset freeze, therefore, does not prevent a person or entity designated in the annexes to resolution 1737(2006) and to this resolution from making payments due under a contract entered into force before that person or entity was listed in cases covered by paragraph 15.

This resolution, building upon resolutions 1696(2006) and 1737(2006), sends a unanimous and unambiguous signal to the Government and people of Iran. To both, we say that we prefer and are committed to the path of cooperation. But we say, also, that the path of proliferation by Iran is not one that the international community can accept. We want Iran to make the right choice - cooperation with the international community, which requires the removal of any doubt that Iran could develop nuclear weapons. The resolve of the Council is clear. Iran must make its choice.

Mr. De La Sablière (**France**):

...

Nobody in this Council wishes to deny Iran its rights or to prevent the Iranian people from benefiting from nuclear energy for peaceful purposes. All States parties to the Treaty on the Non-proliferation of Nuclear Weapons (NPT) have the right to the peaceful use of nuclear energy as long as they meet the non-proliferation obligations derived from articles I, II and III of the NPT. What the international community asks of Iran is that it fulfil these non-proliferation obligations. It is unacceptable that the Iranian authorities find pretexts to shirk their commitments made under the NPT.

By adopting resolution 1737(2006), the Security Council clearly indicated that it would suspend the sanctions put in place if Iran reverted to the complete suspension of all its enrichment and reprocessing activities. It also warned Iran, however, that it would take further measures, should Iran persist in its refusal to meet the demands of the international community.

The last report of the Director General of the IAEA[104] clearly showed that the Iranian leaders did not make the choice that the international community had hoped for. In the circumstances, the Security Council had no choice but to act.

The measures that the Security Council has adopted today are proportionate to Iran's actions. They are reversible. They are in line with the approach of progressively increasing the pressure applied by the Council for more than a year, in order to persuade the Iranian leaders to return to the conditions for negotiation and to restrict the development of the sensitive programmes undertaken.

[104] Doc. 47.

...

[8] These measures have been established in order to exert effective pressure on the Iranian authorities, while seeking to penalize the Iranian people as little as possible...

...

Mr. Wolff (**United States of America**): The United States is pleased that the Security Council has once again unanimously taken action against what is clearly a grave threat to international peace and security. The Iranian leadership's continued defiance of the Council in failing to comply with resolutions 1696(2006) and 1737(2006) requires that we uphold our responsibilities defined in the Charter of this esteemed body and take necessary action. While we hope that Iran responds to this resolution by complying with its international legal obligations, the United States is fully prepared to support additional measures in 60 days should Iran choose another course.

...

[9] The unanimous adoption today of resolution 1747(2007) sends a clear and unambiguous message to Iran: the regime's continued pursuit of a nuclear-weapons capability, in violation of its treaty obligations as well as its obligations as a State Member of the United Nations, will only further isolate Iran and make it less, not more, secure.

In the light of that history, it is not only appropriate, but the responsibility of the Security Council, to act. And we have done so in a careful and deliberate manner...

Iran called the Council's decisions invalid and an extralegal act, and vowed that the new resolution would not be an obstacle in the way of Iran's nuclear progress. Sadly, Iran continues to defy the will of the international community, the decisions of this Council and its obligations under international law. For that reason it is entirely appropriate and necessary that we have adopted stronger measures to persuade the regime to make its country more secure by abandoning its pursuit of nuclear weapons. Should Iran choose a different path, this resolution makes clear that we are prepared and willing to adopt additional measures. Indeed, in the face of Iran's continued defiance, the United States expects that the Council will continue to incrementally increase pressure on the Iranian Government.

Let me be clear, though, to the Iranian people: these measures that we are adopting today are in no way meant to punish the civilian population of Iran. Resolution 1747(2007) is properly tailored to target Iranian institutions and officials that support Iran's nuclear and missile programmes...

...

The decisions of the Iranian leadership, however, required the Council to act. It is our solemn responsibility to take measures which will not only halt the development of Iran's nuclear weapons programme, but encourage the leadership of Iran to choose a different path, which will benefit the entire Iranian nation - including its Government-professed aspiration for nuclear energy.

...

The Iranian leadership has claimed that this Council seeks to deprive Iran of its right to peaceful nuclear energy - and we may hear that again today. That is simply not true. The six Governments, including my own, that have been trying in vain to get to negotiations with the Iranians over the past year recognize Iran's right to peaceful, civil nuclear energy in conformity with all articles and obligations of the NPT...

[10] Iran's rejection of this offer sends a deeply troubling signal to the entire international community. Nonetheless, my Government also associates itself with the statement read by the United Kingdom reaffirming our offer and willingness to resolve this issue through negotiations.

The current path chosen by Iran's leadership poses a direct challenge to the very principles on which the United Nations was founded. Iran's leadership openly proclaims that the Council is 'illegal' and that its resolutions are 'torn pieces of paper'.[105] Iran's Supreme Leader has pledged that Iran would undertake 'illegal acts' if the Council proceeded with the adoption of this resolution. Article 2 of the Charter makes clear that all Members shall refrain in their international relations from the threat or use of force against the territorial integrity or political independence of any State. Calls by Iran's leaders to have Israel, a State Member of the United Nations, 'wiped off the map' stand in stark contrast to everything for which this body stands. That contrast is amplified by Iran's continued well-known role as one of the world's leading State sponsors of terrorism.

...

Mr. Churkin (**Russian Federation**): Russia voted in favour of the draft resolution submitted to the Security Council. The text was the outcome of the collective efforts of all the members of the Security Council and the concrete result of intensive consultations and complicated compromises. We are pleased to note that the intensive process of working on the text, in which the views expressed and proposals made by members of the Council were taken on board, has led to a text that is much more balanced and coherent in terms of the goals it sets out to achieve, compared to the initial draft.

The restrictions introduced by the resolution on cooperation with Iran, like those contained in the provisions of resolution 1737(2006), are aimed at eliminating the concerns that the International Atomic Energy Agency (IAEA) still has on the Iranian nuclear programme. These restrictions are in no way aimed at punishing Iran. The Council's decision has sent an unequivocal message to Tehran on the need for full cooperation with the IAEA and the Security Council. At the same time, the content of resolution 1747(2007) is unambiguous in that the door to negotiations with Iran remains open.

[11] ...

Another very important point: these measures, just as in resolution 1737(2006), have been imposed in accordance with Article 41 of the Charter and consequently preclude the possibility of the use of force. One of the provisions of the resolution stipulates that any further steps taken by the Security Council, if necessary, will also be exclusively peaceful ones. We remain convinced that the effective resolution of the Iranian nuclear problem can be achieved only through political and diplomatic efforts.

We deem of great significance the fact that the new resolution does not in any way alter the provisions of paragraph 15 of resolution 1737(2006). The freezing of financial activities will therefore not prevent payments from being made by the natural or legal persons listed in the annexes to resolution 1737(2006) or in the resolution just adopted, payments under contracts entered into before the aforementioned persons were included on the list on the grounds outlined in paragraph 15 of resolution 1737(2006). In other words, the activities authorized by the Security Council in the area of trade and economic cooperation can continue.

...

---

[105] —— 'Iran sanctions go to UN council' *BBC News* (15 March 2007), news.bbc.co.uk/2/hi/middle_east/6452545. stm.

Mr. Wang Guangya (**China**):

...

Developments related to Iran's nuclear programme are currently a source of concern. China respects and recognizes Iran's right to the peaceful use of nuclear energy. However, we are also disappointed that the Iranian side has failed to respond positively to the requests of the International Atomic Energy Agency and the Security Council. Under these circumstances, we support the Security Council's taking of further, appropriate actions aimed at urging the Iranian side to suspend enrichment-related activities in order to bring the process back onto the negotiation track.

At the same time, China believes that any measure taken should aim at safeguarding the international non-proliferation mechanism and at maintaining international and regional peace and stability. Actions taken by the Security Council should be appropriate, incremental and proportionate. They should help enhance diplomatic efforts rather than aggravate conflicts and lead to confrontation. Given that the resolution that has just been adopted basically reflected the views of China that I have just expressed, we voted in favour of it.

It needs to be pointed out that the purpose of the new resolution is not to punish Iran but to urge it to return to negotiations and reactivate diplomatic efforts. The relevant sanctions measures should neither harm the Iranian people nor affect normal economic, trade and financial exchanges between Iran and other countries...

[12] The new resolution and the sanctions measures in resolution 1737(2006) are all reversible. If Iran suspends its enrichment-related and reprocessing activities and complies with the relevant resolutions of the International Atomic Energy Agency (IAEA) and the Security Council, the Security Council shall suspend, and even terminate, the sanctions measures.

... we should bear in mind the following principles in seeking solutions to the Iran nuclear issue.

First, in handling the Iran nuclear issue, safeguarding international non-proliferation mechanisms and maintaining international and regional peace and stability remain the premise and ultimate objective. No actions should deviate from that goal.

Secondly, it is essential to keep the process on the path of dialogue and negotiation and to insist on seeking a peaceful solution through political and diplomatic efforts. It is therefore particularly important to reinforce diplomatic efforts outside the Security Council.

Thirdly, we should firmly safeguard the international non-proliferation mechanism. The IAEA remains the main framework for solving the Iran nuclear issue. Its authority and role should therefore be safeguarded and strengthened.

Fourthly, it is necessary to handle, in a balanced manner, the relations between the peaceful use of nuclear energy and non-proliferation. The international community should recognize Iran's right to the peaceful use of nuclear energy. Iran also has the obligation to accept effective supervision by the IAEA and to resolve outstanding issues through cooperation with the IAEA, so as to prove the peaceful nature of its nuclear programme and establish international confidence in that regard.

Fifthly, all the parties concerned should act on the basis of equality and mutual respect, strengthen dialogue and communication, increase trust, reduce doubts and remove each other's concerns, so as to create the necessary atmosphere and conditions for the settlement of this issue.

Sixthly, the current urgent task for all the parties is to show full flexibility and creatively seek to resume negotiations. The June 2006 proposal put forward by the six countries is still on the table. The time-out proposal by IAEA Director General ElBaradei and the establishment of a mechanism for talks that includes Iran also deserve our consideration.

...

[13] Mr. Verbeke (**Belgium**): Belgium voted in favour of resolution 1747(2007) and welcomes its unanimous adoption. Belgium regrets that Iran has not met the requirements of the Security Council by suspending its uranium-enrichment activities as well as its work on all heavy-water-related projects. Belgium deplores the lack of cooperation and transparency on the part of Iran that led the International Atomic Energy Agency to conclude, on 22 January [*sic*], that it was not in a position to provide assurances about the absence of undeclared nuclear material and activities in Iran or the exclusively peaceful purpose of its nuclear programme.

The new resolution serves to demonstrate the resolve of the international community to monitor the integrity of the nuclear non-proliferation regime and also reaffirms its desire to create the framework within which to search for a negotiated solution.

In that regard, Belgium launches a strong appeal to Iran to pay due heed to the offer made to it in June 2006, in order to implement a long-term and lasting agreement.

The new resolution reflects the unanimous resolve expressed by the Security Council, as stated in resolution 1737(2006) and reaffirmed in the current resolution, to take appropriate additional measures since Iran has ignored the requirements of the Security Council and the International Atomic Energy Agency. We attach particular importance to the principles of proportionality and reversibility that are provided for within the resolution. Those principles reflect the [14] resolve of the Council, while indicating to Iran that another path remains open.

...

Mr. Motaki (**Islamic Republic of Iran**): This is the fourth time in the last 12 months that, in an unwarranted move orchestrated by a few of its permanent members, the Security Council is being abused to take an unlawful, unnecessary and unjustifiable action against the peaceful nuclear programme of the Islamic Republic of Iran, which presents no threat to international peace and security and therefore falls outside the Council's Charter-based mandate.

As we have stressed time and again, Iran's nuclear programme is completely peaceful. We have expressed our readiness, taken unprecedented steps and offered several serious proposals to address and allay any possible concern in that regard. Indeed, there has been no doubt on our part from the beginning, nor should there be any on the part of the Council, that all the schemes of the sponsors of the resolution are dictated by narrow national considerations and are aimed at depriving the Iranian people of their inalienable rights, rather than emanating from any so-called proliferation concerns.

In order to give this scheme a semblance of international legitimacy, its initiators first manipulated the Board of Governors of the International Atomic Energy Agency (IAEA) and - as they acknowledged themselves - coerced some of its members to vote against Iran on the Board, and then have taken advantage of their substantial economic and political power to pressure and manipulate the Security Council to adopt three unwarranted resolutions within 8 months.

Undoubtedly, those resolutions cannot indicate universal acceptance, particularly when the heads of State of the nearly two thirds of the States Members of the United

Nations that also belong to the Non-Aligned Movement and the Organization of the Islamic Conference (OIC) supported Iran's position as recently as September 2006[106] and expressed concern about the policies pursued within the Security Council. Those resolutions do not even reflect the views of the Council's own 15 members, since most of them were not thoroughly informed about - let alone engaged in - the discussions held in secret meetings where only a few parties, among them non-Council members, made decisions for the entire Council.

This is not the first time that the Security Council has asked Iran to relinquish its rights...

...

[15] There is every reason to assert that the Security Council's consideration of the Iranian peaceful nuclear programme has no legal basis, since the referral of the case to the Council and then the adoption of resolutions fail to meet the minimum standards of legality. Iran's peaceful nuclear activities cannot, by any stretch of law, fact or logic, be characterized as a threat to peace. Rather, certain members of the Security Council decided to hijack the case from the IAEA, the principal specialized technical organ in charge of the issue, and to politicize it.

How can Iran's peaceful nuclear programme be considered in the Security Council while Iran has carried out all its obligations and cooperated to the fullest extent possible, far more than it is obliged to do in accordance with its treaty obligations, namely those under the Treaty on the Non-Proliferation of Nuclear Weapons (NPT) and the Safeguards Agreement?[107] Is it not simply because the IAEA could not find any diversion from lawful and peaceful purposes? How could one expect the IAEA to prove a negative fact?

In order to achieve the politically motivated and unlawful goal of depriving Iran of its inalienable right to nuclear technology, attempts have been made to manufacture evidence. According to a recent report in an American newspaper, 'most United States intelligence shared with the United Nations nuclear watchdog agency has proved inaccurate and none has led to significant discoveries inside Iran'. The same news article also quotes a senior IAEA official as saying 'since 2002, pretty much all the intelligence that's come to us has proved to be wrong'.

However, in order to enable the IAEA to reach this conclusion, Iran had to implement transparency measures outside all IAEA safeguards and protocols and allow the IAEA inspectors to make over 20 visits to its sensitive military sites which had no connection whatsoever with its nuclear programme.

Would any member of this Council agree to do likewise? Are the permanent members of this Council even prepared to inform the international public of the number of centrifuges they own? In fact, over the last four years, the IAEA has conducted more than 2,100 person-days of scrutiny of all Iranian nuclear facilities. All reports by the IAEA since November 2003 until now have been indicative of the peaceful nature of the [16] Iranian nuclear programme. The Agency confirmed in 2003, and has maintained since then, that to date, there is no evidence that the previously undeclared nuclear material and activities were related to a nuclear weapons programme.

On several occasions, the Agency concluded that all the declared nuclear material in Iran has been accounted for, and therefore such material is not diverted to prohibited activities. As recently as February 2007, the IAEA Director General stated in his report

---

[106] Doc. 146.
[107] Doc. 4.

(S/2007/100, annex, enclosure) that 'pursuant to its NPT Safeguards Agreement, Iran has been providing the Agency with access to declared nuclear material and facilities, and has provided the required nuclear material accountancy reports in connection with such material and facilities'. The same report also indicates that 'the Agency is able to verify the non-diversion of declared nuclear material in Iran'. The Director General also indicated to the Board of Governors on 5 March 2007 that the Agency has seen no 'industrial capacity to produce weapon-usable nuclear material, which is an important consideration in assessing the risk'.[108]

It is very unfortunate that the Security Council, under the manifest pressure of a few of its permanent members, persists in trying to deprive a nation of its 'inalienable right' to develop nuclear technology for peaceful purposes, while that nation has met, and continues to honour, its international obligations. The Security Council's decision to try to coerce Iran into suspension of its peaceful nuclear programme is a gross violation of Article 25 of the Charter of the United Nations and contradicts the Iranian people's right to development and right to education.

While Member States have agreed, in accordance with Article 25 of the Charter, to accept and carry out the decisions of the Security Council in accordance with the present Charter, the Security Council cannot pressure countries into submitting either to its decisions taken in bad faith or to its demands negating the fundamental purposes and principles of the Charter of the United Nations.

Likewise, as the International Court of Justice held in its 1971 Advisory Opinion,[109] Member States are required to comply with its decisions only if they are in accordance with the Charter of the United Nations. Does the Charter authorize the Security Council to require States Members of the United Nations to give up their basic rights emanating from treaties? To do that would violate established principles of international treaty law and the principle set forth in the Preamble to the Charter, namely, to establish conditions under which justice and respect for treaty obligations are to be maintained.

Who could deny that depriving a whole nation of higher education in specific fields and of the benefits of nuclear technology for humanitarian and civil uses is contrary to the basic right of all people to education and development? Is not that an alarmingly discriminatory approach vis-à-vis knowledge and development? How could an organ of the United Nations, established to maintain peace and security, be manipulated by certain States not only to act contrary to the fundamental purposes and principles of the Charter, but also to aggravate an issue that could be easily resolved into an international crisis? However, it is evident that such an approach will strengthen the resolve of developing countries to expedite their independence-seeking efforts and attain even greater scientific and technological achievements.

Although those who voted in favour of the resolution just adopted concerning Iran's peaceful nuclear programme did not even bother to listen to my country's positions and explanations before the vote, I would like to highlight a number of elements of that resolution for the record and for the awakened global public opinion.

First, by establishing sanctions, the resolution is punishing a country that, according to the IAEA, has never diverted its nuclear programme. The resolution punishes a country that has been a committed party to the NPT, with all of its nuclear facilities monitored by

---

[108] UN News Center Press Release, 'UN atomic watchdog agency reports stalemate over Iran's nuclear programme' 5 March 2007.
[109] *Legal Consequences for States of the Continued Presence of South Africa in Namibia (South West Africa) notwithstanding Security Council Resolution 276(1970)* [1971] ICJ Rep 16.

IAEA inspectors and their cameras. The resolution imposes sanctions on a country that has fulfilled all of its commitments under the NPT and the IAEA safeguards, and demands nothing more than its inalienable rights under the Treaty. Could there be any better way to undermine an important multilateral instrument that deals directly with international peace and security? Is not this action by the Security Council, in and of itself, a grave threat to international peace and security?

Secondly, the resolution clearly departs from the stated claims of its sponsors. By targeting my country's defence, economic and educational institutions, it is pursuing objectives far beyond Iran's peaceful nuclear [17] programme. The sanctions provided for in the resolution are clearly targeting an independent, proud and tireless nation with thousands of years of culture and civilization. What can the harming of hundreds of thousands of depositors in Bank Sepah, which has an 80-year history in Iran, mean other than a confrontation with ordinary Iranians?

Thirdly, the resolution has been adopted at a time when not only have all rational proposals and initiatives to return to a negotiated solution been neglected, but also certain countries have not even allowed such proposals to be presented. Iran has always been ready for time-bound and unconditional negotiations aimed at finding a mutually acceptable solution. Iran has done its best to achieve that objective and has presented numerous proposals to provide necessary assurances about the peaceful nature of its nuclear programme. In the past several weeks, other proposals have been advanced, each of which could have provided an opportunity to break the current stalemate and to lead to a rational and just resolution. The only interpretation that can be made of the rush to adopt this resolution and prevent negotiations is that there are ulterior motives on the part of the sponsors and a lack of political will to find solutions.

Finally, the resolution has been adopted against Iran's peaceful nuclear programme even as the major nuclear powers continue to flout the persistent demand of the international community for nuclear disarmament and instead jeopardize international peace and security by developing new generations of those weapons and threatening to use them.

...

It has been clear from the outset that there are only two alternatives in dealing with Iran's peaceful nuclear programme: cooperation and interaction, or confrontation and conflict. The Islamic Republic of Iran, confident of the peaceful nature of its nuclear programme, has always insisted on the first alternative. Iran does not seek confrontation, nor does it want anything beyond its inalienable rights. I can assure the Council that pressure and intimidation will not change Iranian policy. If certain countries have pinned their hopes on the possibility that repeated resolutions would weaken the resolve of the great Iranian nation, they should not doubt that they have once again faced a catastrophic intelligence and analytical failure vis-à-vis the Iranian people's Islamic revolution.

...

Document 18: Security Council Debate on Resolution 1803(2008)

S/PV.5848, 3 March 2008

...

[2] Mr. Khazaee (**Islamic Republic of Iran**): The international community is once again witnessing the credibility of the Security Council, whose primary responsibility is to maintain international peace and security, being readily downgraded to a mere tool of the national foreign policy of just a few countries. The Council once more has been pushed to take unlawful action against a proud and resolute nation merely because that nation is defending its legal rights enshrined in international instruments. Today's action by some members of the Security Council against Iran's peaceful nuclear programme, along with the measures taken in this regard in the past, do not meet the minimum standards of legitimacy and legality for the following reasons.

First, Iran's peaceful nuclear programme was brought to the Security Council in violation of the Agency's Statute. Iran had not violated, and therefore had not been in non-compliance with, its comprehensive safeguards agreement[110] under the Treaty on the Non-Proliferation of Nuclear Weapons (NPT). Iran signed the additional protocol[111] in 2003, and began its voluntary implementation. That continued for two and a half years. Iran was therefore not obliged to implement its provisions prior to 2003. Our country accepted the modified Code 3.1 of the subsidiary arrangement in 2003 and had no obligation to implement it prior to that date. Therefore, Iran was only obliged, according to the comprehensive safeguards agreement, to inform the International Atomic Energy Agency (IAEA) 180 days prior to feeding nuclear material into its facilities. We informed the IAEA about the uranium conversion facility by inviting the Agency's Director General to visit in the year 2000 - that is, four years prior to its operation in 2004 and four years before Iran was obliged to do so.

Secondly, Iran's nuclear programme has been, is and will remain absolutely peaceful and in no way poses any threat to international peace and security, and therefore does not fall within the purview of the Security Council. There is solid evidence and concrete arguments attesting to the exclusively peaceful nature of Iran's nuclear programme. In that regard, I would like to draw the Council's attention to the following three points.

The peaceful nature of Iran's nuclear programme has been confirmed by each and every IAEA report in the past several years, including the most recent one, which clearly stresses that

> 'The Agency has been able to continue to verify the non-diversion of declared nuclear material in Iran. Iran has provided the Agency with access to declared nuclear material and has [3] provided the required nuclear material accountancy reports'.[112]

As the latest example, the IAEA report of 22 February 2008 clearly attests to the exclusively peaceful nature of the nuclear programme of the Islamic Republic of Iran, both in the past and at present, and serves to strongly and unambiguously support our country's long-standing position that the allegations raised by a few States against the peaceful nuclear programme of the Islamic Republic of Iran have been entirely

---

[110] Doc. 4.
[111] Doc. 5.
[112] Doc. 51.

groundless. In the work plan concluded between Iran and the IAEA in August 2007,[113] it was also emphasized that

'The Agency has been able to verify the non-diversion of the declared nuclear materials at the enrichment facilities in Iran and has therefore concluded that it remains in peaceful use.'

On the basis of ideological and strategic grounds, Iran categorically rejects the development, stockpiling and use of nuclear weapons, as well as all other weapons of mass destruction. That fundamental position has been reiterated by every senior Iranian official on numerous occasions. The Supreme Leader of the Islamic Republic of Iran has strongly stressed that position before through a religious verdict - a fatwa - and once again reiterated the same principled position during Mr. ElBaradei's recent visit to Tehran. The President of the Islamic Republic of Iran has emphasized repeatedly that Iran's nuclear programme has been and will remain absolutely peaceful, and that Iran is a leading country in international efforts to oppose nuclear weapons and all other weapons of mass destruction.

The IAEA Director General has stressed in his various statements that 'the Agency does not have any data or evidence indicating that Iran is trying to develop nuclear weapons'. He has also said that 'there is no evidence Iran's enrichment of uranium is intended for a military nuclear programme'. In the wake of the national intelligence estimate report of the United States,[114] which reversed many of its previous baseless allegations against Iran's nuclear programme, the IAEA Director General stressed that Iran had been 'vindicated in saying it has not been working on a weapons programme'.

Thirdly, in addition, the actions of the Security Council are unjustifiable because the main pretext on the basis of which consideration of Iran's peaceful nuclear programme was imposed on the Security Council - namely, the outstanding issues - is now resolved and closed. The sponsors of today's resolution have argued in the past that Iran's peaceful nuclear programme should be dealt with by the Security Council due to unresolved outstanding questions. In order not to leave any stone unturned in its cooperation with the IAEA and to remove this much ballyhooed yet baseless pretext, Iran agreed to work with the Agency on a work plan to address and resolve the outstanding issues. In that regard, the text of the 'Understandings of the Islamic Republic of Iran and the IAEA on the Modalities of Resolution of the Outstanding Issues' was negotiated and finally concluded in August 2007.

...

[4] Finally, the latest report by the Agency, circulated on 22 February 2008, clearly declared the resolution and closure of all outstanding issues and emphasized in its paragraph 53 that 'The Agency has been able to conclude that answers provided by Iran, in accordance to the work plan, are consistent with its findings' and 'considers those questions no longer outstanding'. Additionally, the IAEA Director General declared the resolution of all outstanding issues in his remarks after the release of the report and said, 'We have managed to clarify all the remaining outstanding issues, including the most important issue, which is the scope and nature of Iran's enrichment programme'.[115]

---

[113] Doc. 6.
[114] Doc. 138.
[115] UN News Centre, 'Outstanding issues remain for Iran, despite progress – UN atomic watchdog chief', 22 February 2008, www.un.org/apps/news/storyAr.asp?NewsID=25731&Cr=iran&Cr1=. The report continues: 'But the agency has yet to get to the bottom of the country's alleged past weaponization studies, he said'.

While it was estimated that at least 18 months would be needed for the work plan to be implemented, Iran's unwavering and full cooperation with the Agency made it possible for the work plan to be implemented in less than six months.

It is worth mentioning that, based on the initial agreement with the Agency, we were only supposed to address the past remaining issues. Nevertheless, as a sign of good will and in line with its robust cooperation with the IAEA, the Islamic Republic of Iran considered the present issues as well. As a result, two important legal documents - the 'Safeguards Approach Document' and 'Facility Attachment' for Fuel Enrichment Plant in Natanz - were negotiated, concluded and finally put into force on 30 September 2007. Accordingly, the implementation of those documents has provided necessary assurances for the verification of enrichment activities in Iran for the present time and in the future.

By resolving the outstanding issues with regard to its past activities, on the one hand, and, on the other, by conducting all its present activities, including enrichment, under the full and continuous monitoring of the Agency on the basis of the IAEA Statute, the NPT and the comprehensive safeguards agreement, the Islamic Republic of Iran has removed any so-called concerns or ambiguities with regard to its peaceful nuclear activities in the past and present.

Now that the work plan has been fully implemented and the outstanding issues have been resolved, there exists no justification for the continuation of the politically motivated and misleading call of 'lack of confidence' by a few countries, countries whose number hardly amounts to four among 192 Member States of the United Nations but who always mischievously proclaim themselves to be speaking on behalf of the international community or the whole world.

The IAEA Director General said on 10 September 2007 that 'Resolving all outstanding verification issues ... would go a long way towards building the confidence of the international community in the peaceful nature of Iran's past nuclear programme.'

Indeed, those who did not want to allow the Agency to discharge its technical duties spared no efforts to undermine the momentum generated by the conclusion and implementation of the work plan and resorted to a systematic and relentless campaign of false claims, propaganda, intimidation and pressure aimed at the Agency, its Director General, some members of the Security Council and the work plan. This unhealthy and ill-intended campaign prompted a senior official of the IAEA to stress that 'Since 2002, pretty much all the intelligence that's come to us [from the US] has proved to be wrong'. The so-called alleged-studies issue is an example of such a fabrication and misinformation campaign.

While those baseless allegations - the alleged study - had not been an outstanding issue between Iran and the IAEA, a very organized and pre-planned propaganda campaign began even before the release of the latest IAEA report in order to eclipse the landmark accomplishment that Iran has made in its cooperation with the Agency in resolving the outstanding issues.

As stressed in the work plan, 'Iran reiterated that it considers the ... alleged studies as politically motivated and baseless allegations ... [but] as a sign of good will and cooperation with the Agency, [stated that] upon receiving all related documents [Iran] will review and inform the Agency of its assessment.'

The IAEA reports, particularly the most recent one, together with the statements of the Agency's officials, clearly indicate that the Iranian nation is committed to its international obligations and, at the same time, persistent in pursuing and exercising its legal rights.

...

[5] Undoubtedly, the full implementation of the work plan, and thus the resolution and closure of the outstanding issues, have eliminated the most basic pretexts and allegations on the basis of which Iran's peaceful nuclear programme was referred to the Security Council. The Security Council's involvement and the actions it has taken so far in that regard have been unwarranted and unconstructive, and have only damaged the credibility of the IAEA.

Iran's peaceful nuclear programme should be dealt with solely by the Agency. I wish to draw the Security Council's attention to the very important point that, based on the very last paragraph of the work plan,

> '[t]he Agency and Iran agreed that after the implementation of the above work plan and the agreed modalities for resolving the outstanding issues, the implementation of safeguards in Iran will be conducted in a routine manner'.

Therefore, the consideration of Iran's peaceful nuclear programme in no way falls within the purview of the Security Council. In fact, based on the IAEA reports and as a result of Iran's cooperation and the closure of the outstanding questions, not only does there remain no single reason or shred of legality for any new action by the Council, but also the illegality of the previous actions of the Council have become more abundantly clear.

Much has been said about suspension. Iran cannot and will not accept a requirement which is legally defective and politically coercive. History tells us that no amount of pressure, intimidation and threat will be able to coerce our nation into giving up its basic and legal rights. We have never attempted to impose our will on others; equally, we will never allow others to impose their unjust demands on us. We do not consider the call for suspension legitimate for, among others, the following reasons.

First, as we have stressed over and over again, no Government has the desire or the authority to suspend the exercise of the legal rights of its nation. Any demand from a nation to do so would be politically incorrect and legally flawed.

Second, neither in the IAEA's Statute, nor in the NPT safeguards, nor even in the Additional Protocol are enrichment and reprocessing prohibited or restricted. There is even no limit for the level of enrichment in the said documents.

Third, in all resolutions of the Board of Governors of the IAEA, suspension was considered to be a non-legally binding, voluntary and confidence-building measure.

Fourth, suspension was in place for more than two years and the IAEA, in each and every report from November 2003 to February 2006,[116] repeatedly verified that Iran had fully suspended what it had agreed to suspend. During that period, it became clear that those insisting on suspension were indeed aiming to prolong and ultimately perpetuate it, and consequently to prevent the Iranian nation from exercising its legal rights.

Fifth, the attempt to make the suspension mandatory through the Security Council has been, from the outset, against the fundamental principles of international law, the non-proliferation Treaty and IAEA Board resolutions. The Security Council's resolutions that made the suspension mandatory also flout the stated position of the overwhelming majority of the international community.

Sixth, unquestionably, with the resolution of the outstanding issues, with the IAEA's repeated conclusion of non-diversion in Iran's nuclear activities and with Iran's nuclear activities under the full and continuous monitoring of the Agency, there remains no pretext for the illegal request for suspension.

---

[116] Doc. 35-Doc. 42.

Seventh, the Security Council's decision to coerce Iran into suspension of its peaceful nuclear programme is also a gross violation of Article 25 of the [6] Charter. While Member States have agreed, in accordance with the said Article, to accept and carry out the decisions of the Security Council in accordance with the Charter, the Security Council cannot coerce countries into submitting either to its decisions taken in bad faith or to its demands negating the fundamental purposes and principles of the Charter.

Eighth, we need to enrich uranium to provide fuel for the tens of nuclear reactors that we are building or planning to build in order to meet the growing needs of our country for energy. There has never been nor will there ever be guarantees that our needs for fuel will be completely provided for by foreign sources. It is worth mentioning that there is no single document that serves as a legally binding international instrument for the assurance of nuclear supplies to guarantee fuel for nuclear power plants.

...

[7] Mr. Kumalo (**South Africa**): South Africa regrets that the sponsors of the draft resolution have persisted with the same substantive text that they had tabled before the latest report of the Director General of the International Atomic Energy Agency (IAEA) was even issued and hence, the draft resolution appears not to adequately take into account the progress made on the basis of the work plan agreed between the IAEA and Iran.

Moreover, the adoption of the new draft resolution, which imposes further punitive sanctions, could apparently not even be postponed until the IAEA Board of Governors had a full opportunity to consider the matter and take account of the verbal update of the Director General of the IAEA. That gives the international community the impression that the verification work and important progress made by the Agency is virtually irrelevant to the sponsors of this draft resolution.

The rationale for bringing the Iran issue to the Security Council in the first place was, we were told, to reinforce the decisions of the IAEA and to enhance its authority, and yet the current draft resolution does not accurately reflect what is happening at the IAEA. We are seriously concerned about the implications of this situation for the credibility of the Security Council, and the only reason we will vote in favour of the resolution is to preserve the previous decisions of the Council that Iran has not fully implemented.

The IAEA is the only international authority that can verify and provide the necessary assurances as to the peaceful nature of Iran's nuclear programme. It is therefore unfortunate that the Security Council gives the impression that it is in such great haste to decide on a series of further punitive sanctions that it does not wish even to consider the significant progress being made through the IAEA to provide the international community with important factual information on the implementation of the Nuclear Non-Proliferation Treaty (NPT) safeguards in Iran.

The report by the IAEA Director General issued on 22 February 2008 clearly shows that all outstanding safeguards issues, which are also included in the work plan between the IAEA and Iran, have been clarified due to the cooperation between Iran and the IAEA. The IAEA has thus far not found any evidence of diversion, and all material has been accounted for. Furthermore, those issues that originally gave rise to serious concern [8] resulting in the demand for the confidence-building measures, including suspending the uranium enrichment programme, have now also been clarified.

On the basis of the factual situation available to us we also have to recognize that since the adoption of resolution 1747(2007)[117] in March of last year, which South Africa

---

[117] Doc. 12.

supported, the situation has further changed following the release of the United States National Intelligence Estimate (NIE), which concluded that Iran does not have a current nuclear weapons programme. The NIE seems consistent with the IAEA's findings to date.

To the extent that all the outstanding issues have now been clarified, at least there ought to be increased confidence in the peaceful nature of the Iranian nuclear programme. It is important to allow the verification process to proceed on its current course.

Also, given the context of the recent allegations of weaponization activities, the need for continued factual and reliable information about Iran's current nuclear activities, based on increased access by and cooperation with the IAEA, can be said to be all the more important.

It is important not to jeopardize any of the gains made. Rather, we should seek to build on the progress made through systematic and continued verification work by the IAEA. This approach will help to establish the facts and encourage negotiations among concerned parties with a view to reducing tension and further escalation. Given the confidence deficit that existed earlier, we need to move forward in a responsible and balanced manner because we are dealing with a highly sensitive matter that can have serious implications in a volatile region.

...

The suspension of enrichment activities may under no circumstances become a goal in itself. In addition, it is incumbent on the Council to assure Iran that the call for suspension is not a smokescreen for any indefinite suspension or termination. In this regard, it would also be important to terminate the sanctions once the IAEA has addressed the remaining issues.

We would have preferred that the resolution not contain the controversial provision that allows for searches of certain Iranian vessels and aircraft, even subject to very strict limitations, as this could spark confrontation and further threaten international peace and security. Furthermore, the restrictions on dual-use goods and on loans and credits must not be allowed to have a negative impact on the civilian population of Iran. Members of the Security Council that will vote in favour of the current resolution, including South Africa, have a special obligation to the Iranian people and must exercise the highest degree of scrutiny and oversight of the implementation of sanctions to ensure that there are no unintended consequences and that the focus remains solely on the nuclear programme.

Whilst we have decided to vote for this resolution, it is imperative that we should now work creatively to defuse the confrontation in order to allow for a resumption of negotiations towards a sustainable, peaceful solution of this issue.

Finally, South Africa wishes to reaffirm the principle that once the peaceful nature of the Iran nuclear programme has been establish, Iran will enjoy the rights and responsibilities that any member of the NPT also enjoys.

Mr. Dabbashi (**Libyan Arab Jamahiriya**):

...

[9] Non-proliferation and disarmament together form a single comprehensive issue which should be dealt with without selectivity. All States without exception must submit their nuclear facilities to the International Atomic Energy Agency (IAEA) safeguards regime. We deplore the fact that the Security Council has not attached adequate importance to the issue of Israel's nuclear weapons, in spite of the fact that the Israelis are refusing to accede to the NPT or to submit their facilities to the IAEA safeguards regime.

...

... The Council's selectivity has given rise to questions about the Council's true objectives.

Our commitment to nuclear non-proliferation must not make us forget the right of all States parties to the NPT - including the Islamic Republic of Iran - to use nuclear energy for peaceful purposes and to acquire and develop related technology. The 22 February 2008 report of the IAEA Director General shows that essential progress has been made on the Iranian nuclear issue and that the majority of pending issues have been resolved. It also shows that there is now greater clarity with regard to Iran's declared nuclear programme. It was our hope that those positive developments would be taken into account and that negotiations and diplomatic contacts would be continuing with a view to resolving contentious issues and with a view to reinforcing the status of the IAEA as the appropriate body to deal with this problem.

For our part, we did not agree with other Council members about the usefulness of a resolution imposing additional sanctions on Iran, or that this would help us achieve a solution; it might instead cause the situation to deteriorate. We had asked that the text reflect the content of the latest report of the IAEA Director General and that the draft resolution address the Iranian nuclear programme in the context of concerns related to the Middle East in general.

Because the countries that formulated the text of the draft resolution before us have taken into consideration some of the concerns we share with other members - and while, although the majority of Council members consider that it is useful to adopt a draft resolution of this kind, we do not share that view - we have decided to join the unanimous opinion in the Council and to vote in favour of the draft resolution, so that the Security Council can speak with a single voice.

...

[10] Mr. Natalegawa (**Indonesia**):

...

In determining the right course of action with regard to the issue under discussion, Indonesia has been guided by the important information contained in the latest report of the Director General of IAEA, issued on 22 February 2008, which revealed several key findings.

...

We have carefully considered both the report and the draft resolution before the Council today. With regard to the outstanding issues, we note that the Agency considered that all remaining outstanding issues contained in the work plan, with the exception [11] of one issue, have been resolved. The report stated that, contrary to the decisions of the Security Council, Iran has not suspended its enrichment-related activities and, in addition, has started the development of new-generation centrifuges and continued its construction of the IR-40 reactor and its operation of the heavy water production plant. For the remaining issue - that is, the alleged weaponization studies - the report of the IAEA clearly noted that the Agency has not detected the use of nuclear material. However, the report also stated that the Agency is not yet in a position to determine the full nature of Iran's nuclear programme. It implies, therefore, that some specific demands stipulated in resolutions 1737(2006) and 1747(2007) have not been met. However, it is important to note that notable progress has been made in resolving the outstanding issues between Iran and the IAEA, as demanded by those resolutions.

We have been keen to ensure that there is synergy and complementarity between the report and the IAEA's efforts generally, on the one hand, and the letter and spirit of the draft resolution, on the other. We cannot fail to note the well-calibrated nature of the report - recognizing important progress in its cooperation with the Agency as well as the facts of Iran's lack of compliance with Security Council resolutions. It depicts well the complexity and the mixed picture of the issue. It had been our expectation that the draft resolution would reflect those complex dynamics and mixed findings and not succumb to an overly one-dimensional characterization of where we are today.

We note that the additional sanctions in the present draft resolution have been described as being incremental, targeted at non-proliferation areas and reversible, and that the Council would suspend its implementation should Iran curtail all enrichmentrelated and reprocessing activities, including research and development, as verified by the IAEA.

However, Indonesia remains to be convinced of the efficacy of adopting additional sanctions at this juncture. Essentially, we are not convinced that more sanctions - however incremental, well-targeted and reversible - would move us forward in resolving the question of Iran's nuclear programme. Will they instead have a potential negative impact at a time when progress is being made? We wonder, therefore, whether imposing more sanctions at this juncture is the most sensible approach. We need to pose the question whether imposing more sanctions is the most sensible course of action to instil confidence and trust and engender cooperation between all the parties concerned. It is our belief that, ultimately, lack of confidence and trust lies at the heart of the matter. We must avoid more of the same.

It is our expectation that Iran will continue to engage actively with the Agency in order to build confidence about the scope and nature of its nuclear programme. Such a development is not without relevance to our deliberations today. After all, the Iran dossier was referred to the Council to encourage that country to resolve outstanding verification issues with the IAEA and to restore the international community's confidence in its nuclear programme. While yet to be completed, that has begun and is making progress.

The suspension of enrichment-related activities is an instrument. It is a means to an end. It is not, as we understand it, an end by itself, isolated from developments in Iran's cooperation with the IAEA. The IAEA-Iran work plan constitutes a platform to restore the confidence of the international community. Any interruption of that confidence-building process will only threaten to unravel the important gains that have been made.

The NPT guarantees the inalienable right of all States parties to develop, research, produce and use nuclear energy for peaceful purposes without discrimination and in accordance with the Treaty. Nonetheless, we are often trapped in a vicious cycle, as there is no guarantee given to non-nuclear States regarding the security of supply of nuclear technology and materials for peaceful purposes. They remain prone to suspicion in their attempts to exercise their rights.

In order to put an end to that cycle, it is imperative for all of us to move forward and in a more creative and constructive manner. We must revive and renew the initiative to establish a multilateral arrangement, as part and parcel of the NPT, to guarantee the security of supply of nuclear technology and materials, including highly enriched uranium. Such an arrangement would provide certainty, as well as assurances, to Iran, and eventually put an end to the existing suspicions - thereby removing any reason for anyone to question the peaceful nature of Iran's current enrichment process.

[12] As a faithful State party to the NPT, Indonesia is always of the view that the three pillars of the NPT should be pursued in a balanced and nondiscriminatory manner. We have

consistently expressed our view that we should not only emphasize the nonproliferation obligations of non-nuclear-weapon States, but that we must also require nuclear-weapon States to comply fully with their nuclear disarmament obligations under article VI of the NPT, on which there has barely been any progress so far.

We are aware that resolution 1747(2007) provides for the possibility of further appropriate measures in the event of Iranian non-compliance. There is, however, nothing automatic about such measures. Further decisions will be needed - hence our deliberations today. Above all, it is important to recognize that the conditions prevailing today are different than those on the eve of the adoption of resolution 1747(2007). The strategic goals of resolutions 1737(2006) and 1747(2007) are being achieved. Iran is cooperating with the IAEA. At this juncture, more sanctions are not the best course.

For those considerations and reasons, Indonesia will abstain on the draft resolution before us today.

The President: It is my understanding that the Council is ready to proceed to the vote on the draft resolution before it (S/2008/141). Unless I hear any objection, I shall put the draft resolution to the vote now.

There being no objection, it is so decided.

A vote was taken by show of hands.

In favour: Belgium, Burkina Faso, China, Costa Rica, Croatia, France, Italy, Libyan Arab Jamahiriya, Panama, Russian Federation, South Africa, United Kingdom of Great Britain and Northern Ireland, United States of America, Viet Nam

Against: None

Abstaining: Indonesia

The President: The result of the voting is as follows: 14 votes in favour, none against and 1 abstention. The draft resolution has been adopted as resolution 1803(2008).[118]

I shall now give the floor to those members of the Council who wish to make statements following the voting.

Sir John Sawers (**United Kingdom**): I would like to begin by reading out the text of a statement which has been agreed by the Foreign Ministers of China, France, Germany, Russia, the United Kingdom and the United States of America, with the support of the High Representative of the European Union (EU). The statement reads as follows:

'Today the United Nations Security Council adopted resolution 1803(2008), reflecting the international community's ongoing serious concerns about the proliferation risks of the Iranian nuclear programme. This is the third time that the United Nations Security Council has sent a strong message of international resolve to Iran by adopting a sanctions resolution under Article 41 of Chapter VII of the Charter of the United Nations on Iran's nuclear programme. We deplore Iran's continued failure to comply with its United Nations Security Council and IAEA Board requirements, in particular by expanding its enrichment-related activities. We note the progress made in implementing the IAEA-Iran work plan and the IAEA's serious concerns about the 'alleged studies', which are critical to an assessment of a possible military dimension to Iran's nuclear programme. We call upon Iran to heed the requirement of the United Nations Security Council and the IAEA, including the suspension of its enrichment-related and reprocessing activities.

---

[118] Doc. 13.

'We remain committed to an early negotiated solution to the Iranian nuclear issue and reaffirm our commitment to a dual-track approach. We reconfirm the proposals we presented to Iran in June 2006 and are prepared to further develop them. Our proposals will offer substantial opportunities for political, security and economic benefits to Iran and to the region. We urge Iran to take this opportunity to engage with us all and to find a negotiated way forward. We reiterate our recognition of the right of Iran to develop, research, production and use of nuclear energy for peaceful purposes in conformity with its NPT obligations. We reconfirm that once the confidence of the international community in the exclusively peaceful nature of Iran's nuclear [13] programme is restored it will be treated in the same manner as that of any non-nuclear-weapon State party to the NPT. We remain ready to negotiate future arrangements, modalities and timing in this respect once the conditions for negotiations have been established.

'This will require further diplomatic efforts and innovative approaches. To that end, we have asked Dr. Javier Solana, the High Representative of the European Union for Common Foreign and Security Policy, to meet with Dr. Saeed Jalili, Secretary of Iran's Supreme National Security Council, and to address the interests and concerns of both sides in a manner which can gradually create the conditions for the opening of negotiations.'

That concludes the statement on behalf of the six Foreign Ministers.

I should like now to make some remarks in my national capacity.

First, I welcome the presence of the Permanent Representative of Iran. Many points he has made in his statement are open to clarification, argument and correction, but that would take a long time. Let me confine myself to the following points.

The British Government welcomes the very broad support for this Security Council resolution. Its adoption sends a clear message to the Government and the people of Iran. It underlines yet again that the international community is profoundly concerned that Iran might be intending to use its nuclear programme for military purposes. The United Kingdom does not have confidence that Iran's programme is for exclusively peaceful purposes. On the contrary, to us their nuclear programme only makes sense as part of plan to develop, at the least, a nuclear weapons capability.

This resolution is a necessary response to Iran's continued failure to comply with the requirements of the IAEA Board and the Security Council that, while we try to build confidence in Iran's nuclear intentions, Iran has to suspend all enrichment-related and reprocessing activity and work on all heavy-water-related projects; has to resolve all outstanding questions; and has to implement and ratify the Additional Protocol.

The progress that Iran has made with the IAEA addresses only one of those issues, and then only partially. Iran has refused to answer the most difficult questions about its past programme or to meet IAEA requests to interview named Iranian officials. And, as the IAEA reports, far from suspending its enrichment activities, Iran has intensified its efforts, including by trying to develop a new generation of centrifuges. Overall, Iran has clearly failed to abide by its legal obligations under successive Security Council resolutions.

...

Iran's leaders should listen to what the international community is saying rather than misleading their people by misrepresenting our actions and misrepresenting the reports of the IAEA on their nuclear programme. I commend the efforts of the Director General and the officials of the IAEA, but Iran's failure to do what is required of them, as clearly stated by the IAEA, left us no option but to seek further measures in the Security Council.

These further measures today strengthen the restrictions on individuals and entities closely associated with Iran's proliferation-sensitive nuclear activities and with its ballistic missile programme. They increase vigilance over the activities of Iranian banks, particularly Banks Melli and Saderat, which we believe are engaged in proliferation-sensitive activities; they introduce a provision for careful scrutiny of new commitments for export credits and guarantees to Iran; and they encourage Member States to inspect cargo to and from Iran where there are grounds to believe that prohibited items are being transported.

[14] By adopting this resolution, the Security Council has continued its incremental and proportionate approach, gradually increasing the pressure on Iran to address the widely shared concerns about its nuclear programme...

With this new resolution, the Security Council is reaffirming the clear choice confronting Iran's leaders: to cooperate with the international community and enjoy the benefits of normal relations with the rest of the world or to pursue their nuclear programme in disregard of international concerns and worsen still further their international isolation. The choice is for Iran's leaders to make. The British Government hopes they take the positive path. The Iranian people deserve no less.

Mr. Lacroix (**France**):

...

Why are we here? The Treaty on the Non-Proliferation of Nuclear Weapons (NPT) establishes a regime based on confidence, to which the International Atomic Energy Agency (IAEA) is the keystone. That confidence is necessary to guarantee our security. It is also the condition allowing all to enjoy the peaceful uses of nuclear energy. It is not arbitrary, but based on concrete facts.

Iran concealed a clandestine nuclear programme for 20 years, in violation of its Safeguards Agreement and without a credible civilian use. It developed that programme through a network that serviced military programmes throughout the world. It has revealed no information on its own initiative, and has cooperated with the Agency only sporadically since it was exposed. While the enrichment to make fissile material was being undertaken, Iran was working on various techniques that can be used to develop nuclear weapons. In 1987, Iran also received and preserved a document on the conversion of uranium hexafluoride gas into metallic uranium and on the melding of enriched metallic uranium into hemispherical forms, which has no use other than the manufacture of a nuclear weapon. Iran is also actively developing long-range missiles.

Given that disturbing situation, the international community's requests to restore confidence - requests iterated by the Board of Governors of the IAEA and the Security Council in its resolutions 1696(2006),[119] 1737(2006) and 1747(2007) - are simple and understandable to all. Iran must suspend its sensitive activities, offer full transparency under the Additional Protocol to the IAEA, and shed full light on the outstanding issues.

Bearing in mind the future of the NPT, if anyone can violate its safeguards agreements, refuse to implement the resolutions of the IAEA Board of Governors and the Security Council, and engage in dangerous activities on that basis, the entire regime will be under threat. We cannot afford that while the demand for nuclear energy is greater than ever because global development requires it.

Of course, there is no question of refusing Iran the right to use nuclear energy peacefully when it meets its international obligations. France, which is committed to distributing such energy, is particularly sensitive to that matter, but we must bear in mind the dangers that

---
[119] Doc. 10.

would arise with respect to Iran's implementation of a policy of fait accompli. In that volatile region, it would raise the risk of confrontation, and that is what we wish to avoid above all else.

...

[15] A new and disturbing aspect that is developed at length in the report is that of Iran's presumed militarization activities. The Director General calls them a matter of serious concern. If we are to maintain confidence in the NPT, we have no choice but to adopt sanctions against that country. In that respect, I express the position of the Federal Republic of Germany as well.

...

Mr. Khalilzad (**United States of America**): The United States welcomes the adoption of resolution 1803(2008). Iran's violations of Security Council resolutions not only continue, but are deepening. Instead of suspending its enrichment and reprocessing activities as required by the Council, Iran chose to expand dramatically its number of operating centrifuges and to develop a new generation of centrifuges, testing one of them with nuclear fuel. Iran continues to construct its heavy water research reactor at Arak, a potential source of weapons-useable plutonium, and still has not implemented the Additional Protocol.

Once again, Iran has not made the choice the world had hoped for; once again, the Security Council has no choice but to act. At stake is the security of a vital region of the world and the credibility of the Security Council and the International Atomic Energy Agency (IAEA) as they seek to hold Iran to its nuclear non-proliferation commitments.

...

...We agree with the IAEA that, until Iran declares all of its nuclear activities and ceases its weapons-related work, Iran's nuclear activities cannot be verified as peaceful.

... As long as the Iranian Government continues to be secretive about its nuclear [16] activities, refusing to implement the Additional Protocol, we must inevitably conclude that Iran is hiding weapons work and thereby preserving or establishing options for a nuclear weapons programme. Iran wants us to believe that its nuclear programme is peaceful, but it must be transparent with IAEA inspectors. It should implement the Additional Protocol, as the Council and the IAEA have repeatedly called for.

The latest IAEA report states that Iran is not suspending its sensitive nuclear activities. For almost two years now, this Council has required Iran to suspend all of its enrichment-related, reprocessing and heavy-water-related activities. To increase Iran's incentives to cooperate with the Council, we have imposed sanctions, to which the Council has added once again today. I want to ask the Iranian leaders: if your goal is to generate nuclear power for peaceful purposes, why do you court increasing international isolation, economic pressure and more, for a purported goal more easily and inexpensively obtained with the diplomatic solution we and others offer?

The Iranian ambassador did not answer the questions I have raised. He devoted his remarks to distorting the official record of the IAEA. He stated explicitly that Iran will not comply with the Council's demand to suspend enrichment. Iran continues to make the wrong choice, to choose the path of defiance and to divert attention from its nuclear programme by exploiting the plight of innocent Palestinians and bashing Israel.

...

The United States also supports Russia's supply of fuel for Iran's nuclear power plant in Bushehr. The delivery of that fuel exposes Iran's false claim that it needs to enrich uranium for civil nuclear power. A total of 17 countries generating nuclear power today purchase their fuel on the international market rather than enrich uranium themselves. The Russian offer would provide fuel to Iran in a reliable way and would not contribute to proliferation.

Iran should do what other States have done to eliminate any doubts that their nuclear programme is peaceful. Many States have made the decision to abandon programmes to produce a nuclear weapon; two of them sit on the Security Council today as my colleagues: South Africa and Libya. Other countries that have stepped away from past nuclear weapon aspirations include Brazil, Argentina, Romania, Ukraine and Kazakhstan. Those countries did not see their security diminished as a result of their decisions - indeed, one could easily say that their security has been enhanced - nor did they lose their right to develop nuclear energy. We urge Iran to take the same path that those countries have chosen.

The international community has good reason to be concerned about Iran's activities to acquire a nuclear weapons capability. The present Iranian regime, armed with nuclear weapons, would pose a greater potential danger to the region and to the world. The Iranian Government has been a destabilizing force in the broader Middle East and beyond. Contrary to its statements, Iran has been funding and supporting terrorists and militants for operations in Lebanon, the Palestinian territories, Iraq and Afghanistan. Its assistance has killed countless innocent civilians. The President of Iran has made many reprehensible statements embracing the objective of destroying a Member State of the United Nations.

Because of those factors, the international community cannot allow Iran to develop nuclear weapons. If Iran continues down its current path, it would likely fuel proliferation activities in the region, which, in turn, could cause the demise of the NPT regime itself.

...

[17] Mr. Wang Guangya (**China**):

...

... the Security Council once again adopted a new resolution on the Iranian nuclear issue. Like the previous three resolutions, it is not aimed at punishing Iran, but is aimed at urging Iran's return to the negotiating table and thus reactivating a new round of diplomatic efforts. The sanctions measures are not targeted at the Iranian people and will not affect normal economic and financial activities between Iran and other countries. All the sanctions measures are reversible. That is to say, if Iran suspends uranium enrichment and reprocessing activities and complies with the relevant IAEA and Security Council resolutions, the sanctions will be suspended and even terminated.

China wishes to reiterate that sanctions can never fundamentally resolve the issue. They can only serve as a means to promote reconciliation and negotiations. The best way to resolve the issue remains diplomatic negotiations. We call upon all parties concerned to adopt a highly responsible and constructive attitude, show the necessary flexibility as appropriate, give full play to initiative and creativity and demonstrate determination and sincerity in resuming negotiations.

We call upon the parties to make unremitting efforts to enhance all-round diplomatic endeavours, seek a solution that will not only ensure Iran's right to the peaceful use of nuclear energy but also address the international concern over nuclear non-proliferation, and strive to achieve an early, long-term, comprehensive and proper solution of the Iranian nuclear issue. We call upon Iran to fully comply with the IAEA and Security Council resolutions as soon as possible.

...

Mr. Urbina (**Costa Rica**) (*spoke in Spanish*):

...

[18] Today, as in the past, Costa Rica respects the right of every State to use nuclear energy for peaceful purposes. But we consider this right to be contingent on the fulfilment of all international obligations in this [19] matter. In this respect, the right to enrich uranium is a legitimate activity if its scope and objectives are subject to complete international supervision through absolutely transparent processes. We believe that that is still not the case of the Iranian nuclear programme and for this reason we are obligated to support the resolution that we have voted on today. Despite this context which is we hardly find pleasant, we are very pleased with Iran's stated intentions to continue working with the International Atomic Energy Agency and to meet its requirements. We hope that we will soon see the day in which we can verify that Iran has met all of its obligations, and in which the international community can cooperate with Iran to promote the well-being of its people.

...

[20] Mr. Suescum (**Panama**) (*spoke in Spanish*): Panama regrets that we have had once again to face the decision to impose sanctions on Iran. As we stated during prior negotiations, we hold that the imposition of coercive measures reflects a failure of diplomacy on this issue. I stress that this is a failure by all parties, not only those of us seeking clarity about the nature of the Iranian nuclear programme with a view to making substantive progress towards the resolution of this disturbing situation.

Our decision to vote in favour of today's resolution was based on the following reasoning. Iran has been a State party to the Treaty on the Non-Proliferation of Nuclear Weapons (NPT) since 1970, and as such it must adhere to restrictions on the production, development and proliferation of nuclear weapons. Panama recognizes that, under the NPT, Iran has the right to develop atomic energy for peaceful purposes and to carry out processes that are indispensable to that end, such as uranium enrichment. But the exercise of that right involves equally important obligations, in particular open and transparent inspections by the International Atomic Energy Agency (IAEA) of activities and processes linked to the peaceful use of atomic energy.

...

Despite the noteworthy and commendable progress in the process, Panama believes that until we have comprehensive clarity about the present scope of its nuclear programme, Iran will not have fully met its obligations.

...

[21] The President: I shall now make a statement in my capacity as the representative of the **Russian Federation**.

...

The resolution is in fact a political signal to Iran of the need to cooperate with the international community by implementing the decisions of the Board of Governors of the International Atomic Energy Agency (IAEA) and the Security Council. That signal should be understood in conjunction with the statement issued by the Ministers for Foreign Affairs of the six countries. It is important that the six countries be prepared to formulate additional proposals for talks, something from which Iran and the entire region can only benefit - economically, politically and in terms of security.

...

Another point of principle is that today's decision by the Council, like resolutions 1737(2006) and 1747(2007), was taken under Chapter VII, Article 41, of the Charter of the United Nations. It therefore calls for no use of force whatsoever. There is a provision in the resolution that says that, if necessary, the Council will adopt further measures on an exclusively peaceful basis. We remain convinced that an effective solution to the Iranian nuclear problem can only be found in the political and diplomatic spheres.

...

It is important that the members of the group of six countries show a consistent willingness to engage in constructive cooperation with Iran. The need for that approach has been borne out by the content of our discussion today in the Council and by the results of the vote on the resolution.

Document 19: Security Council Debate on Resolution 1835(2008)

S/PV.5984, 27 September 2008

...

[2] **The President** (*spoke in French*): The Security Council will now begin its consideration of the item on its agenda. The Council is meeting in accordance with the understanding reached in its prior consultations.

Members of the Council have before them document S/2008/624, which contains the text of a draft resolution submitted by Belgium, China, Croatia, France, Germany, Italy, the Russian Federation, the United Kingdom of Great Britain and Northern Ireland and the United States of America.

It is my understand [*sic*] that the Council is ready to proceed to the vote on the draft resolution before it. Unless I hear any objection, I shall put the draft resolution to the vote now.

There being no objection, it is so decided.

I shall now give the floor to members of the Council wishing to make statements before the voting.

Mr. Natalegawa (**Indonesia**):

...

The present draft resolution does not provide for additional sanctions against Iran. If it did, we would not have been able to support it. The draft resolution reaffirms previous statements and resolutions and calls on Iran to comply fully with its obligations under those resolutions.

However, it would not have sufficed to stop there. As a matter of principle, Indonesia attaches the greatest weight to a negotiated solution of the issue. It is our firm belief that negotiations and dialogue offer the best chance for a solution. My delegation therefore appreciates the incorporation of its amendment reaffirming the commitment to a negotiated solution of the issue as part of the dual-track approach. Such a dual-track approach must have the same common objectives and must not cancel one another out. An atmosphere conducive to the negotiations must be nurtured and promoted.

The President (*spoke in French*): The Council will now proceed to the vote on the draft resolution (S/2008/624) before it.

A vote was taken by show of hands.

In favour: Belgium, Burkina Faso, China, Costa Rica, Croatia, France, Indonesia, Italy, Libyan Arab Jamahiriya, Panama, Russian Federation, South[3] Africa, United Kingdom of Great Britain and Northern Ireland, United States of America, Viet Nam

The President (*spoke in French*): There were 15 votes in favour. The draft resolution has been adopted unanimously as resolution 1835(2008).[120]

3. Reports of the 1737 Committee

Document 20: Letter from the Chairman of the Security Council Committee Established Pursuant to Resolution 1737(2006) Addressed to the President of the Security Council

S/2007/780, 31 December 2007

...

Report of the Security Council Committee established pursuant to resolution 1737(2006)

I. Introduction

1. The present report of the Security Council Committee established pursuant to resolution 1737(2006)[121] covers the period from 23 December 2006, when the Committee was established, to 31 December 2007.

...

II. Background information

3. By its resolution 1737 of 23 December 2006, the Security Council imposed certain measures relating to the Islamic Republic of Iran. These included a proliferation sensitive nuclear activities-related and nuclear weapon delivery systems-related embargo and targeted measures; namely, an assets freeze and requirements concerning travel imposed on persons and entities designated in the annex to the resolution and on any additional persons and entities designated by the Security Council or the Committee. The assets freeze also applies to the assets of persons or entities acting on behalf of or at the direction of designated persons or entities and of entities owned or controlled by them. In addition, the Council called upon all States to prevent specialized teaching or training of Iranian nationals in disciplines that would contribute to the Islamic Republic of Iran's proliferation sensitive nuclear activities and the development of nuclear weapon delivery systems.

4. The Security Council Committee established pursuant to resolution 1737(2006) was entrusted with undertaking the tasks set out in paragraph 18 of the resolution: to seek from States information regarding the actions taken by them to implement effectively the relevant measures and whatever further information it might consider useful in that regard; to seek from the International Atomic Energy Agency (IAEA) information regarding the

---

[120] Doc. 14.
[121] Doc. 11.

actions taken by IAEA to implement effectively the relevant measures concerning the technical cooperation provided to the Islamic Republic of Iran by IAEA and whatever further information it might consider useful in that regard; to examine and take appropriate action on information regarding alleged violations of the relevant measures of resolution 1737(2006); to consider and decide upon requests for exemptions from the relevant measures; to determine as may be necessary additional items the supply of which to the Islamic Republic of Iran would be prohibited; to designate as may be necessary additional individuals and entities as subject to the assets freeze and the measures regarding travel; to promulgate guidelines as may be necessary; and to report at least every 90 days to the Security Council.

5. By its resolution 1747 of 24 March 2007,[122] the Council imposed additional measures relating to the Islamic Republic of Iran.

III. Summary of the activities of the Committee

6. At its first formal meeting, on 30 January 2007, the Committee discussed its initial programme of work. In subsequent informal consultations, until mid-year, members of the Committee mostly discussed draft guidelines for the conduct of the Committee's work. The guidelines were adopted at the Committee's second formal meeting, on 30 May 2007. Among other things, the adopted guidelines incorporated the delisting procedure as outlined in Security Council resolution 1730 (2006). The text of the guidelines is available on the Committee web page. In informal consultations held from June onwards, the Committee discussed, and acted upon, various aspects of its mandate.

Information sought and received from the International Atomic Energy Agency

7. In subparagraph 18 (b) of resolution 1737(2006), the Security Council tasked the Committee with seeking from the IAEA secretariat information regarding the actions taken by IAEA to implement effectively the measures imposed by paragraph 16 of the same resolution, which defined the scope of the technical cooperation provided by IAEA to the Islamic Republic of Iran, and whatever further information it might consider useful in that regard. Accordingly, by a letter dated 5 February 2007 addressed to the Director General of IAEA, the Chairman invited the Agency to provide to the Committee, at its earliest convenience, such information. IAEA transmitted its report on 8 March, in which it informed the Committee that the IAEA Board of Governors concurred with the actions proposed in the report of the Director General dated 9 February.[123] Out of 55 projects, 22 would be suspended. Technical cooperation would continue for food, agricultural, medical, safety and humanitarian purposes.

8. On 7 August 2007, given that more than four months had elapsed since the receipt of the IAEA report, the Chairman, in a letter, invited IAEA to provide an update and, as it deemed appropriate, any additional details with respect to the technical assistance of IAEA to the Islamic Republic of Iran and paragraph 5 of its report transmitted on 8 March. In a reply dated 22 August 2007, IAEA informed the Committee that no projects had been added to its technical cooperation programme since the issuance of its first report, and provided an update on technical cooperation and technical assistance activities since 8 March. Six requests for technical cooperation were considered to be covered and had proceeded; five others had not. Twenty-four requests for participation in technical assistance activities were deemed to be in conformity with resolution 1737(2006), whereas a further three requests were not.

---

[122] Doc. 12.
[123] Doc. 46.

Implementation reports received from Member States

9. In paragraph 19 of resolution 1737(2006), the Security Council decided that all States would report to the Committee within 60 days of the adoption of that resolution on the steps they had taken with a view to implementing effectively paragraphs 3, 4, 5, 6, 7, 8, 10, 12 and 17 of the resolution. ...

10. In addition, in paragraph 8 of resolution 1747(2007), the Council called upon all States to report to the Committee within 60 days of the adoption of that resolution on the steps they had taken with a view to implementing effectively paragraphs 2, 4, 5, 6 and 7 of that resolution...

11. ... By the end of the reporting period, the Committee had received 88 reports under resolution 1737(2006) and 72 reports under resolution 1747(2007). Of those, 17 were combined reports under both resolutions. A majority of the States that reported indicated that they already had legislation in place that covered the relevant paragraph(s) of the resolution(s). Most others reported on the steps they had taken or would be taking to put the necessary legal framework into place. All States that submitted reports assured the Committee of their commitment to implementing the resolution(s) and to meeting their obligations as outlined therein. The reports were issued as official United Nations documents, unless a State requested that its report be kept confidential (for details, see appendix).

Notifications and requests for exemptions received from Member States

12. The Security Council, by paragraph 10 of its resolution 1737(2006) and paragraph 2 of its resolution 1747(2007), decided that all States shall notify the Committee of the entry into or transit through their territories of the persons designated in the annexes to those resolutions, as well as any additional persons designated by the Council or the Committee, except where such travel is for activities related directly to the items in subparagraphs 3 (b) (i) and (ii) of resolution 1737(2006). During the reporting period, the Committee received, pursuant to the above-mentioned paragraphs, one notification concerning the travel of a listed individual.

13. Subparagraphs 13 (a) and 13 (b) of resolution 1737(2006) provide exemptions to the assets freeze, for basic expenses and extraordinary expenses respectively, as determined by the relevant States and subject to a Committee decision. In 2007, the Committee received and granted six requests for exemptions under subparagraph 13 (a) and four requests for exemptions under subparagraph 13 (b).

14. Paragraph 15 of resolution 1737(2006) provides for notifications by relevant States to the Committee of the intention to make or receive payments, or to authorize the unfreezing of funds, in connection with contracts entered into prior to the listing of persons and entities in the annexes to resolutions 1737(2006) and 1747(2007). In 2007, the Committee received 30 such notifications...

Ninety-day reports to the Security Council

15. Under the provisions of subparagraph 18 (h) of resolution 1737(2006), the Chairman must report to the Security Council at least every 90 days on the Committee's activities. Accordingly, the Chairman briefed the Council on 23 March, 21 June, 19 September and 18 December 2007.[124]

---

[124] UN Doc S/PV.5646, UN Doc S/PV.5702, UN Doc S/PV.5743, UN Doc S/PV.5807.

Queries and other communications received from Member States

16. During the reporting period, the Committee received four written queries from Member States requesting clarification on certain aspects of the sanctions regime imposed by resolutions 1737(2006) and 1747(2007). As part of its role of monitoring the implementation of the measures imposed by the Council, the Committee responded to each of those requests.

17. The Committee also received a communication from a Member State forwarding, for the Committee's information, a copy of a letter that the same Member State had sent to the Director General of IAEA, transmitting, on behalf of a group of nuclear supplier countries, a list of items, end-users and procurement agents for which those countries, in their national capacity, had denied nuclear-related exports to the Islamic Republic of Iran. ...

Appendix: List of reports, received from Member States pursuant to paragraph 19 of resolution 1737(2006) and paragraph 8 of resolution 1747(2007)

...

Document 21: Letter from the Chairman of the Security Council Committee Established Pursuant to Resolution 1737(2006) Addressed to the President of the Security Council

S/2008/839, 31 December 2008

...

Report of the Security Council Committee established pursuant to resolution 1737(2006)

I. Introduction

1. The present report of the Security Council Committee established pursuant to resolution 1737(2006)[125] covers the period from 1 January to 31 December 2008.

...

II. Background information

4. By its resolution 1737(2006), the Security Council imposed certain measures relating to the Islamic Republic of Iran...

5. The Security Council Committee established pursuant to resolution 1737(2006) was entrusted with undertaking the tasks set out in paragraph 18 of the resolution...

6. By its resolution 1747(2007),[126] the Security Council imposed additional measures relating to the Islamic Republic of Iran. These included a ban on the export of arms and related material from the Islamic Republic of Iran, the designation of additional persons as subject to the assets freeze and to the travel notification requirement, and the designation of additional entities as subject to the assets freeze. In addition, the Council called upon all States to exercise vigilance and restraint in the supply of the seven categories of conventional weapons as defined for the purposes of the United Nations Register of

---

[125] Doc. 11.
[126] Doc. 12.

Conventional Arms and related services to the Islamic Republic of Iran, and called upon all States and international financial institutions not to enter into new commitments for grants, financial assistance and concessional loans to the Government of the Islamic Republic of Iran, except for humanitarian and development purposes.

7. By its resolution 1803(2008),[127] the Security Council imposed further measures relating to the Islamic Republic of Iran. These included the broadening of the scope of the proliferation-sensitive nuclear activities and nuclear weapons delivery systems-related embargo, the introduction of a travel ban on persons designated in an annex to the resolution as well as on any additional persons designated by the Council or the Committee, and the expansion of the lists of persons and entities subject to the assets freeze and of persons subject to the travel notification requirement.

8. In addition, the Security Council called upon all States to exercise vigilance with regard to publicly provided financial support for trade with the Islamic Republic of Iran and activities of their financial institutions with banks in the Islamic Republic of Iran, and, in accordance with States' national legal authorities and legislation and consistent with international law, in particular the law of the sea and relevant civil aviation agreements, to inspect the cargoes to and from the Islamic Republic of Iran of aircraft and vessels, at their airports and seaports, owned or operated by two Iranian companies, provided that there were reasonable grounds to believe that the aircraft or vessel was transporting goods prohibited under resolution 1737(2006), resolution 1747(2007) or resolution 1803(2008). In cases when the aforementioned inspection of cargoes is undertaken, the Council requires all States to submit to it within five working days a written report on the inspection.

9. By its resolution 1803(2008), the Security Council also broadened the scope of the Committee's mandate as set out in paragraph 18 of resolution 1737(2006) to include the measures imposed by resolutions 1747(2007) and 1803(2008).

10. By its resolution 1835(2008),[128] the Security Council reaffirmed resolutions 1737(2006), 1747(2007) and 1803(2008), as well as resolution 1696(2006), and also reaffirmed its commitment to an early negotiated solution through a dual-track approach to the Iranian nuclear issue and welcomed the continuing efforts in that regard. The Council also called upon the Islamic Republic of Iran to comply fully and without delay with its obligations under the four aforementioned resolutions and to meet the requirements of the IAEA Board of Governors.

III. Summary of the activities of the Committee
…

Information sought and received from the International Atomic Energy Agency
…

14. … In a letter dated 18 April 2008, IAEA informed the Committee that no projects had been added to its technical cooperation programme with the Islamic Republic of Iran since the issuance of its report, and provided an update on technical cooperation and technical assistance activities since 22 August 2007. Three requests for technical cooperation had been considered to be covered and had proceeded; two others had not. Forty-four requests for participation in technical assistance activities had been deemed to be in conformity with resolution 1737(2006), whereas a further eight requests had not.

---

[127] Doc. 13.
[128] Doc. 14.

Implementation reports, briefings and other communications received from Member States

...

18. By the end of the reporting period, the Committee had received 90 reports pursuant to resolution 1737(2006), 77 reports pursuant to resolution 1747(2007) and 63 reports pursuant to resolution 1803(2008). Of those reports, some were combined under two or three resolutions. The reports were issued as official United Nations documents, unless a State requested that its report be kept confidential (see appendix for details).

...

21. Also in connection with paragraph 10 of resolution 1803(2008), two letters addressed to the President of the Security Council and subsequently issued as documents of the Council — the first submitted jointly by three Member States on 1 August (S/2008/520) and the second submitted by the Islamic Republic of Iran on 15 August (S/2008/554) — were circulated to the members of the Committee for their information. The letter from the three States, which was copied to the Chairman of the Committee, contained a list of banks domiciled in the Islamic Republic of Iran and their branches and subsidiaries abroad. The list was intended to assist States in their implementation of paragraph 10 of resolution 1803(2008). The letter from the Islamic Republic of Iran was a direct response to the letter from the three States.

Notifications and requests for exemptions received from Member States and IAEA

22. By paragraph 5 of its resolution 1737(2006), the Security Council required States to notify the Committee of the supply, sale or transfer of all items, materials, equipment, goods and technology covered by document S/2006/814 the export of which to the Islamic Republic of Iran is not prohibited by subparagraph 3 (b) of resolution 1737(2006). During the period under review, the Committee received eight notifications of the supply of items relevant to the construction of the nuclear power plant in Bushehr, Islamic Republic of Iran, with reference to paragraph 5. During informal consultations on 15 October 2008, the Committee also received a briefing from a State in connection with a project, which fell within the scope of the provisions on IAEA cooperation as described in paragraph 16 of resolution 1737(2006), aimed at strengthening the effectiveness of the regulatory oversight of the safety at that nuclear power plant.

23. Subparagraphs 13 (a) and 13 (b) of resolution 1737(2006) provide for exemptions to the assets freeze, for basic expenses and extraordinary expenses respectively, as determined by the relevant States and subject to a Committee decision. In 2008, the Committee received and granted two requests for exemptions under subparagraph 13 (b).

24. Subparagraph 13 (d) of resolution 1737(2006) provides for an exemption to the assets freeze for activities directly related to the items specified in subparagraphs 3 (b) (i) and (ii) of the resolution, which have been notified by the relevant States to the Committee. In 2008, the Committee received one such notification from IAEA.

25. Paragraph 15 of resolution 1737(2006) provides for an exemption to the assets freeze for making or receiving payments, or authorizing the unfreezing of funds, in connection with contracts entered into prior to the listing of persons and entities referred to in the annexes to resolutions 1737(2006), 1747(2007) and 1803(2008), which have been notified by the relevant States to the Committee. In 2008, the Committee received four such notifications.

Ninety-day reports to the Security Council

26. Under the provisions of subparagraph 18 (h) of resolution 1737(2006), the Chairman must report to the Security Council at least every 90 days on the Committee's activities. Accordingly, the Chairman briefed the Council on 17 March, 13 June, 11 September and 10 December 2008 (see S/PV.5853, S/PV.5909, S/PV.5973 and S/PV.6036).

Responses to queries received from Member States

27. As part of its role of monitoring the implementation of the measures imposed by the Security Council by resolutions 1737(2006), 1747(2007) and 1803(2008), the Committee responded to four written queries received from Member States.

IV. Violations and alleged violations of the sanctions regime

28. During informal consultations on 28 April 2008, it was brought to the Committee's attention that, as reported in the media, a Government had made a public statement that there had been a contravention of resolutions 1747(2007) and 1803(2008) on its territory with respect to the export ban on arms and related material from the Islamic Republic of Iran. On 9 May 2008, the Committee approved the dispatch of letters to the States concerned seeking clarifications and additional information. The Committee received a reply, dated 20 June 2008, from only the State that had made the announcement, providing an explanation of the actions taken by that State to address the situation and containing assurances that that State would continue to fully implement the relevant resolutions.

Appendix: List of reports received from Member States pursuant to paragraph 19 of resolution 1737(2006), paragraph 8 of resolution 1747(2007) and paragraph 13 of resolution 1803(2008)

	Reports pursuant to resolution 1737(2006)	*Reports pursuant to resolution 1747(2007)*	*Reports pursuant to resolution 1803(2008)*
Albania	S/AC.50/2007/9		
Algeria	S/AC.50/2007/65 (combined report)		
Andorra	S/AC.50/2007/50		
Argentina	S/AC.50/2007/57	S/AC.50/2007/57/Add.1 and 2	S/AC.50/2008/60
Australia	S/AC.50/2007/27	S/AC.50/2007/70	S/AC.50/2008/19
Austria	S/AC.50/2007/11	S/AC.50/2007/66	S/AC.50/2008/2
Azerbaijan	S/AC.50/2007/107 (combined report)		S/AC.50/2008/44
Bahrain	S/AC.50/2007/67	S/AC.50/2007/121	S/AC.50/2008/12 and Add.1
Bangladesh	S/AC.50/2007/47		
Belarus	S/AC.50/2007/41	S/AC.50/2007/77	S/AC.50/2008/16
Belgium	S/AC.50/2007/10	S/AC.50/2007/74	S/AC.50/2008/14
Brazil	S/AC.50/2007/26	S/AC.50/2007/82	S/AC.50/2008/63
Brunei Darussalam	S/AC.50/2008/1 (combined report)		S/AC.50/2008/64
Bulgaria	S/AC.50/2007/2 and Add.1	S/AC.50/2007/108 and Add.1	S/AC.50/2008/11
Cambodia	S/AC.50/2007/125		

	Reports pursuant to resolution 1737(2006)	*Reports pursuant to resolution 1747(2007)*	*Reports pursuant to resolution 1803(2008)*
Canada	S/AC.50/2007/33	S/AC.50/2007/75	S/AC.50/2008/5
China	S/AC.50/2007/22	S/AC.50/2007/99	S/AC.50/2008/18
Costa Rica	S/AC.50/2007/71 (combined report)		
Croatia	S/AC.50/2007/15	S/AC.50/2007/117	S/AC.50/2008/61
Cuba	S/AC.50/2007/38	S/AC.50/2007/89	S/AC.50/2008/38
Cyprus	S/AC.50/2007/128 (combined report)		S/AC.50/2008/65
Czech Republic	S/AC.50/2007/14		
Denmark	S/AC.50/2007/13	S/AC.50/2007/85	
Ecuador	S/AC.50/2007/129 (combined report)		
Egypt	S/AC.50/2007/59	S/AC.50/2007/68	S/AC.50/2008/3
Estonia	S/AC.50/2007/49	S/AC.50/2007/113	
Finland	S/AC.50/2007/19	S/AC.50/2007/97	S/AC.50/2008/26
France	S/AC.50/2007/17	S/AC.50/2007/84	S/AC.50/2008/39
Georgia	S/AC.50/2007/29		
Germany	S/AC.50/2007/37	S/AC.50/2007/98	S/AC.50/2008/15
Germany (on behalf of the European Union)	S/AC.50/2007/28		
	S/AC.50/2007/105 (combined report)		
Ghana	S/AC.50/2007/136		
Greece	S/AC.50/2007/60	S/AC.50/2007/122	
Grenada	S/AC.50/2007/140		
Guatemala	S/AC.50/2007/100 (combined report)		S/AC.50/2008/33
Hungary	S/AC.50/2007/81 (combined report)		S/AC.50/2008/59
India	S/AC.50/2007/20	S/AC.50/2007/123	S/AC.50/2008/49
Indonesia	S/AC.50/2007/5		S/AC.50/2008/10
Israel	S/AC.50/2007/141(combined report)		
Italy	S/AC.50/2007/25	S/AC.50/2007/103	S/AC.50/2008/47
Jamaica			S/AC.50/2008/21
Japan	S/AC.50/2007/16	S/AC.50/2007/79	S/AC.50/2008/24
Jordan	S/AC.50/2007/119 (combined report)		S/AC.50/2008/17
Kazakhstan	S/AC.50/2007/39	S/AC.50/2007/102	S/AC.50/2008/36
Kuwait	S/AC.50/2007/118 (combined report)		S/AC.50/2008/57 and Add. 1
Kyrgyzstan	S/AC.50/2007/53	S/AC.50/2008/50	S/AC.50/2008/53
Latvia	S/AC.50/2007/62	S/AC.50/2007/91	
Libyan Arab Jamahiriya	S/AC.50/2007/61	S/AC.50/2007/69	S/AC.50/2008/51
Liechtenstein	S/AC.50/2007/31		S/AC.50/2008/27
Lithuania	S/AC.50/2007/34	S/AC.50/2007/90	S/AC.50/2008/55
Luxembourg	S/AC.50/2007/64		
Malta	S/AC.50/2007/7	S/AC.50/2007/63	S/AC.50/2008/35
Mauritius	S/AC.50/2007/35 and Add.1	S/AC.50/2007/106	S/AC.50/2008/58

	Reports pursuant to resolution 1737(2006)	Reports pursuant to resolution 1747(2007)	Reports pursuant to resolution 1803(2008)
Mexico	S/AC.50/2007/58	S/AC.50/2007/94	S/AC.50/2008/45
Monaco	S/AC.50/2007/130	S/AC.50/2007/126	
Netherlands	S/AC.50/2007/48	S/AC.50/2007/73	S/AC.50/2008/32
New Zealand	S/AC.50/2007/36	S/AC.50/2007/132	S/AC.50/2008/22
Niger	S/AC.50/2007/135 (combined report)		
Norway	S/AC.50/2007/6	S/AC.50/2007/93	S/AC.50/2008/4
Oman	S/AC.50/2008/62		
Pakistan	S/AC.50/2007/12	S/AC.50/2007/96	S/AC.50/2008/6
Panama	S/AC.50/2007/139 (combined report)		
Peru	S/AC.50/2007/44	S/AC.50/2007/86	S/AC.50/2008/41
Philippines	S/AC.50/2007/137 (combined report)		
Poland	S/AC.50/2007/43	S/AC.50/2007/95	S/AC.50/2008/37
Portugal	S/AC.50/2007/56	S/AC.50/2007/111	S/AC.50/2008/30
Qatar	S/AC.50/2007/24 and Add.1	S/AC.50/2007/87	S/AC.50/2008/25
Republic of Korea	S/AC.50/2007/51	S/AC.50/2007/115	S/AC.50/2008/28
Republic of Moldova	S/AC.50/2007/127 (combined report)		
Romania	S/AC.50/2007/30	S/AC.50/2007/101	S/AC.50/2008/52
Russian Federation	S/AC.50/2007/8 and Add.1	S/AC.50/2007/92 and Add.1	S/AC.50/2008/13 and Add.1
Saudi Arabia	S/AC.50/2007/120		S/AC.50/2008/56
Serbia	S/AC.50/2007/52	S/AC.50/2007/131	
Singapore	S/AC.50/2007/45	S/AC.50/2007/116	S/AC.50/2008/43
Slovakia	S/AC.50/2007/42	S/AC.50/2007/78	S/AC.50/2008/9
Slovenia	S/AC.50/2007/23		S/AC.50/2008/54
South Africa	S/AC.50/2007/4	S/AC.50/2008/40	
Spain	S/AC.50/2007/55	S/AC.50/2007/112	S/AC.50/2008/46
Sri Lanka		S/AC.50/2007/133	
Suriname	S/AC.50/2007/138 (combined report)		
Sweden	S/AC.50/2007/21	S/AC.50/2007/83	
Switzerland	S/AC.50/2007/40	S/AC.50/2007/109	S/AC.50/2008/20
Thailand	Not published	Not published	S/AC.50/2008/29
The former Yugoslav Republic of Macedonia	S/AC.50/2007/1	S/AC.50/2007/114	S/AC.50/2008/42
Turkey	S/AC.50/2007/32		
Ukraine	S/AC.50/2007/80 and Add.1 (combined report)		S/AC.50/2008/7
United Arab Emirates	S/AC.50/2007/46	S/AC.50/2007/104	
United Kingdom of Great Britain and Northern Ireland	S/AC.50/2007/3	S/AC.50/2007/72	S/AC.50/2008/31
United States of America	S/AC.50/2007/18	S/AC.50/2007/88	S/AC.50/2008/34

	Reports pursuant to resolution 1737(2006)	*Reports pursuant to resolution 1747(2007)*	*Reports pursuant to resolution 1803(2008)*
Uruguay	S/AC.50/2007/134 and Add.1		S/AC.50/2008/8
Uzbekistan	S/AC.50/2007/124 (combined report)		S/AC.50/2008/23
Viet Nam	S/AC.50/2007/54	S/AC.50/2007/110	S/AC.50/2008/48
Yemen	S/AC.50/2007/76		

IAEA DOCUMENTS

1. Statements and Resolutions of the Board of Governors on Implemntation of the NPT Safeguards Agreement in the Islamic Republic of Iran and Related Resolutions

Document 22: Statement by the Board (issued by the Chairwoman)

19 June 2003

On the basis of our discussions, I am confident that I express the broad sense of the Board in stating the following points:

The Board expressed its appreciation for the 6 June report of the Director General,[129] which provides a factual and objective description of developments since March in relation to safeguards issues in the Islamic Republic of Iran, which need to be clarified, and actions that need to be taken.

The Board commended the Secretariat for the extensive verification activities which it has undertaken and expressed full support for its on-going efforts to resolve outstanding questions. The Board shared the concern expressed by the Director General in his report at the number of Iran's past failures to report material, facilities and activities as required by its safeguards obligations. Noting the Iranian actions taken thus far to correct these failures, the Board urged Iran promptly to rectify all safeguards problems identified in the report and resolve questions that remain open.

The Board welcomed Iran's reaffirmed commitment to full transparency and expected Iran to grant the Agency all access deemed necessary by the Agency in order to create the necessary confidence in the international community. Noting that the enrichment plant is under IAEA safeguards, the Board encouraged Iran, pending the resolution of related outstanding issues, not to introduce nuclear material at the pilot enrichment plant, as a confidence-building measure.

The Board called on Iran to co-operate fully with the Agency in its on-going work. Specifically, the Board took note of the Director General's 16 June Introductory Statement which called on Iran to permit the Agency to take environmental samples at the particular location where allegations about enrichment activities exists.

The Board welcomed Iran's readiness to look positively at signing and ratifying an additional protocol,[130] and urged Iran to promptly and unconditionally conclude and implement an additional protocol to its Safeguards Agreement,[131] in order to enhance the Agency's ability to provide credible assurances regarding the peaceful nature of Iran's nuclear activities, particularly the absence of undeclared material and activities.

The Board requested the Director General to provide a further report on the situation whenever appropriate.

---

[129] Doc. 33.
[130] Doc. 5.
[131] Doc. 4.

Document 23: Implementation of the NPT Safeguards Agreement in the Islamic Republic of Iran

Resolution GOV/2003/69, 12 September 2003

The Board of Governors,

(a) *Recalling* the Director General's report of 6 June 2003 (GOV/2003/40),[132] which expressed concern over failures by the Islamic Republic of Iran to report material, facilities and activities as it was obliged to do pursuant to its safeguards agreement,[133] and noted that the Secretariat continues to investigate a number of unresolved issues,

(b) *Recalling* also recent statements by Iranian authorities recommitting Iran to full NPT and IAEA safeguards compliance and renouncing Iranian interest in nuclear weapons,

(c) *Acknowledging* Iran's decision to start negotiations for the conclusion of an additional protocol,[134] but noting it does not meet the Board's 19 June request that Iran promptly and unconditionally sign and implement such a Protocol,

(d) *Noting* with appreciation the Director General's report of 26 August 2003 (GOV/2003/63),[135] on the implementation of safeguards in Iran, and acknowledging that as a result of intensive inspection activities in Iran by the Agency since February, the Agency now has a better, although still incomplete, understanding of Iran's nuclear programme,

(e) *Commending* the Secretariat for its continuing efforts to resolve all outstanding safeguards issues and sharing the view of the Director General that much essential work remains to be completed urgently to enable the Agency to draw conclusions on the programme,

(f) *Noting* the interim nature of the report of the Director General and calling on Iran to further enhance cooperation and provide full transparency to allow the Agency to fully understand and verify all aspects of Iran's nuclear programme, including the full history of its enrichment programme,

(g) *Concerned* by the statement of the Director General that information and access were at times slow in coming and incremental, that some of the information was in contrast to that previously provided by Iran, and that there remain a number of important outstanding issues that require urgent resolution,

(h) *Noting* with concern:

– that the Agency environmental sampling at Natanz has revealed the presence of two types of high enriched uranium, which requires additional work to enable the Agency to arrive at a conclusion;

– that IAEA inspectors found considerable modifications had been made to the premises at the Kalaye Electric Company prior to inspections that may impact on the accuracy of the environmental sampling;

– that some of Iran's statements to the IAEA have undergone significant and material changes, and that the number of outstanding issues has increased since the report;

---

[132] Doc. 33.
[133] Doc. 4.
[134] Doc. 5.
[135] Doc. 34.

– that despite the Board's statement in June 2003[136] encouraging Iran, as a confidence-building measure, not to introduce nuclear material into its pilot centrifuge enrichment cascade at Natanz, Iran has introduced such material;

(i) *Expressing* grave concern that, more than one year after initial IAEA inquiries to Iran about undeclared activities, Iran has still not enabled the IAEA to provide the assurances required by Member States that all nuclear material in Iran is declared and submitted to Agency safeguards and that there are no undeclared nuclear activities in Iran,

(j) *Mindful* of Iran's heavy responsibility to the international community regarding the transparency of its extensive nuclear activities,

(k) *Recognising* the basic and inalienable right of all Member States to develop atomic energy for peaceful purpose,

(l) *Stressing* the need for effective safeguards in order to prevent the use of nuclear material for prohibited purposes in contravention of safeguards agreements, and underlining the vital importance of effective safeguards for facilitating cooperation in the field of peaceful uses of nuclear energy,

1. *Calls* on Iran to provide accelerated cooperation and full transparency to allow the Agency to provide at an early date the assurances required by Member States;

2. *Calls* on Iran to ensure there are no further failures to report material, facilities and activities that Iran is obliged to report pursuant to its safeguards agreement;

3. *Reiterates* the Board's statement in June 2003 encouraging Iran not to introduce nuclear material into its pilot enrichment cascade in Natanz, and in this context calls on Iran to suspend all further uranium enrichment-related activities, including the further introduction of nuclear material into Natanz, and, as a confidence-building measure, any reprocessing activities, pending provision by the Director General of the assurances required by Member States, and pending satisfactory application of the provisions of the additional protocol;

4. *Decides* it is essential and urgent in order to ensure IAEA verification of non-diversion of nuclear material that Iran remedy all failures identified by the Agency and cooperate fully with the Agency to ensure verification of compliance with Iran's safeguards agreement by taking all necessary actions by the end of October 2003, including:

(i) providing a full declaration of all imported material and components relevant to the enrichment programme, especially imported equipment and components stated to have been contaminated with high enriched uranium particles, and collaborating with the Agency in identifying the source and date of receipt of such imports and the locations where they have been stored and used in Iran;

(ii) granting unrestricted access, including environmental sampling, for the Agency to whatever locations the Agency deems necessary for the purposes of verification of the correctness and completeness of Iran's declarations;

(iii) resolving questions regarding the conclusion of Agency experts that process testing on gas centrifuges must have been conducted in order for Iran to develop its enrichment technology to its current extent;

(iv) providing complete information regarding the conduct of uranium conversion experiments;

---

[136] Doc. 22.

(v) providing such other information and explanations, and taking such other steps as are deemed necessary by the Agency to resolve all outstanding issues involving nuclear materials and nuclear activities, including environmental sampling results;

5. *Requests* all third countries to cooperate closely and fully with the Agency in the clarification of open questions on the Iranian nuclear programme;

6. *Requests* Iran to work with the Secretariat to promptly and unconditionally sign, ratify and fully implement the additional protocol, and, as a confidence-building measure, henceforth to act in accordance with the additional protocol;

7. *Requests* the Director General to continue his efforts to implement the Agency's safeguards agreement with Iran, and to submit a report in November 2003, or earlier if appropriate, on the implementation of this resolution, enabling the Board to draw definitive conclusions; and

8. *Decides* to remain seized of the matter.

Document 24: Implementation of the NPT Safeguards Agreement in the Islamic Republic of Iran

Resolution GOV/2003/81, 26 November 2003

The Board of Governors,

(a) *Recalling* the Resolution adopted by the Board on 12 September 2003 (GOV/2003/69),[137] in which the Board, inter alia:

– expressed concern over failures by the Islamic Republic of Iran to report material, facilities and activities that Iran is obliged to report pursuant to its Safeguards Agreement;[138]

– decided it was essential and urgent, in order to ensure IAEA verification of non-diversion of nuclear material, that Iran remedy all failures identified by the Agency and cooperate fully with the Agency by taking all necessary actions by the end of October 2003;

– requested Iran to work with the Secretariat to promptly and unconditionally sign, ratify and fully implement the Additional Protocol,[139] and, as a confidence-building measure, to act thenceforth in accordance with the Additional Protocol; and

– called on Iran to suspend all further uranium enrichment-related activities, including the further introduction of nuclear material into Natanz, and any reprocessing activities,

(b) *Welcoming* the Agreed Statement between the Foreign Ministers of France, Germany and the United Kingdom and the Secretary of the Iranian Supreme National Security Council issued in Tehran on 21 October,

(c) *Noting* with appreciation the Director General's report of 10 November 2003 (GOV/2003/75),[140] on the implementation of safeguards in Iran,

---

[137] Doc. 23.
[138] Doc. 4.
[139] Doc. 5.
[140] Doc. 35.

(d) *Commending* the Director General and the Secretariat for their professional and impartial efforts to implement the Safeguards Agreement with Iran and to resolve all outstanding safeguards issues in Iran, in pursuance of the Agency's mandate and of the implementation, inter alia, of the Resolution adopted by the Board on 12 September 2003 (GOV/2003/69),

(e) *Acknowledging* that Vice-President Aghazadeh of the Islamic Republic of Iran has reaffirmed his country's decision to provide a full picture of its nuclear activities and has also reaffirmed his country's decision to implement a policy of cooperation and full transparency,

(f) *Noting* with deep concern that Iran has failed in a number of instances over an extended period of time to meet its obligations under its Safeguards Agreement with respect to the reporting of nuclear material, and its processing and use, as well as the declaration of facilities where such material has been processed and stored, as set out in paragraph 48 of the Director General's report,

(g) *Noting* in particular, with the gravest concern, that Iran enriched uranium and separated plutonium in undeclared facilities, in the absence of IAEA safeguards,

(h) *Noting* also, with equal concern, that there has been in the past a pattern of concealment resulting in breaches of safeguard obligations and that the new information disclosed by Iran and reported by the Director General includes much more that is contradictory to information previously provided by Iran,

(i) *Noting* that the Director General, in his opening statement, indicated that Iran has begun cooperating more actively with the IAEA and has given assurances that it is committed to a policy of full disclosure,

(j) *Recognising* that, in addition to the corrective actions already taken, Iran has undertaken to present all nuclear material for Agency verification during its forthcoming inspections,

(k) *Emphasising* that, in order to restore confidence, Iranian cooperation and transparency will need to be complete and sustained so that the Agency can resolve all outstanding issues and, over time, provide and maintain the assurances required by Member States,

(l) *Noting* with satisfaction that Iran has indicated that it is prepared to sign the Additional Protocol, and that, pending its entry into force, Iran will act in accordance with the provisions of that Protocol,

(m) *Noting* that the Director General, in his opening statement, reported that Iran has decided to suspend enrichment-related and reprocessing activities,

(n) *Stressing* that the voluntary suspension by Iran of all its uranium enrichment-related activities and reprocessing activities remains of key importance to rebuilding international confidence,

(o) *Recognising* the inalienable right of States to the development and practical application of atomic energy for peaceful purposes, including the production of electric power, with due consideration for the needs of developing countries,

(p) *Stressing* the need for effective safeguards in order to prevent the use of nuclear material for prohibited purposes in contravention of safeguards agreements, and underlining the vital importance of effective safeguards for facilitating cooperation in the field of peaceful uses of nuclear energy,

1. *Welcomes* Iran's offer of active cooperation and openness and its positive response to the demands of the Board in the resolution adopted by Governors

on 12 September 2003 (GOV/2003/69) and underlines that, in proceeding, the Board considers it essential that the declarations that have now been made by Iran amount to the correct, complete and final picture of Iran's past and present nuclear programme, to be verified by the Agency;

2. *Strongly deplores* Iran's past failures and breaches of its obligation to comply with the provisions of its Safeguards Agreement, as reported by the Director General; and urges Iran to adhere strictly to its obligations under its Safeguards Agreement in both letter and spirit;

3. *Notes* the statement by the Director General that Iran has taken the specific actions deemed essential and urgent and requested of it in paragraph 4 of the Resolution adopted by the Board on 12 September 2003 (GOV/2003/69);

4. *Requests* the Director General to take all steps necessary to confirm that the information provided by Iran on its past and present nuclear activities is correct and complete as well as to resolve such issues as remain outstanding;

5. *Endorses* the view of the Director General that, to achieve this, the Agency must have a particularly robust verification system in place: an Additional Protocol, coupled with a policy of full transparency and openness on the part of Iran, is indispensable;

6. *Reiterates* that the urgent, full and close co-operation with the Agency of all third countries is essential in the clarification of outstanding questions concerning Iran's nuclear programme;

7. *Calls* on Iran to undertake and complete the taking of all necessary corrective measures on an urgent basis, to sustain full cooperation with the Agency in implementing Iran's commitment to full disclosure and unrestricted access, and thus to provide the transparency and openness that are indispensable for the Agency to complete the considerable work necessary to provide and maintain the assurances required by Member States;

8. *Decides* that, should any further serious Iranian failures come to light, the Board of Governors would meet immediately to consider, in the light of the circumstances and of advice from the Director General, all options at its disposal, in accordance with the IAEA Statute and Iran's Safeguards Agreement;

9. *Notes* with satisfaction the decision of Iran to conclude an Additional Protocol to its Safeguards Agreement, and re-emphasises the importance of Iran moving swiftly to ratification and also of Iran acting as if the Protocol were in force in the interim, including by making all declarations required within the required timeframe;

10. *Welcomes* Iran's decision voluntarily to suspend all enrichment-related and reprocessing activities and requests Iran to adhere to it, in a complete and verifiable manner; and also endorses the Director General's acceptance of Iran's invitation to verify implementation of that decision and report thereon;

11. *Requests* the Director General to submit a comprehensive report on the implementation of this resolution by mid-February 2004, for consideration by the March Board of Governors, or to report earlier if appropriate; and

12. *Decides* to remain seized of the matter.

Document 25: Implementation of the NPT Safeguards Agreement in the Islamic Republic of Iran

Resolution GOV/2004/21, 13 March 2004

The Board of Governors,

(a) *Recalling* the resolutions adopted by the Board on 26 November 2003 (GOV/2003/81),[141] and on 12 September 2003 (GOV/2003/69)[142] and the statement by the Board of 19 June 2003 (GOV/OR.1072),[143]

(b) *Noting* with appreciation the Director General's report of 24 February 2004 (GOV/2004/11),[144] on the implementation of safeguards in Iran,

(c) *Commending* the Director General and the Secretariat for their continuing efforts to implement the Safeguards Agreement with Iran[145] and to resolve all outstanding issues in Iran,

(d) *Noting* with satisfaction that Iran signed the Additional Protocol on 18 December 2003[146] and that, in its communication to the Director General of 10 November 2003, Iran committed itself to acting in accordance with the provisions of the Protocol with effect from that date; but also noting that the Protocol has not yet been ratified as called for in the Board's resolutions of 26 November 2003 (GOV/2003/81) and 12 September 2003 (GOV/2003/69),

(e) *Noting* the decision by Iran of 24 February 2004 to extend the scope of its suspension of enrichment-related and reprocessing activities, and its confirmation that the suspension applied to all facilities in Iran,

(f) *Noting* with serious concern that the declarations made by Iran in October 2003 did not amount to the complete and final picture of Iran's past and present nuclear programme considered essential by the Board's November 2003 resolution, in that the Agency has since uncovered a number of omissions - e.g., a more advanced centrifuge design than previously declared, including associated research, manufacturing and testing activities; two mass spectrometers used in the laser enrichment programme; and designs for the construction of hot cells at the Arak heavy water research reactor - which require further investigation, not least as they may point to nuclear activities not so far acknowledged by Iran,

(g) *Noting* with equal concern that Iran has not resolved all questions regarding the development of its enrichment technology to its current extent, and that a number of other questions remain unresolved, including the sources of all HEU contamination in Iran; the location, extent, and nature of work undertaken on the basis of the advanced centrifuge design; the nature, extent and purpose of activities involving the planned heavy-water reactor; and evidence to support claims regarding the purpose of polonium-210 experiments, and

(h) *Noting* with concern, also in light of the Director General's report of 20 February 2004 (GOV/2004/12), that, although the timelines are different, Iran's and Libya's conversion and centrifuge programmes share several common elements, including technology largely obtained from the same foreign sources,

---

[141] Doc. 24.
[142] Doc. 23.
[143] Doc. 60.
[144] Doc. 36.
[145] Doc. 4.
[146] Doc. 5.

1. *Recognizes* that the Director General reports Iran to have been actively cooperating with the Agency in providing access to locations requested by the Agency, but, as Iran's cooperation so far has fallen short of what is required, calls on Iran to continue and intensify its cooperation, in particular through the prompt and proactive provision of detailed and accurate information on every aspect of Iran's past and present nuclear activities;

2. *Welcomes* Iran's signature of the Additional Protocol; urges its prompt ratification; underlines the Board's understanding that, in its communication to the Director General of 10 November 2003, Iran voluntarily committed itself to acting in accordance with the provisions of the Protocol with effect from that date; and stresses the importance of Iran complying with the deadline for declarations envisaged in Article 3 of the Protocol;

3. *Recalls* that in its resolutions of 26 November 2003 and 12 September 2003 the Board called on Iran to suspend all enrichment-related and reprocessing activities, notes that Iran's voluntary decisions of 29 December 2003 and 24 February 2004 constitute useful steps in this respect, calls on Iran to extend the application of this commitment to all such activities throughout Iran, and requests the Director General to verify the full implementation of these steps;

4. *Deplores* that Iran, as detailed in the report by the Director General, omitted any reference, in its letter of 21 October 2003 which was to have provided the 'full scope of Iranian nuclear activities' and a 'complete centrifuge R&D chronology', to its possession of P-2 centrifuge design drawings and to associated research, manufacturing, and mechanical testing activities - which the Director General describes as 'a matter of serious concern, particularly in view of the importance and sensitivity of those activities';

5. *Echoes* the concern expressed by the Director General over the issue of the purpose of Iran's activities related to experiments on the production and intended use of polonium-210, in the absence of information to support Iran's statements in this regard;

6. *Calls* on Iran to be pro-active in taking all necessary steps on an urgent basis to resolve all outstanding issues, including the issue of LEU and HEU contamination at the Kalaye Electric Company workshop and Natanz; the issue of the nature and scope of Iran's laser isotope enrichment research; and the issue of the experiments on the production of polonium-210;

7. *Notes* with appreciation that the Agency is investigating the supply routes and sources of technology and related equipment, and nuclear and non-nuclear materials, found in Iran, and reiterates that the urgent, full and close cooperation with the Agency of all third countries is essential in the clarification of outstanding questions concerning Iran's nuclear programme, including the acquisition of nuclear technology from foreign sources; and also appreciates any cooperation in this regard as may already have been extended to the Agency;

8. *Requests* the Director General to report on these issues before the end of May, as well as on the implementation of this and prior resolutions on Iran, for consideration by the June Board of Governors - or to report earlier if appropriate;

9. *Decides* to defer until its June meeting, and after receipt of the report of the Director General referred to above, consideration of progress in verifying Iran's declarations, and of how to respond to the above-mentioned omissions; and

10. *Decides* to remain seized of the matter.

Document 26: Implementation of the NPT Safeguards Agreement in the Islamic Republic of Iran

Resolution GOV/2004/49, 18 June 2004

The Board of Governors,

(a) *Recalling* the resolutions adopted by the Board on 13 March 2004 (GOV/2004/21),[147] 26 November 2003 (GOV/2003/81),[148] and on 12 September 2003 (GOV/2003/69)[149] and the statement by the Board of 19 June 2003 (GOV/OR.1072),[150]

(b) *Noting* with appreciation the Director General's report of 1 June 2004 (GOV/2004/34),[151] on the implementation of safeguards in Iran,

(c) *Reiterating* its appreciation that Iran has continued to act as if its Additional Protocol[152] were in force, and noting with satisfaction that Iran has submitted to the Agency the initial declarations pursuant to that Protocol,

(d) *Noting*, however, that Iran has yet to ratify the Protocol as called for in previous Board resolutions,

(e) *Recalling* Iran's voluntary decisions to suspend all enrichment-related and reprocessing activities and to permit the Agency to verify that suspension; noting with concern that, as detailed in the Director General's report, this verification was delayed in some cases, and that the suspension is not yet comprehensive because of the continued production of centrifuge equipment; also noting with concern that Iran's decision to proceed with the generation of UF_6 is at variance with the Agency's previous understanding as to the scope of Iran's decision regarding suspension; and further noting that Iran has withheld 10 assembled centrifuge rotors for research activities,

(f) *Encouraged* by the Director General's assessment that there has been good progress on the actions agreed during the Director General's visit to Tehran in early April 2004 and that the Agency continues to make progress in gaining a comprehensive understanding of Iran's nuclear programme, but noting with concern that after almost two years from when Iran's undeclared programme came to the Agency's knowledge a number of questions remain outstanding, and in particular two questions that are key to understanding the extent and nature of Iran's enrichment programme: the sources of all HEU contamination in Iran and the extent and nature of work undertaken on the basis of the P-2 advanced centrifuge design,

(g) *Noting* in this context with serious concern that important information about the P-2 centrifuge programme has often been forthcoming only after repeated requests, and in some cases has been incomplete and continues to lack the necessary clarity and also that the information provided to date relating to contamination issues has not been adequate to resolve this complex matter,

(h) *Noting* with appreciation that the Agency has received some information from other states that may be helpful in resolving some contamination questions,

---

[147] Doc. 25.
[148] Doc. 24.
[149] Doc. 23.
[150] Doc. 60.
[151] Doc. 37.
[152] Doc. 5.

(i) *Noting* with concern that the Agency's investigations have revealed further omissions in the statements made by Iran, including in the October declaration, in particular concerning the importation of P-2 components from abroad and concerning laser enrichment tests, which have produced samples enriched up to 15%, and also that Agency experts have raised questions and doubts regarding the explanations provided by Iran concerning those programmes, which require further clarification,

(j) *Recognising* the inalienable right of states to the development and practical application of atomic energy for peaceful purposes, including the production of electric power, consistent with their treaty obligations, with due consideration for the needs of the developing countries,

(k) *Stressing* the need for effective safeguards in order to prevent the use of nuclear material for prohibited purposes in contravention of safeguards agreements and underlining the vital importance of effective safeguards for facilitating cooperation in the field of nuclear energy, and

(l) *Acknowledging* the statement by the Director General on 14 June that it is essential for the integrity and credibility of the inspection process to bring these issues to a close within the next few months,

1. *Acknowledges* that Iranian cooperation has resulted in Agency access to all requested locations, including four workshops belonging to the Defence Industries Organisation;

2. *Deplores*, at the same time, the fact that, overall, as indicated by the Director General's written and oral reports, Iran's cooperation has not been as full, timely and proactive as it should have been, and, in particular, that Iran postponed until mid-April visits originally scheduled for mid-March - including visits of Agency centrifuge experts to a number of locations involved in Iran's P-2 centrifuge enrichment programme - resulting in some cases in a delay in the taking of environmental samples and their analysis;

3. *Underlines* that, with the passage of time, it is becoming ever more important that Iran work proactively to enable the Agency to gain a full understanding of Iran's enrichment programme by providing all relevant information, as well as by providing prompt access to all relevant places, data and persons; and calls on Iran to continue and intensify its cooperation so that the Agency may provide the international community with required assurances about Iran's nuclear activities;

4. *Calls* on Iran to take all necessary steps on an urgent basis to help resolve all outstanding questions, especially that of LEU and HEU contamination found at various locations in Iran, including by providing additional relevant information about the origin of the components in question and explanations about the presence of a cluster of 36% HEU particles; and also the question of the nature and scope of Iran's P-2 centrifuge programme, including by providing full documentation and explanations at the request of the Agency;

5. *Welcomes* Iran's submission of the declarations under Articles 2 and 3 of its Additional Protocol; and stresses the importance of Iran complying with the deadlines for further declarations required by Articles 2 and 3 of the Protocol, and that all such declarations should be correct and complete;

6. *Emphasises* the importance of Iran continuing to act in accordance with the provisions of the Additional Protocol to provide reassurance to the international

community about the nature of Iran's nuclear programme; and urges Iran to ratify without delay its Protocol;

7. *Recalls* that in previous resolutions the Board called on Iran to suspend all enrichment-related and reprocessing activities; welcomes Iran's voluntary decisions in that respect; regrets that those commitments have not been comprehensively implemented and calls on Iran immediately to correct all remaining shortcomings, and to remove the existing variance in relation to the Agency's understanding of the scope of Iran's decisions regarding suspension, including by refraining from the production of UF_6 and from all production of centrifuge components, as well as to enable the Agency to verify fully the suspension;

8. In the context of Iran's voluntary decisions to suspend all enrichment-related and reprocessing activities, *calls* on Iran, as a further confidence-building measure, voluntarily to reconsider its decision to begin production testing at the Uranium Conversion Facility and also, as an additional confidence building measure, to reconsider its decision to start construction of a research reactor moderated by heavy water, as the reversal of those decisions would make it easier for Iran to restore international confidence undermined by past reports of undeclared nuclear activities in Iran;

9. *Recalls* that the full and prompt cooperation with the Agency of all third countries is essential in the clarification of certain outstanding questions, notably contamination;

10. *Commends* the Director General and the Secretariat for their professional and impartial efforts to implement Iran's safeguards agreement,[153] and, pending its entry into force, Iran's Additional Protocol, as well as to verify Iran's suspension of enrichment-related and reprocessing activities, and to investigate supply routes and sources;

11. *Requests* the Director General to report well in advance of the September Board - or earlier if appropriate - on these issues as well as on the implementation of this and prior resolutions on Iran; and

12. *Decides* to remain seized of the matter.

Document 27: Implementation of the NPT Safeguards Agreement in the Islamic Republic of Iran

Resolution GOV/2004/79, 18 September 2004

The Board of Governors

(a) *Recalling* the resolutions adopted by the Board on 18 June 2004 (GOV/2004/49),[154] 13 March 2004 (GOV/2004/21),[155] 26 November 2003 (GOV/2003/81),[156] and on 12 September 2003 (GOV/2003/69)[157] and the statement by the Board of 19 June 2003 (GOV/OR.1072),[158]

---

[153] Doc. 4.
[154] Doc. 26.
[155] Doc. 25.
[156] Doc. 24.
[157] Doc. 23.
[158] Doc. 60.

(b) *Noting* with appreciation the Director General's report of 1 September 2004 (GOV/2004/60),[159] on the implementation of safeguards in Iran,

(c) *Noting* the Director General's assessment that the Agency is making steady progress towards understanding Iran's nuclear programmes, but that further work is still required on a number of questions and issues, notably contamination and the scope of the P2 centrifuge programme, and that there are other issues that will also require further follow-up, for example the timeframe of Iran's plutonium separation experiments,

(d) *Noting* with serious concern that, as detailed in the Director General's report, Iran has not heeded repeated calls from the Board to suspend, as a confidence building measure, all enrichment-related and reprocessing activities,

(e) *Also concerned* that, at its Uranium Conversion Facility, Iran is planning to introduce 37 tonnes of yellowcake, as this would run counter to the request made of Iran by the Board in resolution GOV/2004/49,

(f) *Recognising* the right of states to the development and practical application of atomic energy for peaceful purposes, including the production of electric power, consistent with their Treaty obligations, with due consideration for the needs of the developing countries, and

(g) *Stressing* the need for effective safeguards to prevent nuclear material being used for prohibited purposes, in contravention of agreements, and underlining the vital importance of effective safeguards for facilitating cooperation in the field of nuclear energy,

1. *Strongly* urges that Iran respond positively to the Director General's findings on the provision of access and information by taking such steps as are required by the Agency and/or requested by the Board in relation to the implementation of Iran's Safeguards Agreement,[160] including the provision of prompt access to locations and personnel, and by providing further information and explanations when required by the Agency and proactively, to assist the Agency to understand the full extent and nature of Iran's enrichment programme and to take all steps within its power to clarify the outstanding issues before the Board's 25 November meeting, specifically including the sources and reasons for enriched uranium contamination, and the import, manufacture, and use of centrifuges;

2. *Emphasises* the continuing importance of Iran acting in accordance with all provisions of the Additional Protocol[161] including by providing all access required in a timely manner; and urges Iran once again to ratify its Protocol without delay;

3. *Deeply regrets* that the implementation of Iranian voluntary decisions to suspend enrichment-related and reprocessing activities, notified to the Agency on 29 December 2003 and 24 February 2004, fell significantly short of the Agency's understanding of the scope of those commitments and also that Iran has since reversed some of those decisions; stresses that such suspension would provide the Board with additional confidence in Iran's future activities; and considers it necessary, to promote confidence, that Iran immediately suspend all enrichment-related activities, including the manufacture or import of centrifuge components, the assembly and testing of centrifuges, and the production of feed material, including through tests or production at the UCF, under Agency verification so that this could be confirmed in the reports requested in paragraphs 7 and 8 below;

---

[159] Doc. 38.

4. *Calls* again on Iran, as a further confidence-building measure, voluntarily to reconsider its decision to start construction of a research reactor moderated by heavy water;

5. *Underlines* the need for the full and prompt cooperation with the Agency of third countries in relation to the clarification of outstanding issues, and expresses appreciation for the cooperation received by the Agency to date;

6. *Appreciates* the professional and impartial efforts of the Director General and the Secretariat to implement Iran's NPT Safeguards Agreement, and, pending its entry into force, Iran's Additional Protocol, as well as to verify Iran's suspension of enrichment-related and reprocessing activities, and to investigate supply routes and sources;

7. *Requests* the Director General to submit in advance of the November Board:
   • a report on the implementation of this resolution;
   • a recapitulation of the Agency's findings on the Iranian nuclear programme since September 2002, as well as a full account of past and present Iranian cooperation with the Agency, including the timing of declarations, and a record of the development of all aspects of the programme, as well as a detailed analysis of the implications of those findings in relation to Iran's implementation of its Safeguards Agreement;

8. *Also requests* the Director General to submit in advance of the November Board a report on Iran's response to the requests made of it by the Board in previous resolutions, especially requests relating to full suspension of all enrichment-related and reprocessing activities;

9. *Decides* that at its November session it will decide whether or not further steps are appropriate in relation to:
   • Iran's obligations under its NPT Safeguards Agreement;
   • the requests made of Iran, as confidence building measures, by the Board in this and previous resolutions;
   and to remain seized of the matter.

Document 28: Implementation of the NPT Safeguards Agreement in the Islamic Republic of Iran

Resolution GOV/2004/90, 29 November 2004

The Board of Governors,

(a) *Recalling* the resolutions adopted by the Board on 18 September 2004 (GOV/2004/79),[162] 18 June 2004 (GOV/2004/49),[163] 13 March 2004 (GOV/2004/21),[164] 26 November 2003 (GOV/2003/81)[165] and on 12 September 2003 (GOV/2003/69)[166] and the statement by the Board of 19 June 2003 (GOV/OR.1072),[167]

---

[160] Doc. 4.
[161] Doc. 5.
[162] Doc. 27.
[163] Doc. 26.
[164] Doc. 25.
[165] Doc. 24.
[166] Doc. 23.
[167] Doc. 60.

(b) *Noting* with appreciation the Director General's report of 15 November 2004 (GOV/2004/83)[168] on the implementation of Iran's NPT Safeguards Agreement (INFCIRC 214),[169]

(c) *Noting* specifically the Director General's assessment that Iranian practices up to October 2003 resulted in many breaches of Iran's obligations to comply with its Safeguards Agreement, but that good progress has been made since that time in Iran's correction of those breaches and in the Agency's ability to confirm certain aspects of Iran's current declarations,

(d) *Also noting* specifically the Director General's assessment that all the declared nuclear material in Iran has been accounted for, and that such material is not diverted to prohibited activities, but that the Agency is not yet in a position to conclude that there are no undeclared nuclear materials or activities in Iran,

(e) *Recalling* the Board's previous requests to Iran to suspend all enrichment related and reprocessing activities as a voluntary confidence building measure,

(f) *Noting* with concern that Iran has continued enrichment related activities, including the production of UF_6 up to 22 November 2004, in spite of the request made by the Board in September that Iran immediately suspend all such activities,

(g) *Noting* with interest the agreement between Iran, France, Germany and the UK with the support of the High Representative of the EU, made public on 15 November (INFCIRC 637),[170] in which Iran states its decision to continue and extend its suspension of all enrichment related and reprocessing activities; and noting with satisfaction that, pursuant to this agreement, notification of this decision was sent by Iran to the Director General on 14 November with the Agency invited to verify the suspension with effect from 22 November 2004,

(h) *Recognizing* that this suspension is a voluntary confidence building measure, not a legal obligation,

(i) *Recognizing* the right of states to the development and practical application of atomic energy for peaceful purposes, including the production of electric power, consistent with their Treaty obligations, with due consideration for the needs of the developing countries,

(j) *Stressing* the need for effective safeguards to prevent nuclear material being used for prohibited purposes, in contravention of agreements, and underlining the vital importance of effective safeguards for facilitating cooperation in the field of nuclear energy, and

(k) *Commending* the Director General and the Secretariat for the work they have done to date to resolve all questions relevant to safeguards implementation in Iran,

> 1. *Welcomes* the fact that Iran has decided to continue and extend its suspension of all enrichment related and reprocessing activities, and underlines that the full and sustained implementation of this suspension, which is a voluntary, non-legally-binding, confidence building measure, to be verified by the Agency, is essential to addressing outstanding issues;

> 2. *Welcomes* the Director General's statements of 25 and 29 November 2004 that the above decision has been put into effect, and requests the Director General to continue verifying that the suspension remains in place and to inform Board members should the suspension not be fully sustained, or should the Agency

---

[168] Doc. 39.
[169] Doc. 4.
[170] Doc. 8.

be prevented from verifying all elements of the suspension, for as long as the suspension is in force;

3. *Welcomes* Iran's continuing voluntary commitment to act in accordance with the provisions of the Additional Protocol,[171] as a confidence building measure that facilitates the resolution of the questions that have arisen, and calls on Iran once again to ratify its Protocol soon;

4. *Reaffirms* its strong concern that Iran's policy of concealment up to October 2003 has resulted in many breaches of Iran's obligations to comply with its NPT Safeguards Agreement; at the same time acknowledges the corrective measures described in the Director General's report;

5. *Welcomes* the Director General's intention to pursue his investigations into the remaining outstanding issues, in particular the origin of contamination and the extent of Iran's centrifuge programme, as well as the full implementation of Iran's Safeguards Agreement and Additional Protocol, with a view to providing credible assurances regarding the absence of undeclared nuclear material and activities in Iran;

6. *Underlines* the continuing importance of Iran extending full and prompt cooperation to the Director General in the above pursuit, and requests Iran as a confidence building measure to provide any access deemed necessary by the Agency in accordance with the Additional Protocol; and

7. *Requests* the Director General to report to the Board on his findings, as appropriate.

Document 29: Implementation of the NPT Safeguards Agreement in the Islamic Republic of Iran and Related Board Resolutions

Resolution GOV/2005/64, 11 August 2005

The Board of Governors,

(a) *Recalling* the resolutions adopted by the Board on 29 November 2004 (GOV/2004/90),[172] 18 September 2004 (GOV/2004/79),[173] 18 June 2004 (GOV/2004/49),[174] 13 March 2004 (GOV/2004/21),[175] 26 November 2003 (GOV/2003/81)[176] and on 12 September 2003 (GOV/2003/69)[177] and the statement by the Board of 19 June 2003 (GOV/OR.1072),[178]

(b) *Recalling* that in the resolution adopted on 18 September 2004 (GOV/2004/79) the Board considered it necessary, to promote confidence, that Iran immediately suspend all enrichment-related activities, including the production of feed material, including through tests or production at the UCF,

---

[171] Doc. 5.
[172] Doc. 28.
[173] Doc. 27.
[174] Doc. 26.
[175] Doc. 25.
[176] Doc. 24.
[177] Doc. 23.
[178] Doc. 60.

(c) *Recalling* that in its resolution adopted on 29 November 2004 (GOV/2004/90) the Board noted with interest the agreement between Iran, France, Germany and the UK with the support of the High Representative of the EU, made public on 15 November 2004 (INFCIRC/637),[179]

(d) *Reaffirming* that, as underlined in the resolution adopted on 29 November 2004 (GOV/2004/90), the full and sustained implementation of the suspension notified by Iran to the Director General on 14 November, as a further voluntary, non-legally binding confidence-building measure, to be verified by the Agency, is essential to addressing outstanding issues,

(e) *Noting* that outstanding issues relating to Iran's nuclear programme have yet to be resolved, and that the Agency is not yet in a position to conclude that there are no undeclared nuclear materials or activities in Iran,

(f) *Recalling* the Director General's assessment in GOV/2004/83[180] that all the declared nuclear material in Iran had been accounted for, and that such material had not been diverted to prohibited activities,

(g) *Recognising* the right of states to the development and practical application of atomic energy for peaceful purposes, including the production of electric power, consistent with their Treaty obligations, with due consideration for the needs of developing countries, and

(h) *Stressing* the need for effective safeguards to prevent nuclear material being used for prohibited purposes, in contravention of legally binding agreements, and underlining the vital importance of effective safeguards for facilitating cooperation in the field of nuclear energy,

1. *Expresses* serious concern at the 1 August 2005 notification to the IAEA[181] that Iran had decided to resume the uranium conversion activities at the Uranium Conversion Facility in Esfahan, at the Director General's report that on 8 August Iran started to feed uranium ore concentrate into the first part of the process line at this facility and at the Director General's report that on 10 August Iran removed the seals on the process lines and the UF_4 at this facility;

2. *Underlines* the importance of rectifying the situation resulting from the developments reported by the Director General and also of allowing for further discussions in relation to that situation;

3. *Urges* Iran to re-establish full suspension of all enrichment related activities including the production of feed material, including through tests or production at the Uranium Conversion Facility, on the same voluntary, non-legally binding basis as requested in previous Board resolutions, and to permit the Director General to re-instate the seals that have been removed at that facility;

4. *Requests* the Director General to continue to monitor closely the situation and to inform the Board of any further developments as appropriate;

5. *Requests* the Director General to provide a comprehensive report on the implementation of Iran's NPT Safeguards Agreement[182] and this resolution by 3 September 2005; and

6. *Decides* to remain seized of the matter.

---

[179] Doc. 8.
[180] Doc. 39.
[181] Doc. 107.
[182] Doc. 4.

Document 30: Implementation of the NPT Safeguards Agreement in the Islamic Republic of Iran

Resolution GOV/2005/77, 24 September 2005

The Board of Governors,

(a) *Recalling* the resolutions adopted by the Board on 11 August 2005 (GOV/2005/64),[183]

29 November 2004 (GOV/2004/90),[184] 18 September 2004 (GOV/2004/79),[185] 18 June 2004 (GOV/2004/49,[186] 13 March 2004 (GOV/2004/21),[187] 26 November 2003 (GOV/2003/81)[188] and on 12 September 2003 (GOV/2003/69),[189] the statement of the Board of 19 June 2003 (GOV/OR.1072)[190] and the Chairman of the Board's conclusions of March 2005 (GOV/OR.1122) and of June 2005 (GOV/OR.1130),[191]

(b) *Recalling* that Article IV of the Treaty on the Non Proliferation of Nuclear Weapons stipulates that nothing in the Treaty shall be interpreted as affecting the inalienable rights of all the Parties to the Treaty to develop research, production and use of nuclear energy for peaceful purposes without discrimination and in conformity with Articles I and II of the Treaty,

(c) *Commending* the Director General and the Secretariat for their professional and impartial efforts to implement the Safeguards Agreement[192] in Iran, to resolve outstanding safeguards issues in Iran and to verify the implementation by Iran of the suspension,

(d) *Recalling* Iran's failures in a number of instances over an extended period of time to meet its obligations under its NPT Safeguards Agreement (INFCIRC/214) with respect to the reporting of nuclear material, its processing and its use, as well as the declaration of facilities where such material had been processed and stored, as reported by the Director General in his report GOV/2003/75 dated 10 November 2003[193] and confirmed in GOV/2005/67,[194] dated 2 September 2005,

(e) *Recalling* also that, as deplored by the Board in its resolution GOV/2003/81, Iran's policy of concealment has resulted in many breaches of its obligation to comply with its Safeguards Agreement,

(f) *Recalling* that the Director General in his report to the Board on 2 September 2005 noted that good progress has been made in Iran's correction of the breaches and in the Agency's ability to confirm certain aspects of Iran's current declarations,

(g) *Noting* that, as reported by the Director General, the Agency is not yet in a position to clarify some important outstanding issues after two and a half years of intensive inspections and investigation and that Iran's full transparency is indispensable and overdue,

---

[183] Doc. 29.
[184] Doc. 28.
[185] Doc. 27.
[186] Doc. 26.
[187] Doc. 25.
[188] Doc. 24.
[189] Doc. 23.
[190] Doc. 60.
[191] Doc. 74.
[192] Doc. 4.
[193] Doc. 35.
[194] Doc. 40.

(h) *Uncertain* of Iran's motives in failing to make important declarations over an extended period of time and in pursuing a policy of concealment up to October 2003,

(i) *Concerned* by continuing gaps in the Agency's understanding of proliferation sensitive aspects of Iran's nuclear programme,

(j) *Recalling* the emphasis placed in past resolutions on the importance of confidence building measures and that past resolutions have reaffirmed that the full and sustained implementation of the suspension notified to the Director General on 14 November 2004, as a voluntary, non legally binding confidence building measure, to be verified by the Agency, is essential to addressing outstanding issues,

(k) *Deploring* the fact that Iran has to date failed to heed the call by the Board in its resolution of 11 August 2005 to re-establish full suspension of all enrichment related activities including the production of feed material, including through tests or production at the Uranium Conversion Facility,

(l) *Also concerned* that Iran has to date failed to heed repeated calls to ratify the Additional Protocol[195] and to reconsider its decision to construct a research reactor moderated by heavy water, as these measures would have helped build confidence in the exclusively peaceful nature of Iran's nuclear programme,

(m) *Noting* that the Director General reported that the Agency 'continues to follow up on information pertaining to Iran's nuclear programme and activities that could be relevant to that programme' and that 'the Agency's legal authority to pursue the verification of possible nuclear weapons related activity is limited' (GOV/2005/67),

(n) *Endorsing* the Director General's description of this as a special verification case, and

(o) *Noting* that the Agency is still not in a position to conclude that there are no undeclared nuclear materials or activities in Iran,

1. *Finds* that Iran's many failures and breaches of its obligations to comply with its NPT Safeguards Agreement, as detailed in GOV/2003/75, constitute non compliance in the context of Article XII.C of the Agency's Statute;[196]

2. *Finds* also that the history of concealment of Iran's nuclear activities referred to in the Director General's report, the nature of these activities, issues brought to light in the course of the Agency's verification of declarations made by Iran since September 2002 and the resulting absence of confidence that Iran's nuclear programme is exclusively for peaceful purposes have given rise to questions that are within the competence of the Security Council, as the organ bearing the main responsibility for the maintenance of international peace and security;

3. *Requests* the Director General to continue his efforts to implement this and previous Resolutions and to report again, including any further developments on the issues raised in his report of 2 September 2005 (GOV/2005/67) to the Board. The Board will address the timing and content of the report required under Article XII.C and the notification required under Article III.B.4;

4. In order to help the Director General to resolve outstanding questions and provide the necessary assurances, *urges* Iran:

(i) To implement transparency measures, as requested by the Director General in his report, which extend beyond the formal requirements of the Safeguards Agreement and Additional Protocol, and include access to

---

[195] Doc. 5.
[196] Doc. 3.

individuals, documentation relating to procurement, dual use equipment, certain military owned workshops and research and development locations;

(ii) To re-establish full and sustained suspension of all enrichment-related activity, as in GOV/2005/64, and reprocessing activity;

(iii) To reconsider the construction of a research reactor moderated by heavy water;

(iv) Promptly to ratify and implement in full the Additional Protocol;

(v) Pending completion of the ratification of the Additional Protocol to continue to act in accordance with the provisions of the Additional Protocol, which Iran signed on 18 December 2003;

5. *Calls* on Iran to observe fully its commitments and to return to the negotiating process that has made good progress in the last two years;

6. *Requests* the Director General to continue his efforts to implement the Agency's Safeguards Agreement with Iran, to implement provisionally the Additional Protocol to that Agreement, and to pursue additional transparency measures required for the Agency to be able to reconstruct the history and nature of all aspects of Iran's past nuclear activities, and to compensate for the confidence deficit created; and

7. *Decides* to remain seized of the matter.

Document 31: IAEA Board of Governors' Chairman's Conclusion

24 November 2005

All comments will be duly reflected in the summary records of the meeting. Therefore, I will not sum up the discussion in detail.

The Board took note of the Director General's report on the implementation of the NPT safeguards agreement[197] in the Islamic Republic of Iran contained in document GOV/2005/87.[198]

Some Members stated that only modest progress had been made since September towards resolving questions arising from Iran's multiple failures, over an extended period of time, to declare nuclear material and activities in accordance with its safeguards obligations. They emphasized that cooperation on the part of Iran remained inadequate and that the continuing absence of full transparency was a matter of the utmost concern. They called on Iran to provide full transparency, beyond the provisions of Iran's NPT safeguards agreement and additional protocol,[199] including providing information and documentation related to P-1 and P-2 centrifuges and dual-use equipment, as well as facilitating visits to relevant military-owned workshops and R&D locations. They expressed concern about the document which relates to the casting and machining of enriched uranium metal into hemispherical forms and requested that the Director General give priority to its investigation.

---

[197] Doc. 4.
[198] Doc. 41.
[199] Doc. 5.

Some Members continued to attach the highest importance to the full suspension of all enrichment-related activities while outstanding issues were addressed and confidence in the exclusively peaceful nature of Iran's nuclear programme established. They expressed their regret that Iran continued to operate the UCF and was still pursuing construction of a heavy water research reactor. They recalled the Board's resolution of 24 September 2005[200] and stated that at present the window of opportunity should remain open for Iran to adopt a responsive attitude to implement the confidence-building measures called for by the Board, to refrain from any further unilateral move, such as resumption of enrichment activities at Natanz, which could aggravate the situation, and to respond faithfully to requests made in previous Board resolutions, before the Board would address the timing and content of communications to the Security Council envisaged in that resolution. Calls were made for Iran to resume the negotiating process with the EU-3 and support was expressed for the EU-3 effort to broaden the basis for an international consensus through additional elements in the negotiating process such as the recent Russian proposal.

Some Members noted that Iran had been implementing the additional protocol and had been more forthcoming in respect of transparency measures. Iran had facilitated access to additional documentation, individuals and sites. They expressed their appreciation for all initiatives by other Member States aimed at facilitating the speedy conclusion of the Iranian nuclear issue within the framework of the Agency. They recognized that the Agency's work on verifying the peaceful nuclear programme of Iran is ongoing and encouraged Iran's further cooperation as a confidence-building measure. It was emphasized that those who have information on illicit supply networks, especially the countries from which these networks operated or sourced technology, should share all such information with the Agency and empower the Agency in every way possible to gain an understanding of how these networks operate. They reiterated the basic and inalienable right of all Member States to develop atomic energy for peaceful purposes in conformity with their respective legal obligations. They referred to the link between non-proliferation and disarmament and reiterated deep concern over the slow pace of progress towards nuclear disarmament. They re-emphasized the distinction between voluntary confidence building measures and legally binding safeguards obligations. They encouraged the resumption of negotiations and cooperation between Iran and the EU-3 to promote mutual confidence with a view to facilitating the Agency's work on Iran's nuclear programme. The importance of restraint and flexibility by all parties was noted.

Some Members emphasized that addressing the issue of the implementation of the NPT safeguards agreement of Iran was closely linked to the establishment of a nuclear-weapon-free zone in the Middle East, and reference was made in this regard to the Teheran Declaration of 2003.[201] The importance of the implementation of international resolutions in relation to this matter was stressed.

The Board reiterated its call that Iran ratify its additional protocol as a matter of urgency. The Board also reiterated its support for the resumption of negotiations between Iran and the EU-3. The Board encouraged Iran to provide further additional supporting documentation as requested by the Agency and to expand the transparency measures provided to the Agency. One Member State requested that the implementation of Iran's NPT safeguards agreement be formally included on the agenda for the next Board meeting and that the Director General provide a follow-up written report to the Board in advance of that meeting.

---

[200] Doc. 30.
[201] Doc. 7.

The Board requested the Director General to continue to keep it informed of developments, as appropriate.

...

Document 32: Implementation of the NPT Safeguards Agreement in the Islamic Republic of Iran

Resolution GOV/2006/14, 4 February 2006

The Board of Governors,

(a) *Recalling* all the resolutions adopted by the Board on Iran's nuclear programme,

(b) *Recalling* also the Director General's reports,

(c) *Recalling* that Article IV of the Treaty on the Non Proliferation of Nuclear Weapons stipulates that nothing in the Treaty shall be interpreted as affecting the inalienable rights of all the Parties to the Treaty to develop research, production and use of nuclear energy for peaceful purposes without discrimination and in conformity with Articles I and II of the Treaty,

(d) *Commending* the Director General and the Secretariat for their professional and impartial efforts to implement the Safeguards Agreement[202] in Iran, to resolve outstanding safeguards issues in Iran and to verify the implementation by Iran of the suspension,

(e) *Recalling* the Director General's description of this as a special verification case,

(f) *Recalling* that in reports referred to above, the Director General noted that after nearly three years of intensive verification activity, the Agency is not yet in a position to clarify some important issues relating to Iran's nuclear programme or to conclude that there are no undeclared nuclear materials or activities in Iran,

(g) *Recalling* Iran's many failures and breaches of its obligations to comply with its NPT Safeguards Agreement and the absence of confidence that Iran's nuclear programme is exclusively for peaceful purposes resulting from the history of concealment of Iran's nuclear activities, the nature of those activities and other issues arising from the Agency's verification of declarations made by Iran since September 2002,

(h) *Recalling* that the Director General has stated that Iran's full transparency is indispensable and overdue for the Agency to be able to clarify outstanding issues (GOV/2005/67),[203]

(i) *Recalling* the requests of the Agency for Iran's cooperation in following up on reports relating to equipment, materials and activities which have applications in the conventional military area and in the civilian sphere as well as in the nuclear military area (as indicated by the Director General in GOV/2005/67),

(j) *Recalling* that in November 2005 the Director General reported (GOV/2005/87)[204] that Iran possesses a document related to the procedural requirements for the reduction of UF_6 to metal in small quantities, and on the casting and machining of enriched, natural and depleted uranium metal into hemispherical forms,

---

[202] Doc. 4.
[203] Doc. 40.
[204] Doc. 41.

(k) *Expressing* serious concerns about Iran's nuclear programme, and agreeing that an extensive period of confidence-building is required from Iran,

(l) *Reaffirming* the Board's resolve to continue to work for a diplomatic solution to the Iranian nuclear issue, and

(m) *Recognising* that a solution to the Iranian issue would contribute to global non-proliferation efforts and to realising the objective of a Middle East free of weapons of mass destruction, including their means of delivery,

1. *Underlines* that outstanding questions can best be resolved and confidence built in the exclusively peaceful nature of Iran's programme by Iran responding positively to the calls for confidence building measures which the Board has made on Iran, and in this context deems it necessary for Iran to:

- re-establish full and sustained suspension of all enrichment-related and reprocessing activities, including research and development, to be verified by the Agency;
- reconsider the construction of a research reactor moderated by heavy water;
- ratify promptly and implement in full the Additional Protocol;[205]
- pending ratification, continue to act in accordance with the provisions of the Additional Protocol which Iran signed on 18 December 2003;
- implement transparency measures, as requested by the Director General, including in GOV/2005/67, which extend beyond the formal requirements of the Safeguards Agreement and Additional Protocol, and include such access to individuals, documentation relating to procurement, dual use equipment, certain military-owned workshops and research and development as the Agency may request in support of its ongoing investigations;

2. *Requests* the Director General to report to the Security Council of the United Nations that these steps are required of Iran by the Board and to report to the Security Council all IAEA reports and resolutions, as adopted, relating to this issue;

3. *Expresses* serious concern that the Agency is not yet in a position to clarify some important issues relating to Iran's nuclear programme, including the fact that Iran has in its possession a document on the production of uranium metal hemispheres, since, as reported by the Secretariat, this process is related to the fabrication of nuclear weapon components; and, noting that the decision to put this document under Agency seal is a positive step, requests Iran to maintain this document under Agency seal and to provide a full copy to the Agency;

4. *Deeply regrets* that, despite repeated calls from the Board for the maintaining of the suspension of all enrichment related and reprocessing activities which the Board has declared essential to addressing outstanding issues, Iran resumed uranium conversion activities at its Isfahan facility on 8 August 2005 and took steps to resume enrichment activities on 10 January 2006;

5. *Calls* on Iran to understand that there is a lack of confidence in Iran's intentions in seeking to develop a fissile material production capability against the background of Iran's record on safeguards as recorded in previous Resolutions, and outstanding issues; and to reconsider its position in relation to confidence-building measures, which are voluntary, and non legally binding, and to adopt

---

[205] Doc. 5.

a constructive approach in relation to negotiations that can result in increased confidence;

6. *Requests* Iran to extend full and prompt cooperation to the Agency, which the Director General deems indispensable and overdue, and in particular to help the Agency clarify possible activities which could have a military nuclear dimension;

7. *Underlines* that the Agency's work on verifying Iran's declarations is ongoing and requests the Director General to continue with his efforts to implement the Agency's Safeguards Agreement with Iran, to implement the Additional Protocol to that Agreement pending its entry into force, with a view to providing credible assurances regarding the absence of undeclared nuclear material and activities in Iran, and to pursue additional transparency measures required for the Agency to be able to resolve outstanding issues and reconstruct the history and nature of all aspects of Iran's past nuclear activities;

8. *Requests* the Director General to report on the implementation of this and previous resolutions to the next regular session of the Board, for its consideration, and immediately thereafter to convey, together with any Resolution from the March Board, that report to the Security Council; and

9. *Decides* to remain seized of the matter.

2. Reports and Statements of the IAEA Director General on Implementation of The NPT Safeguards Agreement in the Islamic Republic of Iran and Relevant Provisions of Security Council Resolutions

Document 33: Implementation of the NPT Safeguards Agreement in the Islamic Republic of Iran, Report by the Director General

GOV/2003/40, 6 June 2003

A. Introduction

1. At the meeting of the Board of Governors on 17 March 2003, the Director General reported on discussions taking place with the Islamic Republic of Iran (hereinafter referred to as Iran) on a number of safeguards issues that needed to be clarified and actions that needed to be taken with regard to the implementation of the Agreement between Iran and the IAEA for the Application of Safeguards in connection with the Treaty on the Non-Proliferation of Nuclear Weapons (the Safeguards Agreement).[206] This report provides further information on the nature of the safeguards issues involved and the actions that need to be taken, and describes developments in this regard since March. More general reporting of safeguards implementation in Iran is not addressed in this document, but in the Safeguards Implementation Reports.

---

[206] Doc. 4.

...

D. Findings and Initial Assessment

32. Iran has failed to meet its obligations under its Safeguards Agreement with respect to the reporting of nuclear material, the subsequent processing and use of that material and the declaration of facilities where the material was stored and processed. These failures, and the actions taken thus far to correct them, can be summarized as follows:

(a) Failure to declare the import of natural uranium in 1991, and its subsequent transfer for further processing. On 15 April 2003, Iran submitted ICRs on the import of the UO_2, UF_4 and UF_6. Iran has still to submit ICRs on the transfer of the material for further processing and use.

(b) Failure to declare the activities involving the subsequent processing and use of the imported natural uranium, including the production and loss of nuclear material, where appropriate, and the production and transfer of waste resulting therefrom. Iran has acknowledged the production of uranium metal, uranyl nitrate, ammonium uranyl carbonate, UO_2 pellets and uranium wastes. Iran must still submit ICRs on these inventory changes.

(c) Failure to declare the facilities where such material (including the waste) was received, stored and processed. On 5 May 2003, Iran provided preliminary design information for the facility JHL. Iran has informed the Agency of the locations where the undeclared processing of the imported natural uranium was conducted (TRR and the Esfahan Nuclear Technology Centre), and provided access to those locations. It has provided the Agency access to the waste storage facility at Esfahan, and has indicated that access would be provided to Anarak, as well as the waste disposal site at Qom.

(d) Failure to provide in a timely manner updated design information for the MIX Facility and for TRR. Iran has agreed to submit updated design information for the two facilities.

(e) Failure to provide in a timely manner information on the waste storage at Esfahan and at Anarak. Iran has informed the Agency of the locations where the waste has been stored or discarded. It has provided the Agency access to the waste storage facility at Esfahan, and has indicated that access will be provided to Anarak.

33. Although the quantities of nuclear material involved have not been large,[207] and the material would need further processing before being suitable for use as the fissile material component of a nuclear explosive device, the number of failures by Iran to report the material, facilities and activities in question in a timely manner as it is obliged to do pursuant to its Safeguards Agreement is a matter of concern. While these failures are in the process of being rectified by Iran, the process of verifying the correctness and completeness of the Iranian declarations is still ongoing.

34. The Agency is continuing to pursue the open questions, including through:

(a) The completion of a more thorough expert analysis of the research and development carried out by Iran in the establishment of its enrichment capabilities. This will require the submission by Iran of a complete chronology of its centrifuge and laser enrichment efforts, including, in particular, a description of all research

---

[207] The total amount of material, approximately 1.8 tonnes, is 0.13 effective kilograms of uranium. This is, however, not insignificant in terms of a State's ability to conduct nuclear research and development activities (footnote in the original).

and development activities carried out prior to the construction of the Natanz facilities. As agreed to by Iran, this process will also involve discussions in Iran between Iranian authorities and Agency enrichment experts on Iran's enrichment programme, and visits by the Agency experts to the facilities under construction at Natanz and other relevant locations.

(b) Further follow-up on information regarding allegations about undeclared enrichment of nuclear material, including, in particular, at the Kalaye Electric Company. This will require permission for the Agency to carry out environmental sampling at the workshop located there.

(c) Further enquiries about the role of uranium metal in Iran's nuclear fuel cycle.

(d) Further enquiries about Iran's programme related to the use of heavy water, including heavy water production and heavy water reactor design and construction.

35. The Director General has repeatedly encouraged Iran to conclude an Additional Protocol.[208] Without such protocols in force, the Agency's ability to provide credible assurances regarding the absence of undeclared nuclear activities is limited. This is particularly the case for States, like Iran, with extensive nuclear activities and advanced fuel cycle technologies. In the view of the Director General, the adherence by Iran to an Additional Protocol would therefore constitute a significant step forward. The Director General will continue to keep the Board informed of developments.

Document 34: Implementation of the NPT Safeguards Agreement in the Islamic Republic of Iran, Report by the Director General

GOV/2003/63, 26 August 2003

...

D. Findings, Assessments and Next Steps

...

48. In its letter of 19 August 2003, Iran acknowledged that it had carried out uranium conversion experiments in the early 1990s, experiments that Iran should have reported in accordance with its obligations under the Safeguards Agreement.[209] Iran has stated, however, that it is taking corrective action in that regard. The Agency will continue its evaluation of the uranium conversion programme.

...

50. Additional work is also required to enable the Agency to arrive at conclusions about Iran's statements that there have been no uranium enrichment activities in Iran involving nuclear material...

...

52. Since the last report was issued, Iran has demonstrated an increased degree of co-operation in relation to the amount and detail of information provided to the Agency and in allowing access requested by the Agency to additional locations and the taking of

---

[208] Doc. 5.
[209] Doc. 4.

associated environmental samples. The decision by Iran to start the negotiations with the Agency for the conclusion of an Additional Protocol[210] is also a positive step. However, it should be noted that information and access were at times slow in coming and incremental, and that, as noted above, some of the information was in contrast to that previously provided by Iran. In addition, as also noted above, there remain a number of important outstanding issues, particularly with regard to Iran's enrichment programme, that require urgent resolution. Continued and accelerated co-operation and full transparency on the part of Iran are essential for the Agency to be in a position to provide at an early date the assurances required by Member States.

...

Document 35: Implementation of the NPT Safeguards Agreement in the Islamic Republic of Iran, Report by the Director General

GOV/2003/75, 10 November 2003

1. This report on safeguards issues in the Islamic Republic of Iran (hereinafter referred to as Iran) responds to paragraph 7 of the Board of Governors' resolution GOV/2003/69 of 12 September 2003.[211] It covers relevant developments from the time of the Director General's visit to Iran on 20-21 February 2003 and Iran's acknowledgement of its centrifuge enrichment programme, but concentrates on the period since his last report (GOV/2003/63 of 23 August 2003).[212] This report begins with the background to the issues in question (Section A) and a chronology of recent events (Section B). Information on the Agency's verification activities is summarized in Section C, organized according to the various technical processes involved (the details of which are set out in Annex 1). Section D provides a summary of the Agency's findings, while Section E sets out its current assessment and next steps. Annexes 2 and 3 to this report contain, respectively, a list of the locations identified to date as relevant to the implementation of safeguards in Iran, and a map showing those locations. Annex 4 is a list of relevant abbreviations and terms used in the text of the report.

...

D. Findings

45. Iran's nuclear programme, as the Agency currently understands it, consists of a practically complete front end of a nuclear fuel cycle, including uranium mining and milling, conversion, enrichment, fuel fabrication, heavy water production, a light water reactor, a heavy water research reactor and associated research and development facilities.

46. Iran has now acknowledged that it has been developing, for 18 years, a uranium centrifuge enrichment programme, and, for 12 years, a laser enrichment programme. In that context, Iran has admitted that it produced small amounts of LEU using both centrifuge and laser enrichment processes, and that it had failed to report a large number of conversion, fabrication and irradiation activities involving nuclear material, including the separation of a small amount of plutonium.

---

[210] Doc. 5.
[211] Doc. 23.
[212] Doc. 34.

47. Based on all information currently available to the Agency, it is clear that Iran has failed in a number of instances over an extended period of time to meet its obligations under its Safeguards Agreement[213] with respect to the reporting of nuclear material and its processing and use, as well as the declaration of facilities where such material has been processed and stored. In his June and August 2003 reports to the Board of Governors (GOV/2003/40[214] and GOV/2003/63), the Director General identified a number of instances of such failures and the corrective actions that were being, or needed to be, taken with respect thereto by Iran.

48. Since the issuance of the Director General's last report, a number of additional failures have been identified. These failures can be summarized as follows:

(a) Failure to report:

(i) the use of imported natural UF_6 for the testing of centrifuges at the Kalaye Electric Company in 1999 and 2002, and the consequent production of enriched and depleted uranium;

(ii) the import of natural uranium metal in 1994 and its subsequent transfer for use in laser enrichment experiments, including the production of enriched uranium, the loss of nuclear material during these operations, and the production and transfer of resulting waste;

(iii) the production of UO_2, UO_3, UF_4, UF_6 and AUC from imported depleted UO_2, depleted U_3O_8 and natural U_3O_8, and the production and transfer of resulting wastes;

(iv) the production of UO_2 targets at ENTC and their irradiation in TRR, the subsequent processing of those targets, including the separation of plutonium, the production and transfer of resulting waste, and the storage of unprocessed irradiated targets at TNRC;

(b) Failure to provide design information for:

(i) the centrifuge testing facility at the Kalaye Electric Company;

(ii) the laser laboratories at TNRC and Lashkar Ab'ad, and locations where resulting wastes were processed and stored, including the waste storage facility at Karaj;

(iii) the facilities at ENTC and TNRC involved in the production of UO_2, UO_3, UF_4, UF_6 and AUC;

(iv) TRR, with respect to the irradiation of uranium targets, and the hot cell facility where the plutonium separation took place, as well as the waste handling facility at TNRC; and

(c) Failure on many occasions to co-operate to facilitate the implementation of safeguards, through concealment.

49. As corrective actions, Iran has undertaken to submit ICRs relevant to all of these activities, to provide design information with respect to the facilities where those activities took place, to present all nuclear material for Agency verification during its forthcoming inspections and to implement a policy of co-operation and full transparency.

E. Assessment and Next Steps

50. The recent disclosures by Iran about its nuclear programme clearly show that, in the past, Iran had concealed many aspects of its nuclear activities, with resultant breaches of its obligation to comply with the provisions of the Safeguards Agreement. Iran's policy

---

[213] Doc. 4.
[214] Doc. 33.

of concealment continued until last month, with co-operation being limited and reactive, and information being slow in coming, changing and contradictory. While most of the breaches identified to date have involved limited quantities of nuclear material, they have dealt with the most sensitive aspects of the nuclear fuel cycle, including enrichment and reprocessing. And although the materials would require further processing before being suitable for weapons purposes, the number of failures by Iran to report in a timely manner the material, facilities and activities in question as it is obliged to do pursuant to its Safeguards Agreement has given rise to serious concerns.

51. Following the Board's adoption of resolution GOV/2003/69, the Government of Iran informed the Director General that it had now adopted a policy of full disclosure and had decided to provide the Agency with a full picture of all of its nuclear activities. Since that time, Iran has shown active co-operation and openness. This is evidenced, in particular, by Iran's granting to the Agency unrestricted access to all locations the Agency requested to visit; by the provision of information and clarifications in relation to the origin of imported equipment and components; and by making individuals available for interviews. This is a welcome development.

52. The Agency will now undertake all the steps necessary to confirm that the information provided by Iran on its past and present nuclear activities is correct and complete. To date, there is no evidence that the previously undeclared nuclear material and activities referred to above were related to a nuclear weapons programme. However, given Iran's past pattern of concealment, it will take some time before the Agency is able to conclude that Iran's nuclear programme is exclusively for peaceful purposes. To that end, the Agency must have a particularly robust verification system in place. An Additional Protocol,[215] coupled with a policy of full transparency and openness on the part of Iran, is indispensable for such a system.

53. In that context, Iran has been requested to continue its policy of active co-operation by answering all of the Agency's questions, and by providing the Agency with access to all locations, information and individuals deemed necessary by the Agency. One issue requiring investigation as a matter of urgency is the source of HEU and LEU contamination. The Agency intends to pursue the matter with a number of countries, whose full co-operation is essential to the resolution of this issue.

54. The recent announcement of Iran's intention to conclude an Additional Protocol, and to act in accordance with the provisions of the Protocol pending its entry into force, is a positive development. The draft Additional Protocol is now being submitted to the Board for its consideration.

55. Iran's decision to suspend its uranium enrichment related and reprocessing activities is also welcome.[216] The Agency intends to verify, in the context of the Safeguards Agreement and the Additional Protocol, the implementation by Iran of this decision.

...

---

[215] Doc. 5.

[216] It should be noted that Iran introduced UF_6 into the first centrifuge at PFEP on 25 June 2003, and, on 19 August 2003, began testing a small ten-machine cascade. On 31 October 2003, Agency inspectors observed that no UF_6 gas was being fed into the centrifuges, although construction and installation work at the site was continuing (footnote in the original).

Document 36: Implementation of the NPT Safeguards Agreement in the Islamic Republic of Iran, Report by the Director General

GOV/2004/11, 24 February 2004

...

B.5.1. Scope of Suspension

58. As reported by the Director General to the November 2003 meeting of the Board, Iran informed him on 10 November 2003 of its decision to suspend enrichment related and reprocessing activities, and that the suspension would cover all activities at the Natanz enrichment facility, the production of all feed material for enrichment and the importation of any enrichment related items.

59. In its Note Verbale of 29 December 2003, Iran further informed the Agency, that, with immediate effect:

- it would suspend the operation and/or testing or any centrifuges, either with or without nuclear material, at PFEP at Natanz;
- it would suspend further introduction of nuclear material into any centrifuges;
- it would suspend installation of new centrifuges at PFEP and installation of centrifuges at the Fuel Enrichment Plant (FEP) at Natanz; and
- it would withdraw nuclear material from any centrifuge enrichment facility if and to the extent practicable.

60. Iran also stated that: it did not currently have any type of gas centrifuge enrichment facility at any location in Iran other than the facility at Natanz that it was now constructing, nor did it have plans to construct, during the suspension period, new facilities capable of isotopic separation; it had dismantled its laser enrichment projects and removed all related equipment; and it was not constructing nor operating any plutonium separation facility.

61. In addition, Iran stated that: during the period of suspension, Iran did not intend to make new contracts for the manufacture of centrifuge machines and their components; the Agency could fully supervise storage of all centrifuge machines assembled during the suspension period; Iran did not intend to import centrifuge machines or their components, or feed material for enrichment processes, during the suspension period; and there was no production of feed material for enrichment processes in Iran.

62. On 24 February 2004, Iran informed the Agency that instructions will be issued by the first week of March to implement the further decisions voluntarily taken by Iran to: (i) suspend the assembly and testing of centrifuges, and (ii) suspend the domestic manufacture of centrifuge components, including those related to the existing contracts, to the furthest extent possible. Iran also informed the Agency that any components that are manufactured under existing contracts that cannot be suspended will be stored and placed under Agency seal. Iran invited the Agency to verify these measures. Iran also confirmed that the suspension of enrichment activities applied to all facilities in Iran.

...

C. Assessment and Next Steps

71. Iran has presented all declared nuclear material to the Agency for its verification. Iran has also provided all of the inventory change reports, material balance reports and physical inventory listings requested by the Agency. While some corrections are required and are still pending, this is partially due to the need to establish the nuclear material

hold-up in dismantled equipment and other problems associated with nuclear material accountancy for past activities. In addition, Iran has submitted design information with respect to facilities, as requested by the Agency, although some of the information needs to be revised and/or supplemented, which Iran has agreed to do.

72. Iran has been actively cooperating with the Agency in providing access to locations requested by the Agency. This included access to workshops situated at military sites. This is welcome. Also welcome is the decision by Iran to expand the scope of suspension to cover remaining enrichment activities, which, in the Agency's view, will contribute to confidence building.

73. Although investigations are ongoing, the Agency has made good progress in verifying Iran's statements regarding the UCF project and the associated experiments and testing activities. The Agency has also been verifying the suspension of those enrichment and reprocessing activities specified in Iran's Note Verbale of 29 December 2003.

74. The omission from Iran's letter of 21 October 2003 of any reference to its possession of the P-2 centrifuge design drawings and associated research, manufacturing and mechanical testing activities is a matter of serious concern, particularly in view of the importance and sensitivity of those activities. It runs counter to Iran's declaration, a document characterized by Iran as providing 'the full scope of Iranian nuclear activities' and a 'complete centrifuge R&D chronology'. The Director General has continued to emphasize to Iran the importance of declaring all the details of Iran's nuclear programme.

75. The Agency has still to resolve the major outstanding issue, of the LEU and HEU contamination found at the Kalaye Electric Company workshop and Natanz, and associated concerns. Until this matter is satisfactorily resolved, it will be very difficult for the Agency to confirm that there has not been any undeclared nuclear material or activities. The Agency is still waiting for Iran to provide requested information detailing the origin of the centrifuge equipment and components, the locations in Iran to which such equipment and components were moved and the associated details of timescales, and the names of individuals involved. The resolution of this issue will depend to a great extent on the cooperation of the country from which the imported items are believed to have originated.

76. Other issues requiring clarification include the nature and scope of Iran's activities in relation to P-2 centrifuges, and the nature and scope of Iran's laser isotope enrichment research and details of the associated equipment. The issue of the purpose of Iran's activities related to the production and intended use of Po-210 remains a concern, in the absence of information to support Iran's statements in this regard.

77. Although the timelines of the conversion and centrifuge programmes of Iran and the Socialist People's Libyan Arab Jamahiriya (Libya) are different, they share several common elements. The basic technology is very similar and was largely obtained from the same foreign sources. As part of verifying the correctness and completeness of the declarations of Iran and Libya, the Agency is investigating, with the support of Member States, whose full cooperation is essential, the supply routes and sources of such technology and related equipment and nuclear and non-nuclear materials.

…

Document 37: Implementation of the NPT Safeguards Agreement in the Islamic Republic of Iran, Report by the Director General

GOV/2004/34, 1 June 2004 and GOV/2004/34 Corr.1, 18 June 2004

...

C. Assessments

43. There has been good progress on the actions agreed during the Director General's visit to Tehran in early April 2004. The Agency welcomes Iran's recent provision of the initial declarations pursuant to its Additional Protocol.[217] Iran has been cooperating with the Agency in providing access to locations in response to Agency requests, including workshops situated at military sites. This is welcome, as is Iran's agreement to provide one-year multiple-entry visas to designated Agency inspectors.

44. The Agency has been able to verify Iran's implementation of its decision to suspend enrichment related and reprocessing activities. However, this verification was delayed in some cases by the discussion of modalities for access to the DIO sites, and is not yet comprehensive because of the continued production of centrifuge equipment by some private companies. Iran's decision to proceed with the generation of UF_6 at UCF through the conduct of hot tests is at variance with the Agency's previous understanding as to the scope of Iran's decision regarding suspension.

45. The Agency continues to make progress in gaining a comprehensive understanding of Iran's nuclear programme, but a number of issues remain outstanding. Two issues, in particular, are key to understanding the extent and nature of Iran's previously undeclared enrichment programme.

46. The first such issue relates to the origin of HEU and LEU contamination found at various locations in Iran. As stated in paragraph 27 above, the information provided to date by Iran has not been adequate to resolve this complex matter and Iran should make every effort to provide any additional information about the origin of the components that could be useful in resolving outstanding questions. The Agency has received some information from other States that may be helpful in resolving some contamination questions, and will equally continue to request those States to make every effort to assist the Agency in resolving this matter.

47. The second issue is the extent of Iran's efforts to import, manufacture and use centrifuges of both the P-1 and the P-2 design. The Agency has gained a fuller understanding of the scale of the programme involving P-1 centrifuges, and the locations of their use. However, important information about the P-2 centrifuge programme has frequently required repeated requests, and in some cases has been incomplete, and continues to lack the necessary clarity.

48. It is important that Iran work proactively to enable the Agency to gain a full understanding of Iran's enrichment programme by providing all relevant information, as well as by providing prompt access to all relevant sites. Iran's postponement until mid-April of the visits originally scheduled for mid-March - including visits of Agency centrifuge experts to a number of locations involved in Iran's P-2 centrifuge enrichment programme - resulted in a delay in the taking of environmental samples and their analysis. It is also important that all other States with relevant information promptly provide such

---
[217] Doc. 5.

information to the Agency. Bringing the two issues referred to in paragraphs 46 and 47 above to a close, after almost two years from when Iran's undeclared programme came to the Agency's knowledge, is of key importance to the Agency's ability to provide the international community with the required assurances about Iran's nuclear activities.

...

Document 38: Implementation of the NPT Safeguards Agreement in the Islamic Republic of Iran, Report by the Director General

GOV/2004/60, 1 September 2004

...

Suspension

47. In its Note Verbale of 29 December 2003, Iran informed the Agency that, with immediate effect, it would suspend:
   • the operation and/or testing of any centrifuges at PFEP at Natanz;
   • further introduction of nuclear material into any centrifuges;
   • installation of new centrifuges at PFEP and installation of centrifuges at FEP.

48. Iran also indicated that it would withdraw nuclear material from any centrifuge enrichment facility if and to the extent practicable. It further stated that:
   • it currently was not constructing any type of gas centrifuge enrichment facility at any location in Iran other than the facility at Natanz, nor did it have plans to construct new facilities capable of isotopic separation during the suspension;
   • it had dismantled its laser enrichment projects and removed all related equipment;
   • it was not constructing or operating any plutonium separation facility;
   • during the period of suspension, it did not intend to make new contracts for the manufacture of centrifuge machines and their components;
   • the Agency could fully supervise storage of all centrifuge machines assembled during the suspension period;
   • Iran did not intend to import centrifuge machines or their components, or feed material for enrichment processes, during the suspension period; and
   • there was no production of feed material for enrichment processes in Iran.

49. On 24 February 2004, Iran invited the Agency to verify its further voluntary decisions to:
   • suspend the assembly and testing of centrifuges; and
   • suspend the domestic manufacture of centrifuge components, including those related to the existing contracts, to the furthest extent possible (and said that any components that were manufactured under existing contracts that could not be suspended would be stored and placed under Agency seal).

50. Iran also confirmed that the suspension of enrichment activities applied to all facilities in Iran.

51. On 21 May 2004, Iran informed the Agency that it had not, at any time, made any undertaking not to produce feed material for the enrichment process, and that its voluntary and temporary suspension did not include suspension of the production of UF_6.

52. As previously indicated in the Director General's report to the Board (GOV/2004/34, para. 42; Annex, paras 60-61), Iran informed the Agency that it was conducting hot tests at UCF that would generate UF_6 product...

53. As indicated above, Iran notified the Agency on 23 June 2004 of its intention to resume, 'under IAEA supervision, manufacturing of centrifuge components and assembly and testing of centrifuges'...

...

C. Findings and Next Steps

56. The Agency welcomes the new information provided recently by Iran in response to the Agency's requests, although the process of providing information needs, in certain instances, to be accelerated. In some cases, such as Iran's clarifications related to its initial declarations pursuant to its Additional Protocol,[218] the provision of new information has been prompt. In other cases, sufficiently detailed information has, despite repeated requests, been provided so late that it has not been possible to include an assessment of its sufficiency and correctness in this report. The Agency also welcomes the cooperation by Iran in providing access to locations in response to Agency requests, including at the Lavisan-Shian site.

57. Although the Agency is not yet in a position to draw definitive conclusions concerning the correctness and completeness of Iran's declarations related to all aspects of its nuclear programme, it continues to make steady progress in understanding the programme. In this regard, the Agency's investigations have reached a point where, with respect to two aspects previously identified by the Agency as requiring investigation (i.e. Iran's declared laser enrichment activities and Iran's declared uranium conversion experiments), further follow-up will be carried out as a routine safeguards implementation matter.

58. Two issues remain key to understanding the extent and nature of Iran's enrichment programme:

> • The first issue relates to the origin of uranium contamination found at various locations in Iran....
> • The second issue relates to the extent of Iran's efforts to import, manufacture and use centrifuges of both the P-1 and P-2 design...

59. There are other issues that will also require further follow-up, for example the timeframe of Iran's plutonium separation experiments.

60. The Agency has been able to verify Iran's suspension of enrichment related activities at specific facilities and sites, and has been able to confirm that it has not observed, to date, any activities at those locations inconsistent with its understanding of Iran's current suspension undertakings.

61. It is important for Iran to support the Agency's efforts to gain a full understanding of all remaining issues by continuing to provide access to locations, personnel and information relevant to safeguards implementation in response to Agency requests - as well as by proactively providing any additional information that could enhance the Agency's understanding of Iran's nuclear programme.

62. The Agency welcomes the cooperation of other States in response to Agency requests, which is key to the Agency's ability to resolve some of the outstanding issues. Information received to date from other States has proven useful in understanding aspects of the uranium contamination found in Iran. The Agency will continue to request States to actively assist the Agency in resolving these issues.

...

[218] Doc. 5.

Document 39: Implementation of the NPT Safeguards Agreement in the Islamic Republic of Iran, Report by the Director General

GOV/2004/83, 15 November 2004

...

C. Current Overall Assessment

106. Iran has made substantial efforts over the past two decades to master an independent nuclear fuel cycle. To that end, Iran has conducted experiments to acquire the know-how for almost every aspect of the fuel cycle. Iran's current nuclear programme, as the Agency understands it, is aimed, upon completion, at an independent front end of the nuclear fuel cycle, including uranium mining and milling, conversion, enrichment, fuel fabrication, a light water reactor, heavy water production, a heavy water research reactor and associated R&D facilities. Iran has also performed some laboratory scale experiments related to the reprocessing of irradiated fuel, and is carrying out R&D in the treatment, storage and disposal of radioactive waste.

107. Many aspects of Iran's nuclear fuel cycle activities and experiments, particularly in the areas of uranium enrichment, uranium conversion and plutonium separation, were not declared to the Agency in accordance with Iran's obligations under its Safeguards Agreement.[219] Iran's policy of concealment continued until October 2003, and has resulted in many breaches of its obligation to comply with that Agreement. Since that time, good progress has been made in Iran's correction of those breaches and in the Agency's ability to confirm certain aspects of Iran's current declarations, which will be followed up as a routine safeguards implementation matter.

108. There remain two important issues relevant to the Agency's investigation in order to provide assurance that there are no undeclared enrichment activities in Iran: the origin of LEU and HEU particle contamination found at various locations in Iran; and the extent of Iran's efforts to import, manufacture and use centrifuges of both the P-1 and P-2 designs.

109. With respect to the first issue, contamination, since the issuance of the last report to the Board, the Agency and the State from which most of the imported P-1 centrifuges originated have, in a cooperative effort, continued to share their respective analytical results. These results generally do not contradict the results from samples taken in Iran. The Agency's current overall assessment with respect to this issue is that the environmental sampling data available to date tends, on balance, to support Iran's statement about the foreign origin of much of the observed contamination. However, other possible explanations cannot be excluded at this point in time, and the Agency is continuing this investigation in an effort to confirm the actual source of contamination. Independent sampling and analysis may enable the Agency to confirm the correctness of statements made by Iran in this regard. Consultations with the State concerned on this matter are progressing, and agreement can be expected shortly on the appropriate modalities for such sampling.

110. With respect to the second issue, further investigation is required into the clandestine supply network in order for the Agency to be able to conclude its assessment on the extent of Iran's centrifuge enrichment programme, taking into account additional information that Iran has provided on its meetings with network intermediaries. A number of States have provided significant support to the Agency through the supply of information on Iran's use of intermediaries for procurement. In addition, consultations are

---

[219] Doc. 4.

under way with the State from which the P-1 and P-2 centrifuge technology obtained by Iran originated. One aspect of this investigation is related to Iran's statement that it did not pursue any work on the P-2 design between 1995 and 2002, as the reasons given by Iran for the apparent gap do not provide sufficient assurance that there were no related activities carried out during that period.

111. The Agency is still assessing other aspects of Iran's past nuclear programme, including statements made by it about plutonium separation experiments, in particular with respect to the dates they were carried out. In addition, while Iran has provided preliminary design information on the IR-40 heavy water research reactor, the construction of which should commence in 2004, the Agency has raised some questions regarding Iran's attempts to acquire manipulators and lead glass windows for the hot cells. With respect to the latter issue, in October and November 2004, Iran provided some clarifications, which are now being assessed.

112. All the declared nuclear material in Iran has been accounted for, and therefore such material is not diverted to prohibited activities. The Agency is, however, not yet in a position to conclude that there are no undeclared nuclear materials or activities in Iran. The process of drawing such a conclusion, after an Additional Protocol is in force, is normally a time consuming process. In view of the past undeclared nature of significant aspects of Iran's nuclear programme, and its past pattern of concealment, however, this conclusion can be expected to take longer than in normal circumstances. To expedite this process, Iran's active cooperation in the implementation of its Safeguards Agreement and Additional Protocol,[220] and full transparency, are indispensable. The assistance and cooperation of other States, as indicated above, is also essential to the resolution of the outstanding issues.

113. The Agency continues to follow up on open source reports relevant to Iran's nuclear programme. In this regard, it should be noted that the focus of Agency Safeguards Agreements and Additional Protocols is nuclear material, and that, absent some nexus to nuclear material, the Agency's legal authority to pursue the verification of possible nuclear weapons related activity is limited. However, in accordance with its practice in connection with its evaluation of other States' nuclear programmes, the Agency has continued to pursue, with Iran's cooperation, open source reports relating to dual use equipment and materials which have applications in the conventional military area and in the civilian sphere as well as in the nuclear military area. Iran has permitted the Agency, as a confidence building measure, to visit a number of defence related sites, including Kolahdouz and Lavisan. While the Agency found no nuclear related activities at Kolahdouz, it is still assessing information (and awaiting some additional information) in relation to the Lavisan site. The Agency is also still waiting to receive permission to visit the Parchin site.

…

II. OTHER REQUESTS BY THE BOARD: SUSPENSION

115. As reflected in paragraph 8 of GOV/2004/79,[221] the Board of Governors has requested the Director General to submit a report on 'Iran's responses to the requests made of it by the Board in previous resolutions, especially requests relating to full suspension of all enrichment related and reprocessing activities'.

116. The Board of Governors has adopted five resolutions, and approved one summary of the Chairman, in which it has made a number of requests of Iran. These requests may be summarized as falling within one or more of the following:

[220] Doc. 5.
[221] Doc. 27.

a. Requests that Iran comply with its obligations under its Safeguards Agreement, resolve all outstanding issues (including those related to LEU and HEU contamination, the nature and scope of Iran's P-2 centrifuge and laser enrichment programmes and the Po-210 experiments), take corrective measures and provide the access to locations and personnel and to information required of it under its Safeguards Agreement, including by providing full declarations on its past and present nuclear programme, in particular its enrichment programme and with respect to its conversion experiments, and by permitting environmental sampling;

b. Requests that Iran sign, ratify and fully implement a Protocol Additional to its Safeguards Agreement, based on the Model Additional Protocol, and, as a confidence-building measure, to act in accordance with the Additional Protocol pending its entry into force, including by complying with the deadline for declarations envisaged in Article 3 of the Protocol;

c. Requests for transparency and cooperation with the Agency; and

d. Requests that Iran suspend all enrichment related and reprocessing activities, including that it reconsider its decisions to begin production testing at UCF; associated with these requests are the Board's requests that Iran not introduce nuclear material into PFEP and that it reconsider its decision to begin production testing at UCF and its decision to start construction of a heavy water research reactor.

117. Section I of this report addresses Iran's response to the requests referred to in sub-paragraphs (a) through (c) above. In Section II, Iran's responses to the requests of the Board in connection with the suspension by Iran of enrichment related and reprocessing activities, summarized in sub-paragraph (d) above, are discussed.

A. Scope of suspension

118. As reflected in the Chairman's summary of the Board's deliberations on this matter in June 2003, the Board at that time 'encouraged Iran, pending the resolution of related outstanding issues, not to introduce nuclear material at the pilot enrichment plant as a confidence building measure.' On 12 September 2003, in resolution GOV/2003/69,[222] the Board reiterated this statement and, in that context, called on Iran 'to suspend all further uranium enrichment related activities, including the further introduction of nuclear material into Natanz, and, as a confidence building measure, any reprocessing activities, pending provision by the Director General of the assurances required by Member States, and pending satisfactory application of the provisions of the additional protocol.'

119. On 10 November 2003, the Iranian Government informed the Director General that it had decided to suspend, with effect from that date, all enrichment related and reprocessing activities in Iran, and specifically: to suspend all activities on the site of Natanz, not to produce feed material for enrichment processes and not to import enrichment related items.

120. In its resolution GOV/2003/81,[223] adopted on 26 November 2003, the Board welcomed Iran's decision voluntarily to suspend all enrichment related and reprocessing activities, requested Iran to adhere to it in a complete and verifiable manner, and endorsed the Director General's acceptance of Iran's invitation to verify implementation of that decision and report thereon.

121. In a Note Verbale dated 29 December 2003, Iran informed the Agency that:

• it would suspend the operation and/or testing of any centrifuges, either with or without nuclear material, at PFEP;

[222] Doc. 23.
[223] Doc. 24.

• it would suspend further introduction of nuclear material into any centrifuges;
• it would suspend installation of new centrifuges at PFEP and installation of centrifuges at the FEP; and
• it would withdraw nuclear material from any centrifuge enrichment facility if and to the extent practicable.

122. In its Note Verbale, Iran stated further: that it did not currently have any type of gas centrifuge enrichment facility at any location in Iran other than the facility at Natanz that it was now constructing, nor did it have plans to construct, during the suspension period, new facilities capable of isotopic separation; that it had dismantled its laser enrichment projects and removed all related equipment; and that it was not constructing or operating any plutonium separation facility.

123. Iran also stated in its Note Verbale that, during the period of suspension: Iran did not intend to make new contracts for the manufacture of centrifuge machines and their components; the Agency could fully supervise storage of all centrifuge machines assembled during the suspension period; Iran did not intend to import centrifuge machines or their components, or feed material for enrichment processes, during the suspension period; and '[t]here is no production of feed material for enrichment processes in Iran.'

124. On 24 February 2004, Iran informed the Agency that instructions would be issued by the first week of March to implement the further decisions voluntarily taken by Iran to: (i) suspend the assembly and testing of centrifuges, and (ii) suspend the domestic manufacture of centrifuge components, including those related to the existing contracts, to the furthest extent possible. Iran also informed the Agency that any components that were manufactured under existing contracts that could not be suspended would be stored and placed under Agency seal. Iran invited the Agency to verify these measures. Iran also confirmed that the suspension of enrichment activities applied to all facilities in Iran.

125. In resolution GOV/2004/21, adopted on 13 March 2004,[224] the Board called on Iran to extend the application of its commitment on suspension to 'all enrichment related and reprocessing activities throughout Iran, and requested the Director General to verify the full implementation of these steps.'

126. On 15 March 2004, Iran notified the Agency that the Agency's verification of the suspension of centrifuge component production could begin as of 10 April 2004. However, due to disputes between the AEOI and some of its private contractors, three private companies would continue with centrifuge component production.

127. In a letter dated 29 April 2004, Iran informed the Agency that it intended to conduct hot tests of the UF_6 production line at UCF. On 7 May 2004, the Agency wrote to Iran, informing it that, given the amounts of nuclear material involved, the hot testing of UCF with UF_6 gas would technically amount to the production of feed material for enrichment processes. In a letter dated 18 May 2004, Iran informed the Agency that 'Iran has not, at any time, made any undertaking not to produce feed material for the enrichment process. The decision taken for voluntary and temporary suspension is based on clearly defined scope which does not include suspension of production of UF_6.'

128. On 21 May 2004, Iran and the Agency were able to reach agreement on the Agency's proposal regarding the frequency of visits during the following twelve months for Agency verification of the suspension of the production of gas centrifuge enrichment components at the nine sites declared by Iran as having been engaged in such activities.

---

[224] Doc. 25.

129. On 18 June 2004, in resolution GOV/2004/49,[225] the Board called on Iran 'immediately to correct all remaining shortcomings, and to remove the existing variance in relation to the Agency's understanding of the scope of Iran's decisions regarding suspension, including by refraining from the production of UF_6 and from all production of centrifuge components, as well as to enable the Agency to verify fully the suspension.' In the context of Iran's voluntary decisions to suspend all enrichment related and reprocessing activities, the Board also called on Iran, 'as a further confidence building measure, voluntarily to reconsider its decision to begin production testing at [UCF] and also, as an additional confidence building measure, to reconsider its decision to start construction of a research reactor moderated by heavy water, as the reversal of those decisions would make it easier for Iran to restore international confidence undermined by past reports of undeclared nuclear activities in Iran.'

130. On 23 June 2004, the Director General received a letter from Iran informing him that Iran 'plan[ned] to suspend implementation of the expanded voluntary measures conveyed in [its] Note dated 24 February 2004' and that Iran 'thus, intend[ed] to resume, under IAEA supervision, manufacturing of centrifuge components and assembly and testing of centrifuges as of 29 June 2004.' In the letter, Iran requested the Agency 'to take steps that may be necessary to enable resumption of such operations as of 29 June.' On 29 June 2004, the Agency received a letter forwarding a list of seals which would be removed from material, components and equipment related to centrifuge component manufacturing and assembling. In a letter dated 29 June 2004, the Agency acknowledged receipt of Iran's letter and agreed to the removal of the seals by the operator in the absence of Agency inspectors.

131. On 18 September 2004, the Board of Governors adopted resolution GOV/2004/79, in which it requested Iran, inter alia, to 'immediately suspend all enrichment-related activities, including the manufacture or import of centrifuge components, the assembly and testing of centrifuges and the production of feed material, including through tests or production at the UCF, under Agency verification.' The Board also called again on Iran 'as a further confidence building measure, voluntarily to reconsider its decision to start construction of a research reactor moderated by heavy water.'

132. In a letter dated 14 November 2004, the Government of Iran notified the Director General that, in the context of an agreement reached on 14 November 2004 between the Government of Iran and the Governments of France, Germany and the United Kingdom, and the High Representative of the European Union,[226] Iran had 'decided, on a voluntary basis and as further confidence building measure, to continue and extend its suspension to include all enrichment related and reprocessing activities, and specifically: the manufacture and import of gas centrifuges and their components; the assembly, installation, testing or operation of gas centrifuges; and all tests and production for conversion at any uranium conversion installation'. In its letter, Iran 'recall[ed] and reconfirm[ed] that Iran does not have any reprocessing activity' or 'any activity for undertaking plutonium separation, or for constructing or operating any plutonium separation installation'. In addition, Iran stated that 'material at Isfahan UCF will be brought to a safe, secure and stable state, not beyond UF_4, in coordination with the Agency.' Iran invited the Agency to verify this suspension starting from 22 November 2004.

---

[225] Doc. 26.
[226] Doc. 8.

Document 40: Implementation of the NPT Safeguards Agreement in the Islamic Republic of Iran, Report by the Director General

GOV/2005/67, 2 September 2005

...

C. Current overall assessment

42. The Director General provided in paragraphs 106-114 of GOV/2004/83[227] a detailed overall assessment of Iran's nuclear programme and the Agency's efforts to verify Iran's declarations with respect to that programme. As indicated in that report, Iran has made substantial efforts over the past two decades to master an independent nuclear fuel cycle, and, to that end, had conducted experiments to acquire the know-how for almost every aspect of the fuel cycle. Many aspects of Iran's fuel cycle activities and experiments, particularly in the areas of uranium enrichment, uranium conversion and plutonium research, had not been declared to the Agency in accordance with Iran's obligations under its Safeguards Agreement.[228] Iran's policy of concealment continued until October 2003, and resulted in many breaches of its obligation to comply with that Agreement (summarized in paragraph 4 above).

43. Since October 2003, good progress has been made in Iran's correction of the breaches, and in the Agency's ability to confirm certain aspects of Iran's current declarations, which will be followed up as a routine safeguards implementation matter (particularly in connection with conversion activities, laser enrichment, fuel fabrication and the heavy water research reactor programme).

44. Two important issues were identified in the Director General's November 2004 report as relevant to the Agency's efforts to provide assurance that there are no undeclared enrichment activities in Iran, specifically: the origin of LEU and HEU particle contamination found at various locations in Iran; and the extent of Iran's efforts to import, manufacture and use centrifuges of both the P-1 and P-2 designs.

...

48. The Agency is still assessing other aspects of Iran's past nuclear programme, including: statements made by it about plutonium research, in particular with respect to the dates they were carried out; Iran's activities at Gchine; and Iran's activities involving polonium.

...

50. In view of the fact that the Agency is not yet in a position to clarify some important outstanding issues after two and a half years of intensive inspections and investigation, Iran's full transparency is indispensable and overdue. Given Iran's past concealment efforts over many years, such transparency measures should extend beyond the formal requirements of the Safeguards Agreement and Additional Protocol[229] and include access to individuals, documentation related to procurement, dual use equipment, certain military owned workshops and research and development locations. Without such transparency measures, the Agency's ability to reconstruct, in particular, the chronology of enrichment research and development, which is essential for the Agency to verify the correctness and completeness of the statements made by Iran, will be restricted.

[227] Doc. 39.
[228] Doc. 4.
[229] Doc. 5.

51. As indicated to the Board in November 2004, all the declared nuclear material in Iran has been accounted for, and therefore such material is not diverted to prohibited activities. The Agency is, however, still not in a position to conclude that there are no undeclared nuclear materials or activities in Iran. The process of drawing such a conclusion, after an Additional Protocol is in force, under normal circumstances, is a time consuming process. In view of the past undeclared nature of significant aspects of Iran's nuclear programme, and its past pattern of concealment, this conclusion can be expected to take longer than in normal circumstances.

...

D. Suspension

53. Pursuant to the Board's resolution on 29 November 2004 (GOV/2004/90),[230] and previous resolutions, the Agency has continued its activities to verify and monitor all elements of Iran's voluntary suspension of all enrichment related and reprocessing activities.

...

57. On 9 May 2005, during a DIV at FEP [fuel enrichment plant], Agency inspectors observed some construction work being carried out in the underground cascade hall of Building A and in the ventilation building above the cascade hall foreseen in the design information for FEP submitted by Iran. Iran has described this work as civil construction, not covered by its voluntary suspension undertaking. In subsequent DIVs, the Agency has noted that this construction work is continuing.

58. The Agency also continued its verification of Iran's voluntary suspension of conversion activities at UCF...

59. On 1 August 2005, Iran informed the Agency of its decision to resume uranium activities at UCF.[231] The Agency installed additional surveillance equipment at UCF between 8 and 10 August 2005. On 8 August 2005, Iran started to feed UOC into the first part of the process line and on 10 August removed the Agency seals from the remaining parts of the process line. The UF_6 remained under Agency seal.

...

Document 41: Implementation of the NPT Safeguards Agreement in the Islamic Republic of Iran, Report by the Director General

GOV/2005/87, 18 November 2005

...

6. The documents recently made available to the Agency related mainly to the 1987 offer; many of them dated from the late 1970s and early to mid-1980s. The documents included: detailed drawings of the P-1 centrifuge components and assemblies; technical specifications supporting component manufacture and centrifuge assembly; and technical documents relating to centrifuge operational performance. In addition, they included cascade schematic drawings for various sizes of research and development (R&D) cascades, together with the equipment needed for cascade operation (e.g. cooling water circuit needs

---

[230] Doc. 28.
[231] Doc. 107.

and special valve consoles). The documents also included a drawing showing a cascade layout for 6 cascades of 168 machines each and a small plant of 2000 centrifuges arranged in the same hall. Also among the documents was one related to the procedural requirements for the reduction of UF_6 to metal in small quantities, and on the casting and machining of enriched, natural and depleted uranium metal into hemispherical forms, with respect to which Iran stated that it had been provided on the initiative of the procurement network, and not at the request of the Atomic Energy Organization of Iran (AEOI).

...

B. Current overall assessment

20. In the September 2005 report to the Board of Governors, it was noted that, in light of the difficulty of establishing a definitive conclusion with respect to all of the contamination, it was important to make progress on the issue of the scope and chronology of Iran's P-1 and P-2 programmes (see paras 44-47 of GOV/2005/67).[232] Since that time, Iran has been more forthcoming in providing access to additional documentation related to the 1987 offer and permitting interviews with individuals who had been involved in discussions with the procurement network. However, there still remain issues to be resolved in connection with the genesis of the mid-1990s offer. The Agency is still seeking additional assurance that no P-2 programme was conducted between 1995 and 2002. The Agency is currently reviewing the new information provided by Iran on the P-1 and P-2 enrichment programmes and has emphasized to Iran the importance of providing the additional requested supporting documentation.

21. As also noted in the previous report to the Board, in order to clarify some of the outstanding issues related to Iran's enrichment programme, Iran's full transparency is indispensable and overdue. Transparency measures should include the provision of information and documentation related to the procurement of dual use equipment, and permitting visits to relevant military owned workshops and R&D locations associated with the Physics Research Centre and the Lavisan-Shian site. In this regard, the Agency welcomes the access provided to the Parchin site. The Agency, however, is still awaiting additional information and permission to undertake additional visits. These should also include interviews on the acquisition of certain dual use materials and equipment, and the taking of environmental samples from the above locations.

...

Document 42: Implementation of the NPT Safeguards Agreement in the Islamic Republic of Iran, Report by the Director General

GOV/2006/15 (also circulated as S/2006/150), 27 February 2006

...

A.5. Voluntary Implementation of the Additional Protocol

30. Iran has continued to facilitate access under its Safeguards Agreement[233] as requested by the Agency and, until 6 February 2006, implemented the Additional Protocol[234]

---

[232] Doc. 40.
[233] Doc. 4.
[234] Doc. 5.

as if it were in force, including by providing, in a timely manner, the requisite declarations and access to locations. Since November 2005, the Agency has conducted complementary access at three locations.

31. On 6 February 2006, Iran informed the Agency, inter alia, that:

'1. As stipulated in Para 7 of INFCIRC/666,[235] from the date of this letter, our commitment on implementing safeguards measures will only be based on the NPT Safeguards Agreement between the Islamic Republic of Iran and the Agency (INFCIRC/214).

2. From the date of this letter, all voluntarily suspended non-legally binding measures including the provisions of the Additional Protocol and even beyond that will be suspended.

Therefore based on the above mentioned, it is requested the following measures be taken by the Agency:

a. The Agency's inspector presence in the Islamic Republic of Iran for the verification activities should be scheduled only on the basis of the Safeguards Agreement.

b. All the Agency's containment and surveillance measures which were in place beyond the normal Agency safeguards measures should be removed by mid February 2006.

c. From now on, the regular channels of communication (code 1.1 of the Subsidiary Arrangement) should only be through the Permanent Mission of the Islamic Republic of Iran to the IAEA in Vienna.'

...

A.7. Suspension

41. In a letter dated 3 January 2006, Iran informed the Agency that it had decided to resume, as from 9 January 2006, 'those R&D on the peaceful nuclear energy programme which ha[d] been suspended as part of its expanded voluntary and non-legally binding suspension'.[236] On 7 January 2006, the Agency received a letter from Iran requesting that the Agency remove seals applied at Natanz, Farayand Technique and Pars Trash for the monitoring of suspension of enrichment related activities.[237] The seals were removed by Iran on 10 and 11 January 2006 in the presence of Agency inspectors.

...

B. Current overall assessment

...

48. Two important issues were identified in the Director General's November 2004 report[238] as relevant to the Agency's efforts to provide assurance that there are no undeclared enrichment activities in Iran, specifically: the origin of LEU and HEU particle contamination found at various locations in Iran; and the extent of Iran's efforts to import, manufacture and use centrifuges of both the P-1 and P-2 designs.

49. With respect to the first issue - contamination - as indicated above, based on the information currently available to the Agency, the results of the environmental sample analysis tend, on balance, to support Iran's statement about the foreign origin of most of the observed HEU contamination. It is still not possible at this time, however, to establish a definitive conclusion with respect to all of the contamination, particularly the LEU

---

[235] Doc. 113.
[236] GOV/INF/2006/1.
[237] GOV/INF/2006/2.
[238] Doc. 39.

contamination. This underscores the importance of additional information on the scope and chronology of Iran's P-1 and P-2 centrifuge programmes, which could greatly contribute to the resolution of the remaining contamination issues.

50. With respect to the second issue - the P-1 and P-2 centrifuge programmes - although some progress has been made since November 2004 in the verification of statements by Iran regarding the chronology of its centrifuge enrichment programme, the Agency has not yet been able to verify the correctness and completeness of Iran's statements concerning those programmes…

…

52. The Agency continues to follow up on all information pertaining to Iran's nuclear programme and activities…

53. As indicated to the Board in November 2004, and again in September 2005,[239] all the declared nuclear material in Iran has been accounted for. Although the Agency has not seen any diversion of nuclear material to nuclear weapons or other nuclear explosive devices, the Agency is not at this point in time in a position to conclude that there are no undeclared nuclear materials or activities in Iran. The process of drawing such a conclusion, under normal circumstances, is a time consuming process even with an Additional Protocol in force. In the case of Iran, this conclusion can be expected to take even longer in light of the undeclared nature of Iran's past nuclear programme, and in particular because of the inadequacy of information available on its centrifuge enrichment programme, the existence of a generic document related to the fabrication of nuclear weapon components, and the lack of clarification about the role of the military in Iran's nuclear programme, including, as mentioned above, about recent information available to the Agency concerning alleged weapon studies that could involve nuclear material.

54. It is regrettable, and a matter of concern, that the above uncertainties related to the scope and nature of Iran's nuclear programme have not been clarified after three years of intensive Agency verification. In order to clarify these uncertainties, Iran's full transparency is still essential. Without full transparency that extends beyond the formal legal requirements of the Safeguards Agreement and Additional Protocol - transparency that could only be achieved through Iran's active cooperation - the Agency's ability to reconstruct the history of Iran's past programme and to verify the correctness and completeness of the statements made by Iran, particularly with regard to its centrifuge enrichment programme, will be limited, and questions about the past and current direction of Iran's nuclear programme will continue to be raised. Such transparency should primarily include access to, and cooperation by, relevant individuals; access to documentation related to procurement and dual use equipment; and access to certain military owned workshops and R&D locations that the Agency may need to visit in the future as part of its investigation.

…

---

[239] Doc. 40.

Document 43: Implementation of the NPT Safeguards Agreement in the Islamic Republic of Iran, Report by the Director General

GOV/2006/27 (also circulated as S/2006/270), 28 April 2006

...

A.8. Suspension

30. In a letter dated 3 January 2006, Iran informed the Agency that it had decided to resume, as from 9 January 2006, "those R&D on the peaceful nuclear energy programme which ha[d] been suspended as part of its expanded voluntary and non-legally binding suspension".

31. In February 2006, Iran started enrichment tests at PFEP by feeding UF6 gas into a single P-1 machine, and later into 10-machine and 20-machine cascades. During March 2006, a 164-machine cascade was completed, and tests of the cascade using UF6 were begun. On 13 April 2006, Iran declared to the Agency that an enrichment level of 3.6% had been achieved. On 18 April 2006, the Agency took samples at PFEP, the results of which tend to confirm as of that date the enrichment level declared by Iran. On that day, UF6 gas was again being fed into the 164-machine cascade, and two additional 164-machine cascades were under construction. The enrichment process at PFEP, including the feed and withdrawal stations, is covered by Agency safeguards containment and surveillance measures.

32. The current uranium conversion campaign at UCF, which was initiated in November 2005, is still ongoing and is expected to be finished in April 2006. Since September 2005, approximately 110 tonnes of UF6 has been produced at UCF, all of which remains under Agency containment and surveillance.

B. Current overall assessment

33. All the nuclear material declared by Iran to the Agency is accounted for. Apart from the small quantities previously reported to the Board, the Agency has found no other undeclared nuclear material in Iran. However, gaps remain in the Agency's knowledge with respect to the scope and content of Iran's centrifuge programme. Because of this, and other gaps in the Agency's knowledge, including the role of the military in Iran's nuclear programme, the Agency is unable to make progress in its efforts to provide assurance about the absence of undeclared nuclear material and activities in Iran.

34. After more than three years of Agency efforts to seek clarity about all aspects of Iran's nuclear programme, the existing gaps in knowledge continue to be a matter of concern. Any progress in that regard requires full transparency and active cooperation by Iran - transparency that goes beyond the measures prescribed in the Safeguards Agreement[240] and Additional Protocol[241] - if the Agency is to be able to understand fully the twenty years of undeclared nuclear activities by Iran. Iran continues to facilitate the implementation of the Safeguards Agreement and had, until February 2006, acted on a voluntary basis as if the Additional Protocol were in force. Until February 2006, Iran had also agreed to some transparency measures requested by the Agency, including access to certain military sites. Additional transparency measures, including access to documentation, dual use equipment and relevant individuals, are, however, still needed for the Agency to be able to verify the

---

[240] Doc. 4.
[241] Doc. 5.

scope and nature of Iran's enrichment programme, the purpose and use of the dual use equipment and materials purchased by the PHRC, and the alleged studies which could have a military nuclear dimension.

35. Regrettably, these transparency measures are not yet forthcoming. With Iran's decision to cease implementing the provisions of the Additional Protocol, and to confine Agency verification to the implementation of the Safeguards Agreement, the Agency's ability to make progress in clarifying these issues, and to confirm the absence of undeclared nuclear material and activities, will be further limited, and Agency access to activities not involving nuclear material (such as research into laser isotope separation and the production of sensitive components of the nuclear fuel cycle) will be restricted.

36. While the results of Agency safeguards activities may influence the nature and scope of the confidence building measures that the Board requests Iran to take, it is important to note that safeguards obligations and confidence building measures are different, distinct and not interchangeable. The implementation of confidence building measures is no substitute for the full implementation at all times of safeguards obligations. In this context, it is also important to note that the Agency's safeguards judgements and conclusions in the case of Iran, as in all other cases, are based on verifiable information available to the Agency, and are therefore, of necessity, limited to past and present nuclear activities. The Agency cannot make a judgement about, or reach a conclusion on, future compliance or intentions.

…

Document 44: Implementation of the NPT Safeguards Agreement in the Islamic Republic of Iran, Report by the Director General

GOV/2006/53 (also circulated as S/2006/702), 31 August 2006

…

G. Summary

27. Iran has been providing the Agency with access to nuclear material and facilities, and has provided the required reports. Although Iran has provided the Agency with some information concerning product assays at PFEP, Iran continues to decline Agency access to certain operating records at PFEP.

28. Iran has not addressed the long outstanding verification issues or provided the necessary transparency to remove uncertainties associated with some of its activities. Iran has not suspended its enrichment related activities; nor has Iran acted in accordance with the provisions of the Additional Protocol. [242]

…

---

[242] Doc. 5.

Document 45: Implementation of the NPT Safeguards Agreement in the Islamic Republic of Iran, Report by the Director General

GOV/2006/64, 14 November 2006

...

G. Summary

20. Iran has been providing the Agency with access to declared nuclear material and facilities, and has provided the required nuclear material accountancy reports in connection with such material and facilities. However, Iran has not provided the Agency with full access to operating records at PFEP.

21. While the Agency is able to verify the non-diversion of declared nuclear material in Iran, the Agency will remain unable to make further progress in its efforts to verify the absence of undeclared nuclear material and activities in Iran unless Iran addresses the long outstanding verification issues, including through the implementation of the Additional Protocol,[243] and provides the necessary transparency. Progress in this regard is a prerequisite for the Agency to be able to confirm the peaceful nature of Iran's nuclear programme.

...

Document 46: Cooperation between the Islamic Republic of Iran and the Agency in the light of United Nations Security Council Resolution 1737(2006), Report by the Director General

GOV/2007/7, 9 February 2007

A. Background

1. On 23 December 2006, the Security Council, acting under Article 41 of Chapter VII, 'Action with respect to Threats to the Peace, Breaches of the Peace, and Acts of Aggression' of the Charter of the United Nations (the Charter), adopted resolution 1737(2006)[244] (the resolution). Pursuant to Article 48(2) of the Charter the decisions of the Security Council for the maintenance of international peace and security 'shall be carried out by the Members of the United Nations directly and through their action in the appropriate international agencies of which they are members'. In addition, the Agreement governing the relationship between the United Nations and the Agency provides that 'the Agency shall consider any resolution relating to the Agency adopted by the General Assembly or by a Council of the United Nations'. It will therefore be necessary for Member States of the Agency to consider the resolution and the Agency's ensuing obligations thereunder.

B. Obligations under Security Council resolution 1737(2006)

2. The resolution, inter alia in operative paragraphs 3 and 4, requires the taking of measures to prevent the supply, sale or transfer to, or for the use in or benefit of, Iran of all items, materials equipment, goods and technology which could contribute to Iran's

---

[243] Doc. 5.
[244] Doc. 11.

enrichment related, reprocessing or heavy water related activities, or to the development of nuclear weapon delivery systems and of specified items, materials, equipment, goods and technology listed in United Nations Security Council documents S/2006/814 and S/2006/815, as well as of any other additional items that may be determined by the Security Council or the Committee established pursuant to operative paragraph 18of the resolution. Also, pursuant to operative paragraph 5 of the resolution, the Agency has to be informed within ten days in cases of the supply, sale or transfer to Iran of those items, materials, equipment, goods and technology listed in document S/2006/814 in respect of which the export to Iran is not prohibited. At the same time, the resolution exempts specific equipment and fuel assemblies for light water reactors from the restrictions mentioned above. While operative paragraph 10 requires Member States to exercise vigilance regarding the entry into or transit through their territories of persons specified in that paragraph, operative paragraph 11 requires Member States to grant to such persons entry into their territories to attend Agency meetings designed to meet the objectives of the resolution.

3. The resolution further provides, in its operative paragraph 6, that all Member States (and through their actions as set out in paragraph 1 above, the Agency) take the necessary measures to prevent the provision to Iran of any technical assistance or training, financial assistance, investment, brokering or other services and the transfer of financial resources or services, related to the supply, sale, transfer, manufacture or use of the prohibited items, materials, equipment, goods and technology specified inoperative paragraphs 3 and 4 of the resolution.

4. In addition to this general prohibition on technical assistance relating to proliferation sensitive nuclear activities, the resolution, in its operative paragraph 16, specifically addresses the Agency and provides that technical cooperation provided to Iran by the IAEA or under its auspices shall only be for food, agricultural, medical, safety or other humanitarian purposes, or where it is necessary for projects directly related to the items specified in subparagraphs 3(b)(i) and (ii) of the resolution (i.e. equipment and fuel assemblies for light water reactors), but that no such technical cooperation shall be provided that relates to the proliferation sensitive nuclear activities set out in operative paragraph 2 of the resolution. The Committee established pursuant to operative paragraph 18 of the resolution is tasked, inter alia, to seek from the Secretariat of the Agency information regarding the actions taken by the Agency to implement effectively the measures provided for in operative paragraph 16 of the resolution and whatever further information it may consider useful in this regard. Taking into account the drafting history of the resolution, given the standard terminology traditionally used in the Agency in the context of defining its technical cooperation programme and the fact that the resolution clearly distinguishes on the one hand between technical assistance in the general sense in operative paragraph 6 and on the other hand technical cooperation in the specific Agency context in operative paragraph 16, it is the Secretariat's judgement that the activities of the Agency dealt with by operative paragraph 16 pertain only to activities in the context of projects implemented through the Agency's Technical Cooperation Programme.

5. In light of the above provisions of operative paragraph 6 no technical assistance outside the Technical Cooperation Programme,[245]can be provided to Iran that relates to the proliferation sensitive nuclear activities specified in the resolution. Technical assistance, however, can be provided to Iran when after a case-by-case screening by the Secretariat

---

[245] For example, the activities carried out in the framework of coordinated research projects (footnote in the original).

upon receipt of a request for specific assistance, it is found to be in conformity with the provisions of operative paragraph 6 of the resolution. The Secretariat has evaluated, and established the necessary internal procedures to keep under review, all its technical assistance activities to ensure that none of them contribute to Iran's proliferation sensitive nuclear activities specified in the resolution.[246]

C. Evaluation of technical cooperation provided to Iran

6. In respect of technical cooperation, the Director General undertook in his letter of 27 December 2006 to the Chairman of the Board of Governors, that the Secretariat 'will evaluate all IAEA technical cooperation projects for Iran in the light of resolution 1737(2006) and will prepare a report including a list of the projects which could, in the Secretariat's judgement, continue to be implemented'. The Director General also stated that, pending completion of the Secretariat's evaluation, and until the Board takes the required decision, it would be ensured that, 'any technical cooperation provided to Iran by the Agency, or under its auspices, will be limited to activities that are, prima facie, in the Secretariat's judgement authorized by the aforementioned resolution.'

7. The Secretariat has evaluated the technical cooperation provided to Iran by the Agency, in the context of the resolution. The Secretariat has also established the necessary procedures to keep the programme under review. The recommendations resulting from the evaluation are provided in the attached Annex and are based on the following considerations:

(i) No technical cooperation may be provided to Iran that relates to the proliferation of sensitive nuclear activities specified in the resolution.

(ii) Technical cooperation by the Agency may continue to be provided only if it is for food, agricultural, medical, safety or other humanitarian purposes, or where it relates to light water reactors as specified in operative paragraphs 3(b)(i) and (ii) of the resolution.

(iii) The phrase 'technical cooperation provided to Iran by the IAEA' in the resolution is understood to include any and all technical cooperation to Iran by the Agency whether through national, regional or interregional projects contained in the Agency's Technical Cooperation Programme.

(iv) The phrase 'under its auspices' is understood to mean any and all technical cooperation provided by the Agency to Iran in the context of agreements, arrangements or events which the Agency supports or co-organizes, to which the Agency is a party, and/or for which the Agency is a sponsor or co-sponsor.

(v) The term 'safety' is understood to mean activities that may have a direct impact on the protection of people and the environment against radiation risks. This includes the safety of nuclear installations, radiation safety, the safety of radioactive waste and safety in the transport of radioactive material.

(vi) The phrase 'or other humanitarian purposes' is understood to mean all activities directly related to basic human needs and human welfare other than those specifically mentioned in operative paragraph 16 of the resolution.

(vii) To the extent that nuclear security may have a direct impact on the safety of people and the environment, relevant nuclear security related technical cooperation projects may continue to be carried out.

---

[246] As a result, Iran's participation in three such activities will require a case-by-case assessment (footnote in the original).

(viii) As regards technical cooperation projects with disparate purposes and activities, the Secretariat will implement the activities on a case-by-case basis for those purposes which are in conformity with the provisions of operative paragraph 16 of the resolution.

8. There are, at present, fifteen national technical cooperation projects for Iran as well as thirty-four regional and six interregional technical cooperation projects in which Iran participates or is eligible to participate.[247] The Secretariat reached the following conclusions regarding the technical cooperation provided to Iran by the Agency or under its auspices[248]:

(i) Technical cooperation to Iran may proceed through eleven national projects and twenty regional and two interregional projects.

(ii) Technical cooperation to Iran may not proceed through one national project and ten regional and one interregional projects with disparate activities except for those specific activities that, after a case-by-case screening by the Secretariat upon receipt of a request for specific assistance, are found to be in conformity with the provisions of operative paragraph 16 of the resolution.

(iii) Technical cooperation to Iran may not proceed through three national projects and four regional and three interregional projects.

9. Pending action by the Board, and as indicated by the Director General in his letter to the Chairman of the Board of 27 December 2006, the Secretariat has placed on hold three fellowships, one Individual participation in a training course and the procurement of fifteen items and shipments under projects INT0081, RAS0042, RAS4025, RAS2011, IRA8015, as well as all technical cooperation projects referred to in paragraph 8(iii) above.

D. Actions by the Secretariat

10. The Secretariat will continue to keep all its technical assistance activities under review to ensure that none contribute to Iran's proliferation sensitive nuclear activities as specified in the resolution.

11. Subject to the concurrence by the Board, the Secretariat will implement the technical cooperation to Iran as specified in paragraphs 7 and 8 above.

12. Obligations to third parties arising out of technical assistance activities and technical cooperation projects that are being put on hold are being kept under review by the Secretariat and will be addressed in accordance with the terms of the relevant contracts.

13. In accordance with operative paragraph 18(b) of the resolution, the Secretariat will provide information that may be required by the Committee established pursuant to the resolution.

E. Recommended Action by the Board

14. It is recommended that the Board:

(i) take note of the resolution; and

(ii) concur with the Secretariat's understanding of the actions required of the Agency by Member States, in respect of the cooperation between Iran and the Agency as contained in paragraphs 10 to 13 above.

Annex

... (omitted)

---

[247] In addition, thirty-six national, regional and interregional technical cooperation projects in which Iran participated or was eligible to participate are under closure pending finalization of the standard administrative requirements. There are no current or future activities for or involving Iran under these projects (footnote in the original).

[248] The current conclusions are limited to activities and projects foreseen at present. Should future developments warrant a change to these conclusions, the Board will be consulted (footnote in the original).

Document 47: Implementation of the NPT Safeguards Agreement and Relevant Provisions of Security Council Resolution 1737(2006) in the Islamic Republic of Iran, Report by the Director General

GOV/2007/8 (also circulated as S/2007/100), 22 February 2007

...

G. Summary

26. Pursuant to its NPT Safeguards Agreement,[249] Iran has been providing the Agency with access to declared nuclear material and facilities, and has provided the required nuclear material accountancy reports in connection with such material and facilities.

27. The Agency is able to verify the non-diversion of declared nuclear material in Iran. The Agency remains unable, however, to make further progress in its efforts to verify fully the past development of Iran's nuclear programme and certain aspects relevant to its scope and nature. Hence, the Agency is unable to verify the absence of undeclared nuclear material and activities in Iran unless Iran addresses the long outstanding verification issues through the implementation of the Additional Protocol (which it signed on 18 December 2003, but has not yet brought into force)[250] and the required transparency measures.

28. Iran has not suspended its enrichment related activities. Iran has continued with the operation of PFEP. It has also continued with the construction of FEP, including the installation of cascades, and has transferred UF to FEP. Iran has also continued with its heavy water related projects. Construction 6of the IR-40 Reactor, and operation of the Heavy Water Production Plant, are continuing. In contrast, there has been no indication of reprocessing related activities at any declared sites in Iran.

29. As underscored by the Director General at the meeting of the Board of Governors in November 2006 (GOV/OR. 1174, paras 86-94), given the existence in Iran of activities undeclared to the Agency for 20 years, it is necessary for Iran to enable the Agency, through maximum cooperation and transparency, to fully reconstruct the history of Iran's nuclear programme. Without such cooperation and transparency, the Agency will not be able to provide assurances about the absence of undeclared nuclear material and activities in Iran or about the exclusively peaceful nature of that programme.

...

Document 48: Implementation of the NPT Safeguards Agreement and Relevant Provisions of Security Council Resolutions in the Islamic Republic of Iran, Report by the Director General

GOV/2007/22 (also circulated as S/2007/303), 23 May 2007

...

E.2. Design Information

12. On 29 March 2007, Iran informed the Agency that it had 'suspended' the implementation of the modified Code 3.1, which had been 'accepted in 2003, but not yet

---

[249] Doc. 4.
[250] Doc. 5.

ratified by the parliament', and that it would 'revert' to the implementation of the 1976 version of Code 3.1, which only requires the submission of design information for new facilities 'normally not later than 180 days before the facility is scheduled to receive nuclear material for the first time.' In a letter dated 30 March 2007, the Agency requested Iran to reconsider its decision.[251]

13. Iran has taken issue with the Agency's right to verify design information which had been provided by Iran pursuant to the modified Code 3.1 concerning the IR-40 reactor at Arak.[252] The basis for Iran's contention is that, under the 1976 version of Code 3.1, to which it had 'reverted', the verification of such information is not justified, given the preliminary construction stage of the facility (described as 'far beyond receiving nuclear material') and the Agency's previous activities at Arak.

14. In accordance with Article 39 of Iran's Safeguards Agreement,[253] agreed Subsidiary Arrangements cannot be modified unilaterally; nor is there a mechanism in the Safeguards Agreement for the suspension of provisions agreed to in Subsidiary Arrangements. Moreover, Code 3.1 is related to the provision of design information, not to the frequency or timing of verification by the Agency of such information. The Agency's right to verify design information provided to it is a continuing right,[254] which is not dependent on the stage of construction of, or the presence of nuclear material at, a facility.

...

G. Summary

18. Although the Agency is able to verify the non-diversion of declared nuclear material in Iran, the Agency remains unable to make further progress in its efforts to verify certain aspects relevant to the scope and nature of Iran's nuclear programme. Pursuant to its NPT Safeguards Agreement, Iran has been providing the Agency with access to declared nuclear material, and has provided the required nuclear material accountancy reports in connection with declared nuclear material and facilities. Iran has, however, ceased to implement the modified Code 3.1 of the Subsidiary Arrangements with respect to the early provision of design information, and has not permitted the Agency to perform design information verification at the IR-40 reactor.

19. As previously stated, unless Iran addresses the long outstanding verification issues, and implements the Additional Protocol[255] and the required transparency measures, the Agency will not be able to fully reconstruct the history of Iran's nuclear programme and provide assurances about the absence of undeclared nuclear material and activities in Iran or about the exclusively peaceful nature of that programme. It should be noted that because the Agency has not been receiving for over a year information that Iran used to provide, including under the Additional Protocol, the Agency's level of knowledge of certain aspects of Iran's nuclear related activities has deteriorated.

20. Iran has not suspended its enrichment related activities. Iran has continued with the operation of PFEP. It has also continued with the construction of FEP and has started feeding cascades with UF_6. Iran has also continued with its heavy water related projects. Construction of the IR-40 reactor and the operation of the Heavy Water Production Plant are continuing.

...

---

[251] Both letters are reproduced in GOV/INF/2007/8 (footnote in the original).

[252] Iran's letters are dated 13 April 2007, 25 April 2007, and 14 May 2007; the Agency's replies are dated 18 April 2007 (GOV/INF/2007/10) and 7 May 2007 (footnote in the original).

[253] Doc. 4.

[254] GOV/2554/Att.2/Rev. 2 (footnote in the original).

[255] Doc. 5.

Document 49: Implementation of the NPT Safeguards Agreement in the Islamic Republic of Iran, Report by the Director General

GOV/2007/48, 30 August 2007 and GOV/2007/48 Corr.1, 7 September 2007

...

G. Summary

22. The Agency is able to verify the non-diversion of declared nuclear material in Iran. Iran has been providing the Agency with access to declared nuclear material, and has provided the required nuclear material accountancy reports in connection with declared nuclear material and facilities. However, the Agency remains unable to verify certain aspects relevant to the scope and nature of Iran's nuclear programme. It should be noted that since early 2006, the Agency has not received the type of information that Iran had previously been providing, including pursuant to the Additional Protocol,[256] for example information relevant to ongoing advanced centrifuge research.

23. The work plan is a significant step forward. If Iran finally addresses the long outstanding verification issues, the Agency should be in a position to reconstruct the history of Iran's nuclear programme. Naturally, the key to successful implementation of the agreed work plan is Iran's full and active cooperation with the Agency, and its provision to the Agency of all relevant information and access to all relevant documentation and individuals to enable the Agency to resolve all outstanding issues. To this end, the Agency considers it essential that Iran adheres to the time line defined therein and implements all the necessary safeguards and transparency measures, including the measures provided for in the Additional Protocol.

24. Once Iran's past nuclear programme has been clarified, Iran would need to continue to build confidence about the scope and nature of its present and future nuclear programme. Confidence in the exclusively peaceful nature of Iran's nuclear programme requires that the Agency be able to provide assurances not only regarding declared nuclear material, but, equally important, regarding the absence of undeclared nuclear material and activities in Iran, through the implementation of the Additional Protocol. The Director General therefore again urges Iran to ratify and bring into force the Additional Protocol at the earliest possible date, as requested by the Board of Governors and the Security Council.

25. Contrary to the decisions of the Security Council, Iran has not suspended its enrichment related activities, having continued with the operation of PFEP, and with the construction and operation of FEP. Iran is also continuing with its construction of the IR-40 reactor and operation of the Heavy Water Production Plant.

...

---

[256] Doc. 5.

Document 50: Implementation of the NPT Safeguards Agreement and Relevant Provisions of Security Council Resolutions 1737(2006) and 1747(2007) in the Islamic Republic of Iran, Report by the Director General

GOV/2007/58, 15 November 2007

...

F. Summary

39. The Agency has been able to verify the non-diversion of declared nuclear material in Iran. Iran has provided the Agency with access to declared nuclear material, and has provided the required nuclear material accountancy reports in connection with declared nuclear material and activities. Iran concluded a Facility Attachment for FEP. However, it should be noted that, since early 2006, the Agency has not received the type of information that Iran had previously been providing, pursuant to the Additional Protocol[257] and as a transparency measure. As a result, the Agency's knowledge about Iran's current nuclear programme is diminishing.

40. Contrary to the decisions of the Security Council, Iran has not suspended its enrichment related activities, having continued the operation of PFEP and FEP. Iran has also continued the construction of the IR-40 and operation of the Heavy Water Production Plant.

41. There are two remaining major issues relevant to the scope and nature of Iran's nuclear programme: Iran's past and current centrifuge enrichment programme and the alleged studies. The Agency has been able to conclude that answers provided on the declared past P-1 and P-2 centrifuge programmes are consistent with its findings. The Agency will, however, continue to seek corroboration and is continuing to verify the completeness of Iran's declarations. The Agency intends in the next few weeks to focus on the contamination issue as well as the alleged studies and other activities that could have military applications.

42. Iran has provided sufficient access to individuals and has responded in a timely manner to questions and provided clarifications and amplifications on issues raised in the context of the work plan. However, its cooperation has been reactive rather than proactive. As previously stated, Iran's active cooperation and full transparency are indispensable for full and prompt implementation of the work plan.

43. In addition, Iran needs to continue to build confidence about the scope and nature of its present programme. Confidence in the exclusively peaceful nature of Iran's nuclear programme requires that the Agency be able to provide assurances not only regarding declared nuclear material, but, equally importantly, regarding the absence of undeclared nuclear material and activities in Iran. Although the Agency has no concrete information, other than that addressed through the work plan, about possible current undeclared nuclear material and activities in Iran, the Agency is not in a position to provide credible assurances about the absence of undeclared nuclear material and activities in Iran without full implementation of the Additional Protocol. This is especially important in the light of Iran's undeclared activities for almost two decades and the need to restore confidence in the

---

[257] Doc. 5.

exclusively peaceful nature of its nuclear programme. Therefore, the Director General again urges Iran to implement the Additional Protocol at the earliest possible date. The Director General also urges Iran to implement all the confidence building measures required by the Security Council, including the suspension of all enrichment related activities.

...

Document 51: Implementation of the NPT Safeguards Agreement and Relevant Provisions of Security Council Resolutions 1737(2006) and 1747(2007) in the Islamic Republic of Iran, Report by the Director General

GOV/2008/4, 22 February 2008

...

F. Summary

52. The Agency has been able to continue to verify the non-diversion of declared nuclear material in Iran. Iran has provided the Agency with access to declared nuclear material and has provided the required nuclear material accountancy reports in connection with declared nuclear material and activities. Iran has also responded to questions and provided clarifications and amplifications on the issues raised in the context of the work plan, with the exception of the alleged studies. Iran has provided access to individuals in response to the Agency's requests. Although direct access has not been provided to individuals said to be associated with the alleged studies, responses have been provided in writing to some of the Agency's questions.

53. The Agency has been able to conclude that answers provided by Iran, in accordance with the work plan, are consistent with its findings - in the case of the polonium-210 experiments and the Gchine mine - or are not inconsistent with its findings - in the case of the contamination at the technical university and the procurement activities of the former Head of PHRC. Therefore, the Agency considers those questions no longer outstanding at this stage. However, the Agency continues, in accordance with its procedures and practices, to seek corroboration of its findings and to verify these issues as part of its verification of the completeness of Iran's declarations.

54. The one major remaining issue relevant to the nature of Iran's nuclear programme is the alleged studies on the green salt project, high explosives testing and the missile re-entry vehicle. This is a matter of serious concern and critical to an assessment of a possible military dimension to Iran's nuclear programme. The Agency was able to show some relevant documentation to Iran on 3-5 February 2008 and is still examining the allegations made and the statements provided by Iran in response. Iran has maintained that these allegations are baseless and that the data have been fabricated. The Agency's overall assessment requires, inter alia, an understanding of the role of the uranium metal document, and clarifications concerning the procurement activities of some military related institutions still not provided by Iran. The Agency only received authorization to show some further material to Iran on 15 February 2008. Iran has not yet responded to the Agency's request of that same date for Iran to view this additional documentation on the

alleged studies. In light of the above, the Agency is not yet in a position to determine the full nature of Iran's nuclear programme. However, it should be noted that the Agency has not detected the use of nuclear material in connection with the alleged studies, nor does it have credible information in this regard. The Director General has urged Iran to engage actively with the Agency in a more detailed examination of the documents available about the alleged studies which the Agency has been authorized to show to Iran.

55. The Agency has recently received from Iran additional information similar to that which Iran had previously provided pursuant to the Additional Protocol,[258] as well as updated design information. As a result, the Agency's knowledge about Iran's current declared nuclear programme has become clearer. However, this information has been provided on an ad hoc basis and not in a consistent and complete manner. The Director General has continued to urge Iran to implement the Additional Protocol at the earliest possible date and as an important confidence building measure requested by the Board of Governors and affirmed by the Security Council. The Director General has also urged Iran to implement the modified text of its Subsidiary Arrangements General Part, Code 3.1 on the early provision of design information. Iran has expressed its readiness to implement the provisions of the Additional Protocol and the modified text of its Subsidiary Arrangements General Part, Code 3.1, 'if the nuclear file is returned from the Security Council to the IAEA'.

56. Contrary to the decisions of the Security Council, Iran has not suspended its enrichment related activities, having continued the operation of PFEP and FEP. In addition, Iran started the development of new generation centrifuges. Iran has also continued construction of the IR-40 reactor and operation of the Heavy Water Production Plant.

57. With regard to its current programme, Iran needs to continue to build confidence about its scope and nature. Confidence in the exclusively peaceful nature of Iran's nuclear programme requires that the Agency be able to provide assurances not only regarding declared nuclear material, but, equally importantly, regarding the absence of undeclared nuclear material and activities in Iran. With the exception of the issue of the alleged studies, which remains outstanding, the Agency has no concrete information about possible current undeclared nuclear material and activities in Iran. Although Iran has provided some additional detailed information about its current activities on an ad hoc basis, the Agency will not be in a position to make progress towards providing credible assurances about the absence of undeclared nuclear material and activities in Iran before reaching some clarity about the nature of the alleged studies, and without implementation of the Additional Protocol. This is especially important in the light of the many years of undeclared activities in Iran and the confidence deficit created as a result. The Director General therefore urges Iran to implement all necessary measures called for by the Board of Governors and the Security Council to build confidence in the peaceful nature of its nuclear programme.

...

---

[258] Doc. 5.

Document 52: Implementation of the NPT Safeguards Agreement and Relevant Provisions of Security Council Resolutions 1737(2006), 1747(2007) and 1803(2008) in the Islamic Republic of Iran, Report by the Director General

GOV/2008/15, 26 May 2008 (also circulated as S/2008/338, 27 May 2008)

...

F. Summary

26. The Agency has been able to continue to verify the non-diversion of declared nuclear material in Iran. Iran has provided the Agency with access to declared nuclear material and has provided the required nuclear material accountancy reports in connection with declared nuclear material and activities. However, Iran has not implemented the modified text of its Subsidiary Arrangements General Part, Code 3.1 on the early provision of design information.

27. The alleged studies on the green salt project, high explosives testing and the missile re-entry vehicle project remain a matter of serious concern. Clarification of these is critical to an assessment of the nature of Iran's past and present nuclear programme. Iran has agreed to address the alleged studies. However, it maintains that all the allegations are baseless and that the data have been fabricated.

28. The Agency's overall assessment of the nature of Iran's nuclear programme also requires, inter alia, an understanding of the role of the uranium metal document, and clarifications by Iran concerning some procurement activities of military related institutions, which remain outstanding... It should be emphasised, however, that the Agency has not detected the actual use of nuclear material in connection with the alleged studies.

29. Contrary to the decisions of the Security Council, Iran has not suspended its enrichment related activities, having continued the operation of PFEP and FEP and the installation of both new cascades and of new generation centrifuges for test purposes. Iran has also continued with the construction of the IR-40 reactor.

30. The Director General urges Iran to implement all measures required to build confidence in the peaceful nature of its nuclear programme, including the Additional Protocol,[259] at the earliest possible date.

...

A. Documents shown to Iran in connection with the alleged studies

A.1. Green Salt Project

...

A.2. High Explosives Testing

...

A.3. Missile Re-entry Vehicle

...

---

[259] Doc. 5.

Document 53: Implementation of the NPT Safeguards Agreement and Relevant Provisions of Security Council Resolutions 1737(2006) and 1747(2007) in the Islamic Republic of Iran, Report by the Director General

GOV/2008/38, 15 September 2008

...

F. Summary

22. The Agency has been able to continue to verify the non-diversion of declared nuclear material in Iran. Iran has provided the Agency with access to declared nuclear material and has provided the required nuclear material accounting reports in connection with declared nuclear material and activities. However, Iran has not implemented the modified text of its Subsidiary Arrangements General Part, Code 3.1 on the early provision of design information.

23. The Agency, regrettably, has not been able to make any substantive progress on the alleged studies and other associated key remaining issues which remain of serious concern. For the Agency to make progress, an important first step, in connection with the alleged studies, is for Iran to clarify the extent to which information contained in the relevant documentation is factually correct and where, in its view, such information may have been modified or relates to alternative, non-nuclear purposes. Iran needs to provide the Agency with substantive information to support its statements and provide access to relevant documentation and individuals in this regard. Unless Iran provides such transparency, and implements the Additional Protocol,[260] the Agency will not be able to provide credible assurance about the absence of undeclared nuclear material and activities in Iran.

24. Contrary to the decisions of the Security Council, Iran has not suspended its enrichment related activities, having continued the operation of PFEP and FEP, and the installation of new cascades and the operation of new generation centrifuges for test purposes. Iran has also continued with the construction of the IR-40.

...

Document 54: Implementation of the NPT Safeguards Agreement and Relevant Provisions of Security Council Resolutions 1737(2006), 1747(2007) and 1803(2008) in the Islamic Republic of Iran, Report by the Director General

GOV/2008/59, 19 November 2008

...

E. Possible Military Dimensions

15. There remain a number of outstanding issues, identified in the Director General's last report to the Board (GOV/2008/38, para. 14), which give rise to concerns and need

---

[260] Doc. 5.

to be clarified to exclude the existence of possible military dimensions to Iran's nuclear programme. As indicated in the Director General's report, for the Agency to be able to address these concerns and make progress in its efforts to provide assurance about the absence of undeclared nuclear material and activities in Iran, it is essential that Iran, inter alia, provide the information and access necessary to: resolve questions related to the alleged studies; provide more information on the circumstances of the acquisition of the uranium metal document; clarify procurement and R&D activities of military related institutes and companies that could be nuclear related; and clarify the production of nuclear equipment and components by companies belonging to defence industries.

...

17. As indicated in the Director General's previous report, the Agency currently has no information — apart from the uranium metal document — on the actual design or manufacture by Iran of nuclear material components of a nuclear weapon or of certain other key components, such as initiators, or on related nuclear physics studies (GOV/2008/38,[261] para. 21). Nor has the Agency detected the actual use of nuclear material in connection with the alleged studies.

F. Summary

18. The Agency has been able to continue to verify the non-diversion of declared nuclear material in Iran. Iran has provided the Agency with access to declared nuclear material and has provided the required nuclear material accounting reports in connection with declared nuclear material and activities. However, Iran has not implemented the modified text of its Subsidiary Arrangements General Part, Code 3.1 on the early provision of design information. Nor has Iran implemented the Additional Protocol,[262] which is essential for the Agency to provide credible assurance about the absence of undeclared nuclear material and activities.

19. Regrettably, as a result of the lack of cooperation by Iran in connection with the alleged studies and other associated key remaining issues of serious concern, the Agency has not been able to make substantive progress on these issues. For the Agency to make progress, an important first step, in connection with the alleged studies, is for Iran to clarify the extent to which information contained in the relevant documentation is factually correct and where, in its view, such information may have been modified or relates to non-nuclear purposes. Iran needs to provide the Agency with substantive information to support its statements and provide access to relevant documentation and individuals in this regard. Unless Iran provides such transparency, and implements the Additional Protocol, the Agency will not be able to provide credible assurance about the absence of undeclared nuclear material and activities in Iran.

20. Contrary to the decisions of the Security Council, Iran has not suspended its enrichment related activities, having continued the operation of PFEP and FEP and the installation of new cascades and the operation of new generation centrifuges for test purposes. Iran has not provided access to the IR-40, and, therefore, the Agency is not able to verify the current status of its construction.

21. The Director General continues to urge Iran to implement all measures required to build confidence in the exclusively peaceful nature of its nuclear programme at the earliest possible date.

...

---

[261] Doc. 53.
[262] Doc. 5.

Document 55: Implementation of the NPT Safeguards Agreement and Relevant Provisions of Security Council Resolutions 1737(2006), 1747(2007), 1803(2008) and 1835(2008) in the Islamic Republic of Iran, Report by the Director General

GOV/2009/8, 19 February 2009

...

F. Summary

18. The Agency has been able to continue to verify the non-diversion of declared nuclear material in Iran. However, Iran has not implemented the modified text of its Subsidiary Arrangements General Part, Code 3.1, on the early provision of design information and has continued to refuse to permit the Agency to carry out design information verification at IR-40.

19. Contrary to the request of the Board of Governors and the Security Council, Iran has not implemented the Additional Protocol, which is a prerequisite for the Agency to provide credible assurance about the absence of undeclared nuclear material and activities. Nor has it agreed to the Agency's request that Iran provide, as a transparency measure, access to additional locations related, inter alia, to the manufacturing of centrifuges, R&D on uranium enrichment, and uranium mining and milling, as also required by the Security Council.

20. Regrettably, as a result of the continued lack of cooperation by Iran in connection with the remaining issues which give rise to concerns about possible military dimensions of Iran's nuclear programme, the Agency has not made any substantive progress on these issues. As indicated in previous reports of the Director General, for the Agency to make such progress, Iran needs to provide substantive information, and access to relevant documentation, locations and individuals, in connection with all of the outstanding issues. With respect to the alleged studies in particular, an important first step is for Iran to clarify the extent to which information contained in the documentation which Iran was shown, and given the opportunity to study, is factually correct and where, in its view, such information may have been modified or relates to non-nuclear purposes.

21. Unless Iran implements the above transparency measures and the Additional Protocol, as required by the Security Council, the Agency will not be in a position to provide credible assurance about the absence of undeclared nuclear material and activities in Iran. The Director General continues to urge Iran to implement all measures required to build confidence in the exclusively peaceful nature of its nuclear programme at the earliest possible date. The Director General, at the same time, urges Member States which have provided such documentation to the Agency to agree to the Agency's providing copies thereof to Iran.

22. Contrary to the decisions of the Security Council, Iran has not suspended its enrichment related activities or its work on heavy water-related projects, including the construction of the heavy water moderated research reactor, IR-40, and the production of fuel for that reactor.

...

Document 56: Implementation of the NPT Safeguards Agreement and Relevant Provisions of Security Council Resolutions 1737(2006), 1747(2007), 1803(2008) and 1835(2008) in the Islamic Republic of Iran, Report by the Director General

GOV/2009/35, 5 June 2009

1. On 19 February 2009, the Director General reported to the Board of Governors on the implementation of the NPT Safeguards Agreement and relevant provisions of Security Council resolutions 1737 (2006), 1747 (2007), 1803 (2008) and 1835 (2008) in the Islamic Republic of Iran (Iran) (GOV/2009/8).[263] This report covers relevant developments since that date.

A. Current Enrichment Related Activities

2. Since the Director General's previous report, Iran has continued to feed UF_6 into Unit A24, and twelve cascades of Unit A26, at the Fuel Enrichment Plant (FEP). The six other cascades of Unit A26 have been installed and are under vacuum. Iran has also started installation of cascades at Unit A28; seven cascades have been installed and are under vacuum, and installation of another cascade is continuing.[264] Installation work at Units A25 and A27 is also continuing.

3. Iran has estimated that, between 18 November 2008 and 31 May 2009, 5723 kg of UF_6 was fed into the cascades and a total of 500 kg of low enriched UF_6 was produced.[265] The nuclear material at FEP (including the feed, product and tails), as well as all installed cascades, remain under Agency containment and surveillance. Since the last physical inventory verification (PIV), the Agency and Iran have continued to discuss improvements in the facility's accountancy system. In addition, the Agency has informed Iran that, given the increasing number of cascades being installed at FEP and the increased rate of production of LEU at the facility, improvements to the containment and surveillance measures at FEP are required in order for the Agency to continue to fully meet its safeguards objectives. The Agency has proposed a solution and initiated discussions with Iran to that end.

4. Between 15 January 2009 and 23 May 2009, a total of approximately 54 kg of UF_6 was fed into the 10-machine IR-3 cascade, the 10-machine IR-2 cascade and single IR-1, IR-2, IR-2 modified, IR-3 and IR-4 centrifuges at the Pilot Fuel Enrichment Plant (PFEP). The nuclear material at PFEP, as well as the cascade area, remains under Agency containment and surveillance.[266]

5. To date, the results of the environmental samples taken at FEP and PFEP indicate that the plants have been operating as declared (i.e. less than 5.0% U-235 enrichment).[267]

---

[263] Doc. 55.

[264] On 31 May 2009, 4920 centrifuges were being fed with UF_6; 2132 centrifuges were installed and under vacuum, and an additional 169 centrifuges were installed but not under vacuum (footnote in the original).

[265] The Agency has verified that, as of 17 November 2008, 9956 kg of UF had been fed into the cascades and 839 kg of low enriched UF_6 had been produced since the beginning of operations in February 2007 (GOV/2009/8, para. 3) (footnote in the original).

[266] In line with normal safeguards practice, small amounts of nuclear material at the facility (e.g. some waste and samples) are not under containment and surveillance (footnote in the original).

[267] Results are available for samples taken up to 1 February 2009 for FEP and up to 20 April 2008 for PFEP. These results have shown particles of low enriched uranium (with up to 4.4% U-235), natural uranium and depleted uranium (down to 0.4% U-235 enrichment) (footnote in the original).

Since March 2007, 26 unannounced inspections have been conducted at FEP. Twenty-five of these inspections were successfully implemented. For one inspection, carried out on 19 May 2009, access to the facility was not granted by Iran within the agreed time because of an ongoing security drill being carried out at the facility by Iran which had been notified in advance to the Agency. The Agency has initiated discussions with Iran on arrangements in connection with unannounced inspections that would allow the Agency to meet its safeguards objectives within the required timeframe under similar circumstances.

B. Reprocessing Activities

6. The Agency has continued to monitor the use and construction of hot cells at the Tehran Research Reactor (TRR) and the Molybdenum, Iodine and Xenon Radioisotope Production (MIX) Facility. There have been no indications of ongoing reprocessing related activities at those facilities. While Iran has stated that there have been no reprocessing related R&D activities in Iran, the Agency can confirm this only with respect to these two facilities, as the measures of the Additional Protocol are not available.

C. Heavy Water Reactor Related Projects

7. The Agency last visited the Iran Nuclear Research Reactor (IR-40) in August 2008 (GOV/2008/59, para. 9).[268] On 22 April 2009, the Agency again requested access to carry out design information verification (DIV) at the IR-40. In a letter dated 3 May 2009 referring to previous communications concerning the submission of design information, Iran informed the Agency that it would not permit the Agency to carry out the DIV.

8. Iran's refusal to grant the Agency access to IR-40 could adversely impact the Agency's ability to carry out effective safeguards at that facility, and has made it difficult for the Agency to report further on the construction of the reactor, as requested by the Security Council. The completion of the containment structure over the reactor building, and the roofing for the other buildings on the site, makes it impossible to assess further progress on construction inside the buildings without access to the facility. However, satellite imagery suggests that construction is continuing at the reactor site.

9. On 23 May 2009, the Agency conducted an inspection at the Fuel Manufacturing Plant, at which time it was noted that, with the exception of the final quality control testing area, the process line for the production of fuel assemblies for the heavy water reactor fuel had been completed, and that one fuel assembly had been assembled from previously produced fuel rods.

10. Using satellite imagery, the Agency has continued to monitor the status of the Heavy Water Production Plant, which appears to have been operating intermittently since the last report.

D. Other Implementation Issues

D.1. Uranium Conversion

11. Between 8 and 12 March 2009, the Agency conducted a PIV at the Uranium Conversion Facility. During the PIV, Iran presented 345 tonnes of uranium in the form of UF_6 for Agency verification. The Agency is evaluating the results of the PIV.

D.2. Design Information

12. As previously reported to the Board of Governors, the Agency has still not received preliminary design information, as requested by it in December 2007, for the nuclear power plant that is to be built in Darkhovin (GOV/2008/38, para. 11).

13. Iran has not yet implemented the revised Code 3.1 of the Subsidiary Arrangements General Part (GOV/2008/59, para. 9; GOV/2007/22,[269] paras 12-14). Iran is the only State

---

[268] Doc. 54.
[269] Doc. 48.

with significant nuclear activities which has a comprehensive safeguards agreement in force but is not implementing the provisions of the revised Code 3.1 on the early provision of design information. The absence of such information results in late notification to the Agency of the construction of new facilities and changes to the design of existing facilities.

D.3. Other Matters

14. On 1 November 2008, Iran transferred a few kilograms of low enriched UF_6 from PFEP to the Jabr Ibn Hayan Multipurpose Laboratories at the Tehran Nuclear Research Centre. In a letter dated 1 June 2009, Iran clarified that the material will be used in conversion experiments for the manufacturing of targets to be irradiated in the Tehran Research Reactor for the production of UO_2 radioisotopes for medical applications.

15. Iran has informed the Agency that the loading of fuel into the Bushehr Nuclear Power Plant is now scheduled to take place in September/October 2009.

16. Using satellite imagery, the Agency has observed a continuation of ore recovery activities in the area of the Bandar Abbas Uranium Production Plant (UPP) and at the Saghand uranium mine. New construction and modifications to buildings and process plant have also been observed at UPP, the Saghand uranium mine and the Ardakan Yellow Cake Production Plant, although it is difficult to assess the operational status and degree of utilization of these plants.

E. Possible Military Dimensions

17. As detailed in the Director General's previous reports to the Board (most recently in GOV/2009/8, para. 15), there remain a number of outstanding issues which give rise to concerns, and which need to be clarified to exclude the existence of possible military dimensions to Iran's nuclear programme. As indicated in those reports, for the Agency to be able to address these concerns and make progress in its efforts to provide assurance about the absence of undeclared nuclear material and activities in Iran, it is essential that Iran, inter alia, implement the Additional Protocol and provide the information and access requested by the Agency. The Agency has still not received a positive reply from Iran in connection with the Agency's requests for access to relevant information, documentation, locations or individuals.

18. In a letter to Iran dated 29 May 2009, the Agency responded to Iran's letters dated 16 September 2008, 28 November 2008 and 2 March 2009, in which Iran had, inter alia, provided its views on a number of issues referred to in the Director General's reports and questioned the correctness of certain statements contained in the reports attributed to Iran in connection with possible military dimensions to Iran's nuclear programme and statements in relation to the resolution of the issues contained in the Work Plan. In its letter, the Agency explained why the statements in the Director General's reports were correct. The Agency also reiterated its request to meet with relevant Iranian authorities at the earliest possible opportunity, with a view to addressing in a substantive and comprehensive manner the issues that remain outstanding.

F. Summary

19. As has been reported in previous reports, the Agency continues to verify the non-diversion of declared nuclear material in Iran.

20. Iran has not, however, implemented the modified text of its Subsidiary Arrangements General Part, Code 3.1, on the early provision of design information, and has continued to refuse to permit the Agency to carry out design information verification at IR-40.

21. Iran has not suspended its enrichment related activities or its work on heavy water related projects as required by the Security Council.

22. Contrary to the request of the Board of Governors and the requirements of the Security Council, Iran has neither implemented the Additional Protocol nor cooperated with the Agency in connection with the remaining issues which give rise to concerns and which need to be clarified to exclude the possibility of military dimensions to Iran's nuclear programme. Unless Iran implements the Additional Protocol and clarifies the outstanding issues, the Agency will not be in a position to provide credible assurance about the absence of undeclared nuclear material and activities in Iran.

23. The Agency believes that it has provided Iran with sufficient access to documentation in its possession to permit Iran to respond substantively to the questions raised by the Agency. However, the Director General urges Member States which have provided documentation to the Agency to work out new modalities with the Agency so that it could share further information with Iran since the Agency's inability to share additional information with Iran, and to provide copies or, if possible, originals, is making it difficult for the Agency to progress further in its verification.

24. The Director General will continue to report as appropriate.

Document 57: Implementation of the NPT Safeguards Agreement and relevant provisions of Security Council resolutions 1737 (2006), 1747 (2007), 1803 (2008), and 1835 (2008) in the Islamic Republic of Iran

GOV/2009/55, 28 August 2009

1. On 5 June 2009, the Director General reported to the Board of Governors on the implementation of the NPT Safeguards Agreement and relevant provisions of Security Council resolutions 1737(2006), 1747(2007), 1803(2008) and 1835(2008)[270] in the Islamic Republic of Iran (Iran) (GOV/2009/35).[271] This report covers relevant developments since that date.

A. Current Enrichment Related Activities

2. On 12 August 2009, Iran was feeding UF_6 into Unit A24, and ten cascades of Unit A26, at the Fuel Enrichment Plant (FEP) at Natanz.[272] On that day, the eight other cascades of Unit A26 were under vacuum. Iran has continued with the installation of cascades at Unit A28; fourteen cascades have been installed and the installation of another cascade is continuing.[273] All machines installed to date are IR-1 centrifuges. Installation work at Units A25 and A27 is also continuing.

3. Iran has estimated that, between 18 November 2008 and 31 July 2009, 7942 kg of UF_6 was fed into the cascades and a total of 669 kg of low enriched UF_6 was produced.[274]

---

[270] Doc. 11-Doc. 14.

[271] Doc. 56.

[272] There are two cascade halls planned at FEP: Production Hall A and Production Hall B. According to the design information submitted by Iran, eight units (Units A21 to A28) are planned for Production Hall A (see GOV/2008/38, para. 2) (footnote in the original).

[273] On 12 August 2009, 4592 centrifuges were being fed with UF and an additional 3716 centrifuges had been installed (footnote in the original).

[274] The Agency has verified that, as of 17 November 2008, 9956 kg of UF_6 had been fed into the cascades and 839 kg of low enriched UF_6 had been produced since the beginning of operations in February 2007 (GOV/2009/8,…

The nuclear material at FEP (including the feed, product and tails), as well as all installed cascades and the feed and withdrawal stations, are subject to Agency containment and surveillance.[275]

4. As reported earlier, the Agency had informed Iran that, given the increasing number of cascades being installed at FEP and the increased rate of production of low enriched uranium at the facility, improvements to the containment and surveillance measures at FEP were needed for the Agency to continue to fully meet its safeguards objectives for the facility (GOV/2009/35, para. 3). In the course of a series of meetings, Iran and the Agency agreed on the improvements, which were put in place on 12 August 2009. The next physical inventory verification (PIV) at FEP is planned for November 2009. At that time, the Agency will be able to verify the inventory of all nuclear material at the facility and evaluate the nuclear material balance after the cold traps have been cleaned out.

5. Iran and the Agency have also agreed on improvements regarding the provision of accounting and operating records, and on the requirements for timely access for unannounced inspections (GOV/2009/35, para. 5).

6. Between 24 May 2009 and 13 August 2009, a total of approximately 37 kg of UF_6 was fed into a 10-machine IR-4 cascade, a 10-machine IR-2m cascade and single IR-1, IR-2m and IR-4 centrifuges at the Pilot Fuel Enrichment Plant (PFEP). The nuclear material at PFEP, as well as the cascade area and the feed and withdrawal stations, remain under Agency containment and surveillance.

7. The results of the environmental samples taken at FEP and PFEP indicate that both plants have been operating as declared (i.e. less than 5.0% U-235 enrichment).[276] Since the last report, the Agency has successfully conducted three unannounced inspections. A total of 29 unannounced inspections have been conducted at FEP since March 2007.

B. Reprocessing Activities

8. The Agency has continued to monitor the use and construction of hot cells at the Tehran Research Reactor (TRR) and the Molybdenum, Iodine and Xenon Radioisotope Production (MIX) Facility. There have been no indications of ongoing reprocessing related activities at those facilities. While Iran has stated that there have been no reprocessing related R&D activities in Iran, the Agency can confirm this only with respect to these two facilities, as the measures of the Additional Protocol are not available.

C. Heavy Water Reactor Related Projects

9. On 19 June 2009, the Agency requested Iran to update the Design Information Questionnaire (DIQ) for the Fuel Manufacturing Plant (FMP) and the Iran Nuclear Research Reactor (IR-40) to reflect the design features of the fuel assembly verified by the Agency during its May 2009 inspection at FMP (GOV/2009/35, para. 9). Under cover of a letter dated 21 August 2009, Iran submitted an updated DIQ for FMP, which the Agency is now reviewing.

---

para. 3). The Agency has confirmed, through independently calibrated operator load cell readings, that, between 18 November 2008 and 2 August 2009, 7976 kg of UF_6 was fed into the cascades, and a total of 591 kg of low enriched UF_6 product and 6847 kg of UF_6 tails and dump material was off-loaded into UF_6 cylinders. The difference of 538 kg between the input and output figures comprises natural, depleted and low enriched UF_6 arising mainly from hold-up in the various cold traps and is not inconsistent with the design information provided by Iran (footnote in the original).

[275] In line with normal safeguards practice, small amounts of nuclear material at the facility (e.g. some waste and samples) are not under containment and surveillance (footnote in the original).

[276] Results are available for samples taken up to 25 April 2009 for FEP and up to 19 April 2009 for PFEP. These results have shown particles of low enriched uranium (with up to 4.4% U-235), natural uranium and depleted uranium (down to 0.38% U-235 enrichment) (footnote in the original).

10. On 11 August 2009, the Agency conducted both a PIV and design information verification (DIV) at FMP, at which time it was noted that the final quality control equipment had been installed, and the fuel assembly referred to above was undergoing quality control testing. Assessment of the results of the PIV is still pending.

11. On 17 August 2009, Iran, following repeated requests by the Agency, provided the Agency with access to the IR-40 reactor at Arak, at which time the Agency was able to carry out a DIV. The Agency verified that the construction of the facility was ongoing. In particular, the Agency noted that no reactor vessel was yet present. The operator stated that the reactor vessel was still being manufactured, and that it would be installed in 2011. Iran also stated that no hot cell windows or manipulators could be procured from foreign sources and that it was considering producing them domestically. Iran estimated that the civil construction work was about 95% completed and that the plant itself was about 63% completed. The facility at its current stage of construction conforms to the design information provided by Iran as of 24 January 2007. However, Iran still needs to provide updated and more detailed design information, in particular about the nuclear fuel characteristics, fuel handling and transfer equipment and the nuclear material accountancy and control system. The Agency has continued using satellite imagery to monitor the status of the Heavy Water Production Plant, which seems not to have been operating since the last report.

D. Other Implementation Issues

D.1. Uranium Conversion

12. The Agency finalized its assessment of the results of the PIV carried out at the Uranium Conversion Facility (UCF) in March 2009 (GOV/2009/35, para. 11), and has concluded that the inventory of nuclear material at UCF as declared by Iran is consistent with those results, within the measurement uncertainties normally associated with conversion plants of similar throughput. Between 8 March 2009 and 10 August 2009, approximately 11 tonnes of uranium in the form of UF_6 was produced at UCF. This brings the total amount of uranium in the form of UF_6 produced at UCF since March 2004 to approximately 366 tonnes, some of which was transferred to FEP and PFEP, and all of which remains under Agency containment and surveillance. Between March 2009 and 10 August 2009, 159 samples of ammonium diuranate, containing about 2 kg of uranium, were received at UCF from the Bandar Abbas Uranium Production Plant.

13. On 21 July 2009 and 10 August 2009, the Agency conducted design information verification at UCF. The Agency was able to confirm that the facility conforms to the design information provided by Iran.

D.2. Design Information

14. Iran has not yet resumed the implementation of the revised Code 3.1 of the Subsidiary Arrangements General Part on the early provision of design information (GOV/2008/59,[277] para. 9; GOV/2007/22,[278] paras 12–14). Iran is the only State with significant nuclear activities which has a comprehensive safeguards agreement in force but is not implementing the provisions of the revised Code 3.1. The absence of such information results in late notification to the Agency of the construction of new facilities and changes to the design of existing facilities.

15. The Agency has not yet received the requested preliminary design information for the nuclear power plant that is to be built in Darkhovin (GOV/2008/38, para. 11).

---

[277] Doc. 54.
[278] Doc. 48.

D.3. Other Matters

16. In view of the anticipated loading of fuel into the Bushehr Nuclear Power Plant (GOV/2009/35, para. 15), now expected to take place in October/November 2009, the Agency installed a containment and surveillance system at that facility on 22–25 August 2009.

17. In a letter dated 12 July 2009, Iran informed the Agency that it had transferred all nuclear material out of the Uranium Chemical Laboratory at Esfahan and that it did not plan any other nuclear activities in this location and requested the Agency to consider this facility as a decommissioned facility. The Agency has scheduled an inspection to confirm the decommissioned status of this facility.

E. Possible Military Dimensions

18. As referred to in the Director General's previous reports to the Board (most recently in GOV/2009/35, para. 17), there remain a number of outstanding issues which give rise to concerns, and which need to be clarified to exclude the existence of possible military dimensions to Iran's nuclear programme. As indicated in those reports, it is essential that Iran re-engage with the Agency to clarify and bring to a closure questions related to the alleged studies, the circumstances of the acquisition of the uranium metal document, and the procurement and R&D activities of military related institutes and companies that could be nuclear related as well as the production of nuclear related equipment and components by companies belonging to defence industries.

19. It should be noted that, although the Agency has limited means to authenticate independently the documentation that forms the basis of the alleged studies, the information is being critically assessed, in accordance with the Agency's practices, by corroborating it, inter alia, with other information available to the Agency from other sources and from its own findings. A description of all of the documentation available to the Agency about the alleged studies which the Agency has been authorized to share with Iran and which has been sufficiently vetted by the Agency was provided in the Director General's report of May 2008 (GOV/2008/15,[279] Annex A). It should be noted, however, that the constraints placed by some Member States on the availability of information to Iran are making it more difficult for the Agency to conduct detailed discussions with Iran on this matter. Notwithstanding, as the Director General has repeatedly emphasized, the information contained in that documentation appears to have been derived from multiple sources over different periods of time, appears to be generally consistent, and is sufficiently comprehensive and detailed that it needs to be addressed by Iran with a view to removing the doubts which naturally arise, in light of all of the outstanding issues, about the exclusively peaceful nature of Iran's nuclear programme.[280]

20. In connection with the outstanding issues, Iran has provided to the Agency: (a) its overall assessment of the documentation related to the alleged studies (GOV/2008/15, Annex A), and (b) partial replies and a document, in response to specific questions presented by the Agency (GOV/2008/15, Annex B). Iran has indicated further that it has information which could shed more light on the nature of the alleged studies, but has not yet provided it to the Agency (GOV/2008/15, para. 23). In the meantime, the Agency has studied the information provided by Iran thus far, but has not yet been given the opportunity by Iran to discuss its findings in detail owing to Iran's insistence that it had already provided its final responses. In the view of the Agency, however, there are still matters which need to be discussed based on the documents and information provided by Iran itself or which relate

[279] Doc. 52.

[280] GOV/2008/38, para. 16; GOV/2009/35, para. 23 (footnote in the original).

to information which the Agency has independently corroborated. Examples of information included in the documentation that Iran has not disputed as being factually accurate[281] are provided below.

21. Although Iran has challenged the allegation that it has engaged in nuclear related high explosives testing studies, Iran has told the Agency that it has experimented with the civil application of simultaneously functioning multiple detonators (GOV/2008/15, para. 20), and was asked by the Agency to provide it with information which would prove that such work had been for civil and non-nuclear military purposes (GOV/2008/38, para. 17(c)). Iran has not yet shared that information with the Agency. The Agency would also like to discuss with Iran the possible role that a foreign national with explosives expertise (GOV/2008/38, para. 17(d)), whose visit to Iran has been confirmed by the Agency, played in explosives development work.

22. With respect to the letter with handwritten annotations which was part of the documentation related to the alleged green salt project (GOV/2008/15, Annex A.1, Doc. 2), Iran has confirmed the existence of the underlying letter, has shown the original to the Agency and has provided the Agency with a copy of it. The existence of this original demonstrates a direct link between the relevant documentation and Iran. As already requested of Iran, the Agency needs to see further related correspondence and to have access to the individuals named in the letter.

23. In respect to the alleged missile re-entry vehicle studies, the Agency still wishes to visit the civilian workshops which Iran has indicated to the Agency exist and which are identified in the documentation as having been involved in the production of model prototypes of a new payload chamber for a missile (GOV/2008/38, para. 17(e)). In addition, while asserting that the documentation on the alleged missile re-entry vehicle was forged and fabricated, Iran informed the Agency that it was well known that Iran was working on the Shahab-3 missile. In light of that, the Agency has reiterated the need to hold discussions with Iran on the engineering and modelling studies associated with the re-design of the payload chamber referred to in the alleged studies documentation to exclude the possibility that they were for a nuclear payload.

24. In light of the above, the Agency has repeatedly informed Iran that it does not consider that Iran has adequately addressed the substance of the issues, having focused instead on the style and form of presentation of the written documents relevant to the alleged studies and providing limited answers or simple denials in response to other questions. The Agency has therefore requested Iran to provide more substantive responses and to provide the Agency with the opportunity to have detailed discussions with a view to moving forward on these issues, including granting the Agency access to persons, information and locations identified in the documents in order for the Agency to be able to confirm Iran's assertion that these documents are false and fabricated. The Agency has reiterated its willingness to discuss modalities that could enable Iran to demonstrate credibly that the activities referred to in the documentation are not nuclear related, as Iran asserts, while protecting sensitive information related to its conventional military activities.

25. For the Agency to be in a position to progress in its verification of the absence of undeclared nuclear material and activities in Iran, it is essential that Iran take the necessary steps to enable the Agency to clarify and bring to a closure the outstanding issues and implement its Additional Protocol.

---

[281] GOV/2008/15, para. 18 (footnote in the original).

F. Summary

26. The Agency continues to verify the non-diversion of declared nuclear material in Iran. Iran has cooperated with the Agency in improving safeguards measures at FEP and in providing the Agency with access to the IR-40 reactor for purposes of design information verification. Iran has not, however, implemented the modified text of its Subsidiary Arrangements General Part, Code 3.1, on the early provision of design information.

27. Iran has not suspended its enrichment related activities or its work on heavy water related projects as required by the Security Council.

28. Contrary to the requests of the Board of Governors and the Security Council, Iran has neither implemented the Additional Protocol nor cooperated with the Agency in connection with the remaining issues of concern which need to be clarified to exclude the possibility of military dimensions to Iran's nuclear programme. Regrettably, the Agency has not been able to engage Iran in any substantive discussions about these outstanding issues for over a year. The Agency believes that it has provided Iran with sufficient access to documentation in its possession to enable Iran to respond substantively to the questions raised by the Agency. However, the Director General urges Member States which have provided documentation to the Agency to work out new modalities with the Agency so that it could share further documentation with Iran, as appropriate, since the Agency's inability to do so is rendering it difficult for the Agency to progress further in its verification process.

29. It is critical for Iran to implement the Additional Protocol and clarify the outstanding issues in order for the Agency to be in a position to provide credible assurance about the absence of undeclared nuclear material and activities in Iran.

30. The Director General will continue to report as appropriate.

3. Official Records of the IAEA Board of Governors' Meetings on Implementation of the NPT Safeguards Agreement in the Islamic Republic of Iran

Document 58: Consideration of GOV/2003/40

GOV/OR.1070, 18 June 2003

...

87. Mr. GULAM HANIFF (**Malaysia**), **speaking on behalf of the Non-Aligned Movement** Chapter in Vienna,...

...

93. He welcomed the Director General's recent visit to Iran and the subsequent signing of new Subsidiary Arrangements. He also welcomed Iran's constructive initiative in presenting its peaceful nuclear strategy to Member States through its Vice President in May 2003. Iran's decision to allow the Agency to inspect its nuclear facilities even before its official acceptance of the modified Subsidiary Arrangements was to be commended, as were the numerous confidence-building measures it had taken, even allowing visits by

Agency officials to buildings unrelated to any nuclear facility. Moreover, after accepting the modified Subsidiary Arrangements, Iran had allowed six safeguards missions over the preceding three months.

94. The Non-Aligned Movement was of the opinion that the Director General's report contained in document GOV/2003/40[282] did not indicate non-compliance but a failure to report, similar to the cases referred to in paragraph 187 of the SIR. It encouraged both parties to pursue their consultations with a view to making progress in the implementation of safeguards at new facilities. In conclusion, he commended the Director General's efforts in that regard and welcomed Iran's announcement that the Government was considering signing an additional protocol,[283] and its open invitation to developed Member States to participate and co-operate in its nuclear programme.

95. Mr. ALEXANDRIS (**Greece**), **speaking on behalf of the European Union**, the acceding countries, Cyprus, the Czech Republic, Estonia, Hungary, Lithuania, Latvia, Malta, Poland, Slovakia and Slovenia the associated countries Bulgaria, Romania and Turkey, and Norway, said it was regrettable that the extent of Iran's nuclear programme had not been made known earlier to the Agency and the international community. Though any State party to the NPT had the inalienable right, under Article IV thereof, to develop research, production and use of nuclear energy for peaceful purposes, any misuse of civilian nuclear programmes constituted a violation of a State's obligations under that Treaty. It was deeply regrettable that Iran had failed to meet its reporting obligations under its comprehensive safeguards agreement,[284] and its obligations concerning inventory changes. It had also failed to declare facilities where material was stored and processed. The Director General should keep the Board regularly informed on a matter of such grave concern.

...

97. The European Union fully supported the Director General in his efforts to resolve outstanding issues with Iran rapidly and urged that country to address, in full co-operation of the Agency and in a detailed and substantiated manner, the questions which had been raised concerning its nuclear programme, and to take steps to ensure full transparency of that programme and so restore the international community's confidence. It also called on Iran to conclude and implement an additional protocol swiftly and unconditionally.

98. Mr. SALEHI (**Islamic Republic of Iran**) thanked the members of the Non-Aligned Movement for their solidarity and support. His country had not abandoned hope that the matter under discussion could be satisfactorily resolved.

99. The report contained in document GOV/2003/40 could have been more fair and balanced but, given the recent political rhetoric and the directives issued in certain influential capitals, it was perhaps the best that could be expected. However, there was room for hope that not all international organizations had opted for total submission.

...

101. The central issue in the report related to 0.13 effective kilograms of natural uranium which Iran had imported in 1991 to test the various processes at its uranium conversion facility. That facility had been under safeguards ever since construction started, i.e. before Iran had accepted the modified Subsidiary Arrangements. Despite subtle differences in the interpretation of Articles 95 and 34 of the safeguards agreement, Iran had declared the material to the Agency and it was now under full safeguards. However,

---

[282] Doc. 33.
[283] Doc. 5.
[284] Doc. 4.

even if his country were to admit negligence in the delayed declaration of the material in question, which was in any case way below the Agency's inspection thresholds, the SIR for 2002 (document GOV/2003/35) reported several other essential failures. Thus, paragraph 187 stated that 34 facilities (10%) in 15 States had failed to attain fully the quantity component of the inspection goal, and 32 facilities (9%) in 15 States had failed to attain fully the timeliness component. Paragraph 198 indicated that the quantity component of the inspection goal had not been attained for several years at six facilities as the measures foreseen in safeguards approaches could not be implemented. Paragraph 205 stated that it had not been possible to attain the quantity or timeliness components of the inspection goal at six LWRs as spent fuel had been loaded into casks for shipment and had been unavailable for verification during inspections. He also asked whether the hundreds of kilograms of uranium-shielded ammunition that had been transferred into Iraq had been reported either by the latter country or the country of origin. Thus, hardly any Member State could claim to be impeccable. What was important was the willingness of Member States to rectify possible failures. If the aim was to solve problems rather than turning them into international issues with far-reaching repercussions, every effort should be made to avoid the practice of double standards.

102. Questioning the merit of the further enquiries about Iran's programme related to the use of heavy water mentioned in paragraph 34(d) of the report, he asked whether Member States were under any legal obligation to justify any of their peaceful nuclear activities. Was it not the inalienable right of all Member States to acquire peaceful nuclear technology within the framework of the NPT? Iran had fulfilled its obligations under the NPT. Its denunciation of the nuclear option as a matter of principle, and the fact that it had placed its peaceful nuclear facilities under comprehensive safeguards, bore witness to its commitment to a strong NPT. The acquisition, development and use of nuclear weapons were inhuman, immoral, illegal and against Iran's basic principles. Such weapons had no place in its defence doctrine. They neither enhanced its security nor helped rid the Middle East of weapons of mass destruction. However, all provisions of the NPT were of equal importance. Maintaining the balance of rights and obligations enshrined in the Treaty preserved its integrity, enhanced its credibility and promoted the NPT's universality and full implementation thereof. Iran knew that greater capability brought with it more responsibility. It was enforcing its national laws and regulations on the control of nuclear and radioactive material and equipment. Any constructive interaction with other parties in that connection, including the Nuclear Suppliers Group, was welcome.

103. Finally, confidence-building meant acknowledging signs of co-operation, recognizing sincere intentions and using the right language for dialogue. The language of force and threat was not conducive to achieving the common goal. His country was still giving positive consideration to the conclusion of an additional protocol. As a further instance of its policy of transparency, it would raise no objection to the report on the implementation of the NPT safeguards agreement being made public, for it had nothing to hide in any of its peaceful nuclear activities.

104. Mr. TAKASU (**Japan**) said that, while Japan shared the concerns about the number of failures by Iran to report nuclear material, facilities and activities, it had noted the indications in the report that Iran was currently making efforts to take corrective actions in co-operation with the Agency by providing the necessary access and information.

105. He called upon Iran to rectify the outstanding issues as soon as possible by co-operating constructively with the Agency's verification activities. The Iranian authorities

should reply promptly and in a convincing manner to the open questions and should submit specific information on research and development carried out prior to the establishment of Iran's enrichment capabilities, any operations involving the use of nuclear material in connection with its centrifuge enrichment development programme, its reasons for producing uranium metal and developing a laser programme, and the purpose of its programme related to the use of heavy water. Environmental samples were an essential tool to prove the Iranian statement that it had developed its enrichment capabilities and constructed facilities for enrichment without any testing involving the use of nuclear material. Japan was concerned at Iran's lack of co-operation in that regard and hoped that its stated policy of transparency would be translated into concrete co-operation with the Agency. Such co-operation would not only assist the Agency in verifying Iran's declaration, but would also help Iran prove the absence of undeclared nuclear activities and the peaceful nature of its nuclear activities.

106. Though States party to the NPT had an inalienable right to acquire nuclear technology for peaceful purposes, that right did confer obligations. Countries with extensive nuclear activities and advanced fuel cycle technologies had a greater responsibility than others in terms of verification. For its part, Japan was making every effort to enhance transparency and had been one of the first countries to conclude an additional protocol. The Agency's ability to provide credible assurances regarding the absence of undeclared nuclear activities was limited in countries with no additional protocol in force, and he therefore urged Iran to conclude and bring into force an additional protocol without conditions. Such a step would help to convince the international community of the peaceful nature of its nuclear activities.

...

110. Ms. HALL (**Canada**) said that, in view of the press coverage that the issue had attracted, she endorsed the suggestion of the representative of Iran that the report be made public.

111. The Director General's report had established a pattern of failure by Iran to declare information as required by its safeguards agreement. It showed that Iran had been carrying out undeclared nuclear activities using undeclared nuclear material in undeclared nuclear facilities. Iran had only admitted to previously undeclared material, activities and facilities when confronted with evidence from other quarters. Its apparent reluctance to engage the Agency on a more proactive basis was not consistent with its promises of transparency, or in the spirit of co-operation expected under its NPT safeguards agreement.

...

115. The unconditional conclusion and implementation of an additional protocol was the only way for Iran to allay international concern over its nuclear programme. Only through the enhanced authorities provided by an additional protocol could the Agency provide the Board and the world with credible assurances that Iran no longer harboured undeclared nuclear material, activities and facilities.

116. Ms. AL-KHALID (**Kuwait**) expressed satisfaction at the content of the report which, while indicating patterns of failure on the part of Iran, also highlighted corrective measures that country was taking. She welcomed Iran's co-operation with the Agency and urged it to make every effort to resolve the outstanding issues and allay concerns about its nuclear activities. In that connection, she noted with satisfaction that, in February 2003, Iran had accepted modified Subsidiary Arrangements requiring it to inform the Agency of new nuclear facilities and of modifications to existing facilities as soon as a decision in that

regard had been taken. Countries that had signed the NPT had a right to acquire nuclear technology, and the signing by Iran of an additional protocol would dispel any suspicions about the nature of its nuclear programme. Iran was a strategically placed country and had an important role to play in co-operating with other countries of the Middle East to promote peace and stability in the region. Kuwait appreciated Iran's efforts to comply with international agreements and treaties in order to ensure that the NPT regime was fully respected at the regional as well as the international level.

117. Mr. MAYOR (**Switzerland**) said his country shared the Agency's concerns about Iran's failures to meet its obligations under its safeguards agreement with respect to timely reporting. He commended the Director General's efforts to maintain the credibility of the safeguards system in Iran and welcomed the increased transparency on the part of Iran. It should continue its efforts in that direction and take all necessary steps to rectify past omissions. He also urged Iran to sign an additional protocol as soon as possible and called upon the Director General to keep the Board informed of developments.

...

119. Mr. ZHANG Yan (**China**) said that, on the one hand, the report highlighted some safeguards issues that required clarification while, on the other, it indicated that Iran was taking corrective measures, such as allowing Agency inspectors to visit facilities and providing early design information. Every effort should be made for the parties concerned to resolve the issues through dialogue, consultation, co-operation and co-ordination.

120. China had always supported the NPT's objectives and international co-operation on the peaceful uses of nuclear energy. Agency safeguards were an important barrier to nuclear proliferation and his country supported the Agency's efforts to strengthen the safeguards regime. Additional protocols were a useful tool for that purpose and China was the first nuclear-weapon State to have ratified an additional protocol and to have submitted the relevant reports to the Agency. It called on other countries, particularly those with significant nuclear programmes, to sign, ratify and implement additional protocols as soon as possible. Iran should also be encouraged to conclude an additional protocol, which would help allay the international community's concerns.

...

Document 59: Consideration of GOV/2003/40

GOV/OR.1071, 18 June 2003

1. Mr. THIEBAUD (**France**), having thanked the Director General for his factual, detailed and precise report contained in document GOV/2003/40,[285] said that his Government remained concerned over the purpose, scope and technical level of Iran's nuclear programme and he urged that country to pursue a policy of openness and transparency in the interests of dialogue. Though Article IV of the NPT recognized the inalienable right of States to develop nuclear energy for peaceful purposes and to international co-operation in that field, that right was subject to compliance with the safeguards measures provided for in Article III of that Treaty which were essential to create a climate of confidence.

---

[285] Doc. 33.

2. The Director General's report and introductory statement had only served to increase the concerns of the international community, for a series of failures had come to light. Iran had not declared the import of significant quantities of nuclear material, despite the fact that it was explicitly obliged to do so under its safeguards agreement.[286] It had used and processed those materials in an undeclared facility, partly to produce uranium metal, whose role in its declared fuel cycle remained unclear, and partly to conduct a series undeclared processing operations. Although the quantities involved appeared small, the activities in question seemed to pertain to the development of a full fuel cycle.

3. Those failures were serious and raised certain questions, such as what was the intended use of the uranium metal, what were the exact nature and chronology of the undeclared processing activities, what material had been used and produced and in what quantities, what were the exact nature and chronology of the enrichment programme development activities, and how had they been conducted without using uranium. Besides the technical issues, there were questions of strategy such as whether Iran was prepared to commit itself to limiting its enrichment programme and any reprocessing activities to what was required for its nuclear power programme, and what its plans were for the heavy water plant.

4. Iran had committed itself on several occasions to transparency and to co-operating with the Agency. France welcomed those commitments and urged Iran to rectify its failures immediately, responding clearly and promptly to the Agency's questions and granting it access to its facilities and permission to take environmental samples. Iran should comply strictly with its obligations under its safeguards agreement, particularly with regard to the introduction of material in the Natanz pilot plant.

5. France supported the action taken by the Director General and the Secretariat. Iran could not regain the international community's confidence solely by rectifying its past failures, but only by a clear and irreversible commitment to transparency which it could demonstrate by signing, ratifying and implementing an additional protocol[287] without preconditions as soon as possible.

6. Mr. CARRERA DORAL (**Cuba**) took note of the Director General's report and introductory statement which revealed that Iran was fully co-operating with the Agency. The Governor from Malaysia, speaking on behalf of the Non-Aligned Movement, had pointed out how paragraph 187 of the SIR document (GOV/2003/35) indicated that several countries had not met safeguards requirements to some extent, and had highlighted the steps the Iranian authorities had taken to co-operate with the Agency. In March 2003, although the available information on the Iranian nuclear programme had at that time still been preliminary and unconfirmed, a group of countries had already voiced its concerns and urged Iran to sign an additional protocol. Regrettably, one country had stated that even Iran's signing an additional protocol would not dispel its concerns. Those same countries had made Iran's nuclear programme the central focus of the second session of the Preparatory Committee for the 2005 NPT Review Conference only a month later. In May, the Vice President of Iran had explained his country's decisions in detail and had responded to questions from Member States.

7. Cuba recognised the sovereign right of all countries, including Iran, to develop nuclear programmes for peaceful purposes as long as they complied with their obligations. Iran had repeatedly declared that its intentions were peaceful, Agency staff had visited the

---

[286] Doc. 4.
[287] Doc. 5.

country on several occasions, and Cuba had not yet heard any reasoned argument that it was in clear breach of the non-proliferation regime. Thus, the question had to be asked why that country had been singled out in an agenda item, a pattern which should not be followed at future meetings unless circumstances changed.

8. Iran was located close to an unstable area which was still recovering from an unnecessary war fought on the still unconfirmed pretext that a country possessed weapons of mass destruction, including nuclear weapons. Cuba was concerned that Iran was one of the potential targets for attack by the country with the most nuclear weapons, the only country to have used such weapons for military purposes, and the country which had developed the theory of the pre-emptive nuclear strike.

9. As the Director General had point out, the principles of multilateralism had to be upheld, and Cuba believed that the matter should be addressed objectively on the basis of scientific information, avoiding double standards and unilateral declarations and actions. Co-operation should be encouraged, and threatening, confrontational behaviour should be avoided. The Agency was perfectly capable of making a balanced analysis of the situation and proposing the necessary measures, and the matter should not be referred to the Board again unless there was a clear, documented breach of the non-proliferation regime.

10. Mr. BRILL (**United States**), having praised the thoroughness and professionalism of the Agency's efforts to clarify various questions that had arisen about Iran's nuclear activities, said his country was deeply troubled by the Director General's report which uncovered failures to report nuclear material, facilities and activities.

11. With respect to the outstanding issues, the Secretariat should report on the results of its environmental sampling, on its investigation of Iran's centrifuge and heavy water programmes, on Iran's experiments related to the production of uranium metal, an activity without apparent justification in its fuel cycle, and on its isotope production experiments.

12. Iran's claims of complete transparency had proved to be an empty promise in the light of its initial concealment and then reluctant confirmation of various undeclared activities and facilities. The report confirmed that the quantities of nuclear material involved, though small, were not insignificant in terms of a State's ability to conduct research and development activities, and the Agency needed to determine whether undeclared activities had taken place.

13. When the revelations about Iran's nuclear programme had been made during the preceding summer, that country had not demonstrated a willingness to inform the Agency promptly about its activities and had delayed the planned visit by the Agency to the country. It was significant that the sequence of events leading to the Director General's report had been prompted not by reports by Iran to the Agency but by information from open sources. Without those outside revelations, which the Agency deserved credit for pursuing, Iran's extensive nuclear programme might still be proceeding on a largely clandestine basis. That being so, there might be other clandestine facilities which had yet to be revealed.

14. The unresolved questions concerning Iran's nuclear intentions, documented in the Director General's report, were based on facts the Agency had revealed and confirmed and not on United States propaganda, as Iran would like the world to believe. Why, for instance, Iran had engaged in a long-term pattern of safeguards violations and evasions with respect to certain of its nuclear fuel cycle research and development activities if its intentions were peaceful? It was difficult to believe that all the various instances of failure to comply over many years, involving different quantities of nuclear material at different locations, reflected anything but a conscious effort by Iran to avoid those activities being monitored

by the Agency. The Director General had reported that Iran had obtained UF_6 from abroad without reporting the fact and that some of it was now missing. Iran claimed that was due to a leak it had just discovered. In the light of Iran's use of undeclared imported uranium compounds and its practical need to test centrifuges with UF_6 before committing to a large facility like Natanz, it was incumbent on the Iranian authorities to co-operate fully with all Agency efforts to establish what the real facts were. Despite the claims of Iranian officials that they were co-operating fully with the Agency, inspectors had initially been denied access to parts of the Kalaye Electric Company site and then only grudgingly granted some access. They were still being prevented from taking environmental samples. Iran's refusal to permit sampling seemed to imply that it had something to hide. It was also unclear why Iran had tested its capability to make uranium metal using a secret stock of UF_4 at an undeclared location when neither the Bushehr reactor nor the planned heavy water research reactor required uranium metal for fuel. Uranium metal was, however, required to make fissile components for HEU-type nuclear weapons.

…

16. …The Board should urge Iran to refrain from any action which would make it more difficult for the Agency to determine the correctness and completeness of its declarations. Specifically, the Agency should work with Iran to ensure that no new, declared nuclear material was introduced at the Natanz pilot plant while outstanding questions remained, as that might mask evidence of previous undeclared operations.

17. The United States joined other Board members in calling on Iran to sign, ratify and implement an additional protocol without delay or conditions. If its nuclear programme was limited only to peaceful purposes, the additional protocol was a way to demonstrate its commitment to the non-proliferation regime and complete transparency.

18. His country looked forward to receiving further information from the Director General on the Secretariat's progress and expected that the accumulation of further information would point to only one conclusion: that Iran was aggressively pursuing a nuclear weapons programme. The Board should be prepared to meet in special session to consider information when it became available, rather than waiting until September. Finally, he joined others in supporting the release of the Director General's report to the public.

…

21. Mr. O'SHEA (**United Kingdom**) noted the finding in paragraph 32 of the Director General's report that Iran had failed to meet its obligations under its safeguards agreement with respect to the reporting of nuclear material, the subsequent processing and use of that material and the declaration of facilities where the material was stored and processed. Some action had been taken by Iran to correct its failures, but it appeared that they had been taken only in response to the Agency's inquiries, inquiries that the Agency had been able to pursue only once it had received confirmation from a supplier State that nuclear material had been delivered to Iran in 1991. The same paragraph indicated that further action was needed to correct those failures fully. His country strongly endorsed the concern expressed by the Director General and urged Iran to complete the process of rectifying the failures identified as rapidly as possible. Iran's repeated claims to have notified the Agency about the Natanz enrichment facility were not borne out by paragraph 3 of the report, which suggested that the situation was not improving. Where new information had been provided by Iran, that had been done belatedly, in some cases partially, and only after material had been brought to light in other ways. Iran had still not responded to the Agency's inquiries and requests for access. That was not the way to build confidence and future reports should

comment on the quality of Iranian co-operation. Against that background, his country was particularly concerned about the four open questions set forth in paragraph 34.

...

26. Iran currently faced a confidence deficit. The longer questions remained unresolved, the greater that deficit would become. It was essential that Iran answer fully all the Agency's questions, provide all the access the Agency required, and permit the Agency to take all the samples it needed; in other words, that it demonstrate its often stated commitment to transparency. One significant step which would help restore the balance of confidence would be if Iran were to sign, bring into force and implement an additional protocol.

...

28. Mr. ABDENUR (**Brazil**) took note with concern of the information in the Director General's report regarding Iran's failure to meet its reporting obligations under its safeguards agreement. He also noted that those failures were being rectified by Iran and that the process of verifying the Iranian declarations was still ongoing. The statement by the representative of Iran that the acquisition, development or use of nuclear weapons had no place in his country's defence doctrine was heartening. Brazil called on the Government of Iran to abide by its obligations under the NPT and to co-operate fully with the Agency, inter alia, through the provision of all information deemed necessary and through the granting of unrestricted access to any location or installation that the Agency might wish to verify, even if they contained no nuclear material. Furthermore, it encouraged the Agency to proceed with its work to verify the Iranian declarations, and to perform all activities required to provide credible assurances of the absence of undeclared nuclear material or activities in Iran. Finally, he looked forward to receiving additional information on the results of those activities.

...

30. Mr. MINTY (**South Africa**) said that his country recognized and supported the legitimate right of all States to utilize the atom for peaceful purposes. Ownership of capabilities that could be used to develop nuclear weapons placed a special responsibility on the States concerned. It was incumbent on such States to build confidence within the international community so as to remove any concerns about nuclear weapons proliferation. That required full transparency, which implied total co-operation with the Agency. Such considerations applied particularly to States that had developed full nuclear fuel cycles.

31. South Africa had noted the concern expressed by the Director General in relation to the failures mentioned in his report and welcomed the fact that they were in the process of being rectified by Iran. It commended Iran for having invited the Director General to visit the country to discuss its plans for the use of nuclear power, and for allowing him and his team to visit a number of facilities. South Africa was confident that the subsequent enhanced co-operation between the Government of Iran and the Agency would continue and that the remaining questions would be clarified soon. It was encouraged by Iran's readiness to conclude an additional protocol and hoped that would be done as soon as possible. Finally, it was fully supportive of the actions undertaken by the Agency to date and looked forward to an early resolution of the matter.

...

36. Ms. STOKES (**Australia**)...

37. The Director General's report revealed a persistent pattern of apparent failures by Iran to meet its obligations under its safeguards agreement. Several of those failures had still not been remedied and it was thus difficult to have confidences yet that Iran had

declared all its nuclear activities and was totally committed to nuclear non-proliferation. Furthermore, Iran had not granted the Agency access to certain facilities to conduct its investigations, claiming it was not obliged to do so in the absence of an additional protocol. That position was difficult to reconcile with its profession of openness.

38. Australia called on Iran to rectify promptly the safeguards problems identified in the Director General's report and any other problem that might emerge in the course of the Agency's work in Iran, and to respond immediately to all the questions put to it by the Agency. The fact that Iran had not taken an earlier opportunity to demonstrate transparency in respect of its nuclear plans and had not involved the Agency in the design and construction of its new facilities inevitably raised questions about its intentions. It should give its complete co-operation to the Agency, granting all access deemed necessary, and it should refrain from introducing nuclear material at the pilot enrichment plant until the outstanding issues relating to it had been resolved.

39. Because Iran had extensive nuclear activities and advanced nuclear fuel cycle technologies, it should conclude and implement an additional protocol as a matter of urgency and without any preconditions. Moreover, because it was located in a region of political sensitivity, it should show particular restraint in the development of proliferation-sensitive technologies such as uranium enrichment.

...

42. Mr. BERDENNIKOV (**Russian Federation**) said that his country had taken note of the Director General's comments to the effect that corrective action was being taken in co-operation with the Iranian authorities, and that the work to verify the correctness and completeness of Iran's declaration in order to ensure that all its nuclear material had been declared and was under safeguards was still in progress. That work included technical discussions, inspections and sampling and, understandably, would take time. The Russian Federation fully supported the Agency's efforts and was convinced that its actions and conclusions would be objective. His country was working with Iran to promote the early signature of an additional protocol by that country, which it should do without delay and unconditionally. Such a step would be very much in Iran's best interests, as well as strengthening the non-proliferation regime, and would facilitate more active co-operation between Iran and the Agency. It was essential that Iran was entirely open about its nuclear activities and that it co-operate fully and unconditionally with the Agency. Issues relating to implementation of Iran's safeguards agreement needed to be examined and resolved in a climate of co-operation and mutual understanding, with no attempt to introduce controversial elements. Confrontation would in no way facilitate the speedy resolution of the existing problems and would only complicate the situation.

...

46. Mr. Chung-ha SUH (**Republic of Korea**) said that, though the Vice President of Iran had claimed on 6 May that Iran's nuclear programme was peaceful in intent, the Director General's report stated that that country had failed to meet obligations arising out of its safeguards agreement with the Agency in several respects, and that there were still unanswered questions. The inalienable right of States party to the NPT to use nuclear energy for peaceful purposes was guaranteed only if they complied with their NPT obligations. Unfortunately, the line that separated the use of nuclear energy for peaceful purposes from its use for the development of weapons programmes was very fine, hence the importance of transparency.

47. He urged Iran to take the steps requested of it in the Director General's report and to increase the transparency of its nuclear programme by co-operating fully with the Agency. In particular, it should conclude and implement an additional protocol without delay as an earnest of the peaceful nature of its nuclear programme.

48. Mr. SALEHI (**Islamic Republic of Iran**) expressed dismay at the inappropriateness of certain of the comments which had been made and their obvious political motivation.

49. It had been implied that his country was engaged in clandestine radioisotope separation operations. The purpose of those activities was to produce radioisotopes for use in nuclear medicine, as had been made clear in a paper published in 2001.

50. It had been claimed that his country had clandestinely developed an enrichment facility. However, the Uranium Conversion Facility under construction in Esfahan had been declared in 2000 and it was known that that facility would produce UF_6. It should be obvious that the UF_6 would be fed into an enrichment plant. He also questioned the legal basis for forbidding the introduction of nuclear material at the Natanz pilot fuel enrichment plant, pointing out that that facility was not yet under Agency safeguards.

51. He noted that, while an explicit report had been made to the Board about his country's failure to meet certain of its obligations, to his knowledge no such reports had been submitted on other Member States which had committed similar failures.

52. His country had been asked to justify why, when it had such large oil reserves, it needed nuclear power plants, but it was its sovereign right to take such decisions and it was not obliged to justify itself, merely to report.

53. When powerful countries took the attitude that might was right, they assumed the roles of both judge and prosecutor. They could make accusations against other countries, but neglect to answer accusations against themselves. Those same powerful countries could, with impunity, reject the CTBT, plan the resumption of nuclear weapons testing, openly contemplate the use of nuclear weapons in conventional conflicts, name non-nuclear-weapon States party to the NPT as possible targets of nuclear weapon attacks, and even seek to nuclearize outer space.

54. His country had been co-operative and forthcoming. It was also positively considering the conclusion of an additional protocol. For the good of the international community, it wished to see the process which the Agency had initiated continued unhindered. However, some countries seemed not to want the problem to be solved, but rather to exploit it for their own ends. Iran would not allow them to do that.

55. The DIRECTOR GENERAL said that he had drawn three conclusions from the discussion with which he believed all would agree.

56. Firstly, the Secretariat had to be conspicuous in fulfilling its obligations under the NPT and comparable legal instruments. The non-proliferation regime had changed in the preceding decade and the public had become more sensitized to non-proliferation issues. The discussion in the meeting had been about failures in reporting.

57. Secondly, Iran should be encouraged, in the interests of confidence-building, to continue co-operating fully and transparently with the Secretariat. The objective was not to cling to legalities but to build confidence through transparency.

58. Thirdly, the issue under discussion should be resolved as soon as possible.

59. The Secretariat would continue to work diligently over the coming months to ensure that the verification system was effective and comprehensive and created the necessary confidence. For that, full transparency was needed. He had frequently emphasized the importance of additional protocols, not only in connection with Iran but

more generally, and in particular with regard to countries with significant nuclear activities. Without additional protocols the Secretariat's hands were tied. Besides additional protocols, however, there needed to be transparency - a sign that a country had nothing to hide. It was in the interests of each country to be as transparent as possible because that was the way to create confidence.

...

Document 60: Consideration of GOV/2003/40 (continued)

GOV/OR.1072, 19 June 2003

The Chairperson summed up discussion on the issue.[288]

...

60. Mr. SALEHI (**Islamic Republic of Iran**) objected to the unusual manner in which the summing-up had been crafted and brought before the Board. His country found the summing-up neither fair nor balanced. It had already indicated that its pilot enrichment plant was under safeguards and the Board, in encouraging Iran to delay the introduction of nuclear material, implicitly cast doubt on the Agency's ability to safeguard that facility. The summing-up should reflect the statements delivered in a balanced manner, yet only four countries had referred in their statements to the notion of not introducing nuclear material at the plant. The summing-up implicitly and explicitly denied and undermined the well-established principle of the inalienable right of all countries to the peaceful use of nuclear technology. Several statements had been made on behalf of the Non-Aligned Movement pointing out the readiness of the Islamic Republic of Iran to co-operate with the Agency. However, few if any of the points made had been reflected in the summing-up. He requested that the Director General's final words on the subject be published either as an attachment to the summing-up or separately.

61. The Islamic Republic of Iran would not associate itself with the Board's statement. It hoped that eventually the issue would be resolved and that the underlying political motivations would be dispelled.

62. The CHAIRPERSON said she took it that the Board wished her summing-up to be made public.

63. It was so decided.

...

Document 61: Consideration of GOV/2003/63

GOV/OR.1077, 9 September 2003

...

78. The CHAIRPERSON recalled that the Board had last considered the matter of the implementation of the NPT safeguards agreement[289] by Iran in June of that year, and

---

[288] Doc. 22 paras 52-58.
[289] Doc. 4.

had requested the Director General to provide a further report on the situation whenever appropriate.

...

81. Mr. MORENO (**Italy**), **speaking on behalf of the European Union**, the acceding countries Cyprus, the Czech Republic, Estonia, Hungary, Latvia, Lithuania, Malta, Poland, Slovakia and Slovenia, and the associated countries Bulgaria, Iceland, Norway, Romania and Turkey, said that although the report showed that there had been increased co-operation on the part of Iran, some questions remained unresolved and gave cause for concern as far as non-proliferation was concerned...

...

83. He called on Iran to accelerate its co-operation with the Agency, to respond without delay and in detail to all the Agency's questions, and to ensure full transparency with regard to its nuclear programme.

84. He took note of Iran's positive decision with regard to the additional protocol[290] and requested the Secretariat to provide the necessary legal assistance for its prompt conclusion. Stressing that the text of the standard additional protocol, having been approved by consensus, could not be re-negotiated, he urged that it be concluded unconditionally and without further delay. He appealed to Iran, as a confidence-building measure, to apply the additional protocol's provisions voluntarily in the meantime so that the Agency could provide credible assurances regarding the peaceful nature of that country's nuclear activities, particularly the absence of undeclared nuclear material and activities.

85. Mr. SALEHI (**Islamic Republic of Iran**)...

86. It was clear from the Director General's report that Iran had provided a great deal of detailed information about its peaceful nuclear activities and had granted the requested access to additional locations where environmental samples could be taken. Such a degree of co-operation went beyond his country's legal obligations, and indeed was tantamount to provisional application of the additional protocol. It demonstrated Iran's willingness to dispel the legitimate concerns of the international community and to respond to the calls made by the Board of Governors in June.

87. His delegation was committed to the Board's tradition of consensus, which enabled the Director General to fulfil his responsibilities freely and objectively. Implementation of the NPT safeguards agreement in Iran was an ongoing process; any attempt to hinder it was unwelcome and might undo what had been achieved so far. Also, the use of threatening language was futile. Despite its unprecedented co-operation, Iran had received only increased pressure from a few influential Member States.

88. Iran had consistently honoured its obligations under international treaties, and during the war imposed on it had never succumbed to the temptation to use chemical weapons by way of reprisals. It regarded the NPT as the protector of its right to the peaceful use of nuclear technology. To deny a country's rights while laying undue stress on its obligations was unproductive.

89. Full co-operation with the Agency depended on avoiding politicization of the situation. Politicization had led some elements in his country to question the acceptance of further obligations under the additional protocol, and even to advocate withdrawal from the NPT. Having been subjected to unjustified sanctions on the one hand, while following a policy of transparency beyond its obligations on the other, meant that Iran was having to make great efforts to create a domestic consensus favourable to co-operation with the

---

[290] Doc. 5.

Agency. The report contained in document GOV/2003/63[291] was not conclusive. Analysis results were still outstanding and sufficient time should be allowed for that process to be completed.

90. With regard to concerns about its enrichment activities, he stressed that Iran was fully prepared to take remedial action where necessary to ensure that its programme remained peaceful. Finally, he expressed appreciation for the fact that the Agency's focus on nuclear activities in the country had always been related to treaty obligations, and had never intruded on matters outside its mandate.

91. Ms. KELLY (**Argentina**), expressing support for the work done by the Secretariat on the issue, said that the Director General's latest report only deepened her country's doubts about Iran's nuclear programme, particularly in regard to uranium enrichment. It mentioned contradictions with explanations provided earlier by the Iranian authorities and indicated that full collaboration with Agency inspectors had not been forthcoming. Nevertheless, the report as a whole could be interpreted as showing a greater willingness to co-operate.

...

93. Mr. ZNIBER (**Morocco**) said the increased co-operation shown by Iran and its willingness to sign an additional protocol were encouraging and should help to dissipate any remaining questions regarding the implementation of safeguards in Iran. The concerns of the international community were justified and it was important to reach a satisfactory solution to help strengthen the Agency's credibility and avoid a crisis with unforeseeable consequences.

94. Mr. BRILL (**United States of America**) welcomed the report, but found it less effectively organized and less clear in some respects than the report that had been submitted in June.[292] After a further two months of intensive work, the unanswered questions had only grown both in number and in significance.

95. The United States of America agreed that the Secretariat should continue its efforts to clarify the history, nature and purposes of the Iranian nuclear programme. However, Board members also had a responsibility to look at the facts already established. There was need for serious reflection on the patterns that had emerged to date - which were inconsistent with Iran's safeguards agreement and its professions of transparency. They included: working in secret since the 1980s to develop sophisticated nuclear facilities; stalling and providing the Agency with false information, which had been changed when the original was revealed to be inaccurate; and attempting to cover up the traces of activities in order to avoid detection.

...

97. The report now under discussion added to the already significant list of failures by Iran to meet its safeguards obligations. Contrary to earlier statements, and only in response to damning evidence and repeated Agency enquiries, Iran had now confirmed that it had conducted undeclared uranium conversion experiments on two occasions in the 1990s.

98. The most important open question in the June report related to Iran's enrichment programme...

99. There were also open questions in the June report about laser enrichment. They remained open because, according to paragraph 42, Iran had not allowed Agency inspectors to take environmental samples at a previously unacknowledged key site and had not allowed

---

[291] Doc. 34.
[292] Doc. 33.

them to visit the site until equipment, including a large imported vacuum vessel, had been moved elsewhere.

100. Without detailing other open questions involving, for instance, uranium metal and heavy water, it was clear that the more the Secretariat had probed beneath the surface, the less plausible Iran's explanations had become, leaving even more open questions than had existed in June.

101. Most of the increased co-operation by Iran in the amount and detail of information provided had seemingly come a mere fortnight before the appearance of the Director General's report in an attempt to influence its content and tone. The delay had also possibly been intended to prevent sampling results from the Kalaye Electric Company being available to the current session of the Board. Iran's co-operation with the Agency had been at best selective, episodic and reluctant, characterized by delay, denial of access and misinformation, and could be more accurately described as damage control rather than genuine co-operation.

...

104. Without much conviction, his delegation hoped that the Iranian authorities' recent letter to the Director General to the effect that it was prepared to begin negotiation on an additional protocol was not another delaying tactic. How long would Iran take to accept the provisions of a document already signed by scores of Member States? Would it agree in the interim, as specifically requested by the Director General, to apply additional protocol provisions in an effort to give much-needed reassurance to the international community?

105. The combined evidence in the Director General's two reports showed that Iran had failed in many important ways to meet its NPT safeguards agreement obligations. The more recent report made it clear that the Agency was currently unable to provide assurance to the Board that Iran had not diverted nuclear material to non-peaceful purposes, a situation that would still prevail unless Iran provided continued and accelerated co-operation and full transparency.

106. Based on that evidence the Board had a responsibility to act. The Agency - which included the Board - must preserve the credibility of the global non-proliferation regime by standing firm against all efforts to violate or circumvent NPT obligations. The Board must forthwith send a clear message of political support for the Director General and the Secretariat in their efforts to penetrate the fog of obfuscation, misinformation and delayed admissions in which Iran continued to envelop its nuclear programme. The Agency inspectors, despite their professionalism, hard work and skill, needed help in order to complete their task in a timely manner.

107. Contrary to some accusations, the United States of America was not seeking to politicize the Agency process. It sought to ensure that the Agency met its responsibility to find peaceful solutions to critical non-proliferation issues. It was not politicization to support the NPT or expect its signatories to meet their safeguards obligations.

108. Although his country was convinced that the facts fully justified an immediate finding of Iran's non-compliance with its safeguard obligations, it took note of the desire of other Member States to give Iran a last chance to desist from its evasions. His delegation therefore joined the appeal to Iran to take essential and urgent action to demonstrate that it had done so.

...

110. Mr. BERDENNIKOV (**Russian Federation**) said that document GOV/2003/63 attested to the useful work accomplished by the Secretariat since the Director General had

submitted his report to the Board in June. Russia welcomed the increased degree of co-operation shown by Iran and the fact that Iran had allowed inspectors access to facilities, including the Kalaye Electric Company, and had permitted sample taking. It was clear that the Secretariat needed more time to assess the new information and to analyse the samples.

111. At the same time, it was regrettable that the information and access had been at times slow in coming and incremental, and that some information was in contrast with that previously provided by Iran. Russia hoped that Iran would draw the right conclusions and further strengthen its co-operation with the Agency so that the important unresolved issues could be settled soonest. His delegation assumed that the Agency had at its disposal all the technical and human resources it needed. The Agency was the only international body with the authority to evaluate Iran's compliance with its NPT safeguards obligations.

112. As always, Russia supported the Secretariat's efforts and was convinced that the Agency's conclusions would be objective, justified and impartial. His delegation appealed to Iran to sign immediately and unconditionally an additional protocol and welcomed its decision to begin negotiations with the Agency to that end. Such a step would not only strengthen the worldwide non-proliferation regime but also be in Iran's own best interest and encourage co-operation between that country and the Agency. He urged Iran to ensure complete transparency regarding its past and current nuclear activities, as well as full and unconditional co-operation with the Agency.

113. He urged all interested Member States to help resolve all issues in a spirit of co-operation, dialogue and mutual understanding. Confrontation would not lead to a speedy solution and might serve only to complicate the situation.

114. Mr. ZHANG Huazhu (**China**)...

115. The Director General's objective report on the implementation of Iran's NPT safeguards agreement, while noting increased co-operation by that country with the Agency also pointed to a number of important outstanding issues. China was pleased that Iran had no intention to develop nuclear weapons and that it was prepared to begin negotiation on an additional protocol. Hopefully that process could reach conclusion in the near future. His delegation also hoped that, in co-operation with the Agency and with encouragement from the international community, Iran would take practical steps towards the prompt and peaceful resolution of the nuclear issue. That would not only enhance the credibility of the non-proliferation regime, but also benefit Iran itself.

116. Mr. TAKASU (**Japan**)...

...

118. He urged Iran to take immediately all the measures identified by the Director General so that the Agency could verify its compliance with its safeguards agreement, and to suspend all uranium enrichment activities, pending the resolution of outstanding issues. That would assure the international community of its commitment to the use of nuclear material for strictly peaceful purposes.

119. Convinced that countries with extensive nuclear activities, especially advanced fuel cycle technologies, had a greater responsibility to be transparent in their nuclear activities, Japan had endeavoured to improve the transparency of its programme and had been one of the first countries to implement an additional protocol. Iran should accelerate its efforts to sign unconditionally, ratify and fully implement an additional protocol, and, as a confidence-building measure, should start implementing the relevant provisions forthwith.

...

Document 62: Consideration of GOV/2003/63 (continued)

GOV/OR.1078, 9 September 2003

1. Mr. O'SHEA (**United Kingdom**) said successful and speedy resolution of the Iran issue was crucial to the Agency - and the international - safeguards regime and to the cause of preventing the proliferation of nuclear weapons.

...

11. From all that detail in the Director General's latest report it must be concluded that: firstly, the uncertainty and concern over Iran's nuclear programme, far from having been allayed, had actually grown since June; and, secondly, Iran had failed to demonstrate the full and unqualified co-operation and transparency which the Agency had requested.

12. He was sorry to say that as things stood, Iran's failure to resolve issues since June and the extent of the new questions raised by the Director General's latest report meant that Iran's confidence deficit had increased rather than diminished.

13. Iran must sign and implement all the provisions of the additional protocol[293] immediately. But that was not enough. The facts in the Director General's reports and the extent of the work still to be done before the Agency could provide the assurances required by Member States, were sufficient to justify a conclusion that the Agency was not able to verify that there had been no diversion of nuclear material. However, his Government agreed with others that such a conclusion was premature. It, too, wanted Iran to deliver on its new offers of full co-operation and full transparency so that the Agency could provide a complete, credible and suitably verified account of the Iranian nuclear programme. If that was to happen, the Board must send the strongest possible message to Iran and to the international community that the kind of incomplete and conditional co-operation seen to date was unacceptable. That message must be in the form of a resolution that left Iran in no doubt about the action it needed to take and that the action was essential and urgent under Article 18 of its NPT safeguards agreement, contained in INFCIRC/214.[294]

14. Iran must, by the end of October 2003, do everything necessary to enable the Agency to verify compliance with Iran's safeguards agreement. It must provide a full declaration of the sources and types of all imported material and components relevant to the enrichment programme, and the locations where they had been stored and used in Iran; grant unrestricted access, including environmental sampling, to whatever locations the Agency deemed necessary for verification purposes; resolve questions regarding the conclusion of Agency experts that process testing on gas centrifuges must have been conducted; provide complete information regarding the conduct of uranium conversion experiments; and provide all other information and explanations and take all steps deemed necessary by the Agency to resolve all outstanding issues involving nuclear materials and nuclear activities, including environmental sampling results. In the meantime, Iran should suspend all further uranium enrichment-related activities.

15. It was not yet too late for Iran to take the steps necessary to resolve that issue – but it was the last chance.

16. Ms. HALL (**Canada**) said that when the Board had last taken up the subject of NPT safeguards in Iran at its June meeting, she had noted that the Director General's report had established a pattern of failure by Iran to declare information to the Agency as legally

---

[293] Doc. 5.
[294] Doc. 4.

required. The Director General's second report, contained in document GOV/2003/63, now showed something far more serious, a pattern not merely of failure or omission, but of active evasion and deception on the part of the Iranian authorities.

...

19. In response to international concern, Iran had repeatedly promised transparency. Yet the Agency's efforts to reconstruct the history of the Iranian programme were continually thwarted through slow and incremental co-operation by the Iranian authorities...

20. Her Government would like to believe the assurances offered by Iran that its nuclear programme was entirely peaceful, but Iran's contradictory statements had diminishing credibility. How could the Agency provide assurances of non-diversion of nuclear material when Iran wilfully masked important aspects of its programme? The nature of Iran's nuclear programme, coupled with its evasiveness, only made sense in the context of nuclear weapons ambitions. On the basis of the Director General's June and August reports, her Government was forced to conclude that Iran was in non-compliance with its NPT safeguards agreement. While Canada believed that the Agency should apprise the Security Council of that disturbing situation, in deference to the views of others wishing to give Iran another chance, it was prepared to join the Board in deciding that certain actions by Iran were 'essential and urgent' to resolve doubts about the non-diversion of nuclear material. A strongly worded resolution of concern was the minimum action that the Board of Governors must take at the current time to underline the seriousness of the situation and send a firm, clear message.

...

22. Canada urged Iran, as a sign of the good intentions it professed, to sign an additional protocol without further delay and to move swiftly to ratify and implement it. It was only through the powers provided by the additional protocol that the Agency, the sole competent authority for the verification of compliance with the NPT, could provide the world with the assurances it sought.

...

30. Mr. THIEBAUD (**France**) said ...

31. Serious questions thus remained about the nature and objectives of the Iranian programme, including past activities involving uranium, the history of the centrifuge enrichment programme, and the heavy water reactor programme.

32. France also regretted that Iran had not taken account of the Board's appeal to suspend the introduction of uranium at its pilot enrichment plant in order to contribute to restoring confidence. The Iranian authorities had not shown the full co-operation expected. On the contrary, the Director General's report had noted that information and access had been 'at times slow in coming and incremental'. After months of delay, Iran had finally authorized the taking of samples at the Kalaye Electric Facility, but only after having made considerable modifications which diminished the Agency's ability to verify the Iranian statements. That set of worrying facts ran counter to Iran's repeated commitment to ensure the full transparency of its activities. On the whole, Iran had failed to respond to the Board's questions and requests.

33. Although the Secretariat had not yet completed its investigations, the information available painted a disquieting picture of Iran's nuclear programme and its real objectives. It was essential and urgent for the Board and the international community to have conclusive information about the Iranian nuclear programme and that country's compliance with its international commitments.

34. France was committed to the inalienable right of States, as set out in Article IV of the NPT, to benefit from the development of nuclear technologies. That right was not in question. But it could not be exercised without full compliance with the safeguards measures contained in Article III of the Treaty and in an atmosphere of confidence and transparency. It was up to Iran to restore the confidence of the international community and to reply to all questions concerning its nuclear programme.

35. Noting with appreciation Iran's intention to hold discussions with the Agency on an additional protocol, France called on the Iranian authorities to conclude and implement one unconditionally and without delay. France also urged the Iranian authorities to suspend all enrichment and reprocessing activities pending the resolution of the questions raised by the Agency and satisfactory implementation of the additional protocol. It was essential for Iran to provide the Agency with all necessary information so that the Agency could ascertain whether Iran was in compliance with all its obligations under the safeguards agreement before the following meeting of the Board.

...

38. Mr. MINTY (**South Africa**) said ...

39. South Africa continued to promote international co-operation with regard to peaceful nuclear activities, as envisaged in Article III (3) of the NPT, and also the exchange of scientific information - particularly in Africa - for the further development of peaceful nuclear applications, in accordance with the seventh preambular paragraph of the NPT. Possessing capabilities that could be used to develop nuclear weapons placed a special responsibility on the States concerned to build confidence with the international community, particularly those with full fuel cycles. As the internationally recognized competent authority for verifying compliance with safeguards agreements, the Agency must be able to verify that those capabilities were being used for peaceful purposes only, including through the mechanisms available under the additional protocol.

...

42. His delegation also welcomed Iran's stated intention to begin negotiations with the Agency on an additional protocol, the early conclusion of which would serve as an important confidence-building measure.

...

52. Mr. ABDENUR (**Brazil**) said...

...

54. Brazil was pleased that Iran had indicated it was prepared to start negotiations with the Agency on an additional protocol. That decision was entirely appropriate given that the provisions of the comprehensive safeguards agreement were clearly insufficient to dispel the doubts of the international community as to the peaceful purposes of Iran's nuclear programme.

...

56. Ms. STOKES (**Australia**) expressed concern that...

57. The Director General's reports revealed a disturbing series of safeguards failures and a lack of full co-operation and transparency on Iran's part. Whether the term 'failures' constituted 'non-compliance' called for a judgement as to Iran's intentions based on the significance of the failures (for example, the type and quantity of material and how it had been or may have been used); the plausibility of the explanation provided; and whether the failures appeared to be part of a pattern. Iran's safeguards failures - relating inter alia to uranium enrichment, the irradiation and separation of nuclear material, and the production

of uranium metal - were very serious and of potential proliferation significance. They appeared no less serious than the safeguards failures in Iraq in 1991 and in Romania in 1992 - both of which had been considered non-compliance.

58. According to Article 19 of Iran's safeguards agreement, the Board 'may' make a finding of non-compliance if the Agency 'is not able to verify that there has been no diversion of nuclear material required to be safeguarded'. What then was necessary to support such a finding?

59. Since the start of the Agency's investigations, there had been a pattern not only of safeguards failures but also of actions that were clearly intentional, including delays in sampling, 'modifications' to buildings and the introduction of UF_6 at Natanz contrary to the Board's request. Moreover, Iran had delayed acceptance of the Board's 1992 decision on the early provision of design information for more than 10 years, during which there had been extensive development of its uranium enrichment programme. While any one of those incidents might be explicable in isolation, they were strongly suggestive of systematic safeguards violations in the context of major unresolved issues such as the implausibility of developing centrifuges without practical enrichment experience, the lack of a satisfactory explanation for the presence of HEU, the rewriting of declarations and the discovery of new 'facts' as the Agency produced new information.

60. In Australia's view, there was a strong case for finding that Iran was currently in non-compliance. Nevertheless, given the desire of other Member States to grant Iran a last chance, Australia would join in the call on Iran to take essential and urgent action to remedy its past failures and demonstrate transparency.

...

65. The **DIRECTOR GENERAL** said he was grateful to the Board for the support expressed for the Secretariat's efforts to resolve a very important issue that had implications for the integrity of the non-proliferation regime. One common theme in all the statements - including Iran's - was the call for a joint effort to ensure closure of the matter as soon as possible. It was essential to work together for a peaceful outcome through effective exploitation of the Agency's verification capacity. Moreover, all means at the Agency's disposal should be exhausted before any thought was given to alternative courses of action.

66. The Secretariat's work was exclusively on a technical plane. It did not engage in political assessment. Its job was to verify facts and share its findings with the Board. Obviously, though, inspections took time and, as stated in his report, the point where all available remedies had been used up had not yet been reached. The Secretariat adopted a conservative approach because of its unwillingness to jump to conclusions that were not incontrovertibly supported by the facts. On a matter of such importance as Iran's capability to produce weapons-usable material, it was dangerous to reach hasty conclusions.

...

68. Iran had not been under a legal obligation to declare facilities under construction or the importation of equipment or to provide access to certain sites and locations. However, as he had emphasized to the Iranian authorities - legal rights apart - the issues could not be resolved without full transparency and proactive co-operation because the country's nuclear programme was both very extensive and had been in existence since the mid-1980s. The history of such an extensive programme could not be reconstructed solely on the basis of the safeguards agreement. He was grateful for Iran's recognition of that fact and its facilitation of access to certain sites and environmental sampling.

...

Document 63: Consideration of GOV/2003/63, 68 and Add.1

GOV/OR.1081, 12 September 2003

1. The CHAIRPERSON drew the Board's attention to the fact that the draft resolutions contained in documents GOV/2003/66 and GOV/2003/67 had been withdrawn, and that a new draft resolution had been put forward which was contained in document GOV/2003/68.

2. Mr. SALEHI (**Islamic Republic of Iran**) said that the debate on the issue had revealed two distinctly contrasting approaches. One attempted to circumvent the Agency and refer the matter immediately to the Security Council. The other approach, which was clearly the most popular but would not necessarily win through, sought to sustain the process and allow the Agency to discharge its responsibilities despite political bullying. The Director General had summed up the debate in succinct and compelling terms: the issue was important and needed to be cleared up; it was technical and should remain so; the wish to resolve the matter swiftly was justified, but the Agency's work should be allowed to run its course; although failures had occurred, the important thing was to remedy them and ensure that all activities were under safeguards; to conclude that the Agency was unable to verify the situation would be detrimental to the safeguards system; the reaction of the Board, in form and substance, should reflect the collective view of the entire membership; and, above all, there should not be any jumping to conclusions or jumping the gun...

3. On the preceding day, a number of Governors had stated that time was up and that a final ultimatum should be issued, making spurious claims that there was an imminent and clear danger. Even more scandalously, Governments were being told in private that Iran would be a nuclear threat in six months, in an attempt to turn a safeguards issue into one of international security. The United States was, unsurprisingly, resorting to deception and lies, and might even wield its massive power to crush the perceived culprit. Nothing could quench its thirst for vengeance short of confrontation and war. It was no secret that influential groups in the current United States administration were toying with the idea of invading yet another country as part of a plan to reshape the entire Middle East region.

...

6. ...The draft resolution, on the other hand, aimed at reaching an early deadlock so the issue could be rapidly referred to the Security Council, ending co-operation and fabricating a hasty ruling of non-compliance.

7. As an ultimate act of benevolence, Iran had been granted 45 days to deal with every item on a list of things to be done, a patently impossible task. The demands set out in that list went well beyond its obligations under its safeguards agreement[295] and even under an additional protocol.[296] He asked the Governors from Australia, Canada and Japan to state clearly whether, if the demands in the list were met in full, Iran would at long last be allowed to enjoy its inalienable right to the peaceful use of nuclear energy without restrictions or impediments.

8. For the preceding 24 years, Iran had been subject to the severe sanctions and export restrictions on material and technology related to the peaceful use of nuclear energy. Consequently, it had had no choice but to exercise discretion, as any attempt to procure or

---

[295] Doc. 4.
[296] Doc. 5.

produce what it needed for its peaceful programme had been relentlessly suppressed. If his country had sometimes been slow to co-operate, if there had been occasional discrepancies, or if it had hesitated to adhere to the additional protocol or embrace confidence-building initiatives that was because of its concern over the United States' intention to deprive Iran of the benefits of nuclear energy for good.

9. Iran rejected the ultimatum contained in the draft resolution. The United States had insisted on maintaining the proposed deadline, despite appeals by a large number of States, including some of the co-sponsors, to drop it. That was music to the unilateralists' ears, but spelled disaster for the Agency.

...

13. Ms. STOKES (**Australia**), introducing draft resolution contained in document GOV/2003/68, said that it enjoyed widespread support in all geographic regions. All Member States should be able to endorse the draft's overriding objective, which was to provide full support for the Agency in its work and resolve the issue at hand. She expressed the hope that it would be adopted without a vote.

14. The CHAIRPERSON took it that the Board wished to adopt the draft resolution contained in document GOV/2003/68 without a vote.

15. It was so decided.

16. Mr. GULAM HANIFF (**Malaysia**), **speaking on behalf of the Non-Aligned Movement**, said that operative paragraphs 3 and 4 of the resolution asked Iran to take action which went beyond the provisions of both the NPT and an additional protocol. By setting a deadline at the end of October 2003, the resolution tied the Agency's hands. More importantly, it also meant that Iran's co-operation was no longer required after that date.

17. With regard to operative paragraph 4(ii), a legal interpretation was required of the words 'unrestricted access' in connection with Iran's compliance with its current safeguards agreement. Those words were not even used in the additional protocol.

18. In the view of the Non-Aligned Movement, the words 'definitive conclusions' in operative paragraph 7 did not necessarily mean 'final conclusions' but 'appropriate or precise conclusions'. It therefore considered that it was not the intention of the resolution to forestall or hinder the Agency's required activities in Iran before or after the November 2003 meetings of the Board.

...

27. Mr. ABDENUR (**Brazil**) expressed regret at the Board's failure to reach a compromise on the resolution just adopted. Brazil had misgivings with regard to certain elements of the text. For instance operative paragraph 3 contained a clear inconsistency, and perhaps set a dangerous precedent, in calling for a suspension of enrichment activities in a manner that did not adequately reflect the balance of rights and obligations under NPT safeguards. With regard to operative paragraph 4, though there was clearly an urgent need to clarify all outstanding issues, the Board should not attempt to force the pace of what was, of necessity, a difficult and complex process. The imposition of unduly strict timeframes and deadlines might impede the flexibility required by the Secretariat and would not necessarily help bring the issue to a fully satisfactory outcome, upholding Iran's obligations under the NPT and its safeguards agreement. At the same time, Iran should ensure that the co-operation required under operative paragraph 4 was provided without delay. He noted in that connection the Director General's statement to the effect that the Agency could clarify all outstanding issues in a relatively short period with proactive co-operation. Referring to operative paragraph 7, he said that the Board should retain the

option of drawing definitive conclusions after its November meetings if the information required to draw such conclusions was not available by then. Retaining that option did not detract from the sense of the urgency, nor did it imply that the Board would adopt a complacent attitude if Iran were insufficiently co-operative in implementing the provisions of the resolution.

...

29. Mr. CARRERA DORAL (**Cuba**) said that his country fully supported the approach the Agency had adopted to the issue under discussion and welcomed Iran's constructive and transparent attitude. The Agency should take all necessary steps to ensure that States honoured their safeguards obligations. However, any attempt to prejudge a country's nuclear programme or to politicize discussions relating to it was inadmissible. Only the Agency had the mandate to verify and draw conclusions about a country's nuclear programme on the basis of objective and factual information.

...

31. ... The resolution which had just been adopted issued an ultimatum to Iran and was premature and counterproductive. His country opposed any attempt to violate a State's sovereign right to accede to an international instrument whenever it saw fit. Acceptance of such conduct would set a very undesirable precedent in international relations, undermining the principles of justice and equity...

...

33. Mr. MINTY (**South Africa**)...

34. Although his country had supported the resolution just adopted, it wished to clarify certain points relating to it. Firstly, South Africa was of the view that the intention of operative paragraph 3 was to create a situation in which Iran would build confidence vis-à-vis the international community regarding its nuclear activities. It was held to the position that States had the right under the NPT to conduct nuclear activities for peaceful purposes. It would therefore have preferred less peremptory language in the paragraph in question. Secondly, with regard to the request in operative paragraph 7 for the Director General to a report to the Board in November 2003, he stressed that the Director General's work should not be prejudiced in any way, and it should be remembered that he would have to carry out extensive verification work, possibly also involving other countries. The Board's conclusions should be based on a factual report and it would be inappropriate for it to commit itself in advance to reaching definitive conclusions.

35. It was critical to focus on the central importance of maintaining and enhancing the integrity and credibility of the NPT and of the Agency. The issue was sensitive and complicated and the Board should seek to promote continued and full co-operation between Iran and the Agency.

36. Mr. BERDENNIKOV (**Russian Federation**) said that his country had found it difficult to accept the adoption of the resolution on the Islamic Republic of Iran without a vote since that resolution was flawed. For example, it failed to mention the important statement in the Agency's report that Iran had recently been more co-operative in providing information and allowing access to additional sites. However, the Russian Federation had gone along with the resolution in order to preserve and strengthen the unity of the Board in non-proliferation matters.

37. It was his country's understanding that the resolution gave the Agency and Iran the necessary time to clarify the outstanding issues relating to the latter's nuclear programme and did not establish a deadline. If new information of interest to the Agency came to light after the end of October 2003, nothing should prevent Iran from transmitting it to

the Agency as soon as possible. In the current circumstances, haste and the exertion of pressure on the Agency were inappropriate. The most important thing was to help the latter obtain a clear, objective and comprehensive picture of Iran's nuclear activities. Even from a strictly technical point of view, it would be wrong to speed up laboratory analyses of the environmental samples taken in Iran. The Agency also needed time to work with third countries to clarify certain issues.

38. The Russian Federation was equally of the view that operative paragraph 7 of the resolution did not require either the Agency or the Board to draw definitive conclusions by a particular date and was pleased to note that other members of the Board shared that interpretation. Only when the Director General was in a position to present a full picture to the Board of all aspects of the Iranian programme could any specific conclusions be drawn. To state categorically that the Agency should complete its work by November 2003 would be irresponsible and might place the Board and the Agency in a difficult position. Fortunately, operative paragraph 7 gave the Board and the Agency some flexibility in the matter and the resolution could therefore not be interpreted as an ultimatum.

39. The appeal to Iran in operative paragraph 3 of the resolution to suspend its uranium enrichment activities was without prejudice to the legitimate right of States party to the NPT and Member States of the Agency to develop peaceful nuclear programmes and was intended as a temporary confidence-building measure.

40. The most important features of the resolution were the strong signal the Board had sent to Iran that it should continue and enhance its co-operation with the Agency and ensure full transparency of its nuclear programme, and the appeal for it to sign an additional protocol immediately and unconditionally. He noted with satisfaction that Iran's official response to the Agency on that score had been favourable and trusted that the negotiations would not be unduly lengthy and would be crowned with success.

41. Mr. ZHANG Huazhu (**China**) said that… The issue of Iran's nuclear programme should be addressed through constructive dialogue and co-operation within the framework of safeguards. The international community should work in an objective and equitable manner towards a peaceful solution by encouraging Iran to co-operate further with the Agency…

…

44. Ms. HALL (**Canada**) said that, in the light of the evidence contained in the Director General's report and the contradictions in Iran's account of its nuclear programme, her country was of the opinion that a finding of non-compliance would be warranted, requiring the Agency to refer the matter to the Security Council. However, the resolution just adopted had given Iran one last chance fully to meet its NPT and safeguards obligations. In deciding that certain actions by Iran were 'essential and urgent' to dispel doubts about the non-diversion of nuclear material, the resolution was referring to Iran's obligations under Article 18 of its safeguards agreement. Although the resolution fell short of the finding that Canada had originally advocated, it established measurable benchmarks and sent a firm signal to Iran and to the world. She urged Iran to take the final opportunity offered. Failure to take the action specified in the resolution and to address all concerns fully and satisfactorily would necessarily result in a finding of non-compliance and a report to the Security Council. She also noted that the resolution requested third countries to co-operate closely and fully with the Agency in clarifying outstanding questions. Finally, she looked forward with interest to the Director General's report on the matter at the November 2003 meetings of the Board and requested that the text of the resolution be made public.

45. Mr. BRILL (**United States of America**) said that the facts already established by the Agency about Iran's nuclear programme fully justified an immediate finding of non-compliance. However, in deference to other Member States' wish to give the Agency a last chance to elicit Iran's full and prompt co-operation with its requests, his country had supported the resolution. Despite the differences that had arisen during the lengthy consultations which had led to the drafting of the resolution, differences which persisted with regard to certain parts of it, all Member States should be able to agree with its fundamental purpose, namely to express the Board's full and unambiguous support for the Agency in its efforts to implement Iran's safeguards agreement and obtain answers to the many unanswered questions concerning Iran's programme.

...

47. The United States recognized the right of all Member States that complied with their safeguards agreements to develop atomic energy for peaceful purposes, but none had a right to nuclear energy for putatively or presumably peaceful purposes. Under the NPT, States had the right to use nuclear material for verifiably peaceful purposes, i.e. in conjunction with effective safeguards. To expect the Agency or other parties to the NPT to give a State the benefit of the doubt, or to accept assurances of peaceful intent uncritically, would undermine the non-proliferation regime.

48. The Director General had stressed the need to resolve all outstanding issues as soon as possible in order to reach a definitive conclusion. With that in mind, operative paragraph 4 of the resolution stated that it was essential and urgent for Iran to demonstrate that it had not diverted nuclear material for non-peaceful purposes. That wording reflected Article 18 of Iran's safeguards agreement. Iran had been given until the end of October 2003 to take all necessary actions to allow its compliance with its safeguards agreement to be verified.

...

51. Mr. JENKINS (**United Kingdom**) welcomed the adoption of the resolution which, although it was not to the full satisfaction of the Board, was the best that could be achieved in the time available.

52. In response to comments that had been made, he pointed out that the motives of the United Kingdom in tabling the draft resolution contained in document GOV/2003/66 and in supporting the resolution just adopted had not been political. The United Kingdom did not wish to victimize or bully any State but to enhance the Agency's ability to verify non-diversion of safeguarded nuclear material. Having already failed twice to comply with its safeguards obligations, Iran had also failed to resolve the very serious questions surrounding its nuclear activities and to offer full transparency, thereby seriously undermining the Agency's confidence in its intentions.

53. He expressed the hope that Iran would respond positively and fully to the resolution, in particular to the call to suspend enrichment-related activities, and urged third countries to co-operate to resolve outstanding issues.

...

Document 64: Consideration of GOV/2003/75

GOV/OR.1084, 21 November 2003

...

56. Mr. BRILL (**United States of America**) said...

57. Iran was not a State which had been caught committing a merely technical infraction of its obligations. The breaches by Iran of its obligations had been brazen and systematic. The previous week, at a technical briefing, the Deputy Director General for Safeguards had made it clear that the case of Iran was a most extraordinary one. The case involved egregious conduct by a country that was both a Member State of the Agency and a party to the NPT. Fortunately, the case was an exceptional one, very few other States having done what Iran had done, and the Agency must ensure that it remained an exception and did not become a model for other States to follow.

58. Iran was not a State which had tried in good faith to meet its safeguards obligations but had failed, through an honest mistake or an innocent oversight. The Director General's latest report made it clear that Iran had violated its safeguards obligations for over a decade as a matter of governmental policy; it had systematically and deliberately deceived the Agency and the international community year after year.

59. Iran was not a State which, when informed that its conduct had been inconsistent with its obligations, had taken prompt and conscientious remedial action. When the truth about its secret nuclear programme had begun to emerge, it had immediately adopted a cynical strategy of further denial, delay and deception. In May 2003, a Vice-President of Iran had visited Vienna and addressed the Board. It was interesting to compare the transcript of the discussion in the Board with the verified facts in the Director General's latest report. Clearly, the Iranian representative had been sent to Vienna in order to prevent the Agency from uncovering the truth, and he was not the only Iranian official who had made false statements in recent months in an attempt to maintain the deception practised over so many years.

60. Iran was not a State which, having violated its safeguards obligations and lied in an attempt to cover up its non-compliance, had ultimately accepted responsibility for its actions in a manner which generated confidence regarding its compliance in the future. On the contrary, it had refused to accept any responsibility whatsoever for its actions. Rather than admit that what it had done had been wrong and express regret, it was even now trying to shift the blame to others. In statements to the press, approaches to other governments and explanations given at the technical briefing of the previous week, Iran had claimed that it had 'had to' violate its safeguards agreement[297] for over a decade and had 'had to' lie to the Agency and the international community. All the violations were allegedly someone else's fault. If Iran would not acknowledge that its conduct had been wrong and that it was responsible for its own choices and actions, how much could the international community trust its assurances now?

...

63. The Board should be focusing on what conclusions to draw from the conduct of Iran as described by the Director General. In the Director General's opinion, Iran had committed 'breaches of its obligation to comply with the provisions of the Safeguards Agreement'.

[297] Doc. 4.

Did the phrase 'breaches of its obligation to comply' differ from 'non-compliance with its obligations'? Any objective reader of the Director General's report could be in no doubt that the conduct of Iran, stretching back for well over a decade, constituted non-compliance with its safeguards agreement. If repeated failure to report as required, to declare nuclear facilities as required and to co-operate as required and repeated lying to the Agency did not constitute non-compliance with a safeguards agreement, it was difficult to see what did. If the Board did not conclude that non-compliance had occurred, it would send to States throughout the world the message that they too could disregard their safeguards obligations and pursue weapons of mass destruction (WMD) without fear of repercussions.

64. Iran had established a capability for separating plutonium....

65. ... Iran had surely not embarked on plutonium separation merely in order to produce waste, and it had never said that it intended to produce MOX fuel. That left just one possibility - the pursuit of nuclear weapons.

66. The report under consideration also made it clear that Iran was seeking to enrich uranium through laser technology... The only plausible explanation was that laser enrichment was a short-cut way of producing the relatively limited amounts of HEU needed for nuclear weapons.

67. Following discussions with other delegations, his delegation had no doubt that almost all Board members believed that the actions of Iran constituted non-compliance with its safeguards agreement. However, some members were not willing to say so openly. Some acknowledged that Iran's actions had amounted to non-compliance at the time when those actions had occurred, but they said that Iran had now admitted its failures and taken remedial action. Non-compliance in the past, they asserted, did not constitute non-compliance within the meaning of Article XII.C of the Agency's Statute. In his delegation's view, however, that assertion had no legal basis and was inconsistent with the action taken by the Agency with regard to Romania in 1992, when the then Director General had reported Romania's past non-compliance to the Secretary-General of the United Nations. Moreover, accepting the view of those Board members would create a dangerous precedent: in the future, if a State managed to conceal its safeguards violations for a substantial period, it would enjoy permanent complete immunity from the consequences of its actions if, after being caught or - more disturbingly - once its nuclear programme was fully in place, it agreed to co-operate with the Agency. There would be powerful incentives for concealment. The idea that non-compliance in the past should not be regarded as non-compliance was wrong both on legal and on policy grounds.

...

74. His country fully recognized that Iran had taken a positive step by agreeing to sign an additional protocol[298] and to implement it provisionally pending its entry into force. It welcomed that action and commended Iran for taking it - and also for sharing information with the Agency and granting the Agency greater access to its facilities. However, as the Director General and the Deputy Director General for Safeguards had said the previous week, when a country had both a comprehensive safeguards agreement and an additional protocol in force the Agency depended on that country's attitude being co-operative and transparent - rather than legalistic and argumentative. It was not yet clear whether Iran's attitude would be co-operative and transparent.

75. His country hoped that it would be possible for the Board to draw the 'definitive conclusions' referred to in operative paragraph 7 of the resolution adopted by it on 12

---

[298] Doc. 5.

September without excessive delay. Iran had clearly been in non-compliance with its safeguards obligations. Whether the disclosures which Iran had made and the remedial actions which it had taken or was taking would be sufficient for the conclusion to be drawn that it had brought itself into compliance with those obligations remained unclear; everything would depend on the Secretariat's ongoing verification activities. His delegation looked forward to reviewing the status of those activities at the Board's session in March 2004 or at such earlier time as the progress of those activities might make appropriate.

76. The DIRECTOR GENERAL said that he would like to put the record straight regarding the words 'To date, there is no evidence that …' in paragraph 52 of the report under consideration.

…

78. What the Secretariat had meant in stating that there was 'no evidence' was that it had not uncovered facts and did not possess documents indicating that what Iran had done was linked to a nuclear weapons programme. The Secretariat had not said that it had come to the conclusion that the Iranian nuclear programme was exclusively for peaceful purposes.

…

90. Mr. SALEHI **(Islamic Republic of Iran)** said that the process of peacefully resolving the outstanding issues connected with his country's nuclear programme had got under way. Unfortunately, a few countries appeared to be intent on disrupting that process. They were playing a game to which, however, there might be unexpected reactions. Iran's firm commitment to full co-operation with the Agency would not be strengthened by devious political pressures. The important thing now was to maintain the good will that had been created.

91. Mr. NASERI **(Islamic Republic of Iran)** said that, although the United States was contesting facts and conclusions set out in the Director General's report, it was absolutely clear that Iran was not guilty of non-compliance as envisaged in Article XII.C of the Agency's Statute. That had been firmly established, and it was backed by the opinions of some of the world's most renowned international lawyers. At the same time, his country was unhappy about the use of the word 'breaches' in addition to 'failures' in the report.

92. Some countries were clearly suspicious of Iran's intentions. In that connection, it should be borne in mind that the Agency was not a criminal court empowered to look into motives or intentions; the Agency's job was to determine whether nuclear material had been diverted for military purposes. That having been said, he wished to stress that Iran's intention all along had been to engage in the exclusively peaceful uses of nuclear energy and technology.

93. Iran had not been putting the blame for its failures on others, but it had - justifiably in his view - drawn attention to the major impediments which it had encountered in pursuing its peaceful objectives in the nuclear field. Iran's approaches to various countries in the Western world and even to certain friendly countries elsewhere had been rejected, so that it had become impossible for Iran to exercise its right to enjoy the benefits of the peaceful utilization of nuclear energy and technology. Iran had had no option but to pursue a course that involved 'failures' at a certain stage.

…

97. Mr. O'SHEA **(United Kingdom)** said…

…

104. His delegation believed that the report under consideration pointed to what the Director General had described as a pattern and policy of concealment and justified the Director General in saying that Iran's co-operation had been limited and reactive and that information from the Iranian authorities had been slow in coming and contradictory. As the Director General had noted, a number of the many breaches of Iran's safeguards obligations had related to the most sensitive aspects of the nuclear fuel cycle, including enrichment and reprocessing - processes that were sensitive because they were involved in the production of direct-use nuclear material.

...

106. His Government had considered carefully the question of what action should be taken against Iran, including action vis-à-vis the United Nations Security Council, in the light of the serious Iranian failures set out in the report. It had concluded that its immediate priority should be to build on Iran's new approach and to ensure that it was sustained.

107. His Government was proceeding on the assumption that the declaration by Iran of its past activities was complete and that Iran would in future co-operate fully with the Agency. Should there be any further significant breaches reported by the Agency, or evidence of further concealment, his Government would have no option but to support the submission of a report by the Agency to the Security Council.

108. Accordingly, the United Kingdom believed that:

 – Iran must take all the corrective measures anticipated in the report and give full and sustained co-operation to the Agency in implementing its declared new policy of full disclosure and unrestricted access, so that there could be no doubt about the transparency and openness necessary if the Agency was to undertake the considerable work required in order to provide and maintain safeguards assurances;

 – Board authorization of the additional protocol for Iran must be quickly followed by Iran's formal ratification of the protocol, and in the meantime Iran must act fully in accordance with the protocol's provisions - both in terms of the urgent provision to the Secretariat of the information specified by it and in terms of ensuring access on the basis of the Secretariat's assessment of all of the information then available to it; and

 – the continued complete suspension of all enrichment-related and reprocessing activities must be verified by the Agency.

109. A great deal of work would be involved in: resolving all the outstanding issues (for example, in verifying declarations about Iran's recently acknowledged breaches); answering unresolved questions (for example, questions about contamination with enriched uranium); Iran's provision of comprehensive declarations in accordance with the additional protocol; and then the completion of appropriate follow-up actions. It would take a considerable time for Iran to rebuild a track record of compliance and thus restore international confidence in its nuclear activities. While that process was going on, it was essential that the suspension of enrichment-related and reprocessing activities be fully maintained and verified. In fact, that suspension would have to be maintained until a long-term solution providing all parties with satisfactory assurances about their concerns had been found.

110. Successful rehabilitation of Iran's nuclear reputation should then open the way to a dialogue on the basis for longer-term co-operation.

111. Mr. BERDENNIKOV (**Russian Federation**)...

112. ... For Russia, a key conclusion drawn by the Agency on the basis of information provided by Iran and of the results of verification activities was that to date there was no evidence that Iran's previously undeclared nuclear material and activities had been related to a nuclear weapons programme.

113. His country attached great importance to the decisions of the Iranian leadership to conclude an additional protocol to Iran's safeguards agreement with the Agency and to suspend Iran's uranium enrichment-related and reprocessing activities. It believed that the implementation of those decisions would substantially reduce the concern of the international community regarding Iran's nuclear programme. At the same time, it realized that the Agency would need some time in order to completely clarify all questions, owing primarily to the fact that, for well-known reasons, Iran had in the past concealed certain aspects of its research and design activities relating to the nuclear fuel cycle.

...

Document 65: Consideration of GOV/2003/75 (continued)

GOV/OR.1085, 21 November 2003

1. Ms. HALL (**Canada**) said...

2. ... The Director General, in his introductory statement, had noted that there had been a deliberate counter-effort, spanning many years, to conceal material, facilities and activities that were required to be declared under the safeguards agreement, as well as many breaches and failures to comply with the safeguards agreement, and that it would take some time for the Agency to conclude that Iran's nuclear programme was exclusively for peaceful purposes.

...

4. At the September meetings of the Board, her delegation had said it was forced to conclude that Iran was in non-compliance with its NPT safeguards agreement, and information gathered since by the Agency had confirmed that conclusion. However, the Director General's report[299] also contained information of a more positive nature. In response to the resolution adopted by the Board on 12 September,[300] Iran had allowed access to locations where it had previously been denied and had provided answers and information requested by the Agency. Pending confirmation of the accuracy and completeness of those answers and information, Canada would reserve judgement on Iran's current status with regard to its safeguards agreement.

5. At the previous meeting, the Board had authorized the Director General to conclude and implement an additional protocol[301] with Iran. That would help the Agency to come to a comprehensive understanding of Iran's nuclear programme. She hoped that Iran's readiness to conclude and provisionally implement an additional protocol signified a genuine change of heart. However, Iran had earlier requested deferral of the agenda item concerning its additional protocol, without clear explanation, which suggested that its signature might be conditional. Canada could accept nothing less than Iran's full and unequivocal commitment to the additional protocol and its provisional implementation with immediate effect.

---

[299] Doc. 35.
[300] Doc. 24
[301] Doc. 5.

6. At the Board's request, Iran had also voluntarily suspended all enrichment-related and reprocessing activities. An indefinite continuation of that suspension would greatly assist in restoring global confidence in Iran's intentions, and Canada joined other delegations in approving the Director General's plans to verify Iran's suspension of those activities.

7. She looked forward to receiving confirmation that Iran was co-operating with the Secretariat and that its nuclear programme was solely for peaceful purposes. However, until then, the Board would need to remain vigilant and support the Secretariat's efforts to implement a particularly robust verification system. If such confirmation was not obtained, the Board would have no choice but to find Iran in non-compliance and report the matter to the United Nations Security Council.

...

19. Mr. MORENO (**Italy**), **speaking on behalf of the European Union**, the acceding countries Cyprus, Czech Republic, Estonia, Hungary, Latvia, Lithuania, Malta, Poland, Slovakia and Slovenia, the associated countries Bulgaria, Romania and Turkey, and Norway, said that...

...

22. Ms. KELLY (**Argentina**) said...

...

24. Argentina was prepared to support a conclusion or resolution which clearly stated: (a) that Iran had breached its obligations under its safeguards agreement with the Agency; (b) that under the circumstances all enrichment-related and reprocessing activities must be suspended in accordance with the Board's resolution of 12 September; and (c) that an additional protocol would be signed, ratified and provisionally implemented.

...

26. Mr. CORDEIRO (**Brazil**)...

...

28. The information already gathered on past Iranian nuclear activities showed a record of repeated breaches and failures to declare and report activities and installations related to the most sensitive parts of the nuclear fuel cycle. The Board should make it clear that the international community could not condone such a record - although he noted that the Director General was not reporting a specific finding of non-compliance that could trigger the mechanisms of Article XII.C of the Statute and Article 19 of Iran's safeguards agreement.

...

31. Ms. DÍAZ GARCÍA (**Cuba**), reiterating her country's support for the Agency's role, the multilateral system in general and the non-proliferation principle, emphasized both the obligations and the rights of all Member States under the NPT.

32. The Director General's report made one very important point: there was no evidence or proof that the previously undeclared nuclear material and activities in Iran had been related to a nuclear weapons programme...

...

34. Mr. THIEBAUD (**France**)...

...

36. The international community's firm and constructive action - particularly the Board's resolution of 12 September and the joint declaration following the visit by the Foreign Ministers of France, Germany and the United Kingdom[302] - had produced some

---

[302] Doc. 7.

positive results: Iran had decided to co-operate fully and transparently with the Agency and had already provided the Agency with information on its activities; it had informed the Director General of its desire to sign and ratify an additional protocol and to comply with its provisions even prior to ratification; and it had confirmed its commitment to suspend voluntarily all enrichment-related and reprocessing activities.

37. Rather than refer Iran's serious failures to the Security Council, his Government believed that the Agency should build on the new approach adopted by the Iranian Government and ensure it was sustained - assuming that the declaration provided by Iran on 21 October was complete and that Iran continued to co-operate fully with the Agency. However, should the Director General report serious new failures or evidence of further concealment, the Board would have to meet immediately to examine all the options at its disposal.

…

44. Ms. STOKES (**Australia**) welcomed Iran's recent commitment to comply with its safeguards agreement and said that it was in the interest of all Member States to work to encourage Iran to fulfil that commitment. Nevertheless, the Director General's report had revealed serious violations and the Board could not overlook any non-compliance with safeguards agreements. The Board had to uphold the integrity of the Agency's safeguards system, which was just as important to Iran's national security as it was to the security of all Member States.

45. It would be useful to have an established definition for the term 'non-compliance' that could be used to assess the case in point or any future cases. A decision of non-compliance should largely be technical and based on the facts. Where non-compliance was not obvious a judgement should be made whether the breach in question was sufficiently serious to constitute non-compliance, including the nature of the breach and the kind of nuclear material and activities involved. It should also be recognized that the Board had the option of referring non-compliance to the Security Council.

…

Document 66: Consideration of GOV/2003/75 and 80

GOV/OR.1086, 26 November 2003

1. Mr. JENKINS (**United Kingdom**), introducing the draft resolution contained in document GOV/2003/80, said that it stemmed from an agreed statement of the Foreign Ministers of France, Germany and the United Kingdom and the Secretary of the Iranian Supreme National Security Council issued in Tehran on 21 October 2003,[303] and was the product of extensive consultations. He believed that all views, however diverse, had been taken into account, and that the draft resolution reflected the balance of opinion in the Board in a reasonable and measured way. He thanked all those who had expressed their views for the spirit of trust and mutual confidence which had prevailed throughout the consultations.

2. The draft resolution welcomed the steps the Islamic Republic of Iran had taken since 12 September 2003 when the Board had adopted the resolution contained in

---
[303] Doc. 7.

document GOV/2003/69,[304] namely its offer of active co-operation and openness, its recent declarations on its past and current nuclear activities, its decision to suspend voluntarily all enrichment related and reprocessing activities, and its decision to sign an additional protocol.[305]

3. The draft resolution also strongly deplored Iran's past failures and its breaches of its obligations under its safeguards agreement.[306] It set out in unambiguous terms the actions that needed to be taken by Iran to enable the Director General to confirm that the information provided by it on its past and present nuclear activities was correct and complete and to resolve outstanding issues, as well as the actions that needed to be taken to enable Iran to set about rebuilding the confidence of the international community in the peaceful nature of its nuclear programme.

4. Furthermore, the draft resolution reiterated the Board's earlier appeal to all third countries to co-operate fully and urgently with the Agency in the clarification of outstanding questions.

5. Finally, it made it clear that, should Iran squander the opportunity offered to it to adhere more strictly in future to its obligations under its safeguards agreement both in letter and spirit, the Board would meet immediately to consider, in the light of the circumstances and of advice from the Director General, all options at its disposal in accordance with the Agency's Statute and Iran's safeguards agreement.

6. The draft resolution authored by France, Germany and the United Kingdom enjoyed the support of a broad cross-section of Member States and he expressed the hope that the Board would adopt it unanimously without significant amendment.

...

9. It was so decided.

10. Mr. Chang-beom CHO (**Republic of Korea**), noting that he would have preferred to speak before the adoption of the draft resolution, thanked the Director General for his report contained in document GOV/2003/75[307] and commended the Secretariat on its professionalism.

11. The report showed that Iran had failed to report the existence and processing of nuclear material and to declare the facilities where such material had been processed and stored. It had concealed many aspects of its nuclear activities, including the most sensitive aspects of the nuclear fuel cycle. The Republic of Korea deplored those failures and Iran's breaches of its obligations under its safeguards agreement. Such breaches were cause for grave concern and could set a potentially harmful precedent. He urged Iran to take the necessary corrective measures and implement fully its obligations under its safeguards agreement. The reported change in Iran's policy to openness and co-operation was a source of hope for the future. He also expressed appreciation for the initiative taken by France, Germany and the United Kingdom.

12. The Board had to find a way of dealing with the Secretariat's findings on Iran's past nuclear activities that upheld the credibility of the NPT and the safeguards system and ensured that the issue was resolved in a permanent manner. However, it would be prudent to adopt a more constructive and forward-looking attitude towards a State that had, at least, tried to take corrective measures and had offered full co-operation and transparency. Thus, it was preferable not to take the action provided for in Article XII.C of the Statute but to

---

[304] Doc. 23.
[305] Doc. 5.
[306] Doc. 4.
[307] Doc. 35.

allow Iran more time. In the event of any further serious failures or breaches, the Board should meet immediately to consider what action needed to be taken in accordance with the Agency's Statute and Iran's safeguards agreement.

...

15. Mr. MINTY (**South Africa**) thanked the Director General for his report and the Iranian Government for its extensive co-operation.

...

19. Governors had to act with a very special sense of responsibility, not only as representatives of their Governments but also in view of the responsibility they bore vis-à-vis all members of the Agency and the international community. Thus, hasty statements or pronouncements should not be made on complicated matters. At the Board's meetings in September it had been stated that 'definitive' decisions would be made at the current meeting. That had not been possible for reasons that were known and had been known at the time. The credibility of Governors was affected by their decisions and statements, and he expressed the hope that all Governors would act in a manner which enhanced and did not damage their credibility and that of the Board and the Agency.

...

24. Mr. RAMAKER (**Netherlands**)...

...

25. On the basis of the Director General's report alone, the Netherlands would have had no other choice but to conclude that Iran had failed to comply with its safeguards obligations, which would have led automatically to the matter being referred to the Security Council. However, there were strong arguments in favour of giving Iran the opportunity to prove that its new policy of openness, transparency and co-operation was sincere. Nevertheless, it had to understand that the international community still needed to be convinced that its deliberate failures to comply were truly a thing of the past. A comprehensive and robust verification programme was needed. Though the Netherlands agreed that a report to the Security Council would be premature at the current time, should any further failures come to light it would unequivocally advocate that the Board agree forthwith on a report to the Security Council, as provided for in Article XII.C of the Statute and Article 19 of Iran's safeguards agreement. However, it sincerely hoped that that would not be necessary.

26. Mr. ZHANG Yan (**China**) welcomed the adoption of the resolution and expressed the hope that it would facilitate a resolution of the issue within the framework of the Agency. He commended the Agency's efforts to carry out in-depth verification activities in Iran and encouraged Iran to dispel international concerns by co-operating with the Agency on the clarification of its nuclear activities. The issue should be resolved through dialogue and consultation, while upholding the legitimate right of countries to use nuclear energy for peaceful purposes. Iran's co-operative attitude and the steps it had taken were welcome, and the progress the Agency had made was encouraging. He commended all parties, but in particular France, Germany and the United Kingdom, on their efforts.

27. Board members held many different positions with regard to the implementation of safeguards in Iran, and so it was pleasing that those differences had been overcome and a resolution adopted which engaged broad support. That was evidence of a common desire among Board members to maintain and strengthen the role of the Agency and achieve the objectives of the NPT. He expressed the hope that the resolution that had just been adopted would help promote further dialogue and co-operation between the parties involved, that it would facilitate future safeguards implementation in Iran, further Iran's

policy of transparency and openness, encourage Iran's co-operation with other countries in the peaceful uses of nuclear energy, and eventually lead to a permanent resolution of the issue.

28. Mr. BERDENNIKOV (**Russian Federation**) said that his country had not opposed the adoption of the draft resolution since, in its view, the new level of interaction between Iran and the Agency and the positive response of Iran to the demands made by the Board in the resolution adopted on 12 September were recognized in it. The search for mutually acceptable formulations had involved great efforts on all parts. The result was not quite what many of the participants in the consultations had been striving for. For example, his country had advocated a more balanced approach that took into account, inter alia, a number of rather objective conclusions drawn by the Director General. It believed that the resolution would have gained by containing, for example, a reference to the active co-operation and the openness of Iran in recent weeks, or to the conclusion that there was no proof that previously undeclared activities had been related to a nuclear weapons programme. The resolution spelled out what further action the Agency should take to clarify definitively the outstanding questions concerning Iran's nuclear programme. The Russian Federation counted on those actions being taken in a professional and objective manner without unnecessary politicization.

29. Mr. CABAÑAS RODRÍGUEZ (**Cuba**) said that, from the very start of the negotiations on the resolution just adopted, his country had maintained that the matter should be dealt with within the Board, that Iran was not in non-compliance, that the professionalism of the Director General and the Secretariat should be endorsed, that the inalienable right to use nuclear energy for peaceful purposes should be recognized, and that aggressive language should be avoided and Iran given the opportunity to take a sovereign decision regarding what new commitments it would enter into. His country's views had been taken into account and it hoped that, ultimately, the international non-proliferation regime would be strengthened by the current exercise and not weakened.

...

31. Ms. HALL (**Canada**) said that there should now be no doubt in the mind of any Board member that Iran had a long history of violations of its safeguards agreement with the Agency. Acts which directly contravened an agreement had to be regarded as non-compliance with that agreement. The 2001 Edition of the IAEA Safeguards Glossary defined non-compliance, inter alia, as the failure to declare nuclear material required to be placed under safeguards. Iran had not only failed to declare material but had systematically concealed extensive nuclear facilities and activities over many years. Her country interpreted operative paragraph 2 of the resolution as a recognition of Iran's non-compliance.

32. The Board's statutory duty to inform the United Nations Security Council of non-compliance was an important guarantee of the integrity of the global nuclear non-proliferation regime and had to be respected. The final document of the 2000 NPT Review Conference had emphasized the importance of Agency access to the Security Council, and of the role of the Security Council and the General Assembly in upholding compliance with safeguards agreements and ensuring compliance with safeguards obligations. Canada interpreted operative paragraph 8 of the resolution as a warning to Iran that further serious failures would not be accepted, and that the Board would comply with its statutory obligations if Iran committed further acts of non-compliance or if undeclared past acts of non-compliance came to light. The Board had to remain vigilant and hold Iran to its undertakings. She acknowledged Iran's recent co-operation, but nearly 20 years of failures

could not be overlooked because of a mere month of openness, nor were non-proliferation obligations negotiable.

33. The case of Iran demonstrated that an INFCIRC/153-type safeguards agreement alone, without an additional protocol, was insufficient for the Agency to be able to provide the assurances which the international community needed and expected, and that the task of strengthening the norms and mechanisms which made up the nuclear non-proliferation regime was not yet complete. It also demonstrated the dangers of allowing unimpeded access to the means of engaging in the peaceful use of nuclear energy without first ensuring that the commitment to peaceful use was being fully honoured.

...

40. Mr. SALEHI (**Islamic Republic of Iran**) said that his delegation viewed the resolution just adopted with both realism and mixed feelings. The tone and content of some paragraphs were influenced more by the politics of the past 24 years than by the facts which Iran had reported to the Agency and which were reflected in the Director General's report. The most important conclusion in that report - that there was no evidence that the previously undeclared nuclear material and activities were related to a nuclear weapon programme - had not been incorporated in the resolution which, nevertheless, appeared to have thwarted the persistent attempts to stir up a crisis over Iran's peaceful nuclear programme.

41. His country did not like the Director General's report, but not for the same reasons as the United States and Australia. It disliked it not because it contested the facts and the conclusions contained in it, nor because it wanted to teach the Agency and its staff how to do their jobs, but because, by focusing disproportionately on the past, the report did not adequately reflect the change in policy in Iran that had occurred on 21 October.

42. At the preceding meeting, the Governor from Japan had pointed out that his country was the only victim of nuclear weapons, an important historical fact which all should bear in mind. However, he had then gone beyond the limits of even-handedness and objective analysis in saying that it would be some time before the Agency would be able to determine whether Iran's nuclear programme was exclusively for peaceful purposes. Had the Agency had yet been able to conclude that Japan's nuclear programme was exclusively for peaceful purposes? To imply that the absence of such a conclusion regarding Iran's nuclear programme was technically significant was, particularly at the current early stage, less than objective.

43. Iran's commitment to the non-proliferation of nuclear weapons was absolutely firm and it derived not only from contractual obligations based on a strategic defence doctrine but also from the precepts of Iran's faith. His country was determined to continue working closely with the Agency with a view to resolving all outstanding issues on the basis of the provisions of the additional protocol, and it looked forward to enhancing international confidence and promoting international co-operation in the field of nuclear technology in accordance with the NPT.

44. Iran's peaceful nuclear programme, and its failures to report scientific experiments carried out by it in the nuclear field, should be seen in the context of its post-revolution domestic situation and of international politics. It had had the courage to provide the Agency voluntarily with information and to admit it had failed to report what should have been reported on the basis of its safeguards agreement. It was important to note that Iran's unreported experiments had not been illegal; they had all been legitimate and harmless scientific experiments. The fact that it had not reported them had been a failure. However,

it had demonstrated its sense of responsibility by taking remedial measures, and it would continue to do so in full co-operation with the Agency.

45. His country was not attempting to shirk responsibility, and many countries had shown understanding for its behaviour in the face of the severe restrictions that had been imposed on its access to nuclear technology over the preceding quarter of a century. Moreover, several speakers had emphasized that a balance needed to be struck between the rights and responsibilities of all parties to the non-proliferation regime. The fact that Iran had remained loyal to the NPT and to the objectives of safeguards, despite being unjustifiably deprived of a fundamental right, demonstrated the extent of its commitment to nuclear non-proliferation. Iran had gone to unprecedented lengths in trying to gain the trust of the international community, had disclosed all its past peaceful nuclear activities and had declared its willingness to sign an additional protocol. In return, it expected that steps would be taken to end the distortions regarding its nuclear programme and lift the restrictions imposed on it. For over two decades Iran had been subject to severe illegal sanctions on material and technology for peaceful nuclear activities. As a result, it had had no choice but to become discreet about its legal and peaceful nuclear programme. It had been required to fulfil obligations, but the slightest attempt to procure or produce material to meet its needs had been vigorously suppressed. Until recently, the Atomic Energy Organization of Iran had lacked a safeguards accounting and control system. That was one reason why the results of some of the laboratory-scale research experiments had been reported in international journals but not to the Agency. Iran's position had been described more fully in a paper that would be made available to the Secretariat for circulation as an official document of the Agency.

46. Mr. BRILL (**United States of America**)...

...

47. ... Should it be established that Iran had not come clean about the past, or was still pursuing undisclosed nuclear activities, the Board would immediately meet to consider, in the light of the circumstances, all options at its disposal. Iran should clearly understand that an immediate report to the United Nations Security Council would then be necessary.

48. The Board had also made it clear that Iran should, in order to restore international confidence regarding its nuclear intentions, suspend completely and verifiably all enrichment-related and reprocessing activities. Partial steps would not suffice. The further pursuit of such activities by Iran would leave little doubt about the nature of Iran's recent pledge to turn over a new leaf. In that connection, the Agency should apply a comprehensive definition of enrichment-related and reprocessing activities when verifying Iran's thoroughness in fulfilling that undertaking.

49. In the coming months, Agency inspectors would begin to determine whether Iran had met its obligation to make a complete and correct declaration to the Agency. Like other Board members, the United States hoped that Iran's claimed new commitment to openness was not already waning. Linking implementation of the additional protocol to other issues was unacceptable. NPT-related obligations were not subject to linkage or conditions. The United States had argued that Iran's non-compliance should be reported in accordance with Article XII.C of the Statute. Nevertheless, it believed that the consensus adoption of the resolution demonstrated that the Board remained unified and resolute in its determination to hold Iran to its obligations, especially in the wake of its many broken promises. It hoped that Iran had truly chosen to embark on a new path but, as the Director General had made clear in his report and his introductory statement, no Board member was yet in a position

to conclude that that was indeed so. Such a conclusion could only be arrived at on the basis of extensive verification efforts.

…

Document 67: Introductory Statement by the Director General

GOV/OR.1087, 8 March 2004

…

30. The Board had before it a detailed progress report on the Agency's verification work in the Islamic Republic of Iran. There had been marked progress in Iran's cooperation since October 2003. In particular, Iran had provided Agency inspectors access to requested sites, documentation and personnel, and had suspended uranium enrichment-related and reprocessing activities as a confidence-building measure.

31. However, the declaration made by Iran in October 2003 had not included any reference to its possession of P-2 centrifuge designs and related R&D, and in his view that was at variance with Iran's stated policy of transparency, particularly since the declaration had been characterized as providing 'the full scope of Iranian nuclear activities', including a 'complete centrifuge R&D chronology'.

32. It was vital that, in the coming months, Iran ensure full transparency with respect to all of its nuclear activities by providing all relevant information in full detail and in a prompt manner.

33. It was essential that the Agency receive full cooperation on the part of those countries in which the nuclear technology and equipment in question had originated; such cooperation had already been forthcoming, and he hoped it would continue and expand. That was particularly the case with respect to the major outstanding issue regarding the LEU and HEU contamination found at the Kalaye Electric Company workshop and Natanz. Hopefully, with no new revelations and with the satisfactory resolution of those and other remaining questions, the confidence of the international community would in due course be restored.

…

Document 68: Consideration of GOV/2004/11 and 20

GOV/OR.1094, 13 March 2004

…

4. The CHAIRMAN took it that the Board wished to adopt the draft resolution contained in document GOV/2004/20 without a vote.

5. It was so decided

6. Mr. ZAMANINIA (**Islamic Republic of Iran**) said…

…

9. Although the Director General had referred to a few shortcomings, they could not - to a fair-minded observer - imply a reversal of, detour in or threat to the process now under way. However, the resolution just adopted sought to portray a rather benign situation with progress taking place as a state of high alert. Some minor modifications had been made to the earlier version, thanks to the position of principle of many countries, but the version adopted still represented a serious setback. In that connection, his delegation was grateful to the Vienna Chapter of the Non-Aligned Movement (NAM), and in particular its Chairman, and to the Troika for their efforts to bring the draft text into line with the Director General's report.

...

23. Iran's agreement with three European countries had laid the foundations for a new chapter in the cooperation between Iran and the Agency, opening the way for further Iranian commitments. Iran had been faithful to those commitments, making every effort to ensure that the process of cooperation was efficient, expeditious and exhaustive and would lead to a definitive conclusion. A fair and balanced review of the substantive progress made in resolving major issues since October 2003 attested to that fact.

24. Iran had no doubt that, if the process of cooperation was allowed to continue in a positive context of mutual understanding and cooperation, the questions referred to in the Director General's report would be settled by the next session of the Board. Also, by that time Iran would have provided, to the best of its ability, the additional information requested by the Secretariat to help clarify the complex issue of contamination - an issue identified in the Director General's opening statement as one calling for further cooperation on the part both of Iran and of other parties.

25. In the opinion of Iran, by the Board's next session its obligations and commitments would have been met and the necessary corrective measures completed. That opinion was supported by the opening statement of the Director General, despite his characterization of the P-2 centrifuge issue as 'a setback' - a characterization which the Iranian delegation believed would ultimately prove to be incorrect.

26. The fundamental conclusion constituting the essence of the safeguards system was a conclusion of non-diversion of nuclear material and activities for military purposes. Since November, when the Director General had reported no evidence of diversion, a robust system of verification had been in place in Iran. There was still no evidence of diversion, and there would be no such evidence in the future.

27. It was difficult for some to accept the fact that Iran's nuclear programme was exclusively peaceful; those who had for so long based their policies and approaches on the false perception that Iran was seeking weapons of mass destruction could not change course with ease. However, they might ultimately come to accept the truth, which would be gradually confirmed by the Agency's inspectors.

28. The now public attempts being made to disrupt a healthy process were clearly out of order. There existed a fervent unjustified desire to maintain undue pressure on Iran through the misrepresentation of facts, exaggeration of the importance of minor mistakes and unjustifiable prejudgements. The move to force through a tough resolution had been fuelled primarily by ideological emotions. A great deal of damage had been done, and recovery would required enormous efforts. However, his delegation hoped for a change in the thinking of those with obstinate minds and cold hearts, so that a different spirit would prevail in June and the Board's March session would become just a bad memory.

...

40. Mr. MURPHY (**Ireland**), **speaking on behalf of the European Union**, said that the acceding countries Cyprus, the Czech Republic, Estonia, Hungary, Latvia, Lithuania, Malta, Poland, Slovakia and Slovenia, the candidate countries Bulgaria, Romania and Turkey, the countries of the Stabilization and Association Process and potential candidates Albania, Bosnia-Herzegovina, Croatia, The Former Yugoslav Republic of Macedonia and Serbia and Montenegro, the EFTA countries Iceland and Norway, and members of the European Economic Area associated themselves with his statement.

...

44. It was essential that the declarations made by Iran provide a correct, complete and final picture of its past and present nuclear programme. The European Union had therefore noted with great concern that, in addition to the revelations in previous reports and to the related unanswered questions, the Director General's latest report revealed a number of further omissions by Iran and raised new questions about its nuclear programme. Of particular concern were: The still unresolved issue of the LEU and HEU contamination discovered at the Kalaye Electric Company workshop and at Natanz. The Director General had stated that, until that issue had been satisfactorily resolved, it would be very difficult for the Agency to certify that there had not been any undeclared nuclear material or activities. The European Union had in particular noted with great concern that in the Director General's view the level of contamination suggested the presence of more than just trace quantities of HEU; The issue of the omission from Iran's declaration - a document characterized by Iran as providing 'the full scope of Iranian nuclear activities' and 'a complete centrifuge R&D chronology' - of any reference to Iran's possession of P-2 centrifuge design drawings and to associated research, manufacturing and mechanical testing activities. Such omissions undermined credibility; The issue of the purpose of Iran's activities relating to the production and intended use of polonium-210. The Director General had concluded that further clarification was necessary.

...

49. Ms. HALL (**Canada**) said that the disturbing record of Iran with regard to the implementation of its safeguards agreement had first come to the attention of the Board in March 2003. Since that time, further revelations had increasingly called into question the assurances given by the Iranian Government about the nature of and intentions behind Iran's nuclear programme.

50. In November 2003, despite clear evidence of non-compliance by Iran with its safeguards agreement, the Board had decided against finding Iran in non-compliance, because the Iranian Government had insisted that it did not have ill intentions and that it had made a full declaration of its nuclear activities. In the resolution adopted by it on 26 November 2003, the Board had stated that it considered it 'essential that the declarations that have now been made by Iran amount to the correct, complete and final picture of Iran's past and present nuclear programme'.

51. In his latest report, the Director General informed the Board that Iran's previous declarations had been neither correct nor complete - and apparently not final either. For example, Iran had failed to inform the Agency of its possession of an advanced P-2 gas centrifuge design and its conduct of related development activities - a failure which the Director General had described as 'a matter of serious concern, particularly in view of the importance and sensitivity of those activities.'

...

59. The resolution adopted in November 2003 had put Iran on notice that further safeguards violations would not be tolerated and that the Board would consider 'all options at its disposal' in accordance with the Statute 'should any further serious Iranian failures come to light'. In Canada's view, the Iranian omissions reported by the Director General constituted further serious failures and the Board should act accordingly. However, Canada recognized that the prevailing opinion in the Board was to reserve judgement until its meetings in June, giving Iran a further last chance to cooperate fully and transparently with the Agency and completely suspend its enrichment-related activities. She hoped that all Governors agreed that, if Iran did not take that last chance, the Board would have no option but to fulfil its responsibility under Article XII.C of the Statute.

60. Mr. JENKINS (**United Kingdom**) said his delegation welcomed the signing by Iran of a additional protocol to its safeguards agreement and hoped that Iran would ratify the additional protocol without delay. A lengthy delay would not help Iran to rebuild international confidence in its intentions. In the meantime, Iran should comply with all the provisions of the additional protocol, in accordance with its November 2003 communication to the Director General.

61. Immediate full suspension of all enrichment-related and reprocessing activities in Iran was of the utmost importance for confidence-building. Iran's extended commitment of 24 February had been a useful step in that direction.

62. His delegation welcomed the clarification provided by Iran of its position regarding the suspension which it had announced, and particularly the assurance that the suspension applied to the manufacturing, testing and assembly of centrifuges and their components, 'including those relating to the existing contracts, to the furthest extent possible', and to the whole of Iran. The Secretariat should now consider carefully, together with Iran, how the suspension could be effectively and demonstrably verified.

63. It appeared from the report by the Director General that key information had not been volunteered by Iran; the Agency had had to extract it. That was in contrast to the Agency's experience in the case of Libya, which had proactively offered information and had responded promptly whenever new questions had arisen. Iran needed to intensify its cooperation and become more proactive.

...

67. The Board should discuss all the aforementioned issues in June in the light of a further report by the Director General, which his delegation looked forward to receiving in good time.

68. If that report indicated full cooperation on the part of Iran, good progress towards resolving all outstanding issues and the absence of any further significant Iranian failures, the Board could in June consider whether the conditions existed for it henceforth to deal with the question of safeguards in Iran in accordance with the normal practice pertaining to the implementation of safeguards agreements and additional protocols.

69. Ms. STOKES (**Australia**) said that the report by the Director General showed that Iran was still far from dispelling international concerns about its nuclear programme. Iran had yet to provide satisfactory explanations about some of that programme's most sensitive aspects.

...

73. Countries wishing - like Iran - to benefit from access to advanced technologies needed to be able to assure suppliers that the equipment supplied by them would not be used in a manner contrary to the conditions of supply. As long as serious concerns about

Iran's nuclear programme remained, it would be difficult for suppliers to be confident that advanced technologies provided by them would not be used to support nuclear activities.

74. The declarations to be provided by the Iranian authorities pursuant to the additional protocol that Iran had signed would need to be complete. Moreover, Iran should not wait until those declarations were provided before bringing further significant matters to the Agency's attention; it should act promptly in order that the Agency's verification activities might proceed expeditiously. Iran had accepted Australia's offer of assistance in matters relating to the implementation of its additional protocol, and Australia stood ready to send an expert to Iran as soon as the Iranian authorities proposed suitable dates.

...

78. Given the range and nature of the nuclear activities that had come to light in Iran, the significant outstanding issues under investigation and the new concerns raised in the latest report by the Director General, it was clear that much more work needed to be done before the international community could be confident that Iran's nuclear programme was for exclusively peaceful purposes. Iran and other relevant States should cooperate to the fullest extent with the Agency in its investigations.

...

82. Mr. THIEBAUD (**France**) said...

...

85. While welcoming the decision of the Iranian authorities to suspend Iran's enrichment-related activities and the positive step which they had taken on 24 February by broadening the scope of the suspension, the international community still believed that they should, in order to regain its confidence, unreservedly commit themselves to a comprehensive and unrestricted suspension throughout Iran.

86. Despite the serious failings reported by the Director General, the French authorities believed that the main priority at present was encouragement of the cooperation to which the Iranian Government had committed itself. They hoped that Iran's future actions would justify that belief. His country welcomed the positive steps taken by Iran in accordance with the policy of cooperation and transparency to which it had committed itself in the joint declaration made in Tehran by the Iranian Government and the Ministers of Foreign Affairs of Germany, the United Kingdom and France.[308] Iran should continue taking such steps in order to fully meet the requests made by the Board.

...

90. Mr. HONSOWITZ (**Germany**) said that, although the Board now had a clearer picture of Iran's nuclear programme, some important questions were still unresolved.

...

93. The immediate full suspension of all enrichment-related and reprocessing activities was of utmost importance for enhancing confidence. His country welcomed the extended commitment made by Iran on 24 February 2004 as an important step in the right direction.

...

96. If the report to be provided by the Director General in May indicated full cooperation on the part of Iran, good progress towards resolving all the outstanding issues and no further significant failures, the Board could in June consider whether the conditions existed for it to deal with the question of Iran's nuclear activities in accordance with its normal practice regarding the implementation of safeguards agreements and additional protocols.

[308] Doc. 7

...

107. Mr. BERDENNIKOV (**Russian Federation**) said...

...

112. As could be seen from the Director General's report, the Agency proposed to continue its verification work in Iran with a view to clarifying certain outstanding issues. The Russian Federation, which would support the Director General's approach, was sure that the Iranian authorities would continue their active cooperation with the Agency in a constructive manner, strictly observing the provisions of Iran's safeguards agreements and, as a confidence-building measure, implementing the provisions of the additional protocol. It hoped that intensification of the process of successful cooperation between Iran and the Agency would soon enable the Board to draw appropriate conclusions and close the 'Iran file'.

113. It was in that spirit that his delegation understood operative paragraph 9 of the resolution just adopted.

...

Document 69: Consideration of GOV/2004/34 and Corr.1, GOV/2004/48

GOV/OR.1102, 18 June 2004

1. The CHAIRMAN invited the Board to consider document GOV/2004/48, a draft resolution on implementation of the NPT safeguards agreement[309] in the Islamic Republic of Iran which, he understood, enjoyed wide support.

2. Mr. THIEBAUD (**France**), introducing the draft resolution submitted by his country, Germany and the United Kingdom, said it was based on the Director General's report contained in document GOV/2004/34[310] and the corrigendum thereto. It took note of the positive developments since the previous session of the Board, particularly that Iran had continued to act as if its additional protocol[311] were in force prior to ratification and had submitted the declarations pursuant to that protocol, and also the progress that had been made in understanding outstanding questions and Iran's implementation of confidence-building measures.

3. At the same time, it regretted that Iran's cooperation had not been as full and proactive as it should have been, and noted that some key questions about the Iranian nuclear programme had not been resolved, especially relating to the origin of contamination and the P-2 centrifuge programme.

4. It called on Iran to take all necessary steps on an urgent basis to cooperate and provide the necessary explanations.

5. With regard to the suspension of enrichment-related and reprocessing activities, which were voluntary confidence-building measures, the draft resolution called on Iran to take corrective steps enabling full implementation of those decisions and their full verification. It also invited Iran to take additional measures aimed at restoring confidence.

6. While recognizing the inalienable right of States to civil applications of nuclear energy, the draft resolution underlined the importance of safeguards to ensure that that right was not abused.

[309] Doc. 4.
[310] Doc. 37.
[311] Doc. 5.

7. The draft resolution commended the Director General and the Secretariat for their professional and impartial efforts, and requested the Director General to submit a new report in advance of the September Board.

8. The draft had been the subject of intense consultations over the previous two weeks and reflected a concerted approach. He hoped that it would meet with the Board's approval.

9. The CHAIRMAN took it that the Board wished to adopt the draft resolution contained in document GOV/2004/48 without a vote.

10. It was so decided.

11. The CHAIRMAN also took it that the Board authorized the resolution to be made available to the public and issued as document GOV/2004/49.[312]

12. It was so agreed

13. Mr. GULAM HANIFF (**Malaysia**), **speaking on behalf of NAM**, expressed appreciation for the Director General's report contained in document GOV/2004/34. He noted that the robust verification system in place over the previous seven months had found nothing to contradict the Director General's finding in his November 2003 report to the Board (document GOV/2003/75)[313] of no evidence of diversion of the Iranian nuclear programme for military purposes.

14. NAM welcomed the steps taken by Iran in pursuance of its declared policy of full transparency…

15. Also, the Agency had been able to monitor and verify Iran's implementation of its voluntary decision to suspend enrichment and reprocessing related activities at the Tehran Nuclear Research Centre, Lashkar Ab'ad, Arak, the Kalaye Electric Company workshop, Natanz, and the Uranium Conversion Facility in Esfahan, and had not observed to date any activities inconsistent with Iran's commitments. Given that all Member States had a basic and inalienable right to develop atomic energy for peaceful purposes, Iran's gesture was a voluntary confidence-building measure, intended only to bring about prompt closure of the issue.

16. In monitoring Iran's voluntary suspension of its enrichment and reprocessing related activities the Agency was taking on a new role. The assurances that it could provide were different from those achievable hitherto, including with respect to the detection of the diversion of nuclear material. Any delays or variance in understanding the scope of the suspension should be viewed in that perspective.

17. Accelerated cooperation between Iran and the Agency and the progress made meant that there were now only two outstanding issues and no new revelation of any undeclared activities…

18. Given continuing cooperation, it should be possible to achieve a state of normality with regard to implementation of Iran's safeguards agreement and additional protocol. Any outstanding issues should be resolved solely on technical grounds. In that connection, he emphasized the importance of reaching decisions in the Board through consensus. NAM encouraged positive engagement and dialogue between Member States with a view to prompt closure and removal of the item from the Board's agenda.

19. With regard to the resolution that had just been adopted, it was regrettable that some of NAM's principle concerns and positions had not been reflected. Operative paragraphs 7 and 8 addressed issues beyond the mandate of the Agency. They impinged

---

[312] Doc. 26.
[313] Doc. 35.

on the inalienable right of States to develop and use atomic energy for peaceful purposes through technologies of their choice, and downgraded the importance and the role of safeguards. Mindful of the sovereign rights of States in undertaking further commitments, NAM did not believe that the Board could oblige States to ratify the additional protocol as called for in operative paragraph 6.

20. Mr. FIGUEIREDO (**Angola**), **speaking on behalf of the African Group**, endorsed the points made by the previous speaker and urged the Board not to go beyond the Agency's mandate by demanding that Member States act outside the terms and conditions of its Statute[314] and the NPT.[315]

...

27. Mr. ZAMANINIA (**Islamic Republic of Iran**) thanked the Director General and the Secretariat for their tireless efforts and assured them of his country's commitment to continued cooperation with a view to prompt closure of the issue.

28. More than a year had passed since the Agency had begun its robust inspections in Iran. Most issues had been clarified, and the two remaining questions had almost been resolved. The process had begun in a deliberately charged political atmosphere with allegations of a secret Iranian nuclear weapons programme appearing on almost a daily basis. Those allegations had been repeated so often, albeit primarily by one power with a heavy hand and a huge media arsenal at its disposal, that they had been taken as irrefutable facts. The task had been simply to find the evidence, the smoking gun.

29. The Agency, under enormous pressure that its credibility would be tarnished, had had to take a cautious approach. It had been taught a lesson early on, when it had been asserted in the Director General's report to the November 2003 session of the Board, that 'to date, there is no evidence that the previously undeclared nuclear material and activities … were related to a nuclear weapons programme'. That finding had been the subject of unrestrained attacks and intimidation from a country that had already decided what the facts were or should be. It had not been included in the Board's resolution of 26 November (document GOV/2003/81)[316] despite the insistence of the overwhelming majority of Board members, including the non-aligned. Today, after 670 person-days of intrusive inspections and robust verification that finding continued to be valid.

30. However, the concerns had changed. Now the questions were no longer whether Iran had the bomb because everyone knew the answer was no; not whether Iran had produced or received HEU, but where exactly each particle in the contaminated imported equipment had come from; not whether the infamous P-2 'discovery' was related to a secret nuclear weapons programme conducted at military sites, but when the conclusions of the Agency's inspectors in confirming the accuracy of Iranian accounts could be assessed and finalized; not whether Iran was engaged in systematic deception, but how proactive Iran was rather than responsive with respect to enquiries; not whether Iran had told the inspectors where it had obtained its imported parts, but whether private contractors had been proactive enough in providing the inspectors with a list of all their enquiries; and not whether Iran had been prepared voluntarily to suspend its rightful enrichment activities, but whether Iran, or any other country, was prepared to accept an arbitrarily defined new monopoly.

31. Why had that happened? The Board had been led to believe that Iran's less than full transparency in preceding years had been motivated by a grand scheme to conceal a weapons programme, when in fact it was a nationwide defensive mechanism against

---

[314] Doc. 3.
[315] Doc. 1.
[316] Doc. 24.

unilateral illegal sanctions that covered not only the nuclear field but all aspects of daily life from drug enforcement to civil aviation safety and even humanitarian mine clearing operations. The Board had been led to believe that there must be an ulterior motive for the widespread practice of discrete procurement in all areas where sanctions had been imposed.

32. It was time to set the record straight. Iran was confident that misunderstandings had emerged inadvertently despite the best efforts of the Secretariat and Agency inspectors to provide a correct picture and appreciated the Secretariat's courage in providing a partial correction to the Director General's latest report.

…

39. Pursuant to the agreement with the three European countries in October 2003[317] and as a confidence-building measure, Iran had voluntarily decided to suspend enrichment activities, while stressing its inalienable right to peaceful nuclear technology, including in the field of enrichment. Following a subsequent agreement, Iran had voluntarily expanded the scope of its voluntary measures so as to remove any impediment to speedy normalization of the situation. Iran had categorically indicated the scope of its voluntary confidence-building measures in its letters of 29 December 2003 and 24 February 2004 and had invited the Agency to verify the measures specified therein. Despite many technical and contractual difficulties, Iran had implemented both agreements in their entirety and in good faith and had given the Agency extraordinary and unrestricted access to verify the suspension. Any insinuation to the contrary was totally erroneous. The Director General's latest report confirmed that the Secretariat had witnessed no activity inconsistent with Iran's voluntary decisions. But contractual problems had made timely suspension of the activity of private workshops impossible. Such potential problems, as well as the remedy, had been clearly stated in the letter of 24 February. Since Iran's capability to enrich uranium had been acquired through the hard work of its scientists, despite the multifaceted illegal restrictions it had faced over the previous two and a half decades, it would neither abandon its peaceful technology nor accept artificial, self-serving, politically manipulated criteria applied to exclude Iran from any eventual Agency working group or other mechanism. The balance between rights and obligations under the NPT and the Agency's Statute was the main guarantee of the credibility and sustainability of the nuclear non-proliferation regime. Arbitrary attempts to create new monopolies and deprive NPT States of an important area of peaceful nuclear technology undermined the basic foundations of the very system they purported to strengthen.

40. The foregoing showed how a small and inadvertent mistake or omission by the Secretariat were grist to the mill of the vigilant who wished to select particular words and insert them in the resolution or enjoy a propaganda bonanza. The result had been dramatic conclusions in the Director General's latest report and a resolution alien to the real situation as verified by the inspectors. The Board's grounds for adopting it were less than solid. A few minor changes of wording could not remedy the very serious wrong done by the resolution, not only to Iran, but to the entire process. The blame lay not with the hardworking inspectors, but with those who had systematically ruined the sound and impartial environment required for such serious investigations by daily brainwashing everyone through the media with their flawed prejudgements.

41. Iran, feeling the utmost respect for the impartiality and professionalism of the Agency, had done its best to provide everything needed for prompt closure of the joint

---

[317] Doc. 7.

task upon which they had embarked. That objective, if not already at hand, was highly achievable. The Director General's oral and written reports had made it abundantly clear that the Agency had progressed significantly towards satisfactory clarification of the two outstanding issues concerning the P-2 centrifuge programme and contamination.

...

44. The tone and content of the resolution the Board had just adopted, including its disregard for facts, indicated renewed political will to derail the process. A number of elements in the preambular paragraphs, and operative paragraphs 7 and 8 concerning UF_6 production and construction of a heavy water research reactor, violated the letter and spirit of the NPT and the Agency's Statute. For the first time in the Agency's history a Member State was being asked to suspend the exercise of its right with regard to a declared facility under comprehensive Agency safeguards. He thanked NAM, whose members represented a majority of Board members, for its untiring efforts to prevent the Board from setting a dangerous precedent.

45. In conclusion, he said that Iran, as a national security imperative, was committed to non-proliferation and the peaceful use of nuclear technology. Nuclear weapons had no place in Iran's defence or security doctrine. Hundreds of person-days of intrusive and robust inspections had repeatedly affirmed the correctness of the Agency's original assessment. Further sampling and analyses, which could well be done within the framework of safeguards and the additional protocol, would vindicate Iran's conviction that contamination originated from a foreign source. There was now sufficient evidence for the Agency to begin a normal verification process, under the additional protocol, in a technical rather than political environment. The Iranian authorities would examine their confidence-building measures in the light of the degree of implementation of the reciprocal commitments of their partners and take appropriate decisions.

46. Mr. THIEBAUD (**France**) said the resolution just adopted reflected both the progress made and the remaining points of concern regarding the Iranian nuclear issue. On the positive side, Iran had continued to implement the additional protocol it had signed and which it should ratify without delay. It had moved forward with the action plan agreed with the Director General, had cooperated with the Agency's requests for access, including to military locations, and had duly furnished the initial declarations pursuant to its additional protocol enabling the Agency to gain a better understanding of the country's nuclear programme.

47. Two years after the public revelations about Iran's clandestine activities, the international community still had many proliferation concerns and there had been scant progress on key issues. The origin of the HEU and LEU contamination could not be entirely explained by the information provided by Iran so far, and additional information was needed. There had been no progress on the question of polonium-210 production or plutonium separation experiments. Furthermore, new information on the P-2 centrifuge programme, omitted by Iran in its October 2003 declaration, had suggested the country's intention to develop an extensive centrifuge programme. Also, examination of laser enrichment activities had shown that certain trials had produced 15% enrichment.

48. Although Iran had extended its suspension of enrichment and reprocessing activities, the suspension, requested 10 months previously, was still incomplete, and some production and procurement continued. Iran had refused to place a number of components and centrifuges under seal. Verification of suspension had been possible only after long discussions and Iran's decision to proceed with UF_6 conversion was at variance with the

suspension conditions stipulated by the Agency. The Iranian authorities should suspend such activities and enable full verification by the Agency.

49. While acknowledging the positive steps taken by the Iranian authorities, his country called on them to cooperate fully and without delay with the Board's requests, as laid down in the resolution. With the provision of information from the other States concerned as well, France hoped that all the outstanding questions could be resolved before the year's end. There was no point in prolonging the situation one day longer than necessary.

...

67. Ms. HALL (**Canada**) strongly endorsed the view that it was time the Iranian nuclear issue was resolved. Regrettably, closure was not yet possible given the extent and importance of the unanswered questions identified in the Director General's most recent report. The Board knew from previous reports that Iran had in the past engaged in undeclared nuclear activities. It did not know whether Iran had engaged in further undeclared nuclear activities, or whether it was currently engaged in such activities. The Secretariat was not even in a position to advise the Board whether all safeguarded material in Iran had remained in peaceful use. That was in contrast to the situation in 154 other States, where the Agency had been able to draw either a conclusion on the non-diversion of safeguarded material or a more far-reaching conclusion on the absence of undeclared activities. While her delegation welcomed the provisional implementation of Iran's additional protocol, it was disappointed that there had been no apparent movement towards ratification.

...

70. The Board was struggling to resolve matters of fundamental importance to the future of the nuclear non-proliferation regime and access to, and use of, nuclear energy. The right to use nuclear energy for peaceful purposes was a legitimate right enshrined in Article IV of the NPT. But the NPT also stated that it must be exercised in conformity with Articles I and II of the Treaty...

71. Iran must understand that its history of concealing its nuclear activities, and its subsequent delays, contradictions and imperfect cooperation, had resulted in widespread international concerns about its ultimate nuclear ambitions. Those concerns, based on serious and still unresolved safeguards compliance issues identified by the Agency, were why the Iran issue remained on the Board's agenda. That was why the Board had repeatedly called on Iran to suspend all activities related to enrichment and reprocessing. Only by genuinely and comprehensively observing that suspension, and by reversing its decision to operate the Uranium Conversion Facility and to begin construction of a heavy water research reactor, could Iran restore confidence. Without that confidence, Iran could not hope to enjoy fully the benefits of nuclear energy, or to see successful and early closure of the item.

72. Mr. BRILL (**United States of America**) said...

...

75. The United States supported and welcomed the resolution that the Board had just adopted. It was clear, however, that the resolution could not provide the answer to the problem the Agency and the international community were facing. Recapping key events to date, he said that it had been nearly two years since the public revelations that gave the Agency the initial leads it had needed to being peeling away the layers of concealment Iran had put in place over its clandestine nuclear programme. It had been sixteen months since the Director General had made his February 2003 visit to Tehran in response to those revelations. A year ago the Board had adopted a statement calling on Iran to cooperate

fully with the Agency to resolve all outstanding issues raised by its past failure to report material, facilities and activities as required by its safeguards obligations. The resolution just adopted followed others unanimously adopted in September 2003, November 2003 and March 2004, each urging Iran to intensify and accelerate its cooperation. The September resolution had found it 'essential and urgent' that Iran take by the end of October 2003 all necessary actions to remedy all failures identified by the Agency. Since then, a number of new issues had arisen that were equally important and pressing. It had been seven months since the Foreign Ministers of the United Kingdom, France and Germany had gone to Tehran. Despite the October agreement, Iran had neither cooperated in a way that would make possible the resolution of all outstanding issues, nor fulfilled its suspension commitments. The Agency's Safeguards Implementation Report for 2003 reminded the Board that Iran had engaged in undeclared nuclear activities in breach of its obligation to comply with its safeguards agreement. An important achievement throughout that long process had been that the unity of the Board had been maintained. Agency inspectors had also served the international community very well and thanks to them the world now had a far clearer picture of Iran's nuclear programme.

76. The passage of time was not a neutral factor in proliferation cases. Iran had used delaying tactics as part of an attempt to erase facts before the Agency had been allowed access to investigate nuclear-related activities at the Kalaye Electric Company. It would be naïve, based on that experience, to assume that Iran's interruption of inspections in March or its delay in allowing access to certain workshops involved in its enrichment programme had not been based on similar purposes of sanitation and concealment. Furthermore, Iran had completely levelled facilities at Lavizan Shiyan before Agency inspectors arrived.

77. There was an even deeper level of concern, for while Iran was erasing some facts, it could be creating others. The Director General had repeatedly said that the jury was still out on whether Iran was developing its nuclear technology for peaceful or military purposes. In his Government's view it was dangerous not to believe that Iran had a clandestine military programme. It had spent billions of dollars covertly pursuing every conceivable enrichment technology. The Agency had reported levels of uranium enrichment far above those needed for electricity. Every passing day could bring Iran closer to producing the enriched uranium needed for weapons purposes. In such a scenario, all that Iran needed to do was to continue with its policy of delay, denial and deception, while it created facts beyond the view of inspectors. That approach of course carried a price, in terms of critical Board resolutions and statements of deep concern like the one issued by the G-8 the previous week,[318] but that might be a price Iran calculated it could afford to pay.

…

Document 70: Consideration of GOV/2004/34 and Corr.1, GOV/2004/49

GOV/OR.1103, 18 June 2004

…

7. Mr. BERDENNIKOV (**Russian Federation**) thanked the Director General for his latest report, which was informative, objective and well-balanced.

---

[318] G8 Sea Island Summit Action Plan on Nonproliferation para 4 (9 June 2004), www.g8.utoronto.ca/summit/2004seaisland/nonproliferation.html.

...

10. The Russian Federation had not objected to the adoption without a vote of the draft resolution on the implementation of the NPT safeguards agreement[319] in Iran. The decisions taken by the Board had promoted the maximum cooperation between Iran and the Agency as proven by the good progress made in cooperation between Iran and the Agency since the previous session of the Board and the fact that no new elements of concern had been discovered. His delegation noted with satisfaction that most of the questions put to Iran had been clarified. The few outstanding problems should take only a few months to resolve.

...

15. His country was pleased that the Secretariat had been able to begin verification of Iran's suspension of its enrichment-related and reprocessing activities, but regretted that there had been delays and that the suspension was not yet comprehensive. Complete suspension was essential if confidence was to be restored. Iran should extend its confidence-building measures by reconsidering, and to begin construction of a heavy water research reactor and hopefully reversing, its decision to proceed with the generation of UF_6.

...

18. There was still time for Iran to understand that concealment, delays, evasions and omissions - not to mention intimations of non-cooperation and of retreat from commitments as well as attacks on the professionalism and integrity of an institution cherished and admired by all - were not the best way of inspiring international confidence. A policy of too little too late was bound to be counter-productive.

...

29. The DIRECTOR GENERAL thanked the members of the Board for their unanimous support of the resolution on implementation of the NPT safeguards agreement in Iran and their expressions of confidence in the Secretariat's impartiality, including that made by the delegation of Iran.

30. The resolution not only looked forward to the means for completing the tasks ahead but also clearly registered the steady progress that had been made in a number of areas. The fact that there had been no new revelations was another sign of progress. However, Iran and other involved States would have to cooperate fully with the Agency in the coming months, notably regarding contamination. The information the Agency had received from Iran on the P-2 centrifuge issue had unfortunately arrived only after submission of the report and there had been no time to assess it. He hoped that it would be comprehensive and accurate.

31. The file on Iran could be brought to a close within the next few months, but this needed the full cooperation of Iran with the Agency, giving it access to the sites that it needed to inspect. The restoration of confidence in Iran would require extremely meticulous and systematic work on the part of the Secretariat in order to understand every aspect of its nuclear programme. In particular, the Agency needed to be sure that Iran had declared all of its enrichment activities. It would need satisfactory answers to all outstanding questions before it could provide assurances that Iran's programmes were dedicated solely to peaceful purposes. Even questions about procurement that had not taken place were a cause for concern, as, for example, an interest in procuring 100,000 magnets, which was not consistent with an R&D programme.

32. The problem faced by the Agency on many such issues was a lack of documentation. It could not rely on oral statements alone, which were sometimes subject to misinterpretation.

---

[319] Doc. 4.

Comprehensive and accurate written documents were necessary for the Agency to move forward, especially regarding the P-2 centrifuge issue and laser enrichment levels. With regard to the latter, the Agency had at first been informed that there were no documents in existence, only to discover subsequently that documents were available and, what was more, samples had gone outside the country. That pattern of behaviour had to change. As he had pointed out to Iran on several occasions, Agency questions required comprehensive, accurate and prompt written answers.

...

34. For the time being the jury was still out. The Agency was not able to certify either that Iran's programme was exclusively for peaceful purposes or that it had a military component. He hoped that Iran would respond with a sense of urgency to the concerns of the international community.

...

Document 71: Consideration of GOV/2004/60, GOV/2004/76/Rev.1, GOV/2004/77 and GOV/2004/78

GOV/OR.1109, 18 September 2004

...

4. Mr. THIEBAUD (**France**), introducing the draft resolution contained in document GOV/2004/76/Rev.1, said the text was balanced and focused on approaches which would hopefully allow the Board to progress in resolving the matter.

5. The text expressed appreciation for the impartial efforts of the Director General and the Secretariat to arrive at a complete understanding of Iran's nuclear programme. It noted not only the progress made but also the work that remained to be done on such issues as HEU contamination and the P-2 centrifuge programme. It detailed the actions expected from Iran to enable the Agency to resolve those issues and emphasized the importance of cooperation on the part of Iran.

6. The draft resolution highlighted the importance of transparency and confidence-building measures by Iran, particularly the suspension of all enrichment and reprocessing activities and ratification of its additional protocol.[320] It was incumbent on Iran to create the conditions for confidence. The draft resolution regretted that, despite repeated calls from the Board, Iran had not implemented without reservation the voluntary measures to which it had committed itself, and had in fact reversed some decisions, in particular to suspend the manufacture of components for and the testing of centrifuges, and tests on large quantities of material at its conversion facility. The text, particularly operative paragraphs 3 and 4, specified the steps expected from Iran to restore the confidence of the international community.

7. Operative paragraph 5 of the draft resolution underlined the importance of cooperation with the Agency by third countries in resolving outstanding issues.

8. Operative paragraph 7 requested the Director General to report to the forthcoming November Board on implementation of the resolution, and also to provide a recapitulation of the Agency's findings on the Iranian nuclear programme and an analysis of those findings in

---

[320] Doc. 5.

relation to implementation of the safeguards agreement. Furthermore, operative paragraph 8 requested a specific report from the Director General on Iran's response to the Board's requests concerning confidence-building measures. Finally, operative paragraph 9 made provision for the Board to decide at its November session whether further steps were needed.

9. The provisions of the draft resolution related specifically to Iran's current activities and situation. They should not be interpreted as in any way affecting the right of States Party to the NPT to benefit from the peaceful uses of atomic energy. The co-sponsors were prepared to pursue and intensify dialogue with members of the Board, the Agency and all States Party to the NPT regarding their determination to ensure full enjoyment of the rights laid down in Article IV of the NPT, and were fully aware of the distinction between legal obligations and voluntary confidence-building measures.

10. The co-sponsors had made every effort to take account of the concerns of all delegations and hoped that the text could be adopted by consensus. It was more essential than ever that the international community maintain a unified stance on the application of safeguards in Iran and he appealed to the Board to consider the draft resolution in that spirit.

11. Mr. NAQVI (**Pakistan**), introducing his country's proposed amendments to the draft resolution, contained in document GOV/2004/77, said it was important to reach as soon as possible an equitable settlement consistent with Iran's international obligations, including those to the Agency.

12. Pakistan's first proposed amendment, regarding a new preambular paragraph e-bis, stressed the need to respect the rights and obligations of States under relevant non-proliferation treaties, a fundamental principle of international law and behaviour between States.

13. The second proposed amendment, concerning a new preambular paragraph g-bis, recalled Article III.B.3 of the Statute, which needed reiteration to ensure that the overall balance between rights and obligations was kept firmly in view.

14. The third proposed amendment, a rewording of operative paragraph 5, sought to differentiate between the two situations of States having already voluntarily cooperated with the Agency and others which still had to. Furthermore, it clarified that such cooperation would be extended by all countries consistent with their legal obligations under relevant international treaties. They could not and should not be expected to compromise their national security.

15. In the interest of keeping the Board's effectiveness undiminished and in the light of assurances from the co-sponsors of the draft resolution that they would keep Pakistan's concerns in mind in future, his delegation had decided not to insist on a vote being taken on its proposed amendments.

16. Mr. GULAM HANIFF (**Malaysia**), **speaking on behalf of NAM**, said that, despite also having had serious problems with other paragraphs in the draft resolution, in a spirit of consensus NAM had decided to propose amendments to only operative paragraphs 7 and 8. Those proposals were contained in document GOV/2004/78.

17. As a matter of principle, NAM viewed the legal safeguards obligations of Member States as being separate from voluntary decisions. Whilst safeguards obligations were legally binding, confidence-building measures were voluntary. In his introductory statement, the Director General had underlined that two interrelated but distinct sets of issues were involved in the implementation of Agency safeguards in Iran. However, the text of the draft resolution contained no clear distinction between them. Thus, there was an implication that Member States could be penalized for not adhering to their voluntary gestures. In NAM's view, that went beyond the Agency's mandate and ran the risk of setting a precedent.

18. Mr. JENKINS (**United Kingdom**), invoking the terms of Rule 26 of the Provisional Rules of Procedure of the Board of Governors, moved that the debate on the amendments to the draft resolution proposed by the Governor from Malaysia on behalf of NAM be adjourned. He did so not out of disrespect for those who had proposed them, whose concerns had been fully registered by the co-sponsors in the course of extensive consultations, but in the belief that those concerns were based on misunderstandings. It was not the intention of the co-sponsors to imply that suspension of activities was among the legal obligations of Iran or any other Member State. Moreover, the co-sponsors were convinced that the draft resolution did not contain that implication. It was not their intention to limit the right of Member States under the NPT to benefit from the peaceful uses of nuclear energy, as long as that right was exercised in strict compliance with NPT obligations; nor was it their intention to deter States with nuclear programmes under safeguards from volunteering confidence-building measures at some future date. The draft resolution did not argue, suggest or imply that confidence-building measures were a legal obligation.

19. The CHAIRMAN recalled that, under Rule 26, in addition to the proposer of the motion, two Governors might speak in favour of and two Governors might speak against the motion, after which it should be immediately voted upon.

20. Mr. DE VISSER (**Netherlands**) and Mr. CHRISTENSEN (**Denmark**) supported the motion.

21. Mr. GULAM HANIFF (**Malaysia**) **speaking on behalf of NAM**, spoke against the motion. NAM felt that the Board had exceeded its mandate in dealing with the issue. Although permitted under the Rules of Procedure, the move to adjourn the debate ran contrary to the principles of democracy. It could be perceived as preventing others from speaking their minds on a matter of principle with legal connotations. In tabling its proposed amendments, NAM was exercising the legitimate right of any member of the Board to ensure that its concerns were addressed. Unfortunately, the motion could also be misinterpreted as a tactic of the powerful to silence the weak. Clearly the matter had been highly politicized, which it should not be; that was certainly not the message the Board should be sending out. Whatever the outcome of the motion, he sincerely hoped that confidence would be re-established among Member States in good faith.

22. Mr. CARRERA DORAL (**Cuba**), also speaking against the motion, said that - to ensure transparency - the Board should consider the opinions put forward by a group of delegations and make a judgement thereon. The amendments proposed were the result of extensive negotiations and had been drawn up on the basis of consensus among the NAM countries.

23. The number of speakers permitted under Rule 26 having been exhausted, the CHAIRMAN put the motion of 'no action' on the amendments submitted by Malaysia on behalf of NAM, contained in document GOV/2004/78, proposed by the representative of the United Kingdom to the vote.

24. There were 20 votes in favour and 13 against. The motion was carried.

25. There being no remaining amendments, the CHAIRMAN invited the Board to consider the draft resolution on implementation of the NPT safeguards agreement in the Islamic Republic of Iran contained in document GOV/2004/76/Rev.1. The draft had been the subject of difficult and intensive consultations. While the objectives of all delegations were the same, the various parties had differing views on how to achieve them. He appealed to all members of the Board to send a unified message in the often-quoted 'spirit of Vienna'.

26. The CHAIRMAN took it that the Board wished to adopt the draft resolution contained in document GOV/2004/76/Rev.1 without a vote.

27. It was so decided.

...

30. Mr. GULAM HANIFF (**Malaysia**), **speaking on behalf of NAM**, recalled the previous findings of the Director General that there had been no evidence of diversion of the Iranian nuclear programme for military purposes. He noted that the latest report contained in document GOV/2004/60[321] welcomed the additional information provided by Iran in response to the Agency's requests, including prompt clarifications of its initial declaration pursuant to the additional protocol and the granting of six complementary accesses since the Board's meetings in June 2004. The Agency was continuing to make steady progress towards understanding the Iranian nuclear programme.

...

35. NAM looked forward to the Director General's next report. All issues should be resolved on technical grounds and it was important for the Board to reach consensus decisions so that the Iran item could be removed from its agenda and normality achieved.

36. With regard to the resolution just adopted without a vote, NAM had worked in good faith, and on the basis of principle, to enhance the text of the draft resolution with a view to achieving a consensus that reflected reality. In negotiations with the co-sponsors, NAM had at various times been faced with a 'take it or leave it' situation. That was an unfortunate development, particularly considering that NAM seemed to have been the last group to receive the draft text. The Board needed to review the way it conducted its work to ensure that all groups and members were treated with the respect and courtesy embodied in the 'Vienna spirit'.

37. He underlined that, although NAM had had serious problems with many paragraphs, it had still compromised and sought consensus.

38. With regard to operative paragraphs 7 and 8, NAM had sought to separate the issues so that matters relating to confidence-building measures were not transformed into legal safeguards obligations. As he had said in his introduction to NAM's proposed amendments, the Director General had made the same point in his introductory statement. Iran's voluntary actions should have a definite time-frame and cease when appropriate requirements had been met.

39. Finally, expressing full confidence in the professionalism and impartiality of the Secretariat in carrying out its duties, he stressed that the issue should be resolved within the Agency's mandate.

...

55. Ms. SANDERS (**United States of America**), having thanked the Director General and the Secretariat for their sustained and ongoing efforts in Iran, said...

56. The United States welcomed the adoption of a resolution that made clear to Iran that the Board, representing the broader international community, had exhausted its patience with Iran's continuing refusal to meet its commitments, to comply with Board resolution requests and to cooperate fully with the Agency. The adoption of the resolution was a clear victory for the Agency's safeguards system.

...

58. Iran should not underestimate the Board's resolve to do what was necessary in November. Board members, for their part, should not delay beyond November the fulfilment

---

[321] Doc. 38.

of their responsibilities nor allow Iran to manipulate the Board's will or undermine its commitment to address effectively the threat to the safeguards system. Iran should heed the warning from the Board by taking immediate steps to comply with the requests in the resolution just adopted and in the previous four resolutions. That was essential for Iran to allay international concerns about its nuclear ambitions.

…

62. Her country maintained that Iran was pursuing nuclear weapons in violation of its solemn obligations under Article II of the NPT. Other countries questioned that claim and, unfortunately, that debate detracted attention from the fact that Iran had violated Article III of the NPT. That fact alone was sufficient cause for action. The NPT and the Agency's safeguards system had been set up to provide early warning of diversion of nuclear material, it having been recognized that ostensibly civil nuclear programmes could be used by proliferators to develop the fissile material production capabilities needed for weapons by violating safeguards clandestinely, or openly after withdrawal from NPT. By the time the Agency found nuclear weapons or had concrete proof of a nuclear weapons programme in Iran it would be too late.

63. The Statute obliged the Board to take action in the light of Iran's violation of its NPT safeguards agreement. Sustained and deliberate safeguards concealment by Iran over the course of two decades provided the best indicator of Iran's intent and should trigger the Board to report to the Security Council.

64. There must be consequences for States that wilfully violated their safeguards agreements, especially when the State involved had more often impeded than assisted the subsequent Agency investigation. When a State violated its safeguards obligations systematically over an extended period and secretly pursued sensitive nuclear fuel cycle programmes that could contribute to a nuclear weapons capability, the international response had to be resolute. Such unsafeguarded nuclear fuel cycle activities had to be terminated. Under no circumstances should the Agency allow a State subject to comprehensive safeguards to legitimize previously clandestine programmes by simply placing them under safeguards.

65. It was also appropriate for the Board to require Iran to suspend its sensitive fuel cycle activities. Suspension was directly relevant to the Board's task to determine whether Iran was complying with its commitment that safeguards were being applied to all source and special fissionable material so that the Agency could verify that such material was not diverted to nuclear weapons or other nuclear explosive devices. Given what was known about the Iranian programme, surely no Board member could truly believe that the Board was in a position to certify non-diversion. Iranian operation of sensitive nuclear facilities would only make verification work more difficult.

66. The Board's decision in November 2003[322] to postpone reporting Iran's confirmed safeguards violations to the Security Council had been motivated by the desire to give Iran time to build international confidence through the suspension of its fuel cycle activities. However, Iran had cynically taken full advantage of that opportunity to advance even closer to self-sufficiency in its conversion and enrichment programmes. Iran had made clear repeatedly and explicitly that it had no intention of giving up its fuel cycle pursuits, despite their clandestine origins and the absence of any justification for Iran to seek such technology for nuclear power, and had made little secret of its nuclear ambitions or its disregard for the Board's many requests to suspend uranium enrichment as a way of allaying international concerns.

---

[322] Doc. 24.

67. Iran was advancing to the point where no international body would be able to prevent it from achieving a nuclear weapons capability. It was still not too late to resolve the issue through peaceful diplomatic means, and the United States was committed to seeking such a resolution. However, the Board would have to act decisively in November to show Iran that the world stood resolute against Iran's longstanding and serious safeguards violations, including by making a report to the Security Council. The Council was the appropriate body to address Iran's fuel cycle activities. It would add gravity and urgency to the Board's many requests for Iran to abandon its nuclear weapons aspirations. Iran's failure to cooperate with the Board over the previous two years proved that the Agency needed the Security Council's legal, diplomatic and political weight in order to complete its work in Iran. The Security Council could complement and reinforce the Agency's work, not replace it.

...

70. Mr. BERDENNIKOV (**Russian Federation**) welcomed...

...

74. The Agency's positive assessment of the level of cooperation provided by Iran gave every reason to expect the investigation into Iran's nuclear programme to be concluded shortly. The Secretariat had carried out extensive work and had analysed large amounts of information. The Russian Federation called on Iran to support Agency efforts in that investigation. He expressed the hope that the final outstanding questions would be answered in the Director General's next report to the November Board and that by then everything possible would have been done to build confidence in Iran's nuclear programme. The resolution just adopted made every provision for such an outcome, assuming that Iran took a serious approach to cooperation and the Agency maintained its usual impartiality.

75. A constructive confidence-building step would be for Iran to return to voluntary suspension of all its enrichment-related activities, including the conversion, assembly and testing of centrifuge components. The Russian Federation did not deny the right of non-nuclear States, including Iran, to use atomic energy for peaceful purposes, particularly nuclear power. However, in the current situation, restraint would go a long way to helping the Agency complete its investigations. At the same time, it was illogical, both in practical and economic terms, for Iran to establish its own nuclear fuel cycle capability. It would make sense for a State embarking on the development of nuclear power to have fuel for its civilian power units delivered by partners that already had the necessary technology and to return the spent nuclear fuel to the supplier afterwards. That approach would eliminate many of the international community's reservations.

76. His delegation found that the resolution reflected the situation objectively, was balanced and opened the door to a settlement of the situation.

...

79. Mr. PROUDFOOT (**Canada**) expressed deep concern...

...

84. The Director General's introductory remarks had made a useful distinction between Iran's legal obligations and its undertakings to suspend its enrichment-related activities, as requested by the Board. The Board had not made those requests idly but because of profound misgivings over Iran's undeclared nuclear activities and their implications. Iran had unfortunately failed to follow through on the Board's repeated requests and also on its own undertakings to suspend its enrichment-related activities. The Agency had documented manifold breaches by Iran of its obligations under its safeguards agreement.

The Statute required that such breaches be reported to the Security Council. That was true of any case of non-compliance with a safeguards agreement. Nevertheless, in November 2003 the Board had taken the decision, in the light of Iran's undertakings to suspend its enrichment activities, not to report Iran's non-compliance to the Security Council. Iran's subsequent unilateral re-definition of the scope of its suspension followed by reversal of its undertaking had led his delegation to believe that the time had come for the Board to exercise its statutory duty. Such action was important for the credibility of the Agency and of the multilateral nuclear non-proliferation regime as a whole.

...

106. Mr. JENKINS (**United Kingdom**) said...

...

109. The immediate and full suspension of all enrichment-related and reprocessing activities was of the utmost importance. Iran had never fully suspended all such activities and, following the Board's meetings in June, had chosen to demonstrate its contempt for the latter's opinion by reversing previously announced decisions. International confidence was not something that could be turned on and off like a tap. That suspension should include the commissioning tests and any other production processes at the Uranium Conversion Facility. He also called on Iran to reverse its decision to commence construction of a research reactor moderated with heavy water, given the other reactor alternatives available which did not have the same implications for plutonium production.

...

111. The United Kingdom saw the resolution just adopted as a final call for full, verifiable suspension. If Iran failed to heed that call there might be no option in November but to seek the political backing of the Security Council.

112. Ms. BANKS (**New Zealand**) expressed concern....

...

114. New Zealand acknowledged Iran's right to develop a nuclear energy programme for peaceful purposes, provided it met all its safeguards obligations and ensured the transparency of its activities. However, where international confidence in a country's nuclear programme had been eroded, it was incumbent on the State concerned to rebuild that confidence. In that context, she welcomed Iran's voluntary decision in October 2003, and its further decision in February 2004, to suspend its enrichment-related and reprocessing activities...

...

116. Mr. MINTY (**South Africa**) commended the Agency on its highly professional efforts and the Iranian authorities on their continued cooperation.

...

118. ...If verification continued unhindered and the Agency was able to draw definitive conclusions confirming the correctness and completeness of Iran's declarations on all aspects of its nuclear programme, the Board could bring its consideration of the issue to a close. However, if factual findings of serious concern came to light, the Board would have to reach appropriate conclusions.

...

120. South Africa recognized the inalienable right of all States to utilize the atom for peaceful purposes only, as provided for in Article IV and in conformity with Articles I, II and III of the NPT...

121. States had a responsibility to build confidence with the international community in order to dispel legitimate concerns over nuclear weapons proliferation, which required transparency and full cooperation with the Agency. South Africa welcomed the fact that the Agency had been able to verify Iran's suspension of enrichment-related activities at specific facilities and sites. On the other hand, in the context of confidence-building measures, it could not countenance unwarranted restrictions on access to the peaceful uses of nuclear energy by States which were fully compliant with their NPT obligations. That exacerbated the inequalities already inherent in that Treaty and undermined one of the central bargains contained in it.

...

133. Mr. ZAMANINIA (**Islamic Republic of Iran**)...

134. ... The text of the resolution just adopted was inconsistent and ran counter to the letter and spirit of the Director General's report. It would be a major setback to the credibility of the Agency if the Board were to give in to that destructive tactic.

135. Since September 2003, more inspections had been conducted in Iran than in any other country in the history of Agency verification. Over 800 person days of the most intrusive inspections had produced no smoking gun; in fact, the inspections had further substantiated the Director General's original finding that there was no evidence of a nuclear weapons programme. The Board had been consistently obstructed from recognizing that finding.

136. Iran's standpoint remained unchanged. It continued to hold that, strategically, politically, economically and ethically, it was dangerous, illogical, costly and unacceptable for Iran to develop, possess and use nuclear weapons and other WMDs. Therefore, it had never sought nuclear weapons, but it did insist on its right to all aspects of nuclear technology for peaceful purposes.

137. To provide long-term assurances to the international community, in December 2003 Iran had signed and immediately started implementing an additional protocol. In May 2004, it had in record time produced its original declarations, contained in 1033 pages. Subsequently, Iran had submitted a revised version of those declarations, including detailed information about its R&D programmes over the coming 10 years, as well as export and import declarations. Furthermore, it had allowed 13 complementary accesses to various locations in accordance with the protocol, often at only two hours' notice. In his country's view, implementation of the additional protocol was the best guarantee to the international community of the peaceful nature of Iran's nuclear programme.

138. As a temporary confidence-building measure, Iran had taken the voluntary step of suspending its lawful uranium enrichment activities. It had even expanded those voluntary measures as a result of an agreement with the three European Union countries. For its part, Iran had implemented that agreement fully and had allowed the Agency to verify its voluntary measures. On the other hand, the other side had not met its commitments. The scope of the suspension had thus been readjusted. Once again, Iran had carried out its measures in full, as had been verified by the Agency. He drew particular attention to the non-binding and voluntary nature of those measures.

139. The representative of Australia had claimed that Iran's actions since the June 2004 meetings of the Board had further undermined confidence in its nuclear intentions. The Director General's report, to the contrary, testified to the positive trend of cooperation and the steady progress in investigations towards conclusive corroboration of the correctness and completeness of Iran's declarations...

140. However, the resolution just adopted made no single positive reference to Iranian cooperation. One, qualified, positive reference had been removed from the revised draft. Several important Agency findings - namely, conclusion of the laser enrichment and uranium conversion investigations, and the plausibility of the foreign sources of HEU contamination - had also been omitted from the resolution. He recalled that in November 2003 a vicious campaign had seen to it that there was no reference to the Agency's finding of no evidence of diversion in the resolution contained in document GOV/2003/81. Nevertheless, robust and intrusive inspections had factually substantiated that finding.

141. Total disregard for such important conclusions undermined the integrity and credibility of the Agency's safeguards regime...

142. Responding to the representative of Canada's statement that the Board was duty bound to report past failures to the Security Council, he said that that was a misinterpretation of the Statute, which did not bear legal scrutiny.

143. The statement made by the representative of the United States of America contained little, or nothing, that was new...

Document 72: Consideration of IAEA DG Reports GOV/2004/83 and 89

GOV/OR.1115, 29 November 2004

1. The CHAIRPERSON, drawing attention to the report by the Director General contained in document GOV/2004/83,[323] recalled that a technical briefing on the contents of that report had been held for Member States on 18 November 2004.

2. The DIRECTOR GENERAL recalled...

...

4. ... all measures necessary for the verification of Iran's suspension of enrichment-related activities were now in place...

5. Mr. THIEBAUD (**France**), introducing the draft resolution contained in document GOV/2004/89 **on behalf of France, Germany and the United Kingdom**, said that it was a balanced text which took into account recent developments, including those just described by the Director General.

6. The sponsors felt that the draft resolution gave a balanced account of the breaches by Iran of its obligations, the corrective action which had been taken and the voluntary measures Iran had decided upon in order to regain the confidence of the international community. Those measures related specifically to the current activities and present situation of Iran. They did not relate to legal obligations arising out of safeguards agreements. Also, they should in no way be regarded as affecting the right of all States party to the NPT to benefit from the peaceful uses of the atom, in strict conformity with their commitments.

7. Moreover, sustained implementation of the measures decided upon by Iran was essential for smooth progress in the process of building confidence, resolving the outstanding issues and providing the assurances sought by the international community.

8. The agreement concluded in Paris on 15 November 2004 between Iran, France, Germany and the United Kingdom, with the support of the High Representative of the

---

[323] Doc. 39.

European Union (E3/EU),[324] reaffirmed the commitment of those countries to the NPT. In the agreement, the E3/EU had undertaken to begin negotiations with Iran in December on a long-term agreement. The negotiations would cover political and security issues, technology and cooperation issues and nuclear issues. The process would have two aims: objective assurances, in the long term, of the strictly civilian nature of the Iranian nuclear programme; and progress of cooperation and dialogue in a number of economic, technological and security areas.

9. The sponsors of the draft resolution would engage in the negotiations in a constructive spirit, hoping to build on the gains which had been made, with the support of the European Union and of the other G8 countries.

10. The CHAIRPERSON took it that the Board wished to adopt the draft resolution contained in document GOV/2004/89 without a vote.

11. It was so decided

12. The CHAIRPERSON said that the adopted resolution would be issued as Board document GOV/2004/90.[325] She assumed that the Board agreed to the text of the resolution and the Director General's report (GOV/2004/83) being made public.

13. It was so decided.

14. Mr. DE VISSER (**Netherlands**), **speaking on behalf of the European Union**, said that the candidate countries Bulgaria, Croatia, Romania and Turkey, the countries of the Stabilization and Association Process and potential candidate countries Albania, Bosnia and Herzegovina, The Former Yugoslav Republic of Macedonia and Serbia and Montenegro, and the EFTA countries and European Economic Area members Iceland and Norway aligned themselves with the statement which he was about to make.

...

16. The European Union welcomed the fact that the Agency was making further progress towards a comprehensive understanding of the nature and extent of Iran's nuclear programme, although it was still very concerned about two important issues: the origin of the LEU and HEU contamination at various locations in Iran, and the extent of Iran's efforts to import, manufacture and use P-1 and P-2 centrifuges. It appreciated the way in which Iran had been cooperating with the Agency in order to enable it to perform its verification activities, and particularly the fact that Iran had been continuing to act as though its additional protocol[326] was in force. Once again, it called upon Iran to ratify the additional protocol and permit unrestricted access to all locations as deemed necessary by the Agency.

17. The European Union welcomed the agreement reached with Iran and Iran's decision to completely suspend all enrichment-related and reprocessing activities as a confidence-building measure and to maintain the suspension while negotiations on long-term arrangements were under way. It also welcomed the fact that, pursuant to the agreement, notification of the decision had subsequently been sent by Iran to the Director General. Maintaining the suspension as defined in the agreement was essential, particularly for the negotiations on long-term arrangements that would have to provide objective guarantees of the exclusively peaceful nature of Iran's nuclear programme and allow for a new kind of cooperation between Iran and the European Union. The European Union would work in good faith towards a positive outcome of the negotiations.

---

[324] Doc. 8.
[325] Doc. 28.
[326] Doc. 5.

18. The European Union would like the Director General to monitor the implementation of Iran's suspension decision and to report immediately to the Board if the Agency found evidence that the decision was not being fully implemented or if it was prevented from monitoring all elements of the suspension. It was of the view that in such circumstances the Board would have no choice but to consider the implications of the breaches by Iran of its obligations under its safeguards agreement,[327] as reported in documents GOV/2003/75[328] and GOV/2004/83. Given the gravity of those breaches and the questions to which they gave rise, the European Union was also of the view that in such circumstances it would be appropriate for the Board to act in accordance with the provisions of the Agency's Statute.

...

20. The European Union would endeavour to open the way for a durable cooperative relationship with Iran having political, commercial and technological dimensions. Now that the Director General had reported to the Board that the entry into effect of the full suspension had been verified, it might be recalled that the European Council had agreed that the negotiations with Iran on a trade and cooperation agreement should be resumed.

...

22. Mr. GULAM HANIFF (**Malaysia**), **speaking on behalf of NAM**, said that NAM welcomed the progress made in resolving outstanding issues between Iran and the Agency, particularly since the Board's September session.

23. Although it realized that the Agency was still examining some aspects of Iran's past nuclear programme, NAM was pleased that all declared nuclear material in Iran had been accounted for and not diverted to prohibited activities. It hoped that Iran would continue to cooperate in the implementation of its safeguards agreement.

...

25. NAM welcomed the fact that Iran and the E3/EU had reaffirmed the commitments made in the Tehran Agreed Statement of 21 October 2003[329] and had decided to proceed as outlined in the agreement of 15 November 2004. It would like to see other Member States helping to maintain the environment of cooperation that had been created.

26. NAM also welcomed the decision of Iran - taken voluntarily with a view to building further confidence - to continue and extend its suspension of all enrichment-related and reprocessing activities. However, all States had the inalienable right to develop atomic energy for peaceful purposes, and NAM remained of the view that any voluntary suspension should end when appropriate requirements had been met.

27. At the September meetings of the Board, NAM had sought to ensure that confidence-building measures were not transformed into safeguards obligations, as they were two distinct sets of issues. It was therefore pleased that the distinction had been made in the Director General's report, and it was confident that the Director General would continue to make the distinction.

...

44. Mr. ELDER (**Canada**) thanked the Director General for his report on Iran, which demonstrated a clear record of non-compliance on Iran's part, compounded by what the Director General had called a 'policy of concealment'. The Agency should continue its rigorous verification activities in Iran, and the Board should remain seized of the issue until it had been completely resolved.

...

---

[327] Doc. 4.
[328] Doc. 35.
[329] Doc. 7.

46. The NPT conferred both rights and obligations on its States Party: Article IV of the Treaty enshrined the right of all Parties to use nuclear energy for peaceful purposes in conformity with Articles I and II, and the 2000 NPT Review Conference had broadened that understanding to require conformity with Article III of the Treaty, which required the acceptance of Agency safeguards.[330]

47. Iran had accepted the safeguards but had not honoured its safeguards agreement with the Agency. The Director General's report documented 14 categories of breach of the agreement, relating to diverse aspects of the nuclear programme, over an extended period. Those breaches were surely intentional.

48. Thanks to the efforts of the E3/EU, Iran had been given a last chance to regain the confidence of the international community. Canada offered its guarded support but considered that the process had only just begun. Much would depend on achieving a long-term agreement which would provide objective guarantees about Iran's nuclear programme. Iran must cease enrichment-related and reprocessing activities altogether and must maintain the suspension until the long-term agreement was reached.

...

52. Mr. ZHANG Yan (**China**) welcomed...

...

54. The report showed the way to deal with the Iranian nuclear issue and demonstrated that the Agency was the appropriate venue for doing so...

...

75. Ms. STOKES (**Australia**) said her country welcomed Iran's agreement to suspend all of its enrichment-related and reprocessing activities and hoped it would be fully respected. If there was any indication that that was not the case, the Board must not hold back on the proper exercise of its responsibilities and must take the necessary action in line with the Agency's Statute.

...

77. Her delegation considered that the nature and scale of Iran's breaches and concealment activities constituted non-compliance and should be reported as such. Upholding the non-proliferation regime required effective use of both verification and diplomacy. The two could usefully complement one another, but care should be taken that they did not merge and that diplomatic objectives did not compromise verification outcomes. The two issues - a finding of non-compliance and the way to resolve non-compliance - were quite distinct.

...

80. Ms. SANDERS (**United States of America**) said...

...

82. The United States believed that Iran's violations of its safeguards agreement had triggered a requirement under Article XII.C of the Statute and that the Board must report that non-compliance to the Security Council and General Assembly in order to restore the credibility of the Agency. The Board had deferred fulfilling that statutory obligation the previous year to give diplomatic initiatives a chance to solve the problem presented by Iran's pursuit of enrichment capabilities that it did not need but that would permit it to produce fissile material usable in nuclear weapons, and because of Iran's commitment to suspension and its statement that it had provided a complete picture of its nuclear activities in October 2003. That picture had, however, omitted the critical issue of the P-2

---

[330] NPT/CONF.2000/28 (Parts I and II) p. 8 para 2.

centrifuges, and Iran had been unwilling to honour most of its commitments in that regard over the succeeding year. It had never stopped producing centrifuge components and had continued to challenge the meaning of its suspension commitments, adopting positions on the definition of the activities covered that contrasted markedly with those of its European negotiating partners and that of the Agency. Finally, in mid-2004, Iran had repudiated its earlier promises and had resumed full-scale work on uranium conversion activities designed to produce feedstock for enrichment in the very same centrifuges it had pledged to stop building. It had finally reached an agreement with the E3/EU, recently signed in Paris, recapitulating its former promise to suspend all enrichment-related activities. Even then it had still tried to obfuscate and evade those obligations by using a slightly different definition of suspension from that contained in the Paris agreement in its notification to the Agency of its agreement to suspend. It had further eroded the United States' confidence in its peaceful intentions and good faith by rushing to produce as much centrifuge feedstock as possible before the suspension deadline. Iran had then claimed that the clear description 'assembly, installation, testing or operation' of centrifuges in the Paris agreement did not cover centrifuge research and development, and it had delayed the current proceedings of the Board for some days by insisting on retaining a number of gas centrifuges for 'research and development' work. That difficulty had been overcome through a last-minute compromise which might have as yet unforeseeable implications by setting a precedent for Agency monitoring of suspect sites and equipment in the future, both in Iran and elsewhere. Supposedly Iran had agreed not to conduct testing of gas centrifuges, but given its apparent intent to discuss the issue further at the first round of talks with the Europeans in December, the United States was concerned that the suspension issue might still not be fully resolved. Her Government's clear position was that the United States had joined the consensus on the resolution just adopted on the understanding that Iran had fully and verifiably suspended all enrichment-related activities including any research and development work using gas centrifuges and their components; any such work whatsoever by Iran would constitute a breach of the present agreement.

83. The year-long argument over the suspension issue, as well as Iran's continuing unwillingness to come clean to the Agency, highlighted the challenges of eliciting even the most basic cooperation and fair dealing from Iran, and the United States concurred with the Director General that Iran faced a confidence deficit.

84. As Iran had repeatedly demonstrated bad faith, the United States did not believe its ultimate intentions were peaceful. The United States therefore considered it imperative to hold Iran to its suspension commitment under the Paris agreement and to its safeguards obligations so as to end its enrichment work. Iran's clandestine work on plutonium separation illustrated the developing threat of its plutonium weapons programme, and its heavy water reactor programme had never been addressed. Every step must be taken to prevent further loss of confidence in the efficacy of the NPT regime in dealing with such grave compliance challenges.

85. ... If Iran failed to keep its suspension commitments there should be no further deferral and the safeguards violations should be reported to the Security Council as a potential threat to international peace and security. In the light of Iran's past record, the Board had to insist on such measures as a minimum.

86. Drawing the Board's attention to paragraph 107 of document GOV/2004/83, which reaffirmed the Director General's finding that Iran's previous policy of concealment had resulted in multiple breaches of its obligation to comply with its safeguards agreement,

she said that the United States continued to believe that the Board had a statutory obligation to report such non-compliance to the Security Council. Iran's ongoing activities did indeed represent a growing threat to international peace and security, the Security Council had the clear international legal and political authority to address that threat and to bring that issue to a successful resolution. It had the power to require Iran to take all necessary corrective measures and the authority to require and enforce a suspension of Iran's enrichment-related and reprocessing activities and to strengthen the Agency's ability to continue its investigations in Iran. The United States did not wish to remove the issue of Iran from the Agency but rather hoped that the Security Council would reinforce and complement the Agency's work by lending its political, diplomatic and legal weight to the difficult task of ensuring full cooperation by Iran. The continued failure to report the non-compliance to the Security Council was progressively weakening the integrity of the Board, the Agency's safeguards system, and the NPT regime as a whole.

...

100. Mr. NASSERI (**Islamic Republic of Iran**) said that in his opinion the resolution still had some shortcomings and contained unnecessary references to episodes that lay over a year in the past and had been dealt with in previous resolutions. No amount of recapitulation or repetition of legally loose terminology could change the applicable legal framework, which meant that no interpretation of the Statute or other instruments governing the conduct of the Board provided an option for dealing with the issue outside the framework of routine implementation of safeguards and the additional protocol, let alone for moving it elsewhere. The criterion for invoking the option provided for in the Statute was not amount or duration, but diversion. In the case of Iran there were thus no legal grounds for invoking it.

101. The resolution was a start towards normalization of the case of Iran... Despite unnecessary recapitulations of the pre-October 2003 period, the report now before the Board and the resolution just adopted clearly confirmed the Director General's assessment in November 2003 concerning the absence of any diversion...

...

103. During the past year, Iran had consistently tried to overcome the existing hostile environment and to build confidence through transparency and cooperation with the Agency. It had adopted important confidence-building measures whose voluntary nature was reiterated in the present resolution. The inalienable right of all Parties to use nuclear energy for peaceful purposes under Article IV of the NPT had been fundamental to the acceptance of that Treaty by Iran and the other non-nuclear-weapon States. Iran had taken special care to ensure that its case did not set a precedent which would be unfavourable to developing countries - which was partly why the process had been so complicated and time-consuming.

104. The resolution appeared to have set the stage for a positive and constructive process that would provide mutual objective assurances and guarantees with regard to transparency, non-diversion and access to nuclear technology for peaceful purposes. The adoption of the resolution had been the first important test of the Paris agreement, and France, Germany and the United Kingdom had shown their seriousness during the process if not fully in the outcome. He also wished to thank the Non-Aligned Movement and the Government and delegation of South Africa for their help.

105. Iran and the E3/EU had now embarked on negotiations which would be far more difficult but had far greater potential for achieving concrete results than the previous year's

process. The negotiations would have to address the prolonged attempt - in fact, official policy - of the NSG for over two decades to deprive Iran of access to nuclear technology in total contravention of Article IV of the NPT, particularly its second paragraph.

...

Document 73: GOV/OR.1120

2 March 2005

1. The CHAIRPERSON invited comments on the implementation of safeguards in the Islamic Republic of Iran.[331]

2. Mr. FABER (**Luxembourg**), **speaking on behalf of the European Union**, said that the candidate countries Bulgaria, Romania, Turkey and Croatia, the countries of the Stabilization and Association Process and potential candidate countries Albania, Bosnia and Herzegovina, The Former Yugoslav Republic of Macedonia and Serbia and Montenegro, and the EFTA countries and European Economic Area members Iceland, Liechtenstein and Norway associated themselves with the statement which he was about to make.

...

5. The European Union had continuously supported the search initiated by France, Germany and the United Kingdom for a diplomatic solution to the Iranian nuclear issue. It was currently involved in the follow-up to the Paris agreement.[332] In view of the conclusion of that agreement and the confirmation of implementation of Iran's voluntary decision to suspend all enrichment-related and reprocessing activities, the Council of the European Union had decided that negotiation of a trade and cooperation agreement and parallel negotiation of a political agreement should be resumed.[333] Those negotiations were being actively conducted on the understanding that full suspension was sustained. As the Council had stated, solution of the nuclear issue would open the way for a durable and cooperative long-term relationship between the European Union and Iran.

...

17. Mr. BERDENNIKOV (**Russian Federation**) welcomed...

...

18. A protocol had just recently been signed by the Governments of the Russian Federation and of the Islamic Republic of Iran to supplement the intergovernmental agreement of 25 August 1992 on cooperation in the construction of a nuclear power plant in Iranian territory. Under the protocol, the spent fuel from the Bushehr nuclear power plant would be returned to Russia after a cooling period. All fuel supplied by the Russian Federation would be under Agency safeguards. He hoped that that agreement would make for a stronger international non-proliferation regime.

...

33. Ms. SANDERS (**United States of America**) said... The recitation of events since November 2004 provided a startling list of Iranian attempts to hide and mislead, and to delay the work of Agency inspectors.

...

---

[331] GOV/OR.1119.
[332] Doc. 8.
[333] Doc. 158.

45. Her Government continued to believe that the Board must report Iran's non-compliance with its safeguards agreement to the United Nations Security Council. It had a statutory obligation to do so - but so far had failed to act. It could not ignore its statutory responsibility forever. While the Agency must continue to have a role in investigating Iran's past and ongoing nuclear activities and monitoring its suspension pledge, the Security Council had the international legal and political authority needed to bring the issue to a successful and peaceful resolution. It had the authority to require that Iran take all necessary corrective measures, including the steps called for by the Board that Iran had failed to take, and to enforce a suspension of Iran's enrichment-related and reprocessing activities.

...

50. Mr. NASSERI (**Islamic Republic of Iran**), responding to the - unexpectedly detailed and technical - report given by the Deputy Director General and to Board members' comments, said...

...

58. In conclusion, noting that common sense would favour an agreement reached by political means, he said he would like to stress a number of points: Iran was sincere and serious in its negotiations with the E3/EU, and was intent on continuing its full cooperation with the Agency in order to return to a normal relationship under its safeguards agreement. Suspension was a voluntary measure and hinged upon progress made in the negotiations with the E3/EU. Iran's intention to become a nuclear fuel producer and supplier - for which it had the technology and facilities - and to be a player in the future of the lucrative nuclear market was firm and inalterable. An agreement was envisaged and was being pursued with the E3/EU on the basis of an exchange of firm and objective guarantees. Such an outcome was possible given a political environment conducive to a mutually acceptable agreement. The exchange of guarantees with the E3/EU would provide additional assurances for both sides, would enhance confidence, and thus would contribute positively and effectively to regional stability. Finally, good will and well-intentioned support from other members for the success of the negotiations could be helpful to the process.

...

Document 74: GOV/OR.1130

16 June 2005

...

62. Ms. HUSSAIN (**Malaysia**), **speaking on behalf of the Vienna Chapter of the Non-Aligned Movement**, said...

...

65. The suspension of Iran's enrichment and reprocessing activities was a voluntary and legally non-binding measure which was being fully verified by the Agency. It had helped enhance confidence in Iran's nuclear fuel programme and should not be interpreted in any manner that would restrict the inalienable rights of States to engage in peaceful nuclear activities.

...

74. Mr. PROUDFOOT (**Canada**) said...

75. The recent threats by Iran to resume uranium conversion, contrary to Board resolutions and to its undertakings vis-à-vis the three members of the European Union, had further eroded confidence in the genuineness of its interest in addressing the serious international concerns about its nuclear activities and ambitions. Canada continued to support the efforts of France, Germany and the United Kingdom to negotiate a long-term agreement with Iran, and the Agency's efforts to verify Iran's suspension of sensitive activities. His country did not dispute Iran's right to have a peaceful nuclear programme, but only the permanent cessation of enrichment- and reprocessing-related activities would constitute an objective guarantee of the peaceful nature of Iran's nuclear programme. Without such a cessation, Iran's past - and possibly present - non-compliance would have to be reported to the Security Council.

...

86. Ms. SANDERS (**United States of America**) thanked...

...

89. Any final agreement as envisaged in the Paris agreement had to include an agreement by Iran to provide objective guarantees that its nuclear programme and activities were exclusively peaceful. Those guarantees should include the cessation and dismantling by Iran of all nuclear fuel cycle activities, verified over a significant length of time. Any activity that assisted Iran in getting closer to the ability to produce fissile material should fall within the scope of a cessation and dismantling agreement. Such an agreement should encompass, at a minimum, all uranium conversion, all uranium enrichment, all heavy water-related activities and any plutonium reprocessing activities.

90. To facilitate effective verification of such an agreement, Iran should, as a minimum, ratify and fully implement an additional protocol. There should be clear consequences should it continue to deny or impede access to locations or individuals where the Agency deemed such access necessary. Until such an agreement was reached, Iran should adhere fully to its suspension commitments with no further provocative rhetoric to the contrary...

...

110. The **CHAIRPERSON**, summing up the discussions on the issue, said that some members had expressed appreciation to the Secretariat for its professional and impartial implementation of safeguards in Iran. Several members had noted with satisfaction the progress made in the Agency's continuing investigations into the origin of contamination.

111. On the extent of Iran's centrifuge enrichment programmes, some members had noted that, although Iran had provided some additional information and documentation, that was not sufficient to answer several of the remaining questions. They had called on Iran to provide more detailed information in that regard and further access to the sites and areas of interest to the Agency. Some members had urged Iran to maintain the voluntary commitment to suspend all enrichment-related and reprocessing activities without exceptions. Several members had regarded the monitoring of Iran's suspension of enrichment-related and reprocessing activities as essential to the continuation of the overall verification process.

112. A Member State had expressed its regret that Iran was pursuing the construction of a heavy water research reactor.

113. Several members had welcomed the positive trend in the implementation of the safeguards agreement in the Islamic Republic of Iran, and the fact that remaining questions were expected to be resolved and concluded. They had reiterated the basic and inalienable right of all Member States to develop atomic energy for peaceful purposes. They had re-emphasized the distinction between voluntary confidence-building measures and legally binding safeguards obligations.

114. Support had been expressed for the negotiations currently being undertaken between Iran, France, Germany and the United Kingdom, with the support of the High Representative of the European Union, and the hope had been expressed that an agreement would be reached on long-term arrangements. Some members had recalled the Board's resolutions on the matter and had emphasized the importance of their implementation.

115. The Board had emphasized that it was essential that Iran provide full transparency and proactive cooperation to the Agency by providing in full detail and in a prompt manner all information that could shed light on the outstanding issues, in order to build the required confidence and permit the Agency to complete its assessment of all outstanding issues related to Iran's nuclear programme.

116. The Board had reiterated its call for Iran to ratify its additional protocol as a matter of urgency. The Board had noted that the Director General intended to report progress on that matter to the Board in September.

117. She took it that her summing-up was agreeable to the Board.

118. It was so decided.

Document 75: Consideration of GOV/2005/60, 61, 62, 63 and Rev.1, INFCIRC/648, 649 and 651

GOV/OR.1133, 11 August 2005

1. The CHAIRPERSON said that two additional documents had been circulated to Board members since the preceding meeting. Document GOV/2005/62 contained a report by the Director General informing the Board of certain activities undertaken on 10 August 2005 by Iran. Document GOV/2005/63/Rev.1 contained a draft resolution submitted by France, Germany and the United Kingdom.

2. Mr. THIEBAUD (**France**), introducing the draft resolution contained in document GOV/2005/63/Rev.1, said that France, Germany and the United Kingdom had requested the current special meeting of the Board to examine the situation that had resulted from Iran's announcement that it had decided to resume uranium conversion activities in Esfahan, and they had submitted the resolution contained in document GOV/2005/63/Rev.1 with the object of appealing to Iran to reverse its decision and respect the obligations that it had accepted voluntarily, and the Board's requests.

3. In earlier resolutions, the Board had taken note of the Director General's reports indicating that the Agency was not in a position to resolve the outstanding issues or conclude that there were no undeclared material or activities in Iran. In that context, it had welcomed with satisfaction the decision of the Iranian authorities to suspend all enrichment-related and reprocessing activities - a voluntary decision consistent with the agreement concluded with the Governments of France, Germany and the United Kingdom, with the support of the High Representative of the EU, of which they had informed the Director General on 14 November 2004.[334] The Board had emphasized that maintaining such a suspension was necessary to restore confidence and resolve outstanding issues.

4. It was therefore of particular concern that Iran had informed the Director General on 1 August 2005 that it had decided to resume conversion activities at its facility in Esfahan,

---

[334] Doc. 8.

and that it had begun to implement its decision that very week.[335] Such an action was contrary to the suspension requested by the Board, as the outstanding issues had still not been resolved, new issues had arisen and the Agency was still not in a position to provide assurances that would allow confidence to be restored in the exclusively peaceful nature of Iran's nuclear programme. It was important to recall that the issue facing the Board was not related to bilateral agreements between Iran and the three European countries, but to a situation resulting from Iran's past breaches of its international commitments which therefore affected the entire international community.

5. Whilst recognizing Iran's right to the peaceful use of nuclear energy, the Governments of France, Germany and the United Kingdom believed that Iran's resumption of its conversion activities was all the less warranted since there was no need or possible use for the uranium hexafluoride that could be produced in its nuclear programme. Furthermore, the three countries had just made proposals to Iran for a long-term agreement which reaffirmed Iran's rights under the NPT. They had also offered to support Iran's development of a reliable, economically viable and non-proliferative civil nuclear programme and had offered significant cooperation on economic, technological, political and security issues.

6. Turning to the details of the draft resolution, he noted that the earlier Board resolutions mentioned in the preamble were those which highlighted the importance of the suspension to restore confidence and resolve outstanding issues. With regard to operative paragraph 2, he pointed out that the Governments of the three European countries were willing to continue discussions under the Paris Agreement and were prepared to discuss all proposals or new ideas which would allow a long-term agreement to be reached.

7. The draft resolution focused on the objective of calling on Iran immediately to resume the suspension that it had freely accepted so as to restore confidence, allow outstanding issues to be resolved and allow the negotiation process to continue. France, Germany and the United Kingdom hoped that the draft resolution would respond to the common concerns of Board Members and that it would be adopted by consensus. It was essential that the international community maintained its unity on the issue of safeguards application in Iran and Iran's respect for its international obligations in that regard. He called on all present to consider the draft resolution in that spirit.

8. The CHAIRPERSON took it that the Board was ready to adopt the draft resolution contained in document GOV/2005/63/Rev.1 without a vote.

9. It was so decided.

10. The CHAIRPERSON took it that the Board agreed that the adopted resolution should be made public.

11. It was so decided.

12. The CHAIRPERSON noted that the adopted resolution would be issued as document GOV/2005/64.

13. Mr. JENKINS **(United Kingdom)**, **speaking on behalf of the European Union**, said that the EU would be very glad that the Board had chosen to adopt the resolution without a vote and was very grateful to all Member States that had supported the efforts to achieve that result.

14. Ms. HUSSAIN **(Malaysia)**, **speaking on behalf of the Non-Aligned Movement**, said that, at the start of the series of meetings, NAM had expressed the hope that they would contribute towards a fair and just resolution consistent with Iran's rights and obligations

---

[335] Doc. 107.

under its NPT safeguards agreement[336] and the basic and inalienable rights of all Member States to develop atomic energy for peaceful purposes.

...

43. Mr. NASSERI (**Iran**) said that the debate within the Board had centred around the fact that a non-nuclear-weapon State party to the NPT, which had accepted Agency safeguards, had commenced operation at a safeguarded facility to produce feed for nuclear fuel under full-scope Agency monitoring. The question was how such a situation could have become an issue in the first place? How could the Board have been called upon to react to an action which was in full conformity with the NPT and safeguards?

44. The States which had prompted the current debate and had pressed for the adoption of the draft resolution implied that they had done so in the interests of non-proliferation. Yet those same States either possessed nuclear weapons, relied on them for their security, were the exclusive producers of nuclear fuel, or had steadfastly refused to forgo that capability under any circumstances. How could a small amount of feed material for enrichment to produce nuclear fuel be a matter of concern when a number of the States concerned, including non-nuclear-weapon States, were sitting on many tonnes of separated plutonium which could be directly diverted to nuclear weapons at any time of their choosing? The conventional reply - that such States were in good standing as regards their safeguards commitments - failed to take account of the fact that those States had never been forcefully denied access to nuclear material, equipment, and technology. With only a fraction of the access granted to other States, Iran would be fully transparent and in exemplary standing. It was evident that the motive was to put pressure on Iran, and that the purpose was to move beyond denial to deprivation. Furthermore, the prescription written for Iran would be applied to other developing countries were Iran to yield. Fortunately, Iran would not yield. It would be a nuclear fuel producer and supplier within a decade. Like all other developing countries and NPT parties, Iran had firmly rejected nuclear weapons. All it wished to do was to exercise its right under the NPT, a right it had been denied for over two decades.

...

47. Iran believed in the Agency and the safeguards system. It would continue to work with the Agency, its activities would remain fully under safeguards, and operations at the UCF in Esfahan would remain under full-scope monitoring. The product would be sealed by the Agency, and Iran would fully observe its obligations with regard to its nuclear fuel programme. Thus, there was no cause for concern whatsoever.

...

Document 76: Consideration of GOV/2005/67

GOV/OR.1138, 21 September 2005

...

45. Ms. HUSSAIN (**Malaysia**), **speaking on behalf of the Non-Aligned Movement**, questioned the wisdom of opening the debate on agenda item 6(d) while consultations were still ongoing.

---

[336] Doc. 4.

46. The CHAIRPERSON said that, as the Director General's report had been published on 2 September 2005,[337] she saw no reason for the Board to postpone its consideration of the issue.

47. Mr. JENKINS **(United Kingdom), speaking on behalf of the European Union**, the acceding countries Bulgaria and Romania, the candidate country Croatia, the countries of the Stabilization and Association Process and potential candidates Albania, Bosnia and Herzegovina, the Former Yugoslav Republic of Macedonia and Serbia and Montenegro, the EFTA countries Iceland and Norway, members of the European Economic Area, and Moldova, said…

…

49. The EU had also read with concern that the Agency had made a number of other requests for information or access to individuals or locations which had yet to be granted. The EU took a serious view of the Director General's assessment that full transparency was not only indispensable but overdue and that, given Iran's past concealment efforts over many years, such transparency should extend beyond the formal requirements of the safeguards agreement[338] and additional protocol[339] and include access to individuals, documentation related to procurement, dual use equipment, certain military-owned workshops and research and development locations. He noted that the Agency was still not in position to conclude that there were no undeclared nuclear materials or activities in Iran and that, in view of the past undeclared nature of significant aspects of Iran's nuclear programme, and its past pattern of concealment, that conclusion could be expected to take longer to arrive at than in normal circumstances.

50. Furthermore, Iran had not heeded the call made by the Board on 11 August 2005 for the re-establishment of full suspension of all enrichment-related activities,[340] Iran's additional protocol was still unratified, and it had ignored the Board's request for reconsideration of its decision to construct a research reactor moderated by heavy water.

51. Those were some of the many factors that had led the European Union to the view that it was time for the Board to take stock.

…

54. Clearly, Iran had failed to honour the commitments that had made it possible for the Board to hold back from reporting to the Security Council and others in November 2003[341] the non-compliance reported to it by the Secretariat…

55. The EU had sought to create conditions in which the international community could leave it to the Agency to provide the necessary assurances in the knowledge that, meanwhile, Iran would not be developing a capability to produce fissile material. The development by Iran of the most sensitive parts of the fuel cycle had neither an economic nor a technical rationale. It was therefore regrettable and cause for concern that Iran was showing every sign of being intent on developing a fissile material production capability well before the international community acquired the confidence it needed that Iran's programme was exclusively peaceful in nature. It was that concern that had led the EU to assert that the Board could not simply overlook Iran's failure to fulfil its commitments and its defiance of Board resolutions. The Board had to ask itself whether there was anything that could be done to convince Iran to implement the necessary confidence-building measures

---

[337] Doc. 40.
[338] Doc. 4.
[339] Doc. 5.
[340] Doc. 29.
[341] Doc. 64-Doc. 66.

and grant the Agency the full transparency which the Director-General had described on 19 September 2005 as a prerequisite for the Agency to be able to reconstruct the history and nature of all aspects of Iran's past nuclear activities.

56. The EU believed that the Board should draw the attention of the Security Council to the safeguards breaches and failures first reported to the Board in 2003,[342] and to the questions that had arisen in that connection that were within the competence of the Security Council, in order to give the latter an opportunity to throw its weight and authority behind the Board's resolutions and endorse the Board's calls for confidence-building measures, especially full suspension, and for the full transparency that had first been promised in October 2003. Involving the Security Council was not intended to close off diplomacy but was, on the contrary, intended to facilitate it by reinforcing the message that the international community expected Iran to deliver on its promises of full transparency and full suspension. EU Member States intended to work within the Security Council to ensure a sensible, measured and constructive multilateral approach to the issue. The Agency would remain seized of the matter and the Secretariat's responsibility for implementing Iran's safeguards agreement would be unaltered.

...

62. Mr. SCHULTE (**United States of America**) said...

63. ... Iran's actions had, regrettably, exhausted the Board's forbearance. A country with peaceful intent would fully comply with its NPT commitments, not threaten to withdraw from them; and a country seeking the Board's confidence would suspend activities of concern, not threaten to move to the next stage.

64. The United States agreed with the EU that the time had come to report Iran's non-compliance to the United Nations Security Council. Article XII.C of the Agency's Statute unambiguously required the Board to make such a report. Two years of determined effort had not allowed the Agency to conclude that there were no undeclared nuclear weapons or activities in Iran. Over the same period, the Board's confidence in the peaceful nature of Iran's activities had declined. That, coupled with the scope and nature of Iran's nuclear programme, unexplained connections to the military, extensive efforts at concealment, and the intentional shattering of the Paris agreement provided clear cause to notify the Security Council under Article III.B.4 of the Statute.

65. The goal still was to achieve a peaceful diplomatic solution that would restore confidence in Iran's activities and return it to full compliance with its safeguards obligations. However, Iran's actions and bellicose statements in Tehran, New York and Vienna had shown no flexibility and had only served to deepen concerns about its intentions. Reporting Iran to the Security Council would help make it clear to Iran's leadership that the course they were pursuing would lead to increasing condemnation and isolation and would allow the Security Council to take appropriate steps to strengthen international efforts to achieve a diplomatic solution. The proposed resolution would not remove the issue from the Agency's remit, but would seek the Security Council's help in convincing Iran that it had to take its obligations to the Agency seriously. Thus, reporting Iran's non-compliance would be another essential step in the diplomatic efforts to convince Iran to change course and come back to the negotiating table.

...

67. Mr. BEVEN (**Australia**) said...

...

---

[342] Doc. 33.

74. The United Nations Security Council should be given the opportunity to reinforce the Agency's efforts and enhance its authority, with the ultimate aim of resolving the international community's concerns about Iran's nuclear programme. His country had repeatedly made it clear that it was of the view that the nature and scale of Iran's safeguards breaches and its concealment activities constituted non-compliance and should be reported as such.

75. Since 1992, four States had been reported to the United Nations Security Council under Article XII.C of the Agency's Statute. For two of those States, non-compliance had been in the past and had been resolved. Those cases confirmed that there was no time limit for reporting States to the Security Council. Given the number of unresolved issues regarding Iran's nuclear programme and its safeguards failures and breaches, which the Board had strongly deplored in its November 2003 resolution, and that country's ongoing lack of cooperation with the Agency together with the fact that a number of important issues remained unresolved, the time had come for Iran to be similarly reported. Australia also considered that a strong case existed for notifying the Security Council on the basis of Article III.B.4 of the Statute.

...

77. Mr. PROUDFOOT (**Canada**) said...

...

79. ... However, in the preceding month Iran had unilaterally broken the suspension by resuming uranium conversion and had simultaneously rejected a very attractive offer from the three European countries, thus fracturing the process of dialogue.

80. Thus, the reasons which had led the Board to hold off reporting Iran's non-compliance to the Security Council no longer applied. What was more, having further eroded international confidence in its intentions, Iran had accentuated concerns about the broader implications of its nuclear programme that were relevant to the Security Council's mandate as the body responsible for international peace and security.

81. Canada had never denied Iran's right to the peaceful uses of nuclear energy, but those rights had to be exercised in conformity with international non-proliferation obligations under the NPT. That Iran had chosen to develop proliferation-sensitive aspects of its programme in a clandestine manner, and in doing so had committed multiple acts of non-compliance with its safeguards agreement, cast doubt on its claims that its programme was entirely peaceful. Moreover, the fact that Iran had chosen to pursue activities for which it had no coherent explanation, and which did not correspond to the requirements of an incipient nuclear power programme but which did match the checklist for a nuclear weapons programme, heightened his country's concern, particularly in the context of Iran's policy of concealment and its continuing lack of full transparency.

82. The special Board meeting in August 2005 had again called upon Iran to re-establish the full suspension of its enrichment-related activities, but Iran had ignored that call. The resolution which the Board would be adopting during its current series of meetings would be its eighth on the issue and, in the two and a half years that that issue had been before it, the Board had demonstrated extraordinary forbearance. Since Iran had turned down the Board's latest appeal, the time had come for it to report the matter to the Security Council. In doing so it would be acting within the framework of the Agency and taking a step foreseen, and indeed required, by its Statute. That action was essential for the organization's credibility, as well as for the multilateral nuclear non-proliferation and disarmament regime of which the Agency was a key part.

83. However, the Board would not be divesting itself of responsibility for the implementation of safeguards in Iran. That matter should remain on its agenda. The Board should request the Security Council to reiterate and reinforce the Board's own calls for Iran to re-establish the suspension of its enrichment-related activities and grant the Agency the greater transparency and access which the Director General had indicated was required. Canada urged the Board to take that essential step during the current series of meetings.

...

Document 77: Consideration of GOV/2005/67

GOV/OR.1139, 22 September 2005

...

3. Ms. HUSSAIN (**Malaysia**), **speaking on behalf of the Non-Aligned Movement**, stressed the basic and inalienable right of all Member States to develop atomic energy for peaceful purposes...

4. The suspension of Iran's enrichment and reprocessing activities was a voluntary confidence-building measure which was not legally binding and should not be interpreted in any way as inhibiting or restricting the inalienable right of Member States to develop atomic energy for peaceful purposes.

5. All problematic issues should be resolved through dialogue and peaceful means and NAM therefore encouraged continued dialogue and cooperation between the three European countries and Iran to promote mutual confidence, with a view to facilitating the Agency's work on Iran's nuclear programme. In fostering an environment of cooperation to find a mutually acceptable solution to the issue, NAM appreciated all initiatives including that of South Africa.

6. Recognizing the Agency as the sole competent authority for verification, NAM had full confidence in the professionalism and impartiality of the organization. It strongly believed that all issues related to safeguards and verification, including the Iran issue, should be resolved within the framework of the Agency and on the basis of technical criteria.

...

12. Mr. BERDENNIKOV (**Russian Federation**) thanked the Director General for his comprehensive, objective and professional report which had been prepared exceptionally speedily in response to the resolution adopted by the Board on 11 August 2005.[343] It provided a good basis for calm, objective consideration of all aspects of the situation relating to the Iranian nuclear programme and should facilitate a decision leading to the resolution of the issue by diplomatic means, to the provision of reliable assurances of the peaceful nature of Iran's nuclear programme and the recognition of its right to peaceful uses of nuclear energy.

13. The Director General had concluded that no additional failures had been identified and that good progress had been made in removing the serious concerns over Iran's past nuclear programme. It was significant that one of the two main outstanding issues had been clarified, namely the foreign origin of the HEU contamination. With the active cooperation of the Iranian authorities, the Agency should be able to present to the Board its conclusions regarding the remaining unresolved issues.

...

---

[343] Doc. 29.

15. He stressed the importance of Iran's decision to continue its voluntary suspension of enrichment activities, which was an important confidence-building measure and should be maintained. He also noted Iran's declaration that it was willing to cooperate with the Agency in the carrying out of its verification activities and expressed the hope that that cooperation would meet the Agency's requirements as outlined in the Director General's report. The report provided a good basis for the continuation of the professional and unpoliticized work within the Agency on the Iranian nuclear programme, which should be the aim of the Board. Russia stood ready to work with other Board Members on a draft resolution that would constitute a balanced reaction to the report and would help reduce tension and facilitate resolution. It was important to maintain unity within the Board, which meant finding approaches that were acceptable to all and avoiding controversial decisions. Russia opposed any artificial escalation of the situation, including by referring it to the United Nations Security Council, which would be counter-productive both for the resolution of the Iranian nuclear issue and for the strengthening of the non-proliferation regime.

16. Mr. MÁRQUEZ MARÍN (**Bolivarian Republic of Venezuela**), stressing his country's commitment to the NPT, said that all members of the international community should comply strictly with the principles contained in that Treaty in the interests of peace and a world free from the terrible threat of illicit or destructive use of nuclear energy. As a State from a nuclear-weapon-free zone, Venezuela had consistently maintained that a balanced world, where all members of the international community could exploit their natural resources on an equal footing and where the right to self-determination was respected, could only be built through peaceful means. It had therefore spoken out on many occasions in favour of the inalienable right of States to the peaceful uses of nuclear energy, including the full nuclear fuel cycle and reprocessing.

17. ... The Director General's report showed that there was no evidence that the Iranian nuclear programme contravened the NPT or that Iran was failing to fulfil its obligations under that Treaty. More time was needed, but there was no reason to conclude that the Agency had exhausted its possibilities for handling the issue. The proposal to refer the case to the Security Council was therefore unfounded and could only politicize the issue, and make an early solution more difficult to achieve.

...

19. For an adequate appraisal of the relations between the Agency and Iran in respect of that country's obligations under the NPT and its safeguards agreement, various considerations had to be borne in mind. First among those was the inalienable right of States to pursue the use of nuclear energy for peaceful purposes in accordance with the NPT and relevant international regulations, free from political or other forms of discrimination. Secondly, to apply fairly regulations related to the prevention of proliferation of nuclear weapons, a distinction had to be made between the legal obligations flowing from those regulations and voluntary commitments. The latter should not be interpreted as a relinquishment or restriction of the inalienable right to the peaceful uses of nuclear energy. Furthermore, when assessing States' compliance with their legal obligations, the same criteria and conditions had to be applied to all. Thirdly, considerable progress had been made in the Agency's verification of Iran's nuclear programme since October 2003, with the voluntary assistance of the Iranian Government.

20. The time had come to evaluate the Iranian nuclear programme on an equitable basis, applying the same criteria to all Member States without distinction, exclusion or discrimination, and without the political bias that characterized hegemonic imperialist aspirations. The Director General's report showed that there were no objective reasons for bringing the Iranian issue before the Security Council. In doing so, the Agency would be relinquishing its role, which would be tantamount to acknowledging its inability to handle the issue, despite the fact that it was handling it well. Such a step would be counterproductive, would compromise the Agency's reputation as a reliable and balanced multilateral organization, and would also mean giving in to the pressure exerted by other countries possessing nuclear technology that were trying to maintain exclusive control over fuel and reprocessing, thus perpetuating a dependency relationship that undermined the sovereign right of States to independent development. Taking the issue out of the Agency's hands would also break the consensus that had characterized its approach.

…

55. Mr. CARRERA DORAL (**Cuba**) said that the Director General's report and his introductory statement revealed that the Secretariat had carried out an enormous amount of work in a highly professional manner, involving hundreds of hours of inspection and wide-ranging cooperation on the part of Iran and other Agency Member States, which had resulted in substantial progress towards clarifying the nature of Iran's nuclear programme. The number of outstanding issues had been reduced considerably. Iran continued to comply with its obligations under its safeguards agreement and additional protocol. All materials declared by Iran had been verified and none had been diverted towards prohibited activities. Ignoring those facts and alleging non-compliance on the part of Iran with its obligations under the NPT, a conclusion that had never been drawn by the Agency, and using that as the basis for reporting the issue to the Security Council, was an unacceptable act of political manipulation.

56. It was true that some issues were still pending and their clarification would require considerable effort by all parties concerned. The Agency, as the only body with the competence and the mandate to do that, could then, on the basis of objective and accurate information, draw definitive conclusions on the nature of Iran's nuclear programme. No such conclusions had been drawn thus far.

57. No State had the right to prejudge the nuclear programme of another or to politicize the debate on the matter, which was unfortunately what was happening at present.

58. Cuba firmly defended the sovereign and inalienable right to the peaceful uses of nuclear technology. No State could be required to limit its use of such technology unless its failure to comply with its commitments under the NPT had been demonstrated.

59. Currently, some major powers which had set themselves up as judges of good and evil were exerting pressure to report Iran to the Security Council for alleged non-compliance with the NPT on the basis of subjective and manipulated factors while, at the same time, openly accelerating vertical proliferation of nuclear weapons and conducting programmes to perfect such weapons in order to use them in their pre-emptive strike strategies, which was a clear and flagrant violation of the NPT. Such conduct illustrated the double standards which were being applied in international relations. His country firmly rejected that approach. A State's legal obligations had to be clearly differentiated from political commitments which they made to demonstrate their good faith.

60. Given the progress made in the matter, the professionalism of the Secretariat's work, the spirit of cooperation shown by Iran to date, and the initiative Iran had recently

presented in New York as a step towards increasing the transparency of its enrichment programme, Cuba was more convinced than ever that the issue should be dealt with within the Agency. It firmly opposed the matter being passed on or reported to the Security Council. Quite apart from the lack of any technical or legal basis for such a step, it would be a grave error, since it could put at risk the ongoing progress made by the Agency and undermine the latter's authority.

...

64. Mr. AKHONDZADEH (**Islamic Republic of Iran**) thanked the Director General for his report, and NAM for their cooperation and understanding.

65. A review of the technical and legal aspects of Iran's peaceful nuclear programme could easily lead to the conclusion that the international community had, to a great extent, been misled with biased, politicized and exaggerated information from certain quarters, when the issue should have been dealt with in a purely technical manner within the framework of the Agency. The financial contributions made by certain countries should not be a basis for fabricating false allegations against Member States.

66. The term 'concealment' was incorrect and misleading. Iran's failure to report such activities as the establishment of a nuclear facility, which under its safeguards agreement it was obliged to inform the Agency of through a DIQ form only 180 days before nuclear material was brought into the facility, was not concealment. It was important to remember that, when some of the activities in question had been initiated, the additional protocol had not even existed. The Agency had been informed about the enrichment plant at Natanz and the Uranium Conversion Facility four years before Iran was obliged to do so. Last but not least, the Agency was not legally in a position to judge the intentions of Member States. The term 'concealment' was therefore out of place.

...

76. Iran invited the Director General to visit Tehran to discuss the remaining outstanding issues, and ways to enhance cooperation with a view to enabling the Agency to provide assurances regarding the peaceful nature of its nuclear programme. Several proposals had been presented that could be considered within the framework of negotiations. Only by engaging in negotiations in good faith, free of duress and threats, could confrontation be avoided. Iran was firmly and wholeheartedly prepared to engage in such negotiations. Above all, the process required time. He called on the Board to put the threats back in the drawer, return to the negotiating table and allow the time required to resolve the matter through peaceful means.

Document 78: Consideration of GOV/2005/76

GOV/OR.1141, 24 September 2005

1. Mr. JENKINS (**United Kingdom**), introducing the draft resolution contained in document GOV/2005/76, said that the path that had brought the Board of Governors to where it was now had begun in 2003. Almost two years previously the Director General had reported to the Board that Iran had concealed many aspects of its nuclear activities, with resultant breaches of its obligation to comply with the provisions of its safeguards

agreement.[344] The Board had held back from reporting Iran's non-compliance because that country had committed itself to taking steps to rebuild confidence in the peaceful nature of its programme. It had been hoped that the necessary confidence would be restored through a negotiating process leading to a long-term agreement.

2. The current situation, two years later, was that Iran had gone back on significant confidence-building commitments and there were still important outstanding questions that needed to be clarified. It was against that background that the United Kingdom, France and Germany were submitting the resolution.

3. There was nothing in the resolution that sought to affect the inalienable right of all parties to the NPT to develop nuclear activities for peaceful purposes. The text made it clear that the issue was specific to the circumstances in which the Board found itself in relation to Iran.

4. He underlined that there were grounds for making the report required under Article XII.C of the Agency's Statute and the notification required under Article III.B.4. Operative paragraph 3 explicitly left open the timing and content of such a report and notification, deferring them to a future Board meeting and a separate Board decision. Time might still enable Iran to take the steps necessary to start restoring confidence, as requested by the Board. That operative paragraph would allow Iran to influence when action was taken and the context in which it was received. It kept the issue within the Board and responded to the requests by other delegations to allow time for further diplomatic contacts with Iran.

5. Operative paragraph 4 reiterated past calls to Iran to implement the transparency measures that the Director General considered would be helpful and the confidence-building measures that the Board had requested.

6. Operative paragraph 5 called on Iran to observe fully its commitments and to return to the negotiating process, which was dependent on full respect for those commitments.

7. Operative paragraph 6 made it clear that the Agency continued to have full responsibility for the verification of nuclear declarations made by Iran.

8. The three sponsors hoped that the draft resolution would commend itself to Governors. It enabled the Board to react in an appropriate manner to the situation created by Iran's notification of 1 August to the Director General,[345] which had prompted the Board to express concern on 11 August.[346] It gave Iran an opportunity to heed calls from the Board to rectify the situation and observe fully its commitments.

9. The CHAIRPERSON proposed that the Board proceed to a decision on the draft resolution contained in document GOV/2005/76.

10. At the request of Mr. Márquez Marín (**Bolivarian Republic of Venezuela**), a roll-call vote was taken.

11. Yemen, having been drawn by lot by the Chairperson, was called upon to vote first.

12. The result of the vote was as follows:

In favour: Argentina, Australia, Belgium, Canada, Ecuador, France Germany, Ghana, Hungary, India, Italy, Japan, Republic of Korea, Netherlands, Peru, Poland, Portugal, Singapore, Slovakia, Sweden, United Kingdom of Great Britain and Northern Ireland, United States of America.

Against: Bolivarian Republic of Venezuela.

---

[344] Doc. 4.
[345] Doc. 107.
[346] Doc. 29.

Abstaining: Algeria, Brazil, China, Mexico, Nigeria, Pakistan, Russian Federation, South Africa, Sri Lanka, Tunisia, Vietnam, Yemen.

13. There were 22 votes in favour and 1 against, with 12 abstentions. The draft resolution was adopted.

14. Mr. MÁRQUEZ MARÍN (**Bolivarian Republic of Venezuela**) said that his delegation disagreed with and was deeply uneasy at the procedure that had been followed to precipitate a decision of such importance despite the request for deferment put forward by NAM, China, Brazil, Mexico, the Russian Federation and others, which together constituted the largest group of member countries in the organization. The draft resolution had been distributed in English only a matter of minutes before the preceding meeting, which had made consultation with capitals very difficult, it being the weekend. Such a procedure ran counter to the democratic principles and the policy of consensus that characterized the Agency and had given it the credibility that it enjoyed in the international community.

15. Venezuela had voted against the resolution for several reasons. The resolution laid the groundwork for passing the issue to the United Nations Security Council and taking it outside of the Agency, closing the door to dialogue and negotiation which was how the matter should be dealt with, even though the safeguards procedures described in the Director General's report had uncoverered no diversion in Iran's nuclear programme. Moreover, referring the matter to the Security Council, far from promoting resolution, was likely to complicate the issue and push it towards confrontation. There was no reason to assume that the Agency's role was played out. On the contrary, the Director General, in addition to recognizing the progress made in the verification process, had actually suggested that more time was needed to pursue the investigation, which would require Iran's full support.

16. The approach of the resolution was completely negative and politically biased. It did not take into account the progress made in the application of safeguards over more than two years, during which time Iran had demonstrated its willingness to cooperate with the Agency with a view to clarifying for the international community the true nature of its nuclear programme, had applied the additional protocol[347] though it was not yet ratified, and had voluntarily suspended its enrichment and reprocessing activities. The resolution ignored Iran's willingness to continue cooperating with the Agency to prove to the international community the peaceful intent of its nuclear programme, to which it had a right like all member countries and on which no limits could be imposed.

17. The Director General had not reported definite non-compliance on the part of Iran, even though the Agency was the body with the technical capacity to make such a pronouncement. That fact had been omitted from the resolution just adopted, showing its political bias and thereby setting a precedent that severely affected the technical credibility of the Agency.

18. Opening the door to refer the issue of Iran to the Security Council, and breaking with the practice of consensus, weakened the Agency, which was a highly important multilateral forum in the fight for non-proliferation of nuclear weapons and global disarmament.

19. Ms. HUSSAIN (**Malaysia**), **speaking on behalf of the Non-Aligned Movement**, said that the elements contained in the resolution did not form a complete basis for moving forward in seeking a constructive solution to the issue of Iran's nuclear programme. In view of the serious nature of the issues covered by the resolution, NAM had suggested that time be allowed for negotiations with a view to reaching a consensus decision and that the matter be discussed at the November meetings of the Board. However, its major concerns

---

[347] Doc. 5.

and those of other like-minded States had not been heeded. The draft resolution had been tabled very late the preceding evening, which had made it very difficult for delegations to obtain instructions from their respective capitals for a decision to be taken at the current meeting.

20. The resolution called into question the inalienable right of all States party to the NPT to develop atomic energy for peaceful purposes. It did not make a clear distinction between the legal obligations of Member States under their safeguards agreements and voluntary confidence-building measures. Any referral to the Security Council, whether explicit or implicit, prejudging Iran's non-compliance in the context of Article XII.C of the Statute and without allowing time for the Director General to complete his work and resolve the remaining issues, was not the correct basis for moving forward.

21. In that context, NAM welcomed Iran's readiness to resume negotiations with France, Germany and the United Kingdom and continued to underline the need for patience and restraint from all parties concerned. It was of the firm view that continued negotiations were the best way to move towards a constructive outcome.

22. Mr. SHARAF (Yemen) said that his country had urged that the three European countries and Iran should have more time to pursue their negotiations in order to arrive at a mutually acceptable solution. However, the draft resolution had been tabled hastily at the last minute and had made for division in the Board, instead of reinforcing its unity and promoting consensus. His delegation had been forced to abstain as it found no grounds for voting in favour of the resolution.

...

24. Mr. BERDENNIKOV (**Russian Federation**) said that his country looked upon the resolution as a signal to continue increasing the Agency's cooperation with Iran in order to clear up all outstanding issues with regard to that country's nuclear programme. The Russian Federation was against referring the Iranian issue to the Security Council as it was convinced that the Agency had the potential to settle the problem internally.

25. The Russian Federation had held intensive consultations with all interested parties, unfortunately - owing to a lack of time - without achieving the desired results. His country had been able to abstain in the vote because the draft resolution did not envisage the immediate referral of the Iranian issue, thus leaving open an opportunity to continue efforts to find a satisfactory solution within the Agency.

26. Mr. BUTT (**Pakistan**) said that his country had hoped to see a consensus in the Board on the resolution, despite the complex nature of the issue. It was regrettable that that had not been possible. Pakistan had abstained as it felt that a confrontational approach would not be conducive to regional stability, which was of vital concern to his country. Despite the acrimony of the debate and the action that had followed, Pakistan hoped that the Agency could move forward and resolve - through negotiations - the broader issue of Iran's nuclear programme to the satisfaction of the Board of Governors.

...

30. Ms. FEROUKHI (**Algeria**), **speaking on behalf of her own country and Tunisia**, said that both countries regretted that a consensus had not been reached and the extreme pressure the Board had been subjected to, particularly the countries of NAM. Algeria and Tunisia would remain motivated by the desire to achieve consensus on that important issue which had long-term implications.

31. Both countries also regretted that NAM's request for a delay of one week had not been received favourably. They remained convinced that the time factor was of fundamental

importance for consensus and would have helped avoid a division in the Board which weakened the Agency.

32. The Agency needed to state its willingness to continue and intensify its work in Iran and to consolidate the progress that had been made on outstanding issues.

33. A consensus would have encouraged Iran to implement the resolutions adopted by the Board and could have reinforced the Agency's safeguards system. Both Algeria and Tunisia remained committed to consensus and were convinced that dialogue and negotiations remained the best instruments for the peaceful settlement of the Iranian issue.

34. Mr. MINTY (**South Africa**) protested strongly at the late start of the meeting.

35. The resolution just adopted addressed matters of critical importance. It was precisely because of the importance of those issues that South Africa, both in the context of NAM and in a national capacity, had appealed for more time for the process of dialogue and negotiation to yield positive results, even at such a late stage. The matter could only be resolved if all parties showed the necessary flexibility and commitment to a peaceful settlement.

36. South Africa and many other countries had abstained because of the time constraints imposed by certain parties. Sufficient time had not been allowed to consult on the far-reaching implications of the resolution and to receive the necessary instructions from capitals.

...

42. Mr. WU Hailong (**China**) said...

43. The resolution just adopted by the Board risked taking the settlement of the Iranian nuclear issue outside the framework of the Agency. It failed to reflect in a balanced way the progress made in the Agency's verification activities in Iran. The manner in which the vote had been conducted was not conducive to the unity of the Board. On the other hand, the resolution did urge Iran to implement transparency measures and cooperate fully with the Agency, to resolve outstanding issues in respect of its nuclear activities and to return to the negotiating table. As those elements were not too far removed from the principles and goals that China expressed, it had abstained in the vote.

...

46. Ms. KELLY (**Argentina**) said that her country did not question the right of Iran, or any other State, to develop peaceful nuclear fuel cycle-related activities. The peaceful nature of a nuclear programme was determined, essentially, by punctilious compliance with obligations under the NPT and under the safeguards agreement concluded with the Agency by a Member State. If shortcomings were detected by the Agency, the nuclear programme of the State in question was subject to suspicion pending investigation to determine whether non-compliance had indeed occurred. The Iranian issue was an isolated event relating specifically to that country. Argentina had therefore voted in favour of the resolution which in no way called into question the right of all countries to the peaceful uses of nuclear energy under Agency safeguards. The issue addressed by the resolution lay outside the normal scope of the peaceful nuclear activities of a State under the NPT and Agency safeguards.

47. Her country had always maintained that the central issue was the need for Iran to regain international confidence before beginning conversion and enrichment-related activities. There were still significant doubts regarding Iran's nuclear programme and the most constructive approach was that which had been advocated by the Board on previous

occasions, i.e. the suspension of enrichment activities until Iran had dispelled concerns regarding the peaceful nature of that programme. The European proposal which had been presented to Iran[348] contained reasonable elements which would allow that country to continue its legitimate access to the benefits of nuclear energy. The rejection of that proposal[349] constituted a step backwards in the confidence-building process initiated by Iran in its negotiations with the three European countries. Referring the issue to the Security Council had always been an option for Argentina.

...

53. Mr. LAI NGOC DOAN (**Vietnam**) said it was deplorable that the Board had voted on the resolution, departing from the Agency's usual practice of consensus. His country had always supported non-proliferation efforts. It affirmed the inalienable right of all Member States to use nuclear energy for peaceful purposes and recognized the Agency as the only competent authority for verification and safeguards issues and, in particular, the Iranian issue, which needed to be resolved through dialogue within the framework of the Agency. He encouraged the parties concerned to exercise restraint and engage in dialogue and negotiations with a view to reaching a mutually acceptable solution.

54. Ms. RICHTER RIBEIRO MOURA (**Brazil**) said...

...

56. Brazil would have wished for more time, and a more adequate process, to consider such an important resolution. Referring to operative paragraph 4, subparagraphs (i) and (ii), she said the text could have been improved to reflect properly the legal framework of the safeguards agreements and the additional protocol. Iran was a special case, and Brazil had abstained so as not to create a precedent.

...

61. Mr. SHARMA (**India**) said that he had studied the resolution tabled by the three European countries and there were elements in it which caused his country some difficulty.

62. The resolution recognized that good progress had been made in Iran's correction of the breaches and in the Agency's ability to confirm certain aspects of Iran's current declarations. There was therefore no justification for finding Iran to be non-compliant in the context of Article XII.C of the Agency's Statute. It would also not be accurate to characterize the current situation as a threat to international peace and security.

63. The resolution did address the two major preoccupations of his country. Firstly, India had consistently maintained that more time should be allowed to explore all possible ways of reaching a satisfactory resolution of the issues that had arisen. The draft resolution had conceded as much by deferring to a later date the taking of a decision on how the matter should be handled. Secondly, India was opposed to referring the matter to the Security Council at the current stage because it did not believe that was justified by the circumstances, and the resolution kept the matter within the purview of the Agency itself. India's support for the resolution, despite its reservations, was based on the assumption that the intervening period would be used by all to expand the diplomatic space and address satisfactorily all outstanding issues. The door should be kept open for dialogue and consensus, and confrontation should be avoided.

...

65. Ms. ESPINOSA CANTELLANO (**Mexico**) reaffirmed...

...

---

[348] Doc. 126.
[349] Doc. 108.

69. The Mexican delegation had abstained in the vote on the resolution because it considered that it did not adequately reflect the state of implementation of the safeguards agreement in Iran and was unbalanced. Only the Agency had the required technical competence to determine whether or not there were breaches of obligations under Iran's safeguards agreement and to provide objective information to its members so that they could in turn determine the appropriate steps to take.

70. Having carefully examined the Director General's report contained in document GOV/2005/67,[350] and following a technical and legal analysis of that report, her country believed that the outstanding issues could and should be resolved within the framework of the Agency. Recognizing, as the Director General had done in his report, that Iran was a special case requiring additional measures to those prescribed in the safeguards agreement and the additional protocol, Mexico considered that the decision taken did not establish a precedent whereby failure to comply with procedural rules was sufficient grounds for taking an issue out of the hands of the Agency.

...

72. Mr. SCHULTE (**United States**) agreed that the authority, integrity and credibility of the Agency were very important. That was precisely why it was important that, after years of reports on safeguards failures and breaches, the Board had finally acknowledged what it had known for two years, namely that Iran was non-compliant with its safeguards obligations. He requested that the resolution be publicly released and posted on the public website of the Agency.

...

78. Mr. CARRERA DORAL (**Cuba**) said that his country firmly believed that the resolution just adopted set a dangerous and shameful precedent in the history of the Agency.

79. The precedent was dangerous for two reasons. Firstly, the resolution stated that Iran had violated its NPT commitments, thereby providing a basis for referring the matter to the Security Council at any time. No such statement was made in any of the Director General's reports to the Board, which were based on the verification reports of the Agency's inspectors. On that basis, in the future any of the numerous failures or breaches reported regularly in the SIR could be manipulated and classified as a violation of NPT commitments, even if they had not been reported as such by the Director General. The work of the inspectorate was being misrepresented and the information presented by the Director General was being manipulated. The interpretation of the current situation was malicious and constituted a distortion of the Agency's Statute. Secondly, the case which had been made for referring the issue to the Security Council at any time was based on non-compliance not with legal commitments, but with commitments undertaken voluntarily by Iran as a sign of goodwill. What would happen in the future with other voluntary commitments undertaken by countries, such as under the additional protocol? Mistrust would undermine goodwill and the consequences for the strengthening of the safeguards system, which was so necessary, were unforeseeable.

80. The precedent was shameful because of the distortion and manipulation of information, the double standards applied, the arrogance shown, the underhand methods that had been used and the unjustified haste. How could the spirit of Vienna be invoked in the future? Many Southern countries had practically begged for a deferment of just a few days to be able to consult their capitals and work towards consensus, but that had been refused on procedural grounds.

[350] Doc. 40.

81. In line with his country's moral stance with respect to the fulfilment of commitments undertaken, and in view of the respect that the Agency deserved, the need for strict compliance with the Agency's Statute and his country's attachment to the basic principles of NAM, if Cuba had been able to vote, it would have voted against the resolution, which was unacceptable.

82. Mr. AKHONDZADEH **(Islamic Republic of Iran)** said that the day had been significant and would be remembered as a turning point.

83. For over two years, the Iranian issue had been lingering on the Board's agenda. Over that period, Iran had made unprecedented offers to restore confidence in the peaceful nature of its nuclear programme and had allowed pervasive and intrusive security measures. It had faced up to every challenge and answered every allegation, however unwarranted. As soon as a matter had been resolved, new allegations had been made, based on sketchy evidence which could not even be described as circumstantial, let alone hard and reliable, yet Iran had responded to each and everyone and they had all been proved wrong. No evidence of diversion had been found at all. The sole instance where some evidence had surfaced had been the issue of the contamination, which it had been established was from outside sources. Under normal, fair and reasonable circumstances, since the Agency's latest findings had confirmed Iran's claim in that regard, the case should have been closed, as the remaining questions lay firmly within the realm of routine safeguards verification.

84. However, the Board had done just the reverse. To rake up old and remedied failures in order to claim non-compliance was simply outrageous and had no legal or technical basis whatsoever. No matter how far interpretation of the Statute and the safeguards agreement was stretched, no basis for involving the Security Council could be established. The Agency had confirmed that there was no evidence of diversion. It had stated that work was making good progress. It had noted that, in order to reach the ultimate and very rare conclusion of a clean bill of health under the additional protocol, it needed to carry out more work. Such an entirely positive situation in no way warranted a decision of such an adversarial nature. Most of the contents of the resolution were meaningless and had no substance or foundation whatsoever.

85. There was only one reason the resolution had been passed: its proponents, essentially Western nuclear-weapon States and their allies, were intent on establishing their newly adopted position that non-nuclear-weapon States should, in addition to their existing commitments, forgo once and for all their inalienable right to develop and produce nuclear fuel and power for peaceful purposes. There was no pretext under which the Board could call on a Member State to refrain from a peaceful activity which was totally permissible under the NPT and fully safeguarded and monitored by the Agency. Such a call was wrong and it created a precedent which was even more wrong. If it was heeded, no other State would be immune.

86. Under the Paris agreement,[351] Iran had suspended work at the Uranium Conversion Facility at Esfahan on condition that a mutually acceptable agreement on its fuel enrichment programme could be reached. The proposal by the France, Germany and the United Kingdom calling for elimination of the fuel cycle effectively nullified the Paris agreement. The adoption of the draft resolution also violated the provisions of the Tehran declaration made by the three European countries and Iran. With the involvement of the Security Council, Iran would no longer have any commitment to the voluntary measures it had provisionally adopted under that declaration.

---

[351] Doc. 8.

87. Iran had gone out of its way to seek and find agreement with Europe on the issue, demonstrating maximum flexibility at all times. It had engaged actively in extensive discussions and negotiations in order to settle the matter and avoid an unwanted crisis. Regrettably, and despite the goodwill of many, all efforts had failed. There was simply too much intransigence from its counterparts to accommodate any settlement.

88. Under those circumstances, Iran was prepared to continue its cooperation with the Agency in line with its safeguards obligations, to work with the Agency for the purpose of confidence building and transparency by implementing safeguards to provide continued assurances of non-diversion to nuclear weapons, and to continue negotiations with all States, in particular the three European countries, in the context of the initiative of the President of Iran presented at the United Nations General Assembly in September 2005. However, the approach hitherto of the three European countries of delay and procrastination was not acceptable. Furthermore, their unfounded calls for Iran to cease its peaceful nuclear activities, which betrayed the NPT and created a damaging precedent for all States, should be withdrawn.

89. If the confrontation persisted, Iran would meet that challenge. It would certainly not give up its right to a complete nuclear fuel cycle for its peaceful nuclear programme, and the threat of referral to the Security Council did not affect that decision. Iran did not seek confrontation, it did not welcome a diplomatic impasse, nor did it seek an end to negotiations. However, negotiations under threat were meaningless and not conducive to agreement. Faced with the threat of confrontation, Iran would have no alternative but to pursue and preserve its rights, which it would do resolutely.

...

Document 79: Consideration of GOV/2005/87

GOV/OR.1145, 24 November 2005

...

63. Ms. HUSSAIN (**Malaysia**), **speaking on behalf of the Non-Aligned Movement**, stressed...

...

65. A clear distinction had to be made between the legal obligations of Member States under their respective safeguards agreements and voluntary commitments, in order to ensure that the latter were not turned into the former. The provision of information on dual-use material and equipment was not a legal obligation.

...

69. The Agency was the sole competent authority for verification and NAM had full confidence in its professionalism and impartiality. All issues relating to safeguards and verification, including that of Iran, should be resolved within the framework of the Agency and based on technical grounds, and NAM hoped that all safeguards activities in Iran would soon be implemented in a routine manner.

70. NAM welcomed the fact that all declared nuclear material in Iran had been accounted for by the Agency and that no such material had been diverted to prohibited activities. The Agency's work on verifying Iran's peaceful nuclear programme on the basis of that country's declarations was ongoing and it was crucial that it be concluded. Iran's

continuing cooperation with a view to resolving the remaining issues, which went beyond its legal obligations, was welcome, in particular the confidence-building measures voluntarily undertaken by Iran, including the provisional implementation of the additional protocol.[352] NAM was optimistic that the remaining questions would be resolved promptly.

71. The Agency's legal authority to pursue verification of possible nuclear-weapons-related activity was limited. Any request for additional legal authority had to be negotiated with Member States. Hence the importance of promoting and strengthening the multilateral process. It was encouraging that, since the September 2005 report to the Board,[353] Iran had been more forthcoming on the issue of its P-1 and P-2 centrifuge programmes, providing access to additional documentation relating to the 1987 offer and permitting interviews with individuals. NAM encouraged Iran to provide all supporting documentation requested in order to facilitate the Agency's work. It also welcomed the access provided by Iran to the Parchin site for the second time.

72. Mr. WRIGHT (**United Kingdom**), **speaking on behalf of the European Union**, the acceding countries Bulgaria and Romania, the candidate countries Croatia and Turkey, the countries of the Stabilization and Association Process and potential candidates Albania and Serbia and Montenegro, the EFTA countries Iceland, Liechtenstein and Norway, members of the European Economic Area, and Moldova and Ukraine, said that the EU had taken careful note of the Director General's latest progress report on implementation of Iran's NPT safeguards agreement, contained in document GOV/2005/87,[354] and his introductory statement and it commended the impartiality and professionalism of the Director General and the Secretariat.

...

74. It emerged clearly from the Director General's report that one reason progress had been modest was that cooperation remained inadequate, and that full transparency was indispensable and overdue. It was disturbing that a State that had practiced a policy of concealment for 18 years should be so reluctant to demonstrate that it no longer had anything to hide. Such reluctance made Iran's claim that its nuclear programme was exclusively peaceful ring hollow. The Board should give full support to the Director General's call for full transparency, which should extend beyond the formal requirements of the safeguards agreement[355] and the additional protocol to include the provision of information and documentation related to the procurement of dual-use equipment, and visits to military-owned workshops and R&D locations associated with the Physics Research Centre and the Lavisan-Shian site.

75. The EU was disturbed to see that Iran had admitted to possessing a document related to the casting and machining of enriched uranium metal into hemispherical forms. Such a process had no other application than in the production of nuclear warheads. That document, which had not been included in the information previously handed over to inspectors, raised a set of new questions. The Director General should give priority to investigation of those matters, and Iran should give all necessary access to sites and individuals who might be able to assist.

...

78. The Board should make it clear to Iran that it continued to attach the highest importance to the full suspension of all enrichment-related and reprocessing activities

---

[352] Doc. 5.
[353] Doc. 40.
[354] Doc. 41.
[355] Doc. 4.

while outstanding issues were being addressed i.e. until confidence in the exclusively peaceful nature of Iran's nuclear programme was established. It should repeat its demand for suspension of all activity at the Uranium Conversion Facility and should warn Iran that any resumption of enrichment-related activities at Natanz would seriously aggravate the situation created by the resumption of activity at Esfahan. It should note with concern that Iran was continuing with civil construction at the Natanz enrichment plant, which was not consistent with the spirit of the confidence-building measures undertaken by Iran. It should also express its deep concern that, despite numerous calls, Iran had continued building a research reactor moderated by heavy water. In addition, it should remind Iran that respecting the Board's calls for full suspension would lead to the resumption of talks between Iran and the EU.

79. In its resolution adopted on 24 September 2005,[356] the Board had found that Iran's many failures and breaches of its obligations to comply with its safeguards agreements constituted non-compliance in the context of Article XII.C of the Agency's Statute. The Board had also found that the history of concealment of Iran's nuclear activities, the nature of those activities, issues brought to light in the course of the Agency's verification of declarations made by Iran since September 2002, and the resulting absence of confidence that Iran's nuclear programme was exclusively for peaceful purposes had given rise to questions that were within the competence of the Security Council. The Board had decided to address the timing and content of the communications required by those findings at a later date. It had done that because it saw reason to hope that Iran would take the opportunity to exert a positive influence on the timing and content of those communications to the Security Council by taking the measures urged upon it. With every passing week that hope had become harder to sustain. Only in relation to transparency had Iran taken positive steps, and they had been no more than half-measures. Having listened carefully to the views of many Board members, the EU saw reason to think that the window of opportunity should not be closed immediately, but it would not stay open in all circumstances. The EU expected Iran to adopt a responsive attitude, to implement the confidence-building measures for which the Board had called, to refrain from any further unilateral move that might aggravate the situation and to re-engage in serious discussions on a reasonable basis and in good faith.

80. Mr. WU Hailong (China) said that his country had noted the cooperative measures adopted by Iran since the Board's September 2005 meetings,[357] as well as the outstanding issues that still needed to be clarified, and hoped that Iran would continue to cooperate with the Secretariat to clarify those issues.

81. If not handled well, the Iranian nuclear issue might no longer be manageable within the framework of the Agency or might even spin totally out of control. That would be in the interests of no-one concerned, nor was it conducive to the effectiveness of the NPT regime, the authority of the Agency or regional peace and stability. As long as all parties exercised restraint and demonstrated patience and flexibility, and the international community adopted constructive measures and a constructive attitude, the situation could move in the direction of a final, peaceful settlement.

...

96. Ms. GERVAIS-VIDRICAIRE (**Canada**) said...

...

---

[356] Doc. 30.
[357] Doc. 76-Doc. 78.

99. It was important to recognize that Iran had failed to meet its safeguards obligations. The Director General had presented more than ten reports to the Board detailing repeated failures by Iran to declare its nuclear activities appropriately and to cooperate adequately with safeguards inspectors. The right to the peaceful uses of nuclear energy, guaranteed by Article IV of the NPT, could only be seen in the context of the obligations imposed by Article III of the Treaty, which required that nuclear facilities be subjected to safeguards.

100. Iran wanted the international community to believe that the right to the peaceful uses of nuclear energy was at stake when its nuclear programme came before the Board. That was not true. Iran had created a unique situation for itself through its many failures. Other Agency members dutifully met their safeguards obligations and thus maintained the confidence of the Board and the related right to the peaceful use of nuclear energy. Recently, the Board had found that Iran had not been in compliance with its safeguards obligations, a fact that distinguished it from other members. That finding called into question the confidence that the Board could have in Iran's declarations and in its uses of nuclear energy.

...

103. The Russian Federation, with the full support of the three European countries, had recently made efforts to engage Iran in dialogue. Canada encouraged Iran to take advantage of that opportunity without further delay and to resume discussions with the three European countries on a comprehensive long-term solution. If Iran did not make every effort to rebuild the confidence it had lost, then the Board should move expeditiously to meet the requirements of the Agency's Statute and report Iran's non-compliance to the United Nations Security Council for appropriate action.

104. Mr. BERDENNIKOV (Russian Federation) said...

...

106. The fact that Iran was continuing with its conversion activities was not conducive to an early resolution of the situation. Calls for a moratorium on such activities had been included in the resolutions adopted by the Board of Governors. However, it was important to note Iran's continued implementation of the additional protocol prior to its entry into force and its continuing moratorium on uranium enrichment activities.

107. All States party to the NPT had a right to the peaceful uses of nuclear energy. That right was inseparable from the non-proliferation obligations enshrined in the Treaty. His country called on Iran to focus on clarifying all outstanding issues and restoring the confidence of the international community in the peaceful nature of its nuclear programme through consistent and continuous cooperation with the Agency on the basis of full transparency. Clearly, that would require additional efforts and would take time. In particular, a suitable explanation would be required with regard to the information on Iran's receipt of documents relating to technology for producing uranium metal and machining it into hemispherical forms.

108. His country was convinced that the resumption of dialogue between Iran and the three European countries would help bring about a diplomatic settlement of the Iranian nuclear issue. Since the preceding meetings of the Board, the Russian Federation had taken steps to achieve that objective. As a neighbour and longstanding partner of Iran, Russia was prepared to engage in the broadest possible cooperation with Tehran in order to guarantee supplies of ready-made fuel to meet Iran's legitimate nuclear energy needs. A solution should be possible on such a basis which would ensure predictable stability in the development of nuclear power in Iran and dispel questions about the nature of Iran's nuclear programme.

109. He called on Iran to step up its efforts to resolve outstanding issues and restore confidence. There was still scope for continuing work on those issues within the framework of the Agency. His country noted that the Secretariat would continue to study all relevant information at its disposal and that the Director General would report on the matter as necessary.

...

Document 80: Consideration of GOV/2005/87 (continued)

GOV/OR.1146, 24 November 2005

...

30. Mr. HONSOWITZ (**Germany**) said...

...

34. How should the Board deal with that situation at its current session?

35. Since the adoption of its 24 September 'non-compliance resolution'[358] the Board had an obligation to submit a report to the Security Council. However, many Board members had requested, in September and subsequently, that the Board and the international community be given more time for diplomatic efforts. Also, ideas had been put forward by some Board members, particularly the Russian Federation, which his country had noted and was prepared to pursue.

36. Against that background, despite its persisting concerns, his country was still ready to explore, together with the United Kingdom, France and the High Representative of the European Union, prospects for a new dialogue with Iran and for negotiations on a long-term agreement. At the present stage, his country did not know whether renewed contacts would open up such prospects. Iran would have to adopt a reasonable attitude, demonstrate its readiness to engage in serious discussions and refrain from further unilateral moves which could aggravate the situation. In particular, any threat to start enrichment activities would immediately put an end to the efforts of his country and its partners.

37. Germany continued to hope that a sustainable solution would be found within the Agency framework and remained ready to do all it could to help bring about such a solution.

...

83. Ms. GARCÍA de PÉREZ (**Bolivarian Republic of Venezuela**) said...

...

86. The solution to safeguards implementation in Iran must take into account several key points. Firstly, the need to respect the inalienable right of all States to develop nuclear energy for peaceful purposes without any kind of discrimination and on the basis of the principle established in the NPT. Secondly, the need to make a clear distinction regarding non-compliance by a State between its legal obligations and its voluntary commitments. Thirdly, it was essential to preserve the Agency's capacity and authority to carry out the tasks entrusted to it under the Treaty and which to date it had carried out meticulously, transparently and impartially. Finally, as actors in the process of the development of the peaceful uses of nuclear energy for the benefit of all humanity, Board members could not shirk their responsibility to defend their obligations with absolute integrity.

...

---

[358] Doc. 30.

145. Mr. SCHULTE (**United States of America**) expressed appreciation for the hard work being done by the Director General and the Department of Safeguards regarding Iran's implementation of its safeguards obligations, especially efforts to investigate all unresolved issues, including concerns about possible undeclared nuclear activities, and to verify Iran's suspension commitments which, as the Director General reported, Iran continued to violate.

146. The resolution adopted by the Board two months previously, contained in document GOV/2005/77, had made two important findings. Firstly, Iran's many breaches and failures of its obligations to comply with its safeguards agreement constituted non-compliance in the context of Article XII.C of the Statute. Secondly, Iran's long history of deception and concealment of its nuclear activities, the nature of those activities and the absence of confidence in Iran's peaceful nuclear intentions had given rise to questions that were within the competence of the Security Council. Both findings were sufficient cause to report Iran to the Security Council, but instead the Board had chosen to give Iran time to take positive steps that could then be reflected in the context of that report. With that goal in mind, the resolution had urged Iran to take a number of steps.

...

148. Given Iran's record of wilful disregard for the Board's requests, it would have been appropriate for the Board to adopt at its present meeting a resolution reporting Iran to the Security Council, as required under Articles XII.C and III.B.4 of the Statute. The United States believed that a majority of Board members would have supported such a step even now. However, the United States joined all in seeking a diplomatic solution and supported the request of France, Germany and the United Kingdom to defer for a short period the required report to the Security Council. It did so in the sincere hope that Iran would reverse its course and demonstrate that it would meet its obligations before the report had to be made.

149. Iran had to understand that the report to the Security Council was required and would be made at a time of the Board's choosing. The United States again urged Iran to resume negotiations in good faith with the three European countries on the basis of the Paris agreement. It was clear that those countries were working hard to broaden international consensus about how to address the crisis in confidence that Iran had created. In that context, the United States welcomed Russia's efforts to encourage Iran to return to negotiations and the ideas that Russia had proposed.

...

153. Mr. JENKINS (**United Kingdom**) expressed concern at the continuing inadequacy of Iran's cooperation and said his country took a very serious view of the implications of the ongoing absence of full transparency. It deplored Iran's squandering of a recent opportunity to re-establish full suspension of all enrichment-related activities. Above all, the United Kingdom deeply regretted that, since September, Iran had done so little to exert a positive influence on the timing and content of the communications to the Security Council required by the Board's September resolution, contained in document GOV/2005/77. Although the Secretary of Iran's Supreme National Security Council had written to European ministers, his letter contained no new ideas, only a suggestion of talks about talks. A reply to that letter would be sent shortly in light of the outcome of the present Board meeting. Iran should be under no illusion that patience was wearing thin. The United Kingdom reserved the right to call for the Board to meet in special session if Iran forced it to the view that, without the involvement of the Security Council, the measures for which the Board had called were going to remain unimplemented.

154. With regard to the Director General's report contained in document GOV/2005/87, the United Kingdom had been disturbed to read that the documents recently made available to the Agency included one relating to the casting and machining of enriched, natural and depleted uranium metal into hemispherical forms. The United Kingdom would be grateful to hear what interpretation the Secretariat put on the document. Was it correct that the casting and machining of enriched uranium metal into hemispheres was a crucial step in the production of nuclear warheads and that there was no civil application for uranium metal in that shape? If so, it seemed that the discovery of the document was a further matter that needed to be notified to the Security Council under Article III.B.4 of the Statute. As a preliminary to that, it would be helpful if the Director General could arrange for the document to be seen by experts from the five nuclear-weapon States. It would also be helpful if he could confirm that the Secretariat would be enquiring, as a matter of urgency, into the use that Iran had made of the document and whether it was connected in some way to reports that Iran had been working on warheads, which appeared to be nuclear in nature, for deployment in the Shihab-3 missile.

155. Was the document a warning that there might be other documents in Iran's possession which were relevant to Agency investigations and which Iran had neglected to show the Agency previously? After all, the document should have been shown to the Agency in 2003 when Iran was making declarations that were supposed to be complete. And did Iran's possession of the document put it in breach of Article II of the NPT which stated, inter alia, that non-nuclear-weapon States should undertake not to seek or receive any assistance in the manufacture of nuclear weapons or other nuclear explosive devices?

…

166. Mr. AKHONZADEH **(Islamic Republic of Iran)** expressed appreciation to the members of NAM, in particular Chairperson Hussain from Malaysia, and to other countries for their cooperative and constructive contribution.

167. After two years of intensive cooperation by his country with the Agency, involving an unprecedented 1400 man-days of intrusive inspection and enabling the Agency to have better understanding of Iran's peaceful nuclear programme, there were now only a few remaining issues to resolve. The Director General's report, contained in document GOV/2005/87, clearly showed how much progress had been achieved. Almost all the outstanding issues, in particular the origin of contamination, had been resolved. Thus, Iran believed that there was no justification to keep the issue on the Board's agenda. All safeguards activities in Iran would hopefully soon be implemented in a routine manner.

168. Despite the unjustified resolution adopted by the Board on 24 September, Iran had continued cooperating in good faith with the Agency…

169. Following the smoke created at the previous Board meeting, Iran had made a concerted effort with regard to its cooperation with the Agency. The Director General's report was crystal clear in that regard…

170. Yet despite all that cooperation, a certain State continued to make allegations undermining the achievements of the Agency. He noted that it had become standard practice for the United States of America and terrorist groups supported by it, to fabricate false allegations against Iran immediately prior to Board meetings in order to divert attention away from the considerable progress made…

171. With regard to the issue of the uranium metal hemispheres, he pointed out that the one-and-a-half page document concerned contained simple, unsophisticated information

that could be found in the open literature and on the internet. Furthermore, the information it contained regarding the reduction of uranium hexafluoride to metal was incomprehensible and incomplete compared with the thorough and well-elaborated information and drawings available at the Esfahan Uranium Conversion Facility. The fact that Iran had submitted all documents received from an intermediary to the Agency was a clear indication of its good intentions and full transparency. Such a minor issue should not be allowed to stand in the way of the tremendous progress made thus far. He expressed the conviction that, once the issue had been assessed and a conclusion reached by the Agency, the accuracy and correctness of the information Iran had provided would be vindicated.

...

173. It had always been Iran's intention to make every effort to achieve a negotiated resumption of its enrichment activities. In his address to the General Assembly on 17 September 2005,[359] the President of Iran had made yet another far-reaching guarantee offer by inviting other countries to take part in Iran's enrichment programme. That was the greatest transparency and confidence-building measure ever offered in that regard by a State. In that respect, his delegation appreciated all initiatives by other Member States aimed at facilitating the speedy conclusion of the Iranian nuclear issue in the Agency.

174. With regard to Iran's talks with France, Germany and the United Kingdom, he reiterated that his country had never walked out of negotiations. On the contrary, Iran welcomed consultations with others with a view to facilitating the Agency's work and called on the three European countries to desist from confrontation and instead negotiate in order to reach understanding and agreement. It was his delegation's hope that the Board's present discussions would contribute to an atmosphere conducive to prompt resolution of the issue and further implementation of safeguards in a routine manner.

The Chairman summarized the discussion.[360]

Document 81: GOV/OR.1147

25 November 2005

...

55. Mr. ALOBIDI (**Libyan Arab Jamahiriya**)...

...

57. The Director General's report on implementation of the NPT safeguards agreement in the Islamic Republic of Iran, contained in document GOV/2005/87,[361] indicated that there had been increased cooperation between that country and the Agency but also that outstanding issues needed to be followed up by the Agency, meaning more time was needed for it to complete its work. Those responsible for Iran's nuclear programmes should show more cooperation and transparency in their dealings with the Agency. More steps should be taken to build confidence with both the Agency and the international community.

58. While acknowledging the concerns of some States about the spread of nuclear weapons and the possibility of their falling into irresponsible hands, endangering innocent civilians, he called upon such States not to adopt a double standard, dealing with certain

[359] Doc. 110.
[360] Doc. 31.
[361] Doc. 41.

countries and closing their eyes in respect of others. The Middle East region was a case in point.

59. The relationship between Iran on the one hand and the Agency and the Western countries on the other resembled his country's experience with the Agency and Western States, particularly the United States and the United Kingdom. Doubts and accusations had been the hallmark of that relationship, but steps to build confidence and transparency had ultimately led to an understanding and the voluntary adoption by his country of its decision of 19 December 2003. No threats or blackmail regarding referral of the issue to the Security Council had taken place. Dialogue and transparency had been the sole means of dispersing doubts and fostering equitable relations between Libya and the Agency and Western countries. Accordingly, his country supported dialogue between Iran, the European Union and the Agency, which would open the way for building confidence and reaching agreement on securing for Iran the use of the atom for peaceful purposes. It would likewise dissipate the doubts of the Agency and Member States regarding Iran's nuclear intentions.

…

62. Mr. MINTY (**South Africa**) said that his delegation had noted with concern the statement by the Ambassador of the United Kingdom with regard to the implementation of the NPT safeguards agreement in the Islamic Republic of Iran, in which he had suggested that documents which Iran had provided to the Agency on the casting and machining of enriched, natural and depleted uranium metal into hemispherical forms should be handed over to the five nuclear-weapon States for further study and consideration. South Africa cautioned that the Agency should not give special status to the five nuclear-weapon States which, pursuant to the NPT, should have destroyed their nuclear arsenals. Moreover, the Board was not an NPT structure.

Document 82: Consideration of GOV/2006/11 and 12, GOV/INF/2006/1 and 2, INFCIRC/662 and 665

GOV/OR.1148, 2 February 2006

…

4. The CHAIRMAN said that members had received in writing an update brief dated 31 January 2006 from the Deputy Director General for Safeguards and had been given the opportunity the previous day to obtain clarification from him on any technical issues arising.

5. The DEPUTY DIRECTOR GENERAL FOR SAFEGUARDS said the purpose of the update brief was to provide an update on the developments that had taken place since November 2005 in connection with the implementation of the NPT safeguards agreement in the Islamic Republic of Iran and on the Agency's verification of Iran's voluntary suspension of enrichment-related and reprocessing activities. The brief provided factual information concerning those developments; it did not include any assessments thereof.

6. Iran had continued to facilitate access under its safeguards agreement as requested by the Agency and to act as if the additional protocol were in force, including by providing in a timely manner the requisite declarations and access to locations.

7. As detailed in the Director General's report of 18 November 2005, contained in document GOV/2005/87,[362] during meetings that had taken place in October and November 2005, the Agency had requested Iran to provide additional information on certain aspects of its enrichment programme Responses to some of those requests had been provided during discussions held in Tehran from 25 to 29 January 2006 between Iranian officials and an Agency team headed by himself. That information was currently being assessed.

8. As part of its assessment of the correctness and completeness of Iran's declarations concerning its enrichment activities, the Agency was continuing to investigate the source(s) of LEU particles, and some HEU particles, which had been found at locations where Iran had declared that centrifuge components had been manufactured, used and/or stored.

9. As previously reported to the Board, Iran had shown the Agency in January 2005 a copy of a hand-written one-page document reflecting an offer said to have been made to Iran in 1987 by a foreign intermediary concerning the possible supply of a disassembled centrifuge (including drawings, descriptions and specifications for the production of centrifuges); drawings, specifications and calculations for a "complete plant"; and materials for 2000 centrifuge machines. The document also made reference to: auxiliary vacuum and electric drive equipment; a liquid nitrogen plant; a water treatment and purification plant; a complete set of workshop equipment for mechanical, electrical and electronic support; and uranium reconversion and casting capabilities.

10. On 25 January 2006, Iran had reiterated that the one-page document was the only remaining documentary evidence relevant to the scope and content of the 1987 offer, attributing that to the secret nature of the programme and the management style of the AEOI at that time.

11. Iran had stated that no other written evidence existed, such as meeting minutes, administrative documents, reports, personal notebooks or the like, to substantiate its statements concerning that offer.

12. According to Iran, there had been no contacts with the network between 1987 and mid-1993. Statements made by Iran and by key members of the network about the events leading to the mid-1990s offer were still at variance with each other. In that context, Iran had been asked to provide further clarification of the timing and purpose of certain trips taken by AEOI staff members in the mid-1990s.

13. Iran had been unable to supply any documentation or other information about the meetings that had led to the acquisition of 500 sets of P-1 centrifuge components in the mid-1990s. The Agency was still awaiting clarification of the dates and contents of those shipments.

14. Iran still maintained that, as a result of the discussions held with the intermediaries in the mid-1990s, the intermediaries had supplied only drawings for P-2 centrifuge components (which contained no supporting specifications), and that no P-2 components had been delivered along with the drawings or thereafter. Iran continued to assert that no work had been carried out on P-2 centrifuges during the period 1995 to 2002, and that at no time during that period had it ever discussed with the intermediaries the P-2 centrifuge design, or the possible supply of P-2 centrifuge components. In light of information available to the Agency indicating the possible deliveries of such components, which information had been shared with Iran, Iran had been asked in November 2005 to check again whether any deliveries had been made after 1995.

---

[362] Doc. 41.

15. In connection with the R&D work on a modified P-2 design said by Iran to have been carried out by a contracting company between 2002 and July 2003, Iran had confirmed that the contractor had made enquiries about, and purchased, magnets suitable for the P-2 centrifuge design. The Agency was still awaiting clarification of all of Iran's efforts to acquire such magnets.

16. Iran had shown the Agency more than 60 documents said to have been the drawings, specifications and supporting documentation handed over by the intermediaries, many of which were dated from the early- to mid-1980s. Among those was a 15-page document describing the procedures to metal in small quantities, and the casting of enriched and depleted uranium for the reduction of UF_6 metal into hemispheres, related to the fabrication of nuclear weapon components. It did not, however, include dimensions or other specifications for machined pieces for such components. According to Iran, the document had been provided on the initiative of the network and not at the request of the AEOI. Iran had declined the Agency's request to provide the Agency with a copy of the document, but had permitted the Agency during its visit in January 2006 to examine the document again and to place it under Agency seal.

17. On 1 November 2005, the Agency had been given access to a military site at Parchin with a view to providing assurances regarding the absence of undeclared nuclear material and activities at that site, where several environmental samples had been taken. Final assessment was still pending the results of the analysis of those samples.

18. Since 2004, the Agency had been awaiting additional information and clarifications related to efforts made by the PHRC, which had been established at Lavisan-Shian, to acquire dual-use materials and equipment that could be used in uranium enrichment and conversion activities. The Agency had also requested interviews with the individuals involved in the acquisition of those items. According to Iran, the PHRC had been established in 1989, inter alia, to support and provide scientific advice and services to the Ministry of Defence.

19. On 26 January 2006, Iran had presented to the Agency documentation the Agency had previously requested on efforts by Iran, which it had stated had been unsuccessful, to acquire a number of specific dual-use items (electric drive equipment, power supply equipment and laser equipment, including a dye laser). Iran had stated that, although the documentation suggested the involvement of the PHRC, the equipment had actually been intended for a laboratory at a technical university where the Head of the PHRC worked as a professor. However, Iran had declined to make him available to the Agency for an interview. The Deputy Director General for Safeguards had reiterated the Agency's request to interview the professor, explaining that it was essential for a better understanding of the envisioned and actual use of the equipment, which included balancing machines, mass spectrometers, magnets and fluorine handling equipment (equipment that appeared to be relevant to uranium enrichment).

20. On that same day, the Agency had also presented to Iran a list of high vacuum equipment purchased by the PHRC, and had asked to see, and to take environmental samples from, the equipment in situ. The following day, some of the high vacuum equipment on the Agency's list had been presented at a technical university, and environmental samples had been taken from it.

21. On 26 January 2006, Iran had provided additional clarification about its efforts in 2000 to procure some other dual-use material (high-strength aluminium, special steel, titanium and special oils), as had been discussed in January 2005. High-strength aluminium had been presented to the Agency, and environmental samples had been taken therefrom. Iran had stated that the material had been acquired for aircraft manufacturing, but had not been

used because of its specifications. Iran had agreed to provide additional information on inquiries concerning the purchase of special steels, titanium and special oils. Iran had also presented information on Iran's acquisition of corrosion-resistant steel, valves and filters, which had been made available to the Agency on 31 January 2006 for environmental sampling.

22. On 5 December 2005, the Agency had reiterated its request for a meeting to discuss information that had been made available to the Agency about alleged undeclared studies, known as the Green Salt Project, concerning the conversion of uranium dioxide into UF_4 ('green salt'), as well as tests related to high explosives and the design of a missile re-entry vehicle, all of which could have a military nuclear dimension and which appeared to have administrative interconnections. On 16 December 2005, Iran had replied that the "issues related to baseless allegations." Iran had agreed on 23 January 2006 to a meeting with him for the clarification of the Green Salt Project, but had declined to address the other topics during that meeting. In the course of the meeting, which had taken place on 27 January 2006, the Agency had presented for Iran's review a copy of a process flow diagram related to bench-scale conversion and communications with respect to the project. Iran had reiterated that all national nuclear projects were conducted by the AEOI, that the allegations were baseless and that it would provide further clarifications later.

23. The Agency had continued to verify and monitor all elements of Iran's voluntary suspension of enrichment-related and reprocessing activities.

24. In a letter dated 3 January 2006, Iran had informed the Agency that it had decided to resume, as from 9 January 2006, the R&D on the peaceful nuclear energy programme which had been suspended as part of its expanded voluntary and non-legally binding suspension (reported in document GOV/INF/2006/1). On 7 January 2006, the Agency had received a letter from Iran requesting that the Agency remove seals applied at Natanz, Farayand Technique and Pars Trash for the monitoring of suspension of enrichment-related activities (reported in document GOV/INF/2006/2). The seals had been removed by Iran on 10 and 11 January 2006 in the presence of Agency inspectors.

25. Since the removal of the seals, Iran had started what it referred to as "small-scale R&D". As of 30 January 2006, Agency inspectors had not seen any new installation or assembly of centrifuges, or the feeding of UF_6 material for enrichment. However, substantial renovation of the gas handling system was underway at the PFEP at Natanz, and quality control of components and some rotor testing was being conducted at Farayand Technique and Natanz. Owing to the fact that all centrifuge-related raw materials and components were without Agency seals, the Agency's supervision of the R&D activities being carried out by Iran could not be effective except at PFEP, where containment and surveillance measures were being applied for the enrichment process. The two cylinders at Natanz containing UF_6, from which seals had been removed on 10 January 2006, had been again placed under Agency containment and surveillance on 29 January 2006.

26. The uranium conversion campaign which had commenced at the UCF in Esfahan on 16 November 2005 was continuing and was expected to end in March 2006. All UF produced at the 6 UCF thus far had remained under Agency containment and surveillance.

27. Using satellite imagery, the Agency had continued to monitor the ongoing civil engineering construction of the Iran Nuclear Research Reactor (IR-40) at Arak.

28. Mr. HONSOWITZ (**Germany**), **speaking on behalf of the European countries**...

...

31. In early August 2005, Iran had been offered an ambitious proposal for cooperation with Europe in the political, security and economic fields.[363] That proposal had reaffirmed Iran's rights under the NPT and had included European support for a civilian nuclear programme in Iran as well as proposals for internationally guaranteed supplies of fuel for Iran's nuclear power programme. That offer had been brusquely rejected before it had been handed over. Even before rejecting the offer, Iran had resumed uranium conversion at Esfahan despite repeated requests by the Board for it not to do so. That had been a clear violation of Board resolutions and the commitments that Iran had made in the November 2004 Paris agreement.[364] However, responding to requests by Board members, France, Germany and the United Kingdom had been ready to go the extra mile in search of a negotiated solution. To that end, they had met an Iranian delegation for exploratory talks on 21 December 2005 to see if a basis could be found for resuming negotiations. At that meeting the Europeans had made it clear that a resumption of negotiations would be possible only if Iran refrained from any further erosion of its suspension commitment. A further exploratory meeting on 18 January 2006 had been agreed on.

32. On 3 January 2006, however, Iran had written to the Director General informing him that it would resume enrichment-related activities. That decision, announced prior to the meeting foreseen for 18 January 2006, was a further clear rejection of the diplomatic process which had been launched by France, Germany and the United Kingdom and supported by the international community. It also constituted a further challenge to the authority of the Agency and the non-proliferation regime. In the face of that challenge, the Foreign Ministers of the three European countries and the High Representative of the European Union had met in Berlin on 12 January 2006 and decided to inform the Board that their discussions with Iran had reached an impasse.[365]

33. France, Germany and the United Kingdom continued to be committed to resolving the issue diplomatically. Over the preceding weeks, they had conducted a very broad range of consultations at the highest levels. Those consultations had revealed that their concerns about the nature of the Iranian nuclear programme were widely shared. The consultations had involved all five permanent members of the Security Council and had led to a ministerial meeting in London on 30 January 2006.[366]

34. He emphasized that the existing situation was not a dispute between Iran and Europe, but an issue between Iran and the entire international community represented in the Board. It was not a dispute about Iran's rights under the NPT, which had always been respected and reconfirmed, but about Iran's need to build the necessary confidence in the exclusively peaceful nature of its nuclear programme, in line with its NPT obligations. Nor was it about the Agency transferring responsibility to the Security Council. Rather it was about the credibility of the NPT, the strengthening of the international non-proliferation regime and the authority of the Agency and its decisions. It was not about abandoning diplomatic efforts, but solving a problem within the multilateral system and by peaceful means. The diplomatic endeavours had now entered a new stage; the time had come for the Security Council to become involved in order to reinforce the authority of the Agency's resolutions. Now was not the time for Iranian threats unilaterally to end cooperation with the Agency. Nor was it the time for Iran to further undermine confidence in its intentions.

---

[363] Doc. 126.
[364] Doc. 8.
[365] Doc. 128.
[366] Doc. 129.

What was needed now was for Iran to address the existing international concerns and respect the Board's decisions.

...

36. Mr. BERDENNIKOV (**Russian Federation**) said...

...

38. It was important for the Board to reaffirm its call to Iran to resume a moratorium on all enrichment-related activities, to ratify its additional protocol and continue to implement it until that time, to reconsider its decision to construct a heavy water reactor, and to cooperate in a fully transparent manner with the Agency. Russia was not against a report to the Security Council about the work that the Agency had carried out with regard to Iran and the steps required by Iran to rectify the situation. The Board was not yet asking the Security Council to take any action and was assuming that work on the Iranian issue would continue within the framework of the Agency. He reiterated Russia's deep concern at Iran's decision to resume uranium enrichment R&D which, in its view, seriously exacerbated the situation. The Board would be sending Iran a serious signal about the need to take urgent measures to dispel the tensions surrounding its nuclear programme.

39. Underlining that Russia was ready to cooperate constructively with all interested parties to resolve the matter, he drew attention to the initiative put forward by President Putin at the meeting of the Eurasian Economic Community in St. Petersburg on 25 January 2006, namely to create a network of international centres to provide nuclear fuel cycle services, including uranium enrichment, under Agency control and on the basis of non-discriminatory access. One way of implementing that initiative would be to act on Russia's earlier proposal to Iran and set up a joint Russian-Iranian enterprise for uranium enrichment on Russian territory. That would ensure that Iran's legitimate nuclear energy requirements were met for years to come whilst maintaining the moratorium on all enrichment-related activities.

...

41. Ms. GERVAIS-VIDRICAIRE (**Canada**) said...

...

43. At its current meeting, the Board should focus not on the aforementioned issues, rather on the much more fundamental issue of the credibility deficit that Iran had created for itself and the lack of confidence in the scope and nature of its nuclear programme that that deficit had produced. The Agency had been investigating Iran's nuclear programme for nearly three years, during which time it had uncovered numerous undeclared nuclear sites and activities. Iran's past failures to declare fully its nuclear facilities had been termed a policy of concealment by the Director General. The Board had recognized those failures but had not reported Iran to the Security Council, as required by the Agency's Statute. Instead, it had offered Iran an opportunity to rebuild its credibility through negotiations with France, Germany and the United Kingdom and through full and transparent cooperation with the Agency. Those negotiations had been premised on a set of confidence-building measures, one of which was the full suspension of all enrichment-related activities, including conversion and R&D.

44. On 10 January 2006 Iran had made a choice when, with discussions with the three European countries scheduled to resume only eight days later, it had unilaterally decided to resume enrichment-related R&D and had broken the seals on equipment and materials at three sites associated with its centrifuge enrichment programme. Through its own decisions and actions, Iran had driven the discussions with France, Germany and the

United Kingdom into an impasse. That had been only the last in a series of steps by which Iran had progressively eroded its commitments.

45. In breaking its voluntary suspension on enrichment-related activities, Iran had made recourse to the argument that, according to Article IV of the NPT, it had the right to the peaceful use of nuclear energy. Nobody had denied Iran that right; the negotiated suspension had in no way inhibited Iran's ability to have a civil nuclear programme. However, the rights laid down in Article IV must be seen in the context of obligations. In view of the confidence deficit created by Iran through its many past failures to meet its safeguards obligations as embodied in Article III of the NPT, Canada urged Iran to heed the Board's repeated calls and desist from the most sensitive parts of the fuel cycle until the trust of the Board, and the world, was fully regained.

46. Now that the talks between the three European countries and Iran were at an impasse — an impasse of Iran's own making — the Board must again consider how to address the collective lack of confidence about Iran's nuclear programme. France, Germany and the United Kingdom, together with China, Russia and the United States of America, had agreed on a draft resolution requesting the Director General to report to the Security Council. Canada fully backed such a report. It was time for the Security Council to be brought to bear on the issue. Over the preceding years, Iran had played a game of incremental brinkmanship and had continually pushed ahead with its nuclear programme. A report to the Security Council should not end efforts to resolve the Iran nuclear issue diplomatically, nor should it take the issue away from the Agency. The Agency would continue to play a fundamental role in providing clarity with regard to all outstanding issues. A report to the Security Council would, however, ensure that the forum responsible for international peace and security put its weight behind the Board's resolutions and the Director General's requests in support of a comprehensive and durable diplomatic solution. While Iran's credibility ultimately had to be rebuilt through its interaction with the Agency, the rebuilding process would need to go above and beyond Iran's comprehensive safeguards agreement and additional protocol, which had yet to be ratified. That process would need to include, among other things, the cooperation and transparency measures requested by the Director General in his report of 2 September 2005, contained in document GOV/2005/67.[367] Since Iran had been given every opportunity to take those measures on a voluntary basis, and since at every opportunity it had decided not to, the Board was left with little choice but to report the matter to the Security Council.

47. Mr. WU Hailong (**China**) said...

...

50. China hoped that Iran would resume the suspension of its research on nuclear fuel and other relevant activities and also that it would resume promptly its negotiations with the three European countries. China urged the other parties concerned to remain calm and to exercise restraint, patience and flexibility. That would avoid exacerbating the situation and help to create the necessary atmosphere and conditions for a resumption of negotiations between the three European countries and Iran.

...

52. Mr. SCHULTE (**United States of America**) said that, at their recent meeting in London, the Foreign Ministers of the United States, France, Germany, the United Kingdom, China and Russia and the High Representative of the European Union had issued an important statement noting their serious concerns about Iran's nuclear programme and

---

[367] Doc. 40.

calling on Iran to restore confidence. The Ministers had reaffirmed that it was time for the Agency to report Iran to the Security Council. They had not reached that decision in haste, but after a careful review of Iran's troubling history in pursuing its nuclear ambitions. He reiterated Secretary of State Rice's statement at that meeting to the effect that the international community had come together to say to the Iranians that they needed to find a way to have peaceful nuclear energy, if that was what they desired, but in a way that removed the proliferation risk associated with the current Iranian course.

...

57. The Board of Governors had adopted eight resolutions on Iran since 2003, all of which Iran had ignored or defied. It was time to send a clear and unequivocal message to the Iranian regime about the international community's concerns by reporting the issue to the Security Council. He urged the members of the Board to adopt the resolution tabled by France, Germany and the United Kingdom. The time had come to fulfil the Board's obligation under Article XII.C and report its finding of Iran's non-compliance given in the resolution adopted on 24 September 2005 (document GOV/2005/77).[368]

58. His Government continued to support all efforts to seek a peaceful, diplomatic solution. Reporting the Iran issue to the Security Council would serve to increase the diplomatic tools available to the international community. He stated clearly that the United States was not seeking sanctions or other punitive measures on Iran nor did it seek to harm the Iranian people or deprive Iran of its rights to nuclear energy for peaceful purposes. Nor was the United States seeking to remove the issue from the Board's active consideration. Instead, it was seeking support for the ongoing efforts of the Agency in the form of the weight of the Security Council's authority. The United States was seeking a carefully calibrated approach whereby the Security Council applied escalating measures on Iran in the hope that such an approach might persuade the Iranian leadership to change course.

59. As a first step when the Security Council began to consider the issue in March, the United States expected it to reinforce the decisions of the Board and to strengthen the Agency's continuing role by calling on Iran to cooperate with the Agency, to comply fully and promptly with all Agency Board resolutions and to provide the Agency with the transparency measures it had repeatedly requested.

...

61. Ms. HUSSAIN (**Malaysia**), **speaking on behalf of NAM**, stated that it was the Movement's understanding that the aim of the current Board meeting was not to consider or assess the overall implementation of the NPT safeguards agreement in Iran, which was to be considered at the regular session of the Board beginning on 6 March 2006. Nor was it to consider the timing and content of a report by the Director General in accordance with operative paragraph 3 of the Board's resolution of 24 September 2005, contained in document GOV/2005/77. That would be premature as the Director General was still investigating outstanding issues in preparation for the Board's March meeting.

62. Reaffirming NAM's basic position, she underlined the basic and inalienable right of all Member States, as stipulated in the Statute, to develop research, production and use of atomic energy for peaceful purposes without discrimination and in conformity with their respective legal obligations. Nothing should be interpreted in a way that would inhibit or restrict that right. NAM also reaffirmed the need to respect Member States' choices and decisions in the field of the peaceful uses of nuclear technology and regarding their fuel cycle policies.

...

---

[368] Doc. 30.

64. It was essential to make a clear distinction between the legal obligations of Member States under their respective safeguards agreements and their voluntary commitments. Moreover, their voluntary commitments not [*sic*] be turned into legal safeguards obligations. Member States should not be penalized for not adhering to their voluntary commitments.

65. NAM recognized the Agency as the sole competent authority for verification and had full confidence in its professionalism and impartiality under Dr. ElBaradei's leadership. All Member States should avoid any undue pressure or interference in the Agency's activities, especially its verification process, which would jeopardize its efficiency and credibility. All issues relating to safeguards and verification, including those of Iran, should be resolved within the framework of the Agency and should be based on technical grounds.

...

69. Further, NAM welcomed the cooperation extended by Iran to the Agency over and above its legal obligations, particularly such confidence-building measures voluntarily taken by Iran as the provision of access to military sites and the provisional implementation of the additional protocol. They clearly demonstrated openness and transparency. Any voluntary suspension should end once the appropriate requirements had been met.

70. Any request for additional legal authority for the Agency had to be negotiated by the Member States. In that context, NAM reiterated the importance of the promotion and strengthening of the multilateral process.

...

72. The Foreign Ministers of the NAM troika, namely Malaysia, Cuba and South Africa, had met with their Iranian counterpart in Hermanus, South Africa on 27 January 2006. After the meeting, the Ministers of the NAM troika had reiterated their continuing support for the Agency's ongoing work in clarifying issues relating to Iran's nuclear programme. They had underscored the importance of the ongoing cooperation between Iran and the Agency to that end and urged all the parties concerned to exhaust all efforts, through dialogue and negotiations, to resolve those issues as soon as possible and in an amicable manner. They welcomed Iran's intention to continue negotiations with the three European countries, as well as with the Russian Federation with respect to the latter's proposal on uranium enrichment, and hoped that those negotiations would contribute to achieving a satisfactory solution. She expressed NAM's appreciation of all initiatives by other Member States aimed at encouraging an environment of cooperation and facilitating the speedy conclusion of the issue in the Agency.

73. Finally, NAM urged that a balanced and even-handed approach be taken on the Iranian nuclear issue to avoid any perception of selectivity or bias. Reiterating NAM's support for the establishment in the Middle East of a zone free of all weapons of mass destruction, she said the Movement attached great importance to the implementation of the various resolutions and decisions taken by relevant international forums on the establishment of a nuclear-weapon-free zone in the Middle East.

74. Mr. STELZER (**Austria**) spoke **on behalf of the EU**...

75. The EU also deeply regretted that, despite repeated calls from the Board to maintain the suspension of all enrichment-related and reprocessing activities which the Board had declared essential to addressing outstanding issues, Iran had resumed uranium conversion activities at its Esfahan facility on 8 August 2005 and had taken steps to resume enrichment activities on 10 January 2006.

76. On 30 January 2006, the EU Foreign Ministers had agreed on a number of conclusions on Iran: Firstly, the EU was gravely concerned at the removal of seals at

several nuclear installations, including Natanz, and at Iran's decision to resume enrichment-related activities. It called on Iran to reinstate the seals and re-establish full, sustained and verifiable suspension of all enrichment-related and reprocessing activities as had been called for repeatedly in Board resolutions as an essential confidence-building measure. The EU emphasized the need for Iran to refrain from all such activities until international confidence was restored.

77. Secondly, the dispute was not between Iran and Europe, but between Iran and the international community. The EU did not question Iran's right to use nuclear energy for peaceful purposes in conformity with its obligations under the NPT, a right which it had consistently reaffirmed. The dispute was about Iran's failure to build the necessary confidence as to the exclusively peaceful nature of its programme. That confidence had further eroded as a result of the unilateral steps Iran had taken contrary to its commitments. The Council of the European Union had noted with concern that the Director General had reported that the Agency was not yet in a position to clarify some important issues after two and a half years of intensive inspections and investigation and that Iran's full transparency was indispensable and overdue.

78. Thirdly, in the light of recent Iranian actions, which ran counter to Agency resolutions and were a rejection of the efforts to explore whether a basis could be agreed for resuming negotiations, the EU Member States had concluded that they would work in close coordination to prepare for the forthcoming extraordinary meeting of the Agency Board with a view to involving the Security Council so as to reinforce the Agency's authority in line with the EU conclusions. That step was necessary, appropriate and fully in line with the Board's resolution of September 2005, which had found Iran in non-compliance with its safeguards agreement and that Iran's history of concealment of its nuclear activities and the nature of those activities had given rise to questions within the competence of the Security Council.

79. Fourthly, the EU had reiterated its belief that the issue could still be solved by negotiations. However, that would require a cooperative and transparent approach on the part of the Iranian Government with the Agency and the return to full suspension. The EU remained committed to a diplomatic solution to the Iranian nuclear issue in which the Agency should play a central role. Involvement of the Security Council did not end the Agency's responsibilities; on the contrary, it strengthened them.

...

81. Finally, the Council of the European Union had recalled in that context its support for the establishment of a zone free of weapons of mass destruction in the Middle East, including their means of delivery. The Council had also recalled that in its conclusions of 7 November 2005 it had repeated that the evolution of its long-term relationship with Iran would depend on action by Iran to address effectively all of the EU's areas of concern. The Council regarded Iran's resumption of enrichment-related activities as a negative development that would impact on the overall relationship, which it would review in the light of actions taken by Iran. The Council had reiterated that it was up to Iran to determine, through its own actions, whether its long-term relationship with the EU would improve or deteriorate.

...

83. The EU fully supported the draft resolution on the implementation of the NPT safeguards agreement in the Islamic Republic of Iran, contained in document GOV/2006/12, submitted by France, Germany and the United Kingdom.

84. Mr. AAS (**Norway**)...

...

88. Norway favoured a political and diplomatic solution in which the Agency played a key role. To that end, the Agency's authority needed to be further strengthened. Accordingly, Norway would support a decision to report to the Security Council the Board's decisions regarding the steps Iran was required to take. That would send a clear and constructive message yet at the same time leave the door open for a political solution. He emphasized that informing the Security Council did not mean it was being requested it to take any action. The matter remained in Vienna and a new basis for a diplomatic solution should be found within the framework of the Agency.

...

92. Ms. STOKES (**Australia**)...

...

95. The update brief by the Deputy Director General for Safeguards had informed the Board for the first time of possible undeclared work by Iran known as the Green Salt Project, involving the conversion of uranium dioxide into UF_4. The Agency had asked Iran about that project and about tests related to high explosives and the design of a missile re-entry vehicle, all of which could have a military nuclear dimension and which appeared to have had administrative interconnections. That information, as well as Iran's possession of a document related to the fabrication of nuclear weapons components and the fact that Iran had declined to provide the Agency with a copy of that document, was troubling. Iran's responses to the Agency's questions were unsatisfactory. The update brief confirmed that the Agency was far from resolving outstanding issues and that Iran's cooperation continued to be inadequate.

96. Recalling the Board's 24 September 2005 resolution, which had found Iran to be in non-compliance in the context of Article XII.C. of the Statute, when the Board had decided to address at a later stage the timing and content of the report required under the Statute, Australia considered that the time had now come to report the matter to the Security Council. That would not mean an end to diplomacy. The Statute recognized, however, that the Security Council had a role to play in reinforcing the Agency and its Board of Governors.

...

107. Mr. CARRERA DORAL (**Cuba**) said that developing countries had a recognized right to produce nuclear energy for peaceful purposes under the appropriate safeguards and to carry out all nuclear fuel cycle activities. The NPT was already deeply discriminatory and served to protect the interests of the 'nuclear club'. It was unacceptable that, through arbitrary interpretation of the text not in keeping with the letter and spirit of the Treaty, new elements were being added that discriminated against the developing countries. The Board of Governors must oppose resolutely any attempt by some nuclear powers to limit, for political motivations, the right of the non-nuclear-weapon States to carry out nuclear fuel cycle activities.

108. The nuclear powers that had instigated the current debate were the very same countries that dedicated huge resources daily to improving their large arsenals of nuclear missiles and warheads and making them more deadly, that were flagrantly reneging on their nuclear disarmament obligations and that had recently caused the failure of the NPT Review Conference.

...

110. The Board did not yet have before it a report on the implementation of the NPT safeguards agreement in the Islamic Republic of Iran. That would be made available at the March Board. The current meeting had been convened, like the Board meetings in August 2005, at the request of a group of Member States to analyse alleged failures by Iran to comply with its safeguards agreement. As on that occasion, the meeting had been preceded by a brutal campaign to manipulate public opinion by the transnational media, which served the interests of the very same governments that had instigated consideration of the issue. The matter under discussion was not alleged breaches, which no delegation had been able to substantiate. It was the Iranian Government's sovereign decision to continue its programme to develop nuclear energy for peaceful purposes and to resume the activities that it had voluntarily decided to suspend in 2003 as a confidence-building measure to facilitate the negotiation process which was then under way. Iran had every right to resume its nuclear activities for peaceful purposes, which the Iranian Government had declared would be under strict Agency safeguards.

111. It was being said, on the basis of a selective and tendentious textual interpretation, that under no circumstances should Iran be permitted to undertake nuclear fuel cycle activities, including uranium enrichment even if only for reasons of R&D, because of suspicions that those activities were being pursued for non-peaceful purposes. What was not being said, however, was that for purely political reasons the main suppliers of nuclear technology, the very same countries that had now become fervent accusers, had denied Iran access to that technology, in violation of the NPT.

112. The Agency could not act on the basis of suspicions, but only on concrete and objective facts. In the many reports on the subject provided by the Secretariat, which was the only entity qualified and authorized to do so, there was no evidence or assertion that Iran's nuclear programme was of a non-peaceful nature. Certain facts noted by the Director General in his reports had been deliberately disregarded. They included: the substantial progress made in clarifying the nature of Iran's nuclear programme and the significant decrease in outstanding issues; Iran's increasing cooperation with the Agency; and, Iran's compliance with its obligations under its safeguards agreement, the verification of all declared materials and the confirmation that those were not being diverted to illicit activities. Iran could not be forbidden from undertaking activities of a peaceful nature because of an alleged risk that they might be used for other purposes, when those activities were subject to strict Agency safeguards. Agency safeguards were the internationally recognized system for preventing the diversion of peaceful nuclear activities to military purposes. The acceptance of such treatment would not only set a very negative precedent in terms of international law, but also condemn countries to unacceptable subordination to the monopoly of the nuclear fuel-producing powers. The attempt to submit Iran's peaceful nuclear programme to the consideration of the Security Council was baseless and the shameful application of a double standard.

113. For those reasons and in line with the principles it had always upheld, Cuba strongly opposed any attempt use Iran's sovereign decision as another pretext to condemn that country and to refer the matter in any form whatsoever to the Security Council. If that happened, it would be impossible to prevent the United States and its allies from manipulating the facts in order to force the Security Council to adopt decisions that would jeopardize peace.

...

118. Mr. MÁRQUEZ MARÍN (**Bolivarian Republic of Venezuela**)...

...

122. In particular, Venezuela rejected the discriminatory and unequal way in which some tried to evaluate the performance of countries in the context of the NPT. On the one hand, they were trying to condemn Iran a priori without the evidence required under the safeguards regime and the legal provisions governing it. On the other, they endorsed the serious threat to humanity posed by the large and deadly arsenals of nuclear weapons possessed by the nuclear powers, some of which had moved very little in the direction of total disarmament — the great aspiration of all.

123. His delegation expressed its total disagreement with the proposal to take consideration of Iran's nuclear programme outside the Agency and refer it to the Security Council. Instead of helping to find a negotiated solution, that could lead to confrontation with unpredictable results. That was what had happened with respect to Iraq when the Agency's voice had been disregarded. Moreover, the proposal contravened the principles of legality and objectivity that should characterize the Agency's performance in fulfilling its mission.

124. Article XII.C of the Statute stated that the inspectors should report any non-compliance to the Director General who should transmit the report to the Board of Governors. The Board should report the non-compliance to all members and to the Security Council and General Assembly of the United Nations. Since the inspectors had not declared Iran's non-compliance, there was no legal basis upon which to apply that statutory provision.

125. Non-compliance with the safeguards agreement required proof that nuclear material was being diverted to non-peaceful purposes. The Agency had concluded that no diversion had taken place and had said that all nuclear material had been declared. It had also said that it was still not in a position to determine the presence or absence of other undeclared nuclear material or activities. The resumption of research activities had taken place in the presence and under the control of Agency inspectors, as the Deputy Director General for Safeguards had indicated in his update. Therefore, there was no objective justification for condemning Iran a priori and referring the matter to the Security Council.

...

137. Mr. WIBOWO (**Indonesia**) said...

...

142. In Indonesia's view, there was no need to rush into reporting the issue to the Security Council before the March Board as that could jeopardize the efforts towards those confidence-building measures. It was convinced that the best possible outcome of the current Board meeting would be a consensus to defer a final decision until that meeting. In doing so, the Board would forestall any prejudgements on the Director General's report to the March Board.

143. Consideration should also be given to the fact that any hasty decision to report Iran to the Security Council could further raise tensions in the troubled areas of the Middle East and Central Asia. It was advisable to avoid any unintended political complications in the Middle East and among Muslim countries with regard to the issue of Iran's nuclear programme.

144. A further point to bear in mind was that taking a tougher stance on Iran by bringing its dossier to the Security Council would only give a strong signal that the international community was taking a very discriminatory approach toward it.

Document 83: Consideration of GOV/2006/11 and 12, GOV/INF/2006/1 and 2, INFCIRC/662 and 665

GOV/OR.1149, 2 February 2006

...

26. Mr. SOLTANIEH (**Islamic Republic of Iran**)...

...

30. The facts underlying developments, particularly during the preceding three years, confirmed the exclusively peaceful nature of the Iranian nuclear programme and activities and its full cooperation with the international community. They also showed that the international community had been greatly misled by biased, politicized and exaggerated information. Iranian nuclear issues, which should have been dealt with in a purely technical manner within the framework of the Agency, had been politicized.

31. International developments had had a serious impact on Iranian nuclear policies and activities. They included the failure of the United Nations Conference for the Promotion of International Cooperation in the Peaceful Uses of Nuclear Energy in Geneva, after ten years of preparation, in 1987; the failure, in Vienna in 1987 after seven years of intense deliberations, of the Agency's Committee on Assurances of Supply, which had been entrusted to establish internationally recognized principles and legally binding instruments to assure sustainable nuclear supply; the failure of the United States either to meet its obligation under the contract made prior to 1979 to supply nuclear fuel for the 5 MW Tehran Research Reactor, which was under comprehensive Agency safeguards and produced radioisotopes for application in medicine, agriculture and industry, or to return the millions of dollars received for the fuel; and the fact that Iran, a 10% shareholder in the EURODIF enrichment company in France for three decades, had donated one billion dollars 30 years previously to help the company in times of financial crisis but had not received even a gram of the uranium produced in the factory to use in its research reactor and power plant.

32. Those developments proved that the promotional pillars of the Statute, particularly Article III, and the provisions of Article IV of the NPT were not being implemented. Considering also the continuous sanctions by certain States and countries and the lack of any international legally binding instrument for the assurance of nuclear supply, Iran had no choice but to depend on its own resources and manpower in order to exercise its inalienable right to use nuclear energy for peaceful purposes and be active in the nuclear cycle, particularly enrichment.

...

37. Iran was concerned and disappointed that despite increased cooperation on its part, with the taking of additional steps and transparency measures beyond its legal obligations, despite the application of more stringent safeguards and the resolution of more outstanding questions, the language of the resolutions tabled by the United States of America and the three European countries had become tougher. On the eve of Board meetings, the United States political campaign against Iran had been augmented with baseless allegations. It was disappointing that Iran's active cooperation in granting prompt access to military sites of direct relevance to national security had not been duly reflected in the reports to the Board and the public.

38. Taking into consideration the bitter past history of monopoly and sanctions and the lack of any international legally binding instrument for assurances of nuclear supply; the fact that Iran's suspension was a non-legally binding, confidence-building measure; the existence of scientifically well-justified and technically reliable mechanisms and sophisticated surveillance equipment in the Department of Safeguards capable of verifying declared enrichment activities and enrichment levels and of giving assurances that such activities were exclusively for peaceful purposes; and also the inalienable right of Member States to conduct R&D as stipulated in Article III of the Statute, there was no reason for Iran to sustain its voluntary suspension of R&D on enrichment. That only further deprived its scientists of their inalienable right to work on the nuclear fuel cycle with the aim of producing the fuels it required for its research reactors and nuclear power plants. Additional comprehensive information in that regard could be found in the communications from the Permanent Mission of the Islamic Republic of Iran to the Agency, contained in documents INFCIRC/657 and INFCIRC/665.

39. After more than two and a half years of voluntary suspension, with the triggering issue of contamination having been resolved, the Iranian Government had no reason to further deprive its nation of its inalienable right to research. Thus, on 3 January 2006, the Agency had been informed that Iran would resume R&D on 10 January 2006 and had been asked to conduct timely and necessary preparations. Iran had reiterated that such activities would be conducted in accordance with its safeguards agreement and that they were on a small scale and not planned for nuclear fuel production. However, its suspension of commercial-scale enrichment, begun in 2003, would continue.

40. By way of clarification regarding comments made during the meeting, he noted that the proposal made by France, Germany and the United Kingdom in August 2005[369] had explicitly denied Iran its right to the nuclear fuel cycle, in contravention of the 2004 Paris agreement.[370] In June 2005 in Geneva, the Secretary of the Iranian Supreme National Security Council, Mr. Rohani, had informed the Foreign Ministers of the three European countries that if the European Union's proposal did not include the fuel cycle it would be rejected in advance. Thus, the negotiations based on the Paris agreement had been brought to a halt by the European Union, not by Iran. Since, according to the Paris agreement, suspension was linked to negotiation, Iran was no longer obliged to uphold the bilateral Paris agreement. Subsequently, Dr. Larijani, Mr. Rohani's successor, had taken a positive initiative and invited the three European countries to come back to the negotiating table. Iran had readiness to negotiate with all Member States, particularly France, Germany and the United Kingdom, in order to remove any ambiguities.[371]

...

44. Regarding the oft-used phrase 'non-compliance', he urged members of the Board to review carefully the texts of the Statute and of the safeguards agreement. Many of Iran's activities had been called concealment but, in accordance with its INFCIRC/153 comprehensive safeguards agreement,[372] Iran was obliged to inform the Agency only 180 days before nuclear materials were fed into facilities. Therefore, it had not been obliged to inform the Agency about the Uranium Conversion Facility at Esfahan or enrichment at Natanz. As stipulated in Article XII.C of the Statute, only inspectors having access to sites and confidential information and utilizing advanced surveillance systems would be in a

---

[369] Doc. 126.
[370] Doc. 8.
[371] Doc. 112.
[372] Doc. 4.

position to report non-compliance to the Director General, whereupon the Director General had a duty to transmit that report to the Board of Governors. The Director General had never used the term 'non-compliance'. He had used the term 'failure', but at the same time had reported that corrective measures had been taken.

45. He emphasized that the dispute was not between Iran and the international community. The NAM countries, comprising 100 Agency members, had consistently supported the inalienable right to the peaceful use of nuclear energy and expressed satisfaction with the progress made regarding cooperation between Iran and the Agency. The dispute was politically motivated and was being imposed on Iran, a developing country, by certain countries desirous of continuing their nuclear technology monopoly.

…

Document 84: Consideration of GOV/2006/12/Rev.1

GOV/OR.1150, 4 February 2006

…

4. Mr. MINTY (**South Africa**)…

…

13. It was important to recognize that the issue of Iran's nuclear programme was a unique and special case and any decisions adopted by the Board in that regard should not be viewed as a precedent for future cases. Iran's implementation of certain non-legally binding confidence-building measures was essential to address the outstanding issues. However, the voluntary measures undertaken by Iran should not be equated with the legally binding obligations stemming from Member States' safeguards agreements with the Agency.

…

23. Ms. FEROUKHI (**Algeria**) said that her country continued to support efforts to find a negotiated diplomatic solution within the Agency, which was the only competent international authority in the field of verification. However, it was aware that restoring the confidence which had to accompany Iran's resumption of its nuclear activities was a complex process that took time, involving both objective elements which were measurable and verifiable, and subjective elements based solely on good faith.

24. Referral to the Security Council was hasty and risky. It was hasty because the next series of Board meetings was scheduled for March 2006. That short amount of time could have been used to intensify efforts and facilitate a decision based on the Director General's report. It was risky because past and recent experience had shown that often the Security Council's moral authority had not led to favourable outcomes, in particular in difficult and complex cases. Therefore the Agency risked being exploited, which could damage its impartiality and objectivity and undermine the balance that had to be maintained in carrying out its three main activities: safety and security, verification and the promotion of atomic energy for peaceful purposes.

25. The Agency was at risk of increased politicization, to the detriment of the eminently technical nature of its role, particularly with regard to the promotion of the peaceful uses of atomic energy to accelerate socio-economic development. In that regard, she pointed out that Article IV of the NPT gave States Party the right to have access, without discrimination, to nuclear technology for exclusively peaceful purposes.

26. There was also the risk that Iran would end its cooperation with the Agency under the additional protocol, which it had been applying voluntarily although it was not yet ratified. That would reduce the effectiveness of the Agency's verification activities and, therefore, the multilateral verification system. It would also affect the significant progress that had been acknowledged in the cooperation with Iran as a result of which the Agency had been able to account for all declared nuclear material in Iran and state that it had not detected any new undeclared nuclear activities or diversion to non-peaceful purposes.

...

30. Mr. ZNIBER (**Morocco**)...

...

32. The politicization of some of the issues the Agency dealt with had a negative impact on technical cooperation, inter alia. International non-proliferation efforts would be insufficient if they were not backed up by progress in nuclear disarmament. The NPT was a complete and integrated text; compliance with it was expected of all and should result in permanent and sustainable disarmament. In that regard, there was a need to take pragmatic measures to create a nuclear-weapon-free zone in the Middle East and ensure that all nuclear facilities in the region were subject to safeguards.

...

41. Mr. CARON (**France**)...

42. Introducing the draft resolution contained in document GOV/2006/12/Rev.1, which had been submitted by the Governments of Germany, the United Kingdom and France, he noted that the text had been revised following two days of intense consultations in order to accommodate the comments and requests that had been expressed.

43. The text was in line with previous Board resolutions on the Iranian nuclear programme, specifically that of the preceding September, and reaffirmed the right of States which respected their international commitments to the peaceful uses of nuclear energy. It underscored the quality of the work carried out by the Director General and Secretariat and noted that the Director General had described the issue as a special verification case, which had been requested during consultations. The preamble also recalled the status of the case and Iran's many failures and breaches of its obligations, as well as the absence of confidence in the peaceful aim of the Iranian nuclear programme. Particular mention was made of the information requested by the Agency on activities which could have a military dimension. Finally, in line with the recent conclusions of the Ministers of Foreign Affairs of the European Union, a new paragraph had been included in the preamble pointing out that a solution to the Iranian nuclear file would contribute to the shared objective of freeing the Middle East of weapons of mass destruction.

44. In the operative part, the draft called on Iran to implement the confidence-building measures requested of it by the Board, which were needed to restore confidence. It asked the Director General to report on those requests to the Security Council as well on all previous reports and resolutions on the subject, in accordance with the Statute.

45. The paragraph relating to Iran's possession of a document on the production of uranium hemispheres had been amended to take account of the Deputy Director General's report and proposals from Board members.

46. Next, concern was expressed over the recent Iranian decisions to resume enrichment, which had aggravated the situation created by its resumption of conversion in August.

47. Operative paragraph 5 had been heavily reworked to accommodate requests put forward during consultations and, in particular, to recall the voluntary nature of the confidence-building measures.

48. There had been no requests to modify operative paragraph 6 which, together with the next paragraph, made it as clear as possible that the Agency continued to exercise fully its responsibilities and invited Iran to demonstrate full cooperation.

49. Operative paragraph 7 had been modified following consultations to underline the importance of pursuing the Agency's verification work in Iran.

50. Operative paragraph 8 requested the Director General to report to the Board in March and to transmit that report subsequently to the Security Council. Its formulation had been changed following consultations in order to reaffirm the Board's competence.

51. The resolution offered Iran the possibility to influence the report to be presented by the Director General in March. Extensive consultations had been held in the preceding weeks in Member States' capitals and the draft, by and large, took account of the recommendations which had been made.

52. He expressed the hope that the Board would approve the resolution, which demonstrated the desire to reach a negotiated solution while respecting the multilateral framework of which the Agency was an integral part.

53. Involving the Security Council did not mean the end of diplomatic efforts but opened a new phase which would enable the authority of the Agency and the credibility of the non-proliferation regime to be strengthened, while offering Iran the opportunity to restore the confidence of the international community through its decisions and actions.

54. Mr. CARRERA DORAL (**Cuba**)…

55. Cuba would vote against the draft resolution based on the positions of principle it had expressed in its statement on 2 February 2006.

…

58. The current meetings had been called at the request of a group of powerful Member States to analyse alleged breaches by the Islamic Republic of Iran of its safeguards agreement. Those allegations had not been proven by a single delegation, nor had they been corroborated by a report from the Director General.

…

60. It was obvious once again who was undermining the Agency's credibility and the Board's integrity: the United States and its allies, who cynically and hypocritically remained silent on the subject of Israel's nuclear arsenal and failed to meet their own nuclear disarmament commitments. Unpredictable consequences for international peace and security could ensue from the adoption of the draft resolution and there was a grave danger that it could unleash a war of looting and genocide against Iran.

61. Mr. WIBOWO (**Indonesia**) said…

…

63. The Director General was still conducting investigations to resolve outstanding issues relevant to the implementation of the NPT safeguards agreement in Iran and was preparing a report to be submitted to the March Board. All parties should therefore exercise patience and refrain from any action that could create an unnecessary confrontation. His country held that it was not necessary to rush and report the issue to the Security Council, as that could jeopardize the confidence-building measures. The best possible outcome of the current meeting would be to defer a final decision on reporting Iran to the Security Council until the Board's meetings in March. To report the matter to the Security Council would only give a strong signal that the international community was taking a very different and discriminatory approach towards Iran.

…

65. For the aforementioned reasons, and since the draft resolution did not fully reflect Indonesia's views on the issue, he would be abstaining in the vote in accordance with his Government's instructions.

...

69. The CHAIRMAN proposed that the Board proceed to a decision on the draft resolution contained in document GOV/2006/12/Rev.1.

70. At the request of Mr. Márquez Marín (**Bolivarian Republic of Venezuela**), a roll-call vote was taken.

71. Ecuador, having been drawn by lot by the Chairman, was called upon to vote first.

72. The result of the vote was as follows: In favour: Argentina, Australia, Belgium, Brazil, Canada, China, Colombia, Ecuador, Egypt, France Germany, Ghana, Greece, India, Japan, Republic of Korea, Norway, Portugal, Russian Federation, Singapore, Slovakia, Slovenia, Sri Lanka, Sweden, United Kingdom, United States of America, Yemen. Against: Cuba, Syrian Arab Republic, Bolivarian Republic of Venezuela. Abstaining: Algeria, Belarus, Indonesia, Libyan Arab Jamahiriya, South Africa.

73. There were 27 votes in favour and 3 against, with 5 abstentions.

74. The draft resolution was adopted.

...

83. Mr. PARINI (**Argentina**)...

84. On 24 September 2005,[373] the Board had found that Iran's breaches of its obligations under its safeguards agreement constituted non-compliance in the context of Article XII.C of the Agency's Statute. At that time, the Board had decided to give Iran room to meet the requirements stipulated by the Board to restore confidence in the exclusively peaceful nature of its nuclear programme. Iran's resumption of enrichment activities was incompatible with the maintenance of the suspension stipulated by the Board. Its withdrawal from negotiations and its lack of active cooperation, inter alia, had prompted the Board to inform the Security Council of the steps it had requested of Iran and to draw to that body's attention all the reports and resolutions on that issue. After almost three years of intensive verification activities, the Agency was still not in a position to clarify certain important questions relating to the Iranian nuclear issue or to conclude that there was no undeclared nuclear material in Iran.

...

90. Mr. MÁRQUEZ MARÍN (**Bolivarian Republic of Venezuela**) said...

91. Article XII.C of the Agency's Statute authorized the Board to inform the Security Council and the General Assembly when the Agency's inspectors and the Director General had verified a State's non-compliance with its safeguards obligations and there was evidence of a diversion of that State's nuclear programme to non-peaceful uses. That did not apply in the case of the Iranian nuclear programme which had not been declared non-compliant. Furthermore, the Iranian Government had been cooperating with the Agency's inspectors and had voluntarily accepted the application of the additional protocol despite not yet having ratified it. It was generally known that, over the preceding two and a half years, the Agency had been constantly monitoring the Iranian nuclear programme and the Director General would be presenting his report on that issue at the Board's next series of meetings. Thus, in addition to being illegal, there was no objective basis for a report to the Security Council and that act was clearly politically motivated. It set a precedent which, without doubt, would affect the future of international relations in the nuclear disarmament field, presaging the beginning of a new arms race with unforeseeable consequences.

---

[373] Doc. 30.

92. The untimely and technically unjustified referral of the issue of the Iranian nuclear programme to the Security Council called into question the NPT by infringing its provisions and seriously undermining the executive role of the Agency in the safeguards field, thus compromising the future of nuclear disarmament. That act was in line with the position adopted by the United States Government, which was pressing for a revision of the NPT that would confirm its discriminatory nature and prohibit the majority of countries from producing their own nuclear fuel, while others were permitted to have a complete fuel cycle and augment their nuclear arsenals with new, limited-scope nuclear weapons based on depleted uranium.

93. ...those who accused Iran of violating the NPT without foundation, while they were themselves in brazen non-compliance, lacked moral authority. The NPT not only obliged non-nuclear-weapon States to renounce such weapons, it also required of those States possessing nuclear weapons that they progressively destroy them. In fact, the opposite had occurred. For example, the United States Government had not only not complied with that commitment, as part of its doctrine of preventive strikes it had developed a new generation of more compact nuclear weapons which were being treated as if they were conventional weapons when in fact they were not. Those weapons had been tested in the Iraq and Afghanistan wars. That policy was part of the United States' imperialist attempts to maintain its world hegemony and was consistent with its refusal to ratify the CTBT.

...

108. Mr. ALOBIDI (**Libyan Arab Jamahiriya**)...

...

110. It was the job of the Security Council to consider issues relating to peace, security and justice. The question was whether the Iranian issue had reached such a pitch that it threatened international peace and security. The Director General had still to submit his report on the matter. Moreover, how could the Board refer the matter to the Security Council merely because it had doubts? On the other hand, the Board declined to look into the issue of the Israeli nuclear programme, even though it was known that that country had a nuclear arsenal.

111. The countries of the Middle East had bitter experience in that regard: hasty decisions were taken which had a negative impact on their peoples.

...

128. Mr.WU Hailong (**China**)...

...

130. It was his country's understanding that, in the resolution just adopted, the relevant provisions that pertained to reporting to the Security Council should not be construed as an exercise based on Articles XII.C or III.B of the Statute. On the contrary, their purpose was to enable the Agency better to address the Iranian nuclear issue. It was on that basis that China had voted in favour of the resolution.

...

133. Mr. BERDENNIKOV (**Russian Federation**)...

...

135. The Security Council, in receiving a report now for information purposes on the steps undertaken by the Board, could remain assured that the matter was being resolved through Agency channels without any additional intervention. The Russian Federation viewed the request for the Director General to report to the Security Council on the Board's decision not as an action pursuant to Articles XII.C or III.B.4 of the Statute, but as a step

to ensure that the United Nations had a clear and full picture of the Agency's work on the Iranian nuclear issue and of the steps that the Board was expecting from Tehran. It was on that understanding that the Russian Federation had been able to support its adoption.

136. Mr. SCHULTE (**United States of America**)...

...

138. He agreed with the Governor from Egypt that the report to the Security Council would not divest the Agency of the challenge posed by Iran. The United States continued to expect the Agency's investigation of Iran's nuclear programme to proceed actively and urgently and looked forward to the Director General's March report on the implementation of the current and previous resolutions. He noted that the Director General's report would be conveyed to the Security Council immediately after the Board's meetings in March. By reporting Iran to the Security Council now, the Board was seeking to add the Council's weight to reinforce the Agency's role and its investigation, and to give Iran a further incentive to choose a course of cooperation and negotiation rather than confrontation.

139. The Agency had a specific mandate to deal with nuclear safeguards issues. That mandate was without prejudice to the rights and responsibilities of the Security Council to address matters that raised questions relating to international peace and security, as was the case with Iran. That was why the Agency's Statute expressly contemplated the Security Council's involvement in such instances of non-compliance. And that was why the Board had made it clear in September that such a report was mandatory.

...

145. Mr. SOLTANIEH (**Islamic Republic of Iran**), having offered condolences to the delegates of Egypt, expressed his Government's objection to and deep regret at the hasty and immature decision of the Board, which was entrusted with protecting the rights and privileges of all Member States including non-members of the Board. He also expressed Iran's appreciation to Venezuela, Cuba and Syria for opposing the resolution, and to Algeria, South Africa, Indonesia, Belarus and the Libyan Arab Jamahiriya for abstaining.

...

148. He underlined that the dispute was not between the international community and Iran, since over 100 NAM Member states were opposed to the decision to send the issue outside the framework of the Agency and to the Security Council. Moreover, the resolution was politically motivated since it had no legal or technical grounds. The course of diplomacy had been brought to a halt by certain States and, now that the resolution had been adopted, it was not clear how diplomacy might be resumed.

149. Immediately after the case was reported to the Security Council, the Islamic Republic of Iran would have to enforce the law - passed virtually unanimously by the Iranian parliament in 2005 - to suspend its almost three-year voluntary implementation of the additional protocol and its voluntary suspension of commercial-scale enrichment activities.

150. The Islamic Republic of Iran considered that there was a clear distinction between voluntary measures and legally binding obligations. Thus, it would continue to comply with its legal obligations under the Statute and its NPT safeguards agreement.

Document 85: Consideration of GOV/2006/15

GOV/OR.1155, 8 March 2006

...

21. Mr. SCHULTE (**United States of America**)...

...

27. The Board in February had agreed that the Director General's report should be transmitted to the Security Council immediately after the present discussion. The time had come for the Security Council to act. The Security Council's involvement should reinforce the Agency's role and investigations. As a first step, it should call on Iran to cooperate with the Agency and to take the measures identified by the Board in order to restore confidence. It could also provide the broader authority which the Agency needed in order to investigate Iran's nuclear activities. The Security Council's approach should be well-considered and incremental, proceeding in full consultation with all Council members. It should emphasize that Iran would face consequences if it did not meet its obligations.

...

29. Mr. AAS (**Norway**)...

...

33. All States party to the NPT, including Iran, had the right to use nuclear energy for peaceful purposes in accordance with Article IV of the NPT. Norway remained a strong advocate of that right, which should be applied without discrimination and in conformity with Articles I and II of the Treaty.

...

44. Mr. SUMI (**Japan**)...

...

46. It was important for Iran to restore the confidence of the international community, which had been damaged by Iran's previous non-compliance with its safeguards agreement. To that end, Iran should comply fully with all the resolutions of the Board, including the most recent. It should, in particular, suspend immediately all uranium enrichment-related and reprocessing activities, including research and development activities, continue the provisional implementation of its additional protocol and ratify that instrument as a matter of urgency.

...

53. Mr. CARRERA DORAL (**Cuba**) said that his delegation had voted against the resolution adopted by the Board on 4 February[374] and had warned of the unpredictable consequences that its adoption could have for international peace and security.[375] Cuba's position was based on the principles that, firstly, developing countries had a full and recognized right to produce nuclear energy for peaceful purposes under the appropriate safeguards and to carry out all nuclear fuel cycle activities; secondly, it was unacceptable that, through arbitrary interpretations of the text of the NPT not in keeping with its letter and spirit, new elements were being added that discriminated against countries; thirdly, the Agency was the only international body technically authorized and legally mandated to

---

[374] Doc. 32.
[375] Doc. 84.

determine the nature of a country's nuclear programme; fourthly, there was no evidence or assertion in the various reports provided by the Secretariat that Iran's nuclear programme was of a non-peaceful nature; and finally, it was unacceptable to condemn and attempt to penalize a country for resuming activities it had voluntarily suspended on a temporary basis and was rightfully entitled to conduct.

...

55. Cuba would wholeheartedly defend the legitimate right of all States party to the NPT, without exception, to conduct research on and engage in the production and use of nuclear energy for peaceful purposes, and to receive, without any discrimination whatsoever, the transfer of materials, equipment and scientific and technological information in conformity with Article IV of the NPT.

56. The Agency must preserve its impartiality and take action without giving in to pressure from those that wanted it to function under the umbrella of the Security Council. Intrusive attitudes undermined the principles enshrined in international law and in the Charter of the United Nations. Quoting from paragraph 53 of the Director General's report,[376] which stated that although the Agency had not seen any diversion of nuclear material, it was not yet in a position to conclude that there were no undeclared nuclear materials or activities in Iran, and from paragraph 54 regarding the need to clarify uncertainties, he said that the biased and subjective character of such observations played into the hands of those trying to use the situation for their own political purposes. The Agency would lose credibility if its decisions were made on the basis of suspicion rather than realism and objectivity. In his delegation's view, the real and objective fact was that the Director General's report provided evidence of systematic progress in Iran's cooperation with the Agency despite the unbalanced and unfair resolutions adopted by the Board in September 2005[377] and February 2006. No evidence had been found to justify reporting the issue to the Security Council. There was still scope for maintaining the issue within the framework of the Agency — which should not give up on its commitment to solve that sensitive issue. There were numerous aspects on which the Agency required more time to reach definite conclusions. The Agency should therefore be allowed to do its work without external political pressure, which would only hinder, rather than help, the verification process.

...

99. Mr. JENKINS (**United Kingdom**), **speaking on behalf of France and Germany as well as his own country**, said that they associated themselves with the statement made by the Presidency of the European Union on behalf of 37 members of the Agency.

100. They commended the Director General and the Secretariat for the professionalism and impartiality with which they had continued their efforts to implement the safeguards agreement with Iran. From the Director General's report, it was clear that since November 2005, only modest progress had been made towards resolving the many serious questions to which Agency verification of Iranian declarations had given rise. Among the reasons for that lack of progress were continuing deficiencies in Iranian cooperation. As a result, important aspects of Iran's nuclear programme remained shrouded from view. The Board still could not judge whether what it knew about Iran's centrifuge enrichment programme represented the full picture or simply the tip of the iceberg — and it was the part of the iceberg below water, out of view, that had sunk the Titanic. Puzzling inconsistencies remained with regard to plutonium and polonium experiments and uranium mining. Most

---

[376] Doc. 42.
[377] Doc. 30.

importantly, indications of a possible military dimension to Iran's nuclear programme continued to be a legitimate source of intense concern.

...

102. Because the Director General pointed so clearly in his report to grounds for continuing serious concern, the need for Iran to carry out confidence-building measures remained undiminished. Yet it had failed to implement the measures called for in the Board's February resolution. On the contrary, it had notified the Agency that it was ceasing to suspend its enrichment-related and reprocessing activities and had injected UF_6 into centrifuges at the Natanz Pilot Fuel Enrichment Plant. It had continued civil engineering work at the nuclear research reactor site near Arak. It had not ratified the additional protocol and had notified the Agency that it was ceasing to act in accordance with its provisions. It had declined to discuss further the Agency's request for additional clarifications regarding the procurement efforts of the Physics Research Centre and the latter's relationship with the technical university.

103. Such decisions and actions aggravated the lack of confidence in Iran's intentions. Confidence-building was at the heart of the matter. The issue was not, as often claimed, that of legal rights to use nuclear energy for peaceful purposes. The EU3 Governments had consistently recognized that inalienable right for Iran. However, the secret nature of the nuclear programme that had been pursued for more than 18 years, the fact that it related to the most sensitive parts of the nuclear fuel cycle, and the numerous breaches of Iran's obligation to comply with its safeguards agreement had prompted a crisis of confidence in Iran's intentions.

...

106. The EU3 would like to see the Board reaffirm the need for Iran to implement in full the confidence-building measures that the Board had requested. However, since Iran had consistently disregarded the Board's requests, the time had come for the Security Council to reinforce the authority of the Agency and its resolutions by calling upon Iran to implement the confidence-building measures requested on 4 February. The EU3 expected that the Security Council would take up consideration of the reports and resolutions it had received from the Board and decide, on the basis of the Board's findings, on appropriate action to reinforce the authority of the Agency with a view to clarifying the nature of Iran's programme and convincing Iran of the need to implement the measures requested by the Board, including full transparency.

...

Document 86: Consideration of GOV/2006/15 (continued)

GOV/OR.1156, 8 May 2006

...

6. Mr. OTHMAN (**Syrian Arab Republic**)...

...

9. One should not deal with the Iranian nuclear issue on the basis of what one thought Iran might do at some time in the future. One should base oneself on firmer ground, such as the reports of Agency safeguards inspectors, whose work Iran had consistently been facilitating.

...

60. Mr. SOLTANIEH ((**Islamic Republic of Iran**)...

...

63. In recent years, systematic attempts had been pursued to redefine the NPT as a single-purpose treaty. Undertakings on nuclear disarmament were all but forgotten, and access to material and technology for peaceful use was blocked, while non-proliferation obligations were sharpened unabatedly. The most recent ambitions were to place further, deeper and harsher restrictions on the supply of nuclear technology and to achieve total monopolization of nuclear fuel production. That twisted approach to the world nuclear order betrayed fundamental tenets of nuclear non-proliferation and stretched far beyond the borders of absurdity.

...

71. In sharp contrast to proliferators, Iran had: stated, stressed, confirmed and reiterated that it rejected nuclear weapons and considered their possession immoral, illegitimate and illegal; worked closely with the Agency towards verification of its peaceful nuclear programme; corrected initial failures stemming from the Western embargo on material and technology to the best of its ability; stayed committed to safeguards and applied the additional protocol for three consecutive years; voluntarily suspended its enrichment activity for a sustained period to promote confidence; received full and verified accountancy of its declared material and activity by the Agency; and continued cooperation with the Agency towards the rarely established finding of absence of undeclared material and activity.

72. To warmongers in Washington, however, facts were not relevant; speculations were. Those mind-readers relied on sheer clairvoyance to pass judgement on Iran's intentions. That judgement was then propagated as the basis for action. That was an easy approach, as no evidence was required to question intentions rather than facts.

...

74. The countries supporting the United States in opposing Iran's peaceful nuclear programme could be categorized as follows: some had extended their nuclear arsenals and continuously updated them; some had very recently announced that the use of nuclear weapons in conventional conflict was legitimate and based their military doctrine upon it; and some did not possess nuclear weapons but had permitted the nuclear-weapon States to stockpile nuclear weapons in their territories, or officially supported the military pacts which benefited from nuclear arsenals, and even shared in planning for the use of nuclear weapons.

75. Finding Iran's nuclear programme to be in non-compliance was by far the biggest blunder in the Agency's history, and it would undoubtedly jeopardize the credibility of international organizations and create a serious deviation from their statutory mandate. Such an approach would be detrimental to international peace and security. ...

...

84. The CHAIRMAN, summing up the discussion, said that the Board had taken note of the Director General's report on the implementation of the NPT safeguards agreement in the Islamic Republic of Iran contained in document GOV/2006/15.[378] The Board had expressed its appreciation to the Director General and the Secretariat for their professional and diligent work on that issue.

---

[378] Doc. 42.

85. It had been noted that, in accordance with the Board's resolution contained in document GOV/2006/14,[379] the Director General's report would be conveyed to the Security Council.

86. Some members had expressed their regret at the lack of implementation of the confidence-building measures requested of Iran by the Board in its resolution of 4 February 2006 and had requested the full implementation of those measures, and had further regretted Iran's declaration of 6 February 2006 that it intended to suspend the voluntary implementation of non-legally binding measures, including the additional protocol.

87. Some members had regretted the slow pace of progress since February towards clarifying outstanding questions relating to Iran's nuclear programme. They also had expressed concern at information related to a possible military dimension to Iran's programme. They had regretted that the Agency was still not in a position to conclude that there were no undeclared nuclear materials or activities in Iran. They had called on Iran to provide full transparency, including the provision of additional information and documentation related to the P-1 and P-2 centrifuge programmes and the procurement of dual-use equipment; access to, and cooperation by, relevant individuals; and access to certain military-owned workshops and research and development locations that the Agency might need to visit in the future as part of its investigation.

88. Some members had recognized that Iran had taken corrective measures and had been continuing to provide some transparency measures. They had encouraged Iran to continue its cooperation with the Agency to resolve the remaining issues regarding the scope and nature of Iran's nuclear programme. They had re-emphasized the distinction between voluntary confidence-building measures and legally binding safeguards obligations.

89. They had noted the conclusion in the Director General's report that all declared nuclear material in Iran had been accounted for, and that the Agency had not seen any diversion of nuclear material to nuclear weapons or other nuclear explosive devices. They had recognized that the Agency's work on verifying the correctness and completeness of Iran's declarations was ongoing. They had also noted that the process of drawing a conclusion with regard to the absence of undeclared nuclear materials or activities was a time-consuming process, even with an additional protocol in force.

90. It had been emphasized that the Agency was the sole competent authority for verification and that it should continue its work to resolve the Iranian nuclear issue.

91. The continued need for diplomatic negotiations and dialogue among all parties, covering all relevant issues, had been emphasized as the way to reach a peaceful solution to the Iranian nuclear issue. In that regard, appreciation had been expressed for all initiatives, such as the EU-Iran dialogue and the Russian proposal on a joint venture, aimed at paving the way to a speedy conclusion of the Iranian nuclear issue. Calls had been made for Iran to adopt a responsive attitude towards implementing the confidence-building measures previously called for by the Board. The basic and inalienable right of all Member States to develop nuclear energy for peaceful purposes in conformity with their respective legal obligations had been reiterated.

92. Some members had emphasized the importance of addressing the Iranian nuclear issue within the context of the establishment of a nuclear-weapon-free zone in the region of the Middle East.

---

[379] Doc. 32.

93. The Board had requested the Director General to continue keeping it informed of developments as appropriate.

94. The Chairman's summing-up was accepted

…

Document 87: Consideration of GOV/2006/27 and 38

GOV/OR.1163, 15 June 2006

…

115. **The CHAIRMAN**, summing up the discussion, said that the Board had taken note of the Director General's reports on the implementation of the NPT safeguards agreement in the Islamic Republic of Iran contained in documents GOV/2006/27[380] and GOV/2006/38. The Board had expressed its appreciation to the Director General and the Secretariat for their professional and impartial work on that issue.

116. Some members had regretted the slow pace of progress towards clarifying remaining outstanding questions relating to the scope and nature of Iran's nuclear programme and the diminished nature of Iran's cooperation with the Agency. They had urged Iran to provide full transparency and to implement fully the confidence building measures called for by the Board in order for the Agency to be able to reach a conclusion about the absence of undeclared nuclear material and activities, and in order for the international community to regain confidence in the exclusively peaceful nature of Iran's nuclear programme.

117. Some members had re-emphasized the distinction between voluntary confidence building measures and legally binding safeguards obligations. The basic and inalienable right of all Member States to develop nuclear energy for peaceful purposes in conformity with their respective legal obligations had been reiterated.

118. They had noted the assessment of the Director General that all declared nuclear material in Iran has been accounted for. They had recognized that the Agency's work on verifying the correctness and completeness of Iran's declarations was ongoing. They had also noted that the process of drawing a conclusion with regard to the absence of undeclared nuclear materials and activities was a time-consuming process.

119. It had been emphasized that the Agency was the sole competent authority for verification and that it should continue its work to resolve the Iranian nuclear issue.

120. The continued need for diplomatic negotiations and dialogue among all parties covering all relevant issues had been emphasized as the way to reach a peaceful solution of the Iranian nuclear issue. Appreciation had been expressed for recent efforts in that connection.

121. Some members had emphasized the importance of the establishment of a NWFZ in the region of the Middle East.

122. The Board had requested the Director General to continue keeping it informed of developments as appropriate.

123. The Chairman's summing-up was accepted.

---

[380] Doc. 43.

Document 88: Consideration of GOV/2006/53 (continued)

GOV/OR.1171, 14 September 2006

...

36. Mr. SOLTANIEH (**Islamic Republic of Iran**)...

...

46. The referral of the Iranian nuclear issue to the Security Council merely because of its resumption of voluntarily suspended R&D activities — which had been, and still were, under full safeguards surveillance — had no legal or technical basis and had been motivated solely by political reasons.

47. The recent Agency report in which the Director General[381] had referred to the slow pace of progress on resolving the few remaining issues did not come as a surprise when seen in the light of the inappropriate decision by a few members of the Board to send what was a purely technical matter from the competent technical organization to a security- and politically oriented body. In accordance with legislation passed by its parliament, Iran had then had no choice but to discontinue provisional implementation of the additional protocol and other voluntary measures.

48. The proposal put forward by the group of 5+1 States[382] had been interpreted as a positive step to correct that error; thus, it had been welcomed by his Government. As an expression of goodwill, Iran had announced that it would study the package proposal closely and give its response in due time. While his Government had been in the process of considering all aspects of the package proposal and preparing an appropriate forward-looking response, the Security Council, goaded by certain States, had taken the hasty decision to adopt a resolution, a step which had disappointed most Member States and the international community at large, since it had interfered with the appropriate course of action, namely the search for a negotiated solution instead of confrontation. Nevertheless, Iran had avoided confrontation and had again demonstrated its political goodwill by responding by the previously announced date of 22 August 2006.[383]

...

56. The CHAIRMAN, summing up the discussion, said that the Board had taken note of the Director General's report contained in document GOV/2006/53 on the implementation of the NPT safeguards agreement in the Islamic Republic of Iran, prepared pursuant to United Nations Security Council resolution 1696(2006).[384] The Board had expressed its appreciation to the Director General and the Secretariat for their professional and impartial work on that issue.

57. Some members had expressed regret that, contrary to the resolutions of the Board and the Security Council, no progress had been made towards clarifying outstanding issues relating to the scope and nature of Iran's nuclear programme, and that Iran had not provided the Agency with access to relevant information and individuals, and other transparency measures needed to clarify those issues.

---

[381] Doc. 44.
[382] Doc. 131.
[383] Doc. 114.
[384] Doc. 10.

58. They had expressed deep regret that Iran had not fulfilled the obligations established by Security Council resolution 1696 and requests by the Board related, inter alia, to the suspension of its uranium enrichment-related activities, reconsideration of the construction of a heavy water research reactor and voluntary implementation of the provisions of the additional protocol.

59. They had stated that the quality of cooperation had declined and had urged Iran to provide the Agency with full transparency and to implement fully the measures called for by the Board and Security Council resolution 1696, in order to establish the necessary confidence in the exclusively peaceful nature of Iran's nuclear programme.

60. Some members had re-emphasized the distinction between voluntary confidence-building measures and legally binding safeguards obligations. The basic and inalienable right of all Member States to develop nuclear energy for peaceful purposes in conformity with their respective legal obligations had been reiterated.

61. They had noted the assessment of the Secretariat that all declared nuclear material in Iran had been accounted for. They had recognized that the Agency's work on verifying the correctness and completeness of Iran's declarations had been ongoing. They had encouraged Iran to continue cooperating actively and fully with the Agency within its mandate to resolve outstanding issues.

62. It had been emphasized that the Agency was the sole competent authority for nuclear verification in connection with the NPT, and that it should continue its work to resolve the Iranian nuclear issue.

63. The continued need for negotiations and dialogue among all parties covering all relevant issues had been emphasized as the way to reach a peaceful solution of the Iranian nuclear issue. The six countries' package proposal and the response thereto had been noted in that regard. Appreciation had been expressed for recent efforts in that connection, including meetings between the High Representative of the European Union and the Secretary of the Supreme National Security Council of Iran.

64. Some members had emphasized the importance of the establishment of a nuclear-weapon-free zone in the region of the Middle East.

65. The Board had requested the Director General to continue to keep it informed of developments as appropriate.

66. He asked whether his summing-up was acceptable to the Board.

67. The Chairman's summing-up was accepted.

Document 89: Technical Assistance and Cooperation Committee: The Agency's proposed programme for 2007-2008

GOV/COM.8/OR.144, 20 November 2006

1. The representative of **BOLIVIA**, speaking on behalf of the Group of 77 and China, said that...

...

5. Regarding the proposed technical cooperation programme for 2007–2008, the Group was confident that the Secretariat had developed it in a professional, impartial and non-discriminatory manner, following a well-established process based on Member States'

needs and in line with the Statute and in accordance with the relevant decisions of the Agency's policy-making organs. It was essential for the efficiency and credibility of the Agency that the technical assistance provided through it not be subject to any political, economic, military or other conditions incompatible with the Statute. ...

10. The representative of **MOROCCO**, speaking on behalf of the African Group,...

11. The African Group, which was mindful of Article II of the Statute and believed that the promotion of peaceful uses of atomic energy was a basic objective of the Agency, considered technical assistance to be a key benefit of Agency membership.

...

20. The representative of **CUBA, speaking on behalf of NAM**, said that technical cooperation was an important part of the Agency's work, complementing related development programmes in developing countries.

21. In the final document of the NAM Summit held in Havana, Cuba, from 11 to 16 September 2006, the Heads of State and Government had reaffirmed the inalienable right of developing countries to engage in research on and the production and use of nuclear energy for peaceful purposes without discrimination. Also, they had emphasized the responsibility of developed countries to meet the legitimate needs of developing countries for nuclear power and permit them to participate to the greatest extent possible in the transfer of nuclear equipment, materials and scientific and technical information for peaceful purposes. In addition, they had expressed strong opposition to attempts by any Member State to use the Agency's technical cooperation programmes for political purposes in violation of the Statute.

22. One of the statutory objectives of the Agency was 'to accelerate and enlarge the contribution of atomic energy to peace, health and prosperity throughout the world.' The promotional activities carried out by the Agency pursuant to that objective constituted an important incentive for developing countries to join the Agency.

23. NAM attached great importance to the Revised Guiding Principles and General Operating Rules to Govern the Provision of Technical Assistance by the Agency (INFCIRC/267), which envisaged free access to the peaceful uses of atomic energy and the related technology for all Member States, and to Article III C. of the Statute, which stated that, in carrying out its functions, 'the Agency shall not make assistance to members subject to any political, economic, military, or other conditions incompatible with the provisions of this Statute.'

24. Accordingly, NAM did not wish to see TACC politicized. The deliberations and recommendations of TACC should be based on technical considerations and the related financial requirements.

25. NAM welcomed the assurance given by the Secretariat that all the projects in the proposed programme for 2007–2008 were in conformity with the Statute and the principles contained in document INFCIRC/267 and that none of them violated Security Council or Board resolutions.

26. The representative of **FINLAND, speaking on behalf of the European Union** (EU)...

...

32. With respect to one project in the proposed technical cooperation programme for 2007–2008, the Secretariat had referred to resolutions in which the Board of Governors had stated that it deemed it necessary that the Islamic Republic of Iran reconsider the construction of a research reactor moderated by heavy water and to United Nations Security

Council resolution 1696 of 31 July 2006,[385] in which the Security Council had called upon Iran to take, without further delay, the steps required by the Board in its resolution GOV/2006/14,[386] which were essential for building confidence in the exclusively peaceful purpose of its nuclear programme and resolving outstanding questions. Already in 2004, the Board had - in its resolutions GOV/2004/49[387] and GOV/2004/79[388] - unanimously requested Iran to reconsider the construction of the research reactor at Arak. The EU was concerned that such a reactor would in due course produce significant quantities of plutonium and constitute a significant proliferation risk.

33. It had been the practice in TACC to approve the Agency's proposed technical cooperation programmes in their entirety. However, Agency technical assistance had to be consistent with the decisions of the Board and the Security Council, and Iran had requested funding for a project that it had explicitly been asked to reconsider. Therefore, the EU could not support the provision of technical assistance for that project. It deeply regretted that fact and hoped that Iran would open the way for negotiations by complying with the aforementioned resolutions.

34. The EU also needed full assurances that none of the other new technical cooperation projects would in any way contribute to activities that Iran had been asked by the Board or the Security Council to suspend or reconsider. It was important to remain vigilant so as to ensure that technical cooperation projects were fully consistent with the resolutions of the Board and the Security Council throughout their implementation. The EU had noted what had been stated in that connection by the Deputy Director General for Technical Cooperation during the Board's previous meeting, and it would like the Secretariat to keep the Board informed in that matter.

35. The EU attached great importance to the principle of consensus in the approving of Agency technical cooperation programmes, but it could join in a consensus in favour of the proposed 2007-2008 programme only if it received the aforementioned full assurances and on the understanding that project IRA/9/019 would be removed.

...

62. The representative of **CHINA**...

...

66. His delegation, which understood that some Member States were unhappy about certain projects in the proposed 2007–2008 programme, hoped that the parties concerned would, together with the Secretariat, arrive at an appropriate solution through consultations.

...

69. The representative of **CANADA**,

...

73. However, the programme included six new projects proposed for the Islamic Republic of Iran. Those projects, which — if approved and implemented — would represent a significant increase in the technical assistance being provided to that country through the Agency, required very careful scrutiny given the lack of confidence of the Board and the Security Council as regards the Iranian nuclear programme.

74. In September 2005, the Board had arrived at a finding of non-compliance[389] in terms of Article XII.C of the Statute, which provided the Board with the authority to - inter

---

[385] Doc. 10.
[386] Doc. 32.
[387] Doc. 26.
[388] Doc. 27.
[389] Doc. 30.

alia - curtail technical assistance to a State in non-compliance. The Board had called on the Islamic Republic of Iran to reconsider the construction of the Arak heavy-water research reactor, which was the focus of proposed project IRA/9/019 - a call subsequently made mandatory by Security Council resolution 1696. However, the Islamic Republic of Iran had continued work on the construction of that reactor. Agency technical assistance in support of the reactor's construction, through project IRA/9/019 or any other project, would be inconsistent with the reservations expressed by the Board and the Security Council. The Arak research reactor was a matter of particular concern to Canada, which was not prepared to approve a technical cooperation package that included support for its construction.

75. Besides project IRA/9/019, Canada was concerned about the possibility that other projects proposed for the Islamic Republic of Iran would contribute to its capabilities in the areas of enrichment and reprocessing or support work on constructing the Arak research reactor. Her delegation, which welcomed the assurance given by the Deputy Director General for Technical Cooperation that none of the projects proposed for the Islamic Republic of Iran would contribute to its enrichment and reprocessing capabilities and that the implementation of those projects would be closely monitored, expected any issues likely to impact that assurance to be brought to the Board's attention - including issues relating to the possible implications of other technical cooperation projects for the Arak research reactor.

76. The provision of technical assistance through the Agency should remain free from political judgements inconsistent with the Statute. However, the Board should be especially wary when the prospective recipient country had disregarded decisions of the Board and the Security Council and when many important questions about the scope and nature of that country's nuclear programme were still unanswered. In that connection, it should be recalled that subparagraph E.7 of Article XI of the Statute provided that, before approving a project under that article, the Board should give due consideration to "Such other matters as may be relevant".

77. Canada, which was prepared to support without qualification all other new projects proposed for 2007-2008, hoped that TACC would arrive at an agreement on recommending the proposed 2007-2008 programme for adoption by consensus in the Board.

78. The representative of **AUSTRALIA**...

...

86. In the resolution adopted by it on 24 September 2005, the Board had stated that 'Iran's many failures and breaches of its obligations to comply with its NPT Safeguards Agreement ... constitute non compliance in the context of Article XII.C of the Agency's Statute'. Until investigations of the nuclear activities of the Islamic Republic of Iran were satisfactorily completed, it was appropriate to take a cautious approach regarding technical cooperation with that country, and particularly regarding all technical assistance related to the nuclear fuel cycle. Certainly, TACC, the Board and the Secretariat should avoid acting in a manner inconsistent with resolutions adopted by the Board.

87. In resolution 1696, the Security Council had called upon "all States ... to exercise vigilance and prevent the transfer of any items, materials, goods and technology that could contribute to Iran's enrichment-related and reprocessing activities" and had reinforced the authority of the Agency. TACC and the Board should not endorse activities that would run counter to the requirements of Security Council resolutions.

88. Under the terms of Security Council resolution 1696 and of the relevant Board resolutions, the Agency was entitled to suspend or terminate all assistance that was or might

be related to uranium enrichment or to reprocessing, or to the Arak research reactor, and to defer any decision if the information available to it was inadequate. In that connection, his delegation had taken note of the assurances given by the Deputy Director General for Technical Cooperation during TACC's previous meeting.

89. Projects approved for the Islamic Republic of Iran should be monitored by the Secretariat on a one-house basis, and his delegation welcomed the assurance given that during project delivery the Secretariat would remain alert to issues which might arise relevant to decisions of the Board and the Security Council and bring them to the Board's attention.

90. The representative of the **UNITED STATES OF AMERICA** said...

...

98. The projects proposed by the Islamic Republic of Iran for the 2007-2008 technical cooperation programme required close scrutiny in the light of United Nations Security Council resolution 1696 and the continuing inability of the Director General to confirm the peaceful nature of the Iranian nuclear programme. The United States welcomed the assurance given by the Secretariat that the projects would be implemented in conformity with the relevant Board and Security Council resolutions, and it was his country's understanding that the training provided through them would not further Iran's efforts relating to enrichment, reprocessing or heavy water production. Implementation of the projects should proceed only if the Secretariat kept them under continuous review, until it arrived at a positive conclusion about the Iranian nuclear programme.

99. Project IRA/9/019 pertained to a heavy water-moderated research reactor of continuing concern to the Board and the Security Council. Once completed, the reactor would be capable of producing enough plutonium for one or more nuclear weapons each year. Given past Board decisions, the outstanding questions about the Iranian nuclear programme, and the risk of plutonium being diverted to use in a weapon, his country was joining with other Member States in not approving that project.

100. The United States would like the proposed technical cooperation programme for 2007-2008 to be approved by consensus, and it was prepared to join a consensus in favour of it if project IRA/9/019 was removed - given the Secretariat's assurances regarding the other projects. Approval of those projects by his country did not constitute acceptance of Iran's stated goal of achieving 20 000 MW of nuclear capacity by 2020. Iran had cited that goal in an attempt to justify certain activities, once conducted in secret and now in violation of Security Council resolution 1696. That goal was not credible.

101. The representative of EGYPT...

...

107. His country continued to believe in the approval of Agency technical cooperation programmes by consensus once the technical and financial feasibility of the projects constituting them had been examined by the Secretariat in accordance with agreed rules and principles. Care should be taken to avoid the politicization of technical cooperation activities, as it could have a negative effect on the image of the Agency and its ability to achieve its goals. Attempts by donor countries to exploit the voluntary nature of technical cooperation funding would threaten the credibility of the Agency.

108. The credibility of the non-proliferation regime was already threatened by the application of double standards, and it was important that double standards not be applied in the field of technical cooperation. The proposed 2007-2008 programme included nine projects for a country whose nuclear programme aroused many suspicions and which had

not acceded to the NPT or placed all its nuclear installations under Agency safeguards, in contravention of binding United Nations Security Council resolutions going back 25 years, including resolution 487 of 1981 relating to an action by that country which had threatened international peace and security and the Agency's safeguards system. Why were donor countries not questioning the projects proposed for that country? Technical cooperation with that country had been halted in 1981, pursuant to decisions by the Board and the General Conference, and it had been resumed in 1994 only in the light of circumstances suggesting an intention on the part of that country to abide by the non-proliferation regime - an intention that had still not been acted upon by that country.

...

131. The representative of **JAPAN** said...

...

136. As regards the recommendation for action contained in document GOV/2006/59/ Rev.1, Japan had some difficulty in accepting it in its present form since the Board and the Security Council had called upon the Islamic Republic of Iran to reconsider the construction of the research reactor to which one of the projects proposed for that country related. At the same time, Japan attached great importance to the Board's approving Agency technical cooperation programmes by consensus. His delegation had full confidence in the ability of the Chairman to resolve the issue now before the Committee.

...

139. The representative of **INDONESIA** said...

...

147. As regards the proposed 2007-2008 programme, his delegation believed that Member States were entitled to request any technical assistance which was in accordance with the Agency's Statute and that the Agency technical assistance should not be subject to political, economic, military or other conditions incompatible with the Statute. Accordingly, it could accept that programme in its entirety.

...

151. The representative of **SOUTH AFRICA**...

...

157. Member States should not only pay their full TCF target shares in a timely manner, but also do so without preconditions. They should not seek to micromanage the provision of technical assistance through the Agency. His delegation, which had noted the concerns expressed by some delegations regarding the technical assistance proposed for one particular Member State, had the fullest confidence in the ability of the Secretariat and the Director General to decide on technical cooperation matters in conformity with decisions of the Board and with international law. It would be inappropriate to question the Secretariat's integrity, since such a vote of no-confidence in the Secretariat on - for example - a safeguards-related issue in another forum would have serious repercussions. His delegation therefore endorsed the proposed technical cooperation programme and hoped that it would be approved by consensus.

Document 90: Technical Assistance and Cooperation Committee: The Agency's proposed programme for 2007-2008

GOV/COM.8/OR.145, 21 November 2006

1. The representative of the **SYRIAN ARAB REPUBLIC** said...

...

9. One Member State had requested assistance in strengthening its safety capabilities in connection with the construction of a reactor, the request being indicative of that country's desire to comply with the relevant international safety standards and to ensure transparency during the operation of that reactor, which was to be used for the production of radioisotopes. His delegation was surprised at the lack of confidence in that country's intentions on the part of some TACC members, given the fact that they were not questioning any of the technical cooperation projects proposed for another Member State, located in the same region, which had consistently refused to submit all its nuclear facilities to any kind of Agency supervision. Turning down a technical assistance request from a Member State for political reasons was a clear violation of the Agency's Statute.

10. In his delegation's view, when preparing the programme proposed for 2007–2008 the Department of Technical Cooperation had followed all the relevant rules, and his delegation would like to see that programme approved as it stood.

11. The representative of **INDIA** said...

...

15. In India's view, the Agency's technical cooperation activities should enjoy consensus and be assessed solely in the light of the relevant technical and legal requirements; they should certainly not be politicized.

...

17. The representative of the **LIBYAN ARAB JAMAHIRIYA** said was supporting them through its voluntary contributions to the TCF. It also attached great importance to the statutory provision that assistance to Member States should not be subject to any political, economic, military or other conditions incompatible with the Statute.

...

22. He endorsed the comments made during TACC's previous meeting by the representative of Egypt regarding the application of double standards in the field of technical cooperation. Every Member State had the right to receive technical assistance through the Agency without discrimination.

23. The representative of the **REPUBLIC OF KOREA** said...

...

27. It also believed that all technical cooperation projects should comply with non-proliferation norms and should therefore be consistent with the relevant Board and Security Council resolutions. There were misgivings about one of the projects in the proposed 2007–2008 programme - a project relating to a heavy water-moderated reactor — on the grounds that it might be inconsistent with those resolutions. The decision regarding that project would have to be a prudent one, in the interests of consensus and of facilitating the implementation of all the projects in the proposed 2007-2008 programme and in order to meet all the concerns expressed by the Board and the Security Council.

28. With that qualification, his delegation could go along with the recommendation for action contained in document GOV/2006/59/Rev.1.

29. The representative of **ARGENTINA** said that the Agency's technical cooperation activities, which were contributing to the achievement of sustainable development objectives, derived not only from the Statute but also from the NPT, and they were consequently one of the pillars on which the non-proliferation system rested.

...

32. The representative of **THAILAND** said...

...

38. Thailand, which was strongly of the view that Agency technical assistance should not be subject to any political, economic, military or other conditions incompatible with the provisions of the Statute, had full confidence in the professionalism, integrity and impartiality of the Secretariat and its judgement in ensuring that all proposed technical cooperation projects were consistent with the Statute, the Revised Guiding Principles and General Operating Rules to Govern the Provision of Technical Assistance by the Agency (INFCIRC/267) and the relevant resolutions of the Board of Governors and the United Nations Security Council. It believed that the proposed technical cooperation programme for 2007–2008 should, in line with long-standing practice, be approved by consensus, in the light of the assurances which the Secretariat had given regarding the implementation of all the projects making up that programme. It would be unfortunate if the noble cause of enhancing the well-being of people and hence promoting the attainment of human security through the peaceful uses of nuclear technology were jeopardized by politicization of the Agency's technical cooperation programmes, which normally reflected a shared responsibility of the international community.

39. The representative of **PAKISTAN** said that the Secretariat was to be commended for maintaining, through the Agency's technical cooperation programmes, the reputation of the Agency as a scientific and technical organization contributing to sustainable development.

40. Pakistan, which was strongly of the view that Agency technical assistance should not be subject to any conditions incompatible with the Statute, welcomed the assurance given by the Secretariat that the technical cooperation projects proposed for 2007–2008 had been formulated in conformity with the relevant guiding principles. Also, it was grateful for the briefings given by the Department of Technical Cooperation on the proposed 2007–2008 programme.

...

45. The representative of **FRANCE** said ...

...

50. As to the other new projects proposed for the Islamic Republic of Iran, his delegation had taken note of the information provided by the Secretariat regarding their conformity with Security Council resolution 1696 and was looking forward to the Secretariat's replies to questions posed by a number of countries, including France. It was France's understanding that the implementation of those projects would not contribute to activities of the Islamic Republic of Iran connected with enrichment, reprocessing or the Arak reactor.

51. Clearly, a decision to finance those projects would in no way constitute Agency approval of the nuclear programme of the Islamic Republic of Iran. In particular, without precise information regarding the enrichment programme of the Islamic Republic of Iran,

doubts remained about the reasons given by that country in justifying the programme a posteriori.

52. In requesting the Secretariat to keep the Board informed regarding the implementation of those projects, France, which remained fully committed to the Agency's technical cooperation activities, was not questioning the right of Member States to use nuclear energy for peaceful purposes. What was at stake was consistency in the actions of the Board, and also the credibility of the Agency.

53. The representative of **CUBA** said…

57. The relationship which some delegations claimed to see between the Board's resolutions on safeguards in the Islamic Republic of Iran and the technical assistance proposed for that country was, in Cuba's opinion, based on a tendentious interpretation of those resolutions.

58. Article XII.C of the Statute provided that, if a State had difficulty in complying with a safeguards agreement with the Agency, the Board could penalize it by suspending all or part of the technical assistance that it was receiving through the Agency. However, that was not relevant to the case of the Islamic Republic of Iran. In none of the Board resolutions on safeguards in the Islamic Republic of Iran was such Board action contemplated. If it had been, it would have had to be explicitly referred to.

59. As regards the heavy water-moderated reactor project, the Board's references to it had been exhortations to the Islamic Republic of Iran to reconsider construction of the reactor as a confidence- building measure, and such measures were — as everyone knew — of a voluntary nature. There had been no demand for an end to the construction of the reactor. There could not have been, since such a facility, while admittedly capable of being used to produce plutonium, could produce radioisotopes and high-flux radiation for peaceful applications. Consequently, the sovereign decision of the Islamic Republic of Iran to continue with the construction of the reactor should be respected.

60. Furthermore, the application of Agency safeguards to the reactor should be enough to ensure its utilization for peaceful purposes only.

61. In addition, the purpose of the technical cooperation project requested by the Islamic Republic of Iran was to contribute to the safety of the reactor, not to help in its design or construction.

62. Finally, if those considerations were insufficient, the explanations provided by the Secretariat in recent briefings and the assurances given to TACC the previous day by the Deputy Director General for Technical Cooperation should dispel the genuine concerns of Member States, allowing approval of all the projects proposed for the Islamic Republic of Iran. Any other outcome would inevitably lead to the questioning of proposed projects for other States because of political suspicions, and that should be avoided at all costs as it could have unpredictable consequences for the Agency.

63. Cuba believed that the proposed technical cooperation programme for 2007–2008 should be recommended to the Board for approval in its entirety.

64. The representative of the **UNITED KINGDOM** said…

…

70. The United Kingdom had confidence in the impartiality of the Secretariat, but it was concerned about the inclusion in the proposed technical cooperation programme for 2007–2008 of project IRA/9/019. Recommending that project for approval by the Board would be inconsistent with requests that the Board had made unanimously in the past. His delegation had heard no convincing explanation of why, for the production of medical radioisotopes,

it was necessary to have in Arak an uneconomically large heavy water-moderated reactor capable of producing large quantities of plutonium. The United Kingdom would be unable to join a consensus in favour of the proposed technical cooperation programme if project IRA/9/019 was included in it. Nevertheless, his delegation still hoped that an appropriate adjustment would be made and the tradition of consensus thereby maintained.

...

77. The representative of the **BOLIVARIAN REPUBLIC OF VENEZUELA** said...

...

80. Like many other delegations, her delegation was concerned about the unusual idea of depriving a Member State of its legitimate right to receive, in line with the Statute, assistance for technical cooperation projects that — as had been made clear by the Secretariat, and especially by the Deputy Director General for Technical Cooperation — were technically sound and had peaceful objectives. Depriving a Member State of that right, without legal justification, would not benefit the Agency; it would simply create more despair and confusion in the international community. Her delegation therefore rejected that idea outright. In its view, TACC should take the action recommended in document GOV/2006/59/Rev.1 without hesitation.

...

88. The representative of **MALAYSIA** said...

89. In the light of the Handbook on Implementation and Management Strategies for IAEA Technical Cooperation Projects (document IAEA-MSI-01/01), his delegation believed that there was no basis for rejecting any of the projects in the proposed 2007–2008 technical cooperation programme. It had full confidence in the judgement of the Secretariat that all the projects were in conformity with United Nations Security Council resolution 1696 and that none of them would contribute to enrichment-related or reprocessing activities in the Islamic Republic of Iran. It therefore supported the proposed programme in its entirety.

90. The representative of the **ISLAMIC REPUBLIC OF IRAN** said that, under Article III.A of the Statute, the Agency was authorized to 'encourage and assist research on, and development and practical application of, atomic energy for peaceful purposes throughout the world'. Technical cooperation was the principal means by which the Agency did that and was the main incentive for developing countries to join the Agency.

91. One serious shortcoming of Agency technical cooperation was that the mechanism for funding it was based on voluntary contributions, so that the resources for one of the pillars of the Agency were neither assured nor predictable, whereas safeguards activities were funded from the Regular Budget.

92. In recent decades, developing Member States' expectations in that respect had been totally ignored and donor countries had on a number of occasions interfered in and imposed their politically motivated discriminatory policies on the Secretariat's technical evaluations of project proposals on the pretext that they would be funding the projects in question. That situation should be corrected without further delay.

93. In Article III.C of the Statute it was stated that, in carrying out its functions, the Agency 'shall not make assistance to members subject to any political, economic, military, or other conditions incompatible with the provisions of this Statute' — and virtually the same statement was contained in the Revised Guiding Principles and General Operating Rules to Govern the Provision of Technical Assistance by the Agency (INFCIRC/267).

Moreover, in resolution GC(50)/RES/10.A the General Conference: – encouraged Member States 'to continue requesting Agency safety review services in order to enhance nuclear, radiation, transport and waste safety, and integrated regulatory review missions in order to improve regulatory effectiveness continuously'; – encouraged the Secretariat 'to implement a more integrated assessment process in the establishment of its safety priorities, and to incorporate the insights of this process into all of its review services'; and – encouraged the Secretariat and Member States, if they so desired, 'to make effective use of the Agency's technical cooperation resources for the further enhancement of safety'. Against that background, it was most regrettable that TACC had become politicized.

94. His delegation was disappointed that a few Member States had raised objections to a project which had been proposed by the Secretariat following intensive in-house evaluation. In addition to politicizing TACC, their objections had brought into question the impartiality and professionalism of the Department of Technical Cooperation, jeopardizing the Agency's constructive role in promoting the peaceful utilization of nuclear energy in the safest and most secure manner.

95. The IR 40 heavy water-moderated reactor, now under construction, would replace the 5 MW Tehran Research Reactor when its normal operating lifetime ended. It had been designed principally to produce radioisotopes for medical, agricultural and industrial applications. Potential suppliers had refused to provide his country even with a light water-moderated reactor to replace the Tehran Research Reactor, so it was having to rely on its indigenous capabilities. His country had opted for a heavy water-moderated reactor because such reactors used natural uranium, whereas light water- moderated reactors required uranium enriched to at least 20%. The original fuel of the Tehran Research Reactor, received from the United States of America, had been enriched to 93%. When it had taken its decision in favour of a heavy water-moderated reactor, a decade previously, his country had not known when it would succeed in enriching uranium to the level necessary for a light water- moderated reactor.

96. The Secretariat had been provided with full, detailed information on the design and construction of IR 40, and its representatives had visited both the reactor site and the heavy water production plant, which were under full Agency safeguards.

97. The purpose of project IRA/9/019 was to obtain technical recommendations regarding nuclear safety, not assistance relating to the construction of IR 40 or to its fuel or equipment, and almost half of the project budget would be covered by his country under a government cost-sharing arrangement.

98. The laboratories and hot cells in the vicinity of the Arak reactor were not designed to reprocess the spent fuel, and detailed information regarding them had been submitted to the Secretariat in a design information questionnaire.

99. His country's small reprocessing research project had been terminated more than a decade previously, so that the phrase 'suspension of reprocessing activities' in resolutions of the Board and the United Nations Security Council was meaningless. As the Director General had stated in his latest report, no reprocessing activities were taking place in the Islamic Republic of Iran.

100. The Atomic Energy Organization of Iran was determined to continue constructing the Arak reactor and make it operational as soon as possible, in order to meet the increasing demand for radioisotopes, particularly for cancer treatment.

101. Through project IRA/9/019, the Secretariat's physical presence at the reactor site would be increased, as not only safeguards inspectors but also safety experts would be visiting it. That clearly showed his country's political will to ensure full transparency.

102. If the Islamic Republic of Iran were not a party to the NPT, its nuclear activities would not be the subject of Board agenda items, no resolutions regarding them would have been adopted by the Board, no intrusive inspections of its facilities would have been carried out by the Secretariat, the Iranian nuclear dossier would not have been referred to the United Nations Security Council, and TACC would not be scrutinizing what was a humanitarian project. Anyone doubting that statement should consider the projects proposed for Israel. It was shameful that countries which publicly declared themselves strong proponents of the NPT and its universality, such as Canada and Australia, did not dare to express concerns regarding the provision of technical assistance to a country which was not party to the NPT, which had a long, dark record of violating Agency and United Nations Security Council resolutions and which categorically rejected the NPT and Agency safeguards. Among Israel's nuclear facilities was a heavy water-moderated reactor which was not subject to Agency safeguards and also not being operated in accordance with the Agency's safety standards, and even visits to it by Agency safety experts were rejected, giving rise to serious concerns about possible releases of radionuclides into the environment. It was astonishing that the governments of such countries assumed that the bitter reality could be kept secret from their peoples indefinitely. Sooner or later, those governments would be brought to account and be questioned for deceiving their peoples and the international community as a whole. In the words of an Iranian proverb, 'The sun shall not be hidden behind the clouds forever!'

103. TACC was expected to refrain from engaging in politics and to facilitate technical cooperation between developing and developed countries. Endorsement of all projects in the proposed technical cooperation programme for 2007–2008 would assure developing Member States that the Agency was really serious about promoting the safe and secure application of nuclear energy throughout the world.

...

Document 91: Technical Assistance and Cooperation Committee: The Agency's proposed programme for 2007-2008

(GOV/2006/59/Rev.1, Add.1, and Add.1/Corr.1), GOV/COM.8/OR.147,
22 November 2006

1. The **CHAIRMAN**, summing up, said that...

...

9. Several members had expressed the need for caution regarding technical cooperation with the Islamic Republic of Iran, in light of the recent resolutions of the Board of Governors and the Security Council. They had welcomed the assurances provided by the Secretariat that the proposed projects were in conformity with relevant Board and Security Council resolutions and in particular that they did not contribute to enrichment related or reprocessing activities in Iran and that during implementation of those projects, as with all others, all the requirements of the relevant Board and Security Council resolutions would continue to be conformed with. However, they had expressed particular concern regarding the proposed project IRA/9/019 in light of the resolutions of the Board and the Security Council. They had expressed the view that they were not in a position to join a consensus on the proposed technical cooperation programme if that project were included.

10. Several other members had expressed their confidence that the Secretariat had developed the proposed technical cooperation programme in a professional, impartial and non-discriminatory manner in line with the Agency's Statute and in accordance with the decisions of its Policy-Making Organs and of the Security Council. They had emphasized the relevance of the Revised Guiding Principles approved by the Board and contained in document INFCIRC/267. They had stressed that technical assistance should not be subject to any political, economic, military or other conditions incompatible with the Agency's Statute. They had proposed that the programme as contained in the Secretariat's documents be forwarded to the Board for approval in its entirety. Some had expressed the view that the credibility of the Agency would be damaged if double standards were applied in assessing the Agency's technical cooperation projects.

11. The importance of recommending to the Board the technical cooperation programme by consensus and the need to avoid politicization of the work of the Committee had been stressed by many members.

…

15. The Committee had received the technical cooperation programme for 2007–2008. After considering the programme and following an exchange of views, the Committee had decided to convey the programme to the Board for its consideration.

16. He took it that his summing-up was acceptable.

17. It was so agreed.

18. The representative of **CUBA, speaking on behalf of the NAM**, expressed the Movement's appreciation to the Chairman for his efforts to find consensus. She recalled the NAM's principled position on the inalienable right of developing countries to engage in research, production and use of nuclear energy for peaceful purposes without discrimination. The NAM furthermore emphasized that the promotional activities of the Agency, which were essential in fulfilling its mandate, were accomplished through technical assistance and cooperation and without imposing conditions incompatible with the Agency's Statute.

19. Without prejudice to the assurances given by the Secretariat that all the projects included in the proposed technical cooperation programme for 2007–2008 had been formulated in conformity with the Statute and the Revised Guiding Principles as contained in document INFCIRC/267, and that the projects were not in violation of Security Council or Board of Governors resolutions, the NAM agreed that the Committee forward the proposed programme to the Board of Governors for its consideration.

20. The NAM had exhibited flexibility and readiness to cooperate with all other members on the way forward and had the expectation that when the proposed programme was considered by the Board there would be no repetition of statements and issues already discussed in the Committee. With a view to facilitating the conclusion of the work, the NAM could go along with the proposal that the Board, when it met, could decide to implement the entire programme and defer the decision on project IRA/9/019 without prejudice. The NAM hoped that all members would display a constructive spirit to enable the Agency's proposed programme for technical assistance and cooperation for the period 2007-2008 to be implemented without delay.

21. The representative of **MOROCCO** renewed his delegation's confidence in and support for the Secretariat's impartiality and professionalism, and called on all to refrain from taking measures that might undermine that confidence in the Secretariat. He said that it was very important for all concerned to preserve the Committee as a forum for considering issues of importance to technical cooperation.

Document 92: Report of the Technical Assistance and Cooperation Committee on its meetings held from 20 to 22 November 2006

GOV/2006/65, 22 November 2006

...

12. A number of members expressed the need for caution regarding technical cooperation with the Islamic Republic of Iran, in light of the recent resolutions of the Board of Governors and the Security Council. They welcomed the assurances provided by the Secretariat that the proposed projects are in conformity with relevant Board and Security Council resolutions and in particular that they do not contribute to enrichment-related or reprocessing activities in Iran and that during implementation of these projects, as with all others, the Secretariat will ensure that all the requirements of the relevant Board and Security Council resolutions would continue to be conformed with. However, they expressed particular concern regarding the proposed project IRA/9/019 in light of the resolutions of the Board of Governors and the United Nations Security Council. They expressed the view that they were not in a position to join a consensus on the proposed TC programme if that project were included.

13. A number of other members expressed their confidence that the Secretariat had developed the proposed TC programme in a professional, impartial and non-discriminatory manner in line with the Agency's Statute and in accordance with the decisions of its policy-making organs and of the United Nations Security Council. They emphasized the relevance of the Revised Guiding Principles approved by the Board and contained in document INFCIRC/267. They stressed that technical assistance should not be subject to any political, economic, military or other conditions incompatible with the Agency's Statute. They proposed that the programme as contained in the Secretariat's documents be forwarded to the Board of Governors for approval in its entirety. Several expressed the view that the credibility of the Agency would be damaged if double standards were applied in assessing the Agency's TC projects.

14. The importance of recommending to the Board the TC programme by consensus and the need to avoid politicization of the work of the Committee was stressed by most members.

Document 93: GOV/OR.1173

23 November 2006

...

21. The CHAIRMAN, recalling that the items before the TACC had prompted extensive discussions and difficult negotiations, expressed appreciation for the flexibility and understanding which had enabled a compromise to be reached and proposed that the Board proceed to take decisions on the items referred to it by the TACC.

22. It was so agreed.

23. With regard to Annex 1 of the TACC's report, he took it that the Board approved the Agency's proposed technical cooperation programme for 2007–2008 contained in document GOV/2006/59/Add.1 and Corr.1, with the exception of project IRA/9/019 entitled 'Strengthening Safety Capabilities for the Construction of a Research Reactor' on which no decision was taken.

24. It was so decided.

25. The CHAIRMAN said he understood that, to reflect the decision just taken, the document containing the technical cooperation programme for 2007–2008 just approved would be re-issued with project IRA/9/019 appearing as an annex.

...

123. Ms. KAUPPI **(Finland), speaking on behalf of the European Union**, said...

...

128. The European Union recalled the statement made by its foreign ministers on 17 July 2006 that if Iran did not comply with the Security Council's requirements, the European Union would work for the adoption of measures under Article 41 of the United Nations Charter. The European Union also recalled that in its resolution 1696 the Security Council had expressed its intention to adopt appropriate measures under Article 41 of the Charter if Iran did not comply. Accordingly, the continuation by Iran of its enrichment-related activities had left the European Union no choice but to support consultations on such measures.

...

Document 94: Consideration of GOV/2006/64 (continued)

GOV/OR.1174, 23 November 2006

...

66. Mr. SOLTANIEH **(Islamic Republic of Iran)**...

...

68. Paragraph 7 of the Director General's latest report bore witness to the fact that Iran's assertion that it had no reprocessing activities was correct. There had therefore been no legal basis for either the Board resolutions or Security Council resolution 1696.[390]

69. Iran had fully cooperated in the implementation of comprehensive safeguards in accordance with the agreement contained in document INFCIRC/214.[391] Indeed, Iran had recently sent two communications to the Director General demonstrating its full support for the Agency and to the Director General. The first one related the Agency's request for access to the operating records for product and tail assays at the PFEP. It informed the Agency that the President of the Atomic Energy Organization of Iran (AEOI) had agreed to instruct the operator to provide such access. Although the AEOI had already provided access to those records, which it did not consider an obligation, the decision had been made in a spirit of cooperation with a view to facilitating the work of the Agency. The second communication related to Iran's agreement to an Agency request to resample equipment at a technical university.

70. The threat of armed attack against Iran's peaceful nuclear installations by the United States of America and Israel had increased... Thus, the Agency's Member States

---

[390] Doc. 10.
[391] Doc. 4.

and the international community were expected to take prompt action in dealing with such an urgent case.

...

83. Mr. SOLTANIEH (**Islamic Republic of Iran**) requested the Deputy Director General for Safeguards to inform the Board and the international community how many Member States had received a certificate stating that they had no undeclared nuclear activities. It was a fact that there were only a handful of such countries; even for Japan, it had taken almost 30 years to get that certificate. The media was putting pressure on Iran in that regard without knowing the full details of the process involved.

...

85. Mr. HEINONEN (**Deputy Director General for Safeguards**) said that as at the end of 2005, the Agency had certified the correctness and completeness of the declarations of 24 countries, as reflected in the SIR. He repeated that the Agency was facing a unique situation in Iran where nuclear activities had gone undeclared for two decades. That had hitherto not happened in many countries. As a result, the issues had to be addressed in a unique way.

86. The DIRECTOR GENERAL, underlining what the Deputy Director General of Safeguards had just said, said that the situation with Iran was obviously unique and could not have been foreseen in developing comprehensive safeguards agreements. An NPT (INFCIRC/153-type) safeguards agreement focused on verifying declared nuclear material and nuclear facilities and making sure that nothing had been diverted to nuclear weapons. After the situation with Iraq in 1991, Member States had recognized that focusing on declared activities alone was not sufficient. They had given the Agency additional authority under the additional protocol to verify that there were no indications of undeclared material or activities. The additional protocol helped the Agency to do that in many ways. For example, the Secretariat could visit places that it was not able to visit readily under the safeguards agreement. He hoped to see the additional protocol universally applied because it allowed the Secretariat to provide additional assurances to the board of Governors, which was something it regarded as a service.

87. In the case of Iran, the unique element was that the Agency had not started with a tabula rasa. The Secretariat had started from a situation where it had come to realize that there had been activities for 20 years which it did not know about. Obviously that created a different situation and meant that Iran had to take the initiative to explain what had happened if it wanted to assure the international community that everything in Iran had now been declared. For some time an additional protocol had been operating in Iran, applied provisionally. It had been helpful because, as a result of intensive efforts, the Secretariat had gained considerable understanding of the Iranian programme.

88. What the Secretariat had seen so far, and reported to the Board, was that Iran had knowledge of the entire spectrum of the fuel cycle. That was legitimate under the NPT, but should have been declared to the Agency many years previously. So far, the Secretariat had not yet seen any industrial operating capacity.

89. While the Secretariat had verified that all declared nuclear material and facilities in Iran were under safeguards, it still needed to assure itself, because of the long period of undeclared activities, that there was nothing in Iran that had not been declared to the Agency. When the Secretariat asked questions in Iran, it did so in order to reconstruct the 'history'. What had Iran procured? Who had been involved? What had a certain experiment been for? When and where had it taken place?

90. He emphasized that what the Secretariat was doing was essentially giving a service to Iran and to the international community because it wanted to be able to provide assurance that Iran's programme was exclusively for peaceful purposes. That would begin to build the confidence that had been lost because of the undeclared activities.

91. He made it very clear that the Secretariat did not get involved in future intentions. It reported the facts. It stayed away from future intentions because that was a matter of political risk assessment that it was not requested to do, was not equipped to do, nor was it, in his view, proper for the Secretariat to do.

92. He assured members that in Iran the Secretariat was using all the ability, capacity and authority that it had, as it had also been doing everywhere else. He repeated that much of what the Secretariat had to do had not been foreseen in the authority provided to the Agency under the NPT safeguards agreements, or even the additional protocol in 1995. Basically, he was telling Iran: "If you want to fully restore the confidence of the international community you need to go out of your way to clarify the situation for us and that will require full transparency". Iran had taken a number of transparency measures in the past giving, for example, access to military sites that was not available under normal circumstances. But the Secretariat still needed an explanation of the programme from its inception to the present day clarifying how it had been developed and its scope. That meant meeting people, getting records and having evidence of what had happened. Much of that went beyond the additional protocol, and far beyond the safeguards agreement, so the solution was not going to be found by relying on one legal clause or another. The solution would be for Iran to accord the Secretariat maximum transparency and maximum cooperation so that it could report to Member States that it had checked all the outstanding questions, verified all the information available, visited all the sites that it had been told might be relevant to the programme and that it had no indication of undeclared activities. Of course, as for every other country, such a statement was not a 100% guarantee. The more transparency there was, the more assurance the Secretariat could provide Member States.

...

95. The CHAIRMAN, summing up, said that the Board had taken note of the Director General's report in document GOV/2006/64 on the implementation of the NPT safeguards agreement in the Islamic Republic of Iran.[392] The Board had expressed its appreciation to the Director General and the Secretariat for their professional and impartial work on that issue. 96. Several members had regretted that, contrary to the resolutions of the Board and the Security Council, no progress had been made towards clarifying outstanding questions relating to the scope and nature of Iran's nuclear programme, and they had expressed concern that Iran had not provided the Agency with access to relevant locations, information and individuals or carried out the transparency measures needed to clarify those questions. They had noted that the latest results of environmental sampling carried out by the Agency gave rise to further important issues. They had noted the Director General's assessment that the Agency would remain unable to make further progress in its efforts to verify the absence of undeclared nuclear material and activities in Iran unless Iran addressed the long-outstanding verification issues.

97. Some members had expressed deep regret that Iran had not fulfilled the obligations established by the Security Council in resolution 1696 or the requests by the Board related to, inter alia, the suspension of its uranium enrichment related activities and reconsideration

---

[392] Doc. 45.

of the construction of a heavy water research reactor, and that Iran had instead continued its enrichment activities by installing and running a second 164-machine cascade.

98. They had stated that Iran continued to suffer from a confidence deficit. They had urged Iran to provide the Agency with full transparency and to implement fully the measures called for by the Board and the Security Council, its comprehensive safeguards agreement and the additional protocol in order to establish the necessary confidence in the exclusively peaceful nature of its nuclear programme.

99. Most members had reaffirmed the basic and inalienable right of all Member States to develop nuclear energy for peaceful purposes in conformity with their respective legal obligations. Some had emphasized the distinction between voluntary confidence-building measures and legally binding safeguards obligations.

100. Several members had noted the assessment of the Secretariat that all declared nuclear material in Iran had been accounted for, while recognizing that the Agency's work on verifying the correctness and completeness of Iran's declarations was ongoing. Several members had encouraged Iran to continue cooperating actively and fully with the Agency within its mandate to help resolve outstanding issues.

101. Also, they had reiterated their support for the establishment of a NWFZ in the region of the Middle East. They had stated that any attack or threat of attack against peaceful nuclear facilities posed a great danger and constituted a grave violation of international law.

102. Several members had emphasized that the Agency was the sole competent authority for nuclear verification in connection with the NPT and that the Agency should continue working towards the resolution of the Iranian nuclear issue.

103. The continued need for negotiations and dialogue among all parties covering all relevant issues had been emphasized as the way to reach a solution of the Iranian nuclear issue. The package proposal made by six countries, with the support of the EU High Representative, and the response thereto had been noted in that regard.

104. The Board had noted the information provided by the Director General concerning Iran's agreement to the Agency's request for access in order to take further environmental samples from the equipment already sampled at a technical university and to provide access to operating records of the PFEP.

105. Several members had enquired about the implications of findings in the Director General's report for the compliance of Iran under its comprehensive safeguards agreement. The Director General and the Deputy Director General for Safeguards had responded to those enquiries.

106. The Board had requested the Director General to continue keeping it informed of developments as appropriate.

107. The Chairman's summing-up was accepted.

IRANIAN STATEMENTS AND PROPOSALS

Document 95: Statement by Iran, IAEA 38ᵗʰ General Conference

GC(XXXVIII)/OR.3, 20 September 1994

...

11. Mr. AMROLLAHI (**Islamic Republic of Iran**):

...

15. The Agency's safeguards system, based on the existing agreements between the Agency and Member States, and the Agency's record in implementing safeguards agreements had been successful. The exceptional instances of violation, as in the case of Iraq, should not serve as an excuse for the nuclear-weapon States, particularly the United States, to undermine the Agency's statutory tasks and obligations or to exert pressure to perform unconventional inspections and interfere irresponsibly with and violate the sovereign rights of other countries under the pretext of strengthening safeguards. In order to strengthen the Agency's safeguard system, it was necessary to respect the Agency's mandate and jurisdiction, to refrain from indulging in discrimination and applying double standards, and to maintain a strong stand against the unilateral actions of certain nuclear-weapon States.

16. In that context, the efforts taking place at international level to divert the issue of the proliferation of nuclear weapons to the United Nations Security Council were not only in sharp contrast with the mandate foreseen for the Security Council in the Charter of the United Nations, but could also undermine the effective implementation of Agency safeguards.

17. The Agency, under the pressure of influential powers, had so far not been able to provide a balance between its duty to prevent the proliferation of nuclear weapons and its duty to promote the peaceful applications of nuclear energy. Most parties to the NPT, particularly those which acted more independently, had been deprived of easy access to nuclear material and technology for peaceful purposes. During the preparation of the Convention on Nuclear Safety, the industrialized countries had opposed the inclusion of phrases in the draft that would have facilitated the exchange of the required technical know-how needed by Member States to ensure the safety of their nuclear power plants. Furthermore, the unilateral actions of certain nuclear-weapon States in preventing the transfer of so-called dual-purpose materials and technology, based on arbitrary interpretations, was unacceptable. Such transfers should be devoid of any political aims and objectives and should be negotiated at international level, within the framework of a legitimate and transparent process.

18. The Islamic Republic of Iran had been one of the victims of such gross injustices and, although its nuclear activities had always been approved by the Agency, it had been subjected to strong pressure from the United States and certain other Western countries. Countries such as the United States apparently did not recognize the right of the people of the Third World to enjoy the peaceful applications of nuclear energy.

19. Concerns associated with infringement of national sovereignty as a result of political pressure and the consequent increased difficulty of benefiting from the peaceful

applications of nuclear energy had led some developing countries to cease their co-operation with the Agency and even to renounce the NPT. If the objectives of the developing countries in joining international treaties on nuclear weapons and technology were not met, such countries could not be expected to comply with the provisions of such treaties....

...

21. His country had initiated the nuclear-weapon-free zone plan for the Middle East and had repeatedly emphasized that it should be established in a fair and comprehensive manner. The regional objectives would never be fulfilled and countries in the region would not be encouraged to co-operate, so long as unilateral and discriminatory pressure was applied and Israel's threatening stance continued to be supported by the United States and overlooked by certain countries in the West....

Document 96: Statement by Iran, 1995 Review and Extension Conference of the Parties to the NPT

NPT/Conf.1995/SR.3, 18 April 1995

...

166. Mr. MORADI (**Islamic Republic of Iran**), speaking in exercise of the right of reply, said that he deplored the unjustified and unsubstantiated remarks made by the representative of the United Kingdom about the Islamic Republic of Iran. It was regrettable that, since the beginning of the general debate of such an important Conference, which should help harmonize points of view, certain States were making comments which spread discord.

167. His Government's position on the export control regime was very clear. Recent events demonstrated that disagreements regarding the regime had been accentuated when a small group of supplier States, referring to 'gaps' in the IAEA safeguards system, had decided unilaterally to establish regimes which did not fall within the purview of the Treaty. Taking advantage of their privileged position as supplier States and ignoring the suspicions of the majority of State parties they were taking secret decisions after closed debates and, curiously, were making no distinction between non-nuclear-weapon States parties and non-nuclear weapon States which were not parties to the Treaty, thereby disregarding the inalienable right of non-nuclear-weapon States parties to the Treaty to have access to the peaceful applications of nuclear technology. In recent years, certain countries which controlled exports, such as the United Kingdom, which, moreover, had essentially helped create nuclear capacity in some countries, had tried to justify the discriminatory nature of the export control regime. It was time to review those erroneous principles in order to strengthen the implementation of the Treaty. The States parties to the Treaty which fulfilled their obligations should be able to exercise their inalienable right as stipulated in Article IV of the Treaty and have free access to the peaceful applications of nuclear energy. Certain powers considered themselves to be above the law and were claiming the right to judge the intentions of others, which was in absolute contradiction with the spirit of the Treaty.

Document 97: Statement by Iran, ICJ Oral Proceedings in *Legality of the Use by a State of Nuclear Weapons in Armed Conflict* (Request for Advisory Opinion Submitted by the World Health Organization) and in *Legality of the Threat or Use of Nuclear Weapons* (Request for Advisory Opinion Submitted by the General Assembly of the United Nations)

Verbatim Records CR 95/26, 6 November 1995

...

28. ... I wish to reemphasize that the right to self-defence as provided in Article 51 of the Charter, cannot be invoked to justify use of nuclear weapons. The right to self-defence is limited by the general principles of necessity and proportionality as well as those of international humanitarian law...

...

33. It is quite appropriate here to recall obligations of States arising from the Non-Proliferation Treaty and the régime created by it for achieving in fact nuclear disarmament. The treaty on Non-Proliferation of Nuclear Weapons, which entered into force on 5 March 1970, is an essential measure towards achieving the goal of nuclear disarmament. Its preamble calls for:

Cessation of the manufacture of nuclear weapons, the liquidation of all their existing stockpiles, and the elimination from national arsenals of nuclear weapons and their means of delivery.

Article VI of the Treaty which has been regarded as the most important part of the arrangements between nuclear and non-nuclear parties to the Treaty contains a legally binding commitment on all parties 'To pursue negotiations in good faith on effective measures relating to cessation of the nuclear arms race at an early date and nuclear disarmament.' This article reflects the undertaking of the nuclear powers to end vertical proliferation of nuclear weapons and eventually dismantle their nuclear arsenal as well as the commitment of non-nuclear States to end horizontal proliferation.

...

42. To say the least on the good faith negotiations, unfortunately we feel that nuclear-weapon States' words do not correspond with their deeds. In this respect, I wish to recall the statement made by the Minister for Foreign Affairs of Australia, Senator Evans, before the Court on 30 November 1995, in which he elucidated the aspects of the 'continuous and profound developments' in nuclear technology. It is difficult to believe proclaimed intentions of the nuclear-weapon States to pursue negotiations with good faith while witnessing the ongoing endeavour to acquire ever more destructive, ever more deadly nuclear technology, and ever more efficient delivery systems.

...

Document 98: Statement by Iran, UN General Assembly, Report of the International Atomic Energy Agency

A/51/PV.42, 28 October 1996

Mr. Danesh-Yazdi (Islamic Republic of Iran):

...

The last issue I should like to raise concerns the unjustifiable insistence of some nations on the unilateral evaluation and certification of the activities of other members of the Agency. As was reaffirmed in the Declaration of the 1995 Review and Extension Conference of the Treaty on the Non-Proliferation of Nuclear Weapons (NPT),[393] the IAEA remains the competent authority to verify and assure that the obligations of States Parties to the NPT are being fulfilled and that nothing is done to undermine the authority of the Agency in that regard. My delegation opposes the continued use of unilateral mechanisms for the evaluation, qualification and certification of some member States, since they are not consistent with the letter and spirit of the NPT, the principles of the sovereign equality of States and non-intervention and they undermine the authority of the IAEA.

...

Document 99: Letter Dated 4 February 2002 from the Permanent Representative of the Islamic Republic of Iran to the United Nations addressed to the Secretary-General

A/56/806-S/2002/140, 4 February 2002

...

I wish to refer to the State of the Union address by the President of the United States on 29 January 2002 and express grave disappointment about its overall approach, as well as strong indignation about the parts in which unfounded allegations were made against my country or where the President used profanity when referring to the Islamic Republic of Iran. That these remarks were intended for domestic politics and seeking to substantially increase military spending in the United States are no justification for misrepresenting historic facts and events and one cannot but reject them as diversionary sensationalism.

...

The President of the United States accused the Islamic Republic of Iran of seeking weapons of mass destruction. It is ironic that a United States administration that has systematically engaged in the dismantling and undermining of all international regimes against weapons of mass destruction takes the liberty of levelling unfounded accusations against one of the foremost advocates of such international regimes.

...

In short, this administration has made it abundantly clear that it does not seek transparent and rule-based multilateral regimes on weapons of mass destruction and wishes

---

[393] NPT/CONF.1995/32 Part I, Decision 2, Principles and Objectives for Nuclear Non-Proliferation and Disarmament, para 2.

to remain unhindered not only in developing and proliferating such weapons but more dangerously in levelling self-serving accusations against others.

The Islamic Republic of Iran does not seek weapons of mass destruction and, unlike the United States ally in this region, is a party to the NPT, CWC and BWC and has signed the CTBT. As the only victim of weapons of mass destruction in the last generation, the Iranian people have felt the horror of these weapons and are determined to ensure that no other people will have to go through the same agony. We intend to pursue this objective by advocating and promoting a world free from all these inhuman weapons.

It must be underlined that, unlike the United States, weapons of mass destruction have no place in Iran's defence doctrine. Iran is fully committed to observing all relevant international instruments on prohibition of such weapons and its compliance has been repeatedly verified by the relevant international organizations. At the same time, Iran insists and vigorously pursues its inalienable right to develop its nuclear, chemical and biological industries for peaceful purposes. This right is guaranteed in all relevant international instruments and the deliberate campaign by the United States to arbitrarily deprive Iran of this right is a further violation of these regimes.

...

(*Signed*) Kamal **Kharrazi**
Minister for Foreign Affairs of the Islamic Republic of Iran

Document 100: Statement by Iran, IAEA

46th General Conference, 16 September 2002

...

Our debate, Mr. President, is on the peaceful use of nuclear energy or put in other words the positive features of nuclear technology. We firmly believe that the real motive behind the creation of the Agency was basically the intention of facilitating the transfer of peaceful uses of nuclear technology to the developing member states. So far the Agency has pursed its statutory mandate in this regard very faithfully.

We would, however, like to emphasize the importance of staying the course of upholding the principle of balance between the promotional and verification activities. Loyalty to such a doctrine keeps the Agency within its preordained course.

...

Iran is embarking on a long-term plan, based on the merits of energy mix, to construct nuclear power plants with a total capacity of 6000 MW within two decades. Naturally, such a sizeable project entails with it an all out planning, well in advance, in various fields of nuclear technology such as fuel cycle, safety and waste management. I take this opportunity to invite all the technologically advanced member States to participate in my country's ambitious plan for the construction of nuclear power plants and the associated technologies such as fuel cycle, safety and waste management techniques.

...

Finally, Mr. President, the Islamic Republic of Iran, on the basis of its Islamic tenets, beliefs and human affinity, has always condemned the possession of weapons of mass destruction.

...

Document 101: Statement by Iran, UN General Assembly, General Debate

A/58/PV.12, 25 September 2003

Mr. Kharrazi (Islamic Republic of Iran) (*spoke in Farsi; English text provided by the delegation*):
...

Weapons of mass destruction are among the most potent threats to peace and security at the regional and global levels. The Chemical Weapons Convention, Biological Weapons Convention and the Treaty on the Non-Proliferation of Nuclear Weapons (NPT) are the results of our collective wisdom in our efforts to eliminate the threat of chemical and biological weapons and the spread of nuclear weapons. We believe that more needs to be done. We should do more to make these basic international instruments universal. We should also do more to strengthen verification of their implementation. Finally, we should all work collectively, as mandated by the International Court of Justice, to move towards the total elimination of nuclear weapons.

By adhering to all of these three instruments as an original party, my country has shown its determination to work towards the complete eradication of weapons of mass destruction from the Earth. Our commitment to international regimes on weapons of mass destruction lies not merely in our contractual obligations but, more importantly, in our religious convictions and historical experience. No country has suffered as acutely as mine from the tragic scars left from being victims of such weapons, particularly against the backdrop of a complacent international environment. We are convinced that the pursuit of nuclear weapons and other weapons of mass destruction will not only fail to provide deterrence or enhance security and influence, but will only increase vulnerability. Thus, I can state categorically that for all these reasons, weapons of mass destruction have no place in the defensive strategy of my country. We believe the only option is to work actively towards a global and regional ban on these weapons, and we have thus spared no effort in this regard.

However, the efforts to ban, or strengthen the ban, on weapons of mass destruction should not provide any excuse for denying States the right to develop technology for peaceful purposes. Unfortunately, the political pressure against the Islamic Republic of Iran to relinquish its inalienable right to develop peaceful nuclear technology is mounting, while some nuclear weapon States continue to test and develop advanced tactical nuclear weapons programmes. Furthermore, in defiance of international calls to adhere to the NPT, Israel is continuing, with impunity, its clandestine development of sophisticated nuclear weapons and their delivery systems. All NPT Review and Extension conferences have called for the suspension and freezing of Israel's tactical weapons and nuclear programmes, which are the real threats to international peace and security. They are both considered to be in contravention with the letter and spirit of the Non-Proliferation Treaty.

Iran's nuclear programme is solely for peaceful purposes, specifically for the planned production of 7,000 megawatts of electricity by 2020 for Iran's economic development. Iran will vigorously pursue its peaceful nuclear programme and will not give in to unreasonable, discriminatory and selective demands that go beyond the requirements of non-proliferation under existing International Atomic Energy Agency instruments. At the same time, Iran does not have a nuclear weapons programme, nor does it intend to embark on one. Thus, we have nothing to hide, and in principle have no problem with the Additional Protocol.[394] We are eager to ensure that this step will be utilized solely to enhance confidence and remove all doubts about the peaceful nature of our nuclear programme.

Document 102: Statement by Iran, UN General Assembly, Report of the International Atomic Energy Agency

A/58/PV.53, 3 November 2003

Mr. Zarif (Islamic Republic of Iran):

...

The objectives of the International Atomic Energy Agency, as set out in article II of its statute, include the Agency's seeking to 'accelerate and enlarge the contribution of atomic energy to peace, health and prosperity throughout the world.'

That objective emanates from an important pillar of the non-proliferation regime enshrined in legally binding provisions of the Treaty on the Non-Proliferation of Nuclear Weapons (NPT). In accordance with article IV of the Treaty, States parties undertook to facilitate the fullest possible exchange of equipment, materials and scientific and technological information for the peaceful uses of nuclear energy. Indeed, the inalienable right of all States parties to nuclear technology for peaceful purposes without discrimination constitutes the very foundation of the Treaty.

This inalienable right in itself emanates from two broader propositions. First, scientific and technological achievements are a common heritage of mankind. They must be used for the improvement of the human condition and not abused as instruments of terror and domination...

The second general proposition is the requisite balance between rights and obligations, which is the basis of any sound legal instrument. This balance guarantees the longevity of the legal regime by providing incentives for membership and compliance. The provisions of the NPT and IAEA Statute on the right to nuclear technology and the imperative of cooperation and sharing of the technology among those who have accepted the obligations of non-proliferation testify to the wisdom and understanding of the drafters. However, in practice, we must guard against further entrenchment of the impression that membership in the NPT and the IAEA safeguard regime in fact constitutes an impediment to peaceful use, while non-membership is rewarded by acquiescence, as in the case of the development of one of the largest stockpiles of nuclear weapons in the Middle East. If anything, failure to accept the NPT and the safeguard obligations of IAEA should have made the only outsider to the NPT in the Middle East the subject of most severe restrictions and not provide it with impunity.

The international community as whole has a right to be assured that the nightmare visited upon the people of Hiroshima and Nagasaki will never happen again. The only guarantee of this, obviously, is the total elimination of nuclear weapons, as stipulated by the NPT and the advisory opinion of the International Court of Justice. But as an interim measure, the international community must take all necessary steps to ensure the universality

---

[394] Doc. 5.

of the non-proliferation regime and the IAEA safeguard mechanisms. The IAEA can play a decisive role through vigorously pursuing a balanced and non-discriminatory application of the provisions of the NPT and IAEA safeguards.

Yet it must be emphasized that arbitrary and often politically motivated limitations and restrictions will only impede the ability of the IAEA to conduct its verification responsibilities in an orderly fashion. The logic is simple: such restrictions will not lead to the targets' abandoning of their inalienable right to nuclear technology and accepting marginalization in this important field of human achievement. In all likelihood, it will lead, as it has, to acquisition of the same peaceful technology from unofficial channels and in a less than fully transparent fashion, thus exacerbating mutual suspicions and mistrust.

Like all other members of the NPT, Iran considers the pursuit and development of nuclear technology for peaceful purposes to be its inalienable right, and has thus invested extensive human and material resources in the field. At the same time, as repeatedly stated, nuclear and other weapons of mass destruction have no place in Iran's defence doctrine, not only because of our commitment to our contractual obligations under the NPT and other relevant conventions, but in fact because of a sober strategic calculation.

Yet, illegitimate sanctions have targeted not only Iran's legitimate nuclear programme but in fact the entire industry and all possible sources of supply of material and equipment. What Iran has been able to achieve is primarily the result of the intellect and hard work of Iranian scientists. Regrettably, a politically charged atmosphere of concern was orchestrated concerning this limited peaceful capability, an atmosphere that has little to do with the objectives of non-proliferation.

Following consultations with the Director General of the IAEA and the Foreign Ministers of Britain, France and Germany, possibilities for a different approach emerged, an approach in which Iran's right to peaceful use was recognized and future cooperation in the area of material and technology through confidence-building and transparency promised to replace the past practice of limitations and denials.

Iran therefore decided to take yet other measures in order to remove any doubts about its intentions and to set the stage for mutual confidence and cooperation. On 23 October, we provided a full and consistent picture of Iran's activities in the past, which will certainly enable the Agency to verify not only that all Iranian activities are exclusively in the peaceful domain, in compliance with the NPT, but also that necessary corrective measures have additionally been taken in order to meet every technical requirement of the safeguard system. This will enable us to put the past behind us, to put to rest all the concerns, misplaced as they may have been from the beginning, from our perspective.

As further confidence-building measures for the present, Iran has voluntarily decided to suspend uranium enrichment activities, sign the Additional Protocol[395] and continue to cooperate with the IAEA in accordance with the Protocol, pending its ratification, which will have to be done by the Iranian parliament.

We continue in this trend and are pleased to see that this process has begun to bear fruitful results. We expect that, as we proceed on this track, reciprocal satisfaction of commitments in good faith will open yet further horizons for confidence and cooperation.

---

[395] Doc. 5.

Document 103: Proposal by Iran

Presented to Political and Security Working Group Geneva, 17 January 2005

I - General Principles

1. The E3/EU and Iran restate their respect for each other's sovereign equality and the right to freely choose and develop their political, social, economic and cultural systems.

2. The E3/EU and Iran emphasize their rejection of any threat or use of force against each other's national sovereignty, territorial integrity or political independence. No consideration may be invoked to justify resort to the threat or use of force in contravention of this principle. They will refrain from participating, assisting or supporting any act constituting a threat of force or direct or indirect use of force against each other individually or collectively.

3. The E3/EU and Iran underline the inviolability of their respective internationally recognized boundaries and will reject any attempt to infringe or alter them.

4. The E3/EU and Iran will settle disputes among them by peaceful means in such a manner as not to endanger international peace and security, and justice. They will endeavor in good faith and a spirit of cooperation to reach rapid and equitable solution to all disputes on the basis of international law and will refrain from any action which might aggravate the situation.

5. The E3/EU and Iran will refrain from engaging in, supporting or assisting any intervention, direct or indirect, individual or collective, in their respective internal or external affairs, regardless of their mutual relations. They will in all circumstances refrain from any act of military, or of political, economic or other coercion designed to subordinate to their own interest the exercise by another party of the rights inherent in its sovereignty and thus to secure advantage of any kind. Accordingly, they will refrain from direct or indirect assistance to terrorist or subversive activities against each other.

II. Elimination and Non-Proliferation of Weapons of Mass Destruction

6. Iran and the E3/EU reaffirm their commitment to all relevant international instruments on the elimination and non-proliferation of weapons of mass destruction, and underline the imperative of universal adherence to these instruments.

7. The two sides restate their commitment to elimination as well as countering the proliferation of weapons of mass destruction, nuclear, biological and chemical, through full compliance with their obligations under relevant international disarmament and non-proliferation treaties and agreements.

8. Iran remains committed not to pursue nuclear weapons and other weapons of mass destruction under any circumstances.

9. The E3/EU undertake, individually or collectively, to reject the use or threat of use of nuclear weapons against Iran, and to take all appropriate measures, individually, collectively and through the UNSC to prevent it.

10. The E3/EU and Iran underline the inviolability of peaceful and safeguarded nuclear facilities. They reject any direct or indirect attack or sabotage or threats thereof against Iranian nuclear facilities, which would warrant effective and practical action by the Security Council in accordance with the provisions of the Charter of the United Nations.

11. The two sides share the concern about proliferation of nuclear weapons in the region and in the Middle East and commit themselves to pursue rigorously establishment of Middle East NWFZ.

Ill - Combating Terrorism

12. The E3/EU and Iran condemn terrorism in all its forms and manifestations and affirm their determination to combat it.

13. The E3/EU and Iran decide to intensify and accelerate the exchange of operational information, especially regarding actions or movement of terrorist persons or groups, forged or falsified travel documents, traffic in arms, explosives or sensitive materials, use of communications technologies, and the threat posed by possession of WMD by terrorist groups.

14. Iran and the E3/EU will deny safe heaven to those who finance, plan, support, or commit terrorist acts and prevent them from using their respective territories for those purposes and will cooperate to bring them to justice.

15. Iran and the E3/EU will provide one another the greatest measure of assistance in connection with criminal investigation or criminal proceedings relating to the financing or support of terrorist acts.

16. Iran and the E3/EU will cooperate in preventing the movement of terrorists or terrorist groups by effective border controls and controls on issuance of identity papers and travel documents, and through measures for preventing counterfeiting, forgery of fraudulent use of identity papers and travel documents.

17. Iran and the E3/EU restate their commitment to continue to freeze the funds and other financial assets or economic resources of persons who commit, or attempt to commit, terrorist acts or participate in or facilitate the commission of terrorist acts; of entities owned or controlled directly or indirectly by such persons; and of persons and entities acting on behalf of, or at the direction of such persons and entities, including funds derived or generated from property owned or controlled directly or indirectly by such persons and associated persons and entities.

18. Iran and the E3/EU will cooperate, in conformity with international law, in order to ensure that refugee status is not abused by the perpetrators, organizers or facilitators of terrorist acts, and that claims of political motivations are not recognized as grounds for refusing requests for the extradition of alleged terrorists.

19. Iran and the E3/EU express their determination to scrupulously apply the above and all other provisions of the relevant Security Council resolutions equally to Al Qaeda and MeK and their affiliates and front organizations.

20. The E3/EU and Iran will establish regular contacts between their intelligence services, individually or collectively as appropriate, to ensure the implementation of the above decision, exchange information and define particular areas of cooperation.

IV- Sustainable Partnership on Regional Issues

21. The E3/EU and Iran underline that security and stability of the Persian Gulf region can only be attained through cooperation among countries in the region, and will therefore support the establishment of arrangements for security and cooperation in the Persian Gulf Region with the participation of all countries in the region, under appropriate United Nations umbrella.

22. Iran and the E3/EU underline the imperative of respect for principles of international law and bi-lateral and multilateral treaties in the relations among countries of the Persian Gulf, including respect for sovereignty, territorial integrity, national unity and political independence, rejection of resort to the threat or use of force, non interference in the internal and external affairs, and inviolability of internationally recognized boundaries.

23. The E3/EU and Iran will intensify their consultations with respect to other important regional issues particularly Iraq and Afghanistan, in promoting stability and security in the region. They will lend their full support for the finalization of the political process in these countries including holding of nation-wide elections, aimed at the establishment of democratic, stable and broad-based governments which coexist peacefully with their neighbors.

V - Security and Defense Cooperation

24. The E3/EU and Iran will cooperate in promoting peace and security at the global and regional levels. They recognize that destabilization and threats to peace and security particularly in the Persian Gulf region is of direct consequences for security of both parties and should be avoided.

25. The E3/EU reaffirms the inherent right of Iran to acquire legitimate means for self-defense pursuant to Article 51 of the Charter of the United Nations. The E3/EU decide to remove restrictions against the transfer of conventional armaments and their relevant sensitive dual use goods and technologies to Iran, and ensure that any export control arrangement will not impede bona fide transactions with Iran for legitimate self-defense and civil purposes.

26. Iran and the E3/EU decide to establish a senior expert level group with the participation of their respective military officials to carry out intensive consultations on defense issues, including defense requirements of Iran and the framework of their mutual defense cooperation.

27. The E3/EU and Iran reaffirm that an effective fight against drug-trafficking and terrorism not only require political will but the capacity to do so. The E3/EU recognizes that Iran should be supported as a country in a region which is highly affected by drug-trafficking and terrorism.

28. The E3/EU will remove restrictions and provide military, police and border control assistance to enhance Iran's counter-terrorism and drug enforcement capacities.

29. The E3/EU and Iran will establish a coordination mechanism with the participation of their relevant national and regional agencies including police, enforcement and operational officers responsible for combating terrorism and drug-trafficking, to coordinate their cooperation in these fields and to assess, identify and meet the necessary requirements to enhance Iran's capacities in these areas.

VI- Cooperation in the Area of Export Control

30. The E3/EU and Iran agree that transfer of highly sensitive materials, devices and technology should not contribute to the development and proliferation of weapons of mass destruction, particularly nuclear weapons.

31. Iran undertakes to adopt legal, procedural and other measures to prevent unauthorized access to its nuclear capability and enrichment technology by any individual, group or state and uncontrolled export to other states.

32. The E3/EU and Iran decide to cooperate actively in the area of export control and to exchange expertise and knowledge to assist Iran to put in place an effective national export of control related sensitive material, equipment and technology, and containing enforcement procedures with appropriate penalties which could contribute to the development and proliferation of weapons of mass destruction.

33. Iran and the E3/EU decide to establish a high level expert group for the exchange of expertise in the area of export control and to address any possible problem which may arise with respect to the transfer of any item, including through agreement on practical

measures to be adopted by recipient and suppliers to satisfy the legitimate concerns for the purpose of ensuring the transfer and preventing the denial.

VII. Interim Measures

34. The two sides agree that pending an overall agreement, they will form the mechanisms envisaged above for defense, counter-terrorism, counter-trafficking and export control cooperation, to meet periodically in Iran and Europe beginning immediately and as a matter of priority identify specific measures to be reported to the second meeting of the Steering Committee for implementation.

Document 104: Elements of Objective Guarantees

Presented in the Meeting of Steering Committee, Paris, 23 March 2005

Elements of Objective Guarantees

1. Strong and Mutually Beneficial Relations between Iran and the EU/E3
2. Confinement of the Program
    a. Open Fuel Cycle (No Reprocessing)
    b. Ceiling of Enrichment at LEU Level
    c. Limitation of the Extent of the Program
    d. Immediate Conversion of All Enriched Uranium to Fuel Rods
    e. Incremental and Phased Approach to Implementation
3. Legislative and Regulatory Measures
    a. Additional Protocol[396]
    b. Permanent Ban on the Development, Stockpiling and Use of Nuclear Weapons
    c. Export Controls
4. Enhanced Monitoring
    a. Continued Implementation of the Additional Protocol
    b. Continuous On-Site Presence of IAEA Inspectors, Which Can Include E3/EU Nationals, at the UCF and Natanz.

General Framework for Objective Guarantees, Firm Guarantees, and Firm Commitments

Phase	Action by Iran	Action by E3/EU
1-April to July 2005	• Approval of the additional protocol in the cabinet • policy declaration on Iran's open fuel cycle (no reprocessing) • Presentation of legislation on peaceful use of nuclear technology, including permanent ban on production, stockpiling and use of nuclear weapons to the Majlis • Resumption of the work of the UCF • Storage of UF_6 under agency surveillance	• Declaration of EU Policy to guarantee Iran's access to EU markets and financial and public and private investment resources • Declaration of EU recognition of Iran as a major source of energy supply for Europe • Launching of feasibility studies for building of new nuclear power plants in Iran by E3/EU Members
	•Establishment of a joint counter-terrorism task force, •Establishment of a joint export control task force	

---

[396] Doc. 5.

2	• Presentation of the additional protocol to the Majlis for ratification • Strengthening of legal export control mechanisms • Policy declaration on the ceiling of enrichment at LEU level • Policy declaration on conversion of all enriched uranium to fuel rods • Assembly, installation and testing of 3000 centrifuges in Natanz	• Declaration of EU Policy to guarantee Iran's access to advanced and nuclear technology • Declaration of EU readiness to participate in building new nuclear power plants in Iran • Signing of contracts for construction of nuclear power plants in Iran by E3/EU Members
	•Joint commitment to principles governing relations, •Cooperation on security in the Persian Gulf	
3	• Employing all appropriate measures for adoption of the legislation on peaceful use of nuclear technology, including permanent ban on production, stockpiling and use of nuclear weapons by the Majlis • Allowing continuous on-site presence of IAEA inspectors, which can include E3/EU Nationals, at the UCF and Natanz • Commissioning of the above centrifuges in Natanz • Immediate conversion of the total product of the above to fuel rods • Incremental manufacturing, assembly and installation of centrifuge components up to the numbers envisaged for Natanz	• Normalizing Iran's Status under G8 export control regulations • Firm guarantees on the supply of fuel necessary for Iranian nuclear power reactors to compliment Iran's domestic production • Presentation and active follow up of an EU initiative to establish a zone free from weapons of mass destruction in the Middle East
	• Establishment of a task force on strategic cooperation • Establishment of a task force on defense requirements	
4	• Employing all appropriate measures for ratification of the additional protocol by the Majlis • Commencement of phased commissioning of Natanz • Immediate conversion of the total product of the above to fuel rods	• Conclusion of contracts for defense items • Beginning of construction of new nuclear power plants in Iran by E3/EU Members

Document 105: Proposal Presented to the Meeting of the Steering Committee

London, 29 April 2005

Iran is prepared to continue and intensify negotiations in good faith in the three Working Groups and the Steering Committee and to reach mutually acceptable arrangements on the 'General Framework'.

In order to sustain the process, and as envisaged in the 'General Framework', Iran will take the following measures to implement its Phase 1 and is prepared to engage immediately in negotiations on their details and the modalities for their implementation:

A. During May 2005

• Approval of the Additional Protocol[397] in the Cabinet;

---

[397] Doc. 5.

• Policy Declaration on Iran's open fuel cycle (no reprocessing);

• Presentation of legislation on peaceful use of nuclear technology, including permanent ban on production, stockpiling and use of nuclear weapons to the Majlis.

B. After May 2005

• Resumption of the work of the UCF;

• Storage of UF6 under agency surveillance.

C. Additional Confidence Building Measures:

• For six months, Iran will continue the suspension of all other enrichment related activities and will make every effort in intensive negotiations in the three Working Groups and the Steering Committee to implement each following phase after agreement with E3/EU;

• During this period, Iran will limit the quantity at the UCF to the amount necessary for operation of the facility;

• Iran will begin allowing continuous on-site presence of IAEA inspectors at the UCF, which had originally been envisaged for the Third Phase.

• Iran will allow the Agency to seal the UF6 product if requested by the Agency.

D. Iran is prepared to start the following joint steps:

• Establishment of a joint counter-terrorism task force;

• Establishment of a joint export control task force.

Iran expects E3/EU to complete the implementation of the following steps before the end of 2005:

• Declaration of EU Policy to guarantee Iran's Access to EU markets and financial and public and private investment resources;

• Declaration of EU recognition of Iran as a major source of energy supply for Europe;

• Launching of feasibility studies for building of new nuclear power plants in Iran by E3/EU Members.

Document 106: Statement by Iran's Minister of Foreign Affairs to the Seventh NPT Review Conference

New York, 3 May 2005

...

The inalienable right of the States to develop nuclear technology for peaceful purposes emanates from the universally accepted proposition that scientific and technological achievements are the common heritage of mankind. Nuclear technology has been recognized as a source of energy and a viable option within the sustainable development policies with broad applications in the field of food and agriculture, human health, power generation and industry, water resource management and environment. The promotion of the use of nuclear technology for peaceful purposes has been, therefore, one of the main pillars of the NPT and the main statutory objective of the IAEA.

It is unacceptable that some tend to limit the access to peaceful nuclear technology to an exclusive club of technologically advanced States under the pretext of non-proliferation. This attitude is in clear violation of the letter and spirit of the Treaty and destroys the fundamental balance which exists between the rights and obligations in the Treaty. The

Treaty itself has clearly rejected this attempt in its Article IV by emphasizing that 'nothing in the Treaty shall be interpreted as affecting the inalienable right of all Parties to the Treaty to develop research, produce and use nuclear energy for peaceful purposes without discrimination.'

Let me make it absolutely clear that arbitrary and self-serving criteria and thresholds regarding proliferation-proof and proliferation-prone technologies and countries can and will only undermine the Treaty. Iran, for its part, is determined to pursue all legal areas of nuclear technology, including enrichment, exclusively for peaceful purposes and has been eager to offer assurances and guarantees that they remain permanently peaceful. But, no one should be under the illusion that objective guarantees can theoretically or practically amount to cessation or even long term suspension of legal activities which have been and will be carried out under the fullest and most intrusive IAEA supervision. Cessation of legal activity is no objective guarantee against so-called break-out; it is indeed a historically tested recipe for one.

The implementation of Article IV of the Treaty has been assured by the commitment of the States Parties to Article I and II as well as the implementation of the IAEA safeguards. The IAEA full-scope safeguard system provides the main foundation and basis for preventing the diversion of peaceful nuclear technology to nuclear weapons or other nuclear explosive devices. The IAEA has been recognized by the previous NPT Conferences as 'the competent authority to verify and assure compliance with the safeguards agreements' and to consider and investigate concerns regarding non-compliance.

The difficulty arises and gets worse when, in practice, the non-Parties to the Treaty which are supposed to be under special restrictions have been rewarded at least by acquiescence to have unrestricted access to materials, equipment and technology, while States Parties to the Treaty under the IAEA safeguards have been under extensive restrictions. In the case of the Middle East, provision of such unrestricted access to one non-party to the NPT has effectively contributed to the development of one of the largest stockpiles of nuclear weapons which has endangered regional and global peace and security. Israel has continuously rejected the calls by the internationally community and more particularly the NPT Conferences to accede to the NPT and place its facilities under the IAEA full scope safeguards.

Mr. President,

This conference would be successful if we act together and focus our efforts towards major issues of high importance. Non-proliferation, disarmament and peaceful use are the pillars of the Treaty. The international community has lent this responsibility to each of us to preserve the integrity of the Treaty and promote its implementation.

...

Document 107: Communication Dated 1 August 2005 Received from the Permanent Mission of the Islamic Republic of Iran to the Agency

INFCIRC/648, 1 August 2005

The Permanent Mission of the Islamic Republic of Iran to the United Nations and other International Organizations in Vienna presents its compliments to the Secretariat of the IAEA and has the honour to state the following:

Since early 1980s, Iran's peaceful nuclear program and its inalienable right to nuclear technology have been the subject of the most extensive and intensive campaign of denial, obstruction, intervention and misinformation.

• Valid and binding contracts to build nuclear power plants were unilaterally abrogated;

• Nuclear material rightfully purchased and owned by Iran were illegally withheld;

• exercise of Iran's shareholder's right in several national and multinational nuclear power corporations were obstructed;

• Unjustified and coercive interventions were routinely made in order to undermine, impede and delay the implementation of Iran's nuclear agreements with third parties; and

• Unfounded accusations against Iran's exclusively peaceful nuclear program were systematically publicized.

While Iran's rights under the NPT have continued to be grossly and systematically violated, and while major state parties to the Treaty have persisted in their non-compliance with many of their obligations under Articles I, IV and VI of the Treaty in general, and under paragraph 2 of Article IV vis-a-vis Iran in particular, Iran nevertheless continued diligently to comply with all its obligations under the Treaty. At the same time and merely in order to prevent further illegal and illegitimate restrictions on the exercise of its rights, Iran was forced to be discrete in its legal activities, avoiding to disclose the details of programs, which, in nearly all cases, it was not any way obliged to disclose in accordance with its obligations under its safeguards agreement with the IAEA.[398]

In October 2003, Iran entered into an agreement with France, Germany and the United Kingdom with the explicit expectation to open a new chapter of full transparency, cooperation and access to nuclear and other advanced technologies.[399] Iran agreed to a number of important transparency and voluntary confidence building measures and immediately and fully implemented them.

• It signed and immediately began full implementation of the Additional Protocol;[400]

• It opened its doors to one of the most expansive and intrusive IAEA inspections;

• It provided a detailed account of its peaceful nuclear activities, all of which had been carried out in full conformity with its rights and obligations under the NPT;

• It began and has continuously maintained for the past 20 months a voluntarily suspension of its rightful enrichment of Uranium as a confidence building measure;

• It further expanded in February and November 2004, following agreements with E3/EU in Brussels and Paris respectively, its voluntary suspension to incorporate activities which go well beyond the original Agency's definition of 'enrichment' and even 'enrichment-related' activities.

Iran has worked closely with the Agency, during the course of the last two years, to deal with the issues and questions raised about its peaceful nuclear program. All significant issues, particularly those related to the sources of HEU, have now been resolved. Indeed, except for few questions, mostly speculative, nothing more remains to close this Chapter.

The Agency's thorough inspections of Iran repeatedly confirmed Iran's statement that any amount of inspection and scrutiny will never show the slightest diversion into military activity. The Director-General confirmed in Paragraph 52 of his November 2003 report that 'to date, there is no evidence that the previously undeclared nuclear material and activities

---

[398] Doc. 4.
[399] Doc. 7.
[400] Doc. 5.

referred to above were related to a nuclear weapons programme.' After one more year and over a thousand person-days of the most rigorous inspections, the Director-General again confirmed in Paragraph 112 of his November 2004 report[401] that 'all the declared nuclear material in Iran has been accounted for, and therefore such material is not diverted to prohibited activities.'

Regrettably, Iran received very little, if anything, in return and instead has repeatedly expanded its voluntary confidence building measures only to be reciprocated by broken promises and expanded requests. The October 2003 promises of the E3 on nuclear cooperation and regional security and non-proliferation have yet to be even addressed. The February 2004 commitment by the E3 to 'work actively to gain recognition at the June 2004 Board of the efforts made by Iran, so that the Board works thereafter on the basis of Director-General reporting if and when he deems it necessary, in accordance with the normal practice pertaining to the implementation of Safeguards Agreements and the Additional Protocol', in response to Iran's expansion of its suspension to include assembly and component manufacturing was not fulfilled, until Iran agreed in November 2004 to the expansion of voluntary suspension to include the Uranium Conversion Facility which had been originally defined by the Secretariat of the IAEA as outside the scope of any definition of 'enrichment-related activities'. And the E3/EU has yet to honor its recognition, in the Paris Agreement of November 2004,[402] of 'Iran's rights under the NPT exercised in conformity with its obligations under the Treaty, without discrimination.' After over three months of negotiations following the Paris Agreement, it became evident the E3/EU simply wanted prolonged and fruitless negotiations, thereby prejudicing the exercise of Iran's inalienable right to resume its legal enrichment activities, and did not have the intention or the ability to present its proposals on objective guarantees on peaceful nature of Iran's nuclear program, as well as firm guarantees on economic, technological and nuclear cooperation and firm commitments on security issues.

In a further testament to Iran's desire to ensure the success of the negotiations, so that Iran's rightful nuclear program could also enjoy the support and confidence of the West, Iran suggested to the E3/EU to ask the IAEA to develop technical, legal and monitoring modalities for Iran's enrichment program as objective guarantees to ensure that Iran's nuclear program will remain exclusively for peaceful purposes. While one member of E3/EU accepted the suggestion, lack of consensus among the E3 prevented resort to the IAEA as an authoritative and impartial framework for solving the impasse.

Finally, on March 23, 2005, Iran offered a collection of solutions for objective guarantees suggested by various independent scientist and observers from the United States and Europe.[403] The package included:

...[summary of 23 March 2005 offer]...

Extraneous pressures prevented timely and serious consideration by E3/EU of this proposal which has the potential of providing a framework in which concerns of all sides are reasonably allayed. Even Iran's further effort to salvage the process by suggesting the negotiated commencement of implementation of phase 1 of that proposal on limited resumption of the work of the UCF - which had never had any past alleged failures, and is virtually proliferation free - with additional confidence building and surveillance and monitoring measures was misconstrued by the E3/EU as an ultimatum.

---

[401] Doc. 39.
[402] Doc. 8.
[403] Doc. 104.

In order to correct any wrong perception about an ultimatum and to ensure that no opportunity was spared for an agreed settlement, Iran agreed to extend the period of full suspension for another two months, in response to a commitment made by the E3/EU ministers in Geneva to finally present their comprehensive package for the implementation of the Paris Agreement by the end of July or early August 2005, that is nearly nine months after the Agreement.

Iran made it clear in Geneva that any proposal by the E3/EU must incorporate E3/EU's perception of objective guarantees for the gradual resumption of the Iranian enrichment program, and that any attempt to turn objective guarantees into cessation or long-term suspension were incompatible with the letter and spirit of the Paris Agreement and therefore unacceptable to Iran.

Eager to salvage the negotiations, in a message to the Ministers, Iran offered the most flexible solution to the E3/EU as they were finalizing their package:[404]

• Commencement of the work of Esfahan plant (UCF) at low capacity and under full scope monitoring, while arrangements for import of the feed material and export of the product are worked out with you and other potential partners; (Negotiations on these arrangements have already started and preliminary agreement has been reached.)

• Further negotiations on a mutually acceptable arrangement for an initial limited operation at Natanz or allowing the Agency to develop an optimized arrangement on numbers, monitoring mechanism and other specifics for such an initial limited operation at Natanz;

• Negotiations for full scale operation of Natanz would continue on the premise that it would be synchronized with the fuel requirements of light water reactors.

Against all its sincere efforts and maximum flexibility, Iran has not received a proposal as of today, and all public and diplomatic information, particularly the letter of 29 July 2005 of the E3 Ministers, indicate that the content of the eventual proposal will be totally unacceptable. We have been informed that the proposal not only fails to address Iran's rights for peaceful development of nuclear technology, but even falls far short of correcting the illegal and unjustified restrictions placed on Iran's economic and technological development, let alone providing firm guarantees for economic, technological and nuclear cooperation and firm commitments on security issues. While we had made it crystal clear that no incentive would be sufficient to compromise Iran's inalienable right to all aspects of peaceful nuclear technology, such offers of incentives are in and of themselves demeaning and totally incommensurate with Iran and its vast capabilities, potentials and requirements.

It is now self-evident that negotiations are not proceeding as called for in the Paris Agreement, due to E3/EU policy to protract the negotiations without the slightest attempt to move forward in fulfilling their commitments under the Tehran or Paris Agreements. This protracted continuation is solely geared to serve the purpose of keeping the suspension in place for as long as it takes to make the cessation a fait accompli. This is contrary to the letter and spirit of the Paris Agreement and is not in line with principles of good faith negotiations. After such long period of negotiations and so much that Iran has done to restore confidence and the flexibility that it has shown, there is no pretext for any further delay in the implementation of the first phase of Iran's proposal, by limited resumption of UCF at Esfahan, which is free from any past alleged failures, and is virtually proliferation free. With additional proposed arrangements, it should leave no excuse for anyone.

---

[404] The following proposals do not appear expressly in Iran's proposal, Doc. 105.

It must be underlined that all States party to the NPT, without discrimination, have an inalienable right to produce nuclear energy for peaceful purposes. As this right is 'inalienable', it cannot be undermined or curtailed under any pretext. Any attempt to do so, would be an attempt to undermine a pillar of the Treaty and indeed the Treaty itself.

Iran, like any other Non-Nuclear-Weapon State, has no obligation to negotiate and seek agreement for the exercise of its 'inalienable' right, nor can it be obligated to suspend it. Suspension of Uranium enrichment, or any derivative of such suspension, is a voluntary and temporary confidence-building measure, effectuated by Iran in order to enhance cooperation and close the chapter of denials of access to technology imposed by the west on Iran. It is not an end in itself, nor can be it construed or turned into a permanent abandonment of a perfectly lawful activity, thereby perpetuating, rather than easing, the pattern of denial of access to technology.

The suspension has been in place for nearly 20 months, with all its economic and social ramifications affecting thousands of families. The E3/EU has failed to remove any of its multifaceted restrictions on Iran's access to advanced and nuclear technology. In a twist of logic, it has attempted to prolong the suspension, thereby trying to effectively widen its restrictions instead of fulfilling its commitments of October 2003 and November 2004 to remove them.

As the IAEA Board of Governors has underlined, suspension 'is a voluntary, non-legal binding confidence building measure'. When the Board itself explicitly recognizes that suspension is 'not a legally-binding obligation', no wording by the Board can turn this voluntary measure into an essential element for anything. In fact the Board of Governors has no factual or legal ground, nor any statutory power, to make or enforce such a demand, or impose ramifications as a consequence of it. In light of the above, Iran has decided to resume the uranium conversion activities at the UCF in Esfahan on 1 August 2005.

The Agency is hereby requested to be prepared for the implementation of the Safeguards related activities in a timely manner prior to the resumption of the UCF activities.

The Islamic Republic of Iran wants to ensure that no effort is spared in order to reach a negotiated resumption of its enrichment activities. It is therefore, prepared to continue in good faith and in an expeditious and result-oriented manner, its negotiations with E3/EU. Meanwhile, Iran will continue to maintain its voluntary suspension of all enrichment-related activities. It is to be noted that the UCF was not originally considered by the Agency to be included in such category.

Iran is committed to non-proliferation and elimination of nuclear weapons, and considers nuclear weapons and capability to produce or acquire them as detrimental to its security. Iran will continue to abide by its obligations under the NPT and will continue to work actively for the establishment of a zone free from weapons of mass destruction in the Middle East.

Document 108: Response of the Islamic Republic of Iran to the Framework Agreement Proposed by EU3/EU

(Undated)

The proposal presented by the E3/EU on August 5, 2005[405] is a clear violation of international law and the Charter of the United Nations, the NPT, Tehran Statement[406] and the Paris Agreement of November 15, 2004.[407]

The proposal self-righteously assumes rights and licenses for the E3 which clearly go beyond or even contravene international law and assumes obligations for Iran which have no place in law or practice.

The proposal incorporates to a series of one sided and self service extra-legal demands from Iran, ranging from accepting infringements on its sovereignty to relinquishing its inalienable rights.

• It seeks to intimidate Iran into accepting intrusive and illegal inspections which go well beyond the Safeguards Agreement[408] or the Additional Protocol[409] as well as the provisions of the IAEA Statute and its mandate.

• It asks Iran to abandon most of its peaceful nuclear program

• It also seeks to abandon most of its peaceful nuclear program;

• It also seeks to establish a subjective, discriminatory and baseless set of criteria for Iranian nuclear program.

    − Such criteria would effectively dismantle most of Iran's peaceful nuclear infrastructure;

    − Criteria that if applied globally, would only monopolize the nuclear industry for the Nuclear-Weapon States.

The proposal − in spite of its size − has absolutely no firm guarantees or commitments and does not even incorporate meaningful or serious offers of cooperation to Iran.

• It amounts to an elongated but substantively shortened and self-serving revised version of an offer proposed by E3 and rejected by Iran prior to the Paris Agreement in October 2004 in Vienna.

• In the area of security, the proposal does not go beyond repeating UN Charter principles and previously made general commitments.

    − The proposal even attempts to make E3's commitment to those general principles of international law optional, partial and conditional.

• In the area of technology cooperation it fails to include even an indication − let alone guarantees − of the E3/EU's readiness to abandon or ease its violations of international law and the NPT with regard to Iran's access to technology. For instance, while under the NPT, the E3 is obliged to facilitate Iran's access to technology, the proposal makes a conditional and ambiguous offer 'not to impede'.

• In the area of economic cooperation, it only includes a conditional recital of already existing commitments and arrangements.

---

[405] Doc. 126.
[406] Doc. 7.
[407] Doc. 8
[408] Doc. 4.
[409] Doc. 5.

The proposal not only violates the Paris Agreement, but in fact makes a mockery of that agreement.

• The proposal never even mentions the terms 'objective guarantees', 'firm guarantees' or 'firm commitments', thereby indicating the total departure of its authors from the foundations of the Paris Agreement;

• The proposal equates 'objective guarantees' with termination of Iran's hard gained peaceful nuclear program.

• At the same time, it equates 'firm guarantees and firm commitments' with vague, conditional, and partial restatements of existing obligations.

In sum, the proposal is extremely long on demands from Iran and absurdly short on offers to Iran and it shows the lack of any attempt to even create a semblance of a balance. It amounts to an insult on the Iranian national, for which the E3 must apologize.

Document 109: Communication Dated 12 September 2005 from the Permanent Mission of the Islamic Republic of Iran to the Agency, 'Iranian Nuclear Policy and Activities – Complementary Information to the Report of the Director General (GOV/2005/67)'

INFCIRC/657, 15 September 2005

INTRODUCTION

...

While appreciating the tremendous constructive work by the IAEA, and sincere attempts by Director General, Dr. El Baradei, in resolving the issues, Iran has however serious concerns about the misunderstandings, confusions, misperceptions and the underestimation of great progress so far made by a few members of the Board of Governors trying to remove the purely technical issue from the framework of the Agency. They are trying to underestimate the authority of the Agency by asking the instructions from other international body .This undoubtedly is in contravention of the IAEA statute which considers the IAEA an independent pertinent body in the area of nuclear energy and its authority is already inherited in the Statute. Any attempt in this respect is endangering the multilateralism. This document is prepared with the aim of removing possible ambiguities on the Iranian nuclear activities, using the facts reflected in the various IAEA documents, inspection reports, particularly the Director General's reports to the Board of Governors, list of which are attached.

PART ONE: Short Review of Iran's Past, Present and Future Nuclear Policy & Programs

...

Non-proliferation policy after victory of Islamic Revolution in Iran:

NPT entered into force in Iran in 1974. It was followed by the comprehensive Safeguards Agreement (INFCIRC/214 based on the model agreement INFCIRC/153).[410] After the victory of the Islamic Revolution in 1979, the late Supreme Leader and the

---

[410] Doc. 4.

Founder of Islamic Revolution deplored the nuclear weapons in different occasions in his public addresses. If Iran had the intention to work for nuclear weapons, it should have withdrawn from NPT then. The justified time for withdrawal was immediately after the victory of the revolution, since an overall critical review of all multilateral or bilateral agreements and treaties concluded during last regime, was logical and digestible for the international community. Iran decided to sustain its membership and compliance with NPT safeguards and the IAEA Statute. During the last 26 years the Islamic Republic of Iran has spared no effort in cooperating with the Agency as far as its commitments under the NPT is concerned. Iran is the only Member State which voluntarily invited, in late 80s, the IAEA safeguards inspectors, headed by the DDG, to visit all sites and facilities at their discretion, even those locations not declarable under the Safeguards Agreement. In addition Iran is implementing the Additional Protocol[411] since December 2003, as if it has been ratified.

The impacts of international developments on Iranian nuclear policies:

The international developments, particularly the following ones, have had serious impacts on Iran's nuclear policy, planning and activities:

...

• US was obliged under the contract made prior to 1979 to supply new fuel for Tehran 5 MW Research Reactor, being under the Agency comprehensive Safeguards, producing radioisotope for application in medicine, agriculture and industry. It neither gave the fuel nor the two million dollars received for. Iran had projects with the IAEA on radioisotope production using this reactor. None of the international organizations including the IAEA took any step in redressing the situation and forcing the US to fulfill its contractual and legal obligations which had impeded the peaceful application of nuclear energy.

Considering the aforementioned developments which proves the assertion of the lack of implementation of promotional pillars of Statute of the IAEA as well as provisions of the Article 4 of NPT along with continuous sanctions by certain countries, the Islamic Republic of Iran had no choice other than to depend on its own resources and manpower in order to exercise its inalienable rights to use nuclear energy for peaceful purposes.

PART TWO: Short review of developments prior and after Iranian political nuclear dispute:

Dr. ElBaradei, the Director General paid his first visit to Iran in the year 2000 where he was thoroughly informed about the intention of AEOI in undertaking certain activities in the field of nuclear fuel cycle technology and construction of their facilities such as the Uranium Conversion Facility (UCF). Although Iran then had not yet adhered to the newly modified Subsidiary Arrangement, nevertheless it had willingly submitted the DIQ of Uranium Conversion Facility in Esfahan and other activities on nuclear Fuel Cycle. The Agency received the DIQ of UCF in 2000 that is almost 4 years before Iran was obliged to inform the IAEA under its comprehensive Safeguards Agreement (INFCIRC/214). Therefore the notion of the revelation of undeclared activities such as UCF or concealment is absolutely incorrect.

The Director General was again invited to Iran in 2003 where he visited uranium centrifuge enrichment pilot plant (PFEP) at Natanz on 21st February 2003. In his meeting with Iranian president, he congratulated the scientific achievement. He suggested to Iran to concur with the modified Subsidiary Arrangement and to sign the Additional Protocol. The President gave affirmative response regarding the Subsidiary Arrangement and invited

---

[411] Doc. 5.

the Agency's experts to explore various technical, legal and security dimensions of the Additional Protocol in order to pave the way for decision making process.

There was no doubt for the Director General that the establishment of uranium enrichment facility is not in contravention of the Safeguards obligations and Iran was not obliged to submit the Design Information Questionnaire (DIQ) of the Enrichment Facility in Natanz prior to the visit since according to the comprehensive Safeguards Agreement (INFCIRC/214), Iran has to submit the DIQ only 180 days prior to the introduction of nuclear material to the facility. At meeting of the Board of Governors in March 2003, after DG visit to Iran, the governor of Greece in his statement on behalf of the EU, took note of the important development that the Iranian authorities had agreed to amend the Subsidiary Arrangements of the country's Safeguards Agreement, committing it to providing early design information on relevant facilities (that is Iran was not legally obliged to do so before). At the same meeting, the UK governor said 'while the amendment of Iran's Subsidiary Arrangements following the Director General's visit was welcomed, if they had been amended earlier, Iran would have been required to provide early notification of the enrichment facility'. Therefore Iran had no legal obligation to notify the IAEA about the enrichment facility at Natanz earlier. In fact the Agency became fully aware much sooner than Iran was obliged to report in accordance with its comprehensive agreement, since the Pilot Fuel Enrichment Plant (PFEP) was not fully operational then and even now after about two years is still not operational.

Iran permitted the Agency's inspectors to take environmental samples from the PFEP after DG visited. The results of the analysis indicated the presence of low and high enriched uranium (LEU & HEU) particles. The results created an ambiguity since the PFEP did not have the capability for such enrichment .Therefore Iran decided to share with the IAEA, the highly confidential information regarding the deal on centrifuge components with foreign intermediaries, responsible for delivering used and contaminated items instead the expected brand new ones. Iran declared that the sources of such LEU & HEU are outside of Iran. The information on sample analysis results which required further time consuming technical analysis became an issue to be dealt with in diplomatic circles at Agency headquarter and the Board of Governors. Such delicate confidential information was immediately released to the media. Therefore a purely technical issue at its preliminary analytical stage was used as fuel for political confrontation by a certain country trying to create a dispute in order to justify removal of the issue from the framework of the IAEA, the sole pertinent international organization. In other words, it was determined to impose its unilateral policy though had in other occasions been universally condemned.

The following examples will prove that the exaggeration and continuous allegations such as the 18-year concealment of nuclear activities such as uranium conversion are baseless

...

Sustained & proactive cooperation of Iran with the IAEA and International community

...

d- In an historical and unprecedented gesture, Iran decided to voluntarily and temporarily suspend its enrichment and reprocessing activities in order to give the Agency opportunity to perform its technical activities including sampling and analysis of the contaminated samples at Natanz.

e- Director General in his report to the Board of Governors[412] confirmed that 'Since December 2003, Iran has facilitated in a timely manner Agency access under its Safeguards Agreement and Additional Protocol to nuclear materials and facilities, as well as other locations in the country, and has permitted the Agency to take environmental samples as requested by the Agency.

f- The Director General informed the Board that 'Since October 2003, Iran's cooperation has improved appreciably'.

The following major measures by Iran are the basis of his assessment:

...

IAEA's Performance since the political dispute started:

The Agency performance could be evaluated on the basis of the functions and decisions of the Board of Governors and the Secretariat in brief as follows:

1-Under the political pressure of few western countries, the Board of Governors was in many cases politicized to the extent that the technical issues were scarified and resolutions were mostly beyond the letter and spirit of the Agency's Statute and the NPT. The comparison between the deliberations of Iranian nuclear case and others, by the Board of Governors in this period, will support the assertion that Iran has been discriminated and this technical international body has to great extend been politicized. The historical positions and criticism of the countries of Non-Aligned Movement (NAM) during the meeting of the Board of Governors as well As the 48th Session of the General Conference is a clear indication of the unjustified status quo (Annex 2).

2-The phrase 'Concealment' which was first used by US and later by Secretariat in its reports, are absolutely incorrect and misleading. Lack of reporting of the activities such as establishment of nuclear facility which Iran was obliged to inform the Agency through DIQ form under its Comprehensive Safeguards Agreement (INFCIRC/214),only 180 days before the defined nuclear material are feed in, is not a concealment. It has to be recalled that when some of the activities and design and construction of facilities started, the Additional Protocol even did not exist!! ...The last but not the least is the fact that the Agency is legally neither in position nor it could judge the intention of Member States thus the use of the concealment phraseology is out of context. The Secretariat is mandated to verify the declaration of the State Parties by technical means.

3- Although the Secretariat intended and tried to behave impartially and within the provisions of the comprehensive Safeguards and the Additional Protocol but in number of cases acted beyond them demanding Iran to provide information or to grant access where Iran was not obliged either under the provisions of the comprehensive Safeguards or the Additional Protocol, but under the pretext of the cooperation and transparency requested by the Board of Governors.

4- In few cases where Iran was not in position to fulfill the extraordinary requests due to logistic, time constraint or national security concerns, the Secretariat did reflect the issue to the Board of Governors as if Iran had not fulfilled its legal obligations. The few members of the Board of Governors have to be blamed for opening new chapter of unprecedented activities for the Secretariat such as the non-technical intelligence activities working on networks which are beyond the Statute.

5- In many cases conclusions were made and reported to the Board of Governors, before sampling, analysis and technical investigation be completed. Several resolutions were passed against Iran based on premature information particularly on contaminations

---

[412] Doc. 40 para 36.

in spite of repeated request by Iran in refraining to conclude hastily before the technical investigation is over .The confirmation (Para 12 & 45 of GOV/2005/67) of the Iranian repeated assertion of the foreign source of uranium contamination proves this claim. Iran did reflect it inconveniences on such shortcomings in documents INFCIRC/628 and INFCIRC/630 as well as the statements at the meetings of the Board of Governors (Annex 4).

6- Since the terms 'transparency', 'full cooperation', 'completeness of information', are not defined as far as the scope and limits are concerned, sometimes lengthy debates are made in order to convince individual inspectors, where in the majority of cases that the terms are well defined in the Safeguards Agreement and the Additional Protocol inspections are smooth and effective.

7- In fact the proponents of the resolutions using new terms have to be blamed not the Secretariat. Although many Member States have often admired the patience and cooperation of Iran in this regard, but they have already expressed serious concerns that such practices might turn into new precedence in terminology of the legal obligations in particular Agency's Safeguards.

…

Calling on Iran to extend and continue suspension of its nuclear activities which are under Agency's Safeguards is in contravention of the spirit and the letter of the NPT, Statute of the IAEA as well as the Safeguards Agreements. Few members of the Board of Governors have spared no effort in imposing their discriminatory policy by prolongation of the suspension, although considered in all resolutions as voluntary, non-legally binding, as a confidence building measure, with the aim of total cessation of Iranian nuclear activities.

…

It is of a great concern and disappointment that the more Iran did cooperate and took additional steps mostly beyond its legal obligations, and the more outstanding questions were resolved, and the more stringent Safeguards measures applied; the language of the proposed resolutions by US and EU3 became tougher and the inspections were conducted in much more stringent and robust manner.

The following information exerted [*sic*] from the DG report to the Board of Governors and resolutions supported the assertion regarding the unjust and frustrating trend: In June 2003 Iran was first requested: Not to introduce nuclear material at the pilot enrichment plant as a confidence building measure that is only suspend enrichment process. Gradually in subsequent meetings, September 2003, November 2003, February 2004, March 2004, June 2004, September 2004, November 2004,[413] Iran was requested to expand its voluntary suspension to: testing, assembling of the machines, manufacturing of centrifuge components, production of UF6, and finally to suspend complete uranium conversion at UCF, and not to conduct R&D. Considering the fact that the suspension was recognized even by Agency's resolutions as voluntary, non-legally binding, and as a confidence building measure, therefore these requested measure are in contrary to all provision of the NPT and Agency's Statute.

Special session of Board of Governors (August 2005):

Background:

A-Iran submitted a constructive proposal, based on the Paris agreement, on Objective Guarantees for nuclear activities including the enrichment to remain exclusively peaceful. (Annex-5) The EU3 rejected the proposal.

---

[413] Doc. 22-Doc. 28. There was no IAEA BOG resolution in February 2004.

B- After months of delay, the EU3 gave Iran a proposal which is in full contravention of the spirit and letter of the Paris agreement. In this proposal EU3/EU had exclude the Iran's right to have activities on nuclear fuel cycle. Both Tehran & Paris agreements in 2003[414] and 2004[415] respectively had recognized Iran's right to work on nuclear fuel cycle including enrichment. In accordance with the Paris Agreement, Iran agreed to voluntarily suspend, as a confidence building, non-legally binding measure, its enrichment while the negotiation on mutually acceptable long term arrangement proceeds. Long before the resumption of the activities of the UCF, Iran had in many occasions including at the Ministerial Meeting in Geneva warned that any proposal from EU3 which exclude Iran's inalienable right for nuclear fuel cycle, will be contrary to Paris Agreement thus the shall put the continuation of negotiation in jeopardy. Based on the above mentioned developments and arguments, Iran had no more choice than to resume the UCF activities.

In spite of the Iran's major positive initiatives such as the voluntary suspension, the EU3 took an unjustified hasty step by calling a special session of Board of Governors for a minor issue related to bilateral agreement and proposed a resolution against Iran, the negotiating party! Although in this resolution the it is reiterated that the suspension of nuclear activities including the UCF are voluntary, confidence building, and non-legally binding measures but this unprecedented immature gesture by EU3 has to a great extent poisoned the environment of trust, cooperation and dialogue, so called Vienna spirit.

...

The future perspective based on the Agency's latest overall assessment:

After almost two years robust investigation, samplings and technical analysis, the key issue of the source of HEU contamination is resolved. The DG confirmed the Iranian declaration by saying: 'Based on the information currently available to the Agency, the results of that analysis tend, on balance, to support Iran's statement about the foreign origin of most of the observed HEU contamination'.[416] With the cooperation of the third country the assertion of Iran has once again been confirmed.

DG further reported: corrective measures for failures have been made. All the declared nuclear material in Iran has been accounted for, and therefore such material is not diverted to prohibited activities. Agency will continue its safeguards activities in Iran on a routine manner, implementing the comprehensive safeguards agreement and the Additional Protocol. Iran is determined to continue its full cooperation with Agency in accordance with Safeguards Agreement and the Additional Protocol.

PART THREE: Comments on the DG report (GOV/2005/67)

...

In BRIEF:

Considering the facts that:

• After over 1300 Man-days most robust inspections;

• Full implementation of the Additional Protocol, included performed more than 20 complementary accesses some with short notices of 2 hours or less during the past two years;

• IAEA has confirmed that it has not found any evidence that Iranian nuclear materials and activities are diverted to prohibited purposes; All nuclear materials are accounted for;

---

[414] Doc. 7.
[415] Doc. 8.
[416] Doc. 40 para 12.

• Iran decided to take a major proactive step, suspending voluntarily its enrichment activities, in order to give a chance for the Agency to perform technical analysis of the samples;

• The IAEA has confirmed, as reported by DG (GOV/2005/67), that the sources of HEU contamination are outside of Iran. It is proved that the HEU particles are not resulted from enrichment in Iran;

• Iran is implementing Comprehensive Safeguards Agreement and voluntarily implementing the Additional Protocol as if it has ratified it;

• The bitter past history of monopoly, sanctions as well as the lack of any international legally binding instrument for assurances of nuclear supply; As reflected in NAM declarations and even the resolutions, even the last resolution adopted by the Special Board of Governors, the suspension of all related enrichment activities are a voluntary and non-legally binding as a confidence building measure;

• The existence of scientifically well justified and technically reliable mechanisms and sophisticated surveillance equipment at the IAEA's Safeguards Department, capable of verifying the declared enrichment activities and the levels of enrichment, and giving assurance that such activities are exclusively for peaceful purposes;

• Islamic Republic of Iran has in number of occasions announced that it shall spare no effort to assure the international community that its activities will be exclusively for peaceful purpose.

There is no reason for Iran to sustain its frustrated voluntary suspension of uranium conversion (UCF) and enrichment as the result of which it would further be deprived from its inalienable right to work on nuclear fuel cycle, with the aim of producing required fuels for its research reactors and nuclear power plants.

Conclusion:

Based on the facts and documents referred in this paper, the IAEA Member States, have to facilitate the progressive and constructive process within the framework of the IAEA continue, thus to further assure that the multilateralism and multilateral diplomacy works. At the same time the Member States have to prevent a certain state which has in other occasion implemented unilateral policy in contravention of international law and has ignored serious security concerns of the international community, under the false pretext of existence of the WMD, to take all achievements so far made by the IAEA, as hostage and derail the process to outside of the framework of the IAEA, pushing for confrontation which definitely endanger regional and global security.

Reiterating that Islamic Republic of Iran is fully committed to the principles of nuclear disarmament and non-proliferation and the nuclear weapons option is not in Iran's Defense Doctrine, it declares that it is determined to continue its full cooperation with the IAEA and implementation of its obligations under the Agency's Safeguards provided that Iran is not deprived from its inalienable right for peaceful uses of nuclear energy, including nuclear fuel cycle as envisaged in the Agency's Statute and the NPT.

…

Document 110: Address by Iran's President, UN General Assembly

A/60/PV.10, 17 September 2005

President Ahmadinejad (*spoke in Farsi; English text provided by the delegation*): Today, we have gathered here to exchange views about the world, its future and our common responsibilities towards it. It is obvious that the future of the world is intertwined with its current state and with the prevailing trends, which exhibit signs of hope and despair.

...

Here, I should like to talk briefly about the approach and initiative of the Islamic Republic of Iran on the nuclear issue. Nuclear weapons and their proliferation, on the one hand, and attempts to impose an apartheid regime on access to peaceful nuclear energy, on the other, are two major threats to international tranquility and peace.

...Some powerful States practise a discriminatory approach against access by NPT States parties to material, equipment, and peaceful nuclear technology. In doing so, they intend to impose a nuclear apartheid. We are concerned that once certain powerful States completely control nuclear energy resources and technology, they will deny access to other States and thus deepen the divide between powerful countries and the rest of the international community. When that happens, we shall be divided into light and dark countries.

Regrettably, in the past 30 years, no effective measure has been implemented to facilitate the exercise of the legally recognized right of NPT States parties to have access to and to use peaceful nuclear energy in accordance with article IV. Therefore, the General Assembly should ask the International Atomic Energy Agency - in accordance with article II of its Statute - to report on violations by specific countries that have hindered the implementation of the above article and also to produce practical strategies for its renewed implementation.

It is particularly important to note that the peaceful use of nuclear energy without possession of the nuclear fuel cycle is an empty proposition. Countries and peoples that rely for their fuel on coercive powers and stop at nothing to further their interests may indeed become totally dependent on nuclear power plants. No popularly elected, responsible Government would consider such a situation to be in the interest of its people. The history of dependence on oil in oil-rich countries under domination is an experience that no independent country would be willing to repeat.

...

Allow me, as the elected President of the Iranian people, to outline the other main elements of my country's initiative regarding the nuclear issue.

First, the Islamic Republic of Iran reaffirms its previously and repeatedly stated position that, in accordance with our religious principles, the pursuit of nuclear weapons is prohibited.

Secondly, the Islamic Republic of Iran believes that it is necessary to revitalize the Treaty on the Non-Proliferation of Nuclear Weapons (NPT) and, as I proposed earlier, to create an ad hoc committee to combat nuclear weapons and abolish the apartheid that exists in the field of peaceful nuclear technology.

Thirdly, the fuel cycle of the Islamic Republic of Iran is not technically different from that of other countries that have peaceful nuclear technology. Therefore, as a further confidence-building measure and in order to provide the greatest degree of transparency, the Islamic Republic of Iran is prepared to engage in serious partnerships with the private and public sectors of other countries in the implementation of a uranium enrichment programme in Iran. That represents the most far-reaching step - beyond all requirements of the NPT - proposed by Iran as a further confidence-building measure.

Fourthly, in keeping with Iran's inalienable right to have access to a nuclear fuel cycle, continued interaction and technical and legal cooperation with the International Atomic Energy Agency will be the centrepiece of our nuclear policy. The initiation and the continuation of negotiations with other countries will be carried out in the context of Iran's interaction with the Agency. With that in mind, I have directed the relevant Iranian officials to compile the legal and technical details of Iran's nuclear approach, based on the following considerations.

First, international precedent tells us that nuclear fuel delivery contracts are unreliable, and no legally binding international document or instrument exists to guarantee the delivery of nuclear fuel. On many occasions such bilateral contracts have either been suspended or stopped altogether for political reasons. Therefore, the Islamic Republic of Iran, in its pursuit of peaceful nuclear technology, considers it to be within its legitimate rights to receive objective guarantees for uranium enrichment in the nuclear fuel cycle.

Secondly, in its negotiations with the European Union three, Iran has tried in earnest to demonstrate the solid and legitimate foundations of its nuclear activity in the context of the NPT and to establish mutual trust. The selection of our negotiating partners and the continuation of negotiations with the European Union three will be commensurate with the requirements of our cooperation with the Agency regarding the non-diversion of the process of uranium enrichment to non-peaceful purposes, within the framework of the NPT. In that context, several proposals have been presented that can be considered in the context of the negotiations.

Thirdly, the discriminatory approach with respect to the NPT, focusing on the obligations of States parties while disregarding their rights under the Treaty, should cease.
...

Document 111: Communication Dated 4 November 2005 Received from the Permanent Mission of the Islamic Republic of Iran to the Agency

INFCIRC/661, 17 November 2005

Contradiction and legal problems of the Board of Governors resolution on the implementation of the NPT Safeguard Agreement in the Islamic Republic of Iran September 2005 (GOV/2005/77)

...

Indeed the September resolution[417] was adopted by the Board of Governors as a follow up of the August 2005 resolution[418] of the same body. The main reason for August resolution was the resumption of the activities of the Uranium Conversion Facility (UCF)

[417] Doc. 30.
[418] Doc. 29.

which had been suspended voluntarily as a confidence building measure. The UCF has been under the Agency Safeguards and its DIQ was submitted to the Agency four years prior to the obligatory timeline in accordance with INFCIRC/214.[419] There is neither failure nor outstanding issues reported for this facility. The inspection of this site as reported by the Director General is a routine Safeguard matter. While suspension of the enrichment activities, as clearly indicated in Agency's resolutions is a voluntary confidence building measure and non-legally binding obligation, in the framework of the Paris Agreement[420] Iran voluntarily extended the scope of its suspension to the UCF.

On the issue of non-legally binding nature of the suspension, it should be noted that sustaining the suspension was essential for the resolving of the outstanding issues. As aforementioned, there is neither outstanding issue nor failure reported for the UCF. The outstanding issues were mainly related to the centrifuge enrichment and the origin of contamination, which there have been lots of progress for their resolution; therefore there is no justification for linking the outstanding issues to the UCF. The UCF activity is not related to the enrichment process and was suspended as a voluntary confidence building and non-legally binding measure, so there is no legal bases and justification for issuing such an unfair and imbalanced resolution.

Operative paragraph number 4 of the resolution asks Iran to reconsider the construction of the heavy water reactor, while there is neither outstanding issue nor failure reported for the heavy water reactor and while it's [*sic*] construction is under the Agency Safeguards and its declarations are regularly submitted and updated in accordance with the Additional Protocol[421] that Iran voluntarily implements. There is no legal bases and justification for reconsideration of the decision of Iran to build heavy water reactor. Taking into account this fact that the life of Tehran Research Reactor, which is responsible for production of radioisotopes for the hospitals, is approaching to its end and its productivity is limited, the request of this resolution is in clear contradiction of the promotional objectives of the Agency's statute.

Paragraph I of the resolution is in contravention of the generally recognized principle of International Law. In accordance with the principle of international law and also the provisions of 1969 Vienna Convention, joining, ratification and acceding to the international treaties should be done with clear consent of the states and also stases con not be forced to join the international legally binding instruments. Furthermore ratification of a legally binding instrument is a time consuming process and thus the phrase 'promptly' is unacceptable condition in that paragraph.

Director General in paragraph 50 of his report to the board session in September 2005[422] requested more legal authority for the Agency. He requested that '[Iran's] transparency measures should extend beyond the formal requirements of the Safeguards Agreement and Additional Protocol and include access to individuals, documentation related to procurement, dual use equipment, certain military owned workshops and research and development locations.' but Iran and many other states believe that any increase of legal authority can be done only after negotiation and reaching consensuses among member states and this increase shall not be beyond the boundaries of the Agency's Statute (paragraph 16 of NAM statement to the September 2005 Board of Governors[423]).

---

[419] Doc. 4.
[420] Doc. 8.
[421] Doc. 5.
[422] Doc. 40.
[423] Doc. 77.

Regarding the so called failures, though Iran had a different view regarding the failures, but as it has been expressed in different documents the corrections have already taken place. This fact is also mentioned in the Board resolution itself. Therefore they are in the process of settlement and after two years of robust inspection a balanced approach should have been followed in this regard and take all the remedies and progress into account. The Board itself in different resolutions noted the progress and the different reports by Director General reaffirmed this fact (paragraph 19 and 107 and 43 and 46 of the Report Gov/2004/38).

Paragraph F of the resolution reaffirmed the report of the Director General that 'good progress has been made in Iran's corrections of the breaches and in the Agency's ability to confirm certain aspects of Iran's current declarations'. In the light of paragraph F, Operation paragraph 1 is a contradiction and seeking to constitute Iran's non-compliance with its obligations.

Iran has always viewed the so-called failures as a difference of interpretation of the Safeguards regulations. Despite that, Iran extended a vast and sincere cooperation with the Agency to resolve the outstanding questions. Different reports by the DG and even the current resolution referred to this reality. Returning to the year 2003 by this Board resolution and mentioning the failures and also aggrandizement of them could only emanate from the political motivations and ignoring all the progress that the Agency made in that regard. Besides that the DG in his reports clearly expressed that the Iranian peaceful nuclear activities had no diversions to the prohibited purposes. Neither the DG nor the inspectors have used the term 'non-compliance' regarding the implementation of safeguards in Iran. Therefore the use of the term 'non-compliance' in the Beard resolution is a clear deviation from the objectivities and has no legal basis.

Regarding the paragraph O of the resolution that express 'the Agency is not in a position to conclude that there are no undeclared nuclear materials or activities in Iran', I have to note that the DG in many reports informed the Board that conclusion on the issue that there is a bill of health regarding nuclear activities of member states is a time consuming effort. It may take years for the Agency to provide assurances that there is no undeclared nuclear activity in the territory of every member state. Therefore it is a general term and is not only related to the case of Iran. Bearing in mind this reality the content of paragraph O of the resolution which seeks to attribute this general term only to the case of Iran is an unfair statement. Reports by the D.G. show that until now only handful countries could receive that bill of health from the Agency.

Since the peaceful nuclear activities of the I.R. of Iran had no diversion to the prohibited purposes and the progress made by the Agency after more than 1400 man days inspections and also continuation of the Agency's inspections of peaceful nuclear activities of I.R. Iran there is no room for security concerns regarding the Iranian nuclear activities to justify that the issue is within the competence of security council. Therefore the operative paragraph 2 of the resolution has no legal basis and is a clear indication that the Agency is being manipulated by the political motives. By ignoring the objectivities that reported by the DG this resolution also undermined the efforts and competence of the Agency.

Although the resolution in paragraph B is recalling 'the inalienable rights of all Parties to the NPT to develop, research, production and use of nuclear energy for peaceful purposes without discrimination and in conformity with articles 1 and 2 of the Treaty'. But on the contrary, the operative paragraph 4 provided element that clearly deprives the I.R. of Iran for the implementation of its inalienable rights under the Treaty. Such measures that are stipulated in operative paragraph 4 are also against the purposes and functions of the Agency and its Statute. Paragraph K of the Board resolution requested Iran to suspend the uranium conversion facility which is completely under supervision and surveillance of the Agency and also there is no any outstanding question regarding the same facility and it is under the routine inspection of the Agency. Such a call by the resolution doesn't have even any circumstantial basis.

Paragraph L and sub paragraph 4 (iii) also requested Iran to reconsider the construction of a research reactor moderated by heavy water. It is clear that such a call is beyond the authorities of the Board and in contradiction with all the legal instruments governing the non-proliferation and safeguard activities. The NPT itself and also the outcomes of the review conferences of the Treaty reaffirmed that a state party until its activities are under the monitoring of the Agency should not be deprived from the research and development and the use of nuclear technology particularly the heavy water reactor.

Paragraph 4 (iv) requested Iran 'promptly to ratify and implement in full the Additional Protocol'. It is also clear that such a call goes beyond the authority of the Board and it is also with blind ignorance of the objectivities. The I.R. of Iran signed the protocol in 18 December 2003 and since that time voluntarily implements the protocol. Requesting a state to promptly ratify a legal instrument is not within the authority of the Board and according to the principles of international law it is under the discretion of the state to ratify a legal instrument and the consent of the state is the main condition. One has to note that the ratification of an instrument such as the Additional Protocol in any established legal system is a time consuming process and cannot be done 'promptly' as requested by the resolution.

Document 112: Message of H.E. Dr. Larijani, the Secretary of Supreme Security Council of the Islamic Republic of Iran to the Director General of the IAEA dated February 2, 2006

INFCIRC/666, 3 February 2006

...

Respectfully, regarding the emergency meeting of the IAEA Board of Governors, I find it necessary to draw your attention to the following points:

1. The mere fact that some members of the Board - who have no privilege over the others pre-impose certain decisions on the board, goes against the legal stance and authority of the Board, and the Director General is expected to reflect on this matter.

2. Furthermore, these developments have revealed the political pressures over the Board and will jeopardise the credibility of its decisions.

3. The Board decision to report the issue to the Security Council has no legal and technical basis. Nothing particular has lately happened with regard to the inspections and no change has taken place in relations to the factual circumstances. The Iranian cooperation with the Agency has increased and remaining ambiguities have been resolved.

4. The resumption of R&D activities after two and a half years of suspension cannot provide the ground for taking harsh decisions by the Board and reporting the issue to the Security Council. Those activities are exclusively peaceful and completely within the IAEA

legal framework and their suspension was decided by Iran voluntarily and provisionally.

5. Although your Excellency and other authorities and experts in the Agency are well aware, but just for the record once again I reiterate that nuclear R&D programs and activities have the following characteristics:

– They have clear definitions and technical scope that can be recorded with the cooperation of the IAEA experts.

– They are exclusively in the boundary of peaceful activities and in the framework of the rights of the Member States to the Agency.

– They have are being planned and conducted only for the purpose of gaining the know-how for peaceful nuclear activities.

– They will be conducted under the surveillance of the Agency.

– They will be conducted within a specific timing and plan.

6. I reiterate that as you and the Agency experts confirmed, the Islamic Republic of Iran is committed to the NPT and acts within the framework of the Treaty. It implemented the Additional Protocol[424] voluntarily. In the inspections voluntarily cooperated beyond its obligations and for more than 2 and a half years has suspended its legal and rightful activities. All these initiatives were based on the assumption that the Islamic Republic of Iran had confidence in the European interlocutors and tried to create and strengthen the mutual confidence.

7. In this context, I am afraid to warn that if the interlocutors of Iran want to put pressure on the Board to report the issue to the UN Security Council and this pressures be affective, and the Council would be involved in any way with the Iranian peaceful nuclear activities, it would be the final blow to the confidence of the Islamic Republic of Iran and will totally destroy it. In such a case, the government of the Islamic Republic of Iran is logically and legally bound by the law passed by the parliament would have no other choice but to suspend all the voluntary measures and extra cooperation with the Agency which have so far made. In that case the Agency's monitoring would extensively be limited and all the peaceful nuclear activities being under voluntary suspension would be resumed without any restriction.

8. The Islamic Republic of Iran is not interested in such a situation and considers it as a set back in the resolution of the nuclear issue and believes it as a loss for all the parties including the IAEA. Therefore I request you as the Director General of the IAEA to use all your good offices and capabilities to prevent initiations of such a harmful process.

…

---

[424] Doc. 5.

Document 113: Communication Dated 7 March 2006 received from the Permanent Mission of the Islamic Republic of Iran to the Agency, 'Complementary Information and Clarification Provided by the Islamic Republic of Iran on the Report of the Director General to the Board of Governors on Implementation of Safeguards in the Islamic Republic of Iran' (GOV/2006/15)

INFCIRC/672, 8 March 2006

The purely technical nuclear issue of the Islamic Republic of Iran is politicized. The bias, exaggerated and unjustified information has mislead the international community. Due to technical nature of the issue, it requires details elaboration otherwise will create confusions for non professional individuals. The followings are additional information and clarifications aimed at facilitating better understanding of the scope and nature of the nuclear activities of the Islamic Republic of Iran: It should be recalled that the application of over 3 years Agency's robust inspections system and extraordinary cooperation made by the Islamic Republic of Iran with the Agency is a matter of high importance. It should also be recalled that Iran has fully cooperated in provision of voluminous information, granting many accesses to different locations even military sites, arranging interviews with individuals, submission of non-safeguards related information, permission for taking large number of environmental samples from nuclear and non nuclear sites and even from military sites, over thousands of hours of meetings with experts in understanding the detail of every subject, which arrived to close to over more than 1700 man-days of inspection, therefore the Agency has full understanding on every part of the program and has achieved progress on the matters. The list of numerous progress as well as the achievements are already reflected in various DG's report thus it will be refrained from repetition.

It is expected that the Agency makes outmost efforts based on technical rather than political grounds. However, refraining from entering into details of the DG report (GOV/2006/15),[425] the followings comments are focused on some paragraphs of the report, which have created more confusion:

...

Para 46: As far as the phrase 'concealment and breaches' is concerned, it has to be noted that maximum which has occurred was failure in timely reporting of items which have been proven not being related to prohibited activities. Therefore, the phrase 'resulted in many breaches of its obligations to comply with Agreement' in Para 46, is not justified. It has to be further noted that: The Director General paid his first visit to Iran in the year 2000, where he was thoroughly informed about the intention of the AEOI in undertaking certain activities in the field of nuclear fuel cycle technology and construction of their facilities such as the Uranium Conversion Facility (UCF). Although Iran had not yet adhered to the newly modified Subsidiary Arrangement, nevertheless it had willingly submitted the DIQ of Uranium Conversion Facility in Esfahan. The Agency received the DIQ of UCF in 2000 that is almost 4 years before Iran was obliged to inform the IAEA under its comprehensive Safeguards Agreement (INFCIRC/214). Therefore the notion of the revelation of undeclared activities such as UCF or concealment is absolutely incorrect.

[425] Doc. 42.

The phrase 'Concealment' which was first used by US and later by the Agency Secretariat in its reports is absolutely incorrect and misleading. Lack of reporting of the activities such as establishment of nuclear facility which Iran was obliged to inform the Agency through providing DIQ under its Comprehensive Safeguards Agreement (INFCIRC/214) only 180 days before the defined nuclear material are received by facility, is not a concealment. Even if the construction of the Bushehr Nuclear Power Plant was started almost 25 years ago, but Iran was obliged to report its existence and give specification only 180 days before nuclear material (the fuel) is received in the plant. The same is applied to other facilities such enrichment plant at Natanz, uranium conversion Facility (UCF), which the Agency was informed even four years before Iran was obliged to do so. It has to be noted that the Safeguards Implementation Reports (SIR) of the Agency includes a lot of failures by other Member States which have not been highlighted. The last but not the least, is the fact that the Agency is legally neither in position nor it could judge the intention of Member States, thus the use of the concealment phraseology is out of context.

Para 49: Concerning the issue of HEU and LEU contamination, it has to be noted that Iran has informed the followings from the beginning of 2003:

- Such contaminations are not from Iran's activities, and
- The origin of contaminations is from abroad coming through imported contaminated components. Iran has provided to the Agency extensive sampling, interviews and voluntarily presented all related documents.

After the Agency's evaluation and partial investigations outside Iran, the Agency has concluded in September 2005 that 'the results of the environmental sample analysis tend, on balance, to support Iran's statement about the foreign origin of most of the observed HEU contamination'.[426] The Agency concluded veracity of Iran's statement in this regard after long time. However, during the process of investigation at each stage, the Agency was reporting and concluding base on its preliminary results which proved later to be immature and incorrect. Eventually, the analyses of sampling from components from third country have proved the information received from Iran. The few spots on the spectrum which is the result of problems in mathematical modeling, as the DDG-SG of the Agency informed in the technical briefing on 3rd March 2006, should not create confusions and used as an excuse for leaving the file of P1& P2 opened.

Para 50: Islamic republic of Iran has already provided extensive information on P1& P2 chronology thorough interview with the individuals involved, full access to various sites, swipe sampling, documentation regarding procurement, shipment and detailed confidential information on the interaction with the intermediaries. The Agency should not judge and conclude the issues base on biased and unreliable information, where it has not been provided any documents to Iran to prove if any inconsistencies with the assertion that Iran has already made.

Para 51: Regarding the Agency's question on the work on the P2 design between 1995 and 2002, the followings are some of the reasons that there have not been any works during period 1995-2002 which have been provided to the Agency but not asserted in the report: P-1 was the National Project and not the P-2; Iran did not have any experience on centrifuge enrichment; Iran had not still obtained skills on P-1, thus it was technically a big mistake to jump to move to more advanced model such as P-2, before being mastered on P-1. This was also confirmed by the IAEA eminent enrichment expert; The former President of the Atomic Energy Organization of Iran was strongly of the belief that no work

[426] Doc. 40 para 12.

has to be conducted on P-2 before the achievement on the P-1; The commencement time of P-2 was the time that P-1 was in rather good hand and that the contract with an individual started in 2002; The inquiry of the P-2 items from abroad started in the contract period; The duration of an individual contract proves the assertion of the works conducted on P-2 in the indicated time; The Agency inspectors have already thoroughly reviewed and confirmed the activities done by the individual and its progress report; Had Iran conducted P-2 project during the said period (1995-2002, so called gap), then it should have procured items such as magnets from abroad, for the assembly and operation of even a single P-2 machine. The information that the Agency has obtained from sources including States Parties (date of any inquiry or purchase of magnets by Iran) proves that such measures have not taken place prior to the timing of individual contract in 2002; Had Iran worked on P-2 and obtained achievements, there was no logic to continue the national project and invest on P-1 in Natanz. Unfortunately this logic was not recognized by the Agency in the ground that the issue not to be closed.

Para 52: The legal authority of the Agency has already been well defined in the Safeguards documents such as Comprehensive Safeguards and Additional Protocol, which are the result of intensive negotiations of the Member States considering the provisions of the IAEA Statute and the NPT.

Any additional legal authority therefore has to be negotiated by the member states and adopted as new additional safeguard measure. Therefore, this request by the Secretariat has nothing to do with the nuclear issue of Iran. Thus, the Secretariat should have been able to fulfill its mandate under the said Safeguards provisions.

Though, the request for transparency measures are far beyond the Agency's mandate, and Iran has not any legal obligations in this regard, granted access to several military sites and environmental samples taken in addition to those mentioned in this report. It has to be noted that more than 30 samples taken from military sites and the result of the environmental samples did not indicate the presence of nuclear material at those locations, including Lavizan.

DG reported in Para 102 of GOV/2004/83:[427] '...the vegetation and soil samples collected from the Lavisan-Shian site have been analyzed and reveal no evidence of nuclear material'. Transparency measures were fully made including interviews with several individuals, delivering several documents, visits the equipment. The result of the inspections as reflected in this Para, is a crystal clear indication that over 3 years of continuous allegations by America and terrorist group supported by it, are baseless and the Agency has spent a lot of time and efforts for conducting inspections, sampling, interviews, review the documents which creating political tension among member states and damaging the credibility of the Islamic Republic of Iran and the IAEA which would by no means be easily compensated. It's time to stop such an unjustified trend.

Para 53: It is essential to note that the Agency has been able to conclude the lack of undeclared nuclear material and activities in only 8 countries, most of which are not even the advanced countries in nuclear industry. Thus, it is not fair and justified to blame on Iran in this respect. Although the preamble of this paragraph expresses '... that the Agency has not seen any diversion of nuclear material to nuclear weapons or other nuclear explosive devices', the Agency makes an hypothetical assumption in military oriented activities even not providing evidence on those allegations which the Agency claims 'recent information available to the Agency'.

---

[427] Doc. 39.

Para 54: Expression of 'full transparency' does not have a clear and distinct definition in the nuclear activities. The reason for is the example of Iran that what so ever cooperation beyond its Safeguards Agreement and the Additional Protocol and even beyond that were made available to the Agency, it did not satisfy the Agency by repeating such a request. It is not clear how far it should go and what is the boundary? It should be noted that any transparency measure has to be implemented in such a way that the sovereignty, dignity and national security of Member States be observed. Furthermore, all the requests repeated in this paragraph, had already fulfilled.

Document 114: Response Dated 22 August 2006 of the Islamic Republic of Iran to the package presented on 6 June 2006

A/61/514-S/2006/806, 12 October 2006, also circulated as INFCIRC/685, 8 November 2006

Introduction:

...

The Government of the Islamic Republic of Iran presents its reply to the package offered on June 6, 2006 by Mr. Javier Solana in Tehran[428] following examination by expert groups, on the basis of the above stated precepts and in consideration of the initiative of Mr. Kofi Annan, the United Nations Secretary-General.

1. THE ENGAGEMENT APPROACH:

The Islamic Republic of Iran has declared repeatedly in the past that it sought fair negotiations for resolution of issues. When the package was delivered on June 6th, therefore, Iran adopted an engagement approach, welcomed abolition of threatening language and embarked upon serious consideration of the proposal, in the belief that the two sides can arrive at an agreement founded on international law...

...

... With the adoption of the Security Council Resolution,[429] the resolution of the issue through dialogue and understanding was confronted with a serious challenge.

... The adverse implications of this major misstep are not easily rectifiable as confidence in the intentions of the other side is in serious jeopardy.

You are well aware that no legal, logical or even political justification exists for involvement and action by the Security Council on this issue. To interpret exercise of the 'inalienable rights' of a state as threats against international peace and security is absurd by nature and outrageous as precedence. Particularly as the IAEA Director General Dr. El-Baradai has stated that Iran's nuclear program is no threat to international peace and security.

... Defending the right to conduct research, develop and use the peaceful nuclear energy is not solely Iran's responsibility, but indeed the common responsibility for all parties to the NPT.

We reiterate and reemphasize that Iran's nuclear program has never diverted from its Peaceful course. The issue has, therefore, never been viewed as a matter of security in our perspective. ...

...

[428] Doc. 131.
[429] Doc. 10.

Nuclear fuel is destined as a strategic commodity in the future of world energy. As major European countries continue production of this commodity through heavy investments and large subsidies, Iran too expects that its substantial investments will lead to production so that it would not have to depend on exclusive suppliers in the Self-reliance, however, does not exclude cooperation and partnership. Iran's nuclear program is entirely open to joint investment, operation, development and production. As the President has declared, the Islamic Republic of Iran is prepared to implement its nuclear program through consortium with other countries.[430]

In view of our logical and firm approach for engagement aimed at resolving the nuclear and other issues of mutual interest on the basis of dialogue and international law, and to prove out good intention once again, we present our response despite the negative and destructive message that Security Council Resolution 1969 [*sic*] carried.

2. CONSIDERING THE FACT THAT:

2/1. The Islamic Republic of Iran has planned partial domestic production of its required nuclear fuel for the approved program to supply and produce 20,000 Mega Watts of nuclear power during the next twenty years. Repeated breaches and noncompliance by European countries and the United States of their undertakings under the NPT as well as their contractual obligations in cooperation and transfer of technology, before and after the revolution, their imposed sanctions, their failures to supply, and lack of international guarantees in uninterrupted provision of fuel has left no option except to move to produce part of the required fuel domestically.

2/2. The Islamic Republic of Iran has, relying on its rights stipulated under Article 4 of the NPT made substantial progress in nuclear technology... The Islamic Republic of Iran is, today, considered as a member of the nuclear fuel producing countries and this is an undeniable fact.

2/3. The Islamic Republic of Iran has, from the outset, stressed the need for observing the balance between its rights and its responsibilities under the NPT. Development of its peaceful nuclear program is based on its specific and undeniable rights under the NPT. It cannot accept deprivation from its legal rights in development and use of peaceful nuclear energy including the fuel cycle, and continuing research and development of enrichment process as underscored in the NPT and the IAEA safeguards.

2/4. The Islamic Republic of Iran has, from the outset, been committed to its obligations under the NPT in development of its nuclear program and all its actions and activities have, to date, been conducted with necessary and sufficient transparency in accordance with NPT obligations and under IAEA monitoring.

2/5. The Islamic Republic of Iran believes that the June 6, 2006 proposal has elements which may be useful for a constructive approach. Most important among them:

First-Renewed emphasis on Iran's inalienable rights to develop its nuclear program for peaceful purposes without discrimination in accordance with the NPT;

Second- Readiness for negotiations as a new beginning to reach a 'comprehensive agreement' with Iran.

3. ON THIS BASIS THE ISLAMIC REPUBLIC OF IRAN, FOLLOWING EXPERT REVIEWS, DECLARES THAT:

3/1. Considers the proposal of 6 June 2006 as containing useful foundations and capacities for comprehensive and long-term cooperation between the two sides. The Islamic Republic of Iran has, however, questions and ambiguities regarding guarantees of

---
[430] Doc. 110.

its rights. Through constructive negotiations, the grounds for overall agreement should be prepared.

3/2. Is prepared for removing concerns of the two sides through negotiations and receiving clarifications on the nature, extent, approach, level, duration and depth of issues in the offer such as real and practical cooperation in development of Iran's peaceful nuclear program including light and heavy water reactors, and exercise of Iran's right to achieve nuclear energy inclusive of the fuel cycle and continuation of research and development in uranium enrichment.

3/3. Is ready for 'long term cooperation' in security, economic and political and energy areas in order to achieve 'sustainable security in the region' and 'long term energy security'.

3/4. As always, considers that the resolution of all issues may be possible through negotiation and engagement.

4. IN THE VIEW OF THE ISLAMIC REPUBLIC OF IRAN, THE UNDERLYING IDEA AND PRINCIPLE IN THE OFFERED PACKAGE, A 'RENEWED PROCESS OF NEGOTIATIONS TO ACHIEVE COMPREHENSIVE RESULTS AND AGREEMENTS' AS SUBSTITUTE TO ALL OTHER MEANS TO RESOLVE THE NUCLEAR ISSUE, CONTAINS THE FOLLOWING:

To help peaceful and rapid resolution of the nuclear dispute in the framework of the IAEA and NPT provisions through extension of understanding, bridging the positions, and settling the differences between different sides.

To establish necessary tenets and foundations for confidence building and mutual cooperation in the nuclear field.

To improve and expand relations and mutual cooperation between Iran and other parties in all areas on the basis of mutual respect and trust.

To promote peace and security in the region and scientific, technological and economic progress in Iran.

The Islamic Republic of Iran accepts the core idea of the proposal. As it has always stated, arriving at an understanding in a process of comprehensive negotiation, to resolve the differences and to form the grounds and the basis of expansion of comprehensive and reciprocal relations and cooperation as the only way to approach these issues. We welcome this approach.

At the same time, certain points need to be expressed and stressed:

4/1. The negotiation process, as the means to reach an agreement and settle the issue, should be instituted on an initial basis of confidence. This implies that, in areas of significance, a level of assurance, including particularly in the effectiveness of negotiations, possibility of arriving at an effective outcome within a specific and reasonable time, maintaining stability during the process and avoiding disruptive and destructive action from within and without, and prevalence of a fair, balanced, reasonable and non-coercive environment should be established prior to the negotiations.

This requires discussion and understanding. The Proposal is devoid of due attention to this necessity.

4/2. Clear evidence and experience gives reason to Iran to remain seriously skeptical towards sincerity of at least some members of the 5+1 in their declared intention to establish comprehensive relations and cooperative exchanges. Iran believes, therefore, that these governments should come forward with assurances, commitments and indications that demonstrate revision in past behavior and absence of intentions to contain Iran or seek a pretext for hostile actions in advance of the negotiations.

In the view of the Islamic Republic of Iran, recent move by the 5+1 to re-open the door to the Security Council and impose a Resolution against Iran, is in clear breach of the proclaimed good faith of this group in pursuing the course of negotiation and understanding to resolve the nuclear issue. This would impede seriously the successful outcome of the negotiation process, unless all its implications are removed and nullified through a clear procedure.

...

In addition, extent and limitations on the authority of each negotiator should be defined and declared formally, as the significance and depth of the issue at hand calls for. It must become clear that the negotiators are entrusted with sufficient authority for bargaining and give and take on sensitive and disputed issues. This implies that the negotiators should be authorized to negotiate and decide on all issues at least on an *ad-referendum* basis.

Beyond all this, the proposal lacks any reference to irreversible and irrevocable guarantees which should be attached to the undertakings. Such guarantees are particularly essential on access to advanced nuclear technology and equipment, erection and commissioning of nuclear power reactors, nuclear fuel supply, and transfer of know-how and technology. For Iran, it should become clear that the undertakings of our counterparts would become permanent, with no right or possibility to their termination or limitation, in the context of export controls, NSG, domestic laws and regulations, and the procedures of the IAEA and the United Nations.

As the package has not dealt with these essentials, the Islamic Republic of Iran has prepared its own specific suggestions ready for negotiation and agreement.

...

5. THE PACKAGE HAS CONSIDERED TWO MAIN PROCESSES TO RESOLVE THE NUCLEAR ISSUE:

...

Based on elements in the package, the nuclear issue is three pronged:

First: Rights and responsibilities of the parties toward each other and the actions they should undertake in accordance with the NPT and the IAEA;

Second: Transparency, normalization and conclusion of the issue at the Agency;

Third: Confidence building by both sides in all areas including security issues.

The Islamic Republic of Iran:

First: Accepts to deal with the above issues as core issues, along with others;

Second: Agrees that the above three issues are inter-linked and for an integrated whole;

Third: Stresses that the issues are reciprocal and mutual and each side should endeavor through common efforts to move the process forward, bearing in mind that maintaining a balance in actions and expectations of each side is essential;

Fourth: Reiterates that resolution of the issues and agreements would be possible if and when all sides limit their expectations and actions to the framework of internationally accepted norms, in particular the NPT. Any expectation and action beyond the above framework would solely be considered through persuasion, understanding and on a voluntary basis.

6. ON THE FIRST AXIS

Iran's firm position is that the process of negotiations and the process of Iran's interaction with the Agency should be based on the three fundamental principles emanating from the NPT by all parties:

...

Since the enrichment and nuclear fuel cycle for peaceful use is one issue under consideration, the producers of the proposed package should clarify whether they recognize the NPT as the basis for determining the scope of this right. And whether, in their view, fuel cycle activities and in particular enrichment for peaceful use is within that scope or not.

...

Furthermore, the proposed package is vague on nuclear cooperation, transfer of nuclear technology, construction of nuclear power plants in Iran and guaranteed supply of required fuel. References are also made, in this respect, which imply the intention to restrict nuclear cooperation to specific areas, and this adds to the ambiguity.

...

The remaining issue is **suspension of Iran's dossier in the Security Council during the negotiation period by the other party, and suspension of enrichment activities by Iran through negotiations.** The Islamic Republic of Iran essentially agrees with consideration of some principles and conditions for further assurances of productive negotiations and considers that as a correct step. At the meantime, the following points have to be emphasized:

7/1. If negotiation is to be considered as a way for mutual understanding and concord, then it is intrinsically in contradiction with tabling the issue at the Security Council. Therefore, cessation of the Security Council involvement and any other gesture that is inconsistent with the principle of 'resolution through negotiation' is self-evident.

7/2. The other party not only violated this principle by engaging the Security Council and passing a resolution, but impaired the basis for the negotiating process. In fact, the veracity of those who proposed the package, in their intention and action became questionable, unless they propose a certain method to nullify its effect.

7/3. The Islamic Republic of Iran cannot accept equating the 5+1 with the Security Council as openly stated through the package. The proper way would be that the UN Security Council, through the due course, takes the Iran's nuclear dossier off its agenda, and resolves that the legal IAEA ways and means, supported by a fair form of negotiation process, is the logical approach to the issue.

7/4. The Islamic Republic of Iran fundamentally rejects the use of the Security Council resolution as a pressure tool to push forward the 5+1 proposal, and considers this practice as distortion and negation of the initial intent, and would not concede to it. Any progress in this course, would only be possible by separation of these two issues, namely disengagement of any negotiations from unjustified resolution of the Security Council.

7/5. It is not clear for the Islamic Republic of Iran that how the suspension of Iran's nuclear activities would help 'to create the right conditions for negotiations'. But it is clear that the other party's insistence on this issue, reminding some parties' inclination towards Iran's weakening and constraint - specially bearing in mind the records of past negotiations with some and past hostilities of some others - would be disturbing for 'the right conditions for negotiations'.

...

7/6. To avoid any suspicion on the Islamic Republic of Iran's intention or accusation of deliberate idling, etc, the Islamic Republic of Iran declares its specific time-frame for this issue of 'creating the right conditions for negotiations' as follows:

> 1. The Islamic Republic of Iran accepts that 'taking bilateral voluntary steps' that show the goodwill on both sides can help create the right atmosphere and course for the negotiation to make it more effective.

2. In this framework, the Islamic Republic of Iran is ready to discuss this issue in the course of negotiations to comprehend each other's reasons and justifications.

3. This step will be conditional on simultaneous steps by other party to show that it does not intend to deprive or limit the Islamic Republic of Iran. These steps specifically include the following:

Termination of Iran's dossier in the Security Council and returning it to the IAEA

Normalization of Iran's nuclear case at the IAEA

The other party commits itself not to pursue the limitation of Iran's peaceful activities as the result of the negotiations, but to aim for achieving the mutually agreed methods to provide more assurances on the peaceful nature and non-diversion of these activities.

All members of the 5+1 accept as a show of goodwill to abandon all restrictions that they practice beyond the legal international norms in different areas.

8) Regarding the second theme, **the issue of 'transparency'**, the Islamic Republic of Iran believes that the negotiation process and the process of interactions between Iran and the IAEA can be based upon acceptance of these principles by all concerned parties:

a) The negotiating parties are entitled to be informed of non-diversion in Iran's peaceful nuclear activities within the NPT and IAEA statute framework as much as possible with a certain timetable.

b) The study and assessment of this issue is to be undertaken by the IAEA in the framework of NPT rules and regulations. The IAEA's approach regarding this issue must be based on technical and in line and legal standards (according to the IAEA statute) with the spirit of cooperation and mutual respect, free from any prolonging of the process, and away from any political inclination or influence, and based on the principle of innocence.

c) The Islamic Republic of Iran would facilitate the necessary working conditions for the IAEA's inspections for clarification of the ambiguities, would provide the utmost cooperation for expedition of its work, and if deemed necessary, would consider voluntary steps towards implementation of the Additional Protocol,[431] given the provision of the legal conditions. Points mentioned in the proposed package, regarding the full cooperation of Iran with the IAEA is related to this theme.

The Islamic Republic of Iran is ready to negotiate on these issues in the framework of the aforementioned principles, and actively participate towards mutual understanding and concord.

The Islamic Republic of Iran underlines that the cooperation with the IAEA, requires drawing up a comprehensive and logical framework for the whole work and related procedures, which is agreed upon by Iran and the IAEA. This framework should comprise certain significant aspects, including:

To be bounded in the framework of technical and legal standards and not to be influenced by political motives and pressures, and not by problematic inclination and intelligent demands of the parties outside the IAEA.

Setting the assessment criteria for the IAEA in a normal and non-discriminatory manner, based on the principle of innocence. In other words, inability to find any affirmative indications after due course of ordinary technical and legal examinations, is to be considered nonexistence of undeclared nuclear activities or materials.

---

[431] Doc. 5.

Setting the reasonable conditions and timetable for conclusion of the work and normalization of Iran's nuclear dossier in the IAEA, and mutual commitment of both sides for fulfillment of the set conditions and schedules.

Suspension of discussion on Iran's nuclear case in the IAEA board of governors until the presentations of the Director General's final report, according to the declared timetable.

The Islamic Republic of Iran will be ready to implement, voluntarily, the Additional Protocol, with provision of legal conditions, if the above mentioned requirements are met, Iran's nuclear case is only pursued in the IAEA, and any intervention of the Security Council or other entities are ceased.

…

9) Regarding the third theme, the issue of 'mutual confidence building', the Islamic Republic of Iran believes that:

9/1. At present time, the majority of the world community, from the security point of view, have confidence in the Islamic Republic of Iran's nuclear plans and intentions, or at least have no particular security worries about them.

9/2. It is necessary to have a clear definition for the term 'international confidence in the exclusively peaceful nature of Iran's civil nuclear program', since this is a very general and vague term. It should be clarified that what the international confidence building standards are. And who are those who do the assessment? What are the criteria and legal basis for the establishment of the international confidence on the exclusively peaceful nature of Iran's civil nuclear program? Are there any criteria beyond the current international rules and treaties in mind? In any case, the Islamic Republic of Iran, sincerely welcomes 'to develop relations and cooperation based on mutual respect and the establishment of international confidence in the exclusively peaceful nature of Iran's civil nuclear program'. However, it is necessary for reassurance, that these two principles be underlined, and the inclusion of other issues as limiting conditions to be avoided.

9/3. Apart from the above-mentioned point, confidence building in the exclusively peaceful nature of Iran's civil nuclear program, meaning acceptable assurance of non-diversion of those activities towards military purposes and use, comprise of two aspects of present and future. That is, the assurance that at the present time, that there are no undeclared nuclear activities and materials, and all declared nuclear activities and materials have a peaceful nature, and are under IAEA supervisions and control. Additionally in the foreseeable future, this situation will continue. The legal supervision of the Agency in its examination of different aspects in Iran's nuclear activities, and its continued regular examinations, are sufficient for the present aspect of confidence building. In the Islamic Republic of Iran's view, what was mentioned in part 8 regarding transparency these, suffices for this purpose. That is, so long as the Agency is active in examining Iran's nuclear activities, and the Islamic Republic of Iran is cooperating with it, and there has been no indication for existence of any undeclared nuclear activities or materials, there should be no reason for distrust.

Regarding the assurances for the future, that the Islamic Republic of Iran would not use its nuclear capability for other than peaceful applications, it is an issue which may apply to many other cases and to many other countries. This has not been addressed in international treaties and legal rules, and naturally should not be a source of concern. In addition, possession of nuclear weapons are not considered as part of Iran' national security doctrine. Notwithstanding, **the Islamic Republic of Iran is ready** to illustrate its goodwill if it receives responsible and logical behavior from the other party, **to guarantee in an appropriate manner, that it would not abandon its membership in IAEA and NPT,** and through this way, commits itself even to the future aspect of confidence building.

9/4. However, all the afore-mentioned points in 9/3 is conditional to the fact that simultaneous mutual confidence-building (for Iran) is being done on security matters. In the Islamic Republic of Iran's view, this comprises of three important matters, as follows:

A) The other party's commitment to seriously follow up the fulfillment of 'the nuclear free zone in the Middle East', particularly the commitment to disarm the Zionist regime from weapons of mass destruction (WMD) and in particular nuclear arms.

B) The other party's commitment to convince the countries of the region (Middle East) who are not yet signatories to NPT, or are not yet implementing the Additional protocol, to accept NPT membership, and to implement the Additional Protocol.

C) The commitment and guarantee of the negotiating partners to prevent and protest all hostile and restrictive acts against the Islamic Republic of Iran including any scientific, technical, political, economic and commercial embargo and any kind of military aggression or threat.

The negotiation process, can help to reach a mutual understanding on ways of balancing those two aspects (9/3 and 9/4), and action plans to be designed and implemented.

10) Part of the proposed package is related to the areas of political and economic cooperation, which is one of the vague and ambiguous aspects of this package. The main idea is not clear here. ...

If we want to give the negotiations a chance for success, the primary principle is that all parties set their actions and expectations according to the ordinary international rules and arrangements.

The question is what are the international rules and orders for these restrictions and embargoes? What is the purpose in their continuation? And why there should be additional demands for their removal? Therefore, as mentioned before, it is necessary to see a change in policies, changing the policy of intimidation, pressure, embargo and restriction against Iran.

...

11) **The Islamic Republic of Iran is ready for a comprehensive and long-term cooperation agreement to achieve 'sustainable development and security in the region',** based on fair terms and conditions, attending to the rights of all countries, and would contribute to the highest extent possible to participate in effective security arrangements in an all-inclusive model, with all its potential as a responsible state, an active member of the international community, having an effective regional role.

On this basis, the Islamic Republic of Iran is ready to have an active role in a cooperation arrangement for **'sustainable energy security'** to have extensive cooperation and partnership with the European countries and other countries of the region.

...

Document 115: Statement by Iran, IAEA 50ᵗʰ General Conference

18 September 2006

...

128. Mr. AGHAZADEH (Islamic Republic of Iran) said ...

...

134. The Board's decision to convey Iran's nuclear issue to the United Nations Security Council[432] had no legal basis and was in contradiction with the Agency's Statute and its practice. How could a programme be considered a 'threat against international peace and security' and conveyed to the Security Council when the Agency, after three years of intrusive and robust inspection and investigation, had not found any evidence of diversion to prohibited purposes? More surprising still had been that the Board should have changed the voluntary and non-legally binding measure to a mandatory obligation; without doubt that signalled a new trend and constituted a deplorable precedent in the history of the Agency.

135. The overwhelming legal opinion of renowned international jurists asserted that the Board was not empowered to make such a judgement or to act beyond its statutory mandate. The Islamic Republic of Iran therefore had no legal obligation to accept such demands. The Agency's purpose and function was both to safeguard and to facilitate peaceful nuclear activities; the two were intertwined. If it were not able to live up to its commitments vis-à-vis the Islamic Republic of Iran, and restricted Iran's access to peaceful nuclear capabilities and undermined its inalienable rights, the Agency would be in breach of its obligations under the Statute and the bilateral safeguards agreement.[433] In such a case, the Islamic Republic of Iran would also have no legal obligation towards the Agency. There should also be no doubt that any hostile action by the Security Council would lead to a limitation of cooperation with the Agency. Such a unilateral approach aggressively pursued by one or two States was bound to cause loss and damage to all.

...

Document 116: Statement by Iran, First Session of the Preparatory Committee for the 2010 NPT Review Conference

1 May 2007

...

Islamic Republic of Iran, suspended all its enrichment activities for about 2.5 years in order to facilitate removal of any ambiguity if any, about its nuclear activities. It is essential to note that the suspension was considered, in all resolutions of the Board of Governors of the IAEA, as voluntary, non-legally binding. Therefore, stopping voluntary suspension could not be considered in any way as a violation. The Director General of the IAEA has repeatedly reported to the Board of Governors that there has been no evidence of diversion

---

[432] Doc. 32.
[433] Doc. 4

of nuclear materials and activities to prohibited purposes and all declared nuclear materials have been accounted for. According to Article XII of the Statute, non-compliance and diversion have to be recognized by the inspectors, and then be reported to DG, where he, thereupon shall report to the Board of Governors. Since none of these legal procedure and requirements have been pursued, therefore the resolution GOV /2006/14[434] of the Board of Governors conveying the nuclear dossier to the United Nations Security Council, did not have legal grounds, consequently the resolutions 1696,[435] 1737[436] and 1747[437] passed, on the basis of the Board of Governors resolution, are unjustified and legally baseless. Certainly if Iran was not party to NPT, it would have not been faced with such unfair situation. Penalizing NPT party on political grounds shall have grave consequences.

...

The path of the Security Council has no sound legal basis for Iran's nuclear issue. Any further steps taken by the Security Council, would surely complicate the situation, is counterproductive for settlement of the issue and put at stake the current efforts and initiatives for resuming the negotiations, for peaceful settlement of this issue.

The Government of the Islamic Republic of Iran continues to be ready to resolve a few of the remaining issues with the Agency, provided that the nuclear dossier, is returned in full in the framework of the IAEA and the United Nations Security Council disengagement is realized. The Islamic Republic of Iran is the responsible State and continues to comply with its obligations under the NPT, but will not stand still in the face of intimidation and threats, and will never give up its inalienable rights for peaceful use of nuclear energy, stipulated in Article IV of the NPT and articles I and 11 of the Agency's Statute.

Document 117: Statement by Iran, UN General Assembly, General Debate

A/62/PV.5, 25 September 2007

President Ahmadinejad (*spoke in Farsi; English text provided by the delegation*):
...

According to the Statute of the IAEA, every member has a number of rights and obligations. In fact, all members have to stay on a peaceful path and, under the supervision of the Agency, assist other members, and they are entitled to be supported by the Agency and have access to the fuel cycle with the help of the Agency and its members.

Thus far, Iran has fulfilled all of its obligations but has been deprived of other members' technical assistance and, even at times, of the Agency's support. For about five years, some of the aforementioned Powers have, by exerting heavy pressure on the IAEA, attempted to prevent the Iranian nation from exercising its rights. They have derailed Iran's nuclear issue from its legal tracks, and have politicized the atmosphere to impose their wishes through taking advantage of all their potential.

The Government of Iran spared no effort to build confidence, but they were not satisfied with anything short of the complete halt of all activities, even those related to

---

[434] Doc. 32.
[435] Doc. 10.
[436] Doc. 11.
[437] Doc. 12.

research and university fields. They only sought to deprive the Iranian people of all their inalienable rights, even to the extent that centres not involved in the fuel cycle or not in need of supervision by the Agency were closed.

After three years of negotiations and attempts to build confidence, the Iranian nation came to the firm belief that the main concern of these Powers is not the possible deviation of Iran's nuclear activities, but is to prevent its scientific progress under that pretext. If this trend continues, there will be no possibility for Iran to enjoy its rights, not even in the next 20 years. Therefore, Iran decided to pursue the issue through its appropriate legal path, one that runs through the IAEA, and to disregard unlawful and political impositions by the arrogant Powers.

In the past two years, abusing the Security Council, the arrogant Powers have repeatedly accused Iran and have even made military threats and imposed illegal sanctions against it. However, by the grace of faith in God and national unity, Iran has moved forward step by step, and now our country is recognized as one with the capacity for industrial-scale fuel cycle production for peaceful uses. Unfortunately, the Security Council, in dealing with this obvious legal issue, was influenced by some bullying Powers and failed to uphold justice and protect the rights of the Iranian people.

Fortunately, the IAEA has recently tried to regain its legal role as supporter of the rights of its members while supervising nuclear activities. We see this as a correct approach adopted by the Agency. Previously, they illegally insisted on politicizing the Iranian nation's nuclear case, but today, because of the resistance of the Iranian nation, the issue is back with the Agency, and I officially announce that, in our opinion, the nuclear issue of Iran is now closed and has turned into an ordinary Agency matter. Today, many important questions have been raised about the nuclear activities of certain Powers within the IAEA, which should be dealt with properly. Of course, Iran has always been, and will be, prepared to have constructive talks with all parties.

...

Document 118: Identical letters dated 22 February 2008 from the Permanent Representative of the Islamic Republic of Iran to the United Nations addressed to the Secretary-General and the President of the Security Council

S/2008/116, 25 February 2008

I have the honour to write to you with regard to the latest report of the IAEA Director General on the peaceful nuclear programme of the Islamic Republic of Iran (GOV/2008/4) issued on 22 February 2008.[438] As you may have already noticed, the said report declares the full implementation of the Work Plan concluded between Iran and IAEA in August 2007 (INFCIRC/711)[439] and, thus, resolution and closure of all outstanding issues. IAEA had already declared on 15 November 2007 (GOV/2007/58)[440] that three out of six outstanding issues were resolved, and the three remaining issues are now declared resolved

---

[438] Doc. 51.
[439] Doc. 6.
[440] Doc. 50.

and closed in the recent report. In this regard, the IAEA Director General has stressed in the report that 'the Agency has been able to conclude that answers provided by Iran, in accordance with the Work Plan, are consistent with its findings' and 'considers those questions no longer outstanding'. Moreover, the Director General, in his remarks after the release of the report, emphasized the resolution of the outstanding issues and stated, 'we have managed to clarify all the remaining outstanding issues, including the most important issue which is the scope and nature of Iran's enrichment programme'.

The report also clearly attests to the exclusively peaceful nature of the nuclear programme of the Islamic Republic of Iran, both in the past and at present, and also serves to strongly and unambiguously support my country's long-standing position that the allegations raised by a certain country against the peaceful nuclear programme of the Islamic Republic of Iran have been entirely groundless. By implementation of the Work Plan and resolution of the outstanding issues, the very pretexts and allegations, on the basis of which unlawful and unfair actions have been taken by the Security Council against Iran's peaceful nuclear programme, have now proved to be baseless and are gone.

It is now clear more than ever that the consideration of Iran's peaceful nuclear programme was imposed on the Security Council by certain countries out of mere political motivations and narrow national interests and on the basis of certain pretexts and allegations which have been totally baseless. The full implementation of the Work Plan, and thus resolution and closure of the outstanding issues as reflected in the recent IAEA Director General's report, has eliminated those pretexts and allegations which served as the basis of referral of Iran's peaceful nuclear programme to the Security Council.

This report, together with other IAEA reports and statements of the Agency officials, well indicate that Iran has been resolute in its cooperation with the Agency and fully transparent in its nuclear activities. It also shows that the Iranian nation is committed to its international obligations and at the same time persistent in pursuing and exercising its legal and inalienable rights. The report also clearly stresses that Iran's cooperation with IAEA has been proactive and far beyond its comprehensive Safeguards Agreement[441] obligations.

The report of the Director General to the Board of Governors of IAEA further stresses that 'the Agency has recently received from Iran additional information similar to that which Iran had previously provided pursuant to the Additional Protocol,[442] as well as updated design information. As a result, the Agency's knowledge about Iran's current declared nuclear programme has become clearer … The Agency has been able to continue to verify the non-diversion of declared nuclear material in Iran. Iran has provided the Agency with access to declared nuclear material and has provided the required nuclear material accountancy reports in connection with declared nuclear material and activities. Iran has also responded to questions and provided clarifications and amplifications on the issues raised in the context of the work plan', and 'has provided access to individuals in response to the Agency's requests'. In this regard, the IAEA Director General stressed in his remarks after the release of the report that 'Iran in the last few months has provided us with visits to many places that enable us to have a clearer picture of Iran's current programme'.

In view of the above and in the wake of the latest report of IAEA, it has become clear that Iran's peaceful nuclear issue should be dealt with by the Agency as the sole pertinent international organization and, as envisaged in the Work Plan, safeguards implementation in Iran has to be in a routine manner from now on. The Security Council should avoid

---

[441] Doc. 4.
[442] Doc. 5.

inflicting more damage to the credibility and authority of IAEA as well as its own credibility by persisting in further illegal and illogical engagement and actions pursued by few countries. The present great achievement that is the conclusion of the Work Plan, which is the fruitful result of an excellent joint intensive cooperation between IAEA and the Islamic Republic of Iran, has to be safeguarded by all United Nations Member States, and the international community at large.

I would appreciate if you would kindly circulate the present letter as a document of the Security Council.

(*Signed*) Mohammad **Khazaee**
Ambassador Permanent Representative

Document 119: Letter Dated 24 March 2008 from the Permanent Representative of the Islamic Republic of Iran to the United Nations Addressed to the Secretary-General

INFCIRC/724, 28 March 2008 (originally circulated as
A/62/767-S/2008/203, 26 March 2008)

...

In view of the unlawful engagement of the Security Council in the issue of the peaceful nuclear activities of the Islamic Republic of Iran and the illegal measures taken in this regard, I would like to draw your Excellency's attention to the following observations with respect to this process and the adopted Security Council resolutions, including the recent one (1803)[443] as well as the damages inflicted on the Islamic Republic of Iran as a result of malicious steps taken by few countries during the last five years:

A) Inalienable and legal rights of the NPT States parties for the use of nuclear energy for peaceful purposes

Given the ever-increasing needs of energy for its young and growing population, like any other State party to the Non-Proliferation Treaty (NPT) and in accordance with Article IV of the Treaty on the inalienable rights of the States parties for the use of nuclear energy for peaceful purposes, the Islamic Republic of Iran has planned and started activities in the field of peaceful uses of nuclear energy since 1957. In this context, the Islamic Republic of Iran has constantly complied with its obligations under the NPT and the Statute of the International Atomic Energy Agency (IAEA) and has never had any prohibited activities; hence, its inalienable rights under the NPT should not be violated by any means.

B) Violation of international law by certain States

Irrational opposition of the United States and the EU3 to Iran's exercising of its inalienable rights to peaceful uses of nuclear technology, and their instrumental manipulation of the international institutions in order to put pressure on the Board of Governors and the Security Council to deprive the Iranian nation of its established and legal rights have constituted a situation in which international law and the Charter of the United Nations have been seriously violated.

---

[443] Doc. 13.

C) Policy of cooperation and interaction with the IAEA

The United States and three European countries (EU3), by providing false and erroneous information to the IAEA [on Iran's peaceful nuclear program], led this international technical and specialized agency to unnecessarily spend its potentials and resources to address this issue during a long period of time and, by doing so, have prevented the Agency from fulfilling its real tasks on important issues such as the prevention of actual proliferation, disarmament, and contemplating a mechanism to effectively verify the nuclear activities of the non-parties to the NPT, particularly the Zionist regime that is continuing to develop nuclear weapons in the region.

From the very beginning, the Islamic Republic of Iran has officially announced that there is no ambiguity in Iran's nuclear activities and its nuclear program is solely for peaceful purposes. By deciding on a policy of cooperation and interaction with the IAEA, and even going beyond its existing legal obligations in this cooperation, Iran has spared no efforts to display the maximum transparency in its activities. On 21 August 2007, Iran and the IAEA reached an understanding on the Modalities of resolution of all Outstanding Issues,[444] which brought about a new round of cooperation between the two sides. This cooperation was aimed at the resolution of the six outstanding issues, the list of which was provided by the Agency to Iran.

Shortly after the emergence of positive results of such a cooperation, which came through the resolution of the first outstanding issue, namely the 'Plutonium', those few countries started their opposition to the Work Plan (Modalities) and began to put pressure on the Agency. In spite of all these pressures and obstacles, Iran and the Agency continued their cooperation and, as a result, all six outstanding issues were declared resolved and closed in the Agency's reports of November 2007 and February 2008.[445] The Director-General of the IAEA in his recent report announced that all six remaining issues are closed in accordance with the Work Plan, and once again stressed that there is no diversion in Iran's nuclear program and, thus, displayed the falseness and invalidity of the US allegations and EU3 accusations against Iran.

The said few countries have tried to call into question the peaceful nature of Iran's nuclear program through the introduction of ambiguities and baseless allegations concerning Iran's nuclear activities. They have unfoundedly tried to accuse Iran of concealment, non-transparency and unlawful behavior, and have even used these allegations as the basis for bringing Iran's nuclear issue to the UNITED NATIONS Security Council and adopting unwarranted and unlawful measures in this regard.

D) Unlawful engagement of the Security Council in the Iranian peaceful nuclear program

Involvement of the Security Council in the Iranian peaceful nuclear program is in full contravention with the organizational, Statutory and safeguards requirements governing the IAEA practices and procedures. Furthermore, the substantive and procedural legal requirements, that are necessary for engaging the Security Council in the issues raised by the Agency, have been totally ignored in this regard. Referring a country's nuclear issue to the Security Council is only possible under certain conditions as described below:

> – According to paragraph C, Article XII of the IAEA Statute, determining the non-compliance (diversion towards military purposes) is the essential pre-condition for referring an issue to the Security Council. This task, according to the same paragraph, is entrusted to the IAEA inspectors who should report it to the Board

---

[444] Doc. 6.
[445] Doc. 50, Doc. 51.

of Governors through the IAEA's Director General. There has never been any reference in the Agency's reports to any non-compliance by Iran or any diversion in its peaceful nuclear activities. More importantly, the IAEA Director General has repeatedly stressed that there has been no diversion of the declared nuclear materials and activities in the Islamic Republic of Iran. This conclusion has been once again reiterated in the very latest report of the IAEA Director General.

– Furthermore, according to article 19 of the Safeguards Agreement between Iran and the IAEA, dated 15 May 1974,[446] any referral of the issue by the Agency to the Security Council in accordance with Paragraph C, Article XII of the Statute of the IAEA, could only be possible 'if the Board, upon examination of relevant information reported to it by the Director General, finds that the Agency is not able to verify that there has been no diversion of nuclear material required to be safeguarded under this Agreement, to nuclear weapons or other nuclear explosive devices'. It is worth mentioning in this regard that the IAEA Director General has constantly stated in all his reports that the Agency has been able to verify that the declared nuclear materials and activities in Iran have not been diverted towards military purposes, and that they have remained absolutely under peaceful use.

– Also the nuclear activities of a country may be reported by the IAEA to the Council in cases where a threat against international peace and security is involved and, consequently, according to Paragraph b (4), Article III of the IAEA's Statute, the Agency would notify the Security Council in this regard. It is noteworthy that contrary to the baseless allegations made by those few States - allegations that have worked as the basis for referring the Iranian nuclear program to the Security Council - none of the IAEA Director General's reports have ever described Iran's nuclear activities as a threat to international peace and security. Rather, they have expressly declared that such activities are peaceful, and that there is no diversion of nuclear materials and activities in Iran.

E) Contradiction of the Security Council resolutions with the Charter of the United Nations and the international law

For the purpose of placing on record and seeking corrective measures, I wish to inform you [in this part of the letter] of my observations with respect to the allegations made against my country and the measures taken through the Security Council resolutions in contradiction to the Charter of the United Nations and in violation of the peremptory norms of international law.

Before dealing with such observations with respect to the said resolutions, in particular the last one, I find it necessary to stress that the engagement of the Security Council in this issue and also the resolutions adopted in this regard have been unlawful. The recent resolution by the Council has been adopted in a situation where the outstanding questions have been completely resolved in accordance with the Work Plan, and the Council not only has paid no attention to this important development, but has acted against it. With regard to the Security Council resolutions against Iran's peaceful nuclear program, including the latest one (1803), I wish to raise the following observations, among others:

1. The United States and the EU3, by putting pressure on, and instrumental exploitation of, the Security Council, brought about a situation in which some measures have been adopted in contradiction to Articles 1, 2 and 24 of the Charter of the United Nations. Iran's peaceful nuclear program has never posed any threat to international peace and security and

---

[446] Doc. 4.

Iran has not violated its obligations according to the Non-Proliferation Treaty (NPT). Not only the IAEA Director General's reports have never contained any such a conclusion, but they have also confirmed the non-diversion of the declared nuclear activities and materials in Iran and their peaceful nature. Therefore, engagement of the Security Council in Iran's nuclear program is clearly contrary to the Charter of the United Nations. The Security Council has never determined Iran's Nuclear Program as a threat to international peace and security under Article 39 of the Charter of the United Nations and, thus, it could not adopt any measures against the Islamic Republic of Iran under Chapter VII of the Charter of the United Nations. Moreover, the Security Council, before resorting to the measures stipulated in Articles 40 and 41 of the Charter of the United Nations must have exhausted all required procedures under Chapter VI of the Charter of the United Nations. Regrettably, with regard to Iran's issue, the Council has acted in contradiction of these requirements.

2. In the said Security Council resolutions it is claimed that the aim of the Council is to strengthen the authority of the IAEA. This claim is not genuine, since for this statement to have any validity, at least, the Council should have acted within the framework of the Agency's regulations and the NPT. The Council, in taking unlawful actions against Iran's peaceful nuclear program, has gone beyond the legal requirements of the NPT, the IAEA Statute and the Safeguards Agreement. While the IAEA Board of Governors has itself emphasized on the 'voluntary and not legally binding' nature of most of its requests for Confidence Building Measures (CBMs), the Security Council that claims to be supporting the authority of the Agency, has acted in contradiction to the Board of Governors and has considered these CBMs as Iran's obligations. Making 'voluntary measures a mandatory requirement' - as it was mentioned in a letter dated 16 March 2006 from the then British Political Director (UK current Permanent Representative to the United Nations) to his American, French and German counterparts - through instrumental use of the Council, has been from the outset for narrow political objectives.

3. The right of the people of Iran to peaceful uses of nuclear technology is a clear example of the realization of 'the right to development', 'right to natural resources' and 'right to self-determination'. Such rights are among the fundamental rights of nations and their breach entails international responsibility for those who have violated them vis-à-vis the nation whose rights have been violated and also towards the international community as a whole. Nations right to the peaceful uses of nuclear energy has been expressly recognized in the Non-Proliferation Treaty. Any action by States or the international organizations to limit such rights constitutes a violation of the fundamental principles of international law including, *inter alia,* non-interference in internal affairs of other States. I wish to emphasize that in the Final Document of the Sixth NPT Review Conference,[447] all State parties to the Treaty confirmed 'that each country's choices and decisions in the field of peaceful uses of nuclear energy should be respected without jeopardizing its policies or international cooperation agreements and arrangements for peaceful uses of nuclear energy and its fuel-cycle policies'. Therefore, the Security Council's actions against Iran are in clear contradiction with the NPT principles and the Agency's Statute.

4. The Security Council, as a United Nations organ created by Member States, is subject to legal requirements, and is obliged to comply with the same international normative rules that the Member States are bound to. The Council shall observe all international norms, in particular the Charter of the United Nations and the peremptory norms of international law, in the process of its decision making and in its taking actions. Needless to say that any

---

[447] NPT/CONF.2000/28 (Parts I and II) para 2.

measure adopted in contradiction to such rules and principles will be void of any legally binding effects. As the International Criminal Tribunal for former Yugoslavia (ICTY) has stated in one of its judgments 'in any case, neither the text nor the spirit of the Charter conceives the Security Council as *legibus solutus* (unbound by law).'[448] Likewise, as the International Court of Justice has held in its 1971 advisory opinion, the Member States are required to comply with Security Council decisions only if they are in accordance with the Charter of the United Nations.

5. In light of the Security Council's declared purposes in the said resolutions on the one side, and the resolution of all outstanding issues related to the nuclear program of the Islamic Republic of Iran in accordance with the Work Plan, on the other, it was logically expected that the Security Council would take into consideration the IAEA Director General's findings and conclusions.

[In the following paragraphs certain specific observations are elaborated with regard to the preambular and operative paragraphs of the latest Council resolution, namely resolution 1803:]

6. *Second preambular paragraph*: While in this paragraph the Security Council has itself referred to Article IV of the NPT, at the same time it violates, by its decisions, the basic rights of a State party to the Treaty. This is in contravention with the purposes and principles of the Charter of the United Nations, according to which the contractual (treaty) obligations should be respected. ...

...

8. *Fourth preambular paragraph*:

– Suspension, which has already been unsuccessfully experienced, was a provisional, voluntary and non-legally binding measure, taken by Iran for two and a half years as a confidence-building measure. The IAEA Director General has clearly declared in his oral report to the Board of Governors on 3 March 2008 that 'the reason for which the nuclear issue of the Islamic Republic of Iran has been referred to the Security Council was the ambiguities related to its enrichment program in the past, and the Agency has been able to clarify the enrichment program (P.1 & P.2 centrifuges) and this issue is no longer considered outstanding'. Therefore, no pretext or justification remains either for the engagement of the Security Council in this regard or any request for suspension. Furthermore, there is nothing in the NPT, the IAEA Statute and the Safeguards Agreement calling for limiting the rights enshrined therein, or for such unwarranted requests.

– As the IAEA Director General has repeatedly stressed in his reports, there are no reprocessing activities in Iran. Therefore, raising a request in the Council resolutions for the suspension of an activity that does not exist has no basis. This explicitly shows that there isn't enough knowledge in the Security Council regarding the Iranian peaceful nuclear activities, and that the IAEA Director Generals' reports have remained unattended by the Council.

– The Arak 40 MW heavy water research reactor will replace the Tehran 5 MW research reactor that is nearing the end of its life. This reactor will produce radio isotopes for medical, agricultural and industrial uses. Such projects are in full conformity with Iran's rights in accordance with the NPT and the Statute of the Agency. Moreover, these projects are carried out completely under the

---

[448] *Prosecutor v. Duško Tadić a/k/a 'Dule'*, ICTY, Case IT-94-1, Decision on the Defence Motion for Interlocutory Appeal on jurisdiction (2 October 1995) para 28.

Comprehensive Safeguards Agreement. Thus, any request for the suspension of these activities is in contradiction of the NPT and the Statute of the Agency.

– The Islamic Republic of Iran voluntarily implemented the Additional Protocol[449] for more than two years and a half, but in response to this positive action and other voluntary measures taken by my country, a few States referred the Iranian peaceful nuclear program to the Security Council. Against this background, naturally the implementation of these voluntary measures could not be continued. The blame in this regard should, indeed, be put on those States that referred the issue to the Security Council, and not on Iran. Based on international law of the treaties and also according to the text of the Additional Protocol, making a decision by States on the ratification and implementation of this protocol is optional and not obligatory. The non-nuclear weapon States parties to the NPT are only legally bound to accept and implement the Comprehensive Safeguards Agreement. The Islamic Republic of Iran has fully complied with its undertakings in accordance with its Safeguards Agreement, and based on the Agency's reports, all its nuclear activities are under the supervision and monitoring of the Agency. In addition, it is noteworthy that the IAEA Director General in his latest report on 22 February 2008, has stated that the additional information that Iran has provided to the Agency is similar to the provision of information based on the Additional Protocol. It is also worth mentioning that in accordance with the official information released by the Agency, 121 states had not yet ratified the Additional Protocol as of 23 November 2007. Therefore, highlighting Iran in this regard has no logic or justification. Requiring a State to implement a treaty or any other international arrangements, while it has not expressed its consent to that treaty or arrangement, contradicts the established principles of international law of treaties. Thus, the Security Council could not oblige Iran to comply with the Additional Protocol's provisions. Undoubtedly, such an approach by the Security Council would jeopardize the well-founded and recognized principle of the law of treaties.

– Confidence building is a two-way road. The Islamic Republic of Iran has, on its part, taken several voluntary confidence building measures including, *inter alia:* signing and voluntary implementation of the Additional Protocol, voluntary suspension of its nuclear activities in the past, accepting 3000 person-day inspections of its nuclear installations and materials, submission of a formal proposal by its president at the United Nations GA for participation of other states and companies in enrichment activities inside Iran, concluding an agreement with the Agency on resolving the outstanding issues, and many other steps in this regard. It is now other States' turn to do their share of confidence buildings.

9- *Fifth preambular paragraph*: The Security Council should be aware that the Islamic Republic of Iran is still continuing the implementation of the code 3.1 of the Subsidiary Arrangement dated 12 February 1976. But, based on its safeguards agreement and its rights, and because of the adoption of unlawful United Nations SC resolution 1747,[450] Iran decided to suspend the implementation of the amended version of code 3.1 of the Subsidiary Arrangement that has not yet been ratified by its parliament. It will continue this suspension pending the full implementation of the provisions of the NPT, especially those

---

[449] Doc. 5.
[450] Doc. 12.

related to the inalienable rights of member states for peaceful uses of nuclear technology stipulated in Article IV of the Treaty, and until the Council ceases its interference in Iran's peaceful nuclear program issue and returns it to the Agency. It should be noted that the Islamic Republic of Iran has implemented the amended version of code 3.1 of the Subsidiary Arrangement since 2003 with the aim of strengthening its cooperation with the Agency.

In principle, the Security Council is considered as a political-executive organ in the structure of the United Nations and shall, therefore, refrain from taking any measures on issues, or in areas, that do not fall within its purview, and must confer such issues to the relevant and competent bodies. The Security Council's prescription with respect to the modified code 3.1 is beyond the Council's mandate and, accordingly, is an obvious instance of *ultra vires*.

10- *Sixth preambular paragraph*: The Security Council claims to be determined to strengthen the Authority of the Agency for resolving the outstanding issues and has welcomed the agreed Work Plan between Iran and the Agency. But in contradiction to this claim, the Council has completely disregarded the results of that Work Plan which was fully implemented and its implementation resulted in the resolution and closure of all six outstanding issues. The Council has also been absolutely negligent to the Director General's request to take into account his report, and just one day after his request, the Council passed the most recent unlawful resolution. Moreover, the Council has asked Iran to complete the Work Plan, while by the resolution of all six outstanding issues and provision of necessary responses to the Agency's questions by Iran, the Work Plan is fully implemented and nothing more remains to be done in this regard. The Council has also pretended that it looks for strengthening the authority of the Agency, while practically it has interfered in technical and legal affairs that fall within the mandate of the IAEA, and has therefore eroded the credibility and authority of the Agency, rather than strengthening it.

11- *Seventh preambular paragraph*: The Security Council expresses its belief that suspension contributes to a diplomatic and negotiated solution. However and ironically, the measures adopted by the Council have been taken prior to examining the procedures envisaged in the Chapter VI of the Charter which are based on negotiation and mediation. The basic question to ponder is; if the Council really believes in negotiation, then, why it raises preconditions for such a negotiation? It should be noted that the Heads of States of the Non-Aligned Movement, who comprise almost two thirds of the United Nations member states, have expressly asked for the beginning of the said negotiation without any preconditions. The Security Council that claims to be representing all member states has been fully inattentive to this request of 118 member of the Non-Aligned Movement.

12. Eighth preambular paragraph: The Council, in the first part of this paragraph, has referred to the proposed Package, while not only it has completely ignored to mention Iran's detailed response to the said Package, but even it did not wait for Iran's response when it adopted resolution 1696 in a hasty manner and only few days before Iran's response to the package was presented. The Council has merely kept on mentioning the Package in its resolutions against Iran's peaceful nuclear program, while it has always ignored Iran's response to the said Package. In the second part of this paragraph, the enjoyment of the Iranian nation of its inalienable rights that is enshrined in the NPT has been conditioned to the restoration of confidence of the international community in the exclusively peaceful nature of Iran's nuclear program. Undoubtedly, conditioning the enjoyment of a State of its contractual or treaty rights to indefinite and subjective criteria is in contradiction to

the recognized rules and principles of the law of treaties. The sponsors of the resolution have not presented any reason or explanation to clarify what action or omission on the part of Iran justifies this discriminatory manner which is contrary to the NPT provisions. On the contrary, the Director General of the IAEA has repeatedly declared that there is no evidence indicating any diversion in Iran's nuclear activities towards military purposes and thus the NPT has not been violated by Iran.

13. *Preambular paragraph 10*: It is not appropriate for the Security Council, in line with discharging its duties in implementing the Charter of the United Nations, to invoke initiatives or mechanisms which are outside the United Nations, such as the Financial Action Task Force (FATF), on which there is no global consensus.

14- *Preambular paragraph 11*: The development of sensitive technologies in Iran is according to the NPT regulations and the IAEA Statute, and is for absolutely peaceful purposes. Therefore, the United Nations Security Council cannot decide against this program or try to limit this inalienable right. Evidently, some developed countries, by establishing closed clubs, try to have an exclusive control over certain sensitive and important technologies that are necessary for the economic development of nations, and spare no efforts to deprive the developing countries from those technologies. These efforts have indeed proved to be futile. Regarding the missile program, as confirmed in the United Nations Secretary General's Report on 'the issue of missile in all its aspects', there are no universally agreed regulations or mechanisms with regard to missiles, and additionally, according to the Charter of the United Nations, the member states have the right to take appropriate measures to defend themselves. The missile program of the Islamic Republic of Iran is solely for defensive purposes and the United Nations Security Council cannot act against the Charter regulations and deprive a member state from this important right, nor can it limit the said right. Above all, there is no relation between the missile program and the nuclear program of the Islamic Republic of Iran, and the Security Council measures in this regard well indicate the hidden political agenda that are pursued by certain permanent members of the Council.

If the aim of the United Nations Security Council resolutions has been to ensure the authority of the IAEA for the resolution of outstanding issues on Iran's peaceful nuclear program, with the recent resolution and closure of these issues and with the removal of any ambiguities in this regard according to the Work Plan and as contained in the recent report of the Director General of the Agency - which stresses for the eleventh time that there has been no diversion in Iran's nuclear program - there remains no pretexts for the United Nations Security Council to take measures in this regard and, thus, the Council should immediately take compensatory measures to remove and correct its past mistakes.

15- *Preambular paragraph 12*: The Security Council has talked about the risk of proliferation by the Iranian peaceful nuclear program, while all nuclear activities in Iran are carried out in accordance with the NPT provisions and under the full monitoring of the IAEA, and the Agency has, time and again, emphasized on the non-diversion of these activities towards military purposes. In this regard, it should be stressed that the requirements of the Board of Governors and the provisions of the said resolutions of the Security Council, due to their unlawfulness, are not implementable, and raising the so-called 'continued failure of Iran' to comply with the said requests lacks any shred of logic or justification. If the United Nations Security Council is really concerned about the proliferation risks, it should act against the vertical proliferation of new nuclear weapons and against the emerging of military doctrines for the possible use of these weapons. It should also act against the continued existence of thousands of nuclear warheads in the arsenals of nuclear weapons States.

While the Council refers in this paragraph to its primary responsibility under the Charter of the United Nations for the maintenance of international peace and security, it has never expressly determined in this or any other previous resolutions that Iran's nuclear program constitutes a threat to international peace and security. The Council's power in determining a situation or dispute as a threat to international peace and security is limited to certain procedural and substantive rules, including those stipulated in the Charter of the United Nations. As the ICTY has mentioned 'the determination that there exists such a threat is not a totally unfettered discretion, as it has to remain, at the very least, within the limits of the Purposes and Principles of the Charter.'[451] In this respect, undoubtedly the Security Council cannot and shall not determine lawful conducts or situations as a threat to international peace and security. In other words, no legitimate conduct by states shall be introduced as an instance of threat to international peace and security and *a priori* the Council cannot adopt any enforcement measures in this regard. All Iranian nuclear activities are carried out in accordance with relevant international treaties, in particular the NPT and the Statute of the IAEA, and in the absence of any violation of the said treaties by Iran, the Council cannot make an artificial linkage between Iran's peaceful nuclear program and international peace and security.

16. *Preambular paragraph 13*: Decisions made by the Security Council under Article 41 of the Charter of the United Nations entail enforcement measures against the targeted State or States. The immediate effect of such decisions is the restriction, suspension, ignoring and/or violating the rights of targeted States. Thus, they would be justified only if the Council could provide sufficient and convincing evidence proving their necessity for maintenance of or restoring international peace and security. There is no doubt that in such cases the Council bears the burden of providing proof, and in the event of failure in doing so, the Council and its members have the concurrent responsibility towards the targeted State or States for any damages caused as the result of the Security Council measures. Taking into consideration that all IAEA Director General's reports have repeatedly declared that there is no evidence or indication on any diversion of the Iranian nuclear program towards military purposes, and given the fact that all outstanding issues have been resolved and closed in the framework of the Work Plan, and in accordance with the relevant international treaties, any measure by the Council to restrict, suspend, modify, ignore or violate the rights of the Iranian nation is not legally justified, and can be brought by Iran [for compensation] before competent fora at an appropriate time . Principally, the purpose of the sanctions of the Security Council should not be punishment, revenge or other hostile actions towards the targeted States, rather, the Council should adopt such measures in order to maintain or restore international peace and security. Nevertheless, the sponsors of the Security Council resolutions against Iran have not elaborated that how the adopted enforcement measures against Iran and Iranian entities and individuals could lead to the maintenance of international peace and security.

17. *Operative paragraph 1*: As mentioned in the above sections 8 and 9, the requests of the Board of Governors and the Security Council from Iran lack any legal basis. Moreover, calling upon Iran to resolve the remaining issues is unjustifiable, since the Islamic Republic of Iran has already resolved all remaining issues within the framework of the Work Plan.

---

[451] *Prosecutor v. Duško Tadić a/k/a 'Dule'*, ICTY, Case IT-94-1, Decision on the Defence Motion for Interlocutory Appeal on jurisdiction (2 October 1995) para 29.

18. *Operative paragraph 2*: It was expected that, following the implementation of the agreements between Iran and the IAEA in the framework of the Work Plan and the resolution of all outstanding issues, the Security Council would take this development into consideration and take appropriate reactions towards it, instead of adopting a new resolution that has damaged that constructive atmosphere and has hurt the credibility of the Agency and that of the Security Council.

19. *Operative paragraphs 3 and 5*: Constraints and bans imposed on the free movement of Iranian nationals are inconsistent with international human rights law and, indeed, any unwarranted violation of these rights entails the concurrent responsibility of the Council and its Members. Taking into consideration the IAEA Director General's reports and the resolution of all outstanding issues in the framework of the Work Plan and the constant declarations on the part of the Agency that there is no evidence for any diversion of the Iranian nuclear program towards military purposes, the Council's measures in this regard are not justified, too. Moreover, no evidence has ever been presented to prove any role by the Iranian nationals who are listed in the annexes of the Security Council resolutions in any undeclared nuclear programmes, simply because there is not such a program in Iran. Such accusations with high gravity against Iranian Government and nationals require a high standard of proof which has never been met, and to date no evidence has been submitted by the sponsors of the resolution in this regard. On the contrary, the IAEA has repeatedly stated that there is no evidence to prove any diversion of the Iranian nuclear program towards military purposes.

20. *Operative paragraph 7*: Freezing, confiscation and seizure of the funds, assets and properties belonging to individuals, only because the Council has decided so, and without any reason, is in violation of the human rights requirements with respect to due process. Depriving individuals from their rights to ownership, without presenting any evidence of any wrongdoings and in the absence of any judicial decisions rendered by the competent courts, would amount to the fragmentation of universal human rights law. The Council has never submitted any convincing evidence indicating the involvement of the targeted Iranian individuals in any military nuclear activities, and has unlawfully requested the freezing of their funds, financial assets and economic resources, a prescription which is contrary to the fundamental principles of international law.

21. *Operative paragraph 8*: All United Nations Member States have the freedom to enjoy their sovereign rights including the right to international trade. In light of the fact that, based on the principles and purposes of the Charter of the United Nations, the United Nations and its organs shall assist all the member States in this respect, therefore, the adopted restrictions by the Council in operative paragraph 8 of resolution 1803, and all other previous related resolutions are contrary to such sovereign rights of Iran, in particular, in a situation where all relevant IAEA Director General's reports have repeatedly declared that there is no evidence to prove any diversion of the Iranian nuclear program towards military purposes, and while all outstanding issues have been resolved and closed. Prohibiting the exportation to Iran of some goods and materials that are used by Iran in fully peaceful and lawful projects which are under the IAEA monitoring, is incompatible with international law and the Charter of the United Nations. Also, applying these sanctions against Iran's defensive missile program, that based on the Charter of the United Nations is a recognized right for all members, is clearly against the provisions of the Charter. Targeting Iran's missile program while it is claimed that the Security Council is concerned about Iran's peaceful nuclear program well indicates the political motives and the hidden agenda of the aforementioned few countries.

Moreover, the inclusion in the said resolution of a list of items developed by some exclusive clubs and closed groups does not have any international legitimacy and will not lead to the recognition of these groups and their recommendations.

22. *Operative paragraph 9*: Including the public commercial transactions in the scope of the Security Council's measures is an obvious instance of flagrant violation of international trade law. The Council in this paragraph, without presenting any convincing evidence to prove that any export credits, insurance guarantees and financial credits have been ever used to contribute to any alleged illegal nuclear activities, has imposed some unlawful restrictions. Although this paragraph is drafted in a non-binding wording, however, it would *per se* negatively affect the economic and financial aspects of international commercial relations.

23. *Operative paragraph 10*: Given the fact that these banks and other Iranian banks do not have any connection to any non-peaceful nuclear activities (as claimed in the Security Council resolution), therefore, limiting their activities means hampering the banking and financial affairs of millions of deposit holders and customers of these banks, and shows that the measures contained in this paragraph, like other measures of the Council against Iran, are aimed at targeting ordinary people.

24. *Operative paragraphs 11 and 12*: While all outstanding issues with respect to Iran's peaceful nuclear program have been resolved in the framework of the Work Plan, and while the IAEA Director General has repeatedly confirmed the non-diversion of the Iranian nuclear program towards military purposes, it is not clear on what grounds the Security Council has prescribed the inspection of the cargos of the Iranian aircrafts and vessels. Moreover, the Council has not made it clear that if the inspections are done merely on baseless and unfounded pretexts, how and through what competent body, the damages inflicted on the Iranian institutions could be remedied. Certainly, the Government of the Islamic Republic of Iran reserves its right to follow the case before the competent fora, and the said countries bear the responsibility for their measures in this regard. Furthermore, this paragraph could not be considered as a basis for the inspections done according to the arrangements that do not enjoy the endorsement of the general United Nations membership, and, undoubtedly, would not legitimize them.

25. *Operative paragraphs 13 and 14*: In light of the above-mentioned observations on the unlawfulness of the measures taken by the Security Council against Iran's peaceful nuclear program, establishing a mechanism named 1737 Committee and calling on other countries to report to that committee is unlawful. Instead of wasting its resources and the United Nations budget on this issue, it would have been much better for the Security Council to allocate its resources and budget to the more essential and immediate issues such as the genocide and the crimes committed on a daily basis by the Zionist regime in the occupied territories of Palestine.

26. *Operative paragraph 15*: While the few countries that are mentioned in this paragraph express their willingness to engage in dialogue and negotiations with Iran, at the same time and contrary to their expression of readiness for negotiations, they adopt unlawful actions against Iran in the Security Council. Putting precondition for negotiation is yet another inconsistency in the actions of these countries, which well indicates their lack of goodwill in this respect. While Iran has always been ready to negotiate about different issues, it has been the other parties to the negations that have blocked this process by putting preconditions, and by their counterproductive and destructive measures. Chapter VI of the Charter of the United Nations clearly deals with the peaceful settlement of dispute among nations, but since the real intent of the sponsors of the United Nations Security

Council resolutions against Iran has not been the settlement of the dispute, and since they have been only trying to exert pressure against the Iranian nation, therefore, they have not paid any attention to the provisions of this Chapter. Hence, their expression of readiness to negotiate, while at the same time a new resolution is adopted against Iran, cannot be considered genuine.

27. *Operative paragraph 17*: The right of a person to have recourse to the court is a fundamental human right which is expressly recognized in the Universal Declaration of Human Rights (1948) and International Covenant on Civil and Political Rights (1966). The Security Council could in no way limit or derogate such rights. The Council's prescription in this paragraph obviously has ignored such rules as *jus cogens* and could in no way be justified. For sure, the conduct of no entity is excluded from judicial review and the Security Council's decisions and the United Nations Member States actions to implement the Council decisions are also not exempted from this general rule. The Council's prescription in this Paragraph is also clearly in contravention of the principle of accountability of the Security Council.

28. *Operative paragraph 18*: Ironically, the sponsors and supporters of the said United Nations Security Council resolution create obligations for the Director General of the IAEA, as an independent body, which is against the letter and spirit of the Agency's Statute and the NPT.

29. *Operative paragraph 19*: The United States and the sponsors of the resolution (EU3) have inserted the issue of suspension under subparagraph (a) of this paragraph, as a precondition, which is in apparent contradiction to their so-called 'goodwill' for resumption of negotiations. The request for suspension has no technical or legal basis. The sponsors of the resolution, under subparagraph (b) and the so-called 'return mechanism', have yet again shown their real intention. In this subparagraph, they have linked the removal of the unlawful sanctions against Iran to the Security Council's decision or, in other words, to the decision of the possessors of the undemocratic and discriminative right of 'veto' in the Security Council. To make this process even more complicated - and in yet another sign of their political motives - the sponsors of the resolution have added the need for the confirmation of the Board of Governors to this process too, while it is the Agency - which has confirmed the non-diversion of Iran's nuclear activities for several times - that must play the main and pivotal role with regard to Iran's nuclear issue. Also, under sub-paragraph (c) the wider extension of sanctions has been predicted as possible new measures of the Security Council. It is obvious that, due to contradiction of these resolutions to the Charter of the United Nations, the Islamic Republic of Iran is not obliged to implement their unlawful demands and, hence, the way offered in those resolutions is wrong and it would be better for the sponsors of the resolution to seek to correct and redress their mistakes.

30. *Operative paragraph 20*: By keeping this issue in the Security Council's agenda, the integrity and credibility of the sole competent technical organization on nuclear activities of all countries, namely the IAEA, has been endangered and weakened. Keeping in the Agenda of the Security Council an issue which fully belongs to the IAEA, particularly after the last report of the IAEA Director General in which all remaining issues have been declared as closed in accordance with the agreed modalities, has no justification and is merely indicating the hidden political objectives of the US and EU3.

31. *Annexes*: With respect to the list of banned individuals, the sponsors have actually included in the said list those who are national heroes of Iran and have defended their country by putting their lives on the line during the 8-year imposed war - the same war

during which the Security Council was incapacitated and unable to take any action against the aggressor. Adding the names of the AEOI personnel and affiliated companies, which are merely involved in peaceful nuclear activities under the IAEA monitoring and in accordance with NPT and IAEA Statute, is another indication of the intention of these certain States to deprive Iran from nuclear energy for peaceful purposes.

Before concluding this part of the letter, I wish to stress that all legal arguments and reasoning raised by my Government in this letter could in no way be construed or interpreted as admitting the legality of the resolutions of the Security Council and the IAEA resolutions. Moreover, none of the above-mentioned points and observations shall be explicitly or implicitly considered as proof or circumstantial evidence to recognize or admit the requirements mentioned in the Security Council and the IAEA resolutions. Furthermore, the Government of the Islamic Republic of Iran reserves its rights to raise and to invoke any other rights, arguments or reasoning in the future. Taking into consideration the above-mentioned points and considerations, the Government of the Islamic Republic of Iran believes that the decisions adopted by the Security Council shall be considered as *ultra vires* and inconsistent with the Charter of the United Nations. Thus, my Government does not consider the said decisions as those that are covered by article 25 of the Charter and, therefore, will not be obliged to implement them.

F) Damages Inflicted:

Since the beginning of this issue, the US and EU3 tried to use the Board of Governors and the Security Council as a tool for advancing their political intention. To this end, they committed numerous breaches of their obligations which in turn resulted in infliction of damages on the Islamic Republic of Iran. Some of the breaches and consequential damages are as follows:

1. Imposing Costs on the Agency: Unnecessary highlighting of Iran's peaceful nuclear activities led to high costs for the Agency, while the Agency is responsible for more important issues like promoting and facilitating the use of nuclear energy for peaceful purposes, implementation of Article IV of the NPT and Articles II, III, and VIII of its Statute, as well as pursuing the disarmament commitments of the nuclear weapon States and establishing a mechanism to verify the nuclear activities of non-NPT members in accordance with Article VI. With confirmation of peaceful nature of Iran's nuclear activities, there remains no doubt that engaging the Board of Governors and then the Security Council in the nuclear activities of Iran was planned to divert the Agency's attention from its main tasks and responsibilities.

2. Violation of Article IV of the NPT: According to this Article, 'Nothing in this Treaty shall be interpreted as affecting the inalienable right of all the parties to the Treaty to develop research, production and use of nuclear energy for peaceful purposes' and 'all parties to the Treaty undertake to facilitate, and have the right to participate in, the fullest possible exchange of equipment, materials, and scientific and technological information for the peaceful uses of nuclear energy.' Unfortunately, the said few States not only failed to honor their commitments under this Article, but have also violated it. They put obstacles and limitations, in order to deny the Iranian nation the chance to exercise its absolute right and to benefit from the fruits of technology that were obtained without any help from abroad. These few States have made their utmost efforts to close the ways to nuclear cooperation with Iran.

3. Making interruption in peaceful nuclear activities of Iran and releasing confidential information: Based on the allegations and claims of these few states, the

Agency called Iran's nuclear issue a 'special case' which required measures beyond the existing legal commitments of Iran. Hence, to date, more than 3000 person-day inspections of nuclear facilities of the Islamic Republic of Iran have been carried out. These wide inspections interrupted the development of various affairs of nuclear facilities. Continued presence of the inspectors in nuclear facilities has hindered the scientists and the personnel of the facilities to do their job in a tranquil environment. In accordance with Article 4 of the Safeguards Agreement between Iran and the IAEA (INFCIRC/214), the safeguards shall be implemented in a manner 'to avoid undue interference in Iran's peaceful nuclear activities, and in particular in the operation of facilities'. In accordance with Article 9, the visits and activities of the Agency shall be arranged 'to reduce to a minimum the possible inconvenience and disturbance to the Government of Iran'. But due to the erroneous information of those few countries which led to the consideration of Iran's nuclear issue as a 'specific' one, measure beyond these provisions were taken and Iran fully cooperated in order to prove its statements. In this regard, certain sensitive and confidential information provided to the Agency for the fulfillment of its functions have been disclosed. The Islamic Republic of Iran in its various letters to the Agency pointed out this issue. In accordance with Articles 5 and 9 of the Safeguards Agreement between Iran and the IAEA, 'the Agency shall take every precaution to protect commercial and industrial secrets and other confidential information coming to its knowledge in the implementation of this Agreement.' If these few countries had allowed the Agency to fulfill its tasks in a normal manner free from their interference, and had not put pressures on the Agency, we would not have been witness to certain problems. These countries presented their political evaluations before the results of the Agency's verification were released, and therefore poisoned the atmosphere. Now after almost 5 years, everyone is witness to the fact that all statements by Iran have proved to be correct and those few countries have been lying.

4. Interruption in Iran's nuclear activities: As mentioned above, one of the measures taken by Iran in order to build confidence and provide transparency in its nuclear activities was the suspension of all enrichment related activities for more than two years and a half. In this regard, some factories were closed, many people were unemployed during this time and the process of planning for meeting our energy needs was disrupted. As a result, lots of human, financial and political damages were inflicted on Iran. Now, given the fact that peaceful nature of Iran's nuclear activities has been proved, this question arises that who should compensate these huge damages?

5. Breach of Article XI of the IAEA Statute on facilitating the technical cooperation projects: The Security Council that has become unlawfully involved in Iran's nuclear activities has interrupted the technical cooperation of the Agency with Iran while the *raison d'etre* of the Agency is to help the Member States in this field. According to Article XI of the Agency's Statute 'Any member or group of members of the Agency desiring to set up any project for research on, or development or practical application of, atomic energy for peaceful purposes may request the assistance of the Agency in securing special fissionable and other materials, services, equipment, and facilities necessary for this purpose' and ' the Agency may also assist any member or group of members to make arrangements to secure necessary financing from outside sources to carry out such projects'. These few countries have damaged the prestige of the Agency by their actions. It goes without saying that the afore-mentioned measure not only breach the Agency's Statue, but also unilateral and destructive actions and imposing sanctions against the Islamic Republic of Iran such as unilateral measure to stop the completion of the Bushehr atomic power plant in the past

and also nullifying other atomic cooperation contracts with European countries as well as impeding the cooperation of relevant companies with Iran by European countries, basically are in contrast with the establishment of the IAEA for the promotion of peaceful uses of nuclear energy, and are in violation of the provisions of both the Agency's Statue and the NPT.

6. Intellectual damages, particularly damage to reputation: The most important damage inflicted on the Islamic Republic of Iran has been the efforts made to hurt its reputation in the international arena. Enlisting the names of some Iranian scientists, authorities and companies for sanctions, has been intended by the co-sponsors to hurt the reputation of these Iranian nationals and entities. Also, these few countries have unfairly and baselessly tried to portray the peace and justice-loving people of Iran as warmonger and have endeavored to tarnish the image of Iran, and indeed all these can be proper grounds to take legal actions by my country and to seek remedy.

If the Islamic Republic of Iran has to be under such illegal pressures solely because of its peaceful nuclear activities; then what shall be the response to the frequent breaches of international obligations by the said few counties with respect to different international issues? Against this background, these countries should, as a minimum step, admit their mistakes, apologize to the great nation of Iran, correct their behavior, and above all, compensate all the damages they have inflicted on the Islamic Republic of Iran. The Islamic republic of Iran and its citizens have the right to resort to legal actions to seek redress against the sponsors of these unlawful actions. These countries should accept the responsibility for their actions and must be held accountable.

And finally, I would like to mention that our societies have been built upon the rule of law, and the desired world of peace and stability that the global community seeks to achieve also needs to be built on the foundation of justice and the rule of law. Placing one country above others and allowing it to use force is a recipe for dictatorship and anarchy. If the domination of power replaces the domination of law, especially in the light of disparities and ongoing injustices in the world, then the international security would be the main victim of this process. Multilateralism is the only lasting option which can confront the main menaces that the common security of the world is facing. Unfortunately, the tendency by certain countries towards unilateral measures has grown more than ever before. If these policies remain unbridled, at the outset of the new millennium, our world would face the greatest challenges that seriously endanger the international peace and security.

The maintenance and strengthening of international peace and security requires, as a first step, our endeavor to ensure a safer world through developing equitable international rules, and through their evenhanded implementation.

Manouchehr Mottaki
Foreign Minister of the Islamic Republic of Iran

Document 120: Iran's Proposed Package for Constructive Negotiations

INFCIRC/729, 13 May 2008 (also circulated as S/2008/397, 17 June 2008)

Stressing on the respect for the principles of justice, abidance by law, recognition of the rights of nations, respect for the sovereignty of states, reinforcement of regional and international peace, abstaining from monopolistic actions and threats, respect for democracy, human values and cultures of different nations; and rejecting the injustice and lawless behaviors towards the rights of nations;

The Islamic Republic of Iran believes that there is an extensive range of issues such as security issues, regional and international developments, nuclear energy, terrorism, democracy, etc. that provide a substantive potential for cooperation.

To the above are added other fields that include drug control, environmental conservation, and economic, technological, commercial - especially energy - cooperation, that provide other excellent possibilities and avenues for constructive cooperation.

Therefore, in view of the developments that have unfolded internationally and across the region, there is a need for a new and a more advanced plan for interaction. In this new round of negotiations, the main objective of the Islamic Republic of Iran is to reach a comprehensive agreement, one that is based on collective goodwill - that will help to establish long-term cooperation between the parties, and will contribute to the sustainability and strength of regional and international security and a just peace.

We also believe that in its later stages, the negotiations have the capacity to invite other capable and interested states to join it and explore the possibility of cooperation within parameters of the package. The main outcome of this new round of negotiations would be an agreement on 'collective commitments' to cooperate on economic, political, regional, international, nuclear and energy security issues.

Therefore, we are willing to start wide-ranging and comprehensive negotiations on the following issues:

A- Political and Security Issues:

1- One of the most important concerns of humanity is the need to protect the rights and dignity of human being and respect for the culture of other nations. A dialogue, for the appropriate realization of this, is necessary.

2- Talks on bolstering a just peace and advancement of democracy in the region and around the world. The talks will be based on:

— Respect for the rights of nations and their national interests.

— Support for the national sovereignty of states - based on democratic methods.

— Prevention of violence and militarism.

— Prevention of terrorism and its contributing factors.

On the above basis, the Islamic Republic of Iran is willing to enter into talks on cooperation to strengthen a just peace and bolster the stability and the advancement of democracy in regions that suffer from instability, militarism, violence and terrorism. Such cooperation can take place in different parts of the world - more specifically in the Middle East, the Balkans, Africa, and Latin America. Cooperation to assist the Palestinian people to find a comprehensive plan - one that is sustainable, democratic and fair - to resolve the 60-year old Palestinian issue can become a symbol of such collaboration.

3- Fighting common security threats, and talks and collective collaborations on combating the factors which contribute to and create security threats, including:
- Terrorism
- Drugs
- Illegal immigration
- Organized crimes

B- Economic Issues:

1- Cooperation on the provision of energy and its security - in the fields of production, provision, transportation and consumption.

2- Cooperation on trade and investment.

3- A common effort to help fight poverty in least developed countries and to reduce the divide between social classes.

4- Reducing the impact of sharp price fluctuations and retooling global monetary and financial arrangements to benefit the nations of the world.

C- The Nuclear Issue:

With regard to the nuclear issue, Iran is ready - in a comprehensive manner, and as an active and influential member of the NPT and the IAEA - to consider the following issues:

1- Obtaining a further assurance about the non-diversion of the nuclear activities of different countries.

2- Establishing enrichment and nuclear fuel production consortiums in different parts of the world - including in Iran.

3- Cooperation to access and utilize peaceful nuclear technology and facilitating its usage by all states.

4- Nuclear disarmament and establishment of a follow up committee.

5- Improved supervision by the IAEA over the nuclear activities of different states.

6- Joint collaboration over nuclear safety and physical protection.

7- An effort to encourage other states to control the export of nuclear material and equipment.

D- Within the parameters of this package, the Islamic Republic of Iran is ready to start serious and targeted negotiations to produce a tangible result. The negotiations can be evaluated after a specific period of time (a maximum of 6 months) to decide about its continuation.

Document 121: Letter Dated 6 June 2008 from the Permanent Representative of the Islamic Republic of Iran to the United Nations Addressed to the President of the Security Council

S/2008/377, 10 June 2008

Upon instructions from my Government and in pursuance of the previous letters of this Mission, including the letters circulated as documents A/61/571-S/2006/884, A/61/954-S/2007/354 and A/62/705-S/2008/117, regarding the blatant violation of the most basic principles of international law by the Israeli regime in making threats against the Islamic Republic of Iran, I wish to draw your attention to the following:

Emboldened by the absence of any action by the Security Council, and in full contempt of the most basic provisions of the Charter of the United Nations, particularly the provisions which call for refraining 'from the threat or use of force against the territorial integrity or political independence of any state, or in any other manner inconsistent with the Purposes of the United Nations', the Israeli regime's officials, in continuation of their aggressive policies and unlawful practices, have relentlessly and in full impunity continued to make threats of resorting to force against the Islamic Republic of Iran under false pretexts.

This Mission has, through previous communications, in particular the above-mentioned letters, brought to the attention of the Secretary-General and the Security Council's Presidents some of the instances in which the Israeli regime has threatened to use force against my country. Once again, as reported by the media on 6 June 2008, the Israeli Deputy Prime Minister and Minister of Transportation, Shaul Mofaz, repeated the same insolent threat of use of force against the Islamic Republic of Iran in an interview with an Israeli newspaper by saying that Israel 'will attack Iran ... attacking Iran, in order to stop its nuclear plans, will be unavoidable'. Such a dangerous threat against a sovereign State and a Member of the United Nations constitutes a manifest violation of international law and contravenes the most fundamental principles of the Charter of the United Nations, and, thus, requires a resolute and clear response on the part of the United Nations, particularly the Security Council.

Threats to resort to force by various officials of the Israeli regime against the Islamic Republic of Iran are indeed a manifestation of a threat to international and regional peace and security by a regime whose policies and practices are based on aggression, State terrorism and defiance of all basic principles of international law.

Regrettably, the inaction of the Security Council in addressing such Israeli policies, and the impunity with which the said regime has been allowed to insist on threatening other countries, has emboldened it to continue and even increase its unlawful behaviours and policies, to the extent that it engages as a matter of routine policy in openly threatening to use force against a Member of the United Nations.

It is well known to the international community that the Israeli regime, which has never been a party to the international instruments on the prohibition of weapons of mass destruction, has clandestinely developed nuclear weapons. Undoubtedly, nuclear weapons in the hands of an irresponsible regime with a long record of war crimes and crimes against humanity poses the most immediate and serious threat that the world and the region are facing.

Contrary to the baseless allegations fabricated by the Zionist regime, the Islamic Republic of Iran has unambiguously and vehemently rejected and opposed all kinds of weapons of mass destruction, including nuclear weapons. As a State party to the Chemical Weapons Convention, the Biological Weapons Convention and the Treaty on the Non-Proliferation of Nuclear Weapons, the Islamic Republic of Iran has on many occasions officially declared that weapons of mass destruction, including nuclear weapons, as the most inhumane weapons, have no place in the defence doctrine of the country.

I wish to reiterate my Government's position that while the Islamic Republic of Iran has no intention to attack any other nations, nonetheless, in accordance with its inherent right under Article 51 of the Charter of the United Nations, it would not hesitate to act in self-defence to respond to any attack against the Iranian nation and to take appropriate defensive measures to protect itself.

I would be grateful if you would bring the present letter to the attention of the members of the Security Council and circulate it as a document of the Council.

(*Signed*) Mohammad **Khazaee**
Ambassador Permanent Representative

Document 122: Iran's Proposal to EU3+3

5 July 2008

In the Name of God
The Compassionate, the Merciful
HE Mr Yang Jiechi, Minister of Foreign Affairs of the People's Republic of China
HE Dr Bernard Kouchner, Minister of Foreign and European Affairs of the French Republic
HE Dr Frank-Walter Steinmeier, Minister of Foreign Affairs of the Federal Republic of Germany
HE Mr Sergei Viktorovich Lavrov, Minister of Foreign Affairs of the Russian Federation
HE Mr David Miliband, Secretary of State for Foreign and Commonwealth Affairs of the United Kingdom of Great Britain and Northern Ireland
HE Dr Condoleezza Rice, Secretary of State of the United States of America
HE Dr Javier Solana, High Representative for the Common Foreign and Security Policy/Secretary-General of the Council of the European Union
The Islamic Republic of Iran, as a sovereign independent country with democratic and Islamic institutions and practice, with great strength and capacity has always played an important role by its constructive behaviour and actions in helping to strengthen peace and stability in the region and resolving international problems. We have offered the other party an opportunity to make good use of this capacity on wide areas of subjects by proposing a package.[452] We made that offer solely for the purpose of demonstrating our good faith and desire to cooperate, and to settle problems arising from unilateralist and unjust behaviours in our region and other parts of the worlds.

This offer was made despite our lack of trust for the duplicitous behaviour of certain big powers. In our view, the choice for working and cooperating with this unique capacity can present an opportunity for consolidation of peace, an end to violence in the region and extrication from the present impasse for those who interpret and apply human rights law and rules on the basis of their self-serving interests and have wreaked irreparable harm on the nations of the region and their own as a result of successive blunders.

It is abundantly clear that the problems are much more complex and far-reaching for some to try to deal with them by outdated ways of the past, based on discriminatory language of the era after World War II.

We need to make it clear that the world has changed and the laws have to be applied equally. Nobody can regard himself above the law or the sole enforcer of the law. The time for negotiating from the condescending position of inequality has come to an end,

---

[452] Doc. 120.

and this will not remain unnoticed in the eyes of intelligent statesmen of our world. The compassionate approach and behaviour of the Islamic Republic of Iran and its successful efforts to consolidate the rule of people and security in the region, especially in Iraq and Afghanistan, and to promote justice and brotherhood in the world are too clear to need further emphasis.

The message of our people is very plain: rule of law, security, peace and prosperity for all. The people of Iran have worked out the plans for the advancement of their country without asking for the help of others. Our past experience has been successful and we have no intention of changing this path. The international community looks with great respect at our logical behaviour and our efforts to strengthen stability.

Repeated support by the Non-Aligned Movement, as a major part of the international community and the Organization of the Islamic Conference for the peaceful nuclear programmes of Iran are clear testaments for the veracity of our claim. IAEA is no exception. It has repeatedly and clearly stated in its reports that they have found no diversion in activities of Iran. While according to the report on the implementation of the Safeguard by the Agency in 2007 concerning undeclared activities and materials, 114 countries including some countries with advanced nuclear technology – such as Germany and Switzerland – were not able to come to a definite conclusion, there seems to be no logic behind attempt to amplify the case of Iran.

...

Proceeding from our desire and conviction to solve all problems by constructive and logical interactions and by taking into our view all our actual strength and capacity, we presented our package without demanding any consideration in lieu of our proposals. Moreover, to demonstrate our good faith, while welcoming Mr Solana and his accompanying delegation we received the proposed package of the six countries plus their idea for dialogue and talks in a form of a Non Paper,[453] and emphasized that we will consider it carefully in light of the talks on 14 June and our shared attitude concerning new initiative and the positive reception for the initiative of the Islamic Republic of Iran in presenting the proposed package and its agreement on the main outlines and general content of the package, I wish to reiterate that the main headings of the proposed packages of Iran and the 3+3 have certain similarities. These similarities can be the basis for comprehensive and broader negotiations.

The policy of the Islamic Republic of Iran is to find common grounds through logical and constructive interactions under equitable conditions. Proceeding from this positive attitude we hope we will be able to come to new solutions, both in terms of form and content. By starting the new round of negotiations and reaching a comprehensive agreement, we will hopefully take a step toward long-term cooperation to promote lasting peace and security in the region and beyond.

...

Manouchehr Mottaki
Minister of Foreign Affairs of the Islamic Republic of Iran

---

[453] Doc. 133.

Document 123: Iran's Response to the EU3+3 Proposal of 12 June

5 August 2008

IN THE NAME OF GOD

Pursuant to Geneva's constructive talks and submitted proposal by the Islamic Republic of Iran on the modality of continued negotiations[454] and in view of the existing commonalities in both proposed plans as stated by the participants in the meeting, an agreement was made for further reflection on both proposals in order to provide each other with a 'clear response'.

The Islamic Republic of Iran with good will, a constructive approach and a strategic determination to continued negotiations has again carefully considered views as expressed in the Geneva meeting to produce a comprehensive agreement for cooperation, one which can address our common concerns and be based on our collective obligations and set an agenda for consulting all interested parties in order to reach an acceptable outcome.

Now the Islamic Republic of Iran is ready to provide a 'clear response' to your proposal at the earliest opportunity while simultaneously expecting to receive your 'clear response' to our questions and ambiguities as well.

Undoubtedly such mutual clarification can pave the way for a speedy and transparent negotiating process with a bright prospect and provide grounds for cooperation.

The second phase in negotiations can commence as early as possible if there is such willingness on your side.

Document 124: Communication Dated 28 September 2008 received from the Permanent Mission of the Islamic Republic of Iran to the Agency

INFCIRC/737, 1 October 2008

Explanatory Comments by the Islamic Republic of Iran on the Report of the IAEA Director General (GOV/2008/38) to the September 2008 Board of Governors

In the Name of God the Most Compassionate the Most Merciful

The Director General reported to the Board of Governors on the Implementation of the NPT Safeguards Agreement in the Islamic Republic of Iran, (GOV/2008/38, 15 September 2008).[455] The followings are some explanatory comments by the Islamic Republic of Iran on the report:

1- The report once again has confirmed in a crystal clear manner that all nuclear material, activities and facilities in the Islamic Republic of Iran are under full surveillance of the IAEA and the Agency is able to continue its verification of the non-diversion of declared nuclear material and activities. The Director General has acknowledged this fact 14 times in 9 different paragraphs of the report.

---

[454] Doc. 120.
[455] Doc. 53.

2- The Islamic Republic of Iran has repeatedly declared that there is no undeclared nuclear activity and material in Iran.

3- Suspension which is an experienced way, was a temporary, voluntary and non-legally binding measure, and had been carried out for more than two years and certainly could have not been indefinitely continued.

4- The 40 megawatt heavy water reactor in Arak (IR 40) will replace the 5 megawatt research reactor of Tehran that its life time will be soon expired. This reactor is to produce radio isotopes for application in medicine, agriculture and industry. The Agency is well aware of the fact that the research reactor in Arak is under the civil construction, at the same time the Agency is aware of the fact that implementation of such a project is in full compliances with the provisions of the NPT and the Agency's statute as well as the Comprehensive Safeguards Agreement.

5- In August 2007, the Islamic Republic of Iran took an initiative for the resolution of outstanding issues with the aim of removing any ambiguities about its peaceful nuclear activities, in the past and present. It should be emphasized that the main objective of conclusion of the Work Plan with the Agency was to resolve outstanding issues once and forever and to prevent entering into an endless process. In this regard, a Work Plan as reflected in the document INFCIRC/711[456] was agreed upon between the Islamic Republic of Iran and the Agency. On the basis of the Work Plan, the Agency provided the Islamic Republic of Iran with a list of six outstanding issues. The list consisted of Research on Plutonium, P1-P2 Centrifuges, Source of Contamination in an equipment of a technical university, Uranium Metal Document, Polonium 210, and Ghachin Mine.

6- Paragraph 5 of Chapter IV of the Work Plan reads: 'The Agency and Iran agreed that after the implementation of the above Work Plan and the agreed modalities for resolving the outstanding issues, the implementation of safeguards in Iran will be conducted in a routine manner.'

7- The Director General in his reports in November 2007 and February 2008 explicitly stated that all six outstanding issues had been resolved and the Islamic Republic of Iran had responded to all questions about the outstanding issues in accordance with the Work Plan. Following the successful implementation of the Work Plan which led to the resolution of all six outstanding issues, the United States having been dissatisfied about the results, began a political campaign on a part of the program entitled the alleged studies. Therefore, by interfering in the work of the IAEA and exerting various political pressures the United States attempted to spoil the cooperative spirit between the Islamic Republic of Iran and the IAEA.

8- One paragraph in the Work Plan which deals with the alleged studies has not categorized it as an outstanding issue, thus the modality for dealing with this part became different from the six outstanding issues. Chapter III of the Work Plan reads: 'As a sign of good will and cooperation with the Agency, upon receiving all related documents, Iran will review and inform the Agency of its assessment.' According to this paragraph the Agency was expected to deliver all documentations to Iran and Iran was only expected to 'inform' the Agency of its assessment and no meeting or presenting written response was not set forth in this regard. Nonetheless Iran based on the good faith and in spirit of cooperation agreed to hold discussions with the IAEA and provided necessary documents to the Agency and has done so.

---

[456] Doc. 6.

9- In spite of the fact that the so called alleged studies documents had not been delivered to Iran, the Islamic Republic of Iran carefully examined all the materials which have been prepared in power point presentations by the US and provided to the IAEA, and informed the Agency of its assessment with the following important points:

– The Agency has not delivered to Iran any official and authenticated document which contained documentary evidence related to Iran with regard to the alleged studies.

– The United States has not handed over original documents to the Agency since it does not have any authenticated document and all it has are forged documents by it. Had the United States provided original documents then Iran could have proved their forgery. The Agency didn't deliver any original documents to Iran and none of documents and materials that were shown to Iran are of authenticity.

– Existing some words in Persian and some Iranian names was the only thing which was used as a basis to attribute these documents to Iran.

– It is evident that anybody who intends to forge a document uses real names to show the material more convincing and internally consistent. The Islamic Republic of Iran however has proved that some of documents produced by the United States not only are not internally consistent but also have clear inconsistency and are in contradiction with typical Iranian standard documentation. In addition, none of these documents bear any classification seals.

– How can one make allegations against a country without provision of original documents with authentity and ask the country concerned to prove its innocence or ask it to provide substantial explanations.

– Iran has explicitly stated that it has not conducted any activities or studies referred to in the 'alleged studies'. Therefore slides and documents produced by the United States are fabricated and baseless allegations attributed to Iran.

– The Agency has explicitly expressed in a written document dated 13 May 2008 that: '… no document establishing the administrative interconnections between 'Green salt' and the other remaining subjects on alleged studies, namely 'Highly explosive Testing' and 'Re-entry Vehicle', have been delivered or presented to Iran by the Agency'. Regrettably this explicit expression of the fact which has not been reflected in the DG report, proves that in contrary to what has been said in the report, the documents related to the alleged studies lack any internal consistency and coherence.

– Taking into account the above-mentioned facts, and that no original document exists on the alleged studies, and there is no valid and documentary evidence purporting to show any linkage between such fabricated allegations and Iran, and no use of any nuclear material in connection to the alleged studies (because do not exist in reality), also bearing in mind the fact that Iran has fulfilled its obligation to provide information to the Agency and its assessment, and the fact that the Director General has already indicated in his report in June and September 2008 that the Agency has no information on the actual design or manufacture by Iran of nuclear material components of a nuclear weapon or of certain other key components, such as initiators, or on related nuclear physics studies, therefore this subject must be closed.

10- Paragraph 2 of chapter IV of the Work Plan reads: 'The Agency agreed to provide Iran with all remaining questions according to the above Work Plan. This means that after receiving the questions, no other questions are left. Iran will provide the Agency with the required clarifications and information.'

11- According to paragraph 2 of chapter IV of the Work Plan and the time frame which stipulated in the Work Plan, the Agency was obliged to provide all questions related to the Work Plan by 15 September 2007. If the Agency was of the view that the alleged studies was among those other few outstanding issues it should have provided questions as it did for other six outstanding issues. Therefore this trend of addressing new and unlimited range of questions cannot be continued and no new question in this regard could be accepted. Of course new questions, if any, could be raised after the implementation of the safeguards in Iran turned into a routine manner, then Iran would be ready to respond in accordance with its legal and safeguards obligations.

12- The first paragraph of chapter IV of the Work Plan reads: 'These modalities cover all remaining issues and the Agency confirmed that there are no other remaining issues and ambiguities regarding Iran's past nuclear program and activities.'

13- If it was intended to raise other issue in addition to the alleged studies (Green Salt, Re-entry Missile, High Explosive test) such as possible military dimension, since all outstanding issues have been incorporated in the exhausted list prepared by the IAEA during the negations, then it should have been raised by the Agency in the course of the negotiations on the Work Plan. One can clearly notice that no item entitled 'possible military dimension' exists in the modalities.

14- In accordance to the first paragraph of chapter IV of the Work Plan which reads that 'These modalities cover all remaining issues and the Agency confirmed that there are no other remaining issues and ambiguities regarding Iran's past nuclear program and activities, introducing a new wording in paragraph 14 of the DG report reading that 'there remain a number of outstanding issues' or in paragraph 23 of the report which reads 'other associated key remaining issues' not only is in contrary to the Work Plan but also is in contradiction to the pervious DG report (GOV/2008/4, Para 54) which acknowledges 'The one major remaining issue relevant to the nature of Iran's nuclear program is the alleged studies'.

15- Paragraph 15 of the report reads: 'Iran reiterated its assertion that the allegations were based on "forged" documents and "fabricated" data, focusing on deficiencies in form and format'. Although Iran has already addressed the substances of the documents and has proved their invalidity, it should be noted that 'form' and 'format' of the documents have their own merits to prove their forgery. It is noteworthy that the Agency had also questioned 'form' and 'format' during the meetings on 7-8 August 2008 about the Iran's responses to the alleged green salt (as it was referred to in para17 (b) of the report). For instance why the copy of the first page is 'folded' or the fonts are different and considered them as inconsistency. Meanwhile in the same paragraph (Para 17b) the Agency has requested Iran to provide the original documents. Similarly the legitimate question is: why Iran shouldn't have the right to ask for receiving the original documents on the alleged studies.

16- In the footnote number 5 of the report, the Agency indicates that the documentation presented to Iran appears to have been derived from multiple sources over different periods of time. The fact is that all documentation listed in the 25 April 2008 letter which has been shown to Iran, except one (document 18) has been provided to the Agency by the US. The single document is composed of 3 pages of graphs which the Agency claims that obtained it from a different source in 2008.

17- In paragraph 14 of the report, regrettably the Agency re-opened an already-concluded issue, an issue which the Agency explicitly announced its conclusion through a written text. The Agency acknowledged in a written communication dated 8 November 2007: 'Iran delivered the 15-page document related to the procedures for the conversion of uranium and its casting. This closes the u-metal issue of the Work Plan.' The Agency re-confirmed the conclusion of this issue in its communication dated 23 November 2008 and further added: "The Agency appreciates Iran for delivering the document and confirms that this action of the Work Plan is completed."

18- In paragraph 17D of the report the reference is made to the document 18, the document which the Agency is considering it as an important document regarding alleged studies. There is no evidence or indication in this document regarding its linkage to Iran or its preparation by Iran. It even does not contain one single word in Persian. The document only contains some English words and 3 hand-drawn graphs drawn by the Agency. This document is shown in order to be judged by the Board of Governors members whether it is fair to make accusation against a country merely on the basis of such an unauthentic and forged document?!

19- Paragraph 17 of the DG's report mentioned about the possibility of foreign assistance in experiments and expressed that it had provided the entailed information. Firstly this is another type of accusation and shows the validity and legitimacy of Iran's concern on possibility of involving the Agency in an endless process. Secondly based on the Work Plan any question and ambiguity should have been provided to Iran by 15 September 2007. Afterwards no question or ambiguity should be raised. Thirdly no detailed information has been provided to Iran. Fourthly the allegation is basically false and forged.

20- In the report there are various false quotations attributed to Iran including:
  – Iran has confirmed some of information on Alleged Studies (Para 15).
  – Iran has confirmed the accuracy of some of such information and confirmed some of alleged activities (Para 16).
  – Iran has asserted some of these studies and considered them as conventional (17e).
  – Iran has not opposed to the accuracy of alleged information (Para 18 of GOV/2008/15).

21- From the beginning, Iran clearly stated and confirmed that it has not conducted any of studies and activities related to the alleged studies and added those are produced and forged by the United States and all are baseless, incorrect and forgery. Therefore these are false attributions to Iran.

22- In Paragraph 3, chapter IV of the Work Plan, the Agency has acknowledged that 'the Agency's delegation is of the view that the agreement on the above issues shall further promote the efficiency of the implementation of safeguards in Iran and its ability to conclude the exclusive peaceful nature of the Iran's nuclear activities'. On this basis while the Work Plan has been implemented, the Agency is obliged to confirm the exclusive peaceful nature of Iran's nuclear activities. The Agency does not have any obligation to comment on the implementation of the Additional Protocol especially due to the fact that the ratification and implementation of an instrument with a voluntary nature is not subject to the Agency's engagement. As a matter of fact more than 100 NPT Member States has not done so yet and only 82 countries ratified and/or implemented the Additional Protocol.

23- Although the Islamic Republic of Iran voluntarily implemented the Additional Protocol for more than two and a half years, a few countries in an opposite direction to this measure and the other voluntary measured carried out by the Islamic Republic of Iran, conveyed Iran's nuclear issue to the United Nations Security Council. Afterwards Iran's voluntary measures were suspended based on the law adopted by the Iranian Parliament. Now it is not Iran but those countries which brought the issue to the UN Security Council should be blamed.

24- Based on the abovementioned facts:

– There is no original document regarding alleged studies.

– There is no documentary evidence regarding linkage of so called alleged studies to Iran.

– Iran has accomplished its undertaking to present its assessment on alleged studies to the Agency.

– As DG stated in its latest reports, the Agency has not detected the actual use of nuclear material in connection with the alleged studies.

– As DG stated in its latest reports, the Agency has no information on the actual design or manufacture by Iran of nuclear material components of a nuclear weapon or of certain other key components.

– According to the Work Plan the Alleged Studies has been concluded.

– Considering provided detailed responses, the Agency is in a position to close so called Alleged Studies.

– Therefore, in accordance with the modalities, implementation of Safeguards in Iran shall be conducted in a routine manner.

– It is obvious that aftermath, Iran in accordance with its legal and safeguards obligations like other member states, would be ready to respond new questions if any.

Document 125: Communication Dated 4 September 2009 received from the Resident Representative of the Islamic Republic of Iran to the Agency Regarding the Implementation of Safeguards in Iran

INFCIRC/768, 4 September 2009

I have the honor to refer to your last report on implementation of Safeguards in the Islamic Republic of Iran (GOV/2009/55)[457] and inform you of the following to be put on the record of the Agency:

...

3. ... I have to recall that the Work Plan was the fruitful result of a political decision by my Government in response to the appeal by Your Excellency to your former Secretary of the Supreme National Security Council. Following extraordinary cooperation of Iran, all six outstanding issues were resolved and you did report to the Board of Governors such an achievement. Now the document GOV/2009/55 explicitly reports that Iran has performed its obligation on the Alleged Studies as it was foreseen in the Work Plan (INFCIRC/711)[458] by providing its assessment on the so-called Alleged Studies. Therefore the Work Plan is completed and the dossier has to be terminated.

...

---

[457] Doc. 57.
[458] Doc. 6.

c) According to the Work Plan agreed between Iran and the agency on 21 August 2007 (INFCIRC/711), the Alleged Studies have been dealt with fully by Iran and the item in the Work Plan is concluded. The expectation of another round of discussion as reflected in your report is absolutely in contravention of the spirit and the letter of such an agreement which both are committed to. ...

Let's have a short glance at the Alleged Studies:

...

b) On the basis of the Work Plan, the Agency provided the Islamic Republic of Iran with a list of six outstanding issues as reflected in part II of INFCIRC/711. The six outstanding issues were: 1) Plutonium Experiments, 2) P1-P2 Centrifuges, 3) Source of Contamination in an equipment of a technical university, 4) Uranium Metal Document, 5) Polonium 210 and 6) Gachine Mine.

c) It was never the understanding of Iran and the IAEA to categorize the so-called 'Alleged Studies' summarily referred to in part III of INFCIRC/711 as an outstanding issue, otherwise the parties should have addressed it in part II of INFCIRC/711. One has to bear in mind the fact that the issues such [*sic*] high explosives and re-entry missile are outside the domain of the statutory mandate.

Moreover, if the so-called Alleged Studies were an outstanding issue, Iran and IAEA should have developed and agreed on a detailed modality for dealing with it as they did with respect to the six outstanding issues addressed in part II of INFCIRC/711. As a result, Iran and IAEA decided to make a short reference to the Alleged Studies in part III of INFCIRC/711 and to agree on a different approach for addressing it as follows:

> Iran reiterated that it considers the following alleged studies as politically motivated and baseless allegations. The Agency will however provide Iran with access to the documentation it has in its possession... As a sign of good will and cooperation, upon receiving all related documents, Iran will review and inform the Agency of its assessment. (Emphasis supplied).[459]

d) According to the above understanding, the Agency was required to submit all documentation to Iran and then Iran was only expected to 'inform the Agency of its assessment'. NO visit, meeting, personal interview, swipe sampling were foreseen for addressing this matter. Notwithstanding the above and based on good faith and in a spirit of cooperation, Iran went beyond the above understanding by agreeing to hold discussions with the IAEA, provide necessary supporting documents and inform the Agency of its assessment. Meanwhile, by refusing to submit all documentation to Iran concerning the so-called Alleged Studies, IAEA did not fulfill its obligation under part III of INFCIRC/711.

e) In your reports of November 2007 and February 2008,[460] Your Excellency explicitly stated that all six outstanding issues have been resolved and the Islamic Republic of Iran has responded to all questions about the outstanding issues in accordance with the Work Plan. Following the successful implementation of the Work Plan which led to the resolution of all six outstanding issues, the Government of the United States being dissatisfied about the results, began a political campaign on a part of the Work Plan entitled the Alleged Studies. Therefore, by interfering in the work of the IAEA and exerting various political pressures the Government of the United States attempted to spoil the cooperative spirit between the Islamic Republic of Iran and the IAEA.

---

[459] Nothing is emphasized in the original.
[460] Doc. 50, Doc. 51.

f) In spite of the fact that the so called Alleged Studies documents had not been delivered to Iran, the Islamic Republic of Iran carefully examined all the materials which have been prepared by US Government for power point presentations by the Agency, and informed the Agency of its assessment. In this context I recall the following important point:

i. the Agency has not delivered to Iran any official and authenticated document which contained documentary evidence related to Iran with regard to the Alleged Studies.

ii. The Government of the United States has not handed over original documents to the Agency since it does not in fact have any authenticated document and all it has are forged documents. The Agency didn't deliver any original documents to Iran and none of the materials that were shown to Iran have authenticity and all proved to be fabricated, baseless allegations and falls attributions to Iran.

iii. How can one make allegations against a country without provision of original documents with authenticity and ask the country concerned to prove its innocence or ask it to provide substantial explanations?

iv. The Agency has explicitly expressed in a written document dated 13 May 2008 that: '... no document establishing the administrative interconnections between "Green Salt" and the other remaining subjects on Alleged Studies, namely "Highly Explosive Testing" and "Re-entry Vehicle", have been delivered or presented to Iran by the Agency'. This written document proves that in fact the documents related to the Alleged Studies lack any internal consistency and coherence in this regard. It is regrettable that this explicit fact expressed by the agency has never been reflected in the DG reports.

g) Taking into account the above-mentioned fact, and that no original document exists on the Alleged Studies, and there is no valid and documentary evidence purporting to show any linkage between such fabricated allegations and Iran, and no use of any nuclear material in connection to the Alleged Studies (because they do not exist in reality), also bearing in mind the fact that Iran has fulfilled its obligation to provide information to the agency, and its assessment, and the fact that Your Excellency have [*sic*] already indicated in his reports in June, September and November 2008[461] that the Agency has no information on the actual design or manufacture by Iran or nuclear material components of a nuclear weapon or of certain other key components, such as initiators, or on related nuclear physics studies, therefore this subject must be closed.

h) If it was intended to raise other issues in addition to the Alleged Studies (Green Salt, Re-entry Missile, High Explosive Test) such as possible military dimension, since all outstanding issues have been incorporated in the exhausted list prepared by the IAEA during the negotiations, then it should have been raised by the Agency in the course of the negotiations on the Work Plan. One can clearly notice that no issue and item entitled 'possible military dimension' exists in the modalities.

i) According to the recent report of GOV/2009/55, the Agency expressed that the authenticity of the documentation that forms the basis of the Alleged Studies cannot be confirmed. This proved the assessment of the Islamic Republic of Iran that the Alleged Studies are politically motivated and baseless allegations.

j) On several occasions you have emphasized that the Agency is not intending to enter into the domain of the national security of Member States. Surprisingly, in this report you

---

[461] Doc. 52-Doc. 54. There was no DG report in June 2008.

have reflected the unjustified previous request by your staff in Tehran, discussing with Iranian military staff the issue of missiles and explosives! This, undoubtedly, is interference in confidential conventional military activities of a Member State, related to its national security, thus the request of your staff is contrary to your declared position;

...

l) In accordance to the first paragraph of chapter IV of the Work Plan which read that 'These modalities cover all remaining issues and the Agency confirmed that there are no other remaining issues and ambiguities regarding Iran's past nuclear program and activities', introducing a new wording in paragraph 18 of the report (GOV/2009/55) reading that 'there remain a number of outstanding issues' or in paragraph 28 of the report which reads 'there remain issues' [*sic*] not only contrary to the Work Plan but also is in contradiction to the DG report (GOV/2008/4, Para 54).

...

Considering the above and your recent report (GOV/2009/55) that confirmed that Iran has completed its obligations on the Alleged Studies by informing the Agency its assessment, and very positive developments and the joint constructive cooperation between Iran and the Agency, you are hereby highly expected to announce that the safeguards implementation in Iran shall be conducted in a routine manner in accordance with the last paragraph of the work Plan (INFCIRC/711)...

A. A. Soltanieh
Ambassador, Resident Representative

STATEMENTS AND PROPOSALS BY THE EU3+3

1. The EU3/EU3+3 Acting Jointly

Document 126: Framework for a Long-term Agreement between the Islamic Republic of Iran and France, Germany & the United Kingdom, with the Support of the High Representative of the European Union

INFCIRC/651, 5 August 2005

I. PREAMBLE

1. The introduction would provide the political chapeau for the overall agreement, setting out the principles on which a long-term relationship between the E3/EU and Iran would be based. The E3/EU propose that it should comprise the following elements.

2. The E3/EU and Iran would:

a. stress the importance of developing relations of trust and co-operation between the E3/EU and Iran for the preservation of international peace and stability;

b. define the relationship between the E3/EU process and the EU/Iran negotiations on a Political Dialogue Agreement and a Trade & Co-operation Agreement as complementary and mutually reinforcing;

c. commit themselves to establishing a long-term relationship in the security and political field based upon shared principles and conditional on both sides' adherence to all the principles and commitments set out in the overall agreement;

d. welcome Iran's commitment that, in accordance with Article II of the Treaty on the Non Proliferation of Nuclear Weapons, it does not and will not seek to acquire nuclear weapons or other weapons of mass destruction;

e. recall that Article IV of the Treaty on the Non Proliferation of Nuclear Weapons stipulates that nothing in the Treaty shall be interpreted as affecting the inalienable rights of all the Parties to the Treaty to develop research, production and use of nuclear energy for peaceful purposes without discrimination and in conformity with Articles I and II of the Treaty;

f. affirm that a final agreement on long-term arrangements providing objective guarantees that Iran's nuclear programme is exclusively for peaceful purposes would lead immediately to a higher state of relations based on a process of collaboration in different areas;

g. underline their determination to strengthen their long-term relationship through an enhanced programme of economic and technological co-operation, particularly through early completion of negotiations between Iran and the European Union on a Trade & Co-operation Agreement, and the associated Political Dialogue Agreement.

II. POLITICAL AND SECURITY CO-OPERATION GENERAL PRINCIPLES

3. This section would define the principles on which the long-term relationship would be based. The E3 and Iran would reaffirm their commitment to the Charter of the United Nations, and recall the United Nations Millennium Declaration and other appropriate international instruments. The E3/EU propose that, within the context of an overall agreement, this section could include, inter alia, the following mutual commitments in conformity with the Charter of the United Nations:

> a. to fulfil in good faith obligations in accordance with the Charter of the United Nations, under the generally recognised principles and rules of international law, and under relevant international agreements;
>
> b. to the principle of the resolution of disputes by peaceful means and in conformity with the principles of justice and international law;
>
> c. to refrain in their international relations from the threat or use of force against the territorial integrity or political independence of any state or in any other manner inconsistent with the Purposes of the United Nations;
>
> d. to the principle of the sovereign equality of all States;
>
> e. to co-operation between States in the various spheres of international relations;
>
> f. to promote respect for and observance and protection of human rights and fundamental freedoms for all without distinction of any kind;
>
> g. to affirm their commitment to prohibiting discrimination on any ground such as race, colour, sex, language, religion, political or other opinion, national or social origin, property, birth or other status; and
>
> h. to establish conditions under which justice and respect for States' obligations under treaties and international law can be maintained;

4. Within the context of an overall agreement and Iran's fulfilment of its obligations under the Treaty on the Non-Proliferation of Nuclear Weapons (NPT), the United Kingdom and France would be prepared to reaffirm to Iran the unilateral security assurances given on 6 April 1995, and referred to in United Nations Security Council Resolution 984 (1995). Specifically:

> a. the United Kingdom and the French Republic would reaffirm to Iran that they will not use nuclear weapons against non-nuclear-weapon States Parties to the Treaty on the Non-Proliferation of Nuclear Weapons except in the case of an invasion or any attack on them, their dependent territories, their armed forces or other troops, their allies or on a State towards which they have a security commitment, carried out or sustained by such a non-nuclear-weapon State in association or alliance with a nuclear-weapon State; and
>
> b. the United Kingdom and the French Republic would recall and reaffirm their intention, as Permanent Members of the Security Council, to seek immediate Security Council action to provide assistance, in accordance with the Charter, to any non-nuclear weapon State, party to Treaty on the Non-Proliferation of Nuclear Weapons, that is a victim of an act of aggression or an object of a threat of aggression in which nuclear weapons are used.

AREAS OF CO-OPERATION OF SPECIAL INTEREST

5. As part of an overall agreement the E3/EU propose that both parties should make commitments in the following areas.

Non-proliferation

6. The E3/EU and Iran would:

a. recall the statement of the President of the United Nations Security Council on 31 January 1992 and United Nations Security Council Resolution 1540 (2004) and reaffirm that the proliferation of nuclear, chemical and biological weapons, as well as their means of delivery, constitutes a threat to international peace and security; express grave concern that illicit trafficking in nuclear, chemical and biological weapons, as well as their means of delivery and related materials, which adds a new dimension to the issue of proliferation of such weapons and also poses a threat to international peace and security; co-operate to take appropriate and effective measures against such activities; and stress the importance of effective national export controls;

b. reaffirm their commitment to abide by security and non-proliferation treaties to which they are party, and recall the need for more consistent monitoring, effective implementation and, where necessary, firmer enforcement of such treaties;

c. stress the importance of universal adherence to and full implementation of and compliance with disarmament and non-proliferation treaties and of the full implementation of the IAEA safeguards agreements and additional protocols; work towards the conclusion of a Fissile Material Cut-Off Treaty; where it has not already been done, conclude an Additional Protocol;[462] become party to the Comprehensive Nuclear Test Ban Treaty; and subscribe to the Hague International Code of Conduct against Ballistic Missile Proliferation;

d. reaffirm their commitment to the objective of an effectively verifiable Middle East zone free of weapons of mass destruction, nuclear, biological and chemical, and their means of delivery, consistent with the resolution on the Middle-East adopted at the 1995 NPT review and extension conference, United Nations Security Council Resolution 687 (1991), and the relevant resolutions of the United Nations General Assembly.

e. confirm that the prevention of proliferation of WMD should not hamper international co-operation for peaceful purposes, in accordance with the relevant international obligations, while underlining that the goal of peaceful utilisation must not be used as a cover for proliferation.

Regional security

7. The E3/EU recognise that they share a number of specific security concerns and interests with Iran and the important role Iran can potentially play in ensuring regional security and stability. As part of an overall agreement, the E3/EU would welcome an expanded dialogue and relationship on these issues. To this end, the E3/EU would, as part of an overall agreement, commit to working with Iran to encourage confidence-building measures and regional security arrangements. Such discussions would take place in close consultation with all the States of the region. The E3/EU and Iran would recognise that any regional security arrangements must take account of the legitimate interests of all the countries in the region, thus contributing to the stability and security of the region as a whole.

8. In this context, the E3/EU would recall their and Iran's past and present contributions to the reconstruction of Afghanistan and Iraq, and reaffirm their determination to strengthen co-operation in these areas, and to work together to support the political process in both

---

[462] Doc. 5.

these countries with the goal of establishing democratic and stable states, based on the rule of law, which coexist with their neighbours, and by preventing any support and encouragement for groups that use violence for political ends.

Terrorism

9. The E3/EU and Iran would commit themselves to supporting the declaration on terrorism proposed by the Secretary General for the United Nations Millennium Summit, recognising that this definition might evolve before or during the Summit itself. This states that 'the targeting and deliberate killing of civilians and non-combatants cannot be justified or legitimised by any cause or grievance, and … that any action which is intended to cause death or serious bodily harm to civilians or non-combatants, when the purpose of such an act, by its nature or context, is to intimidate a population or to compel a government or an international organisation to do or to abstain from any act constitutes an act of terrorism'. To this end, the E3/EU and Iran would commit themselves to:

> a. combat by all means, in accordance with the Charter of the United Nations, threats to international peace and security caused by terrorist acts;
>
> b. complement international co-operation by taking additional measures to prevent and suppress, through all lawful means, the financing and preparation of any act of terrorism, in the framework of full implementation of United Nations Security Council Resolution 1373; and
>
> c. refrain from organising, instigating, assisting or participating in terrorist acts in another State or acquiescing in organised activities in their territories directed towards the commission of such acts.

Combating drug trafficking

10. The E3/EU recognise that Iran has been and will continue to be a key international partner for the EU in stemming the flow of opiates to Europe and therefore commit to developing co-operation on issues related to: illicit drug production, drug trafficking, chemical precursors trafficking, money-laundering, drug demand reduction, preventative and educational measures, treatment and rehabilitation of drug abusers, and assistance in drafting national legislation.

11. In support of this goal the E3/EU will:

> a. actively support efforts to establish an EU Action Plan with Iran, building on the 'EU commitments to action';
>
> b. actively support international programmes designed to tackle Iran's drug problem;
>
> c. take steps with Iran to implement joint projects in close consultation with Afghanistan and Iraq to establish border police structures, training of police officers and border management. As a first step, the E3/EU will focus their co-operation on enhancing capacities for Afghan/Iranian co-operation in the fields of cross-border police co-operation, intensified communication on both sides of the border, as well as the training of customs officers, and on the development of projects on demand and harm reduction in Iran.

IMPLEMENTATION MECHANISM

12. In the course of the negotiation the E3/EU and Iran would establish an appropriate consultation and co-operation mechanism with a view to developing a long-term relationship on political and security issues, taking into account the continuing EU-Iran negotiations on a Political Dialogue Agreement.

13. To this end, the E3/EU propose the creation of a high-level committee on political and security issues, which would be made up of representatives from respective Foreign Affairs and Defence authorities. This Committee, which would meet periodically, would review progress on this part of the agreement and provide a forum for discussing issues of regional, international and mutual interest. The Committee would report regularly to the appropriate EU bodies and to the Government of Iran.

III. LONG-TERM SUPPORT FOR IRAN'S CIVIL NUCLEAR PROGRAMME PRINCIPLES

14. The E3/EU recognise Iran's rights under Article IV of the NPT to develop research, production and use of nuclear energy without discrimination in conformity with its obligations under the NPT.

15. The E3/EU recognise Iran's right to develop a civil nuclear power generation programme to reduce its dependence on oil and gas and to choose the most appropriate mix of energy sources to meet its needs as it perceives them, consistent with its international obligations.

16. The E3/EU therefore declare, within the context of an overall agreement and a mutually acceptable agreement on long-term arrangements, their willingness to support Iran to develop a safe, economically viable and proliferation-proof civil nuclear power generation and research programme that conforms with its energy needs.

17. The E3/EU fully support long-term co-operation in the civil nuclear field between Iran and Russia.

FRAMEWORK

18. Within the context of an overall agreement, co-operation between the E3/EU and Iran in the civil nuclear field would move forward within the following framework:

a. Iran would have access to the international nuclear technologies market where contracts are awarded on the basis of open competitive tendering, recognising the right of companies to determine their own commercial strategies and choices;

b. co-operation would be conditional on Iran's full implementation of its relevant international obligations and commitments, including the long-term arrangements agreed between the E3/EU and Iran, resolution by the IAEA of all questions raised under Iran's Safeguards Agreement and Additional Protocol, and continued co-operation with the IAEA;

c. under United Nations Security Council Resolution 1540, and based on respective national, European and international norms, the E3/EU and Iran are obliged to implement export controls. The E3 would commit themselves to implementing these controls in a non-discriminatory way, bearing in mind the new context that would be created by the confidence building measures and commitments undertaken by Iran under an overall agreement.

IRANIAN ACCESS TO THE INTERNATIONAL NUCLEAR FUEL MARKET AND CO-OPERATION IN NUCLEAR ENERGY

19. In line with these principles, and in the context of an overall agreement and growing confidence between the E3/EU and Iran, the E3 would support the development of Iran's civil nuclear programme in the following areas:

a. in the field of civil nuclear research through implementation of the E3/EU's offer of an expert mission to help identify the requirement for a research reactor in Iran and how best to meet that requirement. The E3/EU would ensure Iran faced no discriminatory obstacles to filling the requirements jointly identified; and

b. in other fields of peaceful use of nuclear energy, excluding fuel-cycle related activity, the E3/EU would commit themselves not to impede participation in open competitive tendering.

20. The E3 Governments also support the development of co-operation in the following main areas, to be included in a final agreement:

a. in fields such as radio-isotope production, basic research and the peaceful use of nuclear energy in the fields of medicine and agriculture, subject to further expert discussion between the two sides;

b. in establishing co-operation between regulatory authorities in the E3/EU and Iran and the IAEA in order to assist with the design and implementation of international standard nuclear safety and security regimes. This could include formalised co-operation between regulators to share developed expertise and offering advice on security aspects such as the implementation of the Convention on the Physical Protection of Nuclear Materials, after Iran's accession to the Convention in its amended version. These areas of co-operation could be refined during the proposed visit of Iranian experts to the E3/EU.

21. To this end, the E3/EU will actively support commencement of negotiations on an agreement between EURATOM and Iran. This would create a framework for closer co-operation between Iran and all EU Member States.

FUEL ASSURANCES

22. The E3/EU recognise that Iran should have sustained access to nuclear fuel for the Light Water Reactors forming Iran's civil nuclear industry. These arrangements are currently provided for through bilateral agreements and contracts with states/companies with which it is engaged in nuclear co-operation. The E3/EU note that under the Iran/Russia agreement on nuclear co-operation, Russia has committed itself formally to supplying nuclear fuel for the life-time of Russian-built reactors in Iran. But the E3/EU stand ready to explore additional ideas in this context.

23. In order to provide Iran with additional assurances that external supplies of fuel could be relied upon in the long term, the E3/EU would propose to develop with Iran a framework which would provide such assurance, without prejudicing any future multilateral arrangements developed under IAEA auspices.

24. Both the E3/EU and Iran would aim to have IAEA (or possibly other international) endorsement for any framework developed, and the IAEA might be invited to monitor the operation of the mechanism and certify its operation on objective principles.

25. Any fuel provided would be under normal market conditions and commercial contracts and subject to proliferation proof arrangements being agreed for safety, transport and security of the fuel, including the return of all spent fuel.

26. The framework could involve a combination of the following mutually reinforcing measures:

a. E3/EU – Iran ad hoc mechanism

27. This would involve establishment of a specific mechanism to be agreed between the E3/EU and Iran should the contracted supplier not be in a position to provide the fuel pursuant to its agreements with Iran for non-commercial reasons not connected with proliferation or safeguards related concerns and Iran faced serious difficulty in procuring the nuclear fuel necessary for the safe and sustained functioning of its Light Water reactors. In such an event, the E3/EU and Iran would immediately convene an ad hoc senior officials meeting to assess the situation, and identify and review relevant measures. The E3/EU

Governments would, in parallel convene a meeting with relevant companies to review what action could be taken to avoid any shortage of energy. The IAEA could, as appropriate, be invited to such meetings for advisory purposes.

28. The mechanism might seek initially to restore fuel supplies from the contracted supplier. If this was not possible, it could seek to identify an alternative fabricator capable of producing the required design of reactor fuel. If no such fabricator could be identified, possibilities would be investigated to establish and licence a new fabrication line, outside Iran, able to meet the future fuel supply needs at market prices. Any such alternative supply mechanism would be dependent on satisfactory arrangements being established for long-term management of spent fuel outside Iran.

29. The E3/EU would commit themselves to exploring ways with industry to provide assured enrichment services at market prices for fuel fabrication outside Iran if the usual enrichment services provider were unable to meet its contractual obligations for non-commercial reasons; how such a commitment would be formally presented remains to be defined.

b. Establishment of a buffer store

30. In order to provide the necessary time for a solution to be found through the E3/EU – Iran ad hoc mechanism without adversely impacting the operation of Iran's nuclear power reactors, the E3/EU commit themselves to assisting in the establishment of a buffer store of fuel, sufficient to maintain supplies at the contracted rate for a period of 5 years. This store would be physically located in a mutually acceptable third country, and would be available to draw from while long-term arrangements are put in place. The E3/EU would welcome early discussion with Iran on establishment, maintenance and use of the buffer store.

c. Multilateral arrangements

31. The E3/EU and Iran would engage with the IAEA and others to develop international mechanisms following on from the ideas identified in the 'Multilateral Nuclear Approaches' report on security of fuel supply.

CONFIDENCE BUILDING

32. The E3/EU reaffirm Iran's inalienable right to the peaceful use of nuclear energy, exercised in conformity with the NPT. In this context, the support of E3 countries for expanding international co-operation in Iran's civil nuclear sector and for the development of a safe, economically viable and proliferation proof civil nuclear power generation and research programme will present Iran with new opportunities.

33. Effective long-term co-operation between Iran and the international community in the civil nuclear field along the lines set out in this document will, however, require the continued building of confidence over a significant period.

34. As Iran will have an assured supply of fuel over the coming years, it will be able to provide the confidence needed by making a binding commitment not to pursue fuel cycle activities other than the construction and operation of light water power and research reactors. This commitment would be reviewed jointly in line with the review mechanism envisaged in Paragraph 58.

35. The E3/EU would expect Iran to invite the IAEA to agree a mechanism to verify the implementation of the final agreement.

36. As an essential element of this mechanism for international confidence building, Iran would undertake to:

a. make a legally binding commitment not to withdraw from the NPT and to keep all Iranian nuclear facilities under IAEA safeguards under all circumstances;

b. ratify its Additional Protocol, in accordance with its existing commitment, by the end of 2005;

c. in the meantime, fully implement the Additional Protocol pending its ratification and to co-operate proactively and in a transparent manner with the IAEA to solve all outstanding issues pursuant to the Safeguards Agreement and Additional Protocol including by allowing IAEA inspectors to visit any site or interview any person they deem relevant to their monitoring of nuclear activity in Iran; and

d. agree arrangements for the supply of fresh fuel from outside Iran and commit to returning all spent fuel elements of Iranian reactors to the original supplier immediately after the minimum cooling down period necessary for transportation.

37. In line with IAEA Board Resolutions,[463] the E3/EU would also expect Iran to stop construction of its Heavy Water Research Reactor at Arak, which gives rise to proliferation concerns. The E3/EU repeat their existing offer to send an expert mission to Iran to help identify research requirements and the most suitable type of equipment to meet those requirements.

38. The E3/EU would work with Iran to establish a group to identify alternative uses for the equipment, installations, facilities and materials whose use, construction, testing or development would not form part of Iran's long-term civil nuclear industry. The group could consider alternative areas of employment for the scientists, technicians and workers currently employed in these facilities.

CONSULTATION MECHANISM

39. The E3/EU and Iran would conduct regular consultations on the peaceful uses of nuclear energy and the development of the Iranian civil nuclear programme through a specific consultation mechanism to be agreed.

IV. ECONOMIC AND TECHNOLOGICAL CO-OPERATION PRINCIPLES

40. The E3/EU consider that an overall agreement would lead to the development of a programme of economic and technological co-operation with Iran, complementing the envisaged EC/Iran Trade & Co-operation Agreement, which will constitute the main vehicle for the long-term development of economic relations between Europe and Iran.

ENERGY CO-OPERATION

41. The E3/EU would recognise the fundamental importance of energy co-operation to their long-term relationship with Iran. As part of an overall agreement:

a. the E3/EU and the European Commission would be prepared to issue a policy declaration that they regard Iran as a long-term source of fossil energy for the European Union and recognise the growing importance of Iranian gas supplies to Europe in the coming years;

b. the E3/EU and the European Commission would commit to developing a strategic energy partnership through the Trade and Co-operation Agreement and in this context through the High Level Working Group on Energy;

c. in the context of the High Level Working Group on Energy and in the framework of the Memorandum of Understanding of 19 October 2002 between the European Commission and the Iranian Ministry of Petroleum on co-operation in the energy

---

[463] Doc. 26, Doc. 27.

sector, the European Commission would explore the possibility of opening the EU-Iran Management and Technology Centre with a view to commissioning joint studies on areas in which the EU and Iran can develop co-operation in the energy sector as well as providing technical support for the implementation of the policy declaration mentioned in Paragraph 41a;

d. the E3/EU and Iran, as well as the Commission, would discuss possible future oil and gas pipeline projects.

PROMOTION OF TRADE AND INVESTMENT

42. The E3/EU recognise the importance of the proposed EC/Iran Trade & Co-operation Agreement to developing the long-term commercial and economic relationship between the EU and Iran, noting that this will facilitate market access, promote commercial exchanges, and open up a wide range of further co-operation activities in the economic, commercial and other fields.

43. As part of any overall agreement the E3/EU would therefore commit themselves to working to bring the current negotiations between Iran and the European Community on a Trade & Co-operation Agreement, and the associated Political Dialogue Agreement, to an early conclusion.

44. The E3/EU and Iran would agree to continue and strengthen mutually beneficial practices in the areas of export credits and investment guarantees, particularly in light of the additional confidence that an overall agreement and a closer political and economic relationship would give to investors and export credit agencies alike.

WTO ACCESSION

45. The E3/EU welcome Iran's successful application to open WTO accession talks, recalling that this has been a significant benefit of the dialogue initiated by the Paris Agreement.[464]

46. The E3/EU confirm their continued political support for Iranian accession to the WTO and their willingness to offer technical support to assist Iran in making the necessary technical adjustments to its economy. Working with the WTO Secretariat and Commission, the E3 would agree to offer assistance to help Iran with WTO compliance, including on tariff structures, technical barriers to trade, rules of origin, intellectual property, and other areas as appropriate.

PROMOTING TRADE AND TRANSFER OF TECHNOLOGY: EXPORT CONTROLS

47. The E3/EU note that enhanced confidence regarding the civilian end-use of goods transferred to Iran, including through the establishment of export control systems, would facilitate decisions on individual licences. The E3/EU also recognise that effective export control systems will make a significant contribution to developing mutually beneficial economic relations and state that they apply international export control regimes and respective national and European regulations on a non-discriminatory basis. The E3/EU therefore agree to convene a joint export control workshop in Tehran, which would allow for exchanges on the implementation of United Nations Security Council Resolution 1540 and national/EC laws.

48. As a follow up the E3/EU is also prepared to offer support to Iran in establishing an efficient system of export controls.

49. Civil aviation. The E3/EU would continue to promote the sale of aircraft parts to Iran and be willing to enter into discussion about open procurement of the sale of civil passenger aircraft to Iran.

---

[464] Doc. 8.

SCIENTIFIC AND TECHNOLOGICAL CO-OPERATION

50. Recognising the benefits of scientific and academic co-operation to both sides, the E3/EU commit to developing long-term scientific co-operation with Iran.

51. In this context, the European Union, through the Commission, would agree to send an expert team to Iran to draw up Iran's 'Scientific Profile', within the context of the EC/Iran Trade & Co-operation Agreement.

52. The E3/EU would agree to facilitate Iran's access to advanced technologies, respecting national law and international commitments regarding export control; they would strengthen existing and encourage new scientific co-operation between scientists, universities and scientific institutes. This co-operation should cover both fundamental and applied research.

53. In the field of environmental technologies, the E3/EU would be prepared to develop co-operation with Iran in the fields of water supply, waste management, protection of natural habitats and preparedness for natural disasters.

54. In the field of communications and information technology, the E3/EU would be prepared to co-operate with Iran to improve internet connection stability.

55. The E3/EU would also be interested in developing and deepening co-operation with Iran through relevant international fora, particularly in the field of air pollution.

56. Education and vocational training. The E3/EU would be prepared, through their relevant agencies, to co-operate with Iran in developing its system of vocational education.

BUILDING A STRUCTURE OF ECONOMIC AND TECHNOLOGICAL CO-OPERATION

57. The E3/EU and Iran would look to invigorate co-operation through a mechanism, to be agreed, to complement any wider EU/Iran structures agreed under the Trade & Co-operation Agreement, and cover other areas of mutual interest, although of lower priority than those set out above, including but not exclusively:

> – Air transport safety. The E3/EU would co-operate in the fields of air traffic management, certification, accident, investigation and airport security.
>
> – Railway transport. The E3/EU would co-operate with Iran in establishing a transport master plan; they will encourage and support co-operation with Iran in the area of railway rolling stock, signalling and high speed technology.
>
> – Maritime transport. The E3/EU would facilitate the negotiation of a maritime transport agreement with Iran.
>
> – Seismology and seismic mapping. The E3 would, through their relevant institutions contribute to a seismic mapping exercise, with a focus on the most densely populated areas of Iran and work to develop co-operation in the fields of risk and disaster management.
>
> – Infrastructure. The E3/EU would facilitate access to European technology related to constructing earthquake resistant buildings.
>
> – Agriculture and food industry. The E3/EU would be prepared to offer co-operation in ecological agriculture, including natural herbicides and pesticides, food safety; and the regulations and trade aspects of sanitary and phytosanitary standards.
>
> – Tourism. The E3/EU would be prepared to assist Iran in developing its reputation as a tourist destination and support co-operation in the development of new tourist resorts.

V. REVIEW MECHANISM

58. The E3/EU and Iran would agree to implement the agreement in good faith. The agreement would be subject to review, at Ministerial level, every ten years. Any change to these arrangements would be subject to explicit agreement by both the E3/EU and Iran.

59. The E3/EU would be willing to circulate the final agreement as an IAEA Information Circular (INFCIRC) and UN Document for information and with a view to possible endorsement by the international community.

Document 127: Op-ed in the Wall Street Journal, 'Iran's Nuclear Policy Requires A Collective Response'

by Philippe Douste-Blazy, Joschka Fischer, Javier Solana and Jack Straw
(EU3 Foreign Ministers), 22 September 2005

...

Two-and-a-half years ago, Iran was forced to admit to the International Atomic Energy Agency (IAEA) that it was building secret installations to enrich uranium and to produce plutonium, which could be used to produce material for such weapons. It was and still is building ballistic missiles that could carry nuclear warheads. Iran appeared to be challenging the non-proliferation system. Subsequent investigations showed that, in the IAEA's words, 'Iran's policy of concealment ... resulted in many breaches of its obligations.' They gave rise to serious concern that Iran's nuclear program may not, as it claims, be for solely peaceful purposes. Under the IAEA's rules, Iran should have been reported to the U.N. Security Council two years ago.

The stakes were high then and they still are. If the process succeeds, the non-proliferation system will emerge with its authority enhanced. But if Iran continues on its path, Central Asia and the Middle East, the world's most volatile areas, may well be destabilized. Other states would be likely to enhance their own capabilities. The NPT will be badly damaged, as will the goal of creating a WMD-free zone in the Middle East, a cause to which we are committed. This helps explain the wide support we have.

Last month, Iran decided to defy the international community by restarting uranium conversion at its plant in Isfahan,[465] a unilateral step halting our talks. Iran claims it is doing no more than enjoying its right to make peaceful use of nuclear technology, in accordance with the NPT. Iran wants to paint this as a dispute between the developed and developing world.

These arguments do not stand up. No one is trying to stop Iran from generating electricity by nuclear power. We do not question Iran's - or any country's - rights under the NPT. This is why, in August, we offered Iran, as part of a long-term agreement, support for its civil nuclear program. But with NPT rights go very clear obligations, and there are serious grounds for concern that Iran's nuclear ambitions may not be exclusively peaceful.

For nearly two decades Iran hid enrichment-related and reprocessing activities which, if successful, would enable it to produce fissile material for a nuclear weapon. Only since 2002, as the extent of its undeclared activities was uncovered, has Iran admitted to them,

---

[465] Doc. 107.

and then only under the pressure of IAEA investigations. Iran initially denied having enriched any nuclear material, but was found to have done so using two separate processes. Iran also claimed it had no outside help for its centrifuge enrichment program. But it was found to have worked with the same secret network that helped Libya and North Korea develop clandestine nuclear weapons programs.

There is no economic logic to the facilities at the center of the dispute - at Isfahan and Natanz - if they are, as Iran claims, solely to produce fuel for nuclear reactors. Iran does not have any nuclear power station in which the fuel it says it wants to produce could be used. It has only one under construction, for which Russia is contracted to supply fuel for 10 years and has offered to supply fuel for the lifetime of the reactor, which can only work safely with Russian fuel. Iran has no license to make the fuel itself, nor is there any economic rationale. We have offered to work with Iran so it has assurances of supply in the event of a procurement problem. Thirty-one countries have nuclear power reactors - the great majority without developing a fuel-cycle industry, demonstrating that this capability is not critical to a civil nuclear industry.

We have pursued talks in good faith. But as well as breaking the Paris Agreement by resuming suspended activities, Iran rejected, without any serious consideration, detailed proposals for a long-term agreement that we presented last month. These were the most far-reaching ideas for relations between Iran and Europe presented since the 1979 Iranian revolution and would provide the foundation for a new relationship based on cooperation.

At the U.N. last week, we publicly and privately restated our willingness to work with Iran in political, economic, scientific and technological areas, and our readiness to explore ways to continue negotiations. We went out of our way to avoid public comment which might raise tensions, despite Iran's breach of the Paris Agreement.[466] But in his speech to the General Assembly on Sept. 17, President Ahmedinejad gave no hint of flexibility, talking of a 'nuclear apartheid' and insisting that Iran would exercise its right to develop fuel cycle technology, regardless of the concerns of the international community.[467]

The spotlight is now on the IAEA Board of Governors to respond. IAEA head Mohammed ElBaradei's latest report concludes that 'after two and a half years of intensive inspections and investigation, Iran's full transparency is indispensable and overdue.' The proliferation risks if Iran continues on its current path are very great. We hope all members of the international community will remain united. Collectively, we are responsible for meeting the challenge.

Document 128: Statement by Germany, United Kingdom, France and the EU High Representative on the Iranian Nuclear Issue

Berlin, 12 January 2006

The Foreign Ministers of Germany, France and Great Britain, Mr Frank-Walter Steinmeier, Mr Jack Straw and Mr Philippe Douste-Blazy, and the EU High Representative Javier Solana met today to consider the situation following Iran's resumption on 9 January of enrichment related activity.

---

[466] Doc. 8.
[467] Doc. 110.

Iran's nuclear activities have been of great concern to the international community since 2003, when Iran was forced to admit to the International Atomic Agency Authority that it was building a secret installation to enrich uranium, which could be used to produce material for nuclear weapons. The IAEA Director General at the time found Iran's policy of concealment had resulted in many breaches of its obligation to comply with the provisions of its Safeguards Agreement.[468] Under the IAEA's rules, this should have been reported to the Security Council then.

We launched our diplomatic initiative because we wanted to offer an opportunity to Iran to address international concerns. Our objective was to give Iran a means to build international confidence that its nuclear programme was for exclusively peaceful purposes, and to develop a sound relationship between Europe and Iran.

Given Iran's documented record of concealment and deception, the need for Iran to build confidence has been and continues to be the heart of the matter. It was Iran's agreement to suspend all enrichment-related and reprocessing activities while negotiations were underway that gave us the confidence to handle the issue within the IAEA framework, rather than refer it to the Security Council. We had strong support from the IAEA Board, which repeatedly urged Iran to suspend these activities and stressed that the maintenance of full suspension was essential.

Last August, Iran resumed uranium conversion at Isfahan, in breach of IAEA Board Resolutions and the commitments she had given us in the Paris Agreement of November 2004.[469]

The IAEA Board reacted by passing a Resolution in September formally finding that Iran was in non-compliance with its Safeguards Agreement, and declaring that the history of concealment of Iran's programme and the nature of its activities gave rise to questions that were within the competence of the Security Council.[470] Since then the IAEA has raised more disturbing questions about Iran's links with the AQ Khan network, which helped build Libya and North Korea's clandestine military nuclear programmes.

Nonetheless, in response to requests from many of our international partners and despite the major setbacks through unilateral Iranian actions, we agreed to delay a report to the Security Council and go the extra mile in search of a negotiated solution. We held a round of exploratory talks in Vienna on 21 December 2005 to see if we could agree a basis for resuming negotiations. We made crystal clear that a resumption of negotiations would only be possible if Iran refrained from any further erosion of the suspension. Iran's decision to restart enrichment activity is a clear rejection of the process the E3/EU and Iran have been engaged in for over two years with the support of the international community.

In addition it constitutes a further challenge to the authority of the IAEA and international community. We have, therefore, decided to inform the IAEA Board of Governors that our discussions with Iran have reached an impasse. The Europeans have negotiated in good faith. Last August we presented the most far reaching proposals for co-operation with Europe in the political, security and economic fields that Iran has received since the Revolution. These reaffirmed Iran's rights under the NPT and included European support for a strictly civilian nuclear programme in Iran, as well as proposals that would have given Iran internationally guaranteed supplies of fuel for its nuclear power programme. But Iran was to refrain from the most sensitive activities until international confidence was restored.

---

[468] Doc. 4.
[469] Doc. 8.
[470] Doc. 30.

Such a step would not affect Iran's ability to develop a civil and nuclear power industry. We proposed that the agreement be reviewed every ten years. The Iranian government summarily rejected our proposal, and all the benefits that would have flowed from it, nor have they taken up proposals by others. The Iranian government now seems intent on turning its back on better relations with the international community, thereby dismissing the prospect for expanded economic, technological and political cooperation with the international community which would bring tremendous benefits for Iran's young, talented and growing population. This is not a dispute between Iran and Europe, but between Iran and the whole international community. Nor is it a dispute about Iran's rights under the NPT. It is about Iran's failure to build the necessary confidence in the exclusively peaceful nature of its nuclear programme.

Iran continues to challenge the authority of the IAEA Board by ignoring its repeated requests and providing only partial co-operation to the IAEA. It is important for the credibility of the NPT and the international non-proliferation system generally, as well as the stability of the region, that the international community responds firmly to this challenge.

We continue to be committed to resolving the issue diplomatically. We shall be consulting closely with our international partners in the coming days and weeks. We believe the time has now come for the Security Council to become involved to reinforce the authority of IAEA Resolutions. We will, therefore, be calling for an Extraordinary IAEA Board meeting with a view for it to take the necessary action to that end.

Document 129: Statement Following Iran Meeting

London, 30 January 2006

The Foreign Ministers of China, France, Germany, Russia, the United Kingdom, the United States of America and the High Representative of the European Union met this evening, 30 January 2006, and agreed the following:

'Ministers:

underlined their commitment to the Treaty on the Non-Proliferation of Nuclear Weapons (NPT) and their determination to prevent the proliferation of nuclear weapons;

shared serious concerns about Iran's nuclear programme, and agreed that an extensive period of confidence-building was required from Iran;

called on Iran to restore in full the suspension of enrichment-related activity, including Research and Development, under the supervision of the International Atomic Energy Agency (IAEA);

agreed that this week's Extraordinary IAEA Board meeting should report to the Security Council its decision on the steps required from Iran, and should also report to the Security Council all IAEA reports and resolutions, as adopted, relating to this issue; agreed that the Security Council should await the Director General's report to the March meeting of the IAEA Board, which would include a report on the implementation of the February Board's Resolution, and any Resolution from the March meeting, before deciding to take action to reinforce the authority of the IAEA process;

confirmed their resolve to continue to work for a diplomatic solution to the Iran problem.'

Document 130: EU Letter Dated 27 February 2006 to the Secretary of the Supreme Council of National Security of Iran

GOV/INF/2006/5, 2 March 2006

Thank you for your suggestion, which you conveyed first to Javier Solana and then to our ambassadors in Tehran, that we should meet before the next IAEA Board meeting to see if we can agree a way forward.

We have always been prepared to explore new ideas. That was why we agreed to a meeting of officials last December, and again before the 4 February Board of Governors meeting, when we reaffirmed our readiness to support Iran's right to peaceful use of nuclear energy. The experience of our discussion over the last three years shows that ministerial level meetings are more productive if they are prepared by officials in advance. These help clear away underlying problems and make agreement at political level more likely. That is why we were ready, even at this late stage, for our political directors to meet with your officials this week.

On this occasion, you have expressed a preference for meeting at ministerial level without prior preparation. We are prepared to do this, to listen to your new ideas and to see if we can make progress towards resuming negotiations. Given that there will be no preparations by officials we thought it would be helpful for you if we set out in advance some of the considerations that will be critical for success.

In our judgement, for such a meeting to be productive, it must conclude with a clear public commitment from Iran to return immediately to the status quo ante, namely:

– that Iran will re-establish full and sustained suspension of all enrichment-related and reprocessing activities, including research and development, to be verified by the Agency, as requested of it by the IAEA Board of Governors on 4 February.

– and that Iran fully cooperate with the IAEA, including resuming voluntary application of the provisions of the Additional Protocol which Iran signed on 18 December 2003.[471]

We would expect agreement on this to be one outcome of any ministerial meeting. Anything short of this would result in a public disagreement, which would set back our shared objectives. But if we can agree on this point, we would look forward to hearing your views on other issues and to see if we can establish further common ground.

We will also have to consult all other important partners which have a stake in this process, including Russia, China and the United States, with whom we agreed on the way forward at our meeting in London on 30 January.[472]

If Iran is prepared to take these steps, then we believe it would help create a more positive atmosphere for discussions at the 6 March Board of Governors meeting, and would also influence how the Security Council proceed with the issue. Of course, other

[471] Doc. 5.
[472] Doc. 129.

important IAEA Board requests remain outstanding which the Board will also need to consider. Our goal remains to achieve a negotiated solution that meets the international community's concerns.

Document 131: Elements of a Long-term Agreement

6 June 2006 (also circulated as UN Doc S/2006/51, 13 July 2006)

Our goal is to develop relations and cooperation with Iran, based on mutual respect and the establishment of international confidence in the exclusively peaceful nature of the nuclear programme of the Islamic Republic of Iran. We propose a fresh start in the negotiation of a comprehensive agreement with Iran. Such an agreement would be deposited with the International Atomic Energy Agency (IAEA) and endorsed in a Security Council resolution.

To create the right conditions for negotiations,

We will:

• Reaffirm Iran's right to develop nuclear energy for peaceful purposes in conformity with its obligations under the Treaty on the Non-Proliferation of Nuclear Weapons (hereinafter, NPT), and in this context reaffirm our support for the development by Iran of a civil nuclear energy programme.

• Commit to support actively the building of new light water reactors in Iran through international joint projects, in accordance with the IAEA statute and NPT.

• Agree to suspend discussion of Iran's nuclear programme in the Security Council upon the resumption of negotiations.

Iran will:

• Commit to addressing all of the outstanding concerns of IAEA through full cooperation with IAEA,

• Suspend all enrichment-related and reprocessing activities to be verified by IAEA, as requested by the IAEA Board of Governors and the Security Council, and commit to continue this during these negotiations.

• Resume the implementation of the Additional Protocol.[473]

Areas of future cooperation to be covered in negotiations on a long-term agreement
NUCLEAR

We will take the following steps:

Iran's rights to nuclear energy

• Reaffirm Iran's inalienable right to nuclear energy for peaceful purposes without discrimination and in conformity with articles I and II of NPT, and cooperate with Iran in the development by Iran of a civil nuclear power programme.

• Negotiate and implement a Euratom/Iran nuclear cooperation agreement.

---

[473] Doc. 5.

Light water reactors

• Actively support the building of new light water power reactors in Iran through international joint projects, in accordance with the IAEA statute and NPT, using state-of-the-art technology, including by authorizing the transfer of necessary goods and the provision of advanced technology to make its power reactors safe against earthquakes.

• Provide cooperation with the management of spent nuclear fuel and radioactive waste through appropriate arrangements.

Research and development in nuclear energy

• Provide a substantive package of research and development cooperation, including possible provision of light water research reactors, notably in the fields of radioisotope production, basic research and nuclear applications in medicine and agriculture.

Fuel guarantees

• Give legally binding, multilayered fuel assurances to Iran, based on:
  – Participation as a partner in an international facility in Russia to provide enrichment services for a reliable supply of fuel to Iran's nuclear reactors. Subject to negotiations, such a facility could enrich all uranium hexaflouride (UF_6) produced in Iran.
  – Establishment on commercial terms of a buffer stock to hold a reserve of up to five years' supply of nuclear fuel dedicated to Iran, with the participation and under supervision of IAEA.
  – Development with IAEA of a standing multilateral mechanism for reliable access to nuclear fuel, based on ideas to be considered at the next meeting of the Board of Governors.

Review of moratorium

The long-term agreement would, with regard to common efforts to build international confidence, contain a clause for review of the agreement in all its aspects, to follow:

• Confirmation by IAEA that all outstanding issues and concerns reported by it, including those activities which could have a military nuclear dimension, have been resolved;

• Confirmation that there are no undeclared nuclear activities or materials in Iran and that international confidence in the exclusively peaceful nature of Iran's civil nuclear programme has been restored.

POLITICAL AND ECONOMIC

Regional security cooperation

Support for a new conference to promote dialogue and cooperation on regional security issues.

International trade and investment

Improving Iran's access to the international economy, markets and capital, through practical support for full integration into international structures, including the World Trade Organization and to create the framework for increased direct investment in Iran and trade with Iran (including a trade and economic cooperation agreement with the European Union). Steps would be taken to improve access to key goods and technology.

Civil aviation

Civil aviation cooperation, including the possible removal of restrictions on United States and European manufacturers in regard to the export of civil aircraft to Iran, thereby widening the prospect of Iran renewing its fleet of civil airliners.

Energy partnership

Establishment of a long-term energy partnership between Iran and the European Union and other willing partners, with concrete and practical applications.

Telecommunications infrastructure

Support for the modernization of Iran's telecommunication infrastructure and advanced Internet provision, including by possible removal of relevant United States and other export restrictions.

High technology cooperation

Cooperation in fields of high technology and other areas to be agreed upon.

Agriculture

Support for agricultural development in Iran, including possible access to United States and European agricultural products, technology and farm equipment.

Document 132: Press Statement by P. Douste-Blazy on Behalf of the Foreign Ministers of China, France, Germany, the Russian Federation, the United Kingdom, the United States of America and the High Representative of the European Union

Paris, 12 July 2006 (also circulated as UN Doc S/2006/573, 26 July 2006)

On the 1st of June, we met in Vienna and agreed a set of far reaching proposals as a basis for negotiation with Iran, stressing however that, should Iran decide not to engage, further steps would have to be taken in the Security Council. This offer was delivered to Tehran on the 6th of June. It includes offers of cooperation in the political, economic and nuclear areas which would be of significant benefit to Iran.[474]

Today, five weeks later, we reviewed the situation, on the basis of a report by Javier Solana who has met three times with Dr Larijani.

The Iranians have given no indication at all that they are ready to engage seriously on the substance of our proposals. Iran has failed to take the steps needed to allow negotiations to begin, specifically the suspension of all enrichment related and reprocessing activities, as required by the IAEA. We express profound disappointment over this situation.

In this context, we have no choice but to return to the United Nations Security Council and take forward the process that was suspended two months ago.

We have agreed to seek a United Nations Security Council Resolution which would make the IAEA-required suspension mandatory.

Should Iran refuse to comply, then we will work for the adoption of measures under Article 41 of Chapter VII of the UN Charter.

Should Iran implement the decisions of the IAEA and the UN Security Council and enter into negotiations, we would be ready to hold back from further action in the UN Security Council.

We urge Iran once again to respond positively to the substantive proposals we made last month.

---

[474] Doc. 131.

Document 133: Letter and Offer of 12 June 2008 delivered to the Islamic Republic of Iran

INFCIRC/730, 1 July 2008 (also circulated as S/2008/393, 17 July 2008)

HE Manuchehr Mottaki
Minister of Foreign Affairs of the Islamic Republic of Iran, Tehran

12 June 2008

Iran is one of the oldest civilisations in the world. Its people are justifiably proud of their history, culture and heritage. It sits at a geographical crossroads. It has vast natural resources and great economic potential, which its people should be reaping to the full.

But in recent years, Iran's relationship with the international community has been overshadowed by growing tension and mistrust, since there remains a lack of confidence in Iran's nuclear programme. We have supported the IAEA's efforts to address this with Iran but successive IAEA reports have concluded that it is not able to provide credible assurances about the absence of undeclared nuclear material and activities in Iran. Two years ago, the IAEA referred the matter to the UN Security Council,[475] which has now passed four Resolutions calling on Iran to comply with its obligations.[476]

We, the Foreign Ministers of China, France, Germany, Russia, the United Kingdom and the United States of America, joined in this endeavour by the European Union High Representative for the Common Foreign and Security Policy, are convinced that it is possible to change the present state of affairs. We hope that Iran's leaders share the same ambition.

In June 2006, we set out an ambitious proposal for a broad-based negotiation.[477] We offered to work with Iran on a modern nuclear energy programme, with a guaranteed fuel supply. We were also prepared to discuss political and economic issues, as well as issues regarding regional security. These proposals were carefully considered and designed to address Iran's essential interests and those of the international community.

Today, bearing in mind the provisions of UN Security Council resolution 1803, we restate our offer to address constructively these important concerns and interests.

Our proposals are attached to this letter. Iran is, of course, free to suggest its own proposals. Formal negotiations can start as soon as Iran's enrichment-related and reprocessing activities are suspended. We want to be clear that we recognise Iran's rights under the international treaties to which it is a signatory. We fully understand the importance of a guaranteed fuel supply for a civil nuclear programme. We have supported the Bushehr facility. But with rights come responsibilities, in particular to restore the confidence of the international community in Iran's programme. We are ready to work with Iran in order to find a way to address Iran's needs and the international community's concerns, and reiterate that once the confidence of the international community in the exclusively peaceful nature of your nuclear programme is restored, it will be treated in the same manner as that of any Non-Nuclear Weapon State party to the Non Proliferation Treaty.

---

[475] Doc. 32.
[476] Doc. 10-Doc. 13.
[477] Doc. 131.

We ask you to consider this letter and our proposals carefully and hope for an early response. The proposals we have made offer substantial opportunities for political, security and economic benefits to Iran and the region. There is a sovereign choice for Iran to make. We hope that you will respond positively; this will increase stability and enhance prosperity for all our people.

HE Mr Yang Jiechi
Minister of Foreign Affairs of the People's Republic of China

HE Dr Bernard Kouchner
Minister of Foreign and European Affairs of the French Republic

HE Dr Frank-Walter Steinmeier
Minister of Foreign Affairs of the Federal Republic of Germany

HE Mr Sergei Viktorovich Lavrov
Minister of Foreign Affairs of the Russian Federation

HE Mr David Miliband
Secretary of State for Foreign and Commonwealth Affairs
of the United Kingdom of Great Britain and Northern Ireland

HE Dr Condoleezza Rice
Secretary of State of the United States of America

HE Dr Javier Solana
High Representative for the Common Foreign and Security Policy

Possible Areas of Cooperation with Iran

In order to seek a comprehensive, long-term and proper solution of the Iranian nuclear issue consistent with relevant UN Security Council resolutions and building further upon the proposal presented to Iran in June 2006, which remains on the table, the elements below are proposed as topics for negotiations between China, France, Germany, Iran, Russia, the United Kingdom, and the United States, joined by the High Representative of the European Union, as long as Iran verifiably suspends its enrichment-related and reprocessing activities, pursuant to OP 15 and OP 19(a) of UNSCR 1803. In the perspective of such negotiations, we also expect Iran to heed the requirements of the UNSC and the IAEA. For their part, China, France, Germany, Russia, the United Kingdom, the United States and the European Union High Representative state their readiness:
  – to recognize Iran's right to develop research, production and use of nuclear energy for peaceful purposes in conformity with its NPT obligations;
  – to treat Iran's nuclear programme in the same manner as that of any Non-nuclear Weapon State Party to the NPT once international confidence in the exclusively peaceful nature of Iran's nuclear programme is restored.

Nuclear Energy
  – Reaffirmation of Iran's right to nuclear energy for exclusively peaceful purposes in conformity with its obligations under the NPT.

– Provision of technological and financial assistance necessary for Iran's peaceful use of nuclear energy, support for the resumption of technical cooperation projects in Iran by the IAEA.

– Support for construction of LWR based on state-of-the-art technology.

- Support for R&D in nuclear energy as international confidence is gradually restored.

– Provision of legally binding nuclear fuel supply guarantees.

– Cooperation with regard to management of spent fuel and radioactive waste.

Political

– Improving the six countries' and the EU's relations with Iran and building up mutual trust.

– Encouragement of direct contact and dialogue with Iran.

– Support Iran in playing an important and constructive role in international affairs.

– Promotion of dialogue and cooperation on non-proliferation, regional security and stabilisation issues.

– Work with Iran and others in the region to encourage confidence-building measures and regional security.

– Establishment of appropriate consultation and co-operation mechanisms.

– Support for a conference on regional security issues.

– Reaffirmation that a solution to the Iranian nuclear issue would contribute to non-proliferation efforts and to realizing the objective of a Middle East free of weapons of mass destruction, including their means of delivery.

– Reaffirmation of the obligation under the UN Charter to refrain in their international relations from the threat or use of force against the territorial integrity or political independence of any state or in any other manner inconsistent with the Charter of the United Nations.

– Cooperation on Afghanistan, including on intensified cooperation in the fight against drug trafficking, support for programmes on the return of Afghan refugees to Afghanistan; cooperation on reconstruction of Afghanistan; cooperation on guarding the Iran-Afghan border.

Economic

Steps towards the normalization of trade and economic relations, such as improving Iran's access to the international economy, markets and capital through practical support for full integration into international structures, including the World Trade Organization, and to create the framework for increased direct investment in Iran and trade with Iran.

Energy Partnership

Steps towards the normalization of cooperation with Iran in the area of energy: establishment of a long-term and wide-ranging strategic energy partnership between Iran and the European Union and other willing partners, with concrete and practical applications/ measures.

Agriculture

– Support for agricultural development in Iran.

– Facilitation of Iran's complete self-sufficiency in food through cooperation in modern technology.

Environment, Infrastructure

– Civilian Projects in the field of environmental protection, infrastructure, science and technology, and high-tech:

– Development of transport infrastructure, including international transport corridors.

– Support for modernisation of Iran's telecommunication infrastructure, including by possible removal of relevant export restrictions.

Civil Aviation

– Civil aviation cooperation, including the possible removal of restrictions on manufacturers exporting aircraft to Iran:

– enabling Iran to renew its civil aviation fleet;

– assisting Iran to ensure that Iranian aircraft meet international safety standards.

Economic, social and human development/humanitarian issues

- Provide, as necessary, assistance to Iran's economic and social development and humanitarian need.

- Cooperation/technical support in education in areas of benefit to Iran:

  • Supporting Iranians to take courses, placements or degrees in areas such as civil engineering, agriculture and environmental studies;

  • Supporting partnerships between Higher Education Institutions e.g. public health, rural livelihoods, joint scientific projects, public administration, history and philosophy.

– Cooperation in the field of development of effective emergency response capabilities (e.g. seismology, earth quake research, disaster control etc.)

– Cooperation within the framework of a 'dialogue among civilizations'.

Implementation mechanism

– Constitution of joint monitoring groups for the implementation of a future agreement.

Document 134: EU3+3 Statement on the Iran Nuclear Program

4 March 2009, INFCIRC/749, 1 April 2009

We thank the Director General for his report on the Implementation of the NPT Safeguards and relevant provisions of UN Security Council Resolutions 1737, 1747, 1803, and 1835 in the Islamic Republic of Iran.

We reaffirm our unity of purpose and strong support for the Agency. We applaud the Secretariat for the professionalism and impartiality with which it has pursued its verification mission and reaffirm that the IAEA plays an essential role in establishing confidence in the exclusively peaceful nature of Iran's nuclear program.

We call upon Iran to meet without delay the requirements of the IAEA Board of Governors and to implement the resolutions of the UN Security Council.

We note the serious concern expressed in the Director General's report and in his introductory statement to this Board about the continued lack of progress in connection with remaining issues which give rise to concerns about possible military dimensions of

Iran's nuclear program. In this regard, we call on Iran to cooperate fully with the IAEA by providing the Agency such access and information that it requests to resolve these issues.

We further call upon Iran to implement and ratify promptly the Additional Protocol and to implement all measures required by the Agency in order to build confidence in the exclusively peaceful nature of Iran's nuclear program.

We remain firmly committed to a comprehensive diplomatic solution, including through direct dialogue, and urge Iran to take this opportunity for engagement with us and thereby maximize opportunities for a negotiated way forward.

Document 135: Statement Following EU3+3 Political Directors' Meeting

London, 8 April 2009

The Political Directors of China, France, Germany, Russia, the United Kingdom, the United States and the European Union met in London today following the important discussions between our leaders in recent days.

The other members of the group warmly welcome the new direction of US policy towards Iran and their decision to participate fully in the E3+3 process and join in any future meetings with representatives of the Islamic Republic of Iran.

We reaffirm our unity of purpose and collective determination through direct diplomacy to resolve our shared concerns about Iran's nuclear programme, in line with the package proposals for cooperation with Iran and in the context of our dual-track strategy.

We recognise once again that Iran has the right to a civilian nuclear programme, but with that comes the responsibility to restore confidence in the exclusively peaceful nature of its nuclear activities in line with the relevant UN Security Council Resolutions.

We strongly urge Iran to take advantage of this opportunity to engage seriously with all of us in a spirit of mutual respect.

To that end, we shall ask Dr Javier Solana, the European Union's High Representative for Common Foreign and Security Policy, to extend an invitation to the Iranian Government to meet representatives of the E3+3, so that together we may find a diplomatic solution to this critical issue.

2. Statements by the United States

Document 136: Statement by Secretary of State Condoleezza Rice, US Support for the EU3

11 March 2005

The United States appreciates the efforts of the European Union 3 (EU-3) and the International Atomic Energy Agency (IAEA) to deal with the Iranian nuclear issue.

President Bush had very good discussions on Iran when he was in Europe which reflect a common view on the way forward.

The Europeans have been very clear with the Iranians that there will have to be certain objective guarantees that Iran is not trying to use a civilian nuclear program to provide cover for a weapons program.

In order to support the EU-3's diplomacy, the President has decided that the U.S. will drop its objection to Iran's application to the World Trade Organization and will consider, on a case-by-case basis, the licensing of spare-parts for Iranian civilian aircraft, in particular from the EU to Iran.

We share the desire of European Governments to secure Iran's adherence to its obligations through peaceful and diplomatic means. Today's announcement demonstrates that we are prepared to take practical steps to support European efforts to this end. The spotlight must remain on Iran, and on Iran's obligation to live up to its international commitments.

We also share with European Governments concerns about Iran's record on human rights and democracy and its support for terrorism. At this moment of historic opportunity, as the U.S. and our allies work together to support progress between the Israelis and the Palestinians, Iran must cease its support for those groups who use violence to oppose Middle East peace.

Document 137: US Statement, 2005 NPT Review Conference

19 May 2005

...In the Middle East, we applaud Libya for choosing to meet its NPT obligations. By doing so, it set an important standard for how countries in violation of their nonproliferation undertakings can voluntarily return to compliance and strengthen global confidence and security. Regrettably, however, since the last RevCon the world also learned of the Iranian regime's broad-based, long-term secret effort to acquire a fissile material production capability. Iran pursued these programs, which could give Iran a nuclear weapons capability, for nearly 20 years and in violation of its NPT and IAEA safeguards undertakings. The security consequences for the Middle East of these developments are grave. We encourage Iran to respond positively to the EU-3, to fully suspend and permanently cease all enrichment-related and reprocessing activities, to dismantle equipment and facilities related to such activities, to bring into force and implement the Additional Protocol, and to cooperate fully with the IAEA to resolve outstanding questions and meet all IAEA Board requests. Iran should provide objective and verifiable guarantees in order to demonstrate that it is not using a purportedly peaceful program to hide a nuclear weapons program or to conduct additional clandestine nuclear work elsewhere in the country. We share the desire of European Governments to secure Iran's adherence to its NPT obligations through peaceful and diplomatic means.

In addition to keeping pressure on North Korea and Iran, what should NPT parties be doing consistent with their Article I and II obligations to help prevent future cases of noncompliance?

Article I requires the nuclear-weapon States not in any way to assist, encourage or induce any non-nuclear weapon state to manufacture or otherwise acquire nuclear weapons or other explosive devices. To fulfill these obligations, the nuclear-weapon States must establish and implement comprehensive and effective export controls, including on dual-use items. The nuclear-weapon States have a special responsibility as they have possessed nuclear weapons infrastructures for decades. Given the interest of certain non-nuclear-weapon States and non-state actors in seeking the means to build nuclear weapons, the nuclear-weapon States must effectively protect against theft or unauthorized transfer of technology, equipment and material useful in the development and manufacture of nuclear weapons. Of course, their stockpiles of weapons and fissile material for weapons must be closely guarded. Article II requires the non-nuclear-weapon States not to manufacture or otherwise acquire nuclear weapons or other nuclear explosive devices and not to seek or receive any assistance in the manufacture of nuclear weapons or other explosive nuclear devices. Fulfillment of this obligation requires that non-nuclear-weapon States refrain from activities designed to develop a nuclear weapons capability. Further, they should provide transparency into their activities sufficient to demonstrate their peaceful purpose, and have in place the necessary laws and regulations to enforce their Article II obligations.

NPT supplier states, both nuclear- and non-nuclear-weapon States, should not authorize the export of any nuclear-related item unless they are satisfied that the transfer would not contribute to the proliferation of nuclear weapons. Adhering to this principle strongly reinforces the nonproliferation objective of the NPT. When in doubt about a possible diversion risk, it is best to forego the export. By doing so, NPT supplier states can avoid inadvertently assisting a possible future NPT violator in acquiring capabilities useful for a nuclear weapons program. If a state has violated the NPT's nonproliferation obligations, then all nuclear cooperation with that state should terminate. If an NPT party is engaged in nuclear weapons-related activities, it is very difficult to ensure that nuclear supply, even if originally intended for peaceful applications, would not be diverted and used in the activities that violate the Treaty.

...

What more can NPT parties do to strengthen Article II's ban on the manufacture or acquisition of nuclear weapons?

First, NPT parties must have strong declaratory policies that establish the necessity of compliance with the NPT. It should be clear that there is zero tolerance for noncompliance with the NPT 's nonproliferation undertakings, and that NPT parties are prepared to take firm and prompt action to hold any violator accountable for its actions. At a minimum, this should entail a cutoff of all nuclear-related cooperation. Such a step is prudent not only to prevent diversion to a possible nuclear weapons program, but it is good policy to terminate peaceful nuclear cooperation with NPT violators. Such benefits should be reserved only for NPT parties in full compliance with the Treaty.

NPT parties should also seek, through appropriate means, to halt the use of nuclear material or equipment acquired or produced by an NPT state as result of a material violation of the NPT's nonproliferation undertakings. These items should be eliminated or returned to the original supplier.

NPT parties should affirm their willingness to report cases of noncompliance with Article II to the UN Security Council. The Council should act promptly in such circumstances to determine a response, particularly when a case constitutes a threat to international peace and security.

Regardless of what measures are imposed against a violator or by whom, it is essential that any lifting of punitive measures be strictly linked to verifiable actions and be phased in over a period of time. Among the actions that must be taken by the noncompliant party are the full implementation of the IAEA Additional Protocol and transparency sufficient to demonstrate that the prior offender's nuclear program has become fully consistent with its NPT obligations. Moreover, NPT parties are fully justified in insisting on certain limits on the offender's future nuclear program, even after full compliance has returned.

Finally, to strengthen the NPT's nonproliferation obligations requires that NPT parties understand that the prohibition in Article II against the manufacture or acquisition of a nuclear weapon must apply to more than just an assembled nuclear weapon. In an extreme case, an NPT party might have manufactured an entire mockup of the non-nuclear shell of a nuclear explosive, while continuing to observe its safeguards obligations on all nuclear material. It would be folly for NPT parties to fail to act in such circumstances. Whether or not there has been a safeguards violation under Article III, it is also important to determine whether all the facts of a case tend to point toward an intent to manufacture or acquire nuclear weapons. Facts indicating that the purpose of such an activity is the acquisition of a nuclear explosive device would tend to show noncompliance with Article II. Examples of activities of concern include: seeking certain fuel cycle facilities of direct relevance to nuclear weapons, such as enrichment or reprocessing, with no clear economic or peaceful justification; clandestine facilities and procurements; committing safeguards violations and failing to cooperation with the IAEA to remedy them; and using denial and deception tactics to conceal nuclear-related activities.

Some might ask how the pursuit of enrichment or reprocessing without an economic justification can be an indicator of a possible Article II violation. Iran provides a case in point. Iran sought to acquire an enrichment program in secret and in violation of its safeguards obligations under the NPT. In light of the willingness of another state to provide fuel for the Bushehr reactor and any future reactor, Iran's enrichment program has no conceivable civil purpose. Moreover, Iran's uranium reserves are too small to provide an independent fuel supply for its nuclear power program, but large enough to support a weapons program. Why, then, has the Iranian regime been pursuing enrichment, and why has it done so clandestinely for almost two decades? It is painfully clear that Iran has not made the strategic decision to abandon its pursuit of a nuclear weapons capability. It is determined to acquire an enrichment plant to give itself the capability to manufacture nuclear weapons, which it could pursue either through further violation of or withdrawal from the NPT. These factors have led the United States to conclude that the intent of these activities is the manufacture of nuclear weapons and that Iran is in violation of Article II.

…

Document 138: National Intelligence Estimate, Iran: Nuclear Intentions and Capabilities

US National Intelligence Council, November 2007

Key Judgments

A. We judge with high confidence that in fall 2003, Tehran halted its nuclear weapons program[478]; we also assess with moderate-to-high confidence that Tehran at a minimum

---

[478] For the purposes of this Estimate, by 'nuclear weapons program' we mean Iran's nuclear weapon design and weaponization work and covert uranium conversion-related and uranium enrichment-related work; we do not mean Iran's declared civil work related to uranium conversion and enrichment (footnote in the original).

is keeping open the option to develop nuclear weapons. We judge with high confidence that the halt, and Tehran's announcement of its decision to suspend its declared uranium enrichment program and sign an Additional Protocol[479] to its Nuclear Non-Proliferation Treaty Safeguards Agreement,[480] was directed primarily in response to increasing international scrutiny and pressure resulting from exposure of Iran's previously undeclared nuclear work.

We assess with high confidence that until fall 2003, Iranian military entities were working under government direction to develop nuclear weapons.

We judge with high confidence that the halt lasted at least several years. (Because of intelligence gaps discussed elsewhere in this Estimate, however, DOE and the NIC assess with only moderate confidence that the halt to those activities represents a halt to Iran's entire nuclear weapons program.)

- We assess with moderate confidence Tehran had not restarted its nuclear weapons program as of mid-2007, but we do not know whether it currently intends to develop nuclear weapons.
- We continue to assess with moderate-to-high confidence that Iran does not currently have a nuclear weapon.
- Tehran's decision to halt its nuclear weapons program suggests it is less determined to develop nuclear weapons than we have been judging since 2005. Our assessment that the program probably was halted primarily in response to international pressure suggests Iran may be more vulnerable to influence on the issue than we judged previously.

B. We continue to assess with low confidence that Iran probably has imported at least some weapons-usable fissile material, but still judge with moderate-to-high confidence it has not obtained enough for a nuclear weapon. We cannot rule out that Iran has acquired from abroad - or will acquire in the future - a nuclear weapon or enough fissile material for a weapon. Barring such acquisitions, if Iran wants to have nuclear weapons it would need to produce sufficient amounts of fissile material indigenously - which we judge with high confidence it has not yet done.

C. We assess centrifuge enrichment is how Iran probably could first produce enough fissile material for a weapon, if it decides to do so. Iran resumed its declared centrifuge enrichment activities in January 2006, despite the continued halt in the nuclear weapons program. Iran made significant progress in 2007 installing centrifuges at Natanz, but we judge with moderate confidence it still faces significant technical problems operating them.

- We judge with moderate confidence that the earliest possible date Iran would be technically capable of producing enough HEU for a weapon is late 2009, but that this is very unlikely.
- We judge with moderate confidence Iran probably would be technically capable of producing enough HEU for a weapon sometime during the 2010-2015 time frame. (INR judges Iran is unlikely to achieve this capability before 2013 because of foreseeable technical and programmatic problems.) All agencies recognize the possibility that this capability may not be attained until after 2015.

D. Iranian entities are continuing to develop a range of technical capabilities that could be applied to producing nuclear weapons, if a decision is made to do so. For example, Iran's civilian uranium enrichment program is continuing. We also assess with

---

[479] Doc. 5.
[480] Doc. 4.

high confidence that since fall 2003, Iran has been conducting research and development projects with commercial and conventional military applications - some of which would also be of limited use for nuclear weapons.

E. We do not have sufficient intelligence to judge confidently whether Tehran is willing to maintain the halt of its nuclear weapons program indefinitely while it weighs its options, or whether it will or already has set specific deadlines or criteria that will prompt it to restart the program.

> • Our assessment that Iran halted the program in 2003 primarily in response to international pressure indicates Tehran's decisions are guided by a cost-benefit approach rather than a rush to a weapon irrespective of the political, economic, and military costs. This, in turn, suggests that some combination of threats of intensified international scrutiny and pressures, along with opportunities for Iran to achieve its security, prestige, and goals for regional influence in other ways, might - if perceived by Iran's leaders as credible - prompt Tehran to extend the current halt to its nuclear weapons program. It is difficult to specify what such a combination might be.

> • We assess with moderate confidence that convincing the Iranian leadership to forgo the eventual development of nuclear weapons will be difficult given the linkage many within the leadership probably see between nuclear weapons development and Iran's key national security and foreign policy objectives, and given Iran's considerable effort from at least the late 1980s to 2003 to develop such weapons. In our judgment, only an Iranian political decision to abandon a nuclear weapons objective would plausibly keep Iran from eventually producing nuclear weapons - and such a decision is inherently reversible.

F. We assess with moderate confidence that Iran probably would use covert facilities - rather than its declared nuclear sites - for the production of highly enriched uranium for a weapon. A growing amount of intelligence indicates Iran was engaged in covert uranium conversion and uranium enrichment activity, but we judge that these efforts probably were halted in response to the fall 2003 halt, and that these efforts probably had not been restarted through at least mid-2007.

G. We judge with high confidence that Iran will not be technically capable of producing and reprocessing enough plutonium for a weapon before about 2015.

H. We assess with high confidence that Iran has the scientific, technical and industrial capacity eventually to produce nuclear weapons if it decides to do so.

Document 139: US Statement, 2010 Review Conference PrepCom

8 May 2009

...

The United States is committed to diplomacy that builds constructive relations and addresses the full range of issues before us, including the need for Iran to take the necessary steps to meet its international obligations and regain the trust of the international community. On April 8, the E3+3 (China, France, Germany, Russia, the UK and the United States) affirmed their shared concerns about Iran's nuclear program and announced their invitation to the government of the Islamic Republic of Iran to meet to pursue a diplomatic solution to this critical issue. The E3+3, including the United States, are ready to meet with Iran if Iran accepts EU High Representative Solana's invitation on the group's behalf.

The President has stated clearly that he support direct diplomacy as the preferred means to resolve the international concerns about Iran's nuclear program. The President also has made clear that we do not dispute Iran's right to nuclear energy for peaceful purposes. <u>But with that right come responsibilities</u>. Iran needs to address the international community's concerns and restore international confidence in the exclusively peaceful nature of Iran's nuclear program.

...

Document 140: Remarks by President Barak Obama on a New Beginning

Cairo, Egypt, 4 June 2009

...

The third source of tension is our shared interest in the rights and responsibilities of nations on nuclear weapons.

This issue has been a source of tension between the United States and the Islamic Republic of Iran. For many years, Iran has defined itself in part by its opposition to my country, and there is in fact a tumultuous history between us. In the middle of the Cold War, the United States played a role in the overthrow of a democratically elected Iranian government. Since the Islamic Revolution, Iran has played a role in acts of hostage-taking and violence against U.S. troops and civilians. This history is well known. Rather than remain trapped in the past, I've made it clear to Iran's leaders and people that my country is prepared to move forward. The question now is not what Iran is against, but rather what future it wants to build.

I recognize it will be hard to overcome decades of mistrust, but we will proceed with courage, rectitude, and resolve. There will be many issues to discuss between our two countries, and we are willing to move forward without preconditions on the basis of mutual respect. But it is clear to all concerned that when it comes to nuclear weapons, we have reached a decisive point. This is not simply about America's interests. It's about preventing a nuclear arms race in the Middle East that could lead this region and the world down a hugely dangerous path.

I understand those who protest that some countries have weapons that others do not. No single nation should pick and choose which nation holds nuclear weapons. And that's why I strongly reaffirmed America's commitment to seek a world in which no nations hold nuclear weapons. And any nation - including Iran - should have the right to access peaceful nuclear power if it complies with its responsibilities under the nuclear Non-Proliferation Treaty. That commitment is at the core of the treaty, and it must be kept for all who fully abide by it. And I'm hopeful that all countries in the region can share in this goal.

3. Statements by the Russian Federation

Document 141: Statement by the Russian Federation, UN General Assembly, Report of the International Atomic Energy Agency

A/58/PV.53, 3 November 2003

Mr. Konuzin (Russian Federation) (*spoke in Russian*):

...

Let me turn now to some aspects of the Agency's activities on which the international community's attention has been focused. We are following developments related to Iran's nuclear programme, and we welcome the steps taken by that country to develop a dialogue with the IAEA in order to resolve pending issues.

We appreciate the work being done now by Tehran and by IAEA experts, which represents progress in the right direction. We believe that in future any problem between the IAEA and Iran should be resolved through cooperation.

It is our expectation that Iran will fully comply with the provisions of the September resolution adopted by the IAEA Board of Governors.[481] We believe that that resolution offers a work plan for the IAEA and Iran to clarify pending issues as soon as possible. We hope that by the next meeting of the Board of Governors, substantial progress will have been made in the implementation of those measures contained in the September resolution, and it is our hope also that this matter will be shifted back from political debate to the more routine track of work between the Agency and a member State.

We welcome Iran's declared readiness to sign the protocol additional to safeguards agreements[482] with the Agency and to refrain from operations involving sensitive elements of the nuclear fuel cycle, especially uranium enrichment experiments. We regard these decisions as a major step forward by the Iranian leadership. It is our feeling that, today, the issue of Iran's nuclear programme is excessively politicized. We hope that it will be possible to move it back within the area of regular International Atomic Energy Agency (IAEA) inspection activities.

At present we see no reason to reduce our cooperation with the Islamic Republic of Iran in the nuclear field, which is fully transparent and does not violate international obligations, either those of Russia or of Iran.

...

---

[481] Doc. 23.
[482] Doc. 5.

Document 142: Statement by the Russian Federation, UN General Assembly, Report of the International Atomic Energy Agency

A/59/PV.47, 1 November 2004

Mr. Dolgov (Russian Federation) (*spoke in Russian*):

...

Allow me to dwell on a few aspects of the Agency's activities that have great resonance around the world. We have been following developments regarding the nuclear programme of the Islamic Republic of Iran and we continue to advocate the resolution of all outstanding questions in that regard through constructive interaction between Iran and the IAEA. We note the importance of prompt Agency action to switch its monitoring activities in that country into normal, routine channels, as is now the case in most States parties to the NPT, and we will work towards attaining that goal in the future. We hope that Iran will fully implement the provisions of the September resolution adopted by the IAEA Board of Governors.[483] We view that resolution as the Board of Governors plan of action, and we hope that by the November meeting of the Board it will be possible to clarify once and for all the questions that the Agency still has concerning past activities of Tehran in this area.

Document 143: Statement by the Russian Federation, UN General Assembly, Report of the International Atomic Energy Agency

A/60/PV.41, 31 October 2005

Mr. Dolgov (Russian Federation) (*spoke in Russian*):

...

Application of the Additional Protocol[484] of the IAEA Safeguards Agreement[485] is a pillar of the Agency's activities, serving as an innovative tool for ensuring the transparency of national nuclear programmes. We believe that universalizing the Additional Protocol will be one of the international community's crucial non-proliferation tasks in the years to come. The Russian Federation will continue to provide assistance in the strengthening of the IAEA safeguards system, including by funding a national programme of scientific and technical support for the Agency's safeguards initiative.

Russia respects the interest of States in developing peaceful nuclear technologies and has cooperated with many countries in that area for a number of years. We advocate the broadest possible cooperation in the area of nuclear energy for development. However, the use of the peaceful atom for the production of nuclear weapons must be reliably and safely prevented. We promote methods of nuclear power development that would provide - as an alternative to the proliferation of sensitive technologies - programmes to provide a reliable supply of nuclear fuel on the basis of international cooperation. We support multilateral

---

[483] Doc. 27.
[484] Doc. 5.
[485] Doc. 4.

frameworks for practical cooperation in that regard, particularly the work on this issue carried out within the IAEA.

...

We view the resolution on the Iranian nuclear programme, adopted on 24 September 2005 by the IAEA Board of Governors,[486] as a signal for continued and more intensive cooperation between the Agency and Iran to clarify the remaining issues. It is our understanding that the Agency's potential is far from being exhausted, and that allows us to keep the settlement process of the Iran issue within the Agency.

We are in favour of more intensive dialogue on this issue among all interested nations. Decisions must be developed that, on the one hand, can remove all doubts about the peaceful nature of Iran's nuclear activity, and on the other, ensure the legitimate requirements of that country. The Russian Federation will cooperate further to solve that task.

...

4. Statements by China

Document 144: Statement by China, UN General Assembly, Report of the International Atomic Energy Agency

A/59/PV.47, 1 November 2004

Mr. Hu Xiaodi (China) (*spoke in Chinese*):

...

On the Iran nuclear issue, China stands for an appropriate resolution - within the framework of the IAEA - through dialogue and consultation. We hope Iran will continue its comprehensive cooperation with the Agency so as to clarify all the outstanding issues and ratify the Additional Protocol[487] as soon as possible. All parties should encourage Iran to continue to adopt measures conducive to enhancing trust and clarifying doubts.

China supports all diplomatic efforts to resolve the Iran nuclear issue at an early date, and is ready to keep in touch with all the parties in that regard. It is our wish and belief that, with the concerted efforts of all parties, the Iran nuclear issue could be resolved properly within the framework of the Agency. Such a result is not only in the interest of all parties concerned but also conducive to the maintenance of the international nuclear non-proliferation regime.

---

[486] Doc. 30.
[487] Doc. 4.

Document 145: Statement by China, UN General Assembly, Report of the International Atomic Energy Agency

A/61/PV.42, 30 October 2006

Mr. Cheng Jingye (China) (*spoke in Chinese*):

...

With regard to the Iran nuclear issue, China - as it has throughout - supports preserving the international nuclear non-proliferation regime, opposes the proliferation of nuclear weapons, advocates a peaceful resolution of the Iran nuclear issue through diplomatic negotiations, and endorses the Agency's active role in that regard.

A peaceful solution through diplomatic negotiations is still the best option, in the common interests of the international community. We hope that the Iranian side will respond to the appeal of the international community by adopting a constructive attitude and creating conditions for the resumption of dialogue. We also hope that the other parties concerned will remain calm and restrained, continue to seek a peaceful resolution and make full use of creative thinking, so as to find effective ways to achieve appropriate solutions to the Iran nuclear issue, rather than taking measures that may complicate the current situation.

China has actively promoted dialogue and will, with the other parties concerned, continue to play a constructive role in the peaceful resolution of the Iran nuclear issue through diplomatic negotiations.

STATEMENTS BY INTERNATIONAL ORGANISATIONS

1. Statements by the Non-Aligned Movement

Document 146: Fourteenth Summit Conference of Heads of State or Government of the Non-Aligned Movement, Havana, Statement on the Islamic Republic of Iran's Nuclear Issue

15-16 September 2006 (also circulated as A/61/472-S/2006/780, 29 September 2006)

1. The Heads of State or Government *reiterated* their principled positions on nuclear disarmament and non-proliferation reflected in the Final Document of XIV Conference of Heads of State or Government of the Non-Aligned Movement, held in Havana, Cuba from 11-16 September 2006. They *considered* the developments regarding the implementation of the NPT safeguards agreement in the Islamic Republic of Iran.[488]

2. The Heads of State or Government *reaffirmed* the basic and inalienable right of all States, to develop research, production and use of atomic energy for peaceful purposes, without any discrimination and in conformity with their respective legal obligations. Therefore, nothing should be interpreted in a way as inhibiting or restricting this right of States to develop atomic energy for peaceful purposes. They *furthermore reaffirmed* that States' choices and decisions in the field of peaceful uses of nuclear technology and its fuel cycle policies must be respected.

3. The Heads of State or Government *recognised* the International Atomic Energy Agency (IAEA) as the sole competent authority for verification of the respective safeguards obligations of Member States and *stressed* that there should be no undue pressure or interference in the Agency's activities, especially its verification process, which would jeopardise the efficiency and credibility of the Agency.

4. The Heads of State or Government *welcomed* the cooperation extended by the Islamic Republic of Iran to the IAEA including those voluntary confidence-building measures undertaken, with a view to resolve the remaining issues. They *noted* the assessment of the IAEA Director-General that all nuclear material declared by Iran had been accounted for. They *noted*, at the same time, that the process for drawing a conclusion with regard to the absence of undeclared material and activities in Iran is an ongoing and time-consuming process. In this regard, the Heads of State or Government *encouraged* Iran to urgently continue to cooperate actively and fully with the IAEA within the Agency's mandate to resolve outstanding issues in order to promote confidence and a peaceful resolution of the issue.

5. The Heads of State or Government *emphasised* the fundamental distinction between the legal obligations of States to their respective safeguards agreements and any confidence building measures voluntarily undertaken to resolve difficult issues, and *believed* that such voluntary undertakings are not legal safeguards obligations.

---

[488] Doc. 4.

6. The Heads of State or Government *considered* the establishment of nuclear-weapons-free zones (NWFZs) as a positive step towards attaining the objective of global nuclear disarmament and reiterated the support for the establishment in the Middle East of a nuclear-weapon-free zone, in accordance with relevant General Assembly and Security Council resolutions. Pending the establishment of such a zone, they *demanded* Israel to accede to the NPT without delay and place promptly all its nuclear facilities under comprehensive IAEA safeguards.

7. The Heads of State or Government *reaffirmed* the inviolability of peaceful nuclear activities and that any attack or threat of attack against peaceful nuclear facilities - operational or under construction - poses a great danger to human beings and the environment, and constitutes a grave violation of international law, principles and purposes of the Charter of the United Nations and regulations of the IAEA. They *recognised* the need for a comprehensive multilaterally negotiated instrument, prohibiting attacks, or threat of attacks on nuclear facilities devoted to peaceful uses of nuclear energy.

8. The Heads of State or Government *strongly believed* that all issues on safeguards and verification, including those of Iran, should be resolved within the IAEA framework, and be based on technical and legal grounds. They *further emphasised* that the Agency should continue its work to resolve the Iranian nuclear issue within its mandate under the Statute of the IAEA.

9. The Heads of State or Government *also strongly believed* that diplomacy and dialogue through peaceful means must continue to find a long term solution to the Iranian nuclear issue. They *expressed* their conviction that the only way to resolve the issue is to resume negotiations without any preconditions and to enhance cooperation with the involvement of all necessary parties to promote international confidence with the view to facilitating Agency's work on resolving the outstanding issues.

Document 147: Fifteenth Ministerial Conference of the Non-Aligned Movement, Tehran, Statement on the Islamic Republic of Iran's Nuclear Issue

27-30 July 2008 (also circulated as INFCIRC/733, 1 August 2008)

1. The Ministers reiterated their principled positions on nuclear disarmament and non-proliferation reflected in the Final Document of the Ministerial Meeting of the Coordinating Bureau of the Non-Aligned Movement, held in Putrajaya, Malaysia, 27-30 May 2006 and the 14th Summit Conference of Heads of State or Government of the Non-Aligned Movement held in Havana, Cuba, 11-16 September 2006.[489] The Ministers also reiterated the Movement's principled position on the Islamic Republic of Iran's nuclear issue as reflected in the NAM Ministerial Statement adopted in Putrajaya on 30 May 2006 and NAM Heads of State or Government Statement adopted in Havana on 16 September 2006. They considered the positive developments in the implementation of the NPT Safeguards Agreement[490] in the Islamic Republic of Iran as reflected in the reports of the Director General of the International Atomic Energy Agency (IAEA).

---

[489] Doc. 146.
[490] Doc. 4.

2. The Ministers reaffirmed the basic and inalienable right of all states to develop research, production and use of atomic energy for peaceful purposes, without any discrimination and in conformity with their respective legal obligations. Therefore, nothing should be interpreted in a way as inhibiting or restricting the right of states to develop atomic energy for peaceful purposes. They furthermore reaffirmed that States' choices and decisions, including those of the Islamic Republic of Iran, in the field of peaceful uses of nuclear technology and its fuel cycle policies must be respected.

3. The Ministers recognized the IAEA as the sole competent authority for verification of the respective safeguards obligations of Member States and stressed that there should be no undue pressure or interference in the Agency's activities, especially its verification process, which would jeopardize the efficiency and credibility of the Agency.

4. The Ministers welcomed the continuing cooperation being extended by the Islamic Republic of Iran to the IAEA including those voluntary CBMs undertaken with a view to resolving all remaining issues, including those as reflected in the latest report of the Director General of the IAEA on 26 May 2008.[491] They welcomed the fact that the IAEA has been able to verify the non-diversion of declared nuclear material in Iran as reflected in the Agency's reports since November 2003 and further noted the assessment of the IAEA Director General in Safeguard Implementation Report (SIR) 2006 that all nuclear material declared by Iran had been accounted for and remains in peaceful activities. They noted at the same time, that the process for drawing a conclusion with regard to the absence of undeclared material and activities in Iran is an ongoing and time consuming process. In this regard, the Ministers further welcomed the modality agreement reached between the Islamic Republic of Iran and the IAEA on 21 August 2007[492] leading to the resolution of the six outstanding issues as a significant step forward towards promoting confidence and a peaceful resolution of the issue. The Ministers took note of the Document INFCIRC/711 in which the Agency and Iran agreed that after the implementation of the Work Plan and the agreed modalities for resolving the outstanding issues, the implementation of safeguards in Iran will be conducted in a routine manner.

5. The Ministers emphasized the fundamental distinction between the legal obligations of states to their respective safeguards agreements and any confidence building measures voluntarily undertaken to resolve difficult issues, and believed that such voluntary undertakings are not legal safeguards obligations.

6. The Ministers considered the establishment of nuclear- weapons-free-zones (NWFZs) as a positive step towards attaining the objective of global nuclear disarmament and reiterated the support for the establishment in the Middle East of a nuclear weapons free zone in accordance with relevant General Assembly and Security Council resolutions. Pending the establishment of such a zone, they demanded Israel to accede unconditionally to the NPT without delay and place promptly all its nuclear facilities under comprehensive IAEA safeguards in accordance with Security Council Resolution 487 (1981).

7. The Ministers reaffirmed the inviolability of peaceful nuclear activities and that any attack or threat of attack against peaceful nuclear facilities - operational or under construction - poses a great danger to human beings and the environment, and constitutes a grave violation of international law, principles and purposes of the Charter of the United Nations and regulations of the IAEA. They recognized the need for a comprehensive multilaterally negotiated instrument prohibiting attacks, or threat of attacks on nuclear facilities devoted to peaceful uses of nuclear energy.

---

[491] Doc. 52.
[492] Doc. 6.

8. The Ministers strongly believed that all safeguards and verification issues, including those of Iran, should be resolved within the IAEA framework, and be based on technical and legal grounds. They further emphasized that the Agency should continue its work to resolve the Iranian nuclear issue within its mandate under the Statute of the IAEA.

9. The Ministers stressed that diplomacy and dialogue through peaceful means must continue to find a comprehensive and long term solution to the Iranian nuclear issue. They expressed their conviction that the only way to resolve the issue is to pursue substantive negotiations without any preconditions among all relevant parties. In this regard, the Ministers welcomed Iran's willingness to commence negotiations on various regional and global issues, including nuclear issues with NAM Member States, particularly those of the region. The Ministers further welcomed the talks between Iran and the six countries held in Geneva in July 2008.

2. Statement by the Organisation of Islamic Conference

Document 148: Resolution No. 9/11-P(IS) on Cooperation by the Islamic Republic of Iran with IAEA

14 March 2008

The Eleventh Session of the Islamic Summit Conference (Session of the Islamic Ummah in the 21st Century), held in Dakar, Republic of Senegal, from 6 to 7 Rabiul Awal 1429h (13-14 March 2008),

Recalling the relevant OIC decisions and resolutions, particularly those adopted in the 10th Session of the Islamic Summit Conference, and the 31st-34th Sessions of the Islamic Conference of Foreign Ministers, as well as declaration of the NAM Ministerial Conference in Malaysia on 30 May, 2006 and Final Communiqués of the 33rd and 34th Sessions of the ICFM;

Reaffirming the inalienable rights of Member States, without discrimination, to develop nuclear energy for peaceful purposes and in conformity with their respective legal obligations;

Reaffirming that nothing in the Non-Proliferation Treaty (NPT) and the International Atomic Energy Agency (IAEA) Statute, shall be interpreted as affecting the inalienable right of all parties to develop and use nuclear energy for peaceful purposes;

1. *Recognizes* that any attempt aimed at limiting the application of peaceful uses of nuclear energy would affect the sustainable development of developing countries.

2. *Rejects* discrimination and double standards in peaceful uses of nuclear energy and any attempt to resort to unilateral action in resolving verification concerns.

3. *Recognizes* the inalienable right of the Islamic Republic of Iran to develop nuclear energy for peaceful purposes, as enshrined in the NPT and the Statute of the IAEA.

4. *Expresses* concern over any unwanted consequences, on the peace and security of the region and beyond, of threats and pressures on Iran by certain circles to renounce its inalienable right to develop nuclear energy for peaceful purposes, and expresses its support and solidarity with that country.

5. *Appreciates* the cooperation of the Islamic Republic of Iran with the IAEA.

6. *Calls* and *supports firmly* the settlement of the issue exclusively by peaceful means and through negotiation without preconditions, in the framework of the IAEA and in accordance with the NPT and the Statute of the IAEA.

7. *Welcomes* the agreed work-plan between the Islamic Republic of Iran and the IAEA resulted in resolving of all remaining outstanding issues, as provided for in the latest report of the Director General of the Agency on the Nuclear Program of the Islamic Republic of Iran and in this context, reaffirms that the safeguard implementation in Iran should be conducted in a routine manner.

8. *Invites* the Islamic Republic of Iran and the IAEA as the sole competent authority of the safeguard obligations of the Member States, to continue their cooperation in accordance with the statute of the IAEA.

9. *Underlines* the importance of making distinction between the technical aspects of the issue and the political objectives of certain countries.

3. Statements by the G7/ G8

Document 149: G7 Summit 1995 Halifax, Chairman's Statement

17 June 1995

...

Middle East and Africa

...

19. We call upon the Government of Iran to participate constructively in regional and world affairs, and to desist from supporting radical groups that seek to destroy the Middle East Peace Process and destabilize the region. We also call on the Iranian Government to reject terrorism and, in particular, to withdraw its support from the continuing threats to the life of Mr. Salman Rushdie and others associated with his work. We call on all States to avoid any collaboration with Iran which might contribute to the acquisition of a nuclear weapons capability.

Document 150: G8 Summit 2000 Okinawa, Conclusions of the Foreign Ministers' Meeting, Miyazaki, Japan

13 July 2000

...

Iran

37. ... We call on Iran to sign with the IAEA an additional safeguards protocol.[493] The G8 calls on Iran to cooperate fully in not developing and in preventing the proliferation of weapons of mass destruction and missiles for their delivery.

...

---

[493] Doc. 4.

Document 151: G8 Summit 2003 Evian, Non Proliferation of Weapons of Mass Destruction, a G8 Declaration

3 June 2003

...

8. We will not ignore the proliferation implications of Iran's advanced nuclear program. We stress the importance of Iran's full compliance with its obligation under the NPT. We urge Iran to sign and implement an IAEA Additional Protocols without delay or conditions. We offer our strongest support to comprehensive IAEA examination of this country's nuclear program.

...

Document 152: G8 Summit 2007 Heiligendamm, Chair's Summary

Heiligendamm, 8 June 2007

...

III. Foreign Policy and Security Issues

...

Iran: We reiterate our profound concerns over the proliferation implications of the Iranian nuclear program. We urge Iran to comply with its international obligations and UNSCR 1696,[494] 1737[495] and 1747,[496] in particular its obligation to suspend all enrichment related activities. We deeply deplore the fact that, as evidenced by the IAEA Director General's latest report to the Security Council,[497] Iran has expanded its enrichment programme. We urge Iran to engage on the proposals put forward in June 2006 on behalf of China, France, Germany, Russia, the United Kingdom and the United States of America[498] and reiterate that we remain committed to a negotiated solution. We call on Iran to meet the requirements for the resumption of negotiations. Should Iran continue not to heed the call of the Security Council, we shall support further appropriate measures as agreed in UNSCR 1747. We also call on Iran to play a more responsible and constructive role in the Middle East region and condemn the threats towards Israel by the Iranian government and the repeated denial of the Holocaust by representatives of the Iranian government.

---

[494] Doc. 10.
[495] Doc. 11.
[496] Doc. 12.
[497] Doc. 48.
[498] Doc. 131.

Document 153: G8 Summit 2008 Hokkaido Toyako, Summit Leaders Declaration

Hokkaido Toyako, 8 July 2008

...

Non Proliferation

...

59. We express our serious concern at the proliferation risks posed by Iran's nuclear programme and Iran's continued failure to meet its international obligations. We urge Iran to fully comply with UNSCRs 1696,[499] 1737,[500] 1747[501] and 1803[502] without further delay, and in particular to suspend all enrichment-related activities. We also urge Iran to fully cooperate with the IAEA, including by providing clarification of the issues contained in the latest report of the IAEA Director General.[503] We firmly support and cooperate with the efforts by China, France, Germany, Russia, the United Kingdom and the United States supported by the High Representative of the EU to resolve the issue innovatively through negotiation, and urge Iran to respond positively to their offer delivered on 14 June 2008.[504] We also commend the efforts by other G8 members, particularly the high-level dialogue by Japan, towards a peaceful and diplomatic resolution of the issue. We welcome the work of the Financial Action Task Force to assist states in implementing their financial obligations under the relevant UNSCRs.

Document 154: G8 Summit 2009, Statement on Political Issues

L'Aquila, 8 July 2009

Iran

Heads of State and Government of the G8 countries continue to be seriously concerned about recent events in Iran. We reiterate our full respect for the sovereignty of Iran. At the same time, we deplore post-electoral violence, which led to the loss of lives of Iranian civilians. Interference with media, unjustified detentions of journalists and recent arrests of foreign nationals are unacceptable. We call upon Iran to solve the situation through democratic dialogue on the basis of the rule of law and we remind it of its obligations under the International Covenant on Civil and Political Rights.

We agreed that Embassies in Iran must be permitted to exercise their functions effectively under the Vienna Convention, without arbitrary restrictions on, or intimidation of, their staff.

We remain committed to finding a diplomatic solution to the issue of Iran's nuclear program and of Iran's continued failure to meet its international obligations. We welcome the readiness of the U.S. to enter into direct talks and the invitation from China, France, Germany, Russia, the United Kingdom and the United States to Iran to restart negotiations,

---

[499] Doc. 10.
[500] Doc. 11.
[501] Doc. 12.
[502] Doc. 13.
[503] Doc. 52.
[504] Doc. 133.

as well as the constructive involvement of other G8 partners in the process. We stress the need for unity of action on the basis of agreed policy. We sincerely hope that Iran will seize this opportunity to give diplomacy a chance to find a negotiated solution to the nuclear issue. At the same time we remain deeply concerned over proliferation risks posed by Iran's nuclear programme. We recognise that Iran has the right to a civilian nuclear programme, but that comes with the responsibility to restore confidence in the exclusively peaceful nature of its nuclear activities. We strongly urge Iran to cooperate fully with the IAEA and to comply with the relevant UNSC Resolutions, without further delay. The G8 meeting on the margin of the United Nations General Assembly opening week next September will be an occasion to take stock of the situation.

We condemn the declarations of President Ahmadinejad denying the Holocaust.

...

4. Documents of the Council of the EU

Document 155: EU Council Conclusions

17 June 2002

IRAN - Council conclusions

The Council restates its continued support for the process of reforms in Iran and, in this context, reaffirms its willingness to strengthen relations between the EU and Iran as agreed in May 2001. To this end, the Council has reached a political agreement on negotiating directives for a Trade and Co-operation Agreement with Iran, which is linked to separate instruments on political dialogue and counter-terrorism. It asks the Commission to take the appropriate steps to launch the negotiations as soon as the directives have been formally adopted.

The Council reiterates its expectations that the negotiation and conclusion of the agreement will help develop economic exchanges and co-operation with Iran, and contribute to the continuation of the process of political and economic reform. The Council expects that the deepening of economic and commercial relations between the EU and Iran should be matched by similar progress in all other aspects of the EU's relations with this country.

The Council wishes to see an intensified political dialogue between the EU and Iran leading to better understanding between the two parties as well as to significant positive developments in the areas of concern to the EU as identified by the Council in 1998:

- The EU calls on Iran to promote and protect human rights and fundamental freedoms,...

- Regarding non-proliferation, the EU encourages Iran to sign, ratify and fully implement relevant international instruments.

- On terrorism, ...

- With regard to the Middle East...

The Council will review progress in these areas.

The EU looks forward to enhance its co-operation with Iran to ensure stability in

Afghanistan. The EU and Iran also have a joint interest in combating drug trafficking and in addressing refugee problems.

The EU is convinced that the launching of negotiations and progress in these matters of concern will contribute to strengthen dialogue and co-operation in all the areas mentioned above. These are interdependent, indissociable and mutually reinforcing elements of the global approach which is the basis for progress in the EU-Iran relations.

Document 156: EU Council Conclusions

16 June 2003

1. The Council discussed developments in relations with Iran following its decision to launch negotiations on agreements concerning trade and co-operation and political dialogue.

...

3. In particular, the Council has taken note with concern of the Report on implementation of the NPT safeguards agreement in the Islamic Republic of Iran submitted by the Director General of IAEA on June 6.[505]

4. The nature of some aspects of Iran's programme raises serious concerns, in particular as regards the closing of the nuclear fuel cycle, especially the uranium centrifuge, announced by President Khatami. The Council stressed the need for Iran to answer timely, fully and adequately all questions raised regarding its nuclear programme. It called on Iran to fully co-operate with the IAEA.

5. The Council called on Iran to conclude and implement urgently and unconditionally an Additional Protocol.[506] This would be a significant step in demonstrating Iran's stated peaceful intentions with regard to its nuclear programme.

Document 157: EU Presidency Conclusions

16/17 October 2003

...

Iran

...

67. The European Council reiterates its grave concern on Iran's nuclear programme and gives its full support to the IAEA Board of Governors Resolution of 12 of September.[507] The Union expects Iran to cooperate fully with the IAEA in its implementation. The European Council renews its call on Iran promptly and unconditionally to sign, to ratify and to implement the IAEA Additional Protocol on Safeguards[508] and to act immediately

---

[505] Doc. 33.
[506] Doc. 4.
[507] Doc. 23.
[508] Doc. 4.

in accordance with it. It also calls on Iran to suspend all uranium enrichment-related and reprocessing activities. The European Council rejects the perspective [*sic*] of nuclear proliferation in the region, which is already far from stable.

68. The European Union remains ready to explore ways to develop a wider cooperation with Iran. This can only be achieved through increased international confidence on the peaceful nature of Iran's nuclear programme and improvements in the areas of human rights, fight against terrorism and Iran's position on the Middle East Peace Process.

...

Document 158: EU Council Conclusions

13 December 2004

...

1. The Council discussed the EU's relations with Iran in the light of the agreement reached with Iran on 15 November 2004[509] following talks with France, Germany and the UK, supported by the High Representative, and the recent meeting of the International Atomic Energy Agency's Board of Governors (25-29 November 2004).[510]

2. The Council welcomed the adoption, without a vote, on 29 November 2004 of the Board of Governors' resolution on Iran's nuclear programme and called on Iran to comply fully with its provisions.[511]

3. The Council welcomed the confirmation by the IAEA that Iran had voluntarily suspended all enrichment-related and reprocessing activities, thus paving the way for negotiations on a long term arrangement, as provided for in the agreement of 15 November 2004. The Council underlined that sustaining the full suspension of all enrichment related and reprocessing activities is essential for the continuation of the overall process.

4. The Council stressed that a long term arrangement resulting from negotiations, which started on 13 December, will have to provide objective guarantees that Iran's nuclear programme is exclusively for peaceful purposes.

5. The Council underlined its full support for the negotiating process and recalled its commitment to contribute to a positive outcome. In light of the IAEA's confirmation of full suspension, it confirmed that the EU would resume negotiations with Iran on a draft EU-Iran Trade and Cooperation Agreement together with parallel negotiations on a political agreement. It confirmed the EU's readiness to explore ways to further develop political and economic co-operation with Iran, following action by Iran to also address the other concerns of the EU regarding the fight against terrorism, human rights and Iran's approach to the Middle East Peace Process.

...

---

[509] Doc. 8
[510] Doc. 72.
[511] Doc. 28.

Document 159: EU Council Conclusions

18 June 2007

The Council deplores the fact that Iran has still not complied with its international obligations as reiterated in United Nations Security Council (UNSC) Resolution 1747.[512] Iran has instead continued to drive forward its nuclear programme as well as further restricting its cooperation with the IAEA thus creating further doubts as to the exclusively peaceful nature of its programme. Whilst reaffirming its commitment to finding a diplomatic solution that addresses the international community's concerns, the Council also reasserts its full support for the UNSC and its resolve, as expressed in Resolution 1747, to adopt further appropriate measures under Article 41 Chapter VII of the United Nations Charter should Iran continue not to comply with its international obligations.

The Council again urges Iran to respond positively to the proposals put forward by the Foreign Ministers of China, France, Germany, Russia, the United Kingdom and the United States of America, with the support of the High Representative of the European Union, in their Statement of 24 March 2007. The Council also reaffirms its support for the exploratory efforts of the High Representative of the EU, Javier Solana with Dr. Ali Larijani and strongly urges Iran to engage constructively in these consultations and to create the necessary conditions for negotiations to resume.

Document 160: EU Council Conclusions

27 April 2009

The EU reaffirms its full and unequivocal support for efforts to find a negotiated long-term solution to the Iranian nuclear issue within the framework of UNSCR 1696, 1737, 1747, 1803 and 1835[513] and its support for the dual-track process.

The EU warmly supports the new direction of US policy towards Iran, which opens a window of opportunity for negotiations on all aspects of Iran's nuclear programme and more broadly for engagement with Iran. The EU welcomes the decision of the US to participate fully in the negotiations together with China, France, Germany, the Russian Federation and the UK supported by the High Representative and join in any future meetings with representatives of the Islamic Republic of Iran. The EU welcomes the efforts by the High Representative Javier Solana, on behalf of the EU and the international community, in view of facilitating the resumption of the negotiating process, in line with the package proposals for cooperation with Iran.

The EU calls upon Iran to seize this opportunity to engage seriously with the international community in a spirit of mutual respect, in order to find a negotiated solution to the nuclear issue which will address Iran's interests, including the development of a civil nuclear power generation programme, as well as the international community's concerns. The evolution of our relations with Iran will also depend on it.

---

[512] Doc. 12.
[513] Doc. 10-Doc. 14.

Iran's nuclear programme remains a matter of grave concern for the international community, since if Iran were to acquire a military nuclear capability, this would constitute an unacceptable threat to security, both regional and international. Iran must restore confidence in an exclusively peaceful nature of its nuclear activities. The EU encourages Iran to comply with its international obligations.

5. Statement by the European Commission

Document 161: Communication from the Commission to the European Parliament and the Council, EU Relations with the Islamic Republic of Iran

COM(2001)71, 7 February 2001

1. Background
Relations with the EU and Member States
At present the EU does not have any contractual relations with Iran, nor is there any significant financial co-operation. An Agreement existed in the time of the Shah, but it lapsed in 1977 before the Islamic Revolution. An EU-Iran dialogue was initiated in 1995. After the election of President Khatami in 1997 this was extended to new areas and became the Comprehensive Dialogue in 1998. A dialogue meeting is held every six months in Troika format.

The Comprehensive Dialogue allows a wide ranging exchange of views on:
- global issues (terrorism, human rights and proliferation),
- regional issues (Iraq, Gulf, Central Asia, the Middle East Peace Process)
- areas of cooperation (drugs, refugees, energy, trade and investment).

The Comprehensive Dialogue has contributed to improving relations but it is clearly limited in scope. It has been complemented by a number of technical working groups between the Commission and Iran, which have served to identify areas of mutual interest and possible co-operation (see section 4 below). However, it is clear that the lack of a contractual framework limits the development of such co-operation.

Relations with Member States have improved considerably since President Khatami was elected in 1997. The Italian Prime Minister visited Teheran in 1997. In 1999, President Khatami visited Italy and France, and the Presidents of Austria and Greece visited Iran in the same year. President Khatami recently visited Germany. Numerous visits by Foreign Ministers and other Ministers have taken place. British-Iranian relations were unblocked in 1998 by the defusing of the Rushdie fatwa issue and Ambassadors were exchanged in mid-1999.

Iran has manifested a strong interest in strengthening relations with the EU, and has shown interest in negotiating a Trade and Co-operation Agreement and an enhanced relationship with the EU is clearly a major policy objective for President Khatami.
…

2. The current situation in Iran

…

3. Trade and Economy

…

4. EC-Iran Cooperation

In October 1998, the Council asked the Commission to establish contacts with Iran to explore possibilities for cooperation. A Commission-Iran Technical Meeting was organised in December 1998 and it was agreed to explore a number of possible areas for co-operation - energy, environment, transport, agriculture, drugs control, refugees and human rights. With the exception of some humanitarian assistance and limited aid for drugs control, there is at present no EC-Iran financial and technical cooperation. In some areas working groups have been set up between the Commission and the Iranian administration.

…

5. EU Interests

…

Under the right circumstances the development of closer EU-Iran relations could help to promote the reform process in Iran and contribute to greater regional stability. Iran has indicated that it is ready to discuss human rights, which is a positive sign since any future contractual relations with Iran would have to include discussion on human rights issues. In addition, Iran is also ready to discuss security issues, including regional security, and has begun to do so with some Member States.

6. Challenges to Co-operation

A number of issues need to be addressed, bilaterally by the EU and Iran and unilaterally by Iran if co-operation is to be deepened and extended to new areas. These concern both political and economic issues. On the political side, these include:

…

Security Issues

Iran's intention to develop weapons of mass destruction, and in particular long-range missiles, is a matter of serious EU concern. The EU encourages Iran to conclude a strengthened safeguards regime with the IAEA. Iran has repeatedly stated that the conclusion of such a regime, like its possible willingness to ratify the Comprehensive Test Ban Treaty (CTBT), should depend on prior removal of international export control measures against its civilian nuclear programme. The EU does not accept such precondition.

All the above areas of concern are raised in the Comprehensive Dialogue.

…

7. Assessment and Recommendations

Provided that the reform process continues, it is clear from the preceding analysis that it is in the mutual interest of the EU and Iran to develop closer ties, politically and economically, as well as in areas like environment, drugs and migration. Given the possibilities of unforeseen reverses in Iran's own political evolution and its weak economic structures, a cautious approach is required and in view of the number of areas which give rise to concern the development of closer relations should be gradual and dependent on progress made by Iran in these areas. The Commission and the Council should regularly review progress in the light of indicators or benchmarks in areas such as the rule of law, rights of minorities, press freedom, the regulatory environment for the economy and Iran's approach to foreign relations and security matters.

In the light of the analysis set out above and the conclusions of the General Affairs Council of 20 November 2000, the Commission recommends to the Council to develop closer relations with Iran on the basis of the following approach. It goes without saying that the scope for promoting bilateral relations will depend on the progress of political, economic and legislative reform in Iran.

- encouragement of political and economic reform through
    - more frequent official and unofficial bilateral contracts
    - development of exchange/co-operation in areas of mutual interest and concern (such as drugs, rule of law, refugees etc)
    - readiness to engage in dialogue on human rights
    - strengthening the CFSP dialogue by deepening the dialogue in areas such as regional security, weapons of mass destruction, nuclear proliferation)
    - seeking appropriate ways of developing people to people contacts
- promotion of bilateral economic relations through
    - negotiation of a Trade and Co-operation Agreement.
    - continuation of Commission – Iran working groups on energy, Trade and investment.

...

If these recommendations are accepted by the Council, the Commission will consider presenting to the Council, in accordance with Article 300(1) of the Treaty, a recommendation to be authorised to open the necessary negotiations.

Selected Bibliography

Acton, James M, 'The Problem with Nuclear Mind Reading' (2009) 51 *Survival* 119

AEI conference, 'The International Atomic Energy Agency: The World's Enforcer or Paper Tiger?' (28 September 2004), transcript and webcast at http://www.aei.org/events/filter. all,eventID.911/event_detail.asp

Afrasiabi, Kaveh, 'Iran, Nuclear Challenges', (2007) XIX *Iranian Journal of International Affairs*

Afrasiabi, Kaveh and Kibaroglu, Mustafa, 'Negotiating Iran's Nuclear Populism' (2005) XII *Brown Journal of World Affairs* 255-268

Alvarez-Verdugo, Milagros, 'Comparing U.S. and E.U. Strategies against Weapons of Mass Destruction: Some Legal Consequences' (2005) 11 *Annual Survey of International and Comparative Law* 119

Banks, William C, 'Introduction: A Second Nuclear Age' (2007) 57 *Syracuse Law Review* 429

Benvenisti, Eyal, 'The US and the Use of Force: Double-edged Hegemony and the Management of Global Emergencies' (2004) 15 *European Journal of International Law* 677

Blix, Hans, 'Disarmament Visions and the Prospects for a WMD-free Zone in the Middle East' (Berlin, 24 June 2008) (on file with the author)

Blix, Hans, Comments made at the conference 'Breaking the U.S.-Iran Stalemate' organized by the National Iranian American Council (Washington, 8 April 2008) (on file with the author)

Blix, Hans, 'Non-proliferation of Weapons of Mass Destruction: The Search for Truth' (2006) 30 *Fletcher Forum of World Affairs* 17

Boroujerdi, Mehrzad, Fine, Todd, 'Iranian Nuclear Miasma' (2007) 57 *Syracuse Law Review* 619

Busch, Nathan E, and Joyner, Daniel H (eds), *Combating Weapons of Mass Destruction* (University of Georgia Press 2009)

Carlson, John, 'Defining Noncompliance: NPT Safeguards Agreements' (8 May 2009)

Carlson, John, Leslie, Russell, and Berriman, Annette 'Nuclear Weaponisation Activities: What Is the Role of IAEA Safeguards?' (undated)

Chubin, Shahram, *Iran's Nuclear Ambitions* (Carnegie Endowment for International Peace, Washington DC 2006)

Crook, John R (ed), 'Contemporary Practice of the United States Relating to International Law: Use of Force and Arms Control: U.S. Concerns About Declining Effectiveness of Nonproliferation Regime' (2005) 99 *American Journal of International Law* 917

Dalton, Richard (ed), 'Iran: Breaking the Nuclear deadlock' Chatham House Report (2008)

Delpech, Thérèse, *Iran and the Bomb, The Abdication of International Responsibility* (translated by Ros Schwartz, Columbia University Press, New York 2007)

Denza, Eileen, 'Non-proliferation of Nuclear Weapons: The European Union and Iran' (2005) 10 *European Foreign Affairs Review* 289

Eichensehr, Kristen, 'Targeting Tehran: Assessing the Lawfulness of Preemptive Strikes against Nuclear Facilities' (2006) 11 *UCLA Journal of International Law and Foreign Affairs* 59

Fidler, David P, 'International Law and Weapons of Mass Destruction: End of the Arms Control Approach?' (2004) 14 *Duke Journal of Comparative and International Law* 39

Fischer, David, *History of the International Atomic Energy Agency, the First forty Years* (IAEA, Vienna 1997)

Ford, Christopher A, 'Compliance Assessment and Compliance Enforcement: the Challenge of Nuclear Noncompliance' (2006) 12 *ILSA Journal of International and Comparative Law* 583

Ford, Christopher A, 'Debating Disarmament: Interpreting Article VI of the treaty on the Non-Proliferation of Nuclear Weapons' (2007) 14 *Nonproliferation Review* 401

Fry, James D, 'Dionysian Disarmament: Security Council WMD Coercive Disarmament Measures and their Legal Implications' (2007-2008) 29 *Michigan Journal of International Law* 197

Gardiner, Sam, 'Et Maintenant en Avant: Preemption and the Planning for Iran' (2007) 57 *Syracuse Law Review* 443

Garvey, Jack I, 'A New Architecture for the Non-Proliferation of Nuclear Weapons' (2008) 12 *Journal of Conflict and Security Law* 339

Goldschmidt, Pierre, 'Exposing Nuclear Non-compliance' (2009) 51 *Survival* 143

Goldschmidt, Pierre, 'IAEA Safeguards: Dealing Preventively with Non-Compliance' (July 2008)

Goldschmidt, Pierre, 'Rule of Law, Politics and Nuclear Nonproliferation' Presentation to the Ecole Internationale de Droit Nucléaire, the University of Montpellier, France (7 September 2007)

Goldschmidt, Pierre, 'Verifying Iran's Nuclear Program: Is the International Community Up to the Task?' Lamont Lecture at the Belfer Center, Harvard University (30 October 2007)

Graham, Thomas, 'National Self-Defense, International Law, and Weapons of Mass Destruction' (2003) 4 *Chicago Journal of International Law* 1

Greig, D W, 'Reciprocity, Proportionality and the Rule of Law' (1993-1994) 34 *Virginia journal of International Law* 295

Grotto, Andrew J, 'Iran, the IAEA and the UN' ASIL Insight (November 2004)

Ingram, Paul, Preliminary analysis of E3/EU proposal to Iran, Basic Occasional Papers on International Security Policy (11 August 2005)

Jahanpour, Farhang, 'Iran's Nuclear Threat: Exploring the Politics', Oxford Research Group (July 2006)

Johnson, Larry D, 'Protecting the World from Weapons of Mass Destruction: Reflections on the High-level Panel Report on Threats, Challenges and Change' (2007-2008) 28 *California Western International Law Journal* 63

Joyner, Daniel H, '*Jus ad Bellum* in the Age of WMD Proliferation' (2008) 40 *George Washington International Law Review* 233

Joyner, Daniel H, *International Law and the Proliferation of Weapons of Mass Destruction* (Oxford University Press, Oxford 2009)

Joyner, Daniel H (ed), *Non-Proliferation Export Controls* (Ashgate 2006)

Kam, Ephraim (ed), *Israel and a Nuclear Iran: Implications for Arms Control, Deterrence, and Defense*, Memorandum No. 94 (Institute for National Security Studies, Tel Aviv 2008)

Kane, Chen Zak, 'Nuclear Decision-Making in Iran: A Rare Glimpse', Middle East Brief, Paper 5 (May 2006)

Kanwar, Vik, 'Two Crises of Confidence: Securing Non-Proliferation and the Rule of Law through Security Council Resolutions' (2009) 35 *Ohio Northern University Law Review* 171

Kerr, Paul K, 'Iran's Nuclear Program: Status', CRS Report for Congress (11 August 2009)

Kibaroglu, Mustafa, 'Good for the Shah, Banned for the Mullahs: The West and Iran's Quest for Nuclear Power' (2006) 60 *Middle East Journal* 207

Kile, Shannon N (ed), *Europe and Iran: Perspectives on Non-proliferation* SIPRI Research Report No. 21 (Oxford University Press, Oxford 2005)

Kittrie, Orde F, 'Averting Catastrophe: Why the Nuclear Nonproliferation Treaty is Losing its Deterrence Capacity and How to Restore It' (2007) 28 *Michigan Journal of International Law* 337

Kittrie, Orde F, 'Emboldened by Impunity: The History and Consequences of Failure to Enforce Iranian Violations of International Law, (2007) 57 *Syracuse Law Review* 519

Leslie, Russell, 'The Good Faith Assumption: Different Paradigmatic Approaches to Nonproliferation Issues' (2008) 15 *Nonproliferation Review* 479

McDonough, Mark, Tracking Nuclear Proliferation: A Guide in Maps and Charts (Carnegie Endowment for International Peace, Washington, DC, 1998)

Miller, Steven E, Proliferation Gamesmanship: Iran and the Politics of Nuclear Confrontation' (2007) 57 *Syracuse Law Review* 551

Müller, Harald, 'WMD Crisis: Law Instead of Lawless Self-Help' WMDC Publication No. 37 (August 2005)

Müller, Harald, 'National and International Export Control Systems and Supplier States' Commitments under the NPT' Programme for Promoting Nuclear Non-Proliferation (September 2006) 8 *Issue Review*

O'Connell, Mary Ellen and Alevra-Chen, Maria, 'The Ban on the Bomb - and Bombing: Iran, the U.S., and the International Law of Self-Defense,' (2007) 57 *Syracuse Law Review* 497

Ogilvie-White, Tanya, 'International Responses to Iranian Nuclear Defiance: The Non-Aligned Movement and the Issue of Non-Compliance' (2007) 18 *European Journal of International Law* 453

Perkovich, George and Acton, James M (eds), *Abolishing Nuclear Weapons: a Debate* (Carnegie Endowment for International Peace, Washington DC 2009)

Perkovich, George, 'Defining Iran's Nuclear Rights' *Proliferation Analysis* (7 October 2006)

Roberts, Guy B, 'The Counterproliferation Self-Help Paradigm: A Legal Regime for Enforcing the Norm Prohibiting the Proliferation of Weapons of Mass Destruction' (1998-1999) 27 *Denver Journal of International Law and Policy* 483

Rockefeller, Mark L, 'The "Imminent Threat" Requirement for the Use of Preemptive Military Force: Is it Time for a Non-Temporal Standard?' (2004-2005) 13 *Denver Journal of International Law and Policy* 131

Samore, Gary, 'Meeting Iran's Nuclear Challenge' WMDC Publication No 21 (undated, probably 2005)

Scheinman, Lawrence, 'Article IV of the NPT: Background, Problems, Some Prospects' WMDC Publication No 5 (June 2004)

Schmitt, Burkard (ed), Effective Non-Proliferation: the European Union and the 2005 NPT review Conference, Chaillot Papers No. 77 (European Union Institute for Security Studies 2005)

Sloss, David, 'It's Not Broken, So Don't Fix It: The International Atomic Energy Agency Safeguards System and the Nuclear Nonproliferation treaty' (1994-1995) 35 *Virginia Journal of International Law* 841

Sokolski, Henry (ed), *Falling Behind: International Scrutiny of the Peaceful Atom* (Strategic Studies Institute, 2008)

Spies, Michael, 'Iran and the Limits of the Nuclear Non-Proliferation Regime' (2006-2007) 22 *American University International Law Review* 401

Squassoni, Sharon, 'Iran's Nuclear Program: Recent Developments', CRS report for Congress (15 August 2003)

Timbie, James, 'Iran's Nuclear Program' (2007) 57 *Syracuse Law Review* 433

Wallerstein, Mitchel B, 'Responding to a Nuclear Iran: A Defense Policy Perspective - Remarks at the Symposium on a Nuclear Iran: The Legal Implications of a Preemptive National Security Strategy' (2007) 57 *Syracuse Law Review* 457

Weapons of Mass Destruction Commission, Final Report, *Weapons of Terror: Freeing the World of Nuclear, Biological and Chemical Arms'* (WMDC, Stockholm, 1 June 2006)

Welsh, Steven C, 'IAEA on Iran: recent and pending action and legal parameters' (2 February 2006)

Welsh, Steven C, 'Iran's Nuclear Program and International Legal Instruments: IAEA Statute' (24 November 2004)

Wood, Thomas W, Milazzo, Matthew D, Reichmuth, Barbara A and Bedell, Jeffrey, 'The Economics of Energy Independence for Iran' (2007) 14 *Nonproliferation Review* 89

Zhang, Xinjun, 'The Riddle of "Inalienable Right" in Article IV of the Treaty on the Non-Proliferation of Nuclear Weapons: Intentional Ambiguity', (2006) 5 *Chinese Journal of International Law* 647

Zlauvinen, Gustavo R, 'Nuclear Non-Proliferation and Unique Issues of Compliance, (2006) 12 *ILSA Journal of International and Comparative Law* 583

Useful websites:

All URLs accessible as of 15 September 2009

1995 NPT Review Conference, http://disarmament.un.org/wmd/npt/1995nptrevconf.html

2000 NPT Review Conference, http://disarmament2.un.org/wmd/npt/finaldoc.html

2010 NPT Conference Preparatory Committee, Third Session, http://www.un.org/disarmament/WMD/Nuclear/NPT2010Prepcom/PrepCom2009/index.html Arms Control Association, http://www.armscontrol.org/country/10/date

British American Security Information Council, http://www.basicint.org/update/iran.htm

Carnegie Endowment, http://www.carnegieendowment.org/npp/index.cfm?fa=view&npp ID=1000089

Center for Defense Information, http://www.cdi.org/news/law/iran.cfm

ENDC, http://quod.lib.umich.edu/cgi/t/text/text-idx?page=browse&c=endc

Federation of American Scientists, http://www.fas.org/nuke/guide/iran/nuke/

French Ministry of Foreign Affairs, http://www.diplomatie.gouv.fr/en/country-files_156/iran_301/the-iranian-nuclear-issue_2724/index.html

Global Security, http://www.globalsecurity.org/military/ops/iran-hotdocs.htm

http://diplomacymonitor.com/stu/dm.nsf/issued?openform&cat=Iran_Nuclear

IAEA, http://www.iaea.org/NewsCenter/Focus/IaeaIran/index.shtml

Institute for National Strategic Studies, http://www.inss.org.il/research.php?cat=3

Iranian UN mission, http://www.un.int/iran/

Iran Watch, http://www.iranwatch.org/

ISIS Nuclear Iran, http://www.isisnucleariran.org/

Nuclear Threat Initiative http://www.nti.org/e_research/profiles/Iran/index.html

Russian Embassy in Tehran, http://www.iran.mid.ru/

Security Council Report, http://www.securitycouncilreport.org

UN Security Council 1737 Committee, http://www.un.org/sc/committees/1737/index.shtml

Weapons of Mass Destruction Commission, http://www.wmdcommission.org

Index